FROMMER'S
DOLLARWISE GUIDE TO THE MID-ATLANTIC STATES

Including Pennsylvania, New Jersey,
Delaware, Maryland, and
Washington, D.C.

**by Patricia Tunison Preston
and John J. Preston**

1988–1989 Edition

Published by Prentice Hall Press
A Division of Simon & Schuster, Inc.
Gulf + Western Building
One Gulf + Western Plaza
New York, New York 10023

ISBN 0–13–218314–5

Manufactured in the United States of America

*Although every effort was made to ensure the accuracy
of price information appearing in this book,
it should be kept in mind that prices
can and do fluctuate in the course of time.*

CONTENTS

MAPS

Acknowledgments

With special thanks to our family and friends for all their encouragement to us in the writing of this, our first book together. We would also like to acknowledge the tremendous help, guidance, and enthusiasm we received from the people of the Mid-Atlantic states, and, in particular, we extend a big "thank you" to the following: Deb Hickok of the Bureau of Travel Development of Pennsylvania; Gigi Dux of the Delaware Development Office; Tom Murphy of the Washington, D.C., Convention and Visitors Bureau; and the Maryland Office of Tourist Development.

Dedicated to our mothers,
Dorothy A. Tunison
and
Katherine Preston

Chapter I

THE MID-ATLANTIC STATES

1. What You'll Find
2. One Trip or Many?
3. Getting There
4. Getting Around
5. Dollarwise Facts and Figures
6. Invitation to Readers
7. How to Save Money on All Your Travels—The $35-A-Day Travel Club

THE BEST OF NORTH AND SOUTH meet and meld in the Mid-Atlantic States—Pennsylvania, New Jersey, Delaware, and Maryland. Much of what is great about our country has evolved from these four states—from Philadelphia's Constitution Hall, where our government was founded, to Baltimore's Fort McHenry, which inspired the words of "The Star-Spangled Banner." Delaware led the way in forging the new nation by being the first state to ratify the Constitution, and New Jersey has given us Liberty State Park, which overlooks the symbol of freedom for all. To complete the picture (and our book), we add the District of Columbia, our capital city.

1. What You'll Find

The Mid-Atlantic states, for the most part, are bordered by the Atlantic, which means a collage of beaches, each with its own personality and attractions—from America's number-one destination, Atlantic City, and Victorian Cape May, both in New Jersey, to the white sands of Ocean City on Maryland's eastern shore, or Delaware's "quiet resorts" that dominate the Delmarva Peninsula. Not to be outdone, Pennsylvania has its own beaches along the Lake Erie shorefront.

These four states and the federal district are also rimmed and divided by picturesque rivers and bays, such as the Delaware, Lehigh, Allegheny, Susquehanna, Brandywine, Chesapeake, and Potomac. Swimming, boating, and whitewater rafting are just a few of the sports that draw visitors to these states.

Vacationers also come to pay homage to the heroes of history, commemo-

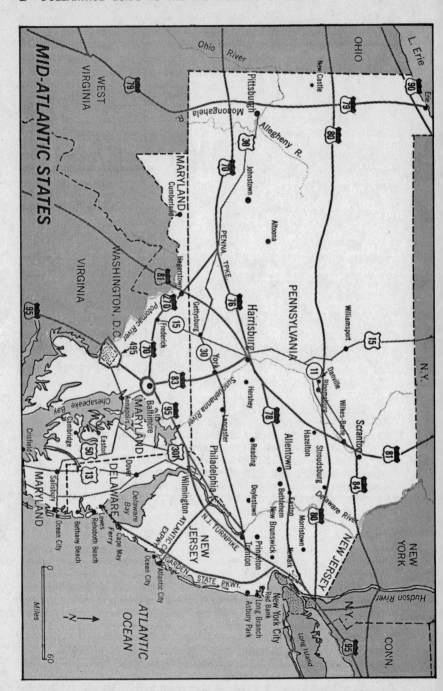

rated on the fields of Gettysburg and Valley Forge in Pennsylvania, Antietam in Maryland, Brandywine in Delaware/Pennsylvania, and Morristown in New Jersey.

Best of all, the Mid-Atlantic region is a medley of places that are synonymous with happy vacation dreams—from the honeymoon resorts of the Pocono Mountains in Pennsylvania, to the dockside crab restaurants of Maryland, the museums that rim Wilmington and Washington, and the outlet shops of New Jersey's suburbs.

Each of these states is a destination in its own right, and could easily merit an individual book. We have grouped them together to give you a handy guide for the whole middle chunk of the eastern seaboard. Many times you'll want to visit adjacent sections of countryside, like western Maryland and southern Pennsylvania; Delaware's beaches and Maryland's Eastern Shore; or nearby cities, such as Wilmington and Philadelphia; Baltimore and Washington, D.C. With other guides, you might have to purchase one or two books; with this book, you can plan a trip without having to worry about state lines . . . just start reading a new chapter.

2. One Trip or Many?

With a total area of more than 64,000 square miles, the Mid-Atlantic states offer months of travel and vacation wonders. The larger cities alone need three or four days, and sometimes a week, to sample the major attractions.

Based on typical one-week vacation segments, here are some compatible combinations:

1. Philadelphia and Bucks County
2. Wilmington and the Brandywine Valley, with historic New Castle
3. The Poconos, alone or with Scranton and Wilkes-Barre, and/or with Columbia and Montour Counties
4. Harrisburg/Hershey and along the Susquehanna to Williamsport
5. Pennsylvania Dutch Country, Hershey, and Harrisburg
6. The Lehigh Valley and the Poconos or Philadelphia
7. Gettysburg, York, Baltimore, and Frederick
8. Pittsburgh, the Laurel Highlands, and Erie
9. Pittsburgh, Johnstown or Altoona, and western Maryland
10. Dover and the Delaware Beaches with Ocean City, Maryland
11. The Eastern Shore of Maryland with Annapolis
12. Baltimore and western Maryland
13. Delaware beaches and Cape May
14. The Jersey shore, including Atlantic City
15. New Jersey's Delaware River shore with Pennsylvania's Bucks County
16. Northern and central New Jersey with eastern Pennsylvania
17. Washington, D.C., on its own or with Baltimore/Annapolis

We could go on and on, but you probably get the picture. Any single one of these destinations makes a perfect weekend trip. It is well to bite off small areas of each state or neighboring states and not attempt to drive hundreds of miles a day. Delaware, the small wonder, is probably the only one of the Mid-Atlantic states that could be toured in a single week. Maryland takes ten days to two weeks. New Jersey can be toured in under two weeks, only if you breeze through the beaches. And Pennsylvania . . . well, this state is larger than all the others put together, twice!

3. Getting There

The Mid-Atlantic states are easy to reach by air, rail, or road. No matter where you live, you'll have no problems getting a flight to the seven major airports located here—Philadelphia, Pittsburgh, Newark, Baltimore, Wilmington, Washington/Dulles, and Washington/National.

Prices, of course, vary with your point of origin, destination, and the type of airfare you choose. To get the best deal, it is wise to consult a travel agent or several carriers, and compare the prices. At the moment, it costs anywhere from $89 to $550 to fly across the U.S. one-way, so airfares really depend on many factors. The lowest prices are usually APEX fares (advance purchase excursions), which require that you book and pay for your ticket at a certain time. You might also have to travel at off-peak times and perhaps during midweek, like Tuesday or Wednesday. Don't be put off by the restrictions, however, as such conditions can usually save you at least 50% off normal fares!

All four Mid-Atlantic states and Washington, D.C., are served daily by regular Amtrak rail service. Like airfares, train prices depend a lot on searching out the best deal. At the moment, Amtrak offers a special "All Aboard America" fare of $198 for round-trip cross-country travel, while the regular coach fare can run as high as $704. Fares change often, so be sure to consult a travel agent or Amtrak when you are planning a trip (tel. toll-free 800/USA-RAIL). In the chapters that follow, we describe the train services available to each location, with appropriate addresses and telephone numbers.

For those who prefer to travel by bus, both Greyhound and Trailways serve the large cities and most smaller towns throughout the Mid-Atlantic region. Depending on when you buy your ticket, your point of origin, and other restrictions, the current one-way fare ranges from $59 to $169 from coast to coast. In each of our chapters, we pinpoint the places that have interstate bus services, including the telephone numbers to call for more information.

By car, you have a choice of roads to bring you to and within the Mid-Atlantic region. Interstate 95, the East Coast's major north-south route, passes through every one of the Mid-Atlantic states and the District of Columbia. From the north or south, you can also follow I-87 or I-81. In an east-west direction, I-80 will bring you to Pennsylvania and New Jersey, and I-70 leads to Maryland and the Washington, D.C., area. As we begin each chapter, we tell you the best roads to follow.

4. Getting Around

The Mid-Atlantic states are ideal for all types of sightseeing. In the chapters that follow, we outline the options available to you regarding local escorted trips, trolley tours, walking tours, river cruising, inclined plane rides, mini-train rides, barge trips, and the like.

In the case of the big cities, we recommend that you take a plane, train, or bus to the city of your choice, and leave your car at home. Cities like Philadelphia, Pittsburgh, Baltimore, and Washington, D.C., have excellent local transport systems and tour services, and can easily be explored on foot as well.

For the smaller cities, the country towns, and the beaches, it is best to bring your own car or to rent a car when you arrive at a major gateway. In each chapter, we describe some of the most scenic roads to take, and we also alert you to places where major car-rental firms maintain depots.

If you don't drive and prefer to see the countryside, then an escorted group tour might be best for you. Some tour companies that specialize in itineraries of this region include **Domenico Tours**, 751 Broadway, Bayonne, NJ 07002 (tel. 201/823-8687 or toll-free 800/554-TOUR); **Casser/Travelcade**, 46 W. 43rd St., New York, NY 10036 (tel. 212/840-6500); and **Blue Bird Tours**, 502 N. Barry St., Olean, NY 14760 (tel. 716/372-5500 or toll-free 800/262-2262). You can contact these operators and ask for their brochures, or go to your travel agent, who will probably have other suggestions as well.

5. Dollarwise Facts and Figures

PRICES IN THIS BOOK: Throughout this guide, we describe the Mid-Atlantic's best lodgings, restaurants, sightseeing attractions, and activities, with the latest prices. As with all Dollarwise books, the prices listed here are for all levels, from expensive to budget, but with an emphasis on moderate choices. These prices are correct now, as we go to press, but probably will go up, due to inflation and other factors, during 1988 and 1989. You may have to add 10% to 20% to the costs we list, as time passes, but, in the main, these prices reflect a price range or barometer. While the cost of a room or a dinner may change by a few dollars, at least you can be guided by the general level of price indicated.

Wherever possible, we have chosen hotels, inns, and restaurants that reflect a bit of history and character of the area you are visiting. By the same token, while we love to tell you about the places that have been in business for 50 or 100 years, we also alert you to what's new, trendy, and different.

WHERE TO STAY: All lodging prices listed on these pages are per-night charges and are based on double-occupancy rates. To estimate the cost of a single, you can usually deduct from $10 to $20 per night off the double rate. However, some hotels, particularly in major beach resorts, do not offer single rates in peak season. In each case, we indicate such factors, and we also advise you of any special considerations, such as reduced weekend rates, surcharges, or minimum-stay requirements.

Double-Occupancy Rates

Super-Deluxe Category	$125 and up
Luxury Lodgings	$80 to $120
Moderate Choices	$40 to $80
Budget Range	$40 and under

The overnight rates quoted in every chapter normally are for room only, except in the case of bed-and-breakfast inns, which provide continental or full breakfasts. Some resort properties also operate on a Modified American Plan (MAP), which means that rates are usually quoted on a per-person basis and include two meals a day. When this applies, we make note of it.

As a rule, the hotels, motor inns, and motels provide rooms with private bath/shower facilities. In the case of some inns or bed-and-breakfast houses, private baths may not come with every room, or rooms with private bath cost more. We tell you when this is the situation.

WHERE TO DINE: A land rich in farmlands, vineyards, fish-bearing waters, and pasturelands, the Mid-Atlantic region offers a wealth of fine dining experiences. This is also the home of Hershey candies, Pocono crunch, saltwater taffy, shoofly pies, Perdue chickens, and Jersey tomatoes, not to mention Amish farm cooking and the crab-cracking seafood houses along Chesapeake Bay.

The restaurants described in this book range from grand hotel dining rooms to country kitchens, as well as rooftop verandas, sailing ships, colonial taverns, courtyard marinas, and restored railroad cars.

In addition to writing about the general décor and ambience of a restaurant, we also specify prices. As a yardstick, we give you the price range for an entree or main course for one person.

Dining Categories

Top Choices	$15 to $20 or more
Moderate Price Range	$10 to $15
Budget Meals	$10 and under

To calculate the price of a full meal with appetizer, dessert, tax, and tips, you can usually double the cost of the entree. So, if your entree is $12, a complete dinner will probably be around the $24 mark for one or about $50 for two.

Since many people do not always order an appetizer or dessert, we have chosen to use entree prices as a barometer. In the majority of cases, the cost of an entree also includes a basket of fresh bread or rolls, house salad, and a choice of vegetables, potato, or pasta appropriate to the entree. If an entree and its accompaniments are enough for you, then a moderately priced meal, with tax and tip, will cost about $15 to $20 per person. Most of the restaurants on the pages that follow fall into the "moderate" category.

Note: The majority of restaurants we have selected offer standard bar services, so we do not go into details about cocktails or wine lists, unless there is something outstanding or unusual. You can assume that alcoholic beverages are available, unless we specify otherwise. In such cases, a "BYOB" (bring your own bottle) policy is usually in effect.

RESERVATIONS: Advance reservations are always recommended for all types of accommodations. In fact, if you like the sound of a certain property, we suggest that you call or write and ask for a brochure, with the most up-to-date rates or any special package deals. Then make a reservation as soon as you can, to avoid disappointment.

As for restaurants, it is always wise to phone ahead and make a reservation. Although we have made every effort to list correct restaurant hours, such data can change from season to season or day to day. You can assume that reservations are in order unless we state that a "no reservations" policy is in effect.

CREDIT CARDS: We use credit cards on our travels and find them very helpful. However, not every credit card is acceptable at every location. While the majority of lodgings and many restaurants do accept all the major cards, some of the smaller places accept only one or two cards, or perhaps none at all. It can be embarrassing if you produce an American Express card and find that only Master Card and Visa are accepted; it can be even worse if you offer your card and are told no credit cards are taken. Likewise, some restaurants take only American Express. So we have collected as much credit-card data as possible. We use the abbreviation "CC" for the words "credit cards." In the case of each hotel, inn, or restaurant, we state if most major CC's are accepted; and, if not, we tell you which ones are. We also abbreviate the names of the credit cards (CC's) for you, as follows:

Credit Cards

American Express	AE
Carte Blanche	CB
Choice	Ch
Diners Club	D
Discover	Disc
MasterCard	MC
Visa	V

Like all the rest of the information in this book, credit-card data can also change. New outlets are constantly being added by most major cards, so if your card is not listed for a certain establishment, do inquire, as it may be in use at the time of your trip. The credit card information that we provide is meant as a guideline only, although establishments that do accept the major cards will likely continue to do so, and places that do not accept any cards will probably keep that policy.

SHOPPING: Shopping for souvenirs is part of the fun of traveling anywhere, and this is certainly true in the Mid-Atlantic region. From the museum shops of Washington and the Brandywine Valley to the country crafts stores of central Pennsylvania, there is lots of good shopping. Special "finds" include the Colonial memorabilia of central Maryland; Civil War artifacts from Gettysburg; the antiques of New Market, Bucks County, Lambertville, and Adamstown; the outlet bargains of Reading or Flemington; and the handmade quilts of the Amish families in Dover and Lancaster County. Whenever there is special shopping unique to an area, we point that out.

In addition, we list some of the sightseeing-cum-shopping experiences, such as the city or country markets in places like Lancaster, Philadelphia, Dover, Baltimore, York, Bloomsburg, Scranton, and Hagerstown.

Other shopping tips include restored landmarks that now house a mulitude of specialty stores, like Baltimore's Harbor Place, the Bourse in Philadelphia, Station Square in Pittsburgh, Everedy Square in Frederick, Modern Tool Square in Erie, Gordon's Alley in Atlantic City, Strawberry Square in Harrisburg, and the Old Post Office in Washington, D.C.

Where possible, we list shopping hours and credit card information.

NIGHTLIFE, SPORTS, ACTIVITIES, AND EVENTS: To round out your travels, we include these categories in most chapters and give you a few suggestions under each heading. For some areas, like the Poconos, the sports and outdoor activity sections are quite extensive.

When a city or area is famous for a special yearly event, like the Miss America Pageant in Atlantic City, the Little League Baseball series in Williamsport, the Civil War Days at Gettysburg, or Christmas in Bethlehem, we give details of how to get tickets and further information.

Last, and certainly not least, we include a "children's corner" in many chapters. The suggestions under this heading will alert you to special theme parks, amusement areas, or museums designed with young travelers in mind.

BON VOYAGE! We wish you happy traveling in the days ahead. Think of us as you come to know and love the Mid-Atlantic region. We look forward to your suggestions and comments.

6. Invitation to Readers

Like all other books in the Dollarwise series, the *Dollarwise Guide to the Mid-Atlantic States* aims to include the establishments that offer the best value-for-money. In achieving this goal, your comments and suggestions can be of tremendous help. If, as a Dollarwise traveler, you find that we've missed an establishment that you consider particularly good value (or even one that's just fun and other readers ought to know about), we'd like to hear about it. We invite you to write to us, so that your suggestion can be included in the next edition of this book. If, on the other hand, by the time you get to a particular destination, you find that a restaurant or lodging is not up to our description (chefs and management do change!), please write and tell us about that as well. The last thing we want is that this book give untimely or misleading information. Any additional travel tips you'd like to add will also be most welcome. And yes, if you find this guide to be especially helpful, we'd naturally like to hear that too. You can be assured that we'll read each and every letter personally, and, although we won't be able to answer each letter individually, we'll certainly be "listening" to what you have to say. Send your comments to Patricia and John Preston, c/o Frommer Books, Prentice Hall Press, One Gulf + Western Plaza, New York, NY 10023-7772.

7. How to Save Money on all Your Travels—The $35-A-Day Travel Club

In this book we'll be looking at how to get your money's worth in the Mid-Atlantic States, but there is a "device" for saving money and determining value on *all* your trips. It's the popular, international $35-A-Day Travel Club, now in its 25th successful year of operation. The Club was formed at the urging of numerous readers of the $$$-A-Day and Dollarwise Guides, who felt that such an organization could provide continuing travel information and a sense of community to value-minded travelers in all parts of the world. And so it does!

In keeping with the budget concept, the annual membership fee is low and is immediately exceeded by the value of your benefits. Upon receipt of $18 (U.S. residents), or $20 U.S. by check drawn on a U.S. bank or via international postal money order in U.S. funds (Canadian, Mexican, and other foreign residents) to cover one year's membership, we will send all new members the following items.

(1) *Any two* of the following books

Please designate in your letter which two you wish to receive:

Frommer's $-A-Day Guides
Europe on $30 a Day
Australia on $25 a Day
Eastern Europe on $25 a Day
England on $40 a Day
Greece including Istanbul and Turkey's Aegean Coast on $30 a Day
Hawaii on $50 a Day
India on $25 a Day
Ireland on $30 a Day
Israel on $30 & $35 a Day
Mexico on $20 a Day (plus Belize and Guatemala)
New York on $50 a Day
New Zealand on $40 a Day
Scandinavia on $50 a Day
Scotland and Wales on $40 a Day
South America on $30 a Day
Spain and Morocco (plus the Canary Is.) on $40 a Day
Turkey on $25 a Day
Washington, D.C., on $40 a Day

Frommer's Dollarwise Guides
Dollarwise Guide to Austria and Hungary
Dollarwise Guide to Belgium, Holland, & Luxembourg
Dollarwise Guide to Bermuda and The Bahamas

Dollarwise Guide to Canada
Dollarwise Guide to the Caribbean
Dollarwise Guide to Egypt
Dollarwise Guide to England and Scotland
Dollarwise Guide to France
Dollarwise Guide to Germany
Dollarwise Guide to Italy
Dollarwise Guide to Japan and Hong Kong
Dollarwise Guide to Portugal, Madeira, and the Azores
Dollarwise Guide to the South Pacific
Dollarwise Guide to Switzerland and Liechtenstein
Dollarwise Guide to Alaska
Dollarwise Guide to California and Las Vegas
Dollarwise Guide to Florida
Dollarwise Guide to the Mid-Atlantic States
Dollarwise Guide to New England
Dollarwise Guide to New York State
Dollarwise Guide to the Northwest
Dollarwise Guide to Skiing USA—East
Dollarwise Guide to Skiing USA—West
Dollarwise Guide to the Southeast and New Orleans
Dollarwise Guide to the Southwest
Dollarwise Guide to Texas
(Dollarwise Guides discuss accommodations and facilities in all price ranges, with emphasis on the medium-priced.)

Frommer's Touring Guides
Egypt
Florence
London
Paris
Venice
(These new, color illustrated guides include walking tours, cultural and historic sites, and other vital travel information.)

Arthur Frommer's New World of Travel 1988
(From America's #1 travel expert, a sourcebook of vacations that cater to the mind, the spirit, and a sense of thrift. Guaranteed to change the way people travel and to save them hundreds of dollars.)

A Shopper's Guide to the Caribbean
(Two experienced Caribbean hands guide you through this shopper's paradise, offering witty insights and helpful tips on the wares and emporia of more than 25 islands.)

Bed & Breakfast—North America
(This guide contains a directory of over 150 organizations that offer bed-and-breakfast referrals and reservations throughout North America. The scenic attractions, businesses, and major schools and universities near the homes of each are also listed.)

Dollarwise Guide to Cruises
(This complete guide covers all the basics of cruising—ports of call, costs, fly-cruise package bargains, cabin selection booking, embarkation and debarkation and describes in detail over 60 or so ships cruising the waters of Alaska, the Caribbean, Mexico, Hawaii, Panama, Canada, and the United States.)

Dollarwise Guide to Skiing Europe
(Describes top ski resorts in Austria, France, Italy, and Switzerland. Illustrated with maps of each resort area plus full-color trail maps.)

Guide to Honeymoon Destinations
(A special guide for that most romantic trip of your life, with full details on planning and choosing the destination that will be just right in the U.S. [California, New England, Hawaii, Florida, New York, South Carolina, etc.], Canada, Mexico, and the Caribbean.)

How to Beat the High Cost of Travel
(This practical guide details how to save money on absolutely all travel items—accommodations, transportation, dining, sightseeing, shopping, taxes, and more. Includes special budget information for seniors, students, singles, and families.)

Marilyn Wood's Wonderful Weekends
(This very selective guide covers the best mini-vacation destinations within a 175-mile radius of New York City. It describes special country inns and other accommodations, restaurants, picnic spots, sights, and activities—all the information needed for a two- or three-day stay.)

Motorist's Phrase Book
(A practical phrase book in French, German, and Spanish designed specifically for the English-speaking motorist touring abroad.)

Swap and Go—Home Exchanging Made Easy
(Two veteran home exchangers explain in detail all the money-saving benefits of a home exchange, and then describe precisely how to do it. Also includes information on home rentals and many tips on low-cost travel.)

The Candy Apple: New York for Kids
(A spirited guide to the wonders of the Big Apple by a savvy New York grandmother with a kid's-eye view to fun. Indispensable for visitors and residents alike.)

Travel Diary and Record Book
(A 96-page diary for personal travel notes plus a section for such vital data as passport and traveler's check numbers, itinerary, postcard list, special people and places to visit, and a reference section with temperature and conversion charts, and world maps with distance zones.)

Where to Stay USA
(By the Council on International Educational Exchange, this extraordinary guide is the first to list accommodations in all 50 states that cost anywhere from $3 to $30 per night.)

(2) A one-year subscription to *The Wonderful World of Budget Travel*

This quarterly eight-page tabloid newspaper keeps you up to date on fast-breaking developments in low-cost travel in all parts of the world bringing you the latest money-saving information—the kind of information you'd have to pay $25 a year to obtain elsewhere. This consumer-conscious publication also features columns of special interest to readers: **Hospitality Exchange** (members all over the world who are willing to provide hospitality to other members as they pass through their home cities); **Share-a-Trip** (offers and requests from members for travel companions who can share costs and help avoid the burdensome single supplement); and **Readers Ask . . . Readers Reply** (travel questions from members to which other members reply with authentic firsthand information).

(3) A copy of *Arthur Frommer's Guide to New York*

This is a pocket-size guide to hotels, restaurants, nightspots, and sightseeing attractions in all price ranges throughout the New York area.

(4) Your personal membership card

Membership entitles you to purchase through the Club all Arthur Frommer publications for a third to a half off their regular retail prices during the term of your membership.

So why not join this hardy band of international budgeteers and participate in its exchange of travel information and hospitality? Simply send your name and address, together with your annual membership fee of $18 (U.S. residents) or $20 U.S. (Canadian, Mexican, and other foreign residents), by check drawn on a U.S. bank or via international postal money order in U.S. funds to: $35-A-Day Travel Club, Inc., Frommer Books, Gulf + Western Building, One Gulf + Western Plaza, New York, NY 10023. And please remember to specify which *two* of the books in section (1) above you wish to receive in your initial package of members' benefits. Or, if you prefer, use the last page of this book, simply checking off the two books you select and enclosing $18 or $20 in U.S. currency.

Once you are a member, there is no obligation to buy additional books. No books will be mailed to you without your specific order.

Chapter II

INTRODUCTION TO PENNSYLVANIA

1. Welcome to the Keystone State
2. Getting to Pennsylvania
3. Getting Around Pennsylvania
4. Useful Facts

"YOU'VE GOT A FRIEND IN PENNSYLVANIA" is more than just a memorable advertising slogan. It is a statement based on the profound beliefs of the state's founder, William Penn. A Quaker from England, Penn sought to establish a colony where friendship would be the code of life.

When he began his "Holy Experiment" on these shores over 300 years ago, Penn had one purpose in mind, religious freedom for all, so that no one group would dominate another. Penn sought to build a land where men and women of all faiths and backgrounds could prosper in harmony. One of the first things Penn did was to sign a peace treaty with the Indians, ensuring that both natives and newcomers would "live friendly together."

It is no wonder that persecuted peoples from all parts of Europe flocked to this new land. The English Quakers arrived first, and then came the Mennonites, Amish, Dunkards, and Moravians from Germany, Switzerland, and France, followed by the Scots-Irish. This melding of nationalities under the banner of friendship helped to shape and develop Pennsylvania into a model for the other colonies, and to make it a true "keystone" for the young nation.

1. Welcome to the Keystone State

The largest of the Mid-Atlantic states, Pennsylvania was named by William Penn in honor of his father; he called it "Penn's Woods" or "Penn's Silvania." The land was part of a grant from King Charles II of England, given in return for money owed by the king to the Penns. The territory had been explored earlier by the Dutch under Henry Hudson in 1609, and settled by both the Dutch and the Swedes before it came under English control in 1664.

When young William Penn arrived in 1682, he personally devised plans for the layout of Philadelphia and fondly christened it "The City of Brotherly Love." He wrote "The Charter of Privileges," a document that called for religious freedom and a liberal penal code, and helped to shape Pennsylvania into a governmental benchmark in the New World.

Just as a rock that holds an arch together is called a keystone, Pennsylvania

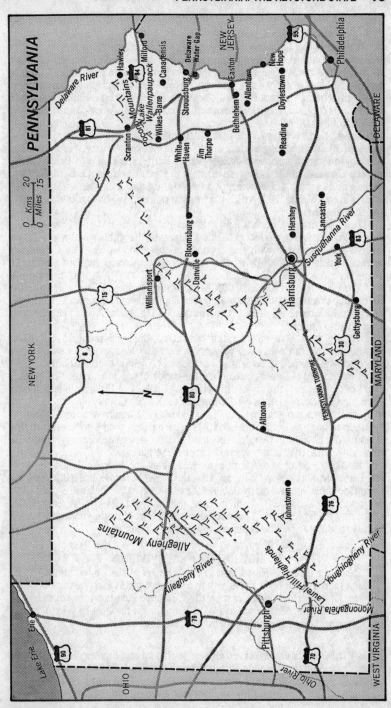

is called the "Keystone State" because it was the pivot in the development of the 13 original colonies into a nation.

Thanks to the ideals of its founder, Pennsylvania not only led the way in granting religious freedom, but it also played a vital role in the formation of our country as it is today. Our founding fathers chose Philadelphia as the Colonial capital, and it was in that city that the Declaration of Independence and our Constitution were written. Home of the symbolic Liberty Bell, Philadelphia was also the first capital of the newly formed United States of America and remained as such until 1800.

In addition to being a force in the birth of our nation, Pennsylvania was the scene of many other significant events in American history, from General Washington's winter encampment at Valley Forge, the Battle of Brandywine, and the Crossing of the Delaware during the Revolution, to the Battle of Gettysburg and Lincoln's Gettysburg Address during the Civil War, and the Battle of Erie in the War of 1812, which gave us the phrase "We have met the enemy, and they are ours."

Pennsylvania has been a leader in our nation's great days of canals, railroading, coal mining, and steel making. Many of the sights we enjoy today as tourists are associated with the heydays of these industries. The Conestoga wagon, which blazed trails to the west, also originated here in Lancaster County.

The home of our fifteenth president, James Buchanan, Pennsylvania produced such diverse personalities as pioneer Daniel Boone, inventor Robert Fulton, novelist James Michener, artist Andrew Wyeth, golfer Arnold Palmer, and singer Mario Lanza.

The sights of this expansive state range from the honeymoon havens of the Poconos to the Little League playing fields at Williamsport, as well as the chocolate-kiss-shaped street lanterns of Hershey, the horse-drawn carriages and colorful hex signs of Lancaster County, the candlelit windows of the "Christmas City" of Bethlehem, the sturdy hill-climbing inclines of Pittsburgh and Johnstown, and the dozens of covered bridges of Columbia County.

Basically rectangular in size, Pennsylvania is 310 miles wide and 180 miles from top to bottom, for a total of 45,308 square miles, with a population of approximately 12 million people. The state charter designates Pennsylvania as a commonwealth, officially only one of four in the nation.

Unlike the other Mid-Atlantic states of Delaware, Maryland, and New Jersey, Pennsylvania does not have an Atlantic Ocean coastline, but it does enjoy a Lake Erie shoreline and many delightful rivers such as the Delaware, Schuylkill (pronounced: Scool-kill), Lehigh, Susquehanna, Allegheny, Monongahela, Ohio, and Youghiogheny. The state also offers ever-changing natural vistas of mighty mountains, verdant valleys, and fertile farmlands.

2. Getting to Pennsylvania

Reaching from the East Coast to the Midwest of the United States, Pennsylvania shares common borders with five different states and two major bodies of water. It is rimmed on the east by the Delaware River; on the south by the states of Delaware, Maryland, and West Virginia; on the west by West Virginia and Ohio; and on the north/northeast by Lake Erie and New York State.

BY CAR: Pennsylvania is served by the fourth-largest highway system in the nation, including the 470-mile Pennsylvania Turnpike (I-76) which sweeps over the southern half of the state. In a similar pattern, I-80 also crosses over the northern half of the state. Other interstates, such as I-95, I-83, I-70, I-81, and

I-79, serve various sections of the state, mostly in north-south directions. To assist you in your travels, we identify the main access routes in each of the chapters that follow.

BY PLANE: Pennsylvania is served by most of the country's national airlines into the major metro areas of Philadelphia, Pittsburgh, Harrisburg, Allentown/Bethlehem/Easton, Wilkes-Barre/Scranton, and Erie. Smaller county airports also handle regional and commuter flights. Each chapter that follows lists the principal airlines serving the areas described.

BY TRAIN: Amtrak offers convenient daily transportation to many Pennsylvania cities, including Philadelphia, Pittsburgh, Harrisburg, Lancaster, Erie, Altoona, and Johnstown. These services include Metroliner trains on the northeast corridor, from New York, Boston, Washington, D.C., and Florida. Trains also traverse the state in an east-west direction, traveling to and from Chicago and points west.

BY BUS: Two major national bus companies, Greyhound and Trailways, travel to all major cities of Pennsylvania such as Philadelphia, Pittsburgh, Erie, Harrisburg, Scranton, Wilkes-Barre, Lancaster, Reading, Altoona, and Johnstown. Buses also are scheduled daily into smaller areas not served by rail, such as the Poconos, the Lehigh Valley, Gettysburg, York, Williamsport, and the counties of Bucks, Columbia, and Montour.

3. Getting Around Pennsylvania

BY CAR: In addition to the primary interstate highways, Pennsylvania is well served with more than 70,000 miles of other roads. Route 30, otherwise known as the Lincoln Highway and originally a stagecoach path, runs in an east-west direction, between Philadelphia and Pittsburgh, and traverses such major destinations as Lancaster, York, Gettysburg, and the Laurel Highlands. In addition, Route 40, the landmark National Pike, covers part of the state's southwest corner, entering from the Maryland border and continuing on to West Virginia, Ohio, and points west.

Route 15, which comes into the state from the Maryland border on the south or from New York State on the north, then runs, for the most part, parallel to the Susquehanna River and is a particularly scenic drive in the center of the state. Route 11 follows a similar Susquehanna path along much of the same territory. To the east, Route 611, which starts as Broad Street in the heart of Philadelphia, travels north through Bucks County and along the Delaware, up into the Poconos, and is another delightfully scenic way to get from one section to another.

BY PLANE: The same major airports that welcome passengers into Pennsylvania also serve the bulk of the intrastate traffic. Daily flights are scheduled between Philadelphia, Wilkes-Barre/Scranton, and Allentown/Bethlehem/Easton airports in the east, and Pittsburgh and Erie to the west, as well as Harrisburg in the center. Smaller regional airports also provide regular commuter flights within all parts of the state.

BY TRAIN: Most of the Amtrak services that bring passengers into the state, as outlined in "Getting To Pennsylvania," also provide connections within the state. Some of the most popular train routes are between Philadelphia and Pittsburgh, or from either of those cities to Lancaster or Harrisburg.

BY BUS: Both Greyhound and Trailways provide regular connections between most major cities and large towns within Pennsylvania. In addition, a number of local and municipal transport authorities operate services within certain cities, counties, or regions. In each of the chapters that follow, such local services are identified and described.

4. Useful Facts

VISITOR INFORMATION: For comprehensive brochures, maps, lists of events, and travel data about the whole state, contact the **Bureau of Travel Development,** Pennsylvania Department of Commerce, 416 Forum Building, Harrisburg, PA 17120 (tel. 717/787-5453 or toll-free 800/VISIT PA). For "Best of Friends," a free vacation guide, write the Bureau, attention Dept. SXA. In the chapters that follow, we also list the individual tourist offices for the various Pennsylvania cities or regions we describe.

CLIMATE: With an elevation that ranges from sea level on its east coast to 3,213 feet in the mountains of the southwestern section of the state, Pennsylvania has an equally varied climate. Here is a sampling of what you can expect:

Weather Statistics

	Av. Temp. Summer	Av. Temp. Winter	Total Annual Rainfall Inches	Total Annual Snow Inches
Philadelphia	74.3°F	35.0°F	35.20	17.8
Harrisburg	74.4°F	34.4°F	33.81	31.2
Scranton/Wilkes-Barre	69.2°F	29.2°F	40.42	38.2
Pittsburgh	69.9°F	29.8°F	38.51	45.4
Erie	69.4°F	28.0°F	45.87	146.7

THE PENNSYLVANIA OUTDOORS: With its mighty mountains and rivers, myriad streams and lakes, and many parklands and preserves, Pennsylvania is an ideal outdoor vacationland. The Pennsylvania Bureau of Travel Development is the best source of information on all types of activities from biking to hiking, as well as boating, swimming, whitewater rafting, skiing, fishing, and hunting, to name a few of the more popular pursuits.

Some sports require special licenses or permits. For full data on fishing seasons, limits, stocking areas, and regulations throughout the state, you should contact the **Pennsylvania Fish Commission,** 3532 Walnut St., P.O. Box 1673, Harrisburg, PA 17105-1673 (tel. 717/657-4518). The cost of a seven-day tourist license is $15.50, and that will entitle you to ply the waters in search of brook trout (the state fish), rainbow and brown trout, coho and chinook salmon, shad, striped bass, pike, pickerel, yellow perch, and many other species.

Pennsylvania is a hunter's haven of more than 1,300,000 prime state game acres, home to everything from black bear, whitetail deer, and turkey, to grouse, pheasant, woodcock, beaver, and hare. Seasons, license fees, and regulations vary for hunting with firearms or bows and arrows, and for trapping. To obtain full information in advance, contact the **Pennsylvania Game**

Commission, 800 Derry St., P.O. Box 1567, Harrisburg, PA 17105-1567 (tel. 717/787-4250).

In addition, Pennsylvania is home to 113 state parks, covering an area of 279,378 acres. You'll find parks in the cities as well as in the countryside; in fact, there's a state park within 25 miles of every resident! Some parks, like Presque Isle at Erie, are known for swimming, boating, and fishing; and others, such as the Ohiopyle at Uniontown, draw people for rafting and canoeing. Most parks also feature hiking, biking, and nature trails, picnicking areas, and camping grounds. For a complete list of Pennsylvania's state parks and their facilities, contact the **Bureau of Travel Development,** Department of Commerce, 416 Forum Building, Harrisburg, PA 17120, or the **Department of Environmental Resources,** P.O. Box 1467, Harrisburg, PA 17120-1467 (tel. 717/387-4255).

Particulars on other sports, such as golf, horseback and mule riding, whitewater rafting, and skiing, are highlighted, wherever appropriate, in each chapter that follows.

BON APPÉTIT: A visit to Pennsylvania means good eating. Although there is no one type of food instantly identified with the whole of Pennsylvania, the vastness of the state provides many special dishes and types of food.

Thanks to its Lake Erie shoreline, Pennsylvania is known for its coho and chinook salmon, perch, and yellow pike. The Delaware River is a big producer of shad, and the Allegheny, Schuylkill, and parts of the Susquehanna are prime bass beds. Other streams and rivers throughout the state offer good rainbow and brown trout, and the northeast is known for its Pocono Mountain brook trout.

Pennsylvania is a big producer of apples and apple products, as well as peaches, cherries, berries, and grapes. You'll delight in sampling wares at farmers' markets in major cities and throughout the countryside. And don't forget that this state is also a major wine-producing region, with more than 20 wineries inviting you to tour their vineyards and sample their vintages, especially in the southeast and the northwestern parts of the state.

In addition, if you are a connoisseur of mushrooms, you'll find bliss here. Pennsylvania grows more than 60% of the country's mushrooms, particularly in the area of Chester and Berks counties in the southeast, where many restaurants specialize in mushroom cookery.

The most famous type of regional food is the traditional Pennsylvania Dutch cuisine, available throughout the state, but especially in the area around Lancaster County. This is hearty eating at its best—heaping platters of fried chicken, spicy sausage, country beef, hickory-smoked ham, pork and sauerkraut, homemade noodles, sweet-and-sour relishes, garden-grown vegetables, pepper cabbage, apple butter, and desserts ranging from shoofly pie and cherrycrumb pie to raspberry tarts.

Other types of ethnic food are equally tempting: from the Moravian sugar cakes, sticky buns, and kiffels of the Lehigh Valley to the cheese steaks and hoagies of the Philadelphia area.

And, to end on a sweet note, Pennsylvania is also the home of Hershey, the chocolate capital of the world.

AREA CODES: Pennsylvania has four area codes within its borders: (215) covers most of the east including the Philadelphia region, Bucks County, Reading, and the Lehigh Valley; (717) is used in the Poconos, Scranton, Wilkes-Barre, Columbia and Montour counties, Williamsport, most of Lancaster County,

Harrisburg, Hershey, York, and Gettysburg; (412) prevails in Pittsburgh; (814) applies in Erie, Altoona, and Johnstown. To avoid confusion, we remind you of each applicable area code at the start of every chapter.

SALES TAX: All hotel room charges, meals, and purchases within the state of Pennsylvania are subject to a 6% sales tax; some other local or county taxes often apply. It is best to check in the course of your travels to see what tax will be added to your bill. One happy note for shoppers is that clothing is exempt from the general 6% sales tax.

PHILADELPHIA

A "GREENE COUNTRIE TOWNE" is the way that William Penn envisioned his new city on the Delaware River in 1682. And if this founding father could see his town today, he'd be mighty proud. Not only has this city retained and revitalized its original parks and historic buildings, but it has aesthetically blended them with gleaming new office skyscrapers and thriving commercial complexes. Cobblestone courtyards and broad tree-lined boulevards exist side by side with bustling transitways.

Years ago, it was true that Philadelphia bore the brunt of W.C. Fields' jokes, but in the 1970s, this spunky settlement said "No more." Spurred by the Bicentennial, concerned citizens stepped forward, and enlightened urban planning came to the fore. Neglected landmarks were restored, derelict halls turned into chic shopping malls, old inns were glamorized, new hotels with skylit atriums sprung up, and a culinary renaissance began that has literally cooked up at least 500 exciting new restaurants.

The recent 1987 "We the People 200" festivities, in celebration of the 200th anniversary of the U.S. Constitution, have served to fuel even more civic pride and creative development in this Mid-Atlantic hub of four million people.

Most of all, Philadelphia is our nation's "Cradle of Liberty"—the home of the Liberty Bell, Independence Hall, and America's "most historic square mile." In many ways, this city has influenced the lives of all Americans, and is a part of each one of us, no matter where we call home.

1. The City of Brotherly Love

Wherever you go in Philadelphia, you can usually look up and see the statue of William Penn proudly surveying his "greene countrie town" from 35 stories atop City Hall. Up until 1986, this was the highest mark on the city skyscape, and no other structure could be built taller than "Billy Penn's hat," but, with the recent topping out of the new 60-story One Liberty Center and the ground-breaking for the Linpro 50-story twin towers, Philadelphia's horizons are rising ever higher. In many ways, reaching for new heights symbolizes the essence of this city from its very first days.

When William Penn chose the name Philadelphia (from the Greek meaning "the City of Brotherly Love") he was seeking new heights in individual freedom and religious harmony. Philadelphia was not only the chief town in the "Holy Experiment" known as Pennsylvania, but it also soon became the focal point of the 13 colonies.

In many ways, Philadelphia's history from 1774 until 1800 is inextricably linked to the lofty ideals of independence urged by our nation's founding fathers. The First Continental Congress convened in this city at Carpenters' Hall in 1774. The Second Continental Congress, which forged America's destiny, met in the Pennsylvania State House, later to become Independence Hall. It was there that the Congress made the fateful decision to prepare the Declaration of Independence, which was then read publicly for the first time in this city's State House Yard on July 8, 1776.

Except for nine months during the British occupation, Philadelphia was the Revolutionary War capital, and later continued as the capital of the fledgling nation. In 1787, the Constitutional Convention met to revise the Articles of Confederation, and, for four months, 55 delegates secretly developed the Constitution of the United States. It was indeed fitting that Philadelphia remained the new nation's capital until 1800.

Although the city is no longer our nation's capital or even the capital of Pennsylvania, it still retains the landmarks and the aura of those early days. As you wander from building to building in the Independence National Historical Park, the cobblestones seem to echo with the footsteps of George Washington, Thomas Jefferson, John Adams, and Ben Franklin. You can walk the same streets, stand in the same doorways, see the same sights, and dine in taverns just like the ones that bid them welcome. Drop into the Betsy Ross House and see the workroom where the first "Stars and Stripes" flag pattern was sewn, and, of course, you can't miss paying your respects to the Liberty Bell.

Visitors to Philadelphia are often surprised that this city has also produced many "firsts" for America: the first hospital, the Philadelphia Hospital; the first university, the University of Pennsylvania; the first mint, the United States Mint; the first stock exchange, and many more, including the nation's first zoo.

Philadelphia is also the gateway to some of the Mid-Atlantic's most inviting countryside. Travel less than 20 miles outside this vibrant city and you are in the heart of three of the top visitor destinations on the East Coast—Valley Forge, the Brandywine Valley (see Chapter XIX), and Bucks County (see Chapter IV).

VISITOR INFORMATION: The **Philadelphia Convention and Visitors Bureau** operates a full-time **Visitors Center** at 1525 John F. Kennedy Blvd., Philadelphia, PA 19102 (tel. 215/636-1666). It's open daily from 9 a.m. to 6 p.m., Memorial Day through Labor Day, and from 9 a.m. to 5 p.m. every other day of the year except Christmas. This central location is the source for all types of brochures, accommodations and restaurant listings, events calendars, and specialized information. It is also the starting point for most bus, trolley, and sightseeing tours of the city. For news of what's happening on a daily basis in Philadelphia, you can also call the 24-hour **Philly Fun Phone** (215/568-7255);

you'll be connected to a two-minute taped message, updated three times a week.

AREA CODE: Unless indicated otherwise, all telephone numbers in this chapter belong to the 215 area code.

2. Getting to Philadelphia

BY PLANE: Philadelphia International Airport, Penrose Avenue, off I-95 (tel. 492-3181), is eight miles southwest of the city center. With more than 1,000 flights a day, this airport is an east-coast gateway, serving arrivals and departures to over 100 U.S. cities, as well as flights to Europe, Canada, Mexico, and the Caribbean, and connections to the Orient.

More than two dozen airlines serve this airport, including such major transcontinental carriers as **American** (tel. 365-4000), **Delta** (tel. 928-1700), **Eastern** (tel. 923-3500), **Northwest** (tel. 922-2900), **Pan American** (tel. 365-1814), **TWA** (tel. 923-2000), **United** (tel. 568-2800), and **USAir** (tel. 563-8055), and international airlines such as **British Airways** (tel. 568-5070), **Air Jamaica** (tel. 545-5705), **Lufthansa** (tel. 800/645-3880), and **Mexicana** (tel. 800/531-7921).

Taxi and **limousine** services stop at all baggage-claim areas. Average cab fare between the airport and city is $15 to $20; the limousine fare is $46. Among the **car-rental** firms that maintain desks at the airport are Avis, Budget, Dollar, Hertz, National, and Thrifty.

If you prefer public transport, a rapid transit link between airport and three major downtown points is operated by **Southeastern Pennsylvania Transportation Authority (SEPTA).** Known as **Philadelphia Airport Rail** (tel. 574-7800), this service operates daily from 6 a.m. to midnight, traveling between terminals B, C, D, or E, to the 30th Street Station at 30th and Market Streets (Gate B, Track 6, upper-level track area); Penn Center/Suburban Station at 16th Street and John F. Kennedy Boulevard (Gate 4B, Track 3); and Market East Station, located just north of Market Street between 10th and 12th Streets (Gates 2B and 4B, Track 3). Travel time is 25 minutes, and the one-way fare is $4 for adults and $2 for children under 12.

BY TRAIN: Philadelphia is the hub of transportation on **Amtrak's** Northeast corridor. Trains from points north, west, and south arrive and depart daily from Amtrak's 30th Street Station, 30th and Market Streets (tel. 824-1600 or toll-free 800/USA-RAIL). This station is located just west of the central downtown region, on the west side of the Schuylkill River. It is within walking distance of Drexel University and the University of Pennsylvania, but you will need a taxi to get to the major downtown hotels. *Note:* Some trains also stop at the North Philadelphia Station, Broad Street and Glenwood Avenue, used mostly by those who live in that area. Do not be confused, however, and get off prematurely. Chances are you'll want the 30th Street Station if your destination is mid-city.

BY BUS: Daily services are provided into Philadelphia by **Greyhound,** 17th and Market Streets (tel. 568-4800); and **Trailways,** 13th and Arch Streets (tel. 569-3100). Both depots are in the central downtown district, near to hotels and major attractions.

BY CAR: Philadelphia is well-served by interstate highways from all directions.

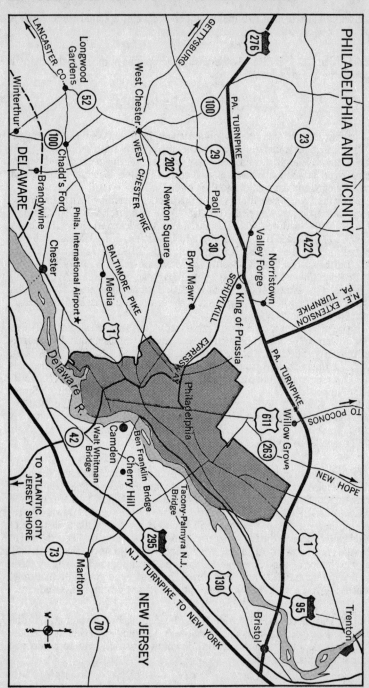

From the north, I-95 leads into the northeastern section of the city, with several exits into midtown, including Route 30 (Vine Street), which takes you into the historic district. Interstate 95 is also the best route from points south. From the east, take I-295 or the New Jersey Turnpike, connecting to I-676, over the Benjamin Franklin Bridge, into the heart of the city. From the west, you can approach via Route 30 or I-76 to the Schuylkill Expressway into the city center. Traffic can be heavy and congested, particularly at morning or evening rush hours. If you are not familiar with the city, try to arrive in the late morning or early afternoon.

3. Overview of the City

Philadelphia is laid out according to a grid system, with the Delaware River on the east and the Schuykill River (pronounced: Scool-kill) cutting through its western side. Most north-south streets, beginning with **Front** (1st Street) on the Delaware, are numbered; while east-west streets are named. **Broad Street,** which is the main artery in the north-south direction, is an exception, and is the equivalent of 14th Street. **Market** is the principal east-west artery, with north-south designations fanning out from this point.

All downtown north-south streets have alternate one-way traffic, with the exception of Broad, which has three lanes in each direction. Market Street is one-way eastbound between 20th and 15th Streets. Westbound motorists should use **John F. Kennedy Boulevard** above 15th Street. Otherwise, traffic patterns are orderly, except that **Chestnut Street** is closed to all traffic other than buses between 8th and 18th Streets, so Chestnut is best avoided as a cross-town artery.

When William Penn designed his "greene countrie towne" over 300 years ago, he created an urban plan that has survived the centuries. The cornerstones of his layout, five park-like squares, still exist today, although the original names have been changed. They are **Penn** (formerly Centre) **Square; Washington** (originally Southeast) **Square; Franklin** (once Northeast) **Square; Logan** (first named Northwest) **Square** or more commonly called **Logan Circle** today; and **Rittenhouse** (which started as Southwest) **Square.** Once you get to know the squares and their surrounding areas, you have a firm grasp on the essence of Philadelphia today.

The main regions of prime interest to visitors are as follows:

THE OLD CITY: Extending east of Franklin and Washington Squares to the Delaware River, the Old City is where Philadelphia began, a cobblestone street area now known as the **Independence National Historical Park.** Sometimes called America's most historic square mile, this is the home of the **Liberty Bell,** the symbol of our country's freedom; **Independence Hall,** where the Declaration of Independence was adopted and the Constitution of the U.S. was written; and dozens of other landmark buildings. Nearby, you can also visit **Penn's Landing,** the spot on the Delaware where William Penn first pulled up his ship to dock; as well as **Society Hill,** a charming old neighborhood of brick walks and Federal houses; and the adjacent Soho-style area of **South Street,** which attracts visitors to its many trendy restaurants, art galleries, and boutiques.

THE CITY HALL AREA: Right in the heart of midtown where Broad Street crosses Market Street is **City Hall.** Standing in the space that was once Centre Square and now known as Penn Square because of the giant statue of William Penn that dominates the top of City Hall, this urban government complex is the focal point of the city's downtown area. Most businesses are located within five

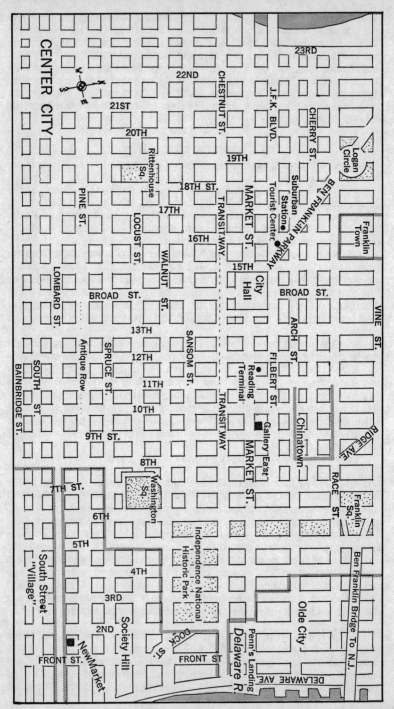

or six blocks of here, as are the leading theaters, department stores, shops, hotels, and restaurants.

RITTENHOUSE SQUARE: A patch of greenery in the city's southwest corner, this tree-lined square is rimmed by a fashionable residential enclave, with graceful brick town houses, chic shops, and stylish restaurants.

LOGAN SQUARE: Now usually called **Logan Circle** because its shape has changed over the years, this parklet is in the center of the Benjamin Franklin Parkway, the wide, shady, and flag-lined boulevard usually compared to the Champs-Élysées. This roadway links City Hall to **Fairmount Park** and is surrounded by many of the town's foremost museums, making Logan Circle the cultural corner of Philadelphia. The adjacent Fairmount Park is full of beautiful old houses, gardens, monuments, and acres of recreational facilities.

Depending on your time, this may be all of Philadelphia that you will see. However, if you are interested in the city's major educational institutions, then you'll want to cross the Schuylkill River westward from Market Street or John F. Kennedy Boulevard. Both the **University of Pennsylvania** and **Drexel University** are located here, and farther westward you'll find a cluster of colleges and top-name schools, ranging from **Villanova** to **Thomas Jefferson University.** This side of the river also holds the city's **Civic Center** and the main rail terminal, **30th Street Station.**

Other sections of the city that are of interest include **Chestnut Hill,** to the northwest, an elite village of revitalized and restored Colonial and 19th-century homes and storefronts; **Germantown,** founded in 1685, and today an area containing some of Philadelphia's oldest houses and a main street that has been declared a National Historic Landmark.

One of the most colorful ethnic neighborhoods is **South Philadelphia,** the part of the city that produced Mario Lanza, Joey Bishop, Fabian, Frankie Avalon, Bobby Rydell, and Chubby Checker. Today it is known for its open-air Italian Market, boccie courts, and a parade of pasta restaurants along Passyunk Avenue. Another popular tourist mecca is Philadelphia's **Chinatown,** located in a compact three-block section of midtown, just two blocks northwest of Independence Mall, and three blocks north and east of City Hall. It may be small, but this Oriental enclave is chock full of fine restaurants and shops.

4. Getting Around Philadelphia

PUBLIC TRANSPORT: For the most part, Philadelphia is an easy city to get around by walking. However, from the Delaware River to the Schuylkill, it is about a three-mile spread, so you will probably want to take some form of public transport to get from section to section.

Buses: The **Southeastern Pennsylvania Transportation Authority (SEPTA)** operates a large fleet of buses throughout the city-center area. The price on most routes is $1.25 and exact change is required.

In addition, of particular interest to visitors, SEPTA runs a **Mid-City Loop Bus,** from 17th Street to 5th Street, with stops on Chestnut Street and Market Street. Operating from 9 a.m. to 6 p.m., this bus also runs late on Wednesday evenings when stores are open, but not on Sunday; the fare is 60¢ and exact change is required. There is also **subway service,** running in an east-west pattern along Market Street and in a north-south direction on Broad Street, but, if you are only staying a short time, it is probably better to opt for the above-ground buses. For complete fare and schedule information, call SEPTA (tel. 574-7800).

Taxis: There are numerous taxis operating throughout the city. You can hail available cabs as they cruise the street or go to areas where taxis frequently line up, such as hotels and the midcity suburban train station at 16th Street and John F. Kennedy Boulevard (across from the Visitor Center). If you prefer to order a cab by phone, call **Liberty Cab** (tel. 365-8414), **Metro Fleet** (tel. 423-3333), **Quality City Cab** (tel. 728-8000), **United Cab** (tel. 625-2881), or **Yellow Cab Co.** (tel. 922-8400).

CAR RENTALS: In addition to the car-rental desks at the airport, you can hire a car at the following downtown locations: **Avis,** 30th Street Station and 1909 Market St. (for either call toll-free 800/331-1212); **Budget,** 21st and Market Streets (tel. 492-9400); **Hertz,** 30th Street Station and 31 S. 19th St. (for either call toll-free 800/654-3131); **National,** 107 Chestnut St. (tel. 925-7723) and 1714 John F. Kennedy Blvd. (tel. 567-1760); and **Thrifty,** 501 N. 22 St. (tel. 564-2220) and 6401 Passyunk Ave. (tel. 365-3900).

PARKING: Although some limited on-street parking is available, particularly after 6 p.m., it is best to park in one of the downtown parking lots or garages. Rates average $2 to $3 an hour, with a maximum of $6 to $8 at most places. In the evenings, many restaurants provide their patrons with free or reduced-rate parking, in conjunction with a neighborhood lot or garage; you should inquire if such arrangements apply when you are making a reservation. It is probably best not to bring your car to this city at all, unless you intend to use it while in Philadelphia. If you do have your car, you can save money by staying at one of the motor-inn hotels that offer ample free parking to guests, such as the Quality Inn—Center City, the Sheraton University City, or Dunfey City Line.

TROLLEY BUSES: During the summer months (May through October), Victorian-style trolley buses take visitors on narrated tours of Fairmount Park. These trips allow on-off boarding, giving you a chance to take time and explore a certain site, and then reboard another trolley at a later time. You can get off at every attraction, or stay on board for the whole 90-minute trip, seeing the sights from your seat. The trolley fare does not include admission charges but does provide discounts at most attractions. This trip operates Wednesday through Sunday, departing every 20 minutes from the Visitors Center, 16th Street and John F. Kennedy Boulevard, between 10 a.m. and 4:40 p.m. In addition, trolleys also depart from the Independence Park Visitor Center, 3rd and Chestnut Streets, from 11 a.m. to 5 p.m. Round-trip fare on either route is $2 for adults and 50¢ for children.

In the December through March period, these trolleys are used for narrated "Town and Country" sightseeing tours, covering the highlights of the Park plus downtown landmarks. Operating from the Visitors Center at 16th Street and John F. Kennedy Boulevard only, these trips last for 2½ hours and depart daily at 10 a.m. and 2 p.m. The fare is $5.50 for adults and $4.50 for children and includes admission to the attractions visited. For further information, inquire at the Visitors Center or call 879-4044.

BUS TOURS: **Romano's Grayline Tours,** 1065 Belvoir Rd., Norristown (tel. 569-3666), offers seven different sightseeing tours of the Philadelphia area, ranging from a three-hour tour of the historic district to an all-day seven-hour excursion around the city with a visit to Valley Forge. Tours are scheduled throughout the year and range from $8.25 to $16.00 for adults and $4.50 to $8.25 for children under 12. In addition, there are usually summer day-trips to Pennsylvania Dutch Country and other areas outside the city. All tours depart from the Visitors Center at 16th Street and John F. Kennedy Boulevard.

WALKING TOURS: To explore the four-block historic district at your own pace with the benefit of a prerecorded commentary, you can rent an AudioWalk and Tour cassette player and tape. Available every day year-round, the narration describes each attraction as you walk from site to site; an illustrated souvenir map also comes with the tape. You can rent the lightweight player and cassette (adaptable for one to eight listeners) for a maximum of three hours from the **AudioWalk and Tour** desk at the Norman Rockwell Museum, 6th and Sansom Streets (tel. 925-1234), located across from Independence Square. The charge is $8 for one person; $12 for two, or $16 for three to eight people. If you prefer to purchase the tape and use your own cassette recorder, the cost is $10.95. CC's accepted: AE, D, MC, and V.

CANDLELIGHT STROLLS: From May through October, you can join in group candlelight walks of the historic district, organized by **Centipede Tours, Inc.,** 1515 Walnut St. (tel. 735-3123). Led by guides in Colonial costume, these walks cover the Old City area (Wednesday and Friday) and Society Hill (Saturday). All tours begin at 6:30 p.m. from the City Tavern, 2nd and Walnut Streets. The charge is $4 for adults and $3.50 for children.

HORSE-AND-CARRIAGE TOURS: To get the feel of Philadelphia as it was in days of old, you may wish to try a narrated **horse-drawn carriage ride.** Operated daily, these tours begin at Independence National Historical Park, 5th and Chestnut Streets, from 9 a.m. to 6 p.m., with later hours in the summer months. The fares range from $10 for 15 minutes to $20 for a half-hour (maximum of four people per carriage). Reservations are not necessary, but if you wish further information, call 923-8516.

BOATING TOURS: The Philadelphia skyline and harbor sights can best be seen from the *Spirit of Philadelphia,* docked at Penn's Landing, off Delaware Avenue at Lombard Street (tel. 923-1419). This is a new 600-passenger ship, air-conditioned and fully carpeted, with two enclosed decks and two open-air decks, offering sightseeing cruises year-round. The trips, which require reservations, run as follows:

● Lunch cruises with buffet and entertainment, Monday through Saturday, from noon to 2 p.m.; the charge is $12.95 for adults, $7.95 for children. On Sunday, a brunch cruise is operated from 1 to 3 p.m., at a cost of $14.95 for adults and $8.95 for children.

● Evening dinner cruises, featuring buffet, dancing, and entertainment, are scheduled daily from 7 p.m. to 10 p.m. The cost is $20.95 per person on weekdays and $23.95 on weekends.

● Moonlight party cruises, with dancing, snacks, and cocktail service, go out on Wednesday from 11 p.m. to 12:30 a.m., and on Friday and Saturday from 11 p.m. to 1:30 a.m. The $10-per-person price includes the food but not the drinks.

AIR TOURS: **Fleet Helicopter Services,** Delaware Avenue and Poplar Street (tel. 282-4100), operates 12- to 15-minute sightseeing excursions over Philadelphia and the Delaware Valley year-round, priced at $29.50 per passenger. Flights normally take off on the hour on weekends and per demand on weekdays. Reservations are necessary in all cases. CC's accepted: MC and V.

5. Where to Stay

Like most big cities, Philadelphia's lodgings are not cheap, especially during midweek, when business traffic is heavy. In recent years, most of the city's prime properties have undergone major renovations, making them more attractive (and more costly) for the average traveler. In addition, new deluxe hotels, like the Four Seasons and the Sheraton Society Hill, have been built in the last five years, raising the average room tab to well over $100 a night.

Some of the more modest hotels, like the Philadelphia Center or the Penn Center Inn, did offer relatively moderate rates, but competition from the grander properties caused them to close their doors in 1986 and 1987. The trend and the demand is for top quality at top prices.

However, do not despair. If you can plan to come over a weekend, you'll find that almost all of Philadelphia's hotels offer very attractive weekend packages, with savings from 30% to 50% or more off normal weekday tariffs. These packages, and their ingredients, do change often, though, so be sure to check in advance for the best deal. The Philadelphia Convention and Visitors Bureau makes it easy for you by publishing a brochure describing all of the hotel packages with prices. Be sure to ask for a copy when requesting travel data (see "Visitor Information" above).

To help you acquaint yourself with the exact locations of the hotels listed below, we are grouping them according to the main sightseeing areas of the city.

HISTORIC DISTRICT AND SOCIETY HILL: The city's newest luxury full-service hotel (opened 1986) is the **Sheraton Society Hill,** 1 Dock St., Philadelphia, PA 19106 (tel. 215/238-6000 or toll-free 800/325-3535), situated at the corner of 2nd and Walnut Streets, just a block away from the Delaware River and four blocks from Independence Hall. With a brick town-house-like façade, this 365-room hotel is designed to reflect the character of the residential streets of Society Hill. The entrance gives a hint of contemporary style, with a four-story atrium lobby, but the overall theme conveys the ambience of a Colonial courtyard. Each guest room features an Early American décor and such standard modern amenities as color cable TV, air conditioning, radio, and direct-dial phone. Doubles range from $142 to $186. Guest facilities include a full-time concierge service, an indoor skylit swimming pool, a health club with exercise room, a cocktail lounge, a video nightclub, a courtyard-style café, and a gourmet dining room, Americus, which serves lunch from 11:30 a.m. to 2 p.m. and dinner from 5 to 10 p.m., with prices in the moderate to expensive range. All major CC's accepted.

If you want to stay in the midst of the historic section, the best choice is the **Holiday Inn—Independence Mall,** 400 Arch St., Philadelphia, PA 19106 (tel. 215/923-8660 or toll-free 800/THE BELL). Situated on the corner of 4th Street, this modern eight-story hotel is across the street from the Friends Meeting House and the U.S. Mint, and within two blocks of the Liberty Bell, Betsy Ross's house, and most of the other top attractions. In keeping with the aura of this historic neighborhood, the lobby has a permanent American Revolutionary Navy exhibit, including 40 specially commissioned paintings. The 364 guest rooms also feature a Colonial theme in furnishings and draperies, although they are also equipped with standard modern conveniences such as color cable TV, direct-dial phone, and air conditioning, plus a choice of two double beds or a king-size bed. Double-occupancy rates range from $82 to $97, and king-leisure rooms from $97 to $103. Guest services include a garage, a lounge with nightly entertainment, a rooftop swimming pool, an all-day café, and Benjamin's, a fine restaurant featuring regional American cuisine in the moderate to expensive range. Lunch is served from 11:30 a.m. to 2 p.m. and dinner from 5:30 to 10 p.m. All major CC's are accepted.

CITY HALL AND MAIN BUSINESS AREA: Three blocks south of City Hall and Wanamaker's is the **Hershey Philadelphia Hotel**, Broad and Locust Streets, Philadelphia, PA 19107 (tel. 215/893-1600 or toll-free 800/533-3131), in the heart of the city's business and shopping districts. If you are interested in the performing arts, this hotel is also within a block of the Academy of Music and the Shubert and Locust Street Theatres. A modern 25-story tower, the Hershey has a four-story atrium lobby and a modern airy look. Each of the 450 rooms offers air conditioning, color cable TV, clock radio, and direct-dial phone in a wide-windowed contemporary setting. Doubles range from $115 to $150. Facilities include an indoor swimming pool, outdoor sundeck, health club, sauna, whirl-pool, and two lounges with entertainment. On the mezzanine level, there is an all-day eatery, the Café Academie, and Sarah's, an art deco restaurant, featuring New Orleans cuisine with a fixed-price dinner priced at $21.95, or an à la carte menu offering entrees from $14.95 to $18.95. The restaurant serves dinner only on Monday through Thursday from 5:30 to 10 p.m. and until 11 p.m. on Friday and Saturday. All major CC's are accepted.

Less than two blocks from the Hershey is the **Holiday Inn—Midtown,** 1305 Walnut St., Philadelphia, PA 19107 (tel. 215/735-9300 or toll-free 800/HOLIDAY), also in this Center City milieu, yet still just seven blocks from Independence Park. A modern high-rise building, this hotel offers 162 contemporary-style rooms, decorated in warm autumn tones and featuring standard amenities as well as free in-room movies and a choice of two double beds or a king-size bed; smoking or non-smoking rooms. Doubles range from $80 to $90, and king-leisure rooms from $92 to $96. Facilities include an outdoor pool, a valet garage, and an all-day moderately priced restaurant, Recipes, that features prime ribs as its specialty. All major CC's are accepted.

Another fairly new (opened 1986) lodging facility is the **Quality Inn—Downtown Suites,** 1010 Race St., Philadelphia, PA 19107 (tel. 215/922-1730 or toll-free 800/228-5151), situated right in the middle of Chinatown. Housed in a converted firehouse, this hotel has 96 all-suite accommodations, offering either three rooms (bedroom, bath, and kitchenette), or four rooms (bedroom, bath, kitchen, and parlor/meeting room). All rooms feature Oriental décor, two telephones, two TVs, free movies, king-size beds, and sofa hide-a-beds (in the larger suites). Double-occupancy rates range from $89 to $109, which includes complimentary continental breakfast. Guests can also enjoy a lounge, health club, sauna, game room, giftshop, and an in-house Chinese restaurant, the Lotus Inn, open daily from noon to 3 p.m. for lunch, and 5 to 11 p.m. for dinner. All major CC's are accepted.

In case you are looking for the landmark Bellevue Stratford Hotel, at the corner of Broad and Walnut Streets, it closed in 1986. The building is now being totally renovated, to transform it into a retail, office, and luxury hotel complex, scheduled to open in mid-1988. The hotel will be managed by Cunard.

LOGAN CIRCLE, MUSEUM ROW, AND FAIRMOUNT PARK: Although relatively young (opened in 1983), the **Four Seasons,** One Logan Square, Philadelphia, PA 19103 (tel. 215/963-1500 or toll-free 800/268-6282), is a splendid example of ageless hotel grandeur. Ideally located overlooking the fountains and sculptures of Logan Square and near the Philadelphia Museum of Art and the gold-domed Cathedral of Sts. Peter and Paul, this modern U-shaped structure has an eight-story façade of Rockville beige granite. The interior is a showcase of imported Italian marble, hand-sewn wool carpeting and Oriental rugs, one-of-a-kind antiques, and light blond woods. There are 377 guest rooms (including non-smoking units), each furnished with reproductions of Philadelphia's Federal period, a mini-bar, and the standard appointments; you'll find an extra telephone in the bathroom, plus thick terry robes and hair dryers. Doubles range from $170 to $210, including little extras like complimentary shoeshines while you sleep. Guest facilities include a complete health spa on the hotel's lower level, consisting of an indoor pool, a spa, massage rooms, and a hair salon; there is also valet parking and a full-time concierge. In addition, the Swann Café serves three meals a day plus afternoon tea. The main restaurant, the Fountain, offers gourmet menus that change daily, with lunch entrees priced from $8 to $12; and dinner at a fixed price of $32.50, including soup, salad, entree, cheese, and dessert. Entrees often include such dishes as rockfish filet; sautéed pork medallions; or sea scallops with red pepper sauce. Lunch is served from 11:30 a.m. to 2:30 p.m. and dinner from 6 to 10:30 p.m. This restaurant also offers daily choices of "alternative cuisine," emphasizing low calories, low fats, low cholesterol, and low sodium. All major CC's are accepted.

Across the street is **The Palace,** 18th Street at Benjamin Franklin Parkway, Philadelphia, PA 19103 (tel. 215/963-2222 or toll-free 800/223-5672), a member of the Trust House–Forte chain. This modern 28-story hotel is a circular tower of 285 suites, many of which have balconies or terraces overlooking the city. The majority of guest units, either one- or two-bedroom suites with living rooms, are furnished in 18th-century English reproductions, carved French beds, antiques, mirrored wet bars, refrigerators, and two color cable TVs with AM/FM radios. The double rates for a one-bedroom suite range from $130 to $160, and a two-bedroom suite from $185; a limited number of studio-style junior suites are also available from $110 a night. In addition, there is a full-time concierge, valet service, outdoor pool and sundeck, a pay parking garage, and an elegant restaurant, the Café Royale, featuring French country cuisine on a fixed-price basis in the expensive bracket. Restaurant hours are noon to 2 p.m. for lunch and from 6 to 10 p.m. for dinner. All major CC's are accepted.

The city's largest hotel is currently the 800-room **Wyndham Franklin Plaza,** Two Franklin Plaza, 17th and Race Streets, Philadelphia, PA 19103 (tel. 215/448-2000 or toll-free 800/448-2111), just off Logan Circle. Built in the early 1980s, this modern tower has a bright and airy four-story lobby with a 70-foot glass atrium, enlivened with leafy potted trees and flowers. The guest rooms are equipped with all the expected deluxe features, including floor-to-ceiling mirrors, a color cable TV with radio, a direct-dial phone, and wide-windowed views of the city. Doubles range from $115 to $135. The hotel maintains a first-class sports center, where you can undergo a stress test and follow with supervised exercise. The center also includes an indoor swimming pool, three squash courts, three racquetball courts, one tennis court, and a one-eighth-mile jogging track. Other facilities include a pay parking garage, the Horizons rooftop lounge with dancing and entertainment, a sidewalk café and coffeeshop, the lobby-level moderately priced Terrace Restaurant, and the clubby enclave, Between Friends, for upscale dining. Lunch is available from 11:30 a.m. to 2:30 p.m. and dinner from 5:30 to 10:30 p.m. All major CC's are accepted.

If you bring your car, one of the best values in town is the **Quality Inn—Center City,** 501 N. 22nd St., Philadelphia, PA 19130 (tel. 215/568-8300 or toll-free 800/228-5151), which provides free outdoor parking for all its guests.

Located one block north of the Benjamin Franklin Parkway, at the entrance to Fairmount Park, this modern four-story hotel is in the heart of the museum district, four blocks from Logan Circle. Formerly an EconoLodge, it has been renovated and refurbished under the Quality Inn banner. Offering a choice of two double beds or a king-size bed, the 283 rooms are individually furnished in bright contemporary colors and feature color cable TV, air conditioning, and direct-dial phone. Double-occupancy rates range from $52 to $72. Guest facilities include an outdoor pool, lounge with live entertainment, and Hemingway's, a moderately priced all-day restaurant with outdoor seating in the summer. In addition, if you just feel like watching TV and ordering a pizza, room service will oblige with a 12-inch round pie delivered to your door (for $3.75). All major CC's are accepted.

RITTENHOUSE SQUARE AREA: Right on the city's most fashionable square is the **The Barclay,** 237 S. 18th St., Rittenhouse Square East, Philadelphia, PA 19103 (tel. 215/545-0300 or toll-free 800/421-6662), now part-condo and part-hotel. An old-world aura will greet you as you step inside the long lobby with its crystal chandeliers, marble floors, classic Oriental rugs, and vases with handmade silk flowers. A similar atmosphere reigns in the 240 guest rooms, mostly furnished with antique reproductions, including canopy beds, four-posters, antique armoires, and chests. More than half the rooms also have refrigerators and all have the standard modern equipment such as color cable TV, air conditioning, and direct-dial phones. Doubles range from $115 to $155. Other facilities include valet parking, a convivial piano-bar lounge, and an elegant restaurant, Le Beau Lieu, known for its haute cuisine. The menu here, with dinner entrees priced in the $17.95 to $19.95 range, includes such specialties as whole Dover sole, braised rabbit, saumon aux champagnes, and lobster Thermidor. Light entrees at lunch fall into the $6.95 to $12.95 price bracket. Lunch is served from noon to 2:30 p.m. and dinner from 6 to 10:30 p.m. daily. All major CC's are accepted.

Just one block east of the square is **The Warwick,** 1701 Locust St. at 17th Street, Philadelphia, PA 19103 (tel. 215/735-6000 or toll-free 800/523-4210), another old-world gem with an English Renaissance décor. The focal point of the antique-filled lobby is a carved Tudor-style marble fireplace, surrounded by a rich array of Oriental rugs. The 180 guest rooms, however, are more modern in style, with bright floral-print furnishings in contemporary designs. A choice of double-, queen-, or king-size beds is offered, and each unit is outfitted with such amenities as a bedside AM/FM radio, a direct-dial telephone, and color cable TV with complimentary movies. Doubles start at $110. Guest services include a full-time concierge desk in the European tradition, a 24-hour café called The Brasserie, and a chic nightspot, the élan Club, open from 4:30 p.m. to 2 a.m. for dining and dancing. There is also a pay parking garage adjacent to the hotel. All major CC's are accepted.

Two blocks northeast of the square is **The Latham,** 17th and Walnut Streets, Philadelphia, PA 19103 (tel. 215/563-7474 or toll-free 800/228-0808), a small and personalized 141-room hotel. Originally an apartment building (for 60 years), this old-world property has been a hotel for the last 20 years. The guest rooms vary in size, but feature handsome reproduction furniture, many with Louis XIV–style writing tables and upholstered armchairs; about a third of the rooms have refrigerators. Doubles range from $130 to $160. Facilities include a lounge with piano bar and a full-service restaurant, Bogart's, specializing in beef and seafood at mostly moderate prices, for lunch (11:30 a.m. to 2:30 p.m.) and dinner (5:30 to 10:30 p.m.). Major CC's are accepted.

Almost midway between Rittenhouse Square and Logan Circle is the **Holi-**

day Inn—Center City, 1800 Market St., Philadelphia, PA 19103 (tel. 215/561-7500 or toll-free 800/HOLIDAY), a handy up-to-date property built in 1971 and completely renovated in 1986. There are 162 units, each offering either two double beds or a king-size bed, with the usual amenities of air conditioning, color cable TV, and a direct-dial phone. Double-occupancy rates range from $77 to $97. Facilities include valet parking, a cocktail lounge, and a moderately priced restaurant, Coffey's. Open all day, this contemporary eatery features stir-fry dishes, Cajun-style blackened meats, and seafoods. All major CC's are accepted.

WEST OF THE SCHUYLKILL RIVER—UNIVERSITY AREA AND THE CITY LINE: The Sheraton University City, 36th and Chestnut Streets, Philadelphia, PA 19104 (tel. 215/387-8000 or toll-free 800/325-3535), is located across the street from the University of Pennsylvania campus, three blocks from Drexel University, and just over six blocks from the Amtrak Station. It is also within walking distance of the city's Civic Center, where many conventions are held, and six miles from the airport. A modern 20-story property, it has 377 rooms, many with views of the Philadelphia skyline. Each unit is outfitted with the usual comforts—air conditioning, a direct-dial phone, color TV, and a hi-fi radio with digital alarm clock. Doubles range from $85 to $98. Facilities include free parking, a heated outdoor swimming pool, a gourmet ice-cream parlor, and Smart Alex, an early-western-theme saloon/restaurant with an eclectic menu of regional American cuisine in the moderate range. Lunch is served from 11:30 a.m. to 2:30 p.m. and dinner from 5:30 to 10:30 p.m. All major CC's are accepted.

A favorite with businesspeople is the Dunfey City Line, City Line Avenue and Monument Road, Philadelphia, PA 19131 (tel. 215/667-0200 or toll-free 800/THE-OMNI), located at the junction of the Schuylkill Expressway (I-76) and Route 1 on the city's western edge. Formerly the Philadelphia Marriott, this is a rambling 705-room motor inn with ten individual wings from two- to five-stories high, all clustered around two outdoor swimming pools and an indoor/outdoor pool. Doubles start at $95. In addition to the trio of pools, facilities include a Polynesian restaurant, two lounges with entertainment and dancing, a 24-hour coffeeshop, free parking, a jogging course, two platform tennis courts, a game room, a barbershop, and a mini-mall of giftshops. All major CC's are accepted.

6. Where to Dine

For many years, Philadelphia cuisine was synonymous with the cheese steak. In case you have never indulged, this is an oversized sandwich, usually on a hot-dog bun, stuffed with quickly cooked lean beef slices, and smothered with fried onions and melted cheese (generally of the Cheez Whiz variety). According to your taste, you can also garnish your cheese steak with hot peppers, mushrooms, tomato sauce, provolone, or other cheeses.

While cheese steaks will always be a Philadelphia tradition, there has also been a happy renaissance in fine dining in this city within the last 15 years. Spurred on by a midtown Restaurant School and some of its more eager and talented alumni, the number of restaurants in and around Philadelphia has now mushroomed to over 500, with more on the way. Housed in Colonial row houses, converted storefronts, on rooftops, or by the harbor, the restaurants of Philadelphia offer a great variety of settings and menus. You'll find traditional seafood houses, restored Colonial taverns, ethnic enclaves, haute and nouvelle cuisine dining rooms, and a diversity of regional eateries, to name a few. Like the hotels, the Philadelphia restaurants are spread throughout the city, so we'll group them by area and at the same time try to give you a cross-section of menu types and price ranges.

Always keep in mind that parking can be a problem. Spaces on the street are hard to come by, and garages and parking lots can be costly. However, many restaurants offer free or reduced-rate parking, especially in the evening. Be sure to inquire about this when you make a reservation (you could save $5 to $10). If a restaurant does not offer parking facilities, then it might be cheaper and more convenient to leave your car wherever it is and use a taxi or public transportation.

HISTORIC OLD CITY AND SOUTH STREET: The culinary delights of this area range from Colonial taverns and contemporary cafes to cheese-steak houses. You'll also find one of America's great seafood restaurants and an inviting blend of ethnic dining spots.

The Top Choices

Most everyone has heard of the **Old Original Bookbinder's,** 125 Walnut St. (tel. 925-7027), a legend in Philadelphia dining and the source for some confusion with its midtown rival, which is simply called Bookbinder's. The story is that the Bookbinder family opened their first seafood restaurant at this location in 1865; when they sold it to the Taxin family in the 1930s, the Bookbinder name was retained as part of the deal. To complicate matters, the Bookbinder family then opened a new restaurant on 15th Street, and also called it by their own family name. This particular "original" restaurant, located between 1st and 2nd Streets, is not only older, but larger and is handy to the Independence Park sights. It is also very expensive. As you walk in, you'll see walls lined with photographs of the celebrities who have dined here, plus displays of antique model fire engines, a preview of the various memorabilia hung throughout the restaurant's four dining areas. The lunch choices change daily, but the price range is normally $4.95 to $8.95 for sandwiches and $10.95 to $22.95 for seafood entrees (such as lobster pot pie, New England cod cakes, or stuffed yellowtail flounder) and steaks, with whole lobsters still higher in price. The huge dinner menu offers entrees in the $16.95 to $40.95 bracket, with most costing between $20 and $30. Seafood lovers think they are in heaven as they savor the lobsters of all sizes (up to four pounds), stone crabs, Dungeness crab, Columbia River king salmon, Dover sole, Scottish finnan haddie, or New England scrod, to name just a few of the selections. For meat eaters, there are generous steaks and veal dishes. All main courses include vegetable and potato. Lunch is served Monday through Friday, from noon to 2:45 p.m.; dinner Monday through Friday, from 2:45 to 10 p.m., on Saturday from noon to 10 p.m., and on Sunday from 1 to 9 p.m. (from 3 p.m. on Sundays in July and August). All major CC's are accepted.

Less than a block away a totally different scene prevails at the **City Tavern,** 2nd and Walnut Streets (tel. 923-6059). The first tavern on this site was built in 1773 and served as a rendezvous point during the days when our forefathers drafted the Constitution. Although the original structure unfortunately was demolished in 1854, the National Park Service faithfully reconstructed it and opened the site as a restaurant in 1975. Great care has been taken to re-create an authentic Colonial atmosphere with a costumed staff and a décor that includes flickering hurricane lamps, open fireplaces, and harpsichord music. Even the recipes hearken back to 18th-century tastes. Lunch, priced from $3.50 to $8.50, features salads (such as colonial salamagundy), sandwiches, and light entrees (like turkey rarebit, or colonial pasty, a combination of meats and herbs in a pastry shell). The dinner entrees, priced from $12.50 to $21, with most under the $15 mark, focus on such choices as sautéed Muscovy duck with elderberry ginger sauce, pheasant in a sauce of truffles and port, Cornish hen with cranberry-orange relish, fricassee of rabbit, salmon stew, lobster pie, and charbroiled steaks. Open daily, lunch is served from 11:30 a.m. to 3:30 p.m. and dinner from 5 to 10 p.m. CC's accepted: AE, MC, and V.

Moderately Priced Dining

The **Head House Inn,** 2nd and Pine Streets (tel. 925-6718), dates back to 1771, although it has only been a restaurant in its present format for the last 20 years. Situated opposite the New Market shopping area, this small and cozy inn has an eclectic décor of church-pew-style booths, cherry and pine tables, solid brass chandeliers, planked floors, 200-year-old oak beams, and chestnut-paneled walls that were once a part of a Colonial barn in Virginia. All the paint colors on the walls are authentic old Philadelphia shades. Lunch, priced from $4.25 to $6.75, offers such choices as omelets, ploughman's cheeseboard and fruit, burgers, sandwiches, crêpes, pasta, and smoked-salmon platters. The price range at dinner is $9.95 to $25.95, with most entrees under $15; the selections include veal Oscar, chicken Cordon Bleu, scallops Dijonnaise, lobster tails, and beef tenderloin en brochette. All main courses come with two vegetables. Lunch is served Monday through Saturday from 11:30 a.m. to 4 p.m.; and dinner Sunday through Thursday from 5 to 10 p.m., and Friday and Saturday until midnight. On Sunday you can also come here for brunch from 11:30 a.m. to 4 p.m. All major CC's are accepted.

Mesquite-grilled seafoods are the specialty of the **Philadelphia Fish & Company Restaurant,** 207 Chestnut St. (tel. 625-8605), located in the historic area between 2nd and 3rd Streets, opposite the Independence Park Visitor Center. This modern eatery offers a simple contemporary setting decorated with framed American wine posters, plus additional seating in the summer on an outside front deck. Lunch primarily features light entrees, sandwiches, and salads, mostly in the under-$5 category. Dinner, priced from $9.95 to $14.95, offers entrees cooked over Texas woods and charcoal, with such choices as mahi-mahi, mako shark, Atlantic bluefish, mixed seafood grill, blackened redfish or bluefish, and Mississippi catfish. All main courses come with appropriate vegetable, potato, or rice, and warm sourdough bread. Lunch is served Monday through Friday from 11 a.m. to 4 p.m., and dinner from 4 to 10 p.m.; on Saturday the hours are noon to 4 p.m. for lunch and 4 to 11 p.m. for dinner, and on Sunday for dinner from 3 to 9 p.m. All major CC's accepted.

Another 20th-century outpost in the historic area is **City Bites,** 212 Walnut St. (tel. 238-1300), a trendy evening spot known for its eclectic contemporary décor and cuisine. Located between 2nd and 3rd Streets, this restaurant is decorated with brightly colored walls and imaginative art, a fitting backdrop that sets the tone for the food. Entree prices range from $5.95 to $13.95 and include hickory-grilled steaks and fish; marinated double breast of chicken with tamari-orange sauce; baby Coho salmon stuffed with brie and spinach; Yucatán white and Louisiana hot sausages; spicy Thai curry of lamb, eggplant, and pecans; and Cajun prime ribs. You can also get homemade meatloaf, deep-dish pizzas, spicy spring rolls, stir-fry dishes, burgers, and innovative omelets (such as smoked salmon with chives). Open Monday through Thursday from 5:30 to 11 p.m., Friday and Saturday from 5:30 p.m. to midnight, and Sunday from 2:30 to 11 p.m. There is also live music Wednesday through Saturday from 10 p.m. to 2 a.m. All major CC's accepted.

On a strip known for dozens of fine restaurants, **Primavera,** 146 South St. (tel. 925-7832), is one of the leaders for fine Italian cuisine. Occupying the first floor of a restored row house between 1st and 2nd Streets, this small dining room serves dinner only, in the $9.95 to $14.95 range for entrees, and $6.50 to $7.25 for homemade pastas. The house specialty is zuppa di pesce for two (clams, mussels, lobster, and filet of fish), but equally good are the scampi, saltimbocca, and salmon in a light cream sauce with tomatoes, yellow squash, and zucchini. All main courses come with two vegetables. Open Tuesday through Thursday from 5:30 to 10:30 p.m., Friday and Saturday until 11 p.m., and Sunday until 9:30 p.m. No CC's are accepted.

Between 3rd and 4th Streets, you'll find **Café Nola,** 328 South St. (tel. 627-2590), a restaurant that manages to blend Cajun-Créole cooking with an Italian flair, in an art deco setting. Lunch focuses on soups, stews, gumbos, and salads, priced mostly in the $3.95 to $6.95 range. In the evening, you'll pay from $12.95 to $18.95 for entrees, although most are pegged under $15. The menu includes jambalaya, rock shrimp étouffée, sesame catfish tenders, blackened prime ribs, crabmeat ravioli, blackened chicken with Créole spaghetti, roast duck and figs poached in champagne, and (Friday only) bouillabaisse-style seafood gumbo. Lunch is served from noon to 3 p.m. and dinner from 5 p.m. to midnight. All major CC's accepted.

The freshest of seafoods at moderate prices is the keystone to success at **Di Nardo's Famous Crabs,** 312 Race St. (tel. 925-5115), located in an old neighborhood between 3rd and 4th Streets and within a block of Elfreth's Alley or the Betsy Ross House. Although this restaurant has been flying in fresh seafood daily for over 15 years, it is a relatively young enterprise compared to its sistereatery of the same name in Wilmington (started in 1938). Lunch consists mainly of shellfish salads, pastas, platters, and crab and fish sandwiches, in the $2.95 to $6.95 price bracket. Crab is king at dinner, with a choice of steamed crabs, crab claws, crab imperial, sautéed crabmeat, and soft-shell crabs. If you don't mind using a mallet and a little effort, the best way to eat your crab is to crack open the hard-shell variety yourself, and pick, crack, pick. If crab is not your passion, then you can also get all types of shellfish, rainbow trout, flounder, cioppino (Italian seafood stew), and steaks. Dinner entrees range from $6.95 to $14.95. Lunch is served Monday through Friday from 11 a.m. to 3 p.m., and dinner from 5 to 11 p.m.; on Saturday, open for dinner only from 5 to 11 p.m.; and on Sunday from 4 to 8 p.m. If you are really enamored with crabs, you can also have your crabs-to-go, for $60 a bushel or $1.50 each. All major CC's are accepted.

A Philadelphia Tradition on South Street

Of the reputed 2,000 cheese-steak houses in Philadelphia, a longtime favorite is **Jim's Steaks,** 400 South St. (tel. 928-1911), a landmark on the corner of South and 4th Streets since 1939. Here you can sample traditional Philadelphia cheese steaks, and the submarine-type sandwiches called hoagies. Most prices are between $2.95 and $4.95. You'll find a cheery art deco tile setting, and walls lined with signed celebrity photos of those famous faces who have eaten here. Open Monday through Thursday from 10 a.m. to 1 a.m.; Friday and Saturday until 3 a.m.; and Sunday from noon to 10 p.m. No CC's accepted.

PENN'S LANDING AND WATERFRONT: One of the prime movers in Philadelphia's restaurant renaissance was **Raymond Haldeman,** 110–112 S. Front St. (tel. 925-9888), a restaurant named for its owner, who also runs a catering business. Located between Chestnut and Walnut Streets, in a riverfront setting, this restored house is furnished with a medley of plants and ferns, and bright white and floral tones, conveying a country-garden ambience. A series of wall mirrors make the restaurant seem larger than it is, although a central courtyard with an herb garden also adds to the spacious feeling, as flute music echoes throughout. The cuisine is French/American, with choices at lunch ranging from smoked duck salad with fresh fruit and raspberry mustard, to hot entrees such as cheese soufflé, pasta primavera, or curried crabmeat tart. Lunch prices fall into the $6.50 to $14.50 category. Dinner entrees, pegged from $12.50 to $22, include such creations as roast chicken breast filled with fresh goat cheese, sun-dried tomatoes, and red pepper jelly; boneless duck with poached pears, pink peppercorns, and ginger sauce; poached salmon with two caviars on a pool of champagne sauce; grilled loin of veal with pistachio sauce; and rack of lamb in phyllo pastry with spinach and pine nuts. You'll hardly have room for the homemade desserts like English trifle or crème brûlée, but do try. Lunch is served Monday through Friday from 11:30 a.m. to 2:30 p.m.; and dinner Monday through Thursday from 5:30 to 10 p.m., and Friday and Saturday until 11 p.m. All major CC's are accepted.

The **Chart House,** 555 S. Delaware Ave. at Penn's Landing (tel. 625-8383), is the city's newest waterfront eatery (opened in 1986). Laid out on three levels, this lovely restaurant is a showcase of curved floor-to-ceiling windows with wraparound views of the harbor and the skyline. Open for dinner only, the entree list is priced from $9.95 to $21.75, with most choices $15 or under. The menu includes baked silver salmon with dill butter, grilled mako shark, and Louisiana channel bass, as well as lobster, flounder, crab, steaks, blue-ribbon prime ribs, and chicken. All main courses entitle you to unlimited helpings from the huge salad bar. Open Monday through Thursday from 5 to 11 p.m.; on Friday and Saturday, from 4 p.m. to midnight; and on Sunday from 4 to 10 p.m. Brunch is also available on Sunday from 11 a.m. to 2 p.m. (priced at $12.95 for adults and $4.95 for children). All major CC's are accepted.

Also on the water is the **Moshulu,** Chestnut Street at Penn's Landing (tel. 925-3237), a 1904 tall ship that was refurbished and turned into a restaurant in 1976. Lunch, priced from $4.95 to $7.95, features mainly sandwiches, salads, and light entrees, such as shrimp Créole, Cajun crêpe, and seafood omelet. The emphasis is on seafood at dinner, with a variety of selections including sole Oscar; cioppino; blackened redfish; and charbroiled sea steaks of salmon, swordfish, halibut; as well as daily specials; and prime ribs and steaks for meat-lovers. The main courses are priced from $10.95 to $18.95 with most choices under $15. Meals are served continuously from 11 a.m. to 11 p.m. Monday through Thursday; until midnight on Friday and Saturday; and on Sunday from 1 to 10 p.m. All major CC's are accepted.

CITY HALL AND MAIN BUSINESS / THEATER AREA: The best of many European and American cuisines can be found in this hub of fine Philadelphia dining.

The Top Choices

Between 15th and 16th Streets is **Le Bec Fin,** 1523 Walnut St. (tel. 567-1000), best described as a French country mansion in the heart of downtown Philadelphia. Over the past 15 years, under the direction of owner-chef Georges Perrier, it has earned a worldwide reputation for fine cuisine. A Louis XVI décor predominates this gracious town-house dining room. With giant crystal chandeliers, damask-covered walls, mirrors, and gilt-framed portraits highlighting the setting, the tables are set with fresh flower arrangements, Cristofle silver, and fine Limoges china. The menu changes seasonally, but the lunch choices usually include such dishes as sweetbreads and snow peas; filet of veal with mustard seeds; or sole sautéed with lemon, capers, and parsley. Lunch is priced at $20 on a fixed-price basis or from $4 to $18 for à la carte selections. Dinner is served only prix-fixe, at $70 for five courses. The menu, which is printed in French, features such specialties as pigeon served with ravioli of eggplant; filet of venison; filet of veal and lamb with two sauces; fricassee of lobster and oysters; and braided bands of salmon and sole. There is a choice of over 30 desserts, such as orange-chocolate mousse, Grand Marnier soufflé, and Alsatian almond tart. Reservations should be made as soon as you arrive in town, if not sooner. Open Monday through Friday for lunch, at two seatings, 11:30 a.m. and 1:30 p.m. Dinner is served Monday through Saturday, with seatings at 6 and 9 p.m. CC's accepted: AE and D.

Another of the leaders in the Philadelphia restaurant renaissance is **Frög,** 1524 Locust St. (tel. 735-8882), the trendy creation of Steve Posas, who also owns City Bites and The Commissary. Located in an old bank building between 15th and 16th Streets, the entrance leads onto a landing, where you can either descend into the piano-wine bar or ascend to a series of dining areas, dramatically lit by recessed pin lights, accented with brass and polished wood, anthuriums and orchids. The main room is influenced by a suspended 20-foot-tall geometric Thai mobile, made of balanced discs and a bamboo rod. If nothing else, it's a conversation starter, although it is also an indication of the Thai-influenced cuisine that is a feature of the kitchen. Lunch is priced from $7.75 to $12.75 for such choices as tri-color primavera; vegetarian mousse with saga bleu; Oriental seafood salad; or petit filet mignon with roasted garlic. The entrees at dinner, priced from $15.50 to $23, include roasted duck breast marinated with citrus and mint; poached tarragon-scented salmon in salmon caviar; grilled swordfish with lemon thyme and fennel butter; roasted scallops with garlic and pine nuts; and sautéed veal with wild mushrooms and cream. Frög desserts, priced $3.25 to $4.25, are especially tempting: hazelnut crunchcake, chocolate truffle cake, frozen praline soufflé, banana walnut pie, orange almond cream torte, and that's only a sampling! The wine list offers a wide range of labels from the Pacific Northwest and Pennsylvania, as well as California and Europe. Open Monday through Friday for lunch from 11:30 a.m. to 2:30 p.m.; and for dinner from 5:30 to 10:30 p.m.; also on Saturday for dinner only from 5:30 to 11:30 p.m., and on Sunday from 5 to 9:30 p.m. In addition, brunch is served on Saturday and Sunday from 11:30 a.m. to 2:45 p.m., and there is piano bar music every night from 5 p.m., except Sunday. If you are wondering where the name Frög originated, as we did, it seems that the owner's mother was always very fond of a restaurant in another city called La Grenouille (French for "Frog"). Major CC's accepted.

And now we come to the "other" great seafood legend in this city, **Book-binder's Seafood House,** 215 S. 15th St. (tel. 545-1137), which celebrated its 50th year at this address in 1985. Operated by the fourth generation of the Bookbinder family, this midtown restaurant is busy, crowded, and noisy, but the food (and attentive service) are worth it. The décor, as can be expected, is nautical with dark, wood-paneled walls and giant fish specimens mounted overhead. Lunch, priced from $3.95 to $11.95, features mainly sandwiches, raw bar selections, stews, and crab cakes; you can also order a lobster, priced according to size, from $18.95. Lobsters are usually the focus at dinner, with the four-pound variety setting you back $39.95, but such a large crustacean can, of course, feed two or more. Other entrees are pegged from $12.95 to $21.95, with most between $15 and $20. Other choices include baked bluefish; whole Jersey flounder; stone crabs; lobster stew, Newburg, or Thermidor; as well as steaks and chops. A favorite starter is the snapper soup laced with sherry, at $3.95 a bowl. Lunch is served Monday through Friday from 11:30 a.m. to 3:30 p.m., and dinner from 3:30 to 11 p.m.; Saturday from 4 p.m. to midnight; and Sunday from noon to 10 p.m. All major CC's are accepted.

A renovated theater between 14th and 15th Streets is the setting for **DiLullo Centro,** 1407 Locust St. (tel. 546-2000), a dazzling rendezvous, known for its gourmet Northern Italian cuisine, in the heart of the theatrical district. Lavishly appointed with Impressionist murals, mirrored walls, and imported marble, this restaurant has four dining rooms with décors that reflect their names, including the Vineyard, Garden, and Courtyard. A muraled elevator leads you to the lower-level Ferrari Lounge, which features piano music nightly. Lunch, priced from $9 to $13.50, offers some unusual pastas (such as quill-shaped pasta or pasta filled with lobster), pan-roasted fish dishes, and light meat entrees. The dinner choices, priced from $12.50 to $21.50, include marinated and grilled pheasant; herb-roasted loin of veal; medallions of salmon in creamy vermouth sauce; filet of Dover sole; and sautéed lobster with ginger. Open for lunch Monday through Friday from 11:45 a.m. to 1:45 p.m.; and for dinner Monday through Saturday from 5:30 to 10:30 p.m. All major CC's are accepted.

A clubby ambiance prevails at **Harry's Bar and Grill,** 22 S. 18th St. (tel. 561-5757), a two-story restaurant housed in a former stationery store off Chestnut Street, and a favorite with neighborhood business executives. The décor is dominated by wood-paneled walls, beveled-edge mirrors, and gilt-framed oil paintings on the lower level, while upstairs features a gallery of horse and dog art. Both the lunch and dinner menu are similar in selection and price, with entrees running from $8.95 to $23.95 at any time of day. The featured dishes are aged prime steaks, sirloin steak tartare, seafood, smoked chicken, and seasonal game dishes, such as squab, mallard duck, and pheasant. Open only on weekdays, lunch is served from 11:30 to 2 p.m., and dinner from 5:30 to 9:30 p.m. All major CC's are accepted.

La Camargue, 1119 Walnut St. (tel. 922-3148), conveys the ambience of a French country château, with its whitewashed walls, etched stained glass, stuffed pheasants, old clocks, and copper pots. Situated between 11th and 12th Streets, directly across from the Forrest Theatre, this restaurant will allow you to have your dinner through the main course, then break to attend the theater, and come back after the performance for a nightcap and your dessert. Lunch is priced from $6 to $16, with most choices under $10, for gourmet omelets, salads, pasta, and light entrees such as red snapper or chicken breast. Entrees at dinner, priced from $15 to $25, range from lobster with light curry sauce, and fresh trout with smoked salmon mousse, to duck breast with fresh peaches, sweetbreads with spinach and cream sauce, veal kidneys, and rack of lamb. Tempting items from the dessert cart add an extra $4 to the tab. Open for lunch Monday through Friday from 11:30 a.m. to 2 p.m.; and for dinner Monday through Saturday from 5:30 to 11 p.m. All major CC's are accepted.

The Garden, 1617 Spruce St. (tel. 546-4455), is an 1870s City Center town house (actually, two houses), between 16th and 17th Streets, with a tree-shaded outdoor brick courtyard and canopied deck. A delightful setting at any time of year, this restaurant was started in 1974 by Kathleen Mulhern, who also owns Harry's Bar, described above. The Garden is similarly a favorite with local executives who find this to be just the spot for "power lunches." Inside there are five dining rooms, on two levels, with a variety of décors ranging from a candlelit Victorian parlor with floral wallpaper to an informal oyster bar. Lunch, priced from $9.95 to $19.95, includes steaks, lobsters, gourmet salads, steak tartare, loin of veal, and chicken breast. There is a similar menu at dinner, with entrees priced from $14.95 to $23.95, and featuring rack of lamb, thin calves' liver, breast of duck with herb-scented oranges, and curried shrimp with chutney, as well as steaks and lobsters. All main courses are accompanied by salad and vegetable. Lunch is served Monday through Friday from 11:30 a.m. to 1:45 p.m.; and dinner Monday through Saturday from 5:30 to 10 p.m. (except July and August, when it is closed both Saturday and Sunday). All major CC's are accepted.

A gallery of paintings by local artists is on view at **L'Aigle d'Or,** 1920 Chestnut St. (tel. 567-0855), a restaurant that offers an international menu every day. Housed in a former bank between 19th and 20th Streets, with its symbol of an Eagle of Gold in the window, this unique eatery is the creation of Danish chef

Soren Arnoldi, who has been honored by the prestigious Chaine des Rôtisseurs for his efforts. Lunch, priced from $8.75 to $12.50, features such dishes as crab quiche, coquilles St-Jacques with three cheeses, Irish chicken in wine and whiskey, or gnocchi (assorted fish and shellfish with potato dumplings and cream-cheese sauce). For dinner, you may wish to start with sashimi, escargots, gravad lax, or scampi ($5 to $7). The ever-changing entrees, in the $12.75 to $19.75 bracket, often include fresh salmon in parchment, Danish farm-style chicken, Greek marinated lamb wrapped in strudel and feta, and beef with truffles and cognac. Lunch is served Monday through Friday from 11:30 a.m. to 3 p.m.; and dinner on Monday through Thursday from 5:30 to 10 p.m., Friday and Saturday until 11 p.m., and Sunday from 4 to 9 p.m. Major CC's are accepted.

Moderately Priced Dining

Sweeping sky-high vistas are the main attraction at the **Top of Centre Square,** 1500 Market St. (tel. 563-9494), between 15th and 16th Streets. Located on the 41st floor of an office building in the center of town, this modern restaurant with bi-level seating offers wraparound views of the city, the two rivers, and New Jersey. Lunch, priced mostly between $5 and $10, focuses on sandwiches, pastas, quiches, and light dishes. Perhaps the best time here is after dark, when the city lights glow and the menu adds a continental flair. Dinner entrees, pegged between $10 and $21, include Coho salmon, shrimp tempura, lobster francese, veal Oscar, and bouillabaisse, as well as prime ribs and steaks. Lunch is served Monday through Friday from 11:30 a.m. to 3 p.m.; dinner Monday through Thursday from 5:30 to 10 p.m.; until midnight on Friday and Saturday; and from 4:30 to 9 p.m. on Sunday. Major CC's are accepted.

Ever since 1947, the **Sansom Street Oyster House,** 1516 Sansom St. (tel. 567-7683), has been a good midtown choice for fresh seafood at moderate prices. Located between 15th and 16th Streets, the décor of this two-room restaurant is simple, with tile floors, old sea scenes on walls, bare wood tables closely packed together, and hand-printed menus that change daily. Lunches tend to be light, in the $3.95 to $9.95 bracket, for sandwiches, seafood stews, and chowders. Dinner offers at least half a dozen types of oysters from the raw bar (60¢ to $1.50 each), and entrees in the $8.95 to $14.95 range. Selections can include whole lobsters, cod steak, St. Peter's fish, tuna steak, blackened redfish, sea trout, oyster pan roast, and mixed seafood platters, plus chicken and filet mignon. Seafoods are prepared grilled, fried, sautéed, or baked, according to your wishes. All main courses come with salad and vegetables. No reservations are taken; and there is a non-smoking section. Open for lunch Monday through Saturday from 11 a.m. to 3 p.m.; and for dinner Monday through Thursday from 3 to 9 p.m.; and until 10 p.m. on Friday and Saturday. Major CC's are accepted.

German and Austrian cuisine is featured at **Hoffmann House,** 1214 Sansom St. (tel. 925-2772), a midtown tradition near 12th Street for over 65 years. With German music gently playing in the background, the charm of Bavaria is also much in evidence as you look around the two dining rooms, from the mounted bear heads and porcelain plates on the walls, sturdy old sideboards, and stained-glass windows to the dark paneled walls that came from the captain's cabin of a German freighter. Lunch choices range from sandwiches made of sausage, sardine, or liverwurst to light dishes, such as smoked pork loin or filet of veal. The midday prices are between $5.75 to $9.75. The dinner entrees, priced from $8.95 to $17, include sautéed loin of venison, braised saddle of rabbit, roast pork with sauerkraut, sauerbraten, weinerschnitzel, weisswurst, and chicken with sweet paprika. Lunch is served Monday through Friday from 11:30 a.m. to 2:30 p.m.; and dinner Monday through Saturday from 5 to 9 p.m. CC's accepted: AE, MC, and V.

Bouillabaisse is the house specialty at **The Fish Market,** 18th and Sansom

Streets (tel. 567-3559), a tri-level contemporary establishment that prides itself on serving gourmet American seafood. Although the ingredients are flown in fresh daily from Maine to the Gulf of Mexico and beyond, you are reminded that this is midtown Philadelphia by wall-size photo murals of the Schuylkill River, Logan Circle, and other city scenes. Lunch, priced from $6.75 to $12, includes Pennsylvania rainbow trout, Norwegian salmon, shrimp and papaya salad, squid-ink pasta with grilled squid, or spinach pasta and lamb. The innovative dinner entrees, priced from $7.25 to $16.50, range from sautéed red Spanish shrimp or Mediterranean seafood salad (shrimp, squid, mussels, and crab) to sea scallops with mussel-saffron cream sauce. Lunch is served Monday through Friday from 11:30 a.m. to 2:30 p.m.; and dinner Monday through Saturday from 5 to 10 p.m., and Sunday from 4 to 9 p.m. Major CC's are accepted.

Many of Philadelphia's new wave of creative chefs owe their training and inspiration to **The Restaurant School,** 2129 Walnut St., (tel. 561-3649), a student- and staff-run dining room, located near 21st Street, two blocks west of Rittenhouse Square. The menu changes every seven weeks at this small 44-seat restaurant, and the quality can fluctuate nightly, but for a $12 fixed-price dinner you really can't beat the value and the experience. Choices often include oven-poached salmon; Cornish game hen; seafood stew with Pernod; grilled chicken suprème with raisins, green peppercorns, and cream; pork chops stuffed with fennel and couscous; and butterflied leg of lamb with a watercress and horseradish sauce. Even though this is primarily a school, there is a full wine list and bar. Open for dinner only, Tuesday through Saturday from 5:30 to 10 p.m., but closed all school holidays. Major CC's are accepted.

A delightful spot for a casual dinner is **Friday, Saturday, Sunday,** 261 S. 21st St. (tel. 546-4232), a three-story corner brick row house between Locust and Spruce. Although the ground-floor dining room is fairly narrow, it seems spacious, thanks to a tent-style décor of plaid and striped canvasses draped from the ceiling, wall mirrors, and light woods. An ever-changing, internationally influenced menu appears on the blackboard each night, offering such selections as stuffed sea trout, duck curry, flounder bonne femme, chicken Dijon, pork loin with apple glaze, salmon with sorrel sauce, and rack of lamb. The entrees range from $10.95 to $18, with appropriate vegetables. Also open for lunch when salads and sandwiches are featured. Hours are Monday through Friday from 11:30 a.m. to 2:30 p.m. for lunch; and Monday through Saturday from 5:30 to 10:30 p.m. for dinner; also Sunday dinner from 5 to 10 p.m. Major CC's are accepted.

Moderate to Budget Meals

Between 17th and 18th Streets, you'll find **The Commissary,** 1710 Sansom St. (tel. 569-2240), actually two restaurants offering meals to suit a range of budgets. Downstairs is a modern self-service eatery featuring soups, salads, pastas, pâtés, and omelets in hearty portions, mostly under $5, with a beer and wine service. Upstairs is the U.S.A. Café , a full-service restaurant with a partiality for Southwestern cuisine. Lunch, priced from $5.95 to $8.95, includes such dishes as duck salad, black-bean pasta, chicken fajitas (chicken in flour tortillas with avocado, refried beans, and fresh tomato salsa), and seafood sandwiches. The entrees at dinner, priced from $6.95 to $13.95, are similar to lunch, with additions such as sautéed flounder with avocado and crabmeat in brandied cream sauce; pan-fried brook trout; blackened prime rib with honey fennel; seafood stew; blackened or grilled tuna or mako shark. The wine list here also features many California boutique labels at moderate prices. The downstairs section is open Monday through Thursday from 8 a.m. to 10 p.m.; on Friday until 11 p.m.; on Saturday from 9 a.m. to midnight; and on Sunday from 10:30 a.m. to 10 p.m. Upstairs is open for lunch Monday through Friday from 11:30 a.m. to 2:30 p.m.; for dinner Monday through Thursday from

5:30 to 10 p.m.; and Friday and Saturday until 11:30 p.m. Major CC's are accepted.

If you are visiting some of the city's museums or taking a stroll in Fairmount Park, then you'll be near **Adrian,** 747 N. 25th St. at Aspen Street (tel. 978-9190), in the city's northwest corner. A little out of the way from midtown, this neighborhood dining spot is worth a cab ride for the good values in fine dining. It's housed in a restored shopfront building and has an authentic pressed-tin ceiling and brick walls lined with paintings by local artists. Fresh flowers and candlelight add to the atmosphere, especially in the evening. Dinner entrees, which change daily, are usually priced in the $8.95 to $13.95 bracket, and include salad, hot breads, vegetable, and potato. Specialties include chicken saltimbocca, steak au poivre, Oriental duck, and sweetbreads. Light lunches are also available during the week with most prices under $5. Open for lunch Monday through Friday from 11:30 a.m. to 2:30 p.m.; and for dinner Monday through Saturday from 6 to 10 p.m. Major CC's are accepted.

An art deco atmosphere and big-band music from the 1950s dominate the scene at **Marabella's,** 1420 Locust St. (tel. 545-1845), a trendy (and sometimes noisy) new restaurant between 14th and 15th Streets, in the heart of the theater district. The mostly black and red décor includes old fashioned jukeboxes and lots of wall mirrors, but the real draw here is an all-day menu with moderate-to-budget prices. At lunchtime, you can get burgers and sandwiches from $3 to $6. The dinner entrees, priced from $5 to $13.50, with most under the $10 mark, include pizzas, grilled swordfish, stuffed shrimp, hot and spicy grilled chicken, tortellini with goat cheese, and filet mignon with mushrooms. Open Monday through Thursday from 11:30 a.m. to 11:30 p.m.; Friday and Saturday from 11:30 a.m. to 12:30 a.m.; and Sunday from 11:30 a.m. to 10 p.m. CC's accepted: AE, MC, and V.

A Midtown Must for Lunch

Hearty and overstuffed sandwiches are the trademark of the **Corned Beef Academy,** 18th Street and John F. Kennedy Boulevard (tel. 568-9696), a lunch favorite with Philadelphians of all ranks. Service is fast (with paper plates and plastic cups) and the food is straightforward, with such deli specialities as lean and sliced-to-order corned beef, roast beef, brisket, and turkey, plus soups and salads. Most midday items are in the $3.95 to $4.95 range. Open for breakfast daily from 7 a.m. to 10 a.m., and for lunch from 11 a.m. to 3:30 p.m. In addition, there are two other locations in the city, at 121 S. 16th St. (tel. 665-0460), and 400 Market St. at 4th Street (tel. 922-2111). No CC's are accepted.

7. The Top Attractions

The focal point of Philadelphia is **Independence National Historical Park,** an area often called "America's most historic square mile." Located just west of the Delaware River, between Walnut and Arch Streets, this four-block-square area is primarily administered by the National Park Service and encompasses over two dozen sites, with the prime attractions being the Liberty Bell and Independence Hall, two of our nation's greatest monuments of freedom.

The **Liberty Bell** is housed in a special glass-enclosed pavilion, located on Market Street, between 5th and 6th Streets. Ranger guides continually greet visitors and give short background talks on the history and significance of the bell. Across the street is **Independence Hall,** 5th and Chestnut Streets, the place where the Declaration of Independence was adopted and the U.S. Constitution was written. Originally built as the State House for the province of Pennsylvania, this building can also be toured with Ranger guides. Both attractions are open daily from 9 a.m. to 5 p.m., with extended hours during the summer. Admission has always been free and continues to be so, as we go to press during the "We The People" celebrations; however, there is a possibility that a $2 admission charge covering both sites may be levied in 1988 or 1989.

Perhaps the best place to start your visit in this historic complex is at the **National Park Service Visitor Center** at 3rd and Chestnut Streets (tel. 597-8974). Here you can pick up brochures that highlight the Park's many historic attractions, and view an introductory film, *Independence*, directed by John Huston. There is a charge of $2 per person (or $5 per family) to see the film, but this one fee also entitles you to admission at six other park sites.

These buildings are:

● The **Graff House**, 7th and Market Streets, is a reconstruction of the house where Thomas Jefferson lived when he wrote the Declaration of Independence; a short film about Jefferson is shown continuously.

● The **Army-Navy Museum**, Chestnut Street between 3rd and 4th Streets. Housed in the replica of the 18th-century home of Quaker merchant Joseph Pemberton, this museum depicts the development of the Army and Navy from 1775 to 1800.

● The **Marine Corps Memorial Museum**, Chestnut Street between 3rd and 4th Streets. This attraction, housed in a reconstructed 1790 building, commemorates the early history of the Marine Corps.

● The **Bishop White House**, 309 Walnut St. Built in 1786–1787, this is the home of the first bishop of the Episcopal Diocese of Pennsylvania.

● The **Todd House**, 4th and Walnut Streets, is the 1775 home of Dolley Payne Todd, who later became Dolley Madison, wife of President James Madison.

● **Franklin Court**, between 3rd and 4th Streets, Chestnut and Market Streets, stands on the site that was once Benjamin Franklin's house, and has been developed as a tribute to him. Your admission ticket entitles you to visit the underground museum, printing shop, and an archeological architecture exhibit. This site also includes the B. Free Franklin Post Office, the only post office open seven days a week.

Other attractions in this historic complex include the **City Tavern**, 2nd and Walnut Streets, a working restaurant in a reconstruction of the famous Revolutionary War tavern where delegates to the First and Second Continental Congresses gathered (see "Where to Dine"); **Carpenters' Hall**, 320 Chestnut St., where the first Continental Congress met in 1774; **Old City Hall**, 5th and Chestnut Streets, home of the first U.S. Supreme Court, 1791–1800; and **Congress Hall**, 6th and Chestnut Streets, where the House and Senate met when Philadelphia was the newborn nation's first capital.

Most of these Independence National Park attractions are open daily from 9 a.m. to 5 p.m., except the City Tavern, which keeps regular restaurant hours and Carpenters' Hall, which is open daily except Monday from 10 a.m. to 4 p.m.

OTHER NEARBY ATTRACTIONS: Betsy Ross House, 239 Arch St. (tel. 627-5343), is the restored 2½-story Colonial home in which Elizabeth ("Betsy") Griscom Ross lived and operated an upholstery shop from 1773 to 1786. It was during that time that she is credited with making the first U.S. flag. Located between 2nd and 3rd Streets, the house is furnished with family artifacts associated with Betsy, who is buried in the adjacent garden. Open daily (except Thanksgiving, Christmas, and New Year's Day) May through October from 9 a.m. to 6 p.m. and during November to March from 9 a.m. to 5 p.m. Admission is free.

Less than a block away is **Elfreth's Alley**, off 2nd Street, between Arch and Race Streets. A registered National Historic Landmark, this narrow cobblestone path is reputed to be the oldest residential street in the nation, lined with 30 houses that were built between 1728 and 1836. Originally occupied by craftspeople and shopkeepers, these homes reflect a variety of architectural styles, and some have Colonial courtyards. It is said that Ben Franklin visited friends at No. 122 often. A **museum** is located in No. 126 and may be visited, daily from 10 a.m. to 4 p.m., but all of the other buildings are privately owned today and not ordinarily open to the public. There is an annual "open house" in June, however, if you want to see more. For full details, contact the **Elfreth's Alley Assn.,** 126 Elfreth's Alley, Philadelphia, PA 19106 (tel. 574-0560).

The **Norman Rockwell Museum,** 601 Walnut St. (tel. 922-4345) at 6th Street, is housed in the Curtis Building, the publishing house where Norman Rockwell used to submit his *Saturday Evening Post* cover drawings each week. This small museum features a display reflecting 47 years of Rockwell's works, including a complete set of his magazine covers from 1916 to 1963. A replica of the artist's studio is also here, as are a variety of his other works. Open daily from 10 a.m. to 4 p.m. Admission charge is $1.50 for adults; children under 12 are admitted free.

Unfortunately, there are no free samples, but you might still enjoy a tour of the **U.S. Mint,** 5th and Arch Streets (tel. 597-7350), the largest operation of its kind in the world. Self-guided tours include audio-visual displays and firsthand observations of the coinage process from a glass-enclosed gallery. Open October through April, Monday through Saturday from 9 a.m. to 4:30 p.m. (except Christmas and New Year's Day); and May through September, daily from 9 a.m. to 4:30 p.m. Admission is free.

Penn's Landing, Delaware River (tel. 923-8181), is a harborfront promenade, between Market and Lombard Streets, which marks the site where William Penn landed in 1682. The 37-acre area is home to a museum, sculpture garden, and restaurants. Several historic ships are also docked here, including the USS *Olympia,* Commodore Dewey's flagship during the Spanish-American War. Open daily, during fall, winter, and spring, from 10 a.m. to 4:30 p.m., and in the summer months from 10 a.m. to 6 p.m. Admission is $2.50 for adults and $1.25 for children under 12.

Society Hill, an area between 6th and Front Streets, and Walnut and South Streets, takes its name from a group of businessmen, the Free Society of Traders, whom Penn persuaded to settle here. Today it's a fashionable section of the old city, just south of Independence Park, where you can stroll among restored Federal, Colonial, and Georgian homes. Two of Philadelphia's finest houses, the **Hill-Physick-Keith House,** 321 S. 4th St. (tel. 925-7866), and the **Powel House,** 244 S. 3rd St. (tel. 627-0364), are open for guided tours, Tuesday through Saturday from 10 a.m. to 4 p.m.; and on Sunday from 1 to 4 p.m. Admission charge in both cases is $2 for adults and $1 for students; and 50¢ for those under age 12.

UPTOWN SIGHTS: Moving uptown, the focal point is **City Hall,** Penn Square, at the juncture of Broad and Market Streets (tel. 567-4476). Built between 1871 and 1901, this landmark building is the seat of the municipal government and has been the tallest structure in Philadelphia for over 100 years. (However, that statistic will change when the new 60-story One Liberty Place office tower opens in 1988.) City Hall is crowned by a giant 37-foot statue of William Penn, believed to be the largest single piece of sculpture on any building in the world, standing atop a 548-foot tower that is visible for miles. One-hour tours of the interior of this grand Beaux Arts hall are offered free, on a first-come basis,

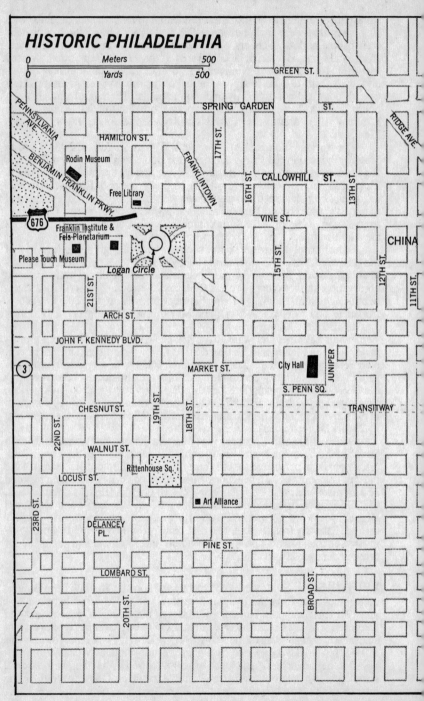

HISTORIC PHILADELPHIA

	Meters	500
0		
0	Yards	500

GREEN ST.

SPRING GARDEN ST.

HAMILTON ST.

PENNSYLVANIA AVE.

Rodin Museum

BENJAMIN FRANKLIN PKWY.

Free Library

17TH ST.

FRANKLINTOWN

CALLOWHILL ST.

16TH ST.

13TH ST.

676

Franklin Institute & Fels Planetarium

VINE ST.

CHINA

Please Touch Museum

Logan Circle

15TH ST.

21ST ST.

ARCH ST.

11TH ST.

12TH ST.

JOHN F. KENNEDY BLVD.

3

MARKET ST.

City Hall

JUNIPER

S. PENN SQ.

CHESNUT ST.

19TH ST.

18TH ST.

TRANSITWAY

22ND ST.

WALNUT ST.

Rittenhouse Sq.

LOCUST ST.

Art Alliance

23RD ST.

DELANCEY PL.

PINE ST.

BROAD ST.

LOMBARD ST.

20TH ST.

RIDGE AVE.

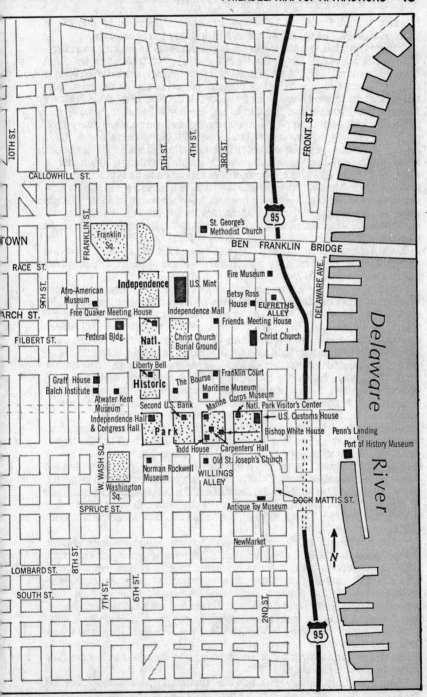

Monday through Friday, at 12:30 p.m. Participants are asked to assemble in Conversation Hall on the second floor, North Broad Street entrance.

From City Hall, you can follow the Benjamin Franklin Parkway in a northwest direction through Logan Circle, and you'll be on "museum row." With flags of all nations waving in the breezes, this wide parkway, sometimes referred to as the Champs-Élysées of Philadelphia, is a perfect setting for the grand institutions that are located here. One of standouts is the **Franklin Institute Science Museum and Planetarium,** 20th Street and Benjamin Franklin Parkway (tel. 564-3375), a four-floor complex that encourages hands-on and do-it-yourself experiences. Among the exhibits that you can see and explore are a Boeing 707, a 350-ton locomotive, and the world's largest walk-through heart. This is also the home of the Benjamin Franklin National Memorial, housing a 30-ton marble statue of its namesake plus a collection of authentic Franklin artifacts and possessions. Open Monday through Saturday from 10 a.m. to 5 p.m., and on Sunday from noon to 5 p.m. General admission is $4 for adults and $3 for children aged 4 to 12. In addition, the Fels Planetarium division presents regular astronomy shows and live constellation shows. The planetarium shows take place on weekdays at 12:30 p.m. and 2 p.m.; Saturday at 10:30 a.m. (for children), noon, 2, 3, and 4 p.m.; and Sunday at 1, 2, 3, and 4 p.m. Live constellation shows are also presented on weekends at 1 p.m. These shows are $1 additional, except the children's show which is 75¢.

Ever since the movie *Rocky,* most visitors recognize the famous set of steps that lead to the **Philadelphia Museum of Art,** 26th Street and Benjamin Franklin Parkway (tel. 763-8100). Once you climb the steps (or take an easier access entrance), you'll see one of the largest and finest collections in the world of American paintings and decorative arts from Colonial times to the present; other galleries include works by such masters as Renoir, Van Gogh, Cézanne, Picasso, Duchamp, and Matisse. In addition, there are collections of tapestries, arms, and armor. Hours are Wednesday through Sunday from 10 a.m. to 5 p.m.; on Tuesday, there is access through hourly guided tours only, from 11 a.m. to 3 p.m. Admission charge is normally $4, but on Sunday it is free between 10 a.m. and 1 p.m., and on Tuesday you can pay whatever you wish.

Other outstanding museums in this area include the **Rodin Museum,** 22nd Street and Benjamin Franklin Parkway (tel. 787-5476), which has the largest collection of Rodin sculptures and drawings outside France (open Tuesday through Sunday from 10 a.m. to 5 p.m., with admission by donation); and the **Academy of Natural Sciences,** 19th Street and Benjamin Franklin Parkway (tel. 299-1000), founded in 1812 and the home of a $2.5 million permanent exhibition on dinosaurs (open Monday through Friday from 10 a.m. to 4 p.m., and Saturday and Sunday from 10 a.m. to 5 p.m.). Admission is $3.50 for adults and $3 for children aged 3 to 12.

The Benjamin Franklin Parkway also leads you into **Fairmount Park,** the world's largest landscaped city park, with 8,700 acres of winding creeks, rustic trails, green meadows, and 100 miles of jogging, bike, and bridle paths. In addition, this park features more than a dozen historical and cultural attractions including some of the nation's finest early American homes which were transferred here from their original sites. These include a Quaker farmhouse, and Federal, Georgian, and Greek Revival homes; as well as gardens, boathouses, America's first zoo (1874), and a Japanese teahouse. Regularly scheduled trolley-bus tours operate around the park, allowing passengers to disembark at various major sites and reboard on a later bus at leisure. (See "Getting Around Philadelphia.")

In South Philadelphia, you'll find the **Mummers Museum,** 2nd Street and Washington Avenue (tel. 336-3050), where "everyday is New Year's." A show-

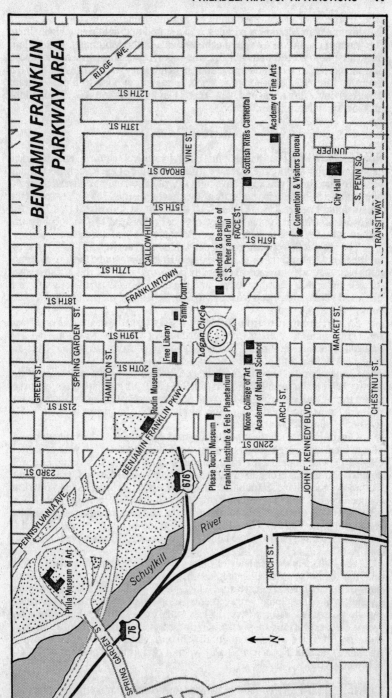

BENJAMIN FRANKLIN PARKWAY AREA

case for the colorful costumed dancers, this museum includes the New Year's suits from recent Mummers parades, and a sound-and-light revue highlighting 300 years of origins, history, and achievements of the Mummers. In addition, there are photo murals dating back to the 1880s, musical instruments, artifacts, and memorabilia, a hall of fame, and research library. Open Tuesday through Saturday from 9:30 a.m. to 5 p.m., and Sunday from noon to 5 p.m. (except Thanksgiving, Christmas, and New Year's Day). Admission is $1.50 for adults and 75¢ for children 12 and under.

8. Nightlife

PERFORMING ARTS: Philadelphia is rich in musical, cultural, and theatrical experiences throughout the year. We'll describe some of the leading performing venues below, but if you don't have time to visit individual box offices, there is a one-stop ticket bureau in the heart of the theater district. It's simply called the **Philadelphia Theatre Ticket Office,** 1500 Locust St. at 15th Street (tel. 735-1903 and 545-1527), and it's open Monday through Friday from 10 a.m. to 5:30 p.m., and on Saturday from 10 a.m. to noon. All major CC's are accepted.

The **Walnut Street Theatre,** 9th and Walnut Streets (tel. 574-3586), was established in 1809 and claims to be the oldest English-language theater in continuous use. A resident theatrical company performs here, but this is also a stage for visiting opera, chamber music, and dance groups. Curtain is usually at 8 p.m. and tickets are priced from $12 to $26, depending on the event. CC's accepted: AE, MC, and V.

Shows en route to or from Broadway often stop at the nearby **Forrest Theatre,** 1114 Walnut St. (tel. 923-1515). Curtain is at 8 p.m., with Wednesday and Saturday matinees at 2 p.m. Tickets range in price from $16 to $35. CC's accepted: AE, MC, and V.

Contemporary, experimental, and off-Broadway works are staged at the **Society Hill Playhouse,** 507 S. 8th St. (tel. 923-0210), an intimate 223-seat house. Open from October through May, with performances Wednesday through Saturday at 8 p.m., and matinees on Sunday at 3 p.m. Ticket prices range from $16 to $19.50. Major CC's are accepted.

One of the city's busiest performing arts centers is the three-theater complex at the **Annenberg Center,** University of Pennsylvania, 3680 Walnut St. (tel. 898-6791). The home of the Philadelphia Drama Guild, this venue also welcomes a continuous program of guest artists such as the Martha Graham Dance Company, the Flying Karamazov Brothers, and the Alvin Ailey American Dance Theatre, as well as touring Broadway shows. Tickets range from $15 to $25, depending on the event and seat location, and performances are scheduled for 7 or 8 p.m. The box office is open from noon to 6 p.m. weekdays and at performance times, starting two hours before curtain. CC's accepted: AE, MC, and V.

The **Philadelphia Academy of Music,** Broad and Locust Streets (tel. 893-1930), is the home of the Philadelphia Orchestra, the Philly Pops, Opera Company of Philadelphia, Pennsylvania Ballet, and the Concerto Soloists Chamber Orchestra of Philadelphia. Engagements by top-name stars and occasional touring shows are also featured here. Tickets range from $5 to $45, but average between $10 and $25 for most events. The box office is open Monday through Saturday from 10 a.m. to 9 p.m. (until 5:30 p.m. when there is no evening performance), and at 1 p.m. on Sunday when a performance is scheduled. CC's accepted: AE, MC, and V.

DINNER THEATER: Broadway classics and contemporary productions are staged year-round at the **Riverfront Dinner Theatre,** Delaware Avenue and Poplar Street (tel. 925-7000). Recent shows have included *The King and I, Annie, Chicago,* and *A Chorus Line.* Buffet dinner is served prior to each performance. Evening shows are staged Tuesday through Sunday, and matinees, Wednesday through Saturday. The price is $23.95 for Saturday evening, and $19.95 for other evenings. Matinees are $16.95. All major CC's are accepted.

DANCING AND MUSIC: Philadelphia has a lively selection of evening entertainment to suit every taste and age group. Here are a few places to start you on your way.

Discos/Dancing: One of the newest hot spots is **Spectacles** at the Sheraton Society Hill, One Dock St. (tel. 238-6000), a trendy video nightclub. Rooftop dancing is featured at **Horizons,** Franklin Plaza Hotel, 16th and Race Streets (tel. 448-2901). Some places charge a cover or "membership" fee, such as **élan,** Warwick Hotel, 17th and Locust Streets (tel. 546-8800), and the **Monte Carlo Living Room,** 2nd and South Streets (tel. 925-2220). Music of the 1950s is on tap at the **Heartthrob Café** at The Bourse, 21 S. 5th St. (tel. 627-0778); and at **Marabella's,** 1420 Locust St. (tel. 545-1845). Jazz and blues sessions are often scheduled on weekends at **Cypress,** 303 S. 11th St. (tel. 238-9967).

CABARET/COMEDY CLUBS: The **Comedy Works,** 126 Chestnut St. (tel. WACKY 97), has shows on Wednesday and Thursday at 9 p.m.; on Friday at 9:30 p.m. and 11 p.m.; and on Saturday from 8 to 11 p.m. If you tire of the comedy, you can always descend to the ground floor to the **Middle East Restaurant** (tel. 922-1003), where belly dancing is featured nightly. Another comedy house is **Going Bananas,** 613 S. 2nd St. (tel. BANANA-1), which stages shows on Friday at 9 and 11:30 p.m., and on Saturday at 8 and 11 p.m. The charges at these clubs usually range from $6 to $10, sometimes with a two-drink minimum.

9. Shopping

Philadelphia is home to the oldest department store in the U.S.A., **John Wanamaker's,** 1300 Market St. (tel. 422-2648), founded in 1861 and occupying an entire city block in the heart of the city next to City Hall. To help you get to know this 12-story emporium, the management provides a self-guided walking tour leaflet. As you traverse the main floor, you'll see a 2,500-pound bronze eagle in the middle of the center aisle. This is not only the emblem of the store, but it has become a local rendezvous spot over the years. The world's largest pipe organ is also located here, and if you happen to stroll by at 11:15 a.m. or 5:15 p.m. (except Sunday), you'll be treated to a short concert. On the eighth floor, there is also a store museum including the original John Wanamaker's office (open Monday through Saturday from noon to 3 p.m.). Shopping hours are Monday through Saturday from 10 a.m. to 7 p.m., with late shopping on Wednesday until 9 p.m.; and on Sunday from 11 a.m. to 6 p.m. CC's accepted: AE, MC, and V.

An old market house and courtyard is the setting of **Head House Square,** 2nd and Pine Streets, in the Society Hill area. Established in 1745 as a shopping center for the convenience of Colonial housewives, this marketplace was renovated in the 1970s, and is now a brick-lined market fair of restaurants and craft vendors of all types. Open on weekends from 10 a.m. to 10 p.m. (except winter). In this section, you'll also find **La Belle Ami,** 562 S. 3rd St. (tel. 928-0418), the designer dress shop owned by entertainer Patti LaBelle.

The Gallery at Market East, 9th and Market Streets (tel. 925-7162), is the nation's largest urban shopping complex, with 200 stores and restaurants.

Spread on four levels, this indoor shopping courtyard features everything from fashions to food shops, and includes Strawbridge & Clothier, another Philadelphia shopping tradition since 1868. Open seven days a week, with hours depending on individual shops.

Across from Independence Hall, you'll find more than 50 shops and restaurants housed in **The Bourse,** 5th and Market Streets (tel. 625-9393), a ten-story landmark constructed between 1893 and 1895 as Philadelphia's first merchant's exchange. Spread out over four levels, the interior includes impressive Corinthian columns, brass and marble staircases, balconies embellished with marble, and wrought-iron and cast-iron rails. The wares for sale range from crafts to designer fashions, fast foods to vintage wines. Open daily, but hours vary among the shops or concessions.

Foods of all types are the attraction at the **Reading Terminal Market,** 12th and Arch Streets (tel. 922-2317). Built in 1893, this markethouse has dozens of vendors selling fresh fruits and vegetables, homemade baked goods and preserves, as well as seafood, barbecued chickens, ice cream, pastas, cheese steaks, and other ethnic specialities. Open Monday through Saturday from 8 a.m. to 6 p.m.

Philadelphia's haven for antique buffs is **Antiques Row,** Pine Street from 9th to 12th Streets. This three-block area includes dozens of stores and curio shops.

Similarly, you'll find **Jewelers' Row** between 7th and 8th Streets, on Sansom Street. This is one of the world's oldest and largest diamond centers, with more than 100 retailers, wholesalers, and craftsmen dealing in precious stones, gold, and silver.

10. Children's Corner

Although there are many activities in Philadelphia that are of interest to children of all ages, there is one that is designed just for children seven years or younger: the **Please Touch Museum,** 210 N. 21st St. (tel. 963-0666). Among the activities in which children can participate are designing colorform murals, performing in a circus, and modeling unusual costumes. There are also computer games, a giant toy elephant, workshops, and theater events. Hours are Tuesday through Saturday from 10 a.m. to 4:30 p.m., and Sunday from 12:30 p.m. to 4:30 p.m. Admission is $3 per person and children should be accompanied by adults.

11. A Trip to Valley Forge

Valley Forge, a 2,800-acre expanse of woodlands and meadows situated 20 miles northwest of downtown Philadelphia, is perhaps the best known site associated with the American Revolution. It was here that Gen. George Washington set up a winter encampment for his Continental Army during the winter of 1777–1778.

A lasting symbol of bravery, courage, and endurance, Valley Forge is a unique Revolutionary landmark, because no shot was ever fired and no battle fought. Nevertheless, thousands of American soldiers died here during that winter, as they struggled to survive against hunger, disease, and the unrelenting forces of nature. On a brighter note, the Valley Forge experience also gave General Washington the opportunity to reorganize and train his impromptu army, which led to ultimate victory.

The focal point of this hollowed stretch of countryside is the **Valley Forge National Historical Park,** Route 23 and North Gulph Road (tel. 215/783-1066). The park is open daily Memorial Day through Labor Day from 8:30 a.m. to 6 p.m., and during the rest of the year from 8:30 a.m. to 5 p.m. The general admission charge has always been free; however, as we go to press, indications are that a flat charge of $1 per person (maximum $3 per vehicle) shortly will be levied—children under 12 and adults over 62 will still be admitted free of charge.

Start your tour at the modern **Visitor Center** at the Park entrance. Here you can see displays, exhibits, and a 15-minute audio-visual program that will provide you with background on the historic Valley Forge encampment. The well-informed staff at the Visitor Center will also equip you with a free map of the grounds that outlines driving, hiking, and biking trails.

You can follow the map on a self-guided tour of your own; or you can rent an audio casette tape outlining the historical sights on the route for a charge of $5.30 for a two-hour period. In addition, narrated bus tours of the park are operated regularly from mid-April through October. The fare is $3.50 for adults and $2.50 for students aged 5 to 16. You can arrange to participate in a tour on arrival at the Visitor Center. For information in advance, contact **Valley Forge Tours,** 1065 Belvoir Rd., Norristown, PA 19401 (tel. 215/783-5788).

Bikes are also available for rental on weekends in mid-April, May, June, September, and October, and daily in June, July, and August. The rates are $2.75 to $3.75 per hour.

No matter how you choose to explore the park, the route will take you past extensive remains and restorations of major forts and lines of earthworks, as well as the Artillery Park, Washington's Headquarters, the quarters of other officers, and the Grand Parade where General von Steuben trained the army. There are also reconstructed huts, memorials, monuments, markers, and three picnic areas.

VISITOR INFORMATION: When you are planning your visit to Valley Forge, be sure to contact the **Valley Forge Convention and Visitors Bureau,** P.O. Box 311, Norristown, PA 19404 (tel. 215/278-3558 or toll-free 800/441-3549). There is also a 24-hour "funline" of recorded information (tel. 215/275-4636). This office will not only supply you with brochures on the Valley Forge Park, but also material on the many other attractions of the surrounding areas, and full data about accommodations, restaurants, events, and activities. If you'd like to visit the office when you are there, it is located on the 6th floor of 1 Montgomery Plaza, Norristown, and is open weekdays from 8:30 a.m. to 5 p.m.

OTHER HIGHLIGHTS OF THE AREA: Once you arrive in Valley Forge country, you'll realize that the park is only one of the attractions in this mélange of well-preserved 18th-century villages, rolling farm fields, and meandering back roads. Here is a sampling of some of the other sights:

Mill Grove, Audubon and Pawlings Roads, Audubon (tel. 666-5593), is the first American home of the world-famous artist/naturalist John James Audubon. Now a museum, this 1762 mansion was Audubon's home for only two years (1804–1806), but it was here that he gained his first impressions of American birds and wildlife on trips into the surrounding forests. Listed on the National Register, the house now serves as a display center for a collection of Audubon works, and the attic has been restored into a studio and taxidermy room, depicting the artist's working quarters when he lived here. With more than 175 species of birds and over 400 species of flowering plants thriving on the grounds, the entire 130-acre estate is a wildlife sanctuary, with miles of trails, feeding stations, nesting boxes, and plantings. Open Tuesday through Sunday from 10 a.m. to 5 p.m. (except Thanksgiving, Christmas, and New Year's Day). No admission charge.

The **Peter Wentz Farmstead,** Schultz Road, off Route 73, Worcester (tel.

584-5104), is a restored Colonial farmhouse, used by General Washington before and after the Battle of Germantown. You can tour the house and an 18th-century kitchen garden. Open Tuesday through Saturday from 10 a.m. to 4 p.m., and on Sunday from 1 to 4 p.m. Admission is free.

For shoppers, the Valley Forge area also includes the historic village of **Skippack,** on Route 73, a charming 18th-century enclave with more than 65 antique shops and boutiques; and the **Court and Plaza,** Route 202 and North Gulph Road, King of Prussia (tel. 265-5727). This is the home of seven major department stores and over 300 smaller shops and restaurants, making it the largest enclosed suburban shopping complex in the U.S. Open Monday through Saturday from 10 a.m. to 9:30 p.m., and on Sunday from noon to 5 p.m.

STAYING OVER: The lodging facilities in Valley Forge country have come a long way since George Washington's time. From dazzling conventional-style hotels to modern motels and restored country inns, you'll find a wide range of accommodations to suit every budget. Here is a sampling:

The **Sheraton Valley Forge Hotel,** North Gulph Road and First Avenue, King of Prussia, PA 19406 (tel. 215/337-2000 or toll-free 800/325-3535), is situated right across from the entrance to the historic park and adjacent to the Valley Forge Convention and Exhibit Center. With 16 floors, 330 rooms, and 79 suites, this modern circular tower is almost a city in itself. The guest rooms offer all the standard amenities and most units also have balconies overlooking the rolling hills and meadows of the countryside. Many visitors opt for one of the hotel's "fantasy" suites, furnished in various décors to reflect such faraway places as Tahiti or Casablanca; or nearby sites such as Olde Philadelphia, Chester County, or Park Avenue, NY; or places distant in time like Camelot or the Wild West. Double-occupancy rates range from $98 to $116 and suites average $170 to $175. Guest facilities include a health club, an outdoor pool, a video-dance nightclub, a café, a deli, a gourmet restaurant, and Lily Langtry's, a theater-restaurant showcasing a Las Vegas–style Follies revue. All major CC's are accepted.

A motel layout prevails at the sprawling **George Washington Lodge,** Route 202 and Warner Road, King of Prussia, PA 19406 (tel. 215/265-6100), situated off Exit 24 of the Pennsylvania Turnpike, and across from the Court and Plaza Shopping complex. Designed with a Colonial façade, this modern inn offers 335 rooms, all on ground level. Each unit is furnished with modern floral prints and a choice of two double beds or a king-size bed. The standard equipment includes wall-to-wall carpeting, color cable TV, a direct-dial phone, and air conditioning. Doubles start at $65. There is an outdoor and an indoor swimming pool, and a tavern-style lounge. All major CC's are accepted.

If you prefer a bed-and-breakfast ambience, then you'll enjoy settling at the **Joseph Ambler Inn,** 1005 Horsham Rd. (Route 463) (Montgomeryville), North Wales, PA 19454 (tel. 215/362-7500), a restored 1734 fieldstone farmhouse on a 13-acre estate. Eight rooms are available in the original house, and an additional seven units have been outfitted in an adjacent cottage. All are decorated with fabrics, antiques, period reproduction furniture, and accessories reflecting the 18th century. Most rooms have stenciled walls, Oriental rugs, and original woodwork, as well as canopy or four-poster beds, old chests, and armoires, and they all have the modern conveniences of a private bath, air conditioning, television, and telephone. Doubles range from $82 to $130 and include a full country egg breakfast. All major CC's are accepted.

WHERE TO DINE: The Valley Forge Convention and Visitors Bureau publishes a very comprehensive restaurant guide for the area. Be sure to ask for it. In the meantime, here are a few suggestions to whet your appetite (in more ways than one!):

The **Baron's Inne,** 499 N. Gulph Rd., King of Prussia (tel. 265-2550), is one of the restaurants nearest to the entrance of the Valley Forge Park. Dating back to the 1800s, this building is named for Baron Freidrich von Steuben, the Prussian General who offered his services to General Washington. The décor is understandably Colonial with assorted bric-a-brac, antiques, and oil paintings, while the menu incorporates some dishes from von Steuben's homeland. For lunch, priced from $5.25 to $7.50, you can expect to find an assortment of hefty sandwiches and salads, as well as such dishes as Wiener Schnitzel and flounder rouladen (with artichokes). The dinner menu features many tableside flambé preparations, such as veal and scallop Nantua (in a shrimp sauce flamed with anisette), and tournedos Rossini; other selections include Swiss sautéed veal, bouillabaisse, crabmeat soufflé, and pork filets garnished with gorgonzola cheese and tomato coulis. Entrees are priced from $14.50 to $18.50 and come with salad, potato, and vegetables. Lunch is served Monday through Friday from 11 a.m. to 2:30 p.m.; and dinner Monday through Thursday from 5 to 10:30 p.m., and on Friday and Saturday until 11 p.m. All major CC's are accepted.

Dating back to 1743, the **Blue Bell Inn,** 601 Skippack Pike, Blue Bell (tel. 646-2010), has had a storied past. Originally titled the White House because of its façade, it was referred to as the White Horse Inn by military troops in 1777. It is said that George Washington stayed here on the second floor, in room number six, since converted into a banquet hall. Whether he recommended the food, we do not know, but we can, especially at dinner. Entrees are priced from $10 to $24, with most under $15. The choices range from rainbow trout amandine, two-pound lobsters, and deviled crab, to frogs' legs, double-rib lamb chops, and Chateaubriand. Main courses come with salad and vegetables of the day. Lunch is served Tuesday through Saturday from noon to 2:30 p.m.; and dinner Tuesday through Friday from 5 to 10 p.m., and Saturday until 10:30 p.m. CC's accepted: AE, MC, and V.

If you want to follow in the footsteps of Pennsylvania's founder, then try the **William Penn Inn,** Route 202 and Sumneytown Pike, Gwynedd (tel. 699-9272), about 10 miles northeast of Valley Forge. According to local history, William Penn came here in 1700 to visit some Quaker friends. Their original house has since been greatly expanded into an elegant restaurant, but the furnishings and the background music impart the ambience of long ago. Lunch items, priced from $4.95 to $10.95, range from sandwiches, salads, quiches, and crêpes, to more Colonial fare such as pot pies, Welsh rarebit in casserole, and steaks. The entrees at dinner are priced from $11 to $25, with most around the $15 mark. Specialties include rack of lamb, Old English mixed grill, roasted tenderloin of pork, prime ribs, lobster tails, and baked capon. All main courses are accompanied by potato and vegetable. Hours for lunch are Monday through Saturday from 11:30 a.m. to 3 p.m.; dinner Monday through Thursday, from 5 to 10 p.m., and Friday and Saturday until 11 p.m.; and on Sunday, brunch from 11 a.m. to 3 p.m. and dinner from 3 to 8 p.m. All major CC's are accepted.

It would be hard to leave this area without a stop at the **Perkiomen Bridge Hotel,** One Main St., Collegeville (tel. 489-9511), about six miles north of Valley Forge on Routes 422 and 29. Tradition has it that the first hotel on this site was built around 1689, and then enlarged in 1701, as it became a stagecoach stop between Philadelphia and Reading. Some say this is America's oldest hotel in continuous operation and in November 1984 it was placed on the National Register of Historic Places. In recent years, it has primarily been a restaurant, although 17 rooms with private bath are currently being outfitted on the second and third floors. Meals are served in the old-world dining room as well as on a patio deck pavilion overlooking the peaceful waters of the Perkiomen Creek. Lunch items, priced from $2.95 to $3.95, focus primarily on burgers, sandwiches, salads, and omelets. The menu at dinner has an Italian slant, with such dishes as chicken cacciatore or parmesan; veal scaloppine or marsala; sirloin steak pizziaola; as well as seafoods, steaks, and surf-and-turf. All entrees, priced from $9.95 to $16.95, with most under $14, come with potato or linguine, salad, and vegetable. Lunch is served Monday through Saturday from 11 a.m. to 2 p.m.; and dinner Monday through Saturday from 4 p.m. to 2 a.m.; and on Sunday from 3 to 8 p.m. CC's accepted: AE, MC, and V.

BUCKS COUNTY

WITH ITS PERVASIVE BUCOLIC CHARM, Bucks County is one of the most popular single-county destinations in the whole Mid-Atlantic region. And for many good reasons. Not only did George Washington sleep here (and cross the Delaware from here), but many famous Americans have lived here over the years, from Pearl Buck and James Michener to Moss Hart, Dorothy Parker, George S. Kaufman, and legions of artists and writers. With all of Pennsylvania in his grasp, William Penn also chose Bucks County as his country retreat in the New World.

A mélange of wooded hillsides, river lowlands, sylvan towpaths, open fields, authentic historic districts, covered bridges, and welcoming country inns, Bucks County offers a magical vacation blend of sightseeing, outdoor activities, and creature comforts. Bounded by the Delaware River on the east, Philadelphia to the south, bustling Montgomery County on the west, and the Lehigh Valley to the north, Bucks County is a 620-square-mile region, just 20 miles wide and 60 miles long. It is compact enough to drive around in a day and yet so diverse that two weeks is hardly enough to see it all.

1. A Bit of Background

Named for Buckingham, England, which was the shire in which William Penn was born, Bucks County first gained prominence because of its location along the Delaware River. In the early 18th century a number of ferries were started from the Bucks side of the river to the New Jersey shores.

The towns that sprung up around these operations were usually named after the men who ran the ferries; thus New Hope was originally called Well's Ferry, then Canby's Ferry, and Coryell's Ferry; and Reigelsville was first referred to as Shenk's Ferry. It was the McConkey Ferry in the lower part of the county that transported General Washington and his troops across the river for the historic Battle of Trenton in December of 1776. This event is still commemorated to this day with the annual re-enactment on Christmas Day of "Washington Crossing the Delaware." Washington Crossing has also been designated as a park and a place name along Route 32.

After the ferries, it was the Delaware Canal that spurred further development in this area during the mid-19th century. The canal, with its towpath running side-by-side along the river, provided a source of transport between Easton and New Jersey. New Hope, in particular, became an important point along the canal as it was the only place where four barges could pass at one time. At that time many mills were also built and operated along the river.

With the advent of the railroads and motorized transport, the ferries, canals, and mills faded into oblivion, but the historic homes and peaceful riverfront lands served to give the county a new lease on life as a colony of artists began to settle in the area. With the opening of the Bucks County Playhouse in 1939, a core of writers and performers also chose this peaceful region as a country retreat.

It didn't take long after that for a nest of country inns to spruce up their façades and for gourmet restaurants to spring up in converted mills or ferry houses throughout the county. Rustic all-purpose general stores have been joined by dozens of antique shops, art galleries, craft centers, and wineries. It's no wonder that tourists flock to Bucks. If all these historic landmarks and aesthetic experiences were not enough, this is also the home of Sesame Place, the children's wonderland presided over by Big Bird.

VISITOR INFORMATION: All types of helpful brochures, maps, accommodations lists, restaurant directories, and a calendar of events can be obtained by contacting the **Bucks County Tourist Commission,** 152 Swamp Rd., Doylestown, PA 18901 (tel. 215/345-4552). If you are visiting the office, it's located adjacent to the Moravian tile works property; Swamp Road is also known locally as Route 313 and is located between Routes 202 and 611. The office is open weekdays from 8:15 a.m. to 4:15 p.m. For specific data about the New Hope area, contact or visit the **New Hope Information Center,** Main and Mechanic Streets, New Hope, PA 18938 (tel. 215/862-5880). Hours for this office are from 9 a.m. to 5:30 p.m. on weekdays and from 10 a.m. to 6 p.m. on weekends.

AREA CODE: Bucks County telephone numbers are all in the 215 area code.

2. Getting to Bucks County

BY CAR: Interstate-95, the main north-south artery along the east coast, passes right through the lower part of Bucks County. The northern half of the county is just a few miles south of I-78 and Route 22, major east-west highways.

BY PLANE: Bucks County can be reached by air via Philadelphia International Airport, less than 20 miles south, where ground transport, including car rental, is readily available (see "Getting to Philadelphia" in Chapter III).

BY BUS: The **Southeastern Pennsylvania Transportation Authority (SEPTA)** offers commuter service throughout the county, from Philadelphia (tel. 215/574-7800). In addition, **West Hunterdon Transit** buses run from Port Authority Terminal in New York City to Route 202, New Hope; for information, call 212/564-8484.

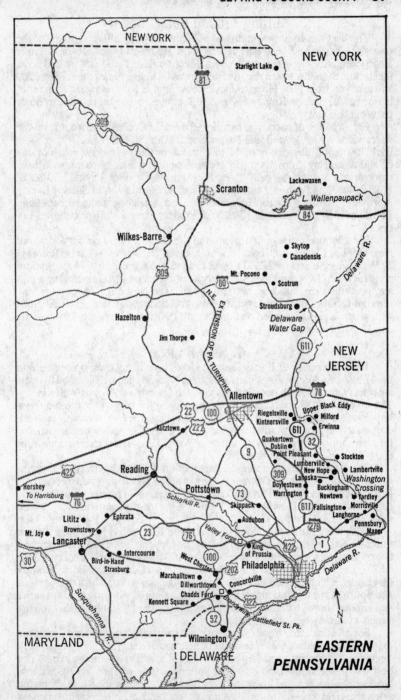

NEW YORK

NEW YORK

Starlight Lake

81

305

Lackawaxen

Scranton

L. Wallenpaupack

84

Wilkes-Barre

309

Skytop

Canadensis

Mt. Pocono

80

Scotrun

Delaware R.

Stroudsburg

Hazelton

*Delaware
Water Gap*

Jim Thorpe

611

NEW
JERSEY

N.E. EXTENSION OF PA. TURNPIKE

78

Allentown

22   100

Upper Black Eddy

Riegelsville   Milford

Kintnersville   Erwinna

611

Kutztown   222

Quakertown   32

9   Dublin

Point Pleasant   Stockton

Lumberville

422   New Hope   Lambertville

Reading   309   Lahaska   *Washington
Crossing*

Hershey   Pottstown   Doylestown   Buckingham

To Harrisburg   Warrington   Newton   Yardley

76   Schuylkill R.   73   611   Fallsington   Morrisville

Skippack   Langhorne

Lititz   Ephrata   Audubon   Pennsbury
Manor

Brownstown   276

Mt. Joy   23   76   Valley Forge   King   422   1

Lancaster   of Prussia

Intercourse   100

30   Bird-in-Hand   West Chester   202   Philadelphia

Strasburg   Marshalltown   Delaware R.

Dillworthtown   Concordville

Chadds Ford

Kennett Square   322

Susquehanna R.   1   Brandywine   Battlefield St. Pk.

52

N

MARYLAND   Wilmington   *EASTERN
PENNSYLVANIA*

DELAWARE

3. Getting Around Bucks County

The best way to get around Bucks County is by car, although many of the towns are easily and best explored by foot. Route 32 (also known as River Road) wends its way in the north-south direction along the Delaware and is the ideal route to follow to see the riverside towns including New Hope. Route 202 will take you from New Hope to Doylestown, and at Doylestown, a number of major roads, such as Routes 611 and 313, converge and branch out to other parts of the county.

For a change of pace, you can view the Bucks County riverfront from the water via the **New Hope Mule Barge,** South Main St. (tel. 862-2842). Dating back 150 years, this one-hour 11-mile canal excursion presents a panorama of sights ranging from riverside cottages and romantic gardens to artists' workshops. It operates daily from May 1 until October 15 at 11:30 a.m., 1, 2, 3, 4:30, and 6 p.m.; and on Wednesday, Saturday, and Sunday during April and October 16 to November 15, on a slightly reduced schedule. The fare is $4.95 for adults, $4.25 for students and $2.75 for children under 12.

For a leisurely nine-mile trip around the Bucks County countryside from New Hope to Lahaska and back, it's "all aboard" the **New Hope Steam Railway,** 32 W. Bridge St. (tel. 862-2707). Save time to explore the New Hope Station, constructed in 1891, and the rolling stock dating back to 1911, including a railway post-office car, caboose, and trolley cars. The 1½-hour ride operates May through October on Saturdays, Sundays, and holidays at 1:30 and 3:30 p.m., with an extra ride scheduled on Sundays at 11:30 a.m. The fare is $5 for adults and $3.50 for children.

4. New Hope

The centerpiece of Bucks County, New Hope first gained prominence in the 1720s when John Wells, a carpenter from Philadelphia, was licensed to operate a ferry and a tavern here and the townland became known as Well's Ferry. The original Old Ferry Tavern still exists today as the core of the building now known as the Logan Inn. The ferry operation across the Delaware was very important to the growth of this town and, as the ferry changed ownership, so also the town took on new names, and thus Well's Ferry later became known as Canby's Ferry and Coryell's Ferry.

The name New Hope was the result of another of the town's resources, grist and lumber mills. In 1790 some of mills burned down and were rebuilt by a local resident, Benjamin Parry. To show his optimism in his new structures, he christened them as "New Hope Mills," and so the town gained still another (and more permanent) name.

With its sylvan setting along the Delaware River, New Hope won fame in the early 20th century as an artist's colony, and, by the 1930s, the area became a haven for actors and writers from New York. Moss Hart and Dorothy Parker had homes here and other luminaries came to perform at the Bucks County Playhouse, which opened in 1939. This creative ambience, which still prevails and flourishes today, has also led to the blossoming of a myriad of art galleries and antique shops. Restored country inns and gourmet restaurants also line the streets of this idyllic riverside retreat.

For all of its attractions, New Hope is a surprisingly small town (no larger than one square mile, with a resident population of only 1500). Parking is very limited and traffic through Main Street moves at a snail's pace on weekends. The best way to see New Hope is to park your car where you are staying or a few blocks from the heart of town and walk back in to explore it on foot. Even the sidewalks tend to be crowded on summer weekends with legions of browsers and shoppers, so do consider a visit during midweek or in the off-season, if this is your first look at New Hope.

WHERE TO STAY AND DINE: The choice of places to stay in or near New Hope is mind-boggling; as you drive on River Road or along Route 202, you'll see many lodging signs and each one looks special in its own way. It is impossible to describe all of them, but we have chosen a cross-section, to give you an idea of the types of accommodations available—from modern 20th-century facilities to landmark inns or bed-and-breakfast homes.

It is always wise to make a reservation before you arrive, especially in the summer months and on weekends at all times. You will find that most establishments fall into the moderate-to-expensive category; and many places have a two-night minimum stay over weekends or three-night minimum during holiday periods. And remember, do not despair if New Hope is booked out. Because Bucks County is relatively small in area, you can stay in Reigelsville, Doylestown, or Newtown and still be within easy striking distance of all the attractions of New Hope.

One of the town's most unexpected pleasures is Pamela Minford's **Hacienda Inn,** 36 West Mechanic St., New Hope, PA 18938 (tel. 215/862-2078), just a block from Main Street in the center of town. Established in 1964, this Iberian-style retreat began as an extension of owner Pam Minford's antique business, in which she specialized in Spanish and Mexican furnishings and art. Today the inn offers 30 guest rooms, all decorated with original pieces selected by Pam. The rooms, which range from studios to suites, are mostly modern, with varying tones of beige and brown, mirrored walls, and lots of hanging plants and fresh flowers, as well as the usual comforts of color TV, a direct-dial phone, and air conditioning. Many units feature kitchenettes, Jacuzzis, fireplaces, spiral staircases, porches, and terrace decks. Outside there is a small garden courtyard and swimming pool. The price for two people ranges from $75 to $180, and that includes complimentary continental breakfast, wine and cheese in the lounge, and a $25 credit in the dining room. Saturday-night stays include a complimentary breakfast brunch buffet on Sunday morning. The Palm Court restaurant, open only for dinner, is worth a visit in its own right, with fine American cuisine (no, not Spanish) and soft piano music in the background. Entrees, which range from $9.95 to $22.95, with most choices under $15, include surf-and-turf; prime ribs; veal Cordon Bleu; breast of chicken with apple stuffing; sautéed frogs' legs, and a velvety seafood au gratin (crab, shrimp, scallops, and lobster). All main courses are accompanied by spinach and green salad, vegetable, and potato. The restaurant is open five nights a week, Wednesday through Saturday, 5 to 10 p.m., and on Sunday from 1 to 9 p.m. Brunch is also served from noon to 3 p.m. (closed January and February). All major CC's accepted.

In contrast, a short distance away is the **Logan Inn,** 10 W. Ferry St., New Hope, PA 18938 (tel. 215/862-5134), said to be New Hope's oldest building (1727), and situated adjacent to Main Street in the heart of town. Unlike some lodgings, this one was originally built as an inn (the Old Ferry Tavern) and has always operated as an inn. Over the years, the guest register has included George Washington who influenced the area's history, as well as stars who came to perform at the nearby playhouse, from Grace Kelly and Helen Hayes to Robert Redford. Current proprietors, Carl Lutz and Arthur Sanders, have taken great care to keep the inn in tiptop shape and have furnished it with an extensive collection of family antiques. The ten guest rooms upstairs (five with private bath and five with shared baths) are a veritable showcase of brass beds, rockers, carved chests, giant armoires, bentwood chairs, and one-of-a-kind pieces. Doubles are $85 with private bath and $75 without. To add to the delights of this wonderful inn, lunch is served in a Victorian-style conservatory, lined with three dozen types of orchids and a variety of thriving leafy plants. Priced from $4.25 to $6.75, lunch usually includes sandwiches, salads, and light dishes. Dinner is served in the house's main dining room, an elegant setting of antique furniture, velvet draperies, original oil paintings, globe lights, and an 1850 grandfather clock. The Italian chef is well versed in American dishes (including an award-winning Bloody Mary soup) as well as Russian and Swedish specialties and a few German recipes that have been in the Lutz family for centuries. Entrees range from $12.75 to $29.75 with most dishes $16 or under, including brook trout amandine, lobster tails, chicken divan, sauerbraten, sea trout in ginger lime sauce, and filet mignon. All main courses are accompanied by potato or rice, vegetable, and mixed green salad. Lunch is served from 11:30 a.m. to 2:30 p.m. and dinner from 6 to 10 p.m. every day except Christmas, New Year's Day, and early January to mid-February. CC's accepted: AE, MC, and V.

Three and a half miles north of midtown is the **Centre Bridge Inn,** Route 32, Box 74, New Hope, PA 18938 (tel. 215/862-2048), right on the Delaware River at the crossroads of Route 263 and River Road (Route 32). Although there has been an inn on this spot since the early 18th century, the current building is the third (the two previous structures were destroyed by fires). The story of the previous inns (including a resident ghost) is well documented on a wall display outside the main dining room. Upstairs there are nine elegant guest rooms, all with canopy, four-poster, or brass beds, wall-high armoires, modern private baths, air conditioning, and many with private fireplaces, outside decks, and views of the river or the countryside. Room rates for two people are $60 to $90 on weekdays and $75 to $115 on weekends, including continental breakfast. The Centre Bridge restaurant offers dining in a candlelight Colonial setting or al fresco on a patio overlooking the river. The cuisine has a French accent, with dinner entrees ranging from duckling and pheasant to rack of lamb, steaks, and seafood. All main courses, priced from $16.95 to $21.95, include salad and a choice of vegetables. Dinner hours are 5:30 to 9 p.m., Monday through Saturday, and from 3 to 9 p.m. on Sunday. Closed Christmas Day. CC's accepted: AE, D, MC, and V.

In the Budget Range

Just a mile west of town is the **New Hope Motel,** 400 W. Bridge St., New Hope, PA 18938 (tel. 215/862-2800), in a peaceful woodland setting off Route 179. For over 30 years, this 28-room facility has offered modern ground-level rooms with private bath, color TV, telephone, air conditioning, and one or two double beds. Open all year, it also has a swimming pool for guests' use during the summer months. Doubles cost $35 to $45. All major CC's accepted.

A Bed-and-Breakfast Choice

About five miles west of New Hope is **Barley Sheaf Farm,** Route 202 (P.O. Box 10), Holicong, PA 18928 (tel. 215/794-5104), a 1740 stone house that is a national historic site and one of the most popular B&B's in Bucks County. Once the home of playwright George S. Kaufman, earlier in this century this house was a gathering spot for visitors from the performing arts world (from the Marx Brothers to Lillian Hellman and S. J. Perlman). Set on a 30-acre working farm, this ivy-covered and mansard-roof house is the domain of Don and Ann Mills, who opened it to guests ten years ago. Six rooms and suites are available upstairs in the main house and three ground-level rooms in an adjoining cottage. All the rooms have queen or double beds, private bath, and antique furnishings; some rooms have fireplaces. Doubles range from $85 to $133, including all taxes. The price also covers a hearty full breakfast (including eggs from the farm, fresh-baked breads, jams, and honey from the hives on the grounds), served in a love-ly Colonial-style room overlooking the garden. Guests facilities include a parlor with TV and a swimming pool in season. Open daily from mid-February until the week before Christmas and then weekends only in January and February until the middle of the month. No CC's accepted.

WHERE TO DINE: New Hope is home to a cluster of fine restaurants, offering various styles, décors, and cuisines. Like the area's lodgings, most restaurants also fall into a moderate-to-expensive price bracket. Reservations are always advisable and imperative on weekends.

Surrounded by the waters of the canal and the river, **Chez Odette,** South River Road and Route 32. (tel. 862-2432), is located on the southern end of town. Operating since 1794 as a restaurant and previously called the Riverside, this spot was last owned by Odette Myrtle, a Broadway and Ziegfeld Follies star (1961–1976). Although Odette is no longer here, lots of her photos and memo-rabilia fill the walls, and entertainment (piano or guitar) is still an important factor here. The crafts and paintings of local artisans are also exhibited and are for sale. The menus are seasonal and change six times a year, with a cuisine that can best be described as "American nouvelle." Lunch, priced from $4.95 to $8.95, features salads, sandwiches, vegetarian and beef burgers, quiches, and tortillas. Dinner entrees include mesquite-grilled steaks, mahi mahi, Cornish game hen, and grilled tofu and Shiitake mushrooms, and cost from $12.95 to $19.95. Lunch is served Monday through Saturday from 11:30 a.m. to 3 p.m.; and dinner Monday through Friday from 5 to 10 p.m., on Saturday until 11 p.m., and on Sunday from 4 to 9 p.m. Sunday brunch is also available from 11 a.m. to 3 p.m. Closed Christmas. Most major CC's accepted.

Views of the water are also an attraction at **The Landing,** 22 N. Main St. (tel. 862-5711), a two-story house that is set back off the street on its own grounds along the river. The décor reflects a bit of old Bucks County with vin-tage prints, a large open fireplace, and antique chandeliers and lamps. Salads, sandwiches, quiches, chili, and pasta dishes are the focus at lunch (in the $3.95 to $6.95 price bracket). Dinner entrees, which change daily, are priced in the $14.95 to $18.95 range, and often include shrimp with a julienne of vegetables, coquilles St-Jacques, and rack of lamb with eggplant and tomato chutney. Lunch is served from 11:30 a.m. to 2:30 p.m. and dinner from 5:30 to 10 p.m. In the summer months, meals are served on the outdoor deck. Open daily (in Jan-uary through March, on Thursday through Sunday only). CC's accepted: D, MC, and V.

Another historic site-turned-restaurant along the river is **Martine's,** 7 East Ferry (tel. 862-2966), a 1792 building that has served this town variously as a salt storehouse, the free library of New Hope and Solebury, and a toll house for Coryell's Ferry. A restaurant for the last ten years, this building still has its origi-nal fireplace and beamed ceilings, along with some modern enhancements like Tiffany lamps, tiled tables, and a relaxing outdoor porch; but the menus are strictly 20th-century. Lunch, priced from $3.95 to $6.95, ranges from stews, sal-ads, and burgers to fondue with steamed vegetables, seafood pastas, gourmet burgers, and pâté and cheese plates. Dinner choices, in the $13 to $16 range, include roast game hen, shrimp florentine, brook trout with fresh spinach and crab stuffing, rack of lamb, and filet mignon with lobster cardinale sauce. Lunch is available from 11:30 a.m. to 2:30 p.m. and dinner from 5:30 to 10 p.m. CC's accepted: CB, D, MC, and V.

The lines are usually outside the door for a table at **Mothers,** 34 N. Main St.

(tel. 862-9354), a trendy and informal dining spot. Composed of two adjoining brick houses in the middle of town, this is the place to come if you like a décor of modern art, small close tables, lots of noise, a background of rock music, and imaginative cuisine. Lunch, from $3.50 to $8, includes tofu burgers, marinated salads, omelets, and crêpes. Dinner entrees, which run from $7.95 to $16.95 with most around the $15 mark, feature stir-fry foods, tasty Cajun and Mexican dishes, gourmet pastas (such as duck pizza), Szechuan linguine, herb-crusted pork loin, and Créole-stuffed trout. Desserts are so cleverly concocted here that baking classes are given regularly by the management. Hours are daily from 11 a.m. to 5 p.m. for lunch and from 5 to 10:30 p.m. for dinner; also breakfast from 8 a.m. to 2 p.m. CC's accepted: AE, MC, and V.

Five miles west of New Hope, in the heart of Peddler's Village, is **Jenny's,** Route 202, Lahaska (tel. 794-5605), a modern restaurant with the décor and ambience of yesteryear. Lunch, priced from $4.95 to $8.95, features sandwiches, salads, crêpes, quiches, burgers, omelets, pastas, and unique dishes like ham, tomato, asparagus, and Cheddar rarebit. Dinner entrees, priced from $11 to $22, include shrimp in champagne sauce, lobster and crab sauté, roast duckling, chicken florentine, and veal, steak, and pasta dishes. Desserts ($2 to $3.50) are also very tempting—from chocolate truffle torte to macadamia nut pie or amaretto mousse. If you have dinner here, you can also enjoy music and dancing Wednesday through Saturday nights. Lunch is served Monday through Saturday from 11:30 a.m. to 3 p.m.; dinner Tuesday through Saturday from 5:30 to 10 p.m., and Sunday from 4:30 to 9 p.m. Sunday brunch is also available from 11 a.m. to 3 p.m. Most major CC's accepted.

Budget Meals

Wildflowers Garden Café, 8 W. Mechanic St. (tel. 862-2241), is an old house with a screened back porch overlooking the canal. Ideal for lunch or light meals, this restaurant is decorated—as its name implies—with lots of wildflowers. Continuous opera music in the background adds to the relaxing ambience. The selection of dishes, priced from $3 to $5.95, includes cream of peanut soup, beef taco salad, and homemade chili. All breads are baked on the premises and include potato and caraway, onion and walnut, and wholewheat with raisins and walnuts. The homemade desserts range from apple-blueberry and cranberry surprise ice creams to Belgian apple waffle cake. BYOB. Open from early morning until 7 p.m. CC's accepted: MC and V.

TOP ATTRACTIONS: A walk around New Hope is a walk through history—no less than 243 properties are included on the National Register of Historic Places. One of the loveliest old houses in the town is the **Parry Mansion,** Main and Ferry Streets (tel. 862-5652), erected in 1784 by a lumber and grist mill owner, Benjamin Parry (the man who is responsible for the name "New Hope"). Parry lived in this fieldstone house until his death in 1839 and it was then occupied only by his direct descendants, five generations of the Parry family, until it was purchased by the New Hope Historical Society in 1966. Now open to the public, this 11-room Georgian Colonial house is decorated in period-style with furnishings from 1775 through 1900. Each room on the first and second floor is restored and decorated to represent the lifestyle of a short span within the 125-year period. Open from May through October, Friday through Monday from 1 to 5 p.m., there is an admission charge of $1.50.

Three miles west of New Hope, you can taste wine produced from Pennsylvania grapes at **Bucks Country Vineyards,** Route 202 (tel. 794-7449). Housed in an old red barn, this winery was started in 1973 and today produces more than

20 varieties of alcoholic and nonalcoholic wines. Visitors are welcome to enjoy the winery, cellars, a wine museum, and the tasting room (which includes cheeses produced at the winery). Hours are Monday through Friday, 11 a.m. to 5 p.m.; Saturdays and holidays, 10 a.m. to 6 p.m.; and Sundays, noon to 6 p.m. Admission and parking are free. An added attraction at the winery is a Broadway Costume Museum, featuring original outfits worn by such stars as Ethel Merman, Mary Martin, Paul Robeson, Richard Burton, and Julie Andrews. Admission charge to the museum is $1.

Self-guided wine tours and tastings (at no charge) are also available at the nearby **Buckingham Valley Vineyard and Winery,** Route 413, Buckingham (tel. 794-7188), just south of Route 202. A small family-owned enterprise, this winery was started in 1966 on 15 acres, and today produces 100,000 bottles a year. Open from Tuesday through Friday from noon to 6 p.m.; Saturday from 10 a.m. to 6 p.m.; and Sunday from noon to 4 p.m. (weekends only in January and February).

NIGHTLIFE: Delightfully situated along the banks of the Delaware River, the **Bucks County Playhouse,** 70 S. Main St., (P.O. Box 313), New Hope, PA 18938 (tel. 862-2041) provides a regular program of Broadway classics, ranging from *A Chorus Line* and *Camelot,* to *Annie* and *Ain't Misbehavin'*. From June through August, performances are nightly (except Monday) plus matinees on Wednesday and Thursday. Schedule varies at other times of the year (closed January through April). A former gristmill with a capacity for almost 500 people, the playhouse should have a particularly special year in 1989 as it celebrates its 50th season. Single ticket prices range from $10 to $15. Parking is $3. CC's accepted: AE, MC, and V.

Next door is **Club Zadar's Video Dance Club,** 50 S. Main St., New Hope (tel. 862-5085). This is a new-wave dance club with large video screen. Open Monday through Saturday from 9 p.m. to 2 a.m. and on Sunday from 2 p.m. to 2 a.m. Admission charge is $4, except Sunday when it is $2.

Broadway shows are also on the playbill at the **Theatre on the Tow Path,** 18–20 W. Mechanic St. (tel. 862-5217). Situated on Ingram's Creek and featuring an outdoor terrace, this theater-restaurant is open year round; shows are scheduled for Friday and Saturday nights, with dinner at 6:30 p.m. and show time at 8:30 p.m. Price of dinner and show is $30 and show only is $10. In addition, the adjacent Towpath Restaurant stages "Folk Soup," a Wednesday evening series of traditional music concerts, at 8 p.m. Prices depend on the attraction but usually range from $3 to $7. CC's accepted: MC and V.

A third choice is **Peddler's Village Dinner Theater,** in the **Cock 'n Bull Restaurant,** Routes 202 and 263, Lahaska (tel. 794-3460), which features a country buffet with a varied program of entertainment ranging from solo performers to Broadway musicals. From July through September, the program commences at 7 p.m. on Thursday, Friday, and Saturday and at 5 p.m. on Sunday, with noon matinees on Wednesday, Thursday, and Saturday. There is also a winter season (January through March) with shows at 7 p.m. on Friday and Saturday plus a Saturday noon matinee. Ticket prices range from $23.50 to $30.50; CC's accepted: AE, MC, and V.

Music and light entertainment are also featured at a number of restaurants in New Hope, including the Palm Court of the **Hacienda,** 36 W. Mechanic St. (tel. 862-2078); **Odette's,** South River Road, Route 32 (tel. 862-2432); and the **Centre Bridge Inn,** North River Road (tel. 862-9139).

SHOPPING: Step back into an 18th-century market atmosphere at **Peddler's Village,** Routes 202 and 263 at Lahaska (tel. 794-7438). With 62 craft shops, antique dealers, taverns, and restaurants, this mélange of Americana is open daily, year round, Monday through Thursday from 10 a.m. to 5:30 p.m.; Friday until 9 p.m.; Saturday until 6 p.m.; and Sunday from noon to 5:30 p.m. Special events staged at the village include a Festival of Flowers in early June, a Teddy Bear's Picnic in mid-July, a Country Bargain Fest in late August, Apple Festival in early November, and a Country Christmas Festival on the first Saturday in December.

In the heart of New Hope you'll find the **Old Franklin Print Shop,** Cannon Square, Main and Ferry Streets (tel. 862-2956). An 1860 hand press is the center of attention here, with daily demonstrations of the art of printing. Items for sale include a large selection of reproduced historical documents, tavern signs, comic posters, book covers, citations, and newspapers, mostly in the $2 to $5 price range. Open Monday through Saturday from 10 a.m. to 5 p.m., and from 1 to 5 p.m. on Sunday. No CC's accepted.

Bucks County is antique territory. More than 50 dealers are located throughout the county, with the greatest concentration (more than 20) in Lahaska and New Hope; the area along Route 202 between New Hope and Lahaska, in fact, is commonly known as "antiques row." A guide and map outlining the antiquing centers can be obtained from the tourist office or by writing directly to the **Bucks County Antiques Dealers Association,** P.O. Box 573, Lahaska, PA 18931.

CHILDREN'S CORNER: A special treat for young travelers in this area is **Quarry Valley Farm,** Street Road, Lahaska (tel. 794-5882), a prototype of a 1700s farm and barnyard with animals. Children can see demonstrations of sheepshearing and cow-milking, as well as working craftsmen, including a blacksmith, a farrier, weavers, and potters. Many of the exhibits are designed for "please touch" experiences. Open from April through December, Monday through Saturday from 10 a.m. to 5:30 p.m.; admission is $3.50 for adults and $2.50 for children under 12.

5. Doylestown

In the heart of Bucks County, Doylestown has been the county seat of this area since 1813. A lot larger than New Hope, Doylestown is a 2.3-square-mile city, with a population of 9,000. Situated less than 15 miles north of Philadelphia, it is also at the intersection of a number of roads that traverse the county including Routes 611, 202, and 313. It is, therefore, a central base for touring the rest of the region.

The city traces its name back to 1745 when William Doyle obtained a license for a public house. Since the pub was at the intersection of some welltraveled Colonial highways, the entire area became known variously as Doyl's Tavern, Doyle's Town, Doyletown, and finally the present Doylestown.

With a mix of Federal and Victorian architecture, Doylestown is home to the county's largest historic district on the National Register (nearly 1,200 buildings). Primarily a residential and professional community, Doylestown was the birthplace of such well-known figures as writer James Michener; anthropologist Dr. Margaret Mead; and archeologist, historian, and inventor Henry Chapman Mercer, who was responsible for the colorful Mercer tiles that decorate so many buildings of the area. A few miles away at Perkasie, author Pearl S. Buck also made her home.

WHERE TO STAY: Like New Hope, Doylestown offers many fine country inns and bed-and-breakfast homes for overnight stays. Although the rates can generally be classified as moderate, there can sometimes be surcharges on weekends and minimum-stay requirements.

The top choice in this area is **The Inn at Fordhook Farm,** 105 New Britain Rd., Doylestown, PA 18901 (tel. 215/345-1766), an 18th-century stone house built as a country retreat by W. Atlee Burpee (founder of the seed company of the same name). Opened as a bed-and-breakfast only since 1985, this gracious home is still owned by the Burpee family and contains original furnishings, fireplaces with colorful Mercer tiles, silver, china, books, and old pictures, all in a setting of a 60-acre private estate with seasonal flower gardens, 200-year-old linden trees, pine forests, woodlands, meadows, and walking paths. Six guest rooms are available upstairs, three with private bath and three with shared bath, and all are furnished with antiques; brass, canopy, or rope beds; and family heirlooms, with lots of fresh flowers and plants. Some bedrooms have working fireplaces and balconies and three rooms have air conditioning. A full farm breakfast is served in the family dining room, which is a showcase of fine linens, silverware, leaded-glass windows, beamed ceiling, and a tiled fireplace with a carved mantle. Afternoon tea is provided in the living room or on the outdoor terrace. Double-occupancy rates, which include both the breakfast and the tea, range from $65 to $90. In addition, a completely renovated carriage house in a carved-chestnut motif, with two bedrooms, two private baths, a full kitchen, and living room, can also be rented by two to four people, at $100 for one couple or $140 for two couples. The inn is located on a quiet country road, 1½ miles west of Doylestown, just beyond the intersection of Routes 202 and 611. The innkeeper is Laurel Raymond; no CC's accepted.

Northeast of town is the **Pear and Partridge Inn,** 4424 Old Easton Rd., Doylestown, PA 18901 (tel. 215/345-7800), located about a half mile off Route 313 (Swamp Road). Nestled along a gentle brook, the original section of this inn was built in 1714, as a grist mill, and it is said that the mill supplied flour to General Washington's troops and lodging for Lafayette and his officers. Not much has changed since then; the scene is early American with huge darkened beams, heavy stone walls, open fireplaces, hanging copper pots, framed needlework, candlelight, and Colonial music. The ten double and twin bedrooms, which purposely do not have telephones or televisions, aim to preserve the Colonial atmosphere, although they do have private and semi-private bathrooms. Rates for two people are from $55 to $75 during weekdays and from $70 to $85 on weekends, including fresh fruit in each room and a substantial continental breakfast. About the only thing with a contemporary tempo here is the kitchen which can best be described as nouvelle American. Lunch, priced from $4.95 to $9.95, features gourmet pizzas, crêpes, pastas, stir-frys, and California cuisine. Dinner entrees focus on blackened Cajun-style sole, grilled swordfish with coconut cream, shrimp and snow crab Oscar, chicken Cordon Bleu, tournedos of beef with grain-mustard sauce, and lobster tails. Priced from $16.95 to $24.95, all entrees come with salad, relishes, and an intermezzo course. There are five separate dining areas, from intimate club rooms to an enclosed patio with a view of the water.

Lunch is served on Tuesday through Saturday from 11:30 a.m. to 3 p.m.; dinner on Tuesday through Saturday from 5:30 to 10 p.m., and on Sunday from 5:30 to 9 p.m. A Sunday brunch buffet is available from 11:30 a.m. to 3 p.m., priced at $14.95 and featuring recipes borrowed from restaurants around the world (from the Claridge in London to Anthony's of Atlanta). Closed Monday and mid-January to early February. Major CC's accepted.

If you prefer to stay right in the heart of town, then try the **Doylestown Inn,** 18 W. State St., Doylestown, PA 18901 (tel. 215/345-6610), a renovated Victorian-style hotel dating back to 1902. There are 22 bedrooms with country furnishings, and each with private bath, air conditioning, and TV. Doubles range from $60 to $70. Other amenities include a tavern and a lounge that features jazz entertainment from Wednesday through Sunday nights. The restaurant, which looks out on to the main thoroughfare of Doylestown, is a showcase of brass fixtures, gold-leafed wall mirrors, crystal chandeliers, hanging plants, and paintings of local scenes. Lunch, priced from $3 to $5.95, includes sandwiches, salads, omelets, and ever-changing daily specials. Dinner items, mostly in the $9 to $14.95 price bracket, range from veal saltimbocca, walnut chicken in brandy cream sauce, seafood stir-fry, and blackened Cajun prime rib to farm-raised Pennsylvania trout. All main courses are accompanied by vegetables and a selection of fresh breads. Open Monday through Saturday for lunch, from 11:30 a.m. to 2:30 p.m.; Sunday from 1 to 4 p.m.; and for dinner Monday through Thursday from 5 to 10 p.m.; Friday and Saturday until midnight, and Sunday from 4 to 9 p.m. Open daily except Christmas. All major CC's accepted.

A Convenient Motor Inn

For those who prefer the more modern lodgings, there is the **Warrington Motor Lodge,** Route 611, North of Route 132, Warrington, PA 18976 (tel. 215/343-0373). Situated on a busy road four miles south of Doylestown, this rambling one-story motel offers 75 units, all with private bath, color TV, direct-dial phone, and air conditioning. Other guest facilities include an outdoor swimming pool, and a fitness room. Doubles start at $55. Most major CC's accepted.

WHERE TO DINE: You'll find a satisfying variety of restaurants in the Doylestown area.

The Top Choices

One of the oldest restaurants in Doylestown is the **Conti Cross Keys Inn,** Easton Highway and Swamp Road (tel. 348-9600 or 348-3539). Built in 1723, and first licensed as the Cross Keys Tavern in 1758, this building also served as one of first tollhouses on the road from Philadelphia to Easton. It was purchased in 1945 by Emily and Frank Conti, emigrants from northern Italy, and has been carried on ever since by three generations of the same family. Although a section of the original tavern remains, the restaurant has expanded over the years and now seats 300, with a choice of four different rooms, from Colonial to art deco motifs. Lunch, priced from $5 to $10, mainly focuses on sandwiches, salads, and pastas. Dinner entrees, priced from $15 to $24.50, are much more elaborate with such choices as lamb Wellington, sweetbreads, monkfish with capers, Dover sole, crab au gratin, lobster tails, and chicken piccante with artichoke hearts. All main courses come with salad, vegetable, and potato. Open Monday through Saturday for lunch from 11:30 a.m. to 3 p.m. and dinner from 3 to 10 p.m. Closed Sundays, Thanksgiving, Christmas, and New Year's Day. All major CC's accepted.

Four miles south of Doylestown is another restaurant with a proud history, **Vincent's Warrington Inn,** 1371 Route 611 and Bristol Road, Warrington (tel. 343-0210). This old stone building, dating back to 1757, was purchased in 1917 by the Coggiola family and is now in the hands of the fourth generation. A Colonial décor prevails throughout, with stone walls, exposed beams, open fireplaces, and early American furnishings. Lunch, priced from $3.95 to $11.95, offers a selection of seafood platters, omelets, sandwiches, salads, and pastas. Dinner selections, priced in the $12.95 to $22.50 bracket, range from bouillabaisse or lobster tails to rack of lamb, garlic steak, and prime ribs. All entrees come with salad, vegetable, and potatoes. There is live piano entertainment

Wednesday through Saturday. Open Monday through Saturday for lunch from 11:30 a.m. to 3 p.m. and for dinner from 6:30 to 11 p.m. Early-bird dinner specials are also featured each evening from 4:30 to 6:30 p.m. Major CC's accepted.

For a countryside setting, drive about ten miles north of Doylestown to the **Lake House Inn,** 1100 Old Bethlehem Rd., Perkasie (tel. 257-5351). Established over 15 years ago, this lovely restaurant overlooks Lake Nockamixon, from the windows of its nautical dining room or from its outdoor deck. Sandwiches, salads, and light seafood fare are featured at lunchtime, in the $4.95 to $12.95 price range. Dinner entrees, priced from $12.95 to $21.95 with most over $15, include such varied dishes as oyster and crab casserole, lobster Newburg in puff pastry, seafood pastas, stir-fried chicken and vegetables, veal Oscar, and beef Wellington. All main courses are accompanied by salad, vegetable, and potato. Lunch is served Tuesday through Saturday from 11:30 a.m. to 2:30 p.m.; and dinner Tuesday through Saturday from 5 to 10 p.m., and Sunday from 3 to 8 p.m. Sunday brunch is also available from 11:30 a.m. to 2:30 p.m. Closed Monday and early January. All major CC's accepted.

Moderately Priced Dining

About 15 miles northwest of Doylestown is Quakertown and the home of the **Benetz Inn,** Route 309 (tel. 536-6315), a restaurant started in 1948 by the parents of the present owner, Frank Benetz. This site today is actually two restaurants, the original Benetz Inn and a new spot with lighter fare called The Cloister. The original inn features a décor and menu with Bavarian and European overtones. The lunchtime menu, priced from $3.95 to $8.95, offers sandwiches, burgers, hot entrees, and a sumptuous salad bar. Dinner entrees, priced from $9.75 to $19.95 with most under $15, range from sauerbraten and spätzle to fresh salmon with Dijon mustard sauce; baby lobster tails; roast young turkey; crab and lobster Wellington; prime ribs; and a signature dish, veal Benetz (with broccoli, provolone cheese, and mushrooms). All main courses come with salad, potato, relishes, and fresh-baked breads. Open for lunch Monday through Friday from 11 a.m. to 2 p.m., and on Saturday from 11 a.m. to 3 p.m.; for dinner Monday through Thursday from 4:30 to 9 p.m., on Friday from 4:30 to 9:30 p.m., and on Saturday from 4 to 9:30 p.m. Sunday hours are from noon to 7:30 p.m.

The Cloister, which has its own separate kitchen and serving staff (attired in monk-style robes), is designed with stained glass and various arches and alcoves, reminiscent of an ancient monastic dwelling. The atmosphere is informal and the menu is geared toward fun, with selections identified with names appropriate to the setting (such as "Sistine Scampi," "Divine Scallops Divan," and "Righteous Ravioli"). Lunch consists mainly of burgers, salads, and sandwiches, in the $2.75 to $6.95 price range. Dinner entrees, which go for $7.95 to $12.95, include prime rib, seafood, and ribs and pasta dishes, all served with salad bar. Hours are Monday from 2 p.m. to midnight; Tuesday through Friday, from noon to midnight; Saturday from 4:30 p.m. to midnight; and Sunday for brunch from 10:15 a.m. to 2 p.m. and dinner from 4 to 9 p.m. All major CC's are accepted in both the Benetz Inn and the Cloister.

If you are anxious to dine in downtown Doylestown, the best choice is **B. Maxwells,** 37 N. Main St. (tel. 348-1027), a two-story Victorian-style restaurant opened in 1984. The décor is a mélange of floral wallpaper, dark wood trim, sconce lamps, smoked-glass windows, brass fixtures, and old-fashioned booth seating. The lunch menu, which is priced from $2.95 to $5.95, features sandwiches, croissantwiches, omelets, and burgers. Dinner focuses on an international range of cuisine, ranging from Cajun dishes, stir-fries, and pastas to steak Diane, flounder amandine, veal parmesan, and chicken marsala. Most dishes are priced from $9.95 to $14.95 and are served with salad or soup, potato, and vegetable. Senior citizen specials are also available most days. Open Monday through Thursday from 11 a.m. to 11 p.m.; and on Friday and Saturday from 11 a.m. to midnight. There is ample parking in the rear of the restaurant. CC's accepted: AE, MC, and V.

Budget Meals
Meyers Family Restaurant, 501 N. West End Blvd. (Route 309), Quakertown (tel. 536-4422), is well known for its friendly atmosphere and its bakeshop full of eat-in or take-out cakes, desserts, cookies, and jams. Salads, sandwiches, and burgers are good choices at lunchtime ($1.95 to $4.95). Dinner entrees, in the $4.95 to $10.95 bracket, include seafood, steaks, chicken, and turkey dishes, served with potato and vegetable. Nightly dinner specials are usually under $5 for such selections as chicken florentine, filet of whitefish, or beef turnover; breakfast is also served each day. Open Sunday through Thursday from 7 a.m. to 10 p.m.; Friday and Saturday from 7 a.m. to 11 p.m., except three days at Christmas; also Sunday brunch from 9 a.m. to 1 p.m. CC's accepted: AE, CB, MC, and V.

TOP ATTRACTIONS: Some of Doylestown's leading sights are associated with a local entrepreneur named Henry Chapman Mercer (1856–1930) who was a master of ceramics and crafts as well as being somewhat of an archeologist and antiquarian. Because so many Mercer-built or -inspired attractions dominate a fairly small area, they are known collectively as "The Mercer Mile." If you stroll along "the mile," here's what you will see:
Fonthill Museum, East Court Street, off Swamp Road (Route 313) (tel. 348-9461), which has the trappings of a medieval castle, was the home Mercer built to exhibit his collection of tiles and prints from around the world. Open Monday through Sunday (except Thanksgiving, Christmas, and New Year's Day), from 10 a.m. to 5 p.m., the inside of the house can be viewed only by guided tours from 10 a.m. to 3:30 p.m., and reservations are suggested. Admission charges are $3 for adults, and $1.50 for students.
The adjacent building with the tile chimneys is the **Moravian Pottery and Tile Works** on Swamp Road (tel. 345-6722), where much of Mercer's work took place. Moorish-shaped, today it is a living-history museum, still producing Mercer tile according to the original methods. Open all year, entrance is free, but tours, conducted every half-hour, cost $2 for adults and $1.50 for students, Wednesday through Sunday from 10 a.m. to 4 p.m.
At the other end of "the mile" you'll come to the **Mercer Museum** on Pine Street at Ashland Street (tel. 345-0210), a monumental building with Gothic, Norman, and Spanish influences. This is a display of more than 40,000 tools representing sixty different crafts and trades. Open from March through December (except for Thanksgiving and Christmas), Monday through Saturday, 10 a.m. to 5 p.m., and Sunday from 1 to 5 p.m. The museum itself is a classic example of Mercer's own use of concrete. Also inside the museum is the Spruance Library, a research collection on Bucks County genealogy and history of trades, crafts, and early industries. It is open year round on Tuesday from 1 to 9 p.m. and Wednesday through Friday from 10 a.m. to 5 p.m. (except for Independence Day, Thanksgiving, Christmas, and New Year's. Admission to both museum and library is $3 for adults, and $1.50 for students.
An attraction of a different nature is the **National Shrine of Our Lady of Czestochowa,** Ferry Road, Beacon Hill, Doylestown (tel. 345-0600). Estab-

lished in 1955, in honor of a religious shrine in Poland, this 240-acre estate is the site of frequent pilgrimages and gatherings of Polish cultural interest. Open Monday through Saturday from 9 a.m. to 5 p.m.; no admission charge.

Green Hills Farm, Pearl S. Buck's 1835 stone farmhouse, at 520 Dublin Rd., off Route 313, Perkasie (tel. 249-0100), is a national landmark, about eight miles northwest of Doylestown. Ten of the house's 19 rooms are on view, furnished with the author's Oriental and American art and antiques, including "The Good Earth Desk" from her attic study in China; her Nobel and Pulitzer prizes are also on display. Two one-hour guided tours are conducted daily from May through September (except Saturdays, Memorial Day, and Labor Day), Monday through Friday at 10:30 a.m. and 2 p.m., and on Sundays at 1:30 and 2:30 p.m. Donation is $4 for adults, $3 for children.

Quakertown Farmers Market, 201 Station Rd., Quakertown (tel. 536-4115), is an antique and flea market that has been a Bucks County institution since 1932. Commonly known as the Q'Mart, this huge (equivalent to the size of two football fields) market contains more than 150 individual stores, shops, factory outlets, and dealers. Open Friday and Saturday from 10 a.m. to 10 p.m. and on Sunday from 11 a.m. to 5 p.m.

6. Along North River Road

River Road, also known as Route 32, follows the flow of the Delaware River along the eastern shoreline of Bucks County. It is an ideal path for a scenic drive at any time of the year. This 60-mile stretch is also a perfect setting for boating, canoeing, swimming, picnicking, tubing, rafting, hiking, and just plain walking. The northern section between New Hope and Riegelsville is a particular delight, with a parade of tree-lined villages, riverside inns, and clusters of country shops.

Heading north from New Hope, you'll pass Lumberville, a village dating back to 1785 when it was built around two sawmills, and the site of the region's only footbridge across the Delaware; Pt. Pleasant, a typical river town dating back to the mid-1700s, and once the site of 28 mills; Erwinna, an important boat-building and repair site during the canal days of the 18th century; Upper Black Eddy, a village located on the longest eddy on the Delaware River and a popular fishing center; Kintnersville, a town bordered by three miles of cliff-like formations; and Riegelsville, dating back to 1774 and the site of one of the first bridges across the river. Every one of these places along the River Road has its own story to tell and each imparts its own special charm to visitors at any time of year.

WHERE TO STAY AND DINE: A turn-of-the-century atmosphere is the keynote of the **Black Bass Inn,** 3774 River Rd. (Route 32), Lumberville, PA 18933 (tel. 215/297-5770). Established in 1745 and in the hands of present owner Herb Ward since 1949, this ivy-covered two-story inn sits right on the banks of the Delaware River. From the moment you walk in, you can feel the ambience of yesteryear—from the antique furniture and old lanterns to the wide-board floors, many-paned windows, and solid pewter bar. Life-size portraits of early British monarchs adorn the walls of the public rooms, showing that the early owners of this inn remained loyal to the Crown. The gallery of royal faces also proves that this is one place in the Delaware Valley where George Washington did not sleep! Each of the upstairs bedrooms has its own personality; and its own name rather than number (such as Place Vendôme in France). The furnishings are an eclectic blend of Federal and Victorian pieces, from four-poster, sleigh, and canopy beds to marble-top dressers and antique quilts. There is a total of ten bedrooms, seven of which share two baths and three suites with private bath. The rooms at the back of the house facing the river have a balcony with cast-iron balustrade. Although the bedrooms have air conditioners, there are no TVs or telephones to detract from the old-world atmosphere. Doubles range from $50 to $70 and suites from $125 to $150. Meals are served in three ground-level dining rooms and a screened-in veranda overlooking the river. Lunch, priced from $6.95 to $9.95, includes a variety of dishes from turkey pot pie to omelets, steaks, or seafood. The menu at dinner is more elaborate, with entrees priced from $14.95 to $19.95 and selections such as rainbow trout stuffed with crab and wild rice; Muscovy duck Normandie; broiled free-range chicken; and lobster pie. Lunch is served Monday through Saturday from noon to 2:30 p.m.; dinner from 5:30 to 10 p.m., and from 3:30 to 8 p.m. on Sunday. A champagne buffet brunch is also available on Sunday ($15.95) from 1 to 3 p.m. CC's accepted: AE, MC, and V.

Just down the road from the Black Bass is the **1740 House,** River Road (Route 32), Lumberville, PA 18933 (tel. 215/297-5611), appropriately named because it dates back to 1740. The inn originally started with five bedrooms but 16 more were added in the north and south wings by owner Harry Nessler in 1967. Today there are 24 guest rooms, all with private bath and air conditioning, and most have private balconies or terraces facing the river. The décor is mostly Colonial, with touches of wicker and rattan. Guest amenities include a well-stocked library, a cozy living room, a card room, an outdoor heated pool, and a brick-lined patio deck for relaxing by the river in the summer sunshine. Double-occupancy rates, which include a buffet or continental breakfast, run from $65 on weekdays to $75 on weekends. The inn does not have a liquor license but guests are invited to bring their own wine or favorite beverages. Dinner is served at one sitting only, 7 p.m., with a menu that ranges from sweetbreads to boned duck, crab imperial, filet of sole, stuffed chicken, and Chateaubriand, in the $14 to $19 price bracket. The inn is open year round, with dinner available on Tuesday through Saturday evenings in the summer, and on a more limited schedule in winter. No CC's accepted.

Set back on its 25 acres of river shoreline, the gracious three-story **EverMay-on-the-Delaware,** River Road, Erwinna, PA 18920 (tel. 215/294-9100), was a popular resort from 1870 until the 1930s, frequented by such notables as the Barrymore family. Today, totally restored and rejuvenated, it is a country inn with the finest Victorian traditions and trappings (from walnut paneling and marble fireplaces to a grand piano, chiming grandfather clocks, and brocade settees). There are 16 guest bedrooms and suites, all with private bath and antique furnishings. Double-occupancy rates, which include continental breakfast and afternoon tea, range from $55 to $90; suites from $135. Dinner is served only on Friday, Saturday, and Sunday evenings at 7:30 p.m. in the elegant high-ceilinged dining room; there is one seating only, usually a six-course meal for a fixed price of $35, including champagne. Open year round; CC's accepted: MC and V.

Dating back to 1830, the **Upper Black Eddy Inn,** River Road, Route 32, Upper Black Eddy, PA 18972 (tel. 215/982-5554), is set back from the river in a farmyard setting. This old red-brick building, known more for its cuisine than its accommodations, offers four guest rooms, with period furnishings and air conditioning, but no private baths; the rates are $45 to $50 per night. The dining room and lounge area, beautifully preserved with dark wood walls, beamed ceilings, and open fireplaces, convey a Colonial ambience. Lunch, priced from $4.50 to $7.95, focuses on such dishes as sausage in puff pastry or crab cakes, and sandwiches and burgers, are available as well. Dinner entrees, which fall into the $12.95 to $22.95 range, include veal Valois; filet of beef chasseur; veal sweetbreads; and English mixed grill. The hours are Wednesday through Saturday, lunch from noon to 2:30 p.m.; dinner Wednesday through Friday from 5 to 9 p.m., Saturday from 5 to 10 p.m., and Sunday from 3 to 8 p.m. Sunday brunch is also served from 1 to 3 p.m. Closed Monday and Tuesday. All major CC's accepted.

With the river flowing in front and the canal behind, the **Riegelsville Inn,** 10–12 Delaware Rd., Riegelsville, PA 18077 (tel. 215/749-2469), stands at a curve in the road just a mile from Bucks County's northern border. Established in 1838, this three-story double-porched house is the pride and joy of innkeepers Fran and Harry Cregar. Highlights of the inn include the bar/lounge with its medley of stained-glass windows, antique ceiling fans, dark wood chairs and benches, gaily upholstered settees, round marble-top and footed tables, and a collection of mantle, wall, and standing clocks (all ticking to slightly different times). Upstairs there are 12 bedrooms, four with private bath and eight with semi-private facilities. Guests can also enjoy the second-floor, glass-enclosed, greenhouse-style veranda overlooking the river and a private TV parlor. Rates range from $45 to $85 and include continental breakfast on the veranda. The dining room downstairs, which incorporates part of the house's original kitchen, features a huge stone fireplace/stove, dark wood walls, Victorian furniture, and crystal chandeliers. A 1914 menu displayed on the wall shows a dinner price of 75¢; times have changed, however, and current dinner entrees, which change daily, now fall into the $14 to $19 price range. Selections usually include various preparations of shrimp, veal, beef, duck, and salmon. Open for lunch and dinner from noon to 2 p.m. and from 5 to 10 p.m.; on Sunday until 9 p.m. Brunch, which features a wide array of home-baked goods, is also available from noon to 2 p.m. on Sunday. The restaurant is closed on Mondays, Tuesdays, Thanksgiving, Christmas, and New Year's Day. CC's accepted: MC and V.

MORE PLACES TO DINE: It's hard to imagine a more idyllic setting for a restaurant than the **Cuttalossa Inn,** River Road, Lumberville (tel. 297-5082), across the road from the river and next to a rippling waterfall. Originally built around 1750, this stone inn was a stopping point for stagecoaches and then a gristmill. Listed on the National Register of Historic Places, it has been masterfully transformed into a top-caliber indoor-outdoor restaurant by Marilyn MacMaster, longtime Bucks County resident and restaurateur. The old millworks now serve as an outdoor veranda, ideal for long summer evenings. The inside rooms, equally well transformed, feature the original flagstone floors, open fireplaces, tables made from old sewing-machine bases, and linens of Colonial raspberry and cranberry tones. The menus change with the seasons but you can always count on creative cuisine and lots of fresh ingredients. Lunch, priced from $5 to $13, usually includes unique omelets (from Reuben to chicken liver or zucchini-pepperoni), quiches, eggs Benedict, and hearty dishes like beef Stroganoff or spinach lasagne. The selections at dinner range from Pekingese-style duckling, freshwater trout with herbed cheese stuffing, and quail stuffed with wild rice to prime steaks, veal, and the "house specialty" of crab imperial with a sauce made from a century-old recipe. All main courses are priced in the $16.95 to $20 bracket and are accompanied by salad, potato, vegetables, and homemade breads. Lunch is available seven days a week from 11 a.m. to 3 p.m.; dinner Monday through Thursday from 5 to 9 p.m., and Friday and Saturday from 5 to 10 p.m. There is a pleasant blend of live background music every night. CC's accepted: AE, MC, and V.

A slight but well-sign-posted detour off the main road will bring you to the **Cascade Inn,** Route 611 and Lehnenberg Road, Kintnersville (tel. 346-7484), at the northern end of Bucks County. In the setting of peaceful pastures, trout ponds, and fountains, this building was a farm and a boardinghouse before it was opened as a restaurant by the Knuth family in 1939. Much of the old farmhouse still remains, including an original dining room, central stone fireplace, wall lanterns, and brass plates. A new L-shaped wing with wide windows overlooks the gardens and cascading waters. Lunch, priced from $5.25 to $8.95, focuses on salads and sandwiches and seafood such as rainbow trout or crab in Dijon sauce. The nearby trout ponds supply much of the dinner choices, with such dishes as trout flambé or trout au brie. Other selections range from grilled shrimp to prime ribs and Chateaubriand. The entrees are priced from $12.95 to $23.95. Hours are Monday through Saturday, lunch from noon to 3 p.m., and dinner from 5 to 9 p.m.; Sunday hours are noon to 7 p.m. All major CC's accepted.

SPORTS AND ACTIVITIES: Much of the outdoor joy of Bucks County is centered along the Delaware River and canal, which meander side by side along the eastern shoreline. This portion of Route 32, also known as River Road, which stretches between Upper Black Eddy and New Hope, is not to be missed, whether you choose to drive, walk, bicycle, or pick a favorite spot and have a picnic.

For those who prefer to be a little more active, **Point Pleasant Canoes,** Route 32, Point Pleasant (tel. 215/297-8181), is a good place to stop. Open from mid-March to mid-November, this company can arrange for you to go tubing (rides of three or four hours from $8 a person), whitewater and leisure rafting (trips of approximately 2½ hours, from $30), canoeing (one to two-hours from $10), and kayaking (from $15 per day) on the Delaware River. If you prefer your adventure to be on land, then this company will also rent bicycles (from $5 an hour); they also organize combination bicycle/boat trips for $20 a day. Operating from April to October, the firm also sets up overnight trips from one day to two weeks in duration. In addition to its main location, a second base is also maintained during the busy summer months (Memorial Day to Labor Day) along the Upper Black Eddy/Riegelsville shoreline (tel. 215/749-2121).

Bucks County is also home to a variety of riverside and lakeland parks, including the **Nockamixon State Park,** west of Route 412 and southeast of Quakertown. This is the county's largest state park, with 5,400 acres and a 1,450-acre lake with 24 miles of shoreline. Activities available here include swimming, fishing, boating, picnicking, hiking, bicycling, and, in the winter months, cross-country skiing. **Tinicum Park** on River Road, just north of Erwinna, sits on the banks of the Delaware River and canal and is an ideal spot for boating, canoeing, hiking, and, in the winter, ice-skating. Other parks lining the river shoreline include the **Ralph Stover State Park** on Tohickon Creek at Point Pleasant (for swimming and picnicking) and the **Theodore Roosevelt State Park** at Upper Black Eddy (for hiking and canoeing). Full information about all the parks in the region can be obtained by contacting the **Bucks County Department of Parks and Recreation,** Core Creek Park, 901 E. Bridgetown Pike, Langhorne, PA 19047 (tel. 215/757-0571 or 348-6114).

7. Washington Crossing Area

History is the keynote to the lower section of Bucks County, an area that contains the Washington Crossing State Park and Pennsbury Manor, the country estate of William Penn. This region is also home to two historic districts, Fallsington and Newtown, and to one of the 20th century's greatest childhood delights, Sesame Place.

WHERE TO STAY: The lodging choices in this region range from 200-year-old inns to the most modern of Bucks County's contemporary hotels.

One of the lodging gems of this area is the **The Brick Hotel,** State Street and Washington Avenue, Newtown, PA 18940 (tel. 215/860-8313), originally built in 1764, and recently restored and renovated (1985). Listed in the National Register of Historic Places, this inn was once owned by Joseph Archambault, an aide to Napoleon Bonaparte, and it is said that George Washington entertained his troops here during the revolution. Whether he did or not, it is a place 20th-century travelers will definitely enjoy. For overnight guests, there are 14 rooms, all beautifully updated with private baths and furnished with antiques (such modern conveniences as televisions are discreetly hidden in old armoire chests). The rooms have shutter-style windows, canopy and four-poster beds, high ceilings, and hand-stenciled decorations on the walls. Doubles range from $70 to $90. Meals are served in a cozy Colonial-style dining room with a large open fireplace or on a glass-enclosed veranda with wraparound porch and views of the main street of Newtown. Lunch choices, mainly in the $3.95 to $4.95 bracket, feature quiches, salads, and sandwiches. Dinner is more of an event, with entrees ranging from $10.95 to $14.95. The menu includes blackened redfish, flounder florentine, shrimp Créole, stuffed roast veal, and a scallops/steak combination. Lunch is available daily from 11:30 a.m. to 4 p.m.; dinner from 4:30 to 10 p.m. on weekdays, until 11 p.m. on Friday and Saturday, and until 9 p.m. on Sunday. Breakfast is also served from 7 to 11 a.m. each day, with brunch on Sunday. All major CC's accepted.

At the other end of the time machine is the **Royce Hotel,** 400 Oxford Valley Rd., Langhorne, PA 19047 (tel. 215/547-4100 or toll-free 800/23 ROYCE), a festive and modern hotel newly opened in 1987. Situated in the lower part of Bucks County, this 14-story tower is at the intersection of I-95 and Route 1; its most noteworthy locator with young travelers, however, is that it is across the street from Sesame Place. The 168 sound-proof rooms have all the modern amenities, including oversized beds, cable TV, direct-dial phone, air conditioning, and AM/FM radio, and many rooms have extra sofa beds. Rates for a double begin at $110. Other facilities include a health club, swimming pool and sauna, a full-service restaurant, and a cocktail lounge with entertainment nightly. All major CC's accepted.

WHERE TO DINE: Two of the area's best restaurants are both located near the Washington Crossing State Park, along the Delaware River, and they both fall into the mostly moderate to expensive price range.

A Colonial atmosphere prevails at the **Washington Crossing Inn,** Routes 32 and 532, Washington Crossing (tel. 493-3634). Although it has been a restaurant for over 50 years (since 1936), this building dates back to 1760 when it was built as a house by William Taylor and the surrounding townland was known as Taylorsville. Much of the early décor has been preserved, including the original fireplace, cherrywood doors, hand-carved mantles, crystal chandeliers, brick floors, copper pots, and a mural of Bucks County in earlier times. Salads, sandwiches, and light fare are featured at lunchtime ($2.95 to $6.95). Dinner entrees, which range from $8.95 to $18.95 with most choices under $15, include breast of capon, calves' liver, beef en brochette, prime ribs, veal saltimbocca, lobster tails, crab au gratin, trout stuffed with crab, and duckling flambé. Each main course is accompanied by salad, vegetable, potato, and freshly baked bread. Lunch is served on Monday and on Wednesday through Saturday from 11:30 a.m. to 3 p.m.; dinner Wednesday through Saturday from 5 to 10 p.m.; Sunday hours are 11 a.m. to 2 p.m. for brunch and 1 to 8 p.m. for dinner. Don't be surprised when you enter the reception area of the restaurant if you hear sounds other than Colonial music; you'll probably be greeted by the resident mascot, a talking parrot named Finbar. CC's accepted: MC and V.

Five miles south is the **Yardley Inn,** Afton and Delaware Avenues, Yardley (tel. 493-3800), a restaurant since 1952, with a contemporary design. Situated just across the road from the Delaware River, this spot offers lovely views from its wraparound enclosed porch and from the wide windows of its dining room. The creative menu features puff-pastry pizzas and omelet soufflés at lunchtime, as well as a large selection of sandwiches and salads ($5 to $9.50). The dinner menu, with entrees priced from $10.50 to $19, includes such dishes as buckwheat pasta with wild mushrooms, seafood ravioli, brook trout, poached salmon, filet of sole stuffed with king crab, and beef medallions with cognac bordelaise. Open daily for lunch Monday through Friday from 11:30 a.m. to 2:30 p.m. and on Saturday and Sunday from 11 a.m. to 3 p.m.; for dinner Monday through Friday from 5:30 to 10:30 p.m., until 11 p.m. on Saturday, and until 8 p.m. on Sunday. All major CC's accepted.

TOP ATTRACTIONS: Just a few miles south of New Hope begins the famous area known as **Washington Crossing Historic Park,** Routes 32 and 532, (tel. 493-4076), where General Washington regrouped his forces and in a blinding snowstorm made the famous crossing of the Delaware River to Trenton on December 25, 1776. Now a 500-acre park, this historic spot contains a Visitor Center and 13 buildings, including the McConkey Ferry Inn (1752), which was the site of the final meeting between General Washington and his staff before leaving for the crossing; an 18th-century farm and industrial complex; the 19th-century village of Taylorsville; and the Durham Boat Barn, which houses four replicas of the cargo boats used for the crossing. On the grounds, you can also explore a 100-acre wildflower preserve and Bowman's Hill, the memorial hilltop "lookout" during the American Revolution. The Visitor Center, which contains a huge painting of George Washington leading his men in the crossing of the Delaware, also offers a free half-hour movie presentation at 9 a.m., 10:30 a.m., noon, 1:30, and 3 p.m. Walking tours of the historic buildings begin promptly after each movie showing (fee for the tours is $1.50 for adults and 50¢ for youth over age 6; under age 6, free). Hours of operation are Monday through Saturday from 9 a.m. to 5 p.m., and Sunday from noon to 5 p.m. The grounds are open daily from 9 a.m. to 8 p.m. or sunset.

For a look at 17th-century lifestyle, be sure to visit **Pennsbury Manor,** 400 Pennsbury Memorial Rd., Morrisville (tel. 946-0400), the reconstructed 1685 plantation country home of William Penn. Built between 1683 and 1700, this historic site is a little off the beaten track, at the southernmost tip of the county on the water, but it is sign-posted from Washington Crossing, about a half-hour away. You can not only tour the manor home but also wander into the adjacent smokehouse and the bake and brew houses, as well as enjoy the garden and orchard setting. Open Tuesday through Saturday from 9 a.m. to 5 p.m., and on Sunday from noon to 5 p.m. Admission charge is $2.50 for adults, $1 for children 6 to 17 years, and children under 6, free.

Five miles northwest of Pennsbury Manor is **Historic Fallsington,** a pre-Revolutionary village with a Visitor Center at 4 Yardley Ave., Fallsington (tel. 295-6567). Three hundred years of architectural history are reflected here, from a 17th-century log cabin to extravagant Victorian buildings of the 19th century. It is said that the village grew up around the Friends Meeting House (1690) and that William Penn worshipped here. Other specimens in this well-preserved Colonial village include two dozen houses, a stagecoach tavern, and a schoolmaster's house. Although you can freely walk around the town at any time, the Visitor Center has limited hours (from 11 a.m. to 4 p.m., Wednesday through

Sunday, from mid-March to mid-November). During this period, tours are conducted of four furnished houses, at 11:15 a.m., 12:30, 1:45, and 3 p.m. The tour fee is $2 for adults, $1 for students to age 18, 50¢ for children under 12, and children under 6 free. A craft shop and antiques store are housed in the same building as the Visitor Center; items on sale range from Colonial decorations to bird houses and grapevine wreaths. The shops are open year round Monday through Saturday from 10 a.m. to 5 p.m., and on Sunday from 11 a.m. to 5 p.m. CC's accepted: MC and V.

The **Newtown Historic District** is also worth a stroll. Founded in 1683, it was one of the earliest place names in the county and served as county seat from 1726 until 1813, and as an important supply depot during the Revolution. No less than 230 of Newtown's structures are listed on the National Register of Historic Places. Among the 18th- and 19th-century architectural gems to be seen are Court Inn (formerly the Half Moon Inn), dating from 1733, a furnished early tavern, and the Newtown Library Company, established in 1760.

The Washington Crossing State Park is also the starting point for a **covered bridge tour** of Bucks County. Of the 36 covered bridges that were built in the county, 13 specimens remain today. Dating back to 1832, most of these covered bridges were built of lattice-type construction, a series of overlapping triangles with no arches or upright beams. The tour takes you first to Van Sant Bridge, slightly southwest of New Hope, and continues northward along River Road and then to the western part of the county. A brochure/map outlining the tour is available free from the Bucks County Tourist Commission.

SHOPPING: One of the most unique shops in this area is **The Patriot,** Route 532, Washington Crossing Historic Park (tel. 493-5411). Built in 1820 as a general store, across the street from the McConkey Ferry Inn, this spot was the focal point of the Colonial village of Taylorsville. Today it is part snackshop and part souvenir emporium, with merchandise for sale ranging from handmade soap, baskets, candles, cast-iron toys, handcrafted brooms, old glass jars, country wood carvings, rag rugs, coonskin caps, and arrowheads to penny candy. Other food items include sandwiches and hot dogs (with Colonial names), ice cream, and hot cider. Open Monday through Saturday from 10 a.m. to 5 p.m. and Sunday from 1 to 5 p.m., with extended hours in summer. CC's accepted: MC and V.

EVENTS: For more than 35 years, a major happening in this area has been the annual Christmas re-enactment of George Washington's crossing the Delaware, the Revolutionary War event that led to victory at the Battle of Trenton. The schedule actually begins in early December and continues throughout the month, with weekend tours, musical concerts, carol singing, and the lighting of a huge community Christmas tree at the intersection of Routes 532 and 32. Other activities include brass ensemble music, candlelight tours, and the illumination of the historic buildings. All the festivities culminate on December 25th, with a riverbank parade and the casting off of the boats for "The Crossing." A complete program and more information is available from the **Washington Crossing Historic Park,** P.O. Box 103, Washington Crossing, PA 18977 (tel. 215/493-4076).

CHILDREN'S CORNER: Sesame Place, Oxford Valley Road, Langhorne (tel. 757-1100), is a four-acre wonderpark designed for Sesame Street fans, as the perfect place to climb, float, glide, bounce, zoom, slide, or roar. Amusements include computer games, water rides, and live entertainment by Big Bird, Bert, Ernie, and other favorites from the TV show. Open daily from 10 a.m. to 5 p.m.

from early May through mid-June and again for the first week of September; daily from 10 a.m. to 8 p.m. from mid-June through the first week of July; daily from 9 a.m. to 8:30 p.m. from the second week of July through the end of August; and on weekends only from mid-September to mid-October, 10 a.m. to 5 p.m. General admission charges are from $9.85 to $10.95 for adults; children, aged 2 to 16, from $12.05 to $13.15; and children under 2 free. Special "Sesame Place Express" rail packages, via Amtrak and express buses, operate from New York, New Jersey, Pennsylvania, Connecticut, Delaware, Maryland, and Washington, D.C., rail terminals; call toll-free 800/USA-RAIL for full details.

Chapter V

THE POCONOS

EIGHT MILLION PEOPLE A YEAR vacation in the Pocono Mountains, making this region the number-one resort destination in Pennsylvania. Situated in the northeast corner of the state, the Poconos are composed of four neighboring counties (Monroe, Pike, Carbon, and Wayne), with an aggregate area of 2,400 square miles, spread out over a panorama of mountainous peaks, rolling hills, glistening lakes, rushing rivers, and gentle valleys.

Although champagne baths and heart-shaped swimming pools have earned the Poconos the title of "honeymoon capital of the world," this multifaceted corner of Pennsylvania is equally popular with families. And best of all, it is a fully fledged resort for all seasons, thriving equally well in the winter ski months, spring blossom time, and fall foliage period, as well as at the height of summer.

1. A Bit of Background

Part of the Appalachian chain, the Pocono Mountains derive their name from the Indian word, "Pocohonne," which means "stream between the mountains." Of course, to this day, there are literally hundreds of streams between the Pocono Mountains, as well as lakes, ponds, and creeks. To top off this idyllic landscape, both the Delaware and Lehigh Rivers add their waters to the scene. The Delaware provides the eastern boundary for the region and the Lehigh flows along part of the western edge.

It is therefore quite natural that water, in all its forms, plays an important part in the Pocono attractions, from swimming at lakeshore beaches to boating, fishing, whitewater rafting, and tubing in the warmer months to skiing, ice skating, snowmobiling, and tobogganing in the winter. Hand-in-hand with watersports, this natural paradise welcomes visitors to enjoy endless walking and hiking trails, picnicking, horseback riding, golfing, and myriad other outdoor activities.

Although the Poconos have been attracting vacationers since the 1700s, it is

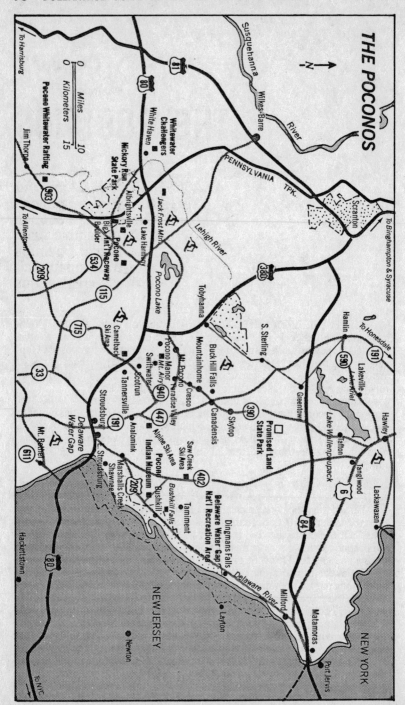

THE POCONOS

only in the last 40 years that the honeymoon industry has taken a firm hold. Resorts of all sizes and shapes have sprung up in the most idyllic and romantic locations, many with a "couples-only" format. This is where the heart-shaped swimming pool originated, not to mention the heart-shaped Jacuzzi and the champagne-glass-shaped whirlpool bath for two. Road signs that say "Caution: Dears crossing" are not unusual, nor are red-velvet furnishings, mirrored ceilings, and "his and her" breakfasts in bed.

Although there are 12 enclaves that cater exclusively to a "couples clientele," there are hundreds of other resorts, hotels, motels, and country inns that welcome couples, families, singles, or groups of all sizes. In this single chapter, it is impossible to give a complete review of all the properties, but we'll give a cross-section of all categories, and in various parts of the region.

For ease of reading (and getting around when you are there), we are breaking this chapter down into four areas. The first section, "Stroudsburg," is often considered the gateway to the region, especially for traffic coming from the east. The main visitor information office and the Delaware Water Gap are also part of this area. Next, we'll take you to the section that can best be described as "The Central Poconos," primarily Monroe County where the greatest concentration of resorts and inns are located, from Mt. Airy Lodge and Mt. Pocono to Skytop. The third part will describe the highlights around "Lake Wallenpaupack" and the fourth will lead you over to the "Western Poconos," where the attractions range from whitewater rafting and mule-riding to the historic district of Jim Thorpe.

2. Getting to the Poconos

BY CAR: The majority of visitors to the Poconos arrive by car, and a car is really an asset if you want to get around. Of course, many of the large resorts are geared to keeping you housed and happy for your entire stay, so you don't have to bring a car. Assuming that you are driving, however, it is useful to know that major highways and interstates criss-cross throughout the 2,400-square-mile area. Both I-80 and I-84 traverse the county in an east-west direction, and I-81 and Route 9 (the Pennsylvania Turnpike Northeast extension) go from north to south. A network of smaller roads also weave in all directions throughout the four counties.

BY BUS: Bus service to the Poconos is operated into Stroudsburg by both Greyhound and Martz Trailways. **Greyhound** maintains a depot at 615 Main St. (tel. 421-4400); and **Martz** stops at 230 Park Ave. (tel. 421-3040). Local **taxis** are available at these terminals. Martz makes an additional stop in Mt. Pocono at 26 Pocono Blvd. (tel. 839-7443). Many of the leading resorts, if advised in advance, will provide a shuttle service from Mt. Pocono to their front doors. At certain times of the year, additional stops may be made at Delaware Water Gap and Jim Thorpe. Check with the bus company of your choice in advance.

BY PLANE: The Poconos are served by two nearby airports, **Wilkes-Barre/Scranton** to the west, and **Allentown-Bethlehem-Easton** in the Lehigh Valley. Both are a maximum of 45 minutes away from major Pocono attractions. In addition, **Newark Airport** in New Jersey is only one hour and 15 minutes away from the heart of the Poconos. **Pocono Limousine Service** (tel. 717/839-2111) operates direct transfers to the Poconos from major airports including Kennedy and LaGuardia in New York, Philadelphia, and Newark, as well as Wilkes Barre/Scranton and Allentown-Bethlehem-Easton.

3. Getting Around the Poconos

BY CAR: The Poconos area is fairly compact and easy to get around by car. From Stroudsburg, it is only an hour's drive to Lake Wallenpaupack or White Haven. For east-west travel, I-80 crosses the region's lower half, while I-84 runs across the northern spread. In addition, many local roads run parallel to the interstates and extend in other directions as well. You can easily base yourself in one location and explore all other parts of the Poconos by taking day trips. Or you may choose to get a feel for different sections by spending a night or two in each of the areas that are outlined on the following pages.

SIGHTSEEING BY PLANE: For an overview of the area, you can take an air tour with **Moyer Aviation,** Pocono Mt. Municipal Airport, Route 611, Mt. Pocono (tel. 839-7161 or 839-6080), located 1½ miles north of Mt. Pocono. Open daily year round, this service offers a variety of small aircraft tours of the area, ranging from 25 to 80 miles in scope and priced from $10 to $25 per person, based on a minimum of two passengers. The planes operate from 8 a.m. to sunset, and reservations are suggested. CC's accepted: MC and V.

VISITOR INFORMATION: Comprehensive brochures and directories on all of the Poconos are available by contacting the **Pocono Mountain Vacation Bureau,** 1004 Main St., Stroudsburg, PA 18360 (tel. 717/421-5791 or toll-free 800/ POCONOS). More specific information on certain areas can also be obtained from the following chambers of commerce and tourist promotion agencies: **Carbon County Tourist Promotion Agency,** P.O. Box 90, Jim Thorpe, PA 18229 (tel. 717/325-3673); **Wayne County Chamber of Commerce,** 865 Main St., Honesdale, PA 18431 (tel. 717/253-1960); **Hawley-Lake Wallenpaupack Chamber of Commerce,** P.O. Box 150, Hawley, PA 18428 (tel. 717/226-3191); **Lake Wallenpaupack Association Inc.,** P.O. Box 398, Hawley, PA 18428 (tel. 717/226-2141); and **Pike County Chamber of Commerce,** Milford, PA 18337 (tel. 717/296-8700).

AREA CODE: All telephone numbers in the Pocono Mountain region are part of the 717 area code, unless otherwise indicated.

4. Stroudsburg Area

Stroudsburg (pop.: 5,100) is the chief town in the Poconos. The main visitor information center is located here and many of the prime roads, such as I-80 and Routes 611, 209, 447, and 191, converge here and branch out to other parts of the region. With a wide main street, Stroudsburg has an assortment of shops and stores (this town was the birthplace of the J.J. Newbury chain). It is named for Col. Jacob Stroud, who settled the area in 1761 and named it Stroudsburg in 1779.

To be precise, there are actually two Stroudsburgs, Stroudsburg and East Stroudsburg, the latter of which is the location of a state university. Both towns are connected by Route 209 and are quite homogenous.

The two Stroudsburgs lie beside the Delaware Water Gap, which is considered the natural Gateway to the Poconos. An attraction in itself, the Gap was formed over the years by slow erosion allowing the Delaware River to chisel a deep crevice through the mountains, leaving walls that tower up to 700 feet above the waterway. It is said that the rock tells a geological story over 400 million years, and the river itself is 150 million years old. In any event, the Delaware Water Gap is a source of great enjoyment for 20th-century visitors.

Fifteen miles northwest of Stroudsburg (on Route 209) is one of the most famous of the Poconos' sightseeing attractions, **Bushkill Falls,** Bushkill Falls Road, Bushkill (tel. 588-6682). Often called the "Niagara Falls of Pennsylvania," this site dates back to 1904 and includes eight falls of various levels, signposted walking trails, a wildlife gallery, shops, free fishing pond, picnicking sites, and paddleboats. Open April through November, 9 a.m. to dusk, the admission charge is $3.50 for adults, $1 for children aged 6 to 12. There is a supplementary charge for the paddleboats of $1.25 per each 15 minutes for two people.

WHERE TO STAY: Rates for Poconos accommodations are at their highest in the summer months and during the ski season. In some cases, a two-night minimum also applies for weekend stays. However, you can often save money by traveling here during midweek periods, rather than on weekends. Many properties also offer package deals throughout the year, with especially good savings during the spring and fall months. Be sure to inquire what special prices may be in effect at the time you plan to visit.

A Grand Old Resort

The **Shawnee Inn,** Shawnee-on-Delaware, PA 18356 (tel. 717/421-1500 or toll-free 800-SHAWNEE), a turn-of-the-century lodge made famous by its previous owner, bandleader Fred Waring. Idyllically set right on the banks of the Delaware River in the shadow of nearby mountains, this hotel is surrounded by a 27-hole golf course. With a Spanish-tile roof and two three-story bedroom wings, this inn has a total of 84 units with private bath and vintage décor, many with panoramic views. Rates are normally quoted on a MAP basis (including full breakfast and dinner) and range from $45 to $85 per person a day, based on double occupancy. If you prefer a room rate only, doubles start at $60 per night. Free activities include indoor and outdoor swimming pools, outdoor tennis, saunas and whirlpool, putting greens, historical walks, ice skating, shuffleboard, boccie, horseshoe games, and jogging trails. Guests also enjoy a 50% discount off the regular $28 golfing greens fees, 33% off ski-lift tickets, and reductions on other activities including the racquet club, horseback riding, and canoe trips. Meals are served in a wide-windowed dining room with views of the river. Most major CC's accepted.

Modern Hotels

A convenient and convivial place to stay is the **Sheraton Pocono Inn,** 1220 W. Main St., Stroudsburg, PA 18360 (tel. 717/424-1930 or toll-free 800/325-3535), situated a mile south of the town center in a quiet wooded setting with a winding stream. Adjacent to I-80 (exit 48) and to major local routes, this modern two-story hotel makes an ideal base for travel throughout the Poconos. The 134 rooms were completely refurbished in late 1986, and offer a choice of two double-, king-, or queen-size beds, with all the standard amenities; many have balconies overlooking an indoor tropical courtyard, and others offer wide picture-window views of the surrounding mountain scenery. Doubles range from $65 to $85. The facilities include indoor and outdoor swimming pools, saunas, a game room, and a nightclub, Whispers, with evening entertainment. The main restaurant, Evergreens, offers a lodge-like motif, with a moderately priced menu. Dinner entrees, from $10.95 to $15.95, include tournedos of beef; roulades of sole; filet of salmon braised with baby shrimp; poached brook trout; and breast of capon with boursin cheese. Meals are served throughout the day from 7 a.m. until 10 p.m. All major CC's accepted.

In the heart of town is the **Best Western Pocono Inn,** 700 Main St.,

Stroudsburg, PA 18360 (tel. 717/421-2200 or toll-free 800/528-1234), a modern four-story motor hotel. Recently updated and refurbished, this facility served as the Pocono Hilton and the Penn-Stroud Town and Country Inn in previous years. A life-size mural map in the lobby depicts a history of the area. The 100 guest rooms have a modern look, each equipped with two double beds, air conditioning, color TV, and a direct-dial phone. Doubles range from $45 to $60. There is also an indoor heated swimming pool, a fitness center, parking facilities, a coffeeshop, a lounge, and a steakhouse, serving moderately priced meals from 11 a.m. to 10 p.m. All major CC's accepted.

A Bed-and-Breakfast Choice

Thirty-five miles northeast of Stroudsburg, along the Delaware, is the **Black Walnut Country Inn,** 509 Fire Tower Rd., Box 9285, Milford, PA 18337 (tel. 717/296-6322). A good base for touring the northern Poconos, this inn is just south of I-84 (exit 10); the other side of the Delaware River marks the New York/New Jersey border. It is located about a mile northeast of the town of Milford and is well sign-posted. As you drive into this 150-acre estate, you'll be charmed by the Tudor stone façade of the house, with its adjacent lake and well-landscaped grounds. A country-style décor prevails inside with a marble fireplace and an assortment of homey furnishings. The 14 guest rooms each have an individual personality, many with antiques and brass beds. Eight rooms have private bathrooms; the rest have shared facilities. Doubles range from $50 to $70 and include a "welcome" glass of sherry, afternoon tea, and a full breakfast served in the wide-windowed dining room overlooking the lake or outside on the patio deck. Guest amenities include paddleboating, fishing, and swimming in the lake; lawn games; and the use of a common parlor with TV and VCR. There are also stables nearby for horseback riding. Stewart Schneider is the innkeeper. Major CC's accepted.

WHERE TO DINE: Top-notch restaurants are a keystone of the Poconos, and in the Stroudsburg area, you'll find an especially international mix of cuisines. Price-wise, all of the selections listed here fall into the mostly moderate category.

A landmark of the area is the **Beaver House,** 1001 N. Ninth St., Stroudsburg (tel. 424-1020), a 40-year-old rustic inn located one mile north of the town center on Route 611. Although the beaver (as in "busy as a beaver") may be the symbol here, lobster and fresh seafood predominate the menu. As you enter this popular enclave of four dining rooms, the lobster tanks by the door offer a preview of what is to follow. The rest of the décor is a mix of nautical and Bavarian, with an eclectic collection of porcelain figurines, old bottles, mugs, jugs, cups, and mounted birds and wildlife; etched glass and curtained booths add to the old-world atmosphere. Lunch, priced from $2.95 to $7.95, focuses mainly on light platters, omelets, salads, and sandwiches. The "main event" of the day is dinner when a selection of one to four lobster dishes are offered, either baked, broiled, steamed, or stuffed. The menu also includes sirloin steaks served ceremoniously on wooden dishes, prime ribs, king crab in the shell, rainbow trout amandine, and duckling. All dishes are priced from $8.95 to $21.95, with most under $15, including a choice of appetizer, soup, potato, vegetable, and dessert. During the course of the evening, chances are you'll be greeted by the congenial host, Joseph Michel, and head chef Thomas Rosemond, both of whom have put in more than 25 years of pleasing customers here. Lunch is served Monday through Friday from 11:30 a.m. to 2 p.m.; dinner Monday through Saturday from 5 to 10:30 p.m., and on Sunday from 1 to 8 p.m. Major CC's accepted.

A Roman villa atmosphere awaits you at **Peppe's Ristorante,** Eagle Valley Mall, East Stroudsburg (tel. 421-4460), situated at the junction of Routes 209 and 447. Although you would ordinarily expect to find only fast food eateries in a shopping center, this is one case when appearances are deceiving. Italian opera plays in the background as you are seated amidst a romantic décor of festive flowers, brick arches, wrought-iron ceiling lanterns, candelabras, and fine linens. Lunch items, priced between $2.95 to $6.95, include sandwiches, burgers, omelets, pasta, and light dishes. The dinner menu features an array of Italian specialties such as scampi; calamari; lobster tail fra diavola; rack of veal stuffed with prosciutto, cheese, and mushrooms; saltimbocca alla Romana; Italian pepper steak; and fresh pastas. The entrees, many of which are prepared tableside, are priced from $9.95 to $16.95, and are accompanied by an intermezzo sorbet, vegetable, and potato or spaghetti. Open Monday through Friday for lunch from 11:30 a.m. to 2:30 p.m.; and for dinner Monday through Friday from 5 to 10 p.m., on Saturday from 4 to 11 p.m., and on Sunday from 12:30 p.m. to 9 p.m. Major CC's accepted.

Gourmet Chinese cuisine is the trademark of **Ho Ho's,** 1863 W. Main St., Stroudsburg (tel. 424-5426), about a mile west of the town center on Route 209. With gentle background music and a Polynesian atmosphere, this restaurant is furnished with caned chairs and a healthy collection of hanging plants and flowering bushes. Open for dinner only, the menu features many of the usual Chinese dishes as well as some specialties, such as velvet crabmeat soup; coconut shrimp; whole crispy bass; sea and earth (scallops sautéed with tender beef); and love nest (shredded chicken and beef tenderloin, marinated and sautéed with seasonal vegetables served in a crispy nest). Soups and appetizers are priced from $1.50 to $5.50, and entrees range from $5.95 to $15.95. Hours are 4 to 10 p.m., Monday through Saturday. CC's accepted: AE, MC, and V.

A landmark railroad station is the setting of the **Dansbury Depot,** Crystal Street, East Stroudsburg (tel. 476-0500). Built in 1864 as a train station and freight house when this town was called Dansbury, this historic building was converted into a restaurant five years ago. The décor is full of vintage railroad memorabilia including pictures, signs, model trains, and an old suitcase or two in the "baggage room." The cuisine is typically American, with salads, quiches, omelets, chili, and burgers for lunch, priced from $3.95 to $5.95. The entrees at dinner, priced in the $8.95 to $15.95 bracket, include stir-fry dishes; Brushy Mountain back ribs; prime beef; game hen with strawberry sauce; duck with brandied orange sauce; Pocono brook trout; and Cajun dishes. Open for lunch from 11:30 a.m. until 2 p.m.; and for dinner from 5:30 to 9 p.m., Monday through Thursday, until 10 p.m. Friday and Saturday, and from 4 until 8:30 p.m. on Sunday. CC's accepted: AE, D, MC, and V.

A SAMPLING OF SPORTS AND ACTIVITIES: A diversity of sports and other activities are available in the Poconos. Here's a sampling of what we found.

Hiking and Trail Walking: National Park rangers conduct a number of programs along the 35-mile **Delaware Water Gap,** maintaining visitor centers from May through October at Kittatinny, off I-80 (tel. 496-4458), and at Dingman's Falls, off Route 209 (tel. 828-7802). Among the activities offered are beach walks, river walks, nature walks, and discovery hikes. Picnicking facilities are also available, as are hourly canoe rentals ($2 per person) and rafting ($5 per person). For advance information, contact the **Delaware Water Gap NRA,** Bushkill, PA 18324 (tel. 717/588-6637).

Swimming: There is a lovely secluded strand at **Smithfield Beach,** just north of Shawnee on River Road; there are also boat and canoe ramps, picnic tables, and restrooms here. Another good spot is at Milford Beach, just north of the toll bridge that crosses the Delaware on Route 209.

Whitewater Rafting: Kittatinny Canoes Inc., Dingmans Ferry (tel. 828-2338 or 828-2700), offers canoe and raft trips that cover the most popular ten-mile section of the Delaware River. These excursions range from 5 to 17 miles in length with varying degrees of difficulty; longer trips are also available. Rates range from $14 per person on weekdays to $16 on weekends. This company can also arrange daily tubing trips from $8 per person and camping from $12 per day or $70 per week. Hours are, mid-April through October, 7 a.m. to 6 p.m. Other outfitters in the area that also arrange canoeing and rafting trips include **Delaware River Canoe Trips,** Delaware Water Gap (tel. 476-0398); **Tri-State Canoe and Boat Rentals,** Shay Lane, Matamoras (tel. 491-4948); and **Shawnee Adventures,** P.O. Box 189, Shawnee-on-Delaware (tel. 424-1139 or toll-free 800/SHAWNEE).

Golfing: The **Cherry Valley Golf Course,** Cherry Valley Road, Stroudsburg (tel. 421-1350) features an 18-hole course, two miles west of the Delaware Water Gap. Greens fees are $7.50 per person midweek and $10 on weekends; cart fees are $14. The **Shawnee Inn and Country Club,** Shawnee-on-Delaware (tel. 421-1500), has three nine-hole courses; greens fees are $28 and cart rentals are $18. Other nearby facilities include 27 holes at **Fernwood Golf Club,** Bushkill (tel. 588-6661) and 18 holes at **Wayne Newton's Tamiment Resort,** Tamiment (tel. 588-6652).

Skiing: With an elevation of 1,350 feet and a vertical drop of 700 feet, **Shawnee Mountain,** Shawnee-on-Delaware (tel. 421-7231), is a leading ski center. There are 20 slopes and trails, seven double chair lifts, a ski-rental shop, and ski school. Midweek lift tickets are priced from $23 and weekend from $25; night-skiing from $15. Other resorts in this area include **Fernwood,** Route 209, Bushkill (tel. 588-6661); **Saw Creek,** off Route 209, Bushkill (tel. 588-9266); and **Tamiment Resort,** Tamiment (tel. 588-6652). These facilities have average vertical drops between 200 and 300 feet and offer lift tickets between $6 and $16.

5. Central Poconos

For our purposes, we are identifying as the "Central Poconos" an area that is west of Stroudsburg, east of White Haven, just south of I-80, and as far north as Skytop. This is primarily Monroe County, although, to be technical, Stroudsburg and the Delaware Water Gap are also part of Monroe. The majority of resorts and honeymoon destinations are clustered in this area, as are a wide selection of hotels, motels, and country inns.

This stretch of Pocono country is also the home of several great ski resorts including Camelback and Alpine Mountain, a variety of fine golf courses, and some of the region's most charming towns, such as Canadensis, Mt. Pocono, Mountainhome, Cresco, and Paradise Valley.

WHERE TO STAY: Many places in this region fall into the classification of "total resort," meaning that guests can "stay put" and enjoy all sorts of sporting activities, entertainment, and two or three meals a day, as part of the daily rate. Rates at most properties will average over $100 per person a day, but that can be classified as a moderate price when you consider all you are getting for your money. Actually, comparing one with the other can be a bit confusing because some places charge more, but then they give more. After glancing through these descriptions, you should contact the **Pocono Mountain Vacation Bureau** and ask to receive a variety of accommodation brochures, so that you compare for yourself.

The Grand Old Resorts

The **Buck Hill Inn,** Buck Hill Falls, PA 18323 (tel. 717/595-7441 or toll-free 800/233-8113), dates back to 1901 when it was built by a group of Quakers as a summer retreat. For years, it flourished as *the* fashionable resort of the Poconos and it still holds its own, especially now that it has just received a $4 million restoration. The public rooms are a showcase of huge native-stone fireplaces, burnished wood floors, and Persian and Oriental carpets; there is also a historical library and a gallery of oil paintings. The 262 guest rooms are located in the main five-story stone lodge and in the adjoining west wing. You have a choice of classic or contemporary décors, but all rooms feature the up-to-date amenities of a private bathroom, air conditioning, color TV, and a direct-dial phone. Some units have canopy beds, mirrored panels, or wet bars, and others have balconies or patios. Rates are $100 to $150 per person per night including full breakfast, dinner, and a plethora of activities. The 5,000-acre estate is a mélange of rolling hills, forests, and cascading streams, an ideal setting for the 27 holes of golf; hiking, biking, and jogging trails; trout fishing; horseback riding; downhill or cross-country skiing; tobogganing; snowmobiling; horse-drawn sleigh rides; and ice skating. Guests can also enjoy an indoor and an outdoor swimming pool; a whirlpool/Jacuzzi; ten tennis courts; and an indoor roller-skating rink. Some activities, such as golf, tennis, fishing, and horseback riding, require a supplementary charge, but most activities are part of the rate. Dinners are served in a choice of two restaurants, with a Swiss chef presiding in the kitchen; and a full program of entertainment is also on tap each evening in the Four Crowns Lounge. All major CC's accepted.

Skytop Lodge, Skytop, PA 18357 (tel. 717/595-7401 or toll-free 800/345-7759), is another gracious old (1928) property, set on 5,500 acres in the heights of the mountains, as its name implies. The rambling gray-stone building started as a private club, and indeed still operates on a membership basis, although it opened to the public for lodging about 15 years ago. There are 192 rooms, not all with private bath, but the majority of double rooms do have private facilities. Most units are furnished with antique reproductions, including a small writing desk, butterfly Windsors, traditional iron lamps, and pine beds, either twin or queen size. Double-occupancy with private bath ranges from $160 to $260, including three meals a day for two people. The rates also cover use of the indoor pool, hiking and fitness trails, shuffleboard, horseshoe pitching, table tennis, archery, miniature golf, cross-country skiing, downhill and cross-country skiing, ice skating, tobogganing, and sledding. Guests also enjoy free movies, dancing, bridge, concerts, picnics, art exhibits, and entertainment. Modest supplementary charges apply for golf, bicycling, trout fishing, paddle tennis, lawn bowling, and tennis. There is also a supervised play area for youngsters, a card room, a library, a glass-enclosed sun porch, and a TV room with a five-foot screen. CC's accepted: AE, MC, and V.

The Largest and Best Known

Mt. Airy Lodge, Mt. Pocono, PA 18344 (tel. 717/839-8811 or toll-free 800/441-4410), is probably the most famous of the Poconos resorts because of the big-name stars it draws to entertain its guests and its catchy advertising jingles. Started over 50 years ago as a boardinghouse with 16 rooms, Mt. Airy has grown to over 600 units, and is now one of the largest and most complete resorts is the east, in a secluded setting off Route 611, surrounded by a private lake and an 18-hole golf course. The bedrooms have all the standard amenities, plus custom interiors; many have balconies. In addition, there is a variety of suites designed just for couples, with such features as heart-shaped whirlpool baths for two; monarch-size or round beds; in-suite indoor-outdoor pools; private sun and lounge patios; and saunas. Rates range from $60 to $125 per person per night including all meals. The amenities available to guests include Olympic indoor and outdoor pools; a private lake with sandy beach; a marina with sailboats and paddleboats; 21 indoor and outdoor tennis courts; golf; team sports; a health club; and such winter sports as skiing, sleighing, ice skating, and snowmobiling. Horseback riding is also available at a supplementary charge. Evening entertainment includes top-name stars, dancing to three bands, and two discos. Major CC's accepted.

A Couple of Country Inns

In a forest setting beside the Brodhead Creek is the **Pine Knob Inn,** Route 447, P.O. Box 275, Canadensis, PA 18325 (tel. 717/595-2532), a two-story pre–Civil War home that has been welcoming guests since the 1880s. Now in the hands of congenial hosts Jim and June Belfie, this charming house offers a cheery blend of antiques, a Steinway piano (which guests are encouraged to play), and paintings by local artists, including the lady of the house herself. There are 18 guest rooms in the main house, 12 of which have private bath. An additional eight rooms with private bath are available in two other renovated 1930s cottages on the grounds. Each bedroom is furnished differently, with country curtains and wall-to-wall carpeting; and most have hobnail spreads or quilts, as well as brass, Victorian carved-oak, or mahogany four-poster beds; needlepoint chairs; rockers; and old-fashioned vanities. The double-occupancy rates range from $60 to $75 per person and that includes a hearty breakfast (with blueberry pancakes, eggs, or French toast) and dinner. And what a dinner it is! Choices usually include apricot rack of lamb; strawberry game hen; Pennsylvania Dutch ham; Pocono mountain trout; shrimp Rosemary on pasta; duckling with orange sauce; coquilles St-Jacques mornay; and prime ribs. Entrees are priced from $10.95 to $18.95, in case you decide to dine here without overnighting. Dinner is served between 6 and 9 p.m. daily to guests, and Tuesday through Saturday for those who come for dinner only. In addition to the candlelit dining room, there is also a cozy bar. The inn is open year round except for several weeks in December at Christmastime. Guest facilities include an outdoor swimming pool, tennis, badminton, shuffleboard, and lawn games. At certain times of the year, creative workshops are offered featuring leading painters and photographers as lecturers. CC's accepted: MC and V.

Down a country road, deep in the mountains, off Route 447, you'll find the **Overlook Inn,** Dutch Hill Road, Canadensis, PA 18325 (tel. 717/595-7519), a three-storied turn-of-the-century structure, which started out as a boarding house. In the capable hands of Bob and Lolly Tupper for the last dozen years, the inn actually incorporates an older (1860s) farmhouse plus a carriage house and small lodge. There is a total of 20 guest rooms with private bath, 12 in the main house and eight in the other two buildings. Country prints and crafts decorate the rooms, which are eclectically furnished with iron bedsteads, pine chests, quilts, oak dressers, and a plant or two. You'll also find a complimentary carafe of wine in your room. In the lobby parlor, there is also usually a huge bowl of apples, to say "welcome." Double-occupancy rates are $60 to $70 per person per day and that includes breakfast and dinner, plus afternoon tea. The inn's amenities include 15 acres of woods and meadows, an outdoor pool, an expansive front porch with rocking chairs, a library stocked with books, games, and a color TV. There are two dining rooms, decorated with paintings by the Tuppers' artist/son Rick. The menu includes veal and capers meunière; brace of quail stuffed with wild rice; rabbit with shallot cream sauce; veal scaloppine alla marsala; brook or rainbow trout, and lobster Thermidor. If you're stopping by just for dinner, the entrees fall into the $13 to $19.50 bracket and include your choices from the salad table, plus potato and vegetable. Dinner is served Monday through Saturday from 6 to 9:30 p.m., and on Sunday from 5 to 8:30 p.m. CC's accepted: AE, MC, and V.

Lodges and Motor Inns

The **Cresent Lodge,** Routes 191 and 940, Paradise Valley, Cresco, PA 18326 (tel. 717/595-7486 or toll-free 800/392-9400), is a small and friendly inn, nestled in a quiet forest setting near the junction of two main roads. A favorite with skiers, this inn is located eight miles from Camelback. Developed by the Dunlop family over the last 40 years, the accommodations consist of 12 rooms and suites in the main lodge and 18 units in motel-style cottages. Each room is wood-paneled, with wall-to-wall carpeting, a telephone, color TV, air conditioning, a tiled bath, and early-American furnishings. Doubles range from $64 to $82 in the lodge; suites from $74 to $94; and individual cottages from $88 to $160. Many of the cottages feature either a kitchenette, private Jacuzzi, fireplace, or garden patio. Guest amenities include an outdoor pool, a disco lounge, and a moderately priced alpine-style restaurant serving dinner from 5:30 to 9 p.m. on weeknights, until 10 p.m. on Friday and Saturday, and until 8 p.m. on Sunday. All major CC's accepted.

The **Comfort Inn,** Route 611, P.O. Box 184, Bartonsville, PA 18321 (tel. 717/476-1500 or toll-free 800/228-5150), is a new (1986) two-story property, located in tree-sheltered grounds near I-80 (exit 46), three miles west of Stroudsburg and six miles east of the Camelback ski area. There are 120 rooms, each with a contemporary décor, a choice of double-, queen-, or king-size beds, and the standard features of air conditioning, color cable TV, and a direct dial-phone. Some rooms also feature individual Jacuzzis or waterbeds. There is an outdoor swimming pool with a hot tub, a cocktail lounge with entertainment on the premises, and restaurants nearby. Doubles range from $45.95 to $89.95. All major CC's accepted.

The **Econo Lodge,** Route 715 and I-80, P.O. Box 131, Tannersville, PA 18372 (tel. 717/629-4100 or toll-free 800/441-2193), is located two miles from Camelback, at exit 45 off I-80. Perched on a hillside amid well-landscaped grounds, this is a three-story chalet-style inn with 88 rooms, about half of which have individual fireplaces. Each unit is equipped with two double beds or a king bed, air conditioning, color cable TV, and a direct-dial phone. Most rooms have lovely mountain views, and some also offer private Jacuzzis or waterbeds. The price for a double ranges from $55.95 to $59.95. Guest facilities include complimentary morning coffee, an outdoor swimming pool, a hot tub, and a game room. All major CC's accepted.

WHERE TO DINE: Try the following establishments while you are in the area.

The Top Choice

The **Pump House Inn,** Skytop Rd., Canadensis, PA 18325 (tel. 717/595-7501), is a delightful country house, high in the mountains. Owned by the Drucquer family, this restaurant is known for its inviting tavern with a fireplace and wide-plank floors, as well as its conversation-piece furnishings, books and antiques from around the world, and an oil-painting collection of sailing ships.

But, most of all, people flock here for the food—a gourmet's delight. Although the menu changes with the seasons, some of the dishes usually featured are apple pecan-stuffed chicken breast; poached Norwegian salmon filet in dill lemon butter sauce; lobster tails with crab stuffing; or rack of lamb. The entree prices run from $12.95 to $22.95, and include salad, potato, vegetable, and hot fruit compote. In addition, the Pump House also has six rooms and suites upstairs and in an adjoining cottage, which are available on a bed-and-breakfast basis. Doubles range from $50 to $65 and suites from $85 to $140. The restaurant is open for dinner, Tuesday through Saturday from 5 to 10 p.m., and on Sunday from 2:30 to 8:30 p.m. All major CC's accepted.

Moderately Priced Dining

A favorite spot for a casual drink or for a fine meal is the **Tannersville Inn,** Route 611, Tannersville (tel. 629-3131), a Pocono landmark enthusiastically run by the Jakubowitz family. The layout includes an old world "saloon," lined with memorabilia reflecting the inn's 155 years of existence. In contrast, there is a modern solarium filled with white wrought-iron furniture and lots of hanging plants. Meals are served here, starting with sandwich lunches and snacks, in the $2.50 to $3.95 price bracket. Dinner entrees, served by candlelight, include surf-and-turf; rainbow trout with wine butter and almonds; bluefish; monkfish; whole Coho salmon; honey-dipped fried chicken; lobster tails; and six types of steaks. All main courses come with salad and potato. The prices run from $8.95 to $18.95, with most choices under $15. Open from 11:30 a.m. to 11 p.m. daily. CC's accepted: AE, MC, and V.

Nestled amid giant old pines, the **Homestead Inn,** Sandspring Drive, Cresco (tel. 595-3171), is a small house-turned-restaurant tucked away in a wooded residential area, off Route 191 near the old Cresco railroad station. Fortunately, it is well signposted, with a striking barn-siding exterior and a giant boulder resting in its front garden. The interior features an early American décor with Wyeth prints on the walls, but the cuisine has been given an international flair by proprietors Drew and Susan Price. Entrees range from steaks and filet au poivre to swordfish and shrimp scampi; roast duckling in Chambord sauce; chicken Dijonnaise; red snapper in tomato basil sauce; baked ham in brown-sugar cinnamon sauce; and fettuccine Alfredo. Prices range from $9.95 to $15.95, and include hot biscuits, salad, and vegetables. Open every evening for dinner from 5 to 10 p.m., and on Sunday from 4 to 9 p.m. (closed Tuesday in winter). All major CC's accepted.

For a taste of Italy, try the **Wine Press Inn,** Star Route, Bartonsville Avenue, Route 611 (tel. 629-4302), where chef-owner Joe Vesce encourages special requests. The décor includes an indoor grape garden, wine casks, and a lobster tank, which foretell a fine wine list and good seafood. Entrees are priced from $9.75 to $16.95 with most under the $15 mark, and include scrod oreganata; shrimp marinara; zuppa di pesce; lobster Guiseppe (served in the shell, Newburg-style, with shrimp and mushrooms); chicken parmigiana; pork scaloppine lemon; and an assortment of steaks and veal dishes. All choices are accompanied by soup and salad bar and vegetable. Open Monday through Thursday (except Tuesday) from 5 to 9 p.m.; Friday and Saturday from 5 to 10:30 p.m.; and Sunday from 4 to 9 p.m. CC's accepted: AE, MC, and V.

A SAMPLING OF SPORTS: You can ride a horse, play golf, go skiing, or indulge in a food-sampling tour or two.

Horseback Riding: More than 60 acres of trails are available at **Carsons Riding Stables,** Route 611, Cresco (tel. 839-9841), one mile south of Mt. Pocono.

This 30-year-old establishment offers three-mile guided rides, every hour on the hour from 10 a.m. to 4 p.m., year round (reservations are suggested; and you should arrive 15 minutes before the ride you wish to take). The rate is $15 per person.

Golf: Pocono Manor Inn and Golf Club, Routes 314 and 940, Pocono Manor (tel. 839-7111), has two championship courses, with greens fees ranging from $13 per course on weekdays to $17 on weekends. Carts are $9 per person for 18 holes. There is also an 18-hole course at **Mt. Airy Lodge,** off Route 611, Mt. Pocono (tel. 839-8811), with midweek greens fee set at $15 for lodge guests and $20 for non-guests; on weekends, the fees are $20 and $25, respectively. Cart rentals are $9.55 per person.

A nine-hole course is also available at **Evergreen Park Golf Course,** Route 314, Analomink (tel. 421-7721), with midweek greens fees starting at $8 and weekend rates from $9. Cart rentals are $8 for nine holes and $13 for 18 holes.

Skiing: The largest of the Pocono ski resorts is **Camelback,** Routes 611 and 715, Tannersville (tel. 629-1661; snow reports toll-free 800/233-8100), at exit 45 on I-80. There is an 800-foot vertical drop, 25 slopes and trails, 11 lifts including six double chairs, two triple chairs and a quad chair, a rental shop, a ski school, and a child care program. Lift tickets range from $23 on weekdays to $26 on weekends, and night-skiing from $16.

Nearby is **Alpine Mountain,** Route 447, Analomink (tel. 595-2150), located nine miles north of I-80. With a 500-foot vertical drop and 14 slopes and trails, this facility also offers a poma lift, a quad chair, two t-bars; a rental shop, and a school. Lift tickets cost $15 at midweek and $19 on weekends.

This area is also the home of **Mt. Airy Lodge,** off Route 611, Mt. Pocono (tel. 839-8811), with a 240-foot vertical drop; and the **Pocono Manor Inn,** Routes 314 and 940, Pocono Manor (tel. 839-7111), with a 250-foot vertical drop.

FOOD-SAMPLING TOURS:

For a change a pace, this region invites you to indulge in some unique food-sampling tours. At **Callie's Candy Kitchen,** Route 390, Mountainhome (tel. 595-2280), you can see candy-in-the-making and enjoy free samples. Started in 1952, this small enterprise turns out over 30 varieties of sweets, from chocolate-covered fresh strawberries and raspberry fudge to two local favorites, Pocono Mountain Bark and Pocono Mountain Crunch. Three miles south is the **Callie's Pretzel Factory,** on Routes 390 and 191, Cresco (tel. 595-3257), a similar operation which produces soft pretzels, with choices ranging from pizza pretzels to garlic, cinnamon, or hot-dog pretzels. There are also 37 varieties of flavored gourmet popcorn. Open from 10 a.m. to 8:30 p.m. in summer and from 10 a.m. to 5 p.m. other times. Tours and samplings are free; all major CC's accepted for purchases.

6. Lake Wallenpaupack

Lake Wallenpaupack is a 13-mile long, 5,700-acre body of water that dominates the Poconos' northern region. With a 52-mile uninterrupted shoreline and a maximum depth of 60 feet, it is a paradise for watersports enthusiasts, honeymooners, campers, photographers, painters, and "just plain folks" who appreciate a new scenic vista at every turn.

Although it looks like a long-time natural wonder, the lake is actually manmade, created for hydro-electric power by the Pennsylvania Power and Light Company in 1926. It was formed from an old Indian Creek of the same name. To the Indians, "Wallenpaupack" meant "the stream of swift and slow water," and to today's traveler, that description is still delightfully accurate.

The chief towns that surround Lake Wallenpaupack are Lakeville, Hawley, Greentown, and South Sterling. Routes 590 and 507 circle the main lake shoreline, and I-84 runs directly south in an east-west direction, for easy access.

WHERE TO STAY AND DINE: Your choices are many in the Lake Wallenpaupack area.

A Classic Couples Retreat

Situated directly on the northern shore of Lake Wallenpaupack is **Cove Haven,** Lakeville, PA 18438 (tel. 717/226-2101 or toll-free 800/233-4141), the quintessential honeymoon resort, where the heart-shaped pool was introduced (1963). Designed totally for couples, this resort attracts a fair share of honeymooners, although 70% of the twosomes who come here can be described as general vacationers of all ages. In addition to the heart-shaped pools, baths, and Jacuzzis, you can also frolic in whirlpools-for-two, designed in the shape of champagne glasses, and Roman-style sunken baths. The décors of most rooms feature rich red carpet on the floors and walls, gold-louvered windows, mirrored headboards and ceilings, and huge round beds. There are eight different types of accommodations, ranging from romantic dimly lit rooms with no windows to harbor-front units with picture windows and private balconies. Most rooms have log-burning fireplaces and refrigerators, as well as the standard amenities of color TV, air conditioning, and a direct-dial phone. Doubles range from $170 to $275 per night, although most people avail of two- or three-night packages. The one price covers three meals a day including "his-and-her breakfasts" in bed, if you wish. Guests also enjoy free access to the nightclub with entertainment and dancing, a roller-skating rink, a gym, heated indoor and outdoor pools, a health club, a spa, and a marina; as well as use of the tennis courts, paddleboats, speedboats, sailboats, water skis, and bicycles. In the winter, you get free ski-lift tickets, tobogganing, and snowmobiling. There is also horseback riding, at a supplementary charge. Cove Haven is one of four Caesar's resorts in the Poconos; the others are **Brookdale-on-the-Lake,** Route 611, P.O. Box 400, Scotrun, PA 18355 (tel. 717/839-8843), for couples and families in the Central Poconos; **Paradise Stream,** Route 940, Mt. Pocono, PA 18344 (tel. 717/226-2101), a couples-only resort in the Central Poconos; and **Pocono Palace,** Route 209, Marshalls Creek, PA 18335 (tel. 717/226-2127), also for couples-only, five miles north of Stroudsburg. All major CC's accepted.

Family Resorts

On the southern shore of Lake Wallenpaupack is the **White Beauty View Resort,** R.D. 2, Box 228C, Greentown, PA 18426 (tel. 717/857-0234 or toll-free 800/233-4130). Started in 1926 by the Guccini family, this 200-acre property consists of a modern six-story tower of 48 hotel rooms right on the lake side of Route 507 and a cluster of rustic chalet-style lodges perched on a hill on the other side of the road. All units have wall-to-wall carpeting, air conditioning, cable color TV, and a direct-dial phone; some of the cottages have kitchenettes and operate on a do-your-own-housekeeping basis. Doubles range from $50 to $60 in the hillside cottages to $65 to $75 a night in the lakeside tower. Housekeeping cottages with one bedroom run from $45 to $95 a night; units with two to five bedrooms are also available. Guest facilities include adult and children's sports programs, and use of an indoor pool, a whirlpool, sauna, a fitness center, an outdoor patio, an indoor game room, plus swimming and boating on the lake. In the winter, there is sledding on the grounds, ice skating on the lake, a private skating pond, and ice fishing. In addition, the complex includes a nightclub, a lounge, the Lakeview Dining Room, and Naldo's, an Italian-American restaurant, featuring moderately priced meals in a rooftop setting overlooking the lake. Naldo's is also open to the public for dinner, Wednesday through Saturday from 5 to 10 p.m., and on Sunday from 4 to 9 p.m. All major CC's accepted.

Ten miles to the north is **The Silver Birches,** Star Route 2, Box 105, Hawley, PA 18428 (tel. 717/226-4388), situated right on the southern shore of the lake on Route 507, and one mile south of Route 6. Operated by the Ehrhardt family since 1943, these accommodations consist of lakeside rooms in the main lodge and several individual motel units. All rooms are paneled, with two double beds, wall-to-wall carpeting, private bath, TV, and air conditioning. Some two-bedroom family units and housekeeping cottages are also available. Rates for regular double-occupancy rooms in the summer start at $38 per person including breakfast and dinner; in the off-season, you can rent a room without meals from $45 a night for two. The price includes use of two swimming pools, a shuffleboard, waterskiing, boating, and badminton. There is an extra charge for rowboats with motors and for sailboats. Meals are served at the adjacent Ehrhardt Lakeside Restaurant, which is also opened to the public for moderately priced lunches and dinners from 11:30 a.m. to 2:30 p.m. and from 5 to 10 p.m. CC's accepted: MC and V.

About ten miles northeast of Lake Wallenpaupack is **The Inn at Woodloch Pines,** R.D. 1, Box 80, Hawley, PA 18428 (tel. 717/685-7121), situated off Route 590 in a secluded tree-shaded setting on Lake Teedyuskung. Long a popular site for time-sharing apartments, this 200-acre property now has 138 units available for overnight guests. There are four types of accommodations, ranging from cottages with motel-style rooms, to two- and three-story lakefront buildings with oversized rooms and suites, many with private balconies. Rates range from $80 to $150 per person per night, although visitors are encouraged to avail of midweek, weekend, or full-week packages. The price includes three meals per day, plus use of a wide variety of facilities including evening entertainment, tennis, volleyball, waterskiing, swimming on the lake beach and in the outdoor pool, cookouts, miniature golf, paddleboats, and a new indoor sports complex with pool, sauna, and exercise room. At certain times of the year, Woodloch is totally booked up to a year in advance, so it is wise to reserve early. Open year round except the last two weeks of December. No CC's accepted.

Country Inns

Two miles north of Lake Wallenpaupack on Route 590 is **Settlers Inn,** 4 Main Ave., Hawley, PA 18428 (tel. 717/226-2993 or 226-2448), dating from 1927. Situated on the eastern edge of the lumbering town of Hawley, this three-story Tudor-style inn thrived in the 1940s and then slowly began to decline. Originally 54 rooms, the hotel was purchased, restored, and refurbished in 1980 by Jeanne and Grant Genzlinger. There are now 16 bedrooms, all with private bath and "early attic" and country-style furnishings. Doubles range from $45 to $60 and entitle you to a hearty continental breakfast. The public rooms include a TV lounge and a homey "Tavern in the Inn" room where you'll find a huge stone fireplace, a rustic bar, and a complimentary cheese board, set out in the early evening for guests who wish to enjoy a cocktail or two. The dining room blends a candlelit Colonial aura with contemporary cuisine. Lunch, priced from $2.50 to $4.95, focuses on sandwiches, burgers, salads, crêpes, and omelets. For dinner, you may wish to start with cream-of-cashew soup or vegetable quiche ($2). Entree choices often feature such choices as roast duckling in bing cherry and port wine sauce; veal Luzerne (with tomatoes and Swiss cheese); scallops wrapped in bacon; baked stuffed shrimp; German-style pot roast; and chicken

Cordon Bleu. The entrees are priced between $9.95 and $15.95, and come with a basket of home-baked treats, salad, and potato. Lunch is served from 11:30 a.m. to 2 p.m., and dinner from 5 to 10 p.m. Open year round (except December 23, 24, and 25). Guests can also enjoy the town park across the street and an on-premises craft shop and art gallery, stocked with the creations of local artisans. All major CC's accepted.

A well-signposted winding road off Route 191 leads you up Huckleberry Mountain to **The French Manor,** P.O. Box 39, South Sterling, PA 18460 (tel. 717/676-3244), a secluded château-style home built by a wealthy businessman in the 1930s. Constructed of oak, cedar, pecky cypress, and stone, with a Spanish slate roof, this mansion is the centerpiece of a 43-acre estate, and was in private hands until 1985 when it was purchased by Dan and Carolyn Balish. Now tastefully transformed into a country inn with a full-time concierge, this property has eight guest rooms, six of which are in the main house and two located in an adjacent carriage house. All rooms have a private bath, except two in the main house which have shared facilities. Each room is individually decorated and named to reflect the ambience of a European city, such as the Venice Room, Florence Room, Monte Carlo Room, and so forth. The emphasis is on fine furnishings and art and there are no distractions, such as TVs or telephones, in the rooms. Rates range from $65 to $90 per person per night and include a continental breakfast with fresh fruit and French toast and a full eight-course dinner. The elegant dining room has two huge fireplaces, a cathedral ceiling, and a French country décor; there is usually a resident piano player providing background music to dine by. In warm weather, guests can enjoy the adjacent outside deck, ideal for viewing the panorama of mountains that surround the estate. Like the setting, the cuisine is mostly French, with a constantly changing selection of entrees (usually beef, veal, lamb, lobster, and other seafoods). There are no menus; you choose only the main course and the chef takes care of the rest, including cold and hot appetizers, soup, salad, sorbet, cheese board with fruit, and dessert cart. Even if you are not overnighting here, you can reserve a table for dinner; the fixed-price per head cost is $38. The only thing missing here is a liquor license, but you are welcome to bring your own bottle. Open Wednesday through Sunday for dinner hours from 6 to 8:30 p.m. CC's accepted: AE, MC, and V.

A SAMPLING OF SPORTS AND ACTIVITIES: Watersports, horseback riding, and camping are featured at Lake Wallenpaupack.

Water sports: On the south shore of the lake is **Pine Crest Boat Rentals,** Route 507, Greentown (717/857-1136), one of the leading watersport centers in the area. Located next to White Beauty View Resort, this is a complete boating facility with a marina, 500 feet of lakefront grounds, and a sailing school on the premises. You can rent all types of ski and family boats, cruising boats, motorboats, catamarans, fishing boats, and sailboats from 13 to 22 feet in length. A two-hour minimum applies for all rentals, with rates ranging from $22 for a sunfish to $42 for a 22-foot Catalina sailboat, for two hours. Open mid-April to September/October.

Horseback riding: There are two horseback-riding facilities near the north shore of the lake. **Double W Ranch and Stables,** off Route 6, Honesdale, (tel. 226-3118), is four miles north of Hawley, on a 170-acre horse farm. Visitors can arrange to go trail riding with a guide, from $11 to $14 per hour, depending on the number of people in the riding group; weekend charges are $1 more per hour. There is a choice of four different trails, meandering through woods, lakelands, meadows, or mountains. Overnight trail rides and hayrides are also organized, by reservation. Open all year, from 9 a.m. to 5 p.m.

You can also arrange to ride at the **RJD Stables,** off Route 590, Hamlin Corners (tel. 698-6996), on the northwest side of the lake. This center offers one-hour trail rides, daily on the hour, from 9 a.m. to 5 p.m., at a cost of $9 per person per hour; two-hour trails for experienced riders can also be arranged, from $18.

Camping: The Pennsylvania Power and Light Company maintains four areas around Lake Wallenpaupack for family camping and recreation, each with its own resident director. Two of the sites are near Greentown on the southern shore, and there is one each near Lakeville and Hawley on the north and east shores, respectively. Campers have access to electricity, coin-operated washing machines and clothes dryers, and hot showers. Open between the last Saturday in April and the third Sunday in October, each area has a small general store, boat rental, docks, launching ramps, and picnic areas.

In the winter, the sites remain open, but only with the restrooms and a frost-free water supply for visitors.

Reservations are advised, but you may also camp on a first-come basis for one to 21 nights. The fees are $9 per night for one to four persons, $1 per night for each additional person; electricity is included in the fee during the summer months. For further information and a brochure describing all four camp sites, contact **Pennsylvania Power and Light Co.,** Mr. Sherwood J. Krum, Lake Wallenpaupack Superintendent, Box 122, Hawley, PA 18428-0122 (tel. 717/226-3702).

Skiing: On the south side of the lake is **Tanglwood,** off Route 390, Tafton (tel. 226-9500), a major resort with a 415-foot vertical drop and ten slopes and trails. There are two double chair lifts, two t-bars, and one beginners' lift. Midweek rates start at $12 and on weekends from $18; there is also night-skiing from $8 on weekdays and $10 on weekends. Other facilities include a cross country center, rentals, lessons, and a ski school.

CHILDREN'S CORNER: More than 60 species of animals from all over the world are displayed in natural settings at **Claws 'n' Paws Wild Animal Park,** Route 590, Lake Ariel (tel. 698-6154). Children are enchanted by the live animal shows and large petting area with tame deer, llamas, and lambs. Other attractions include a wildlife trail devoted exclusively to Pennsylvania animals, a gift shop, a picnic area, and pony rides. Open daily May through late October from 10 a.m. to 6 p.m. Admission charges are $4.95 for adults and $2.95 for youngsters.

7. Western Poconos

Really rural territory awaits you in the western Poconos. As you head west, on I-80 or Route 940, you'll find fewer resorts and man-made attractions, and more natural parklands and open spaces.

Besides the mountains, this section is dominated by the waters of the Lehigh River. Most people come here, in fact, to enjoy whitewater rafting, although skiing, golfing, and hiking are also popular. In addition, this is ideal territory for mule-riding and all-terrain biking. The chief center for most of these sports is White Haven, an outpost of 2,000 residents, named for Josiah White, an 18th-century navigator of the Lehigh.

This remote part of the Poconos is also the home of Jim Thorpe, a charming mountain village (pop.: 5,300), so named in 1954 to honor the famous 1912

Olympic athlete. The real Jim Thorpe never visited here, but his remains were transferred to a 20-ton granite mausoleum at the entrance to the town when the local citizens decided to perpetuate his memory.

Originally called Coalville, then Mauch Chunk (an Indian name meaning "Bear Mountain"), this settlement was once known as the "Switzerland of America" because of its 19th-century architecture, narrow streets, and European layout, but, most of all, for its idyllic location on the Lehigh River, surrounded by broad mountain vistas.

A prominent rail transfer point in the coal era of the 1850s, Jim Thorpe was the home of Asa Packer, a local entrepreneur and philanthropist who started the Lehigh Valley Railroad and Lehigh University (in Bethlehem). Today visitors delight in touring Asa Packer's Italianate mansion as well as other prominent well-preserved buildings of the town.

WHERE TO STAY AND DINE: Unlike the other parts of the Poconos, the western region does not have a huge choice of accommodations, but the places that are here are top notch and each one is distinctive in its own way. In general, rates fall into the moderate category.

The Top Choice

As its name implies, the **Hershey Pocono Resort,** Route 940, P.O. Box 126, White Haven, PA 18661 (tel. 717/443-8411 or toll-free 800/533-3131), brings the sweet magic of "chocolate world" to this part of the state. Located at the intersection of I-80 and Route 9 (the Pennsylvania Turnpike northeast extension), this is a modern three-story 250-room resort in a secluded setting on 300 acres of wooded mountain land. Each of the rooms is furnished in a bright contemporary style with all the usual amenities, and many have balconies or private patios. Doubles in the summer start at $164, including a full breakfast and dinner for two. Most people who stay here, however, avail of a weekend or midweek package plan, particularly in the spring, fall, and winter months. These packages can be as low as $56 per person per night with two meals. One of the most popular weekends is the mid-May **Chocolate Festival,** a three-day event that includes a chocolate treasure hunt, a chocolate fashion show, and many chocolate-tasting experiences. The guest facilities include Olympic-size indoor and outdoor pools, a sauna, tennis courts, archery, shuffleboard, miniature golf, horseshoes, ice skating, sledding, tobogganing, cross-country skiing, and a free shuttle service to the nearby downhill resorts of Jack Frost or Big Boulder. There is a supplementary fee for playing on the hotel's 18-hole golf course or for horseback riding. There is also a "leave the children to us program," full-time activities for youngsters, operated 12 hours a day.

Meals are usually served in the **Treetops Dining Room.** For a change of pace or for people not overnighting at the hotel, there is also a smaller gourmet à la carte restaurant, "A Touch of Vanilla," where entrees range from $11.95 to $19.95. The specialties include hickory-smoked roasted duck; panned chicken with apples and pecans in Cajun sauce; and crab-stuffed brook trout in mushroom cream sherry sauce. Dinner is served Monday through Thursday from 6 to 9 p.m. and Friday and Saturday from 6 to 10 p.m. Other attractions include an old-fashioned ice-cream parlor, a tavern, and lounge with nightly entertainment. All major CC's are accepted.

A Moderately Priced Motor Inn

Nearby is the **Holiday Inn-Pocono,** Route 940, P.O. Box 117, White Haven, PA 18661 (tel. 717/443-8471 or toll-free 800/251-2610). This modern four-story brick hotel has 142 rooms in a wooded hillside setting, just 3½ miles from the two major ski resorts of the area. Each unit is outfitted with all the standard amenities and a choice of two double or king-size beds; nonsmoking rooms are also available. Doubles range from $65 to $85 and meals are extra. The guest facilities include a heated indoor pool, saunas, an indoor tanning deck with sunlamps, a putting green, a lounge with entertainment, and a moderately priced restaurant. All major CC's accepted.

Bed-and-Breakfast in a Mansion

If a tour of the historic Asa Packer Mansion sounds appealing, then you'll be happy to know that you can actually overnight in the adjacent **Harry Packer Mansion,** Packer Hill, Jim Thorpe, PA 18229 (tel. 717/325-8566). Built in 1874, this grand hilltop house was a wedding gift from prominent industrialist Asa Packer to his youngest son, Harold Eldred. Constructed of local brick, stone, New England sandstone, and cast-iron trim, this Second Empire home has an interior that reflects high Victorian grandeur. It is a showcase of walnut wood-work, parquet floors, marble mantles, bronze and polished brass chandeliers, hand-painted ceilings, Tiffany windows, Oriental rugs, and antiques. On the second floor there are three bedrooms delightfully filled with antiques, which are available to overnight guests; plans call for more rooms to be restored on the third floor. The current choice offers two double-occupancy rooms with a shared bath or a suite with a private bath, a master sitting room, and a balcony. Doubles cost $60 each and the suite is $100 per night. The prices include country egg breakfasts. All guests can enjoy the front veranda which overlooks the town of Jim Thorpe, and the distinctive ladies' and gentlemen's parlors. For those who can't stay here, there are tours available, Tuesday through Sunday from noon to 5 p.m.; the cost is $2.50 for adults and $1.50 for children. CC's accepted: MC and V.

WHERE TO DINE: If you are looking for a good spot to eat after you have walked the historic streets of Jim Thorpe, then **The Hotel Switzerland,** 5 Hazard Square (tel. 325-4563), is a fitting find. Reputed to be the oldest remaining structure of the town, dating from the 1830s, this small restaurant will impart a sense of yesteryear from the moment you step inside the door. To the right is a beautifully restored cherry-and-mahogany bar with marble columns and brass fixtures. In the rear is the Victorian Dining Room, a small restaurant furnished with a carved buffet piece, an antique cupboard, ornate wallpaper in cranberry and ivory shades, and a tin ceiling. Lunch items, priced from $2.95 to $4.95, focus mainly on sandwiches, burgers, and platters. Dinner entrees, price from $7.95 to $14.95, include chicken burgundy, sole amandine, and surf-and-turf. All main courses come with salad, potato, and vegetable. Lunch is served daily from 11:30 a.m. to 2:30 p.m., and dinner Thursday through Saturday from 5 to 9:30 p.m. Major CC's are accepted.

If you long for a good steak, then **Richie's,** Route 940, White Haven (443-9528), is the place to go. For over 25 years, Richie (now with son Eric) has catered to skiers, rafters, or vacationers who seek a simple and straightforward meal and a relaxing atmosphere. Besides steaks, the menu offers prime ribs, seafoods, and imported Black Forest ham, in the $9.95 to $16.95 price range. Dinner is served nightly from 4 to 9 p.m. CC's Accepted: AE, D, MC, and V.

A SAMPLING OF SPORTS AND ACTIVITIES: From whitewater rafting to mountain biking and mule riding, you'll find plenty to do in the Poconos.

Whitewater Rafting: Without a doubt, this sport is king in these parts. Anyone can participate, novice or experienced, although most companies have a minimum age requirement of 10 years. In general, they operate from March through June and from September through November. Here are some of the services available:

Lehigh River Rafting, 432 Main St., White Haven (tel. 443-9777 or toll-free 800 647-RAFT), organizes guided whitewater rafting trips, March through November from $38 per adult or $30 for students; wet suits are available in colder weather at a rental charge of $5 to $10 per person. In addition, there is the "Tom Sawyer River Adventure," a slightly easier trek, priced at $22 for adults and $17 for students.

Adjacent to Hickory Run Park, you'll find **Whitewater Rafting Adventure Inc.,** Route 534, Albrightsville (tel. 722-0285). This firm operates raft trips at $37 per person. In addition, there are summer float trips in July and August, priced at $20 per person. Wet suits can be rented for $10 a person.

White Water Challengers, off Route 940, White Haven (tel. 443-9532), offers half-day trips from $23, full-day treks from $39, or overnight packages from $72 per person. This firm operates special programs including a "firstimers" course with instruction. **Jim Thorpe River Adventures Inc.,** Coalport Road, Jim Thorpe (tel. 325-2570), offers similar services.

Golf: The **Hershey Pocono Resort,** Route 940, White Haven (tel. 443-8411) offers an 18-hole PGA course, with weekday greens fees of $15 and weekend rates of $17. Carts can be rented for $18.

Mule Rides: "Mu'-le-teer-ing rides" are conducted by **Pocono Adventures,** Star Route, off Route 903, Jim Thorpe (tel. 325-2036). Open daily year round, this company will lead you through 45,000 acres of backwood trails, various guided treks, including a two-hour beginner's ride over flat easy trails ($20), or a half-day adventurer's ride, up and down mountains in the scenic wilderness ($30). In addition, there are all-day trips including breakfast and dinner at the ranch and lunch on the trail from $70, and overnight treks from $80. This firm also organizes fishing and hunting trips.

Mountain Biking: Described as "all-terrain" vehicles of the bike world, these two-wheelers have fat knobby tires and heavy frames to enable a biker to travel over rock, through mud and sand, and across grassy areas with ease. The bikes have up to 15 speeds for climbing hills and rocky terrain. Rentals of these bikes are offered by **Whitewater Challengers Inc.,** off Route 940, White Haven (tel. 443-9532). The cost is $10 a day with a map outlining two trails, either along the Lehigh or in the mountains, of 10- or 15-mile durations, respectively.

Outdoor Combat Adult Games: Hot Pursuit, off Route 940, White Haven, (tel. 443-9371), organizes "friendly American combat games" in the wilderness of the western Poconos. Described as an adult version of "capture the flag," these games pit teams of two, three, or four players in combative sport. The games are set up from April through mid-December, at a cost of $28 to $30 per person, and $15 in the evening. Reservations are required at least two weeks in advance. Another firm offering a similar service is **Skirmish,** Route 903, Jim Thorpe (tel. 325-3654), charging $30 for a full game or $18 for a shorter version.

Skiing: There are two major ski resorts in the western Poconos. The oldest is **Big Boulder,** Route 903, Lake Harmony (tel. 722-0101), started in the 1950s. This facility has a 475-foot vertical drop, 11 slopes and trails, six double chair lifts, and one beginners' triple chair. Lift tickets cost $20 midweek, $25 on weekends, and $15 at night. Nearby is **Jack Frost Mountain,** Route 115, White Haven, (tel. 443-8425), with a 600-foot vertical drop, 19 slopes and trails, and seven double chair lifts. Lift tickets cost $20 midweek and $25 on weekends. Both resorts offer interchangeable lift tickets, allowing you to ski Jack Frost at day and Boulder at night.

Chapter VI

THE LEHIGH RIVER VALLEY

1. Getting To and Around the Valley
2. Visitor Information
3. Allentown
4. Bethlehem
5. Easton

TWO COUNTIES, Northampton and Lehigh, make up the area known as the Lehigh Valley. The region takes its name from the Lehigh River which meanders in an east-west flow and in a north-south direction, in a fertile valley between Philadelphia and the Poconos.

Although much of Northampton and Lehigh counties are farmland, three cities dominate the region, Allentown, Bethlehem, and Easton, an urban trio rich in historical and natural attractions. Over the centuries, the Lehigh Valley was also influenced by strong Biblical traditions, and that is why you'll find that many roads lead to Nazareth, Egypt, and Emmaus.

1. Getting To and Around the Valley

BY PLANE: The Lehigh Valley has its own airport, named for its three major metropolitan areas, **Allentown-Bethlehem-Easton International Airport** (tel. 264-2831), known as A-B-E for short. It is located between Allentown and Bethlehem, north of both cities at the juncture of Routes 22 and 987 (locally, Airport Road). The following airlines fly scheduled services into A-B-E: **United** (tel. 821-7870 or toll-free 800/241-6522); **USAir** (tel. 437-9801 or toll-free 800/428-4322); **Eastern** (tel. 821-8860 or toll-free 800/327-8376); **Piedmont Henson** (tel. toll-free 800/368-5425); and **Allegheny Commuter** (tel. toll-free 800/428-4253). Almost all hotels and motels operate complimentary shuttle services to and from the airport for their guests. Transfer time from the airport is 6 minutes to Bethlehem, 10 minutes to Allentown, and 15 minutes to Easton.

CAR RENTALS/TAXIS: If you wish to rent a car, depots are maintained at the airport by **Budget** (tel. 266-0666) and **National** (tel. 264-5535). In addition,

Hertz has a rental station at 1400 Waverly Rd. in Easton (tel. 258-9969) and **Thrifty** is at 3320 Airport Rd., Allentown (tel. 264-4588). If you need a cab, call **Quick Taxi** (tel. 434-8132) or **Yellow Cab** (tel. 258-9141).

BY BUS: Service into Allentown is operated by Trailways and Greyhound both of which pull into the **depot** at 27 S. 6th St. and share the same phone number (tel. 434-6188). Bethlehem is served by **Greyhound,** into 3rd St. and Brodhead Ave. (tel. 867-3988). Easton is also reached by either Greyhound or **Trailways,** both stopping at 154 Northampton St. (tel. 253-4126). Local bus service within and among the three cities is operated by **Lehigh and Northampton Transportation Authority,** otherwise known as LANTA (tel. 435-6771 or 258-0479); the fare is 75¢ in peak hours and 50¢ in off-peak.

BY CAR: From the east and west, the cities of Allentown, Bethlehem, and Easton are traversed by Route 22. This area is the last link in the construction of I-78; when this highway is completed in the next year or two, it will make the Lehigh Valley more accessible than ever between New Jersey and Harrisburg and onward points. The Pennsylvania Turnpike's northeast extension, Route 9, also passes west of Allentown in a north-south direction.

2. Visitor Information

The entire area including the cities of Allentown, Bethlehem, and Easton is served by the **Lehigh Valley Convention and Visitors Bureau Inc.,** located at Allentown-Bethlehem-Easton (A-B-E) Airport, International Airport Terminal Building, P.O. Box 2605, Lehigh Valley, PA 18001 (tel. 215/266-0560). In the summer months, this office also operates **information booths** at two points along Route 22 (at North 7th Street, Allentown, and at Route 512, Bethlehem). Both of these visitor centers are open daily from 9 a.m. to 6 p.m. In addition, as you will see on the following pages, all three major cities, Allentown, Bethlehem, and Easton, maintain an individual information center in their respective downtown districts.

AREA CODE: All telephone numbers in the Lehigh Valley region belong to the 215 area code.

3. Allentown

The treasured Liberty Bell of Philadelphia considers Allentown to be its second home. Originally a rural village known as Northamptontowne, this area was chosen by George Washington during Revolutionary War times as a place to hide the Liberty Bell while the British occupied Philadelphia. Fearing that the bell would be melted down for British bullets, a contingent of Washington's men brought it by covered wagon to the basement of a local church in Northamptontowne in 1777. The bell remained here for a year until the colonists retook the City of Brotherly Love and it was safe for the symbol of freedom to return.

It was not until a few years later that the name Allentown was adopted in honor of William Allen, one-time chief justice of Pennsylvania and the official founder of this pleasant Lehigh Valley city.

Located 45 miles north of Philadelphia and surrounded by rich farming territory, Allentown today (pop. 103,000) is the hub of industry and manufacturing; such well-known product names as Kraft, Keebler, Alpo, and Stroh's are all here. Allentown is also the home of Muhlenberg College, founded in 1848 to honor the patriarch of Lutheranism in the U.S.

Bounded on the east by the Lehigh River, Allentown is laid out for the most part on a grid system, with its focus on Hamilton St., which runs in an east-west direction, and 7th St. which extends from north to south. Although the city is currently in the midst of restoring much of its historic residential area, the downtown skyline is dominated by the modern 23-story tower of the Pennsylvania Power and Light Company.

LOCAL VISITOR INFORMATION: Specific data about Allentown can be obtained from the **Allentown-Lehigh Chamber of Commerce,** 462 Walnut St., P.O. Box 1229, Allentown, PA 18105 (tel. 215/437-9661). Open Monday through Friday from 8:30 a.m. to 5 p.m.

WHERE TO STAY: The center of commerce for the Lehigh Valley, Allentown is a hub of business traffic during the week. To encourage weekend visitors, many hotels have developed reduced-rate packages. You can therefore enjoy considerable savings if you travel here on a Friday or Saturday night. Be sure to check with the lodging of your choice to see what special deal may apply at the time of your visit. In general, rates at Allentown hotels and motels can usually be classified as moderate.

The top choice in the downtown area is the **Hamilton Plaza,** 4th and Hamilton Streets, P.O. Box 273, Allentown, PA 18105 (tel. 215/437-9876), a deluxe seven-story property that was completely renovated and refurbished in 1986. The 100 guest rooms, priced from $65, are decorated with graceful pastels and period furniture, and most rooms have wraparound bay windows and views of the city; there are also four theme suites (featuring décors reflecting Bali, an Arabian caravan, Victoriana, and a Stardust motif), priced from $95. All units have air conditioning, color cable TV, an AM/FM clock radio, a direct-dial phone, and a choice of double-, queen-, or king-size beds. The restaurant, one of the finest in the city, is known for its tableside service and conversation-piece décor of fanciful figures and flowers. Dinner entrees are priced from $9.95 to $19.95, with most under $15, and include steak Diane; sautéed veal liver; roast pheasant with chestnuts and wild rice stuffing in rum raisin sauce; salmon en croûte, seafood stew; sweet and sour haddock; and rack of lamb. All main courses are accompanied by salad, sorbet, vegetable, and potato. Flaming coffees and flambé desserts are also a specialty here (bananas Foster and crêpes suzette are each $4.95 per serving). Gentle piano music and extremely cordial wait-persons in tuxedos add to the gracious ambience of this popular dining spot. Dinner is served Monday through Saturday from 5:30 to 10 p.m. and on Sunday from 5 to 9 p.m. Lunch is also available Monday through Saturday from 11 a.m. to 2 p.m. and breakfast from 7 to 10 a.m. daily. A sumptuous brunch is also served on Sunday from 10 a.m. to 2 p.m. at $9.95 for adults and $5.95 for children aged 6 to 12. There is a parking lot at the hotel and valet service is also available. All major CC's are accepted.

In the heart of the downtown shopping district is the **Allentown Hilton,** 904 Hamilton Mall, Allentown, PA 18101 (tel. 215/433-2221), a modern ten-story property with 227 rooms and suites. All guest rooms are decorated in bright pastel contemporary tones with one or two double beds, a direct-dial phone, air conditioning, and color cable TV. Doubles range from $58 to $78 and bi-level suites with spiral staircases from $120. Guest facilities include an indoor swimming pool, a health club, an exercise room and sauna, and parking. The Masterpiece Restaurant is a palette of color on three levels, with mirrored tiles, plants, brass, and menus that feature reproductions of paintings by the world's greatest artists. Lunch, priced from $2.95 to $5.95, offers salads, sandwiches, omelets, quiches, and taco pies. Dinner entrees, priced from $9.95 to $15.95, include such dishes as herb-stuffed double veal chops; boneless breast of duck Dijonnaise; black angus prime ribs; roasted leg of lamb; and rock Cornish game hen with wild rice. All main courses come with salad, vegetable, and potato. There is background piano music on most evenings. Open daily for breakfast from 6:30 to 10:30 a.m.; lunch from 11 a.m. to 2:30 p.m.; dinner from 5:30 to 10 p.m.; and Sunday brunch from 11:30 a.m. to 2:30 p.m. All major CC's accepted.

Just across the street from the A.B.E. airfield is the **Sheraton Jetport,** 3400 Airport Rd., Allentown, PA 18103 (tel. 215/266-1000 or toll-free 800/325-3535), located just off Route 22. Laid out in a T-shape, this modern three-story hotel has 150 rooms and is currently adding 45 more. Each unit has a choice of two double- or one king-size bed, with floor-to-ceiling mirrored closets, air conditioning, color cable TV, a radio/alarm clock, and a direct-dial phone. Doubles start at $70. Guest amenities include a heated indoor pool, a Jacuzzi, a sauna, a courtyard, ample parking, a nightclub that features top 40 hits, and a full-service restaurant called Teddy's. Lunch, priced from $3.95 to $5.95, offers sandwiches, burgers, salads, and omelets; weekdays there is also a $7 lunch buffet. Dinner features a "fresh fish mart" with the catches of the day displayed on ice for you to select your fancy—whether it be a swordfish steak, flounder, shrimp, salmon, or brook trout. If seafood is not your choice, then you can opt for other dishes ranging from prime ribs and steaks to Oriental-style chicken, veal, or vegetable lasagne. All entrees, priced in the $9.95 to $16.95 bracket, entitle you to servings from the salad bar and soft-ice-cream bar. Lunch is available daily from 11 a.m. to 2:30 p.m. and dinner from 5 to 10 p.m. All major CC's accepted.

The **George Washington Lodge,** 1350 MacArthur Rd., Allentown, PA 18052 (tel. 215/433-0131), is located less than a mile north of downtown on Route 145, just south of Route 22 in an area known as Whitehall. There are 226 motel-style rooms, all newly renovated, each with two double beds, color cable TV with free HBO, a direct-dial phone, and air conditioning. Doubles range from $40 to $60. Guest amenities include indoor and outdoor pools, a whirlpool, a sauna, a tavern with nightly entertainment, and a Colonial-motif restaurant called Martha's Tables. Overlooking the park-like setting of nearby Jordan Creek, this dining room features moderate menus daily but is most well known for its "Sinful Sunday Brunches" with dozens of traditional and innovative dishes plus an 18-foot chocolate dessert table, for $12.95 per person. Lunch is available daily from 11 a.m. to 2 p.m.; dinner Monday through Saturday from 5 to 10 p.m., and until 9 p.m. on Sunday. Brunch is served from 11:30 a.m. to 2:30 p.m. All major CC's accepted.

The **Days Inn,** Routes 22 and 309, Allentown, PA 18104 (tel. 215/395-3731 or toll-free 800/325-2525), is conveniently situated near the Pennsylvania Turnpike northeast extension (Route 9) in a westerly direction five miles from downtown. Formerly a Holiday Inn, this rambling mostly one-story property has an alpine style and décor. Offering a variety of bed sizes, each of the 287 rooms has air conditioning, a direct-dial phone, and color cable TV. Doubles range from $52 to $58 and facilities include extensive grounds with parking and an all-day café offering moderately priced meals. In addition, Days Inns operates a smaller 87-room **motel,** one mile north of downtown at 15th Street North off Route 22 (tel. 215/435-7880 or toll-free 800/325-2525), with doubles from $32.99 to $38.99. Most major CC's accepted at both locations.

WHERE TO DINE: In addition to the fine hotel dining rooms, Allentown has a variety of downtown and suburban restaurants, many with historical settings and in the mostly moderate price range.

The aura of Colonial Allentown is alive and well at the **King George Inn,** 3141 Hamilton Blvd. (tel. 435-1723), at Cedar Crest Blvd. (Routes 29 and 229) on the western side of the city. Established as a stagecoach hotel in 1756, this two-story stone house is listed in the National Register and has been in the hands of Cliff and Nancy McDermott since 1970. There are four dining rooms including the original ground-level Hearth Room with beam ceilings, exposed brick walls, and an open fireplace. Upstairs features a glass-enclosed porch setting and the Prince of Wales Tavern with various coats of arms on the walls. Lunch, priced from $2.95 to $6.95, focuses on salads, sandwiches, burgers, and light entrees such as an original recipe devised here called "eggs Napolean" (poached eggs with roast beef and hollandaise on a croissant). Dinner entrees, in the $9.95 to $15.95 price bracket, include steaks, chicken Dijonnaise, veal picatta, lobster, and shrimp Newburg. All main courses are accompanied by salad, potato, or pasta. Open for lunch Monday through Saturday from 11:30 a.m. to 4:30 p.m. and for dinner from 4:30 to 10 p.m., and until midnight on Friday and Saturday; and on Sunday for dinner only from 4 to 9 p.m. All major CC's accepted.

An 18th-century atmosphere is also the keynote of **The Historic 1760 House,** Routes 100 and 222, Trexlertown (tel. 395-2652), five miles west of downtown. Built as a log house in 1731, this building has been operating as a tavern ever since John Trexler applied for a license in 1746. The original structure is incorporated into the present southern half of the building and the northern end dates from 1760. The décor is a medley of glowing hurricane lamps, pewter pitchers, low timber ceilings, and lantern window candles, with brick, log, and stone walls and, of course, a huge central fireplace. Salads, sandwiches, and casseroles are on the menu at lunch, priced from $3.95 to $7.95. Dinner entrees range from $9.95 to $19.95 with most dishes under $15. The selection includes Colonial recipes such as chicken with apricot glaze; roast duckling; and broiled pheasant, as well as a few 20th-century treats like sautéed rainbow trout; Coho salmon with shrimp sauce; seafood au gratin; prime ribs; and pasta. All main courses come with salad, vegetable, potato, or pasta. Open for lunch Monday through Friday from 11:30 a.m. to 2:30 p.m.; for dinner Monday through Saturday from 5 to 10 p.m.; and on Sunday from 4 to 9 p.m. CC's accepted: AE, D, MC, and V.

A restaurant that is especially fun for youngsters is the **Widow Brown's Inn,** 4939 Hamilton Blvd., Wescosville, (tel. 398-1300), about three miles west of downtown. An old-fashioned schoolhouse theme pervades this spot with copybook menu covers, shelves of timeworn textbooks, wall maps, and globes—all that is missing are the teachers and homework! Lunch, priced from $3.95 to $6.95, features salads, burgers, sandwiches, and chalkboard specials. Entrees at dinner, priced in the $7.95 to $15.95 range, include broiled seafood dishes; steaks; veal Cordon Bleu; shrimp and chicken scampi; and vegetable platters. All main courses entitle you to unlimited trips to the unique revolving salad bar, plus potato or pasta. Open for lunch Monday to Friday from 11:30 a.m. to 4 p.m.; for dinner Monday through Thursday from 4:30 to 10:30, on Friday and Saturday from 4:30 to 11 p.m., and on Sunday from 1 to 9 p.m. A second **Widow Brown's Inn** is located six miles north of Easton at Main and Bushkill Streets, Stockertown, (tel. 759-7404). All major CC's accepted.

One of the dining surprises in the downtown area is the **Patio Restaurant** on the lower level of Hess's Department Store, 9th and Hamilton Streets, (tel. 821-

4377), a downtown shopping emporium founded in 1897 by Max Hess and an Allentown institution in its own right. As fine as the store is, however, most people do not expect to find a top-class restaurant in such surroundings, but here we have a real star. Lunch choices, priced in the $3.95 to $5.95 range, include a creative array of salads and sandwiches. The extensive international dinner menu, which is available all day, is priced from $6.95 to $19.95, with most choices under $10. The selections, all prepared to order, include such entrees as lobster tail Newburg in a patty shell; frogs' legs Provencal; salmon steak; stir-fry dishes; seafood tempura; prime ribs; steaks; and vegetable platters. The Patio is also known for its display of irresistible desserts such as strawberry tart, lemon sponge pie, or southern pecan pie ($1.95 to $2.95), and for its extensive cocktail and wine list. Open Monday, Thursday, Friday, and Saturday from 11 a.m. to 8 p.m.; Tuesday and Wednesday from 11 a.m. to 4:30 p.m.; and Sunday from 11:30 a.m. to 5 p.m. All major CC's accepted.

Pennsylvania Dutch cooking and American cuisine are both featured at **Walp's,** 911 Union Blvd., at Airport Road (tel. 437-4841), on the eastern edge of town. Founded over 50 years ago, this restaurant is decorated in a country cupboard theme, with pewter dishes and tankards, stained-glass windows, and curio sideboards. The extensive menu features Wiener schnitzel, Yankee pot roast, smoked sausage, and chicken dumplings, as well as steaks, prime ribs, and seafood including lobster tails. Each main course includes an appetizer, salad, and vegetable. The prices range from $6.95 to $14.95 with most dishes under $10. Desserts (from $1.25), made fresh daily in the on-premises bake shop, include puddings, cakes, and a variety of pies (the shoofly pie is irresistible). Breakfast and lunch are also served, but the greatest values are at dinnertime. Open Monday from 6:30 a.m. to 9 p.m. and Tuesday through Sunday from 6:30 a.m. to 10 p.m. (closed the 4th of July and Christmas). CC's accepted: MC and V.

Devotees of the Pritikin diet will find an oasis of healthy food at **Eating to Win,** Hamilton Boulevard, (tel. 398-7411), two miles west of downtown and adjacent to the Wildwater Kingdom of Dorney Park. Menus here feature dishes that have no sugar, salt, butter, or oil. Lunch, priced in the $1.95 to $4.95 range, includes salads, pitawiches, and pastas. Dinner entrees cost from $4.95 to $8.95 with such selections as chicken à l'orange, vegetable stew, veal parmigiana, red snapper, beef stir-fry, and seafood, or fruit salads. For $2.25 more, you can indulge in a low-calorie and macrobiotic dessert such as fruit crisps or tofu cheesecakes. Natural sodas head the beverage list; no alcohol, wine, or beer. Open daily for lunch from 11 a.m. to 2 p.m. and for dinner from 5 to 10 p.m. CC's accepted: MC and V.

THE TOP ATTRACTIONS: A good place to start a tour of this city is at **Trout Hall,** 414 Walnut St. (tel. 435-4664), Allentown's oldest home, built in 1770 as a summer residence of James Allen, son of William, the city's founder. The property on which the house stands was obtained directly from William Penn by William Allen. Listed in the National Register of Historic Places, this is a fully restored Georgian Colonial stone house, administered by the Lehigh County Historical Society. Volunteer guides will take you throughout the house, telling the story of Allentown through the pictures on the walls and the furnishings on display. You'll see portraits of the city founder and his family as well as early oil paintings of Allentown. Some of the memorabilia includes trundle and rope beds, old-fashioned bed warmers, rare music boxes, needlepoint work, books, toys, and a candlemaker. Open April through November, Tuesday through Saturday from noon to 3 p.m. and on Sunday from 1 to 4 p.m. No admission charge.

The **Liberty Bell Shrine,** 622 Hamilton Mall at Church St. (tel. 435-4232), is probably Allentown's most celebrated sight. Housed in the Zion Reformed Church, this is where the Liberty Bell was brought when Philadelphia fell to the British in September of 1777. Fearing that the redcoats would melt down the bell to make bullets, revolutionary forces carried this symbol of freedom in a covered wagon to Allentown and hid it under the floor of the church until June of 1778, when it was safely returned to Philadelphia as the British evacuated that city. The present church, constructed in 1886, is the fourth to occupy this site. The basement shrine includes a full-size replica of the bell designed in 1962 as part of Allentown's Bicentennial celebration and a 46-foot wall mural depicting the Liberty Bell's trek to Allentown; there are also Colonial artifacts and displays of our nation's earliest flags. Open mid-April through mid-October, Monday through Saturday from noon to 4 p.m. and Sunday from 2 to 4 p.m. Admission is free.

The **Lehigh County Museum,** 5th and Hamilton Streets (tel. 435-4664), will give you a glimpse of the economic, social, and cultural history of the Lehigh Valley. Housed in Allentown's Old Courthouse building, this is a permanent exhibit spotlighting the region's Indian artifacts, mineral and geological findings, the silk industry of the early 1900s, trucking and agricultural traditions, and leading industries of the 20th century. Open Monday through Friday from 9 a.m. to 4 p.m. and on Saturday and Sunday from 1 to 4 p.m. No admission charge.

Less than a block away is the **Allentown Art Museum,** 31 N. Fifth St. (tel. 432-4333), at Court St., a complex of eight galleries on three floors. The exhibits include European and American paintings and graphic arts from the 14th to the 20th centuries, representing everything from Classical Greek and French Impressionistic works to Pennsylvania-Dutch folk art. Other highlights include the Frank Lloyd Wright Library, a children's participation and puppet area, and a series of family musical concerts on Sunday afternoons at 2 p.m. Open Tuesday through Saturday from 10 a.m. to 5 p.m. and on Sunday from 1 to 5 p.m. Admission is free, but a voluntary contribution of $1 is welcomed.

One of the major industries of the area, **The Stroh Brewery,** Routes 22 and 100, Fogelsville (tel. 395-6811), welcomes visitors to tour its facilities which are located six miles northwest of downtown. Originally founded in 1850 in Detroit, Stroh's has several plants in the U.S. but this is its only location in the Mid-Atlantic states. Tours include a view of the brewing and packaging processes, as well as samplings and refreshments in "Strohaus," a visitor center. Tours are given Monday through Friday from noon to 3 p.m. No admission charge.

Ten miles north of Allentown is the **Troxell-Steckel House and Farm Museum,** 4229 Reliance St., Egypt (tel. 435-4664). Built in 1755–1756 by John Peter Troxell and now owned by the Lehigh County Historical Society, this Colonial 2½-story stone farmhouse is an example of German medieval-style architecture brought to Eastern Pennsylvania by early settlers. The adjacent Swiss-style bank barn contains an exhibit of farming implements and carpenter tools on the ground floor; upstairs there are all kinds of carriages, ploughs, sleighs, surrey wagons, and an early omnibus. Hours are Saturday and Sunday from 1 to 4 p.m., from June through October; no admission charge.

NIGHTLIFE: Top Broadway plays are presented by the Pennsylvania Stage Company, at the **J. I. Rodale Theatre,** 837 Linden St. (tel. 433-3394). Once a church, this 274-seat facility opened as a theater in 1977, and is a year-round showcase for professionally produced musicals and dramas. Tickets range from $15 to $20, and the curtain is at 8 p.m. on Tuesday through Saturday, and at 7 p.m. on Sunday, with matinees on Thursday at noon and Sunday at 2 p.m. CC's accepted: MC and V.

On weekends the **Shepherd Hills Dinner Theatre,** 1160 S. Krocks Rd., Wescosville (tel. 398-9666) is also a year-round venue for Broadway musicals and comedies. The admission fee covers the show plus a dinner with full table service featuring entrees of prime ribs, chicken, or seafood, along with salad, vegetables, and dessert. The total cost ranges from $22 to $25, with the highest price on Saturday night. The schedule is Friday at 7 p.m., Saturday at 6 p.m., and Sunday at 5 p.m. CC's accepted: MC and V.

SHOPPING: You can bring home a taste of the Lehigh Valley by stopping at **Josh Early Candies,** 4574 Tilghman Blvd. (tel. 395-4321), a local landmark for more than 50 years. Sold by the piece or the pound, there are 84 varieties of confections ranging from toasted coconut marshmallow fluffs, molasses honey comb, pecan patties, and mint melt aways to chocolate butter creams. Samples are always on the counter to help you decide your choice. Open weekdays from 9 a.m. to 9 p.m. and Sunday from 1 to 6 p.m., Josh Early **also maintains a location** at 3620 Nazareth Pike, Bethlehem (tel. 865-0580). No CC's accepted.

Another local enterprise worth a visit is the **Early American Candle Shop,** 5573 Hamilton Blvd., Wescosville (tel. 395-3995), situated three miles west of Allentown on Route 222. You'll not only see displays of wax creations in all shapes, sizes, and scents, but you can also watch demonstrations of candle-making. Open Monday through Friday from 10 a.m. to 9 p.m., Saturday from 10 a.m. to 5 p.m., and Sunday from noon to 5 p.m. CC's accepted: MC and V.

SPORTS AND ACTIVITIES: Located just west of Allentown, the **Lehigh County Velodrome,** Routes 222 and 100, Trexlertown, (tel. 965-6930), is often referred to as the **"bicycle racing capital** of North America." Built in 1975, this high-speed facility is the home of world-class championships and a regular season of pro-am racing from May through September. Most events take place on Tuesday or Friday nights; tickets range from $2 for general admission to $5 for finish-line seating. If you are a speed cycler yourself, the Velodrome is open for public use in the off-season; the grounds also include free parking, a playground, and a picnic pavilion.

Jogging and Walking: Special circuits for walkers and joggers are part of the layout in **Trexler Memorial Park,** Cedar Crest and Memorial Boulevards (tel. 437-7628), on the city's western edge. Named for Harry Trexler (1854–1933) who established Allentown's park system, a local game preserve, and a national trust for the maintenance of parks, this complex also includes rose gardens, a trout nursery, and picnicking areas. No admission charge.

Skiing: Allentown is just 17 miles from the **Little Gap Ski Area,** Route 145, Palmerton, PA (tel. 215/826-7700). Although technically a part of the Poconos, Little Gap is often considered Lehigh Valley turf. Open from December through March, this resort sports a vertical drop of 803 feet and offers 11 slopes, four lifts, snow-making facilities, night-skiing, and a ski school. Lifts operate from 9 a.m. to 10 p.m. on weekdays and from 8 a.m. to 10 p.m. on Saturday, Sunday and holidays. Lift rates range from $13 to $23 for adults and $11 to $21 for children (aged 12 and under); ski rentals are $12 to $14 for adults and $9 to $10 for children. CC's accepted: AE, MC, and V.

CHILDREN'S CORNER: One of the best-known attractions in the Lehigh Valley is **Dorney Park and Wildwater Kingdom,** 3830 Dorney Park Rd. (tel. 395-3724), two miles west of downtown off Route 222. Over a million people a year flock to this theme-and-water park, which offers three roller coasters, a wave pool, and dozens of rides, shows, and shops. Open on weekends in April, early May and September; Tuesday through Sunday in June; and daily in July and August. The hours are from 11 a.m. to 9 p.m. on most days, with slight variations. Admission to Dorney Park and Wildwater Kingdom is $16.95 for adults and $10 for children aged 3 to 6; reduced-rate admission is also possible to one or the other of these attractions. Parking is $1 per car. CC's accepted: AE, MC and V.

Eight miles north of Allentown is the **Trexler-Lehigh County Game Preserve** on Route 1, off Route 309, Schnecksville, (tel. 799-4171). Founded in 1909 by Harry Trexler who also endowed the city's park system, this 1,500-acre natural expanse is home to camels, bison, deer, elk, and palomino ponies, as well as rare birds and exotic animals. There is also a children's zoo and facilities for picnicking, hiking, and bird-watching. Open daily, Memorial Day through Labor Day from 10 a.m. to 5 p.m.; and Sunday only from 10 a.m. to 5 p.m. in April and May and September through November. Admission charge is $2 for adults and $1 for children aged 2 to 12.

4. Bethlehem

In the heart of the Lehigh Valley between Allentown and Easton is Bethlehem, an area first settled by Moravian missionaries from Europe. Shortly after they arrived, a small group gathered to sing hymns on Christmas Eve of 1741. As they raised their voices to praise Christ's little town of Bethlehem, they also came upon a name for their new community.

Ever since then, America's Bethlehem has prospered. The Moravians built a thriving industrial center along the banks of the Lehigh River and this was followed by the steel mills of the 19th and 20th centuries. Today Bethlehem Steel is still the area's largest employer, with its corporate headquarters dominating a four-mile stretch of the town. Modern Bethlehem is also distinguished by its institutions of higher learning, such as Lehigh University and Moravian College.

But, most of all, this little patch of Pennsylvania is known as "America's Christmas City." As you enter the downtown area, a series of brown signs, each with a shining white star, will lead you to the historic district of America's Bethlehem, still a city of Moravian influence and traditions. Most of all, this is a place where Christmas lives year round in the songs and hearts of the people.

LOCAL VISITOR INFORMATION: Brochures on the attractions of the area are available from the **Bethlehem of Pennsylvania Visitor Center**, 459 Old York Rd., Bethlehem, PA 18018 (tel. 215/868-1513). Housed in the restored Luckenbach Mill (1869), this office regularly publishes a handy newspaper-style tourist brochure called *The Bethlehem Star*. In the centerfold of this paper, you'll find a self-guided walking tour and a map of the historic district. There is also a half-hour orientation film shown here at 11 a.m. and 2 p.m. Open Monday through Friday from 9 a.m. to 5 p.m. and on Saturday from 10 a.m. to 4 p.m. There is a charge for the film of $1.50 for adults and 50¢ for children.

WHERE TO STAY: Bethlehem offers a mix of old-world and modern hotels, all of which fall into the moderately priced category.

The top choice in the downtown area is the **Hotel Bethlehem**, 437 Main St., Bethlehem, PA 18018 (tel. 215/867-3711), a gracious old-world property dating from the 1920s and recently refurbished. Situated in the midst of the historic area, this hotel offers 130 individually furnished rooms, each with air conditioning, multi-channel color cable TV with complimentary HBO, an FM radio, a direct-dial phone, and a choice of bed size. Doubles start at $70, and rooms with Jacuzzis from $75. Guest facilities include free parking in multi-level garage, turn-down service, a beauty salon, a boutique, a gift shop, and a restaurant with a Colonial-style motif, including old lanterns and a mural of old Bethlehem highlights. Lunch, priced between $2.95 and $6.95, focuses on sandwiches, burgers, salads, omelets, quiches, crêpes, and light entrees. Entrees at dinner, priced from $7.95 to $15.95, include such dishes as beef Stroganoff; veal Cordon Bleu or Oscar; chicken Kiev; flounder Veronique; seafood brochettes; and steaks. All main courses come with salad bar, potato, and vegetable. Lunch is served from 11:30 a.m. to 2:30 p.m. and dinner from 5:30 to 10:30 p.m. Breakfast is also served from 7 to 10 a.m., with an unusual carryover from yesteryear which guarantees you'll never have cold toast. Each table has an individual toaster with a basket of freshly baked bread so guests can toast-on-the-spot. All major CC's accepted.

Located three miles north of downtown is the **Holiday Inn,** Routes 22 and 512, Bethlehem, PA 18017 (tel. 215/866-5800 or toll-free 800/HOL-IDAY), a modern two-story property. Completely renovated in 1986, this 195-room hotel features a blend of rich burgundy tones and mirrors in its public rooms. The contemporary-style bedrooms have two double beds or a king-size bed, a direct-dial phone, air conditioning, color TV with free HBO movies, and AM/FM radios. Doubles start at $65, and king-leisure rooms cost from $73 a night. Guest amenities include an outdoor swimming pool, a newly enlarged nightclub, and a restaurant, Krista's, featuring nouvelle American cuisine. Lunch items, priced from $3.95 to $5.95, focus on burgers, sandwiches, and salads. The menu at dinner, in the $9.95 to $18.95 price range, include "chicken Krista" (sautéed with sherry and shrimp); paella; rack of lamb; prime ribs; and lobster tails. All entrees are accompanied by salad and vegetable. Lunch is served from 11:30 a.m. to 2:30 p.m. and dinner from 5 to 10 p.m. All major CC's accepted.

One of the newest hotels in the area is the **Comfort Inn,** 3191 Highfield Dr., Bethlehem, PA 18017 (tel. 215/865-6300 or toll-free 800/228-5150), situated at the intersection of I-78/22 and Route 191, three miles northeast of downtown. This three-story modern property has 116 rooms, each with king, queen, or two double beds, color cable TV with HBO, a direct-dial phone, and air conditioning; and some units have Jacuzzi baths. Doubles range from $39 to $59. Guest facilities include complimentary continental breakfast, a lounge, and a game room. All major CC's accepted.

WHERE TO DINE: Unique settings are part of the dining experience in Bethlehem. In general, the prices at all venues fall into the moderate category.

Bethlehem's top restaurant is also a major sightseeing attraction, the **Sun Inn,** 564 Main St. (tel. 867-1761), in the heart of the historic downtown area. First opened as an inn in 1760, records show that early guests included George Washington, John Hancock, Ethan Allen, John Adams, and the Marquis de Lafayette. Authentically restored in 1982, this Moravian building is furnished with many unique pieces from its early days, such as a ten-leg bench, antique glass from Lititz, and chairs held together with pegs. There are three candlelit dining rooms upstairs, and a Colonial courtyard in back for al fresco dining in the summer. Lunch, priced from $4.95 to $6.95, focuses on sandwiches and quiches, as well as such light dishes as vegetable stir-fry or beef strudel. Dinner is offered at a fixed price $16.95, which entitles you to soup, salad, sorbet, entree of your choice, and coffee or tea. The main courses, which include many 18th-century recipes, range from chicken baked in plum and walnut sauce; stuffed Cornish hen; Pocono salmon trout; and veal with shrimp to marinated lamb on a skewer.

Open Tuesday through Saturday for lunch from 11 a.m. to 3 p.m.; dinner on Wednesday and Thursday from 6 to 9 p.m.; and on Friday and Saturday from 6 to 10 p.m. CC's accepted: AE, MC, and V.

Note: If you can't stay for a meal, you can take a guided tour of the house on Tuesday through Friday from 12:30 p.m. to 4 p.m. and on Saturday from 10 a.m. to 4 p.m. Admission for the tour is $1.50 for adults and $1 for students.

A Victorian atmosphere prevails at the **The Café,** 221 W. Broad St. (tel. 866-1686), a lovely pink house with a sloping mansard roof and gingerbread trim. Eclectically furnished with dark woods and tapestries, there is a lounge bar in the main parlor and a small dining room downstairs and four more distinctive dining rooms upstairs. Lunch consists mainly of innovative salads, croissantwiches, crêpes, and quiches, in the $3 to $4.95 bracket. Dinner entrees, priced from $9.95 to $14.95, include such dishes as chicken cherub (sautéed with ham, hearts of palm, and cheese); Thai shrimp curry; breast of chicken with raspberry or peanut sauce; pasta with seasonal vegetables; and ever-changing beef and veal dishes. A tempting array of homemade cheesecakes and fruit tarts is offered for dessert ($2 to $3); there is also a small bakery shop on the main level, if you prefer to have your sweets-to-go. Open Tuesday through Saturday, for lunch from 11:30 a.m. to 2:30 p.m., and for dinner from 5 to 8:30 p.m. CC's accepted: AE, MC and V.

In the midst of the Lehigh University neighborhood is the **New Street Bridgeworks,** 4 E. 4th St. at New Street (tel. 868-1313), situated in a renovated building near a bridge crossing the Lehigh River. The lively bar area features pictures of locally born celebrities from auto magnate Lee Iacocca to writer H.D. Dolittle. The dining room has a garden atmosphere, with lots of light woods and leafy plants. Lunch, priced from $2.95 to $4.95, consists mainly of burgers, sandwiches, omelets, crêpes, quiches, salads, and fun food. An international menu is featured at dinner with such choices as beef burgundy; veal à la pont (with mushrooms, water chestnuts, and cream sauce); assorted pastas; chicken divan; shrimp stir-fry; and all-American steaks. All entrees, priced from $7.95 to $10.95, include salad, vegetable, and potato or rice. Open daily for lunch from 11:30 a.m. to 3 p.m.; and for dinner Monday through Saturday from 5 to 10 p.m., and on Sunday from 4 to 9 p.m. All major CC's accepted.

THE TOP ATTRACTIONS: Historic Bethlehem's **18th-Century Industrial Area,** 459 Old York Rd., access via Union Boulevard (tel. 691-0603), is the best place to start a tour of this city. Here you will see Bethlehem as it looked in the mid-1700s as a prosperous Moravian settlement along the banks of the Monocacy Creek. You'll see a tannery, a wheat mill, a spring house, a miller's house, and the waterworks, considered to be the first municipal water pumping system in the U.S.; and in every building, interpretative guides demonstrate the crafts and trades of yesteryear. Totally reconstructed and restored, this ten-acre site is listed in the National Register of Historic Places. In the center of the complex is the Luckenbach gristmill which houses the office of the Bethlehem Visitors Center, an ideal place to stock up on maps and brochures. An orientation film is shown daily at 11 a.m. and 2 p.m. Guided tours are also conducted April through December, on Saturday from 10 a.m. to 4 p.m. and on Sunday from noon to 4 p.m.; and from mid-June through Labor Day, also on Tuesday through Friday from 10 a.m. to 4 p.m. Admission is $2.50 for adults and $1 for students.

On the hillside overlooking the industrial area is **Gemein Haus,** the oldest building in Bethlehem, otherwise known as the "community house" or the **Moravian Museum,** 66 W. Church St. (tel. 867-0173). Built in 1741, this five-story white-oak log house is staffed by women in traditional Moravian dress who will guide you through the 15 rooms and tell the story of early Bethlehem. You'll see artifacts reflecting the life and interests of the early settlers, such as Moravian furniture, clocks, silver, musical instruments, art, and needlework. The guides will be quick to tell you that this is the original house, not a renovation and they will also answer questions about the history of the Moravian church back to the 1400s. Open Tuesday through Saturday from 1 to 4 p.m. (closed January and holidays). Admission charge is $1 for adults and 50¢ for children.

In contrast, **The Goundie House,** 501 Main St. (tel. 691-5300), is the first Federal-style brick town house in Bethlehem. Built in 1810, this was the home of John Sebastian Goundie, a prominent Moravian brewer. The ground floor rooms (dining room, hallway, and kitchen) have been restored and are furnished to reflect the 19th century; the upper level rooms are currently being renovated. Open Monday through Saturday from 10 a.m. to 5 p.m. and on Sunday from noon to 4 p.m. No admission charge.

The **Kemerer House,** 427 N. New St. (tel. 868-6868), is a Federal-style building that houses a collection of memorabilia that once belonged to local resident Annie S. Kemerer. Arranged in a private home setting, the objects on display include antique furniture, Oriental rugs, Bohemian glass, Currier and Ives prints, early Bethlehem oil paintings, and locally made grandfather clocks. A modern art gallery is also housed here, featuring monthly exhibits of local, national, and international contemporary artists. Open Monday to Friday from 1 to 4 p.m.; Saturday from 10 a.m. to 4 p.m.; and the second and fourth Sundays of the month from 2 to 4 p.m. (Closed in January). Admission is free.

SHOPPING: An ideal place to buy books on the Moravian traditions and locally made crafts is the **Moravian Bookshop and Cookshop,** 428 Main St. (tel. 866-5481). As its name implies, this eclectic emporium also sells all types of kitchen wares, utensils, and cookbooks. It is also a popular luncheon spot and snackery with tables and chairs scattered among the bookshelves. The array of home-prepared food includes pasta salads, hearty vegetable soups, blueberry or cheddar muffins, and quiches, pies, and pastries (such as Moravian sugar cake, sticky buns, and kiffels). Open Monday, Tuesday, Wednesday, and Friday from 10 a.m. to 7 p.m.; Thursday from 10 a.m. to 8 p.m.; and Saturday from 10 a.m. to 5 p.m. CC's accepted: MC and V.

EVENTS: Over 450 free musical events are part of the program of Bethlehem's annual **Musikfest,** held in mid-August. Drawing guest bands and performers from throughout the U.S. and Europe, this nine-day program features everything from Bach to bluegrass, big bands to brass choirs, as well as vesper concerts, chamber music, ethnic folk dancing, and street balladeers. Concerts generally take place outdoors at various sites spread throughout the city, such as the 18th-century industrial area, the Sun Inn courtyard, the fairgrounds, Main Street, and Broad Street. Admission is free to most daytime attractions, although evening indoor candlelight concerts usually require an admission charge of $6 to $8. A complete schedule and more information are available from the **Bethlehem Musikfest Association,** 556 Main St., Bethlehem, PA 18018 (tel. 215/861-0678).

Christmas at Bethlehem is a month-long celebration of more than 60 events including tree-lighting ceremonies, night-light tours, lantern-light walks, Bach Choir concerts, Christmas pageants, candlelit windows, glittering trees, and the Star of Bethlehem glowing on a nearby mountaintop. Many events are free, although the popular **Night-Light Tours,** which are offered seven nights a week, at 5, 6, 7, 8, and 9 p.m., cost $4 for adults and $1.50 for children (reservations are necessary, tel. 215/868-1513). The mid-December **Bach Choir concerts** also require reservations and cost from $10 a person. You can order tickets from the Bach Choir, 423 Heckwelder Pl., Bethlehem, PA 18018 (tel. 215/866-4382); CC's accepted: MC and V. Further information and a complete program can be obtained from the **Bethlehem Area Chamber of Commerce,** 459 Old York Rd., Bethlehem, PA 18018 (tel. 215/868-1513).

5. Easton

The smallest of the Lehigh Valley cities, Easton (population: 26,000) was founded in 1752 by Thomas Penn, son of William. The name Easton was chosen in honor of the English homestead of the younger Penn's wife, Juliana.

From the beginning, the streets were laid out in a grid pattern, surrounding a central plaza called the "Great Square." The scene of early Indian treaties, the square had its greatest moment when the Declaration of Independence was proclaimed aloud for the first time on July 8, 1776, making Easton one of three cities to share the honor (Philadelphia and Trenton were the other two).

In the 19th century, Easton became one of America's key commercial and transport centers due to its location at the junction of the Lehigh and Delaware Rivers; three canals and five major railroads also came together here. At its prime, Easton served as a valuable conduit between the booming anthracite coal regions of northeastern Pennsylvania and the major east-coast cities of Philadelphia and New York.

A college town, like Allentown and Bethlehem, Easton is the setting of the 110-acre campus of Lafayette College, a landmark in the northern hills overlooking the city. Currently in the process of restoring many of its great 18th- and 19th-century buildings, Easton is also the home of a unique museum that pays tribute to America's canal history.

LOCAL VISITOR INFORMATION: For specific data on Easton, contact the **Two Rivers Area Commerce Council,** 157 S. 4th St., Easton, PA 18042 (tel. 215/253-4211). A visitor center is maintained at this address during the hours of 10 a.m. to 4 p.m. Tuesday through Saturday and from 1 to 4 p.m. on Sunday. Self-guided walking tour folders of the city are also available here, free of charge.

WHERE TO STAY: Like the rest of the city, the hotels of Easton have been undergoing restoration or refurbishment in recent years. You won't find a great choice of accommodations within this city, but the properties listed below offer a warm and eager welcome. In general, prices fall into the moderate category or less.

The top choice is the **Historic Hotel Easton,** 140 Northampton St., Easton, PA 18042 (tel. 215/253-6181), the "grande dame" of the city, dating back to 1927 and newly renovated in 1986. Situated in the heart of downtown and just two blocks from the Delaware River, this 175-room hotel has preserved the aura of earlier times, with the enhancement of modern conveniences. Each of the newly decorated bedrooms has double-, queen-, or king-size beds, reproduction antique furniture, air conditioning, a direct-dial phone, and color cable TV. Doubles start at $65, and small suites with parlors go from $75. Free parking for overnight guests is available adjacent to the ten-story hotel. The in-house Riverside Restaurant is also the best dining spot in town, with a décor of deep blues and reds, classic wood furnishings, gleaming brass, and fine-cut glass. You'll enjoy a touch of the 20th century as tuxedoed waiters enter your order into a computer terminal linked to the kitchen. Lunch, priced from $3.95 to $6.95, consists mainly of salads, omelets, sandwiches, burgers, and light entrees such as scallops Dijonnaise, tortellini, or veal marsala. Dinner entrees range from

$8.95 to $18.95, with most under the $15 mark. The selections include tournedos Henry IV (charbroiled with artichoke hearts and laced with béarnaise sauce); prime ribs; surf-and-turf; lobster tails; and breast of chicken Orleans (with apples, thyme, apple schnapps, and heavy cream). All main courses are accompanied by salad, vegetable, and potato or rice. Lunch is served from noon to 2 p.m. and dinner from 6 to 10 p.m. All major CC's accepted.

Four blocks south of the town center is the **Sheraton-Easton Inn,** 3rd Street and Larry Holmes Drive, Easton, PA 18042 (tel. 215/253-9131 or toll-free 800/325-3535), a modern four-story property near the banks of the Lehigh River and next to a six-film movie theater. Built 15 years ago and completely renovated in 1986, this hotel has 84 rooms of varying pink and aqua tones, some with views of the city and others overlooking the outdoor swimming pool and courtyard. Each guest room has contemporary furnishings, cable color TV, a direct-dial phone, and air conditioning. Doubles range from $63 to $70. Harry's Canal Restaurant, located on the ground floor, conveys an old-Easton atmosphere with a waterfall, stone walls, and Colonial-style furniture. Lunch, priced in the $1.95 to $4.95 bracket, features sandwiches, salads, and burgers. Dinner entrees, priced from $6.95 to $16.95, range from brochette of beef and veal Cordon Bleu to seafood combination plates or Chateaubriand. Prices include salad and vegetables. Lunch is served from 11:30 a.m. to 4 p.m. and dinner from 4 to 10 p.m. All major CC's accepted.

Budget Range

The newest hotel is the **Luxury Budget Inn,** Route 22 at the 25th Street Shopping Center, Easton, PA 18042 (tel. 215/253-0546 or toll-free 800/441-4479). This modern 84-room property is situated about two miles west of the downtown area. Each room has color cable TV with free HBO, a direct-dial phone, air conditioning, and a choice of double-, or king-size beds. Some non-smoking rooms are available and there are several ground-floor rooms. Doubles range from $31.99 to $36.99 and kings from $36.99. Most major CC's accepted.

WHERE TO DINE: Ask any local resident to name a favorite restaurant, and the choice is usually **Mandarin Tang,** 25th Street Shopping Center (tel. 258-5697). Ever since opening in 1984, this Chinese eatery has developed a following both in its dining room and on local television (chef Frank Tang hosts a weekly cooking program that appears on a cable channel). More than 150 dishes are on the menu here, although special orders are equally encouraged. The emphasis is on low salt, high fiber, and lots of healthy vegetables. Lunch choices are priced from $3.95 to $5.95, and the dinner entrees fall into the $4.95 to $15.95 range, with most selections under $8. There is also a sumptuous Sunday brunch buffet at $6.95. House favorites include spicy orange chicken, beef and black-bean sauce, shrimp with walnuts, crispy duck, and lobster Cantonese. No bar service, but you are welcome to bring your own wine (buy it in advance as the liquor store in the adjacent shopping center closes early). Open Monday through Thursday from 11:30 a.m. to 10 p.m.; Friday and Saturday from 11:30 a.m. to 11 p.m.; and Sunday from noon to 10 p.m. On Wednesday night there are cooking demonstrations at 7:30 p.m., which often wind up on the air. CC's accepted: AE, MC, and V.

Budget Meals

You can eat very well in Easton for small bucks. The **Broc'oli Garden,** 40–42 S. 3rd St. (tel. 252-4922) is a local favorite. This buffet-style restaurant features a healthy array of all-you-can-eat soups, salads, casseroles, hot and cold meats, vegetables, cheeses, fruits, breads, and desserts. One price prevails at all times, currently $3.99 for lunch and $5.99 at dinnertime. Open Monday through Saturday from 11 a.m. until 8 p.m., and on Sunday until 3 p.m. Branches of this restaurant are also located in Allentown and Bethlehem. No CC's accepted.

THE TOP ATTRACTIONS: The historic and geographic heart of Easton is its central plaza or "Great Square," situated at the juncture of Northampton Street (which runs east to west) and Third Street (which goes in a north-south direction. This large square was the site of pre-Revolutionary Indian peace treaties held between 1756–1762. Then the Northampton County Courthouse was built here and stood from 1765 until 1862. Most significant of all, this is the spot where the Declaration of Independence was proclaimed verbally on July 8, 1776, along with simultaneous readings in Philadelphia and Trenton, following its formal adoption on July 4. Markers commemorate all of these moments in history, and, in addition, a granite Civil War memorial dedicated to local veterans has stood here since 1900. The square is also used for public gatherings and for outdoor farmers' markets.

The heydays of America's inland waterways are celebrated at the **Canal Museum,** 200 S. Delaware Dr. (tel. 250-6700), situated south of the city at the juncture of the Lehigh and Delaware Rivers on Route 611. This fascinating exhibit invites visitors to step back into the 18th and 19th centuries when 1,200 miles of canals stretched across Pennsylvania, more than any other state, linking cities, villages, mines, factories, and farms. A six-minute video presentation describes the history of canals and locks in the U.S., and particularly the Lehigh and Delaware Canal, the last of the great canals. Exhibits also focus on the people who made their living from the canals and what life was like for them. Open year round, Monday through Saturday from 10 a.m. to 4 p.m. and Sunday from 1 to 5 p.m. Admission charge is $1 for adults and 50¢ for children aged 5 to 12.

If you're between 3 and 103 and want to stay healthy, then plan a visit to **Easton's Weller Center,** 2009 Lehigh St. (tel. 258-8500), a preventive health education complex, with on-going instructional programs for students and adults. Established in 1982, this is one of three centers in the U.S. (the others are in Chicago and Ft. Wayne). Basic health concerns are discussed in small groups with the aid of sophisticated visual aids, three-dimensional exhibits and models, and colorful electronic devices. There are 11 student and five adult programs, with the most popular adult topics being general health, family life, and drug education. Although many programs are designed for groups, the center is also open for walk-ins, from 9 a.m. to 2:30 p.m. in the summer; participation in a 1½-hour adult program costs $3. Call when you reach Easton to see what programs will be in session during your stay.

NIGHTLIFE: Easton's two main hotels, the **Historic Hotel Easton** (tel. 253-6181) and the **Sheraton Inn** (tel. 253-9131), both provide evening music in their lounge area, particularly on weekends. In addition, you can enjoy a wide range of entertainment at the **State Theatre,** 453 Northampton St. (tel. 252-3132). This renovated Beaux Arts building, a former vaudeville palace built in 1926, is a regional center for the performing arts, with an ever-changing program of opera, jazz, blues, chorale, ballet, orchestral, and philharmonic music, as well as top-class plays. Tickets range from $8 to $20, depending on the event, and the curtain is usually at 8 p.m. The box office is open from 10 a.m. to 5 p.m. and, on performance days, from 5 p.m. to curtain time. CC's accepted: MC and V.

SHOPPING: Easton is the home of **Bixler's,** 24 Center Square (tel. 253-3589), an enterprise that is reputed to be America's oldest jeweler and silversmith, founded by Christian Bixler in 1785. The original Bixler was a clockmaker and silversmith, who made over 465 clocks and dozens of silver spoons, many of which are still on display today in the store, as well as 18th-century ledgers and other historical memorabilia. Currently operated by the sixth generation of the same family, Bixler's is still known for its silver and clocks, and also for jewelry, watches, and gifts. Open Monday through Saturday from 9:30 a.m. to 5 p.m., and until 8 p.m. on Tuesday and Friday. CC's accepted: AE, MC, and V. Bixler's also operates a **branch** in Bethlehem at 514 Main St. (tel. 866-8711).

SPORTS AND ACTIVITIES: The **Hugh Moore Park,** 200 S. Delaware Drive (tel. 258-7155), is situated adjacent to the Canal Museum and runs for six miles along the Lehigh River. The meandering expanse includes the Lehigh Canal, locks, a cable suspension bridge, a locktender's house, and other canal structures, many of which have been included in the National Register. Named for a local resident and supporter who founded the Dixie Cup company, the 260-acre park includes picnic sites, a four-mile bike path, two hiking trails, and facilities for boating. Paddleboats, canoes, and bikes can be rented (from $5 an hour). The picnic and park areas are open year round from dawn to dusk. Sports equipment rental is available from Memorial Day weekend through Labor Day, Wednesday through Friday from 11 a.m. to 5 p.m.; Saturday from 11 a.m. to 7:30 p.m., Sunday from 12:30 p.m. to 7:30 p.m.; and in September on weekends only.

Nearby is the starting point for **Canal Boat Rides,** Glendon Road on the Canal (tel. 250-6700). This company offers one-hour rides on a restored section of the Lehigh Canal via an authentic mule-drawn canal boat called *Josiah White*. The craft operates from Memorial Day weekend through Labor Day, Wednesday through Saturday at 11 a.m., 1, 2:30, and 4 p.m.; on Sunday at 1, 2:30, and 4 p.m.; and in September on weekends only at 1, 2:30, and 4 p.m. Tickets are $3 for adults and $1.50 for children aged 5 to 12.

More active sportspeople flock to the **Point Pleasant Canoe Outfitters,** Martins Creek, Route 611 (tel. 258-2606), five miles north of Easton. This is a branch location of the company that maintains a large rafting, tubing, and canoeing operation at Point Pleasant in Bucks County, about 20 miles south (see Chapter IV). This depot primarily provides for multiple-day canoe and rafting trips, and the rental of camping equipment, from Memorial Day to Labor Day only. A 40-mile two-day trip is priced from $28 per person; a three-day 60-mile trip costs from $35 per person; and rafting can be organized from $30 a day for a two-person raft. For a brochure describing all possibilities and prices, contact **Point Pleasant Canoe,** P.O. Box 6, Point Pleasant, PA 18950 (215/297-8181).

Chapter VII

SCRANTON AND WILKES-BARRE

1. Getting There
2. Scranton
3. Wilkes-Barre

NORTHEASTERN PENNSYLVANIA revolves around Scranton and Wilkes-Barre, two industrialized cities barely 15 miles apart and yet totally different. Scranton's architecture is largely European, thanks to its rich ethnic diversity; and Wilkes-Barre is laid out around a public square according to New England traditions.

Although each city has a distinctive history, both Scranton and Wilkes-Barre are linked by common backgrounds as coal mining and railroading centers. And much of their appeal today is based on this shared past—where else would you find a hotel that is a converted railroad station (the Hilton in Scranton) and or a motel complex of re-fitted railcars (the Choo Choo Inn in Wilkes-Barre)?

Scranton and Wilkes-Barre share an airport (located midway between the two cities at Avoca) and are equally considered prime industrial hubs, connected by major interstate highways from north, south, east, and west.

Both cities are at the doorstep to the Poconos and are surrounded by rolling agricultural countryside, gentle rivers, and mountain vistas.

AREA CODE: Both Scranton and Wilkes-Barre are part of the 717 telephone area code.

1. Getting There

BY PLANE: The **Wilkes-Barre–Scranton International Airport** (Avoca Airport), located at Avoca, is the largest and principal airport in northeastern Pennsylvania. Regularly scheduled flights are operated by **Eastern** (tel. 717/825-6416 or toll-free 800/327-8376); **USAir** (tel. 717/825-5641 and toll-free 800/428-4322); **Pocono Airlines** (tel. 717/655-2989); and **Piedmont Henson** (tel. toll-free 800/368-5425), as well as by local commuter lines. For complete information about all services in and out of the airport, call 717/457-5544. Transport into Scranton or Wilkes-Barre is provided by **Airport Limo Service** taxis available at the airport (tel. 654-8545). Several leading car-rental firms maintain desks at the

Wilkes-Barre–Scranton Airport including: **Avis** (tel. 654-3318); **Budget** (tel. 654-8911); **Hertz** (tel. 655-1452); and **National** (tel. 457-5980).

BY BUS: Martz Trailways and Greyhound both link Scranton and Wilkes-Barre to other major cities in Pennsylvania, New York, New Jersey and beyond. In Scranton, the **Martz** depot is located at Lackawanna and Jefferson Avenues (tel. 342-0166); and **Greyhound** is at 23 Lackawanna Ave. (tel. 346-2722). In Wilkes-Barre, Martz Trailways is situated at 46 Public Square (tel. 829-6969); and Greyhound is at 136 S. Pennsylvania Ave. (tel. 823-3125).

BY CAR: At the crossroads of major interstate roads, Scranton and Wilkes-Barre are easy to reach by car. Interstate-84 will bring you directly into Scranton from the east, or you can use the combination of I-80 and northward on I-380. You can take the same route to Wilkes-Barre or continue on I-80 to I-81 and then northward for 20 miles. (Interstate-81 cuts through both cities). From the west, I-80 is the best route to either city, and then northward on I-81. From the south, you can take I-81 directly north or the Pennsylvania Turnpike Northeast Extension (Route 9). From the north, I-81 is the most direct route.

2. Scranton

Mining and railroading were the key industries that led to the blossoming of Scranton in the 19th century. Before that, the area was a quiet agricultural community known by the Indian name of Capoose.

The city owes its present name to two brothers from New Jersey, George and Seldon Scranton, who arrived in this area in the 1840s and helped to develop both the iron-ore and the anthracite-coal industries. The "black diamonds" that the mines produced ultimately shaped the destiny of Scranton for nearly 100 years. With the mines came employment, drawing immigrants from many countries, all contributing to the city's rich cultural heritage and distinctive architecture.

The iron industry also produced the necessary materials for building rails, and fostered a system of land transport to move the coal from the northeastern Pennsylvania mines to major markets, putting Scranton in the forefront of "the railroad age."

Today, although these two industries no longer predominate, both the mines and the railroads serve as tourist attractions—visitors can ride the vintage locomotives, stay in a railroad station that has been converted into a deluxe hotel, see the iron furnaces, or take a coal mine tour (see "The Top Attractions" section in this chapter).

In addition to preserving their mining and railroading traditions, Scrantonians of the 20th century are also known for their community spirit in pooling their resources to attract new businesses. "The Scranton Plan" has brought more than 100 new industrial and manufacturing plants to the area and served as a model for other cities throughout the world.

Currently Scranton (pop. 88,000) is also undertaking a revitalization of its midtown area along Lackawanna Street. Aiming for a 1988 completion date, this $65 million project is transforming dozens of classic (and neglected) buildings into a restored row of trendy shops, skywalks, and pedestrian malls. This ever-growing metropolis on the Lackawanna River is also home to Pennsylvania's newest ski resort, Montage Mountain.

VISITOR INFORMATION: The best source for brochures on sightseeing, accommodations, restaurants, and events is the **Greater Scranton Chamber of Commerce,** Chamber of Commerce Building, 426 Mulberry St., P.O. Box 431,

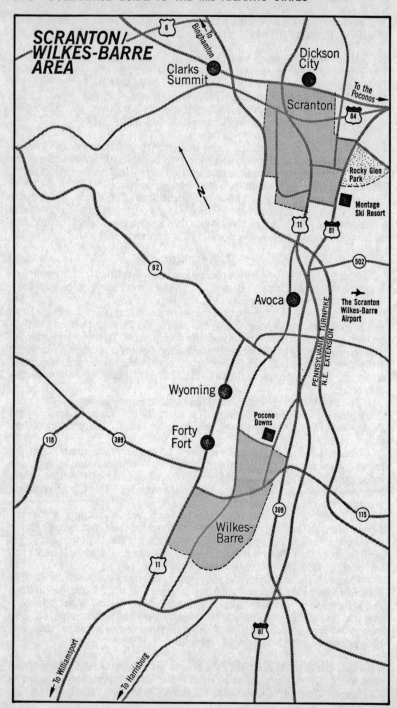

Scranton, PA 18501 (tel. 717/342-7711). Hours are Monday through Friday from 8:30 a.m. to 5 p.m.

GETTING AROUND SCRANTON: Walking is probably the best way to savor the sights of downtown Scranton. There are no formally organized tours, but the Chamber of Commerce is very helpful in mapping out sightseeing suggestions. If you do require public transport, there is a regular city **bus system** known as COLTS (County of Lackawanna Transit System); the fare is 70¢. Taxis are also available from **Red Top Cabs** (tel. 342-3131); **Public Service Taxi** (tel. 344-5000) and **Scranton Yellow Cab** (tel. 342-0138).

WHERE TO STAY: Scranton's hotels are located both in the downtown area and on major routes leading into the city. Prices usually fall into the moderate category. However, reduced-rate packages are offered by many places at certain times of the year, particularly during the ski season at nearby Montage Mountain. Be sure to inquire if any special prices will be in effect at the time of your visit.

Luxury Lodgings

To get a feel for this city's railroading heydays, plan to stay at the **Hilton** at Lackawanna Station, 700 Lackawanna Ave., Scranton, PA 18503 (tel. 717/342-8300), in the heart of downtown. A former Delaware, Lackawanna, and Western Railroad station, this 1908 building was built on a foundation of anthracite coal and has been magnificently restored and transformed (at a cost of $13 million) into a deluxe hotel with 150 rooms (starting at $70 a night for a double). Guest amenities include an indoor swimming pool, a health club, a game room, courtesy transport to and from the airport, free parking, a gift shop, a newsstand, and a barber shop. Conveying the grandeur of yesteryear both inside and out, the hotel façade is made of Indiana limestone and the lobby boasts the original marble columns, terrazzo floors, a stained-glass skylit ceiling, tiled mosaics, brass chandeliers, globe lights, and a still-ticking antique bronze clock. The railroading theme has been carried out onto the guest floors (waiting-room benches near each elevator) and into the restaurants. The Last Stop, a casual eatery for light entrees and fun food (such as tacos, nachos, burgers, croissantwiches, and pizzas, priced from $2.95 to $5.95), is the former platform beside the tracks, which has been enclosed and decorated with a railroad motif, model electric trains, and *Scranton Times* newspaper front pages from the early 1900s. The main dining room, The Phoebe Snow, is named and decorated in tribute to a fabled turn-of-the-century coal-burning locomotive. Lunch, priced from $3.95 to $7.95, features salads, sandwiches, and curry dishes. Entrees at dinner, priced from $10.95 to $17.95, include such varied selections as stuffed pheasant with boursin; veal saltimbocca; rack of lamb; and ragout of lobster and shrimp. Open Monday through Saturday for lunch from 11:30 a.m. to 2:30 p.m. and for dinner from 5 to 10 p.m.; Sunday brunch from 10 a.m. to 2 p.m., and Sunday dinner from 4 to 9 p.m. All major CC's are accepted.

Moderate Choices

Another good downtown property is the newly renovated **Best Western University Inn**, Franklin and Mulberry Streets, Scranton, PA 18503 (tel. 717/346-7061 or toll-free 800/528-1234). This two-story modern motel has 98 rooms, each equipped with two double beds, color cable TV, a direct-dial phone, and air conditioning. Doubles range frcm $50 to $60. Guest facilities include an outdoor swimming pool, free parking, and a full-service restaurant called Number 5 (direct line: 961-1010). The name comes from a No. 5 fire-engine company that served as the inspiration for a sister restaurant in Binghamton, New York. This spot has a homey look, with timeworn books on shelves, pottery, plants, and framed cartoons on brick walls. Lunch, priced from $3.95 to $7.95, consists primarily of salads, sandwiches, gourmet burgers, pasta, omelets, seafood, and petit steaks. The dinner menu, with entrees in the $9.95 to $19.95 bracket, features Greek dishes as well as steaks, prime ribs, seafood, chicken, duckling, veal, and various "you-choose-it" surf-and-turf combinations. All main courses are served with potato or vegetable and soup or salad, plus hot San Francisco sourdough bread. Lunch is available from 11:30 a.m. to 2:30 p.m. and dinner from 5 to 10 p.m. All major CC's are accepted.

A hillside garden atmosphere prevails at **The Inn at Nichols Village,** 1101 Northern Blvd., Clarks Summit, PA 18411 (tel. 717/587-1135), two miles north of the city on Routes 6 and 11. This rambling two-story brick hotel is surrounded by 12 acres of landscaped grounds with a pleasant mix of rhododendrons, hardwood trees, patios, and courtyards. There are 115 modern guest rooms, each with color TV, a phone, and air conditioning. Doubles range from $59 to $75. Other facilities include an indoor pool, saunas, an exercise suite, a tennis court, a game room, and free parking. There are also two restaurants, the moderately priced Sojourner, which serves food all day, and a gourmet enclave called the Ryah House. With an interior of cedar wood and Scandinavian rya rugs, the latter features American traditional and nouvelle cuisine, with such dishes as shrimp and scallops in bourbon sauce; lemon sole with macadamia nuts; duckling breast in brandied pear sauce; and rack of lamb with a port sauce and mustard cream. Prices for entrees range from $10.95 to $19.95; many dishes are prepared at tableside and there is piano music every evening. Open for dinner only from 6 to 10 p.m., Monday through Saturday. Most major CC's are accepted by the hotel and restaurants.

Three miles south of the city is the **Contempri Inn,** 1175 Kane St., Scranton, PA 18505 (tel. 717/348-1000 or toll-free 800/558-5928), located right at the base of the Montage ski slopes. This two-story motel has an alpine décor of light wood and glass, and a ski-lodge ambience. Each of the 104 rooms has oversize or king beds, color cable TV, a radio, a direct-dial phone, and air conditioning. Doubles range from $45 to $55. Other amenities include an outdoor pool and patio, a hot tub, free parking, and a restaurant and disco. Most major CC's accepted.

Budget Range

Another good choice north of the city is the **Summit Inn,** Northern Boulevard, Clarks Summit, PA 18411 (tel. 717/586-1211), on Routes 6 and 11. This two-story semi-Tudor-style motel is built on a hillside, with pleasant views of the surrounding countryside. The 32 units each have two double beds or a king-size bed, color cable TV, air conditioning, and a direct-dial phone. Guests can also avail themselves of complimentary morning coffee, non-smoking rooms, and free parking. Doubles range from $31.99 to $39.99. Most major CC's accepted.

WHERE TO DINE: Thanks to its many ethnic traditions, Scranton is a good eating town. In addition to the hotel dining rooms outlined above, this city has a number of good moderately priced restaurants, some more than 50 years old, geared to please a range of tastes from various European cuisines to seafood houses.

Fish from around the world is the feature at **Cooper's Seafood House,** 701 N. Washington Ave. (tel. 346-6883), a Scranton institution since 1948. Recently expanded and remodeled, this restaurant has an appropriately nautical décor with a ship's motif at its entrance and a replica of a 25-foot blue whale on the ceiling of the main dining room. Fish platters, sandwiches, and salads are featured at lunch (in the $3.95 to $4.95 price bracket). The dinner menu presents a range of unique seafood dishes: from abalone, frogs' legs, and alligator tenderloin to finnan haddie, as well as such popular favorites as king crab legs, lobster tails, and shrimp scampi, plus steaks, chicken, and veal dishes. Main courses, priced from $8.95 to $16.95, include vegetable, potato, or salad. In addition to bountiful seafood, this restaurant is also known for its bar selection of 150 international beers and specialty cocktails. Open Monday to Saturday for lunch from 11 a.m. to 3 p.m. and for dinner from 3 p.m. to midnight. A "no-reservations policy" is followed, so get there early, especially at dinnertime. CC's accepted: AE, D, MC, and V.

If you are in the mood for a touch of France, try **Maxim's,** 426 Mulberry St. (tel. 343-4040), an elegant restaurant on the ground level of the restored Chamber of Commerce Building in midtown. Soft piano music sets the tone here amid a décor of hand-painted scroll ceilings, crystal chandeliers, and floor-length draperies. Lunch, priced from $1.95 to $7.95, consists mostly of salads, burgers, sandwiches, and light platters. The very French choices at dinner include coq au vin, crab au gratin, trout amandine, steak Diane, beef bordelaise, and veal Cordon Bleu. Main courses are priced from $8.95 to $21.95, with most under the $13 mark, and are accompanied by an intermezzo course plus salad, soup, potato, and vegetable or pasta. Open Monday through Saturday for lunch from 11:30 a.m. to 3:30 p.m. and for dinner from 4:30 to 11 p.m.; and Sunday from noon to 10 p.m. CC's accepted: AE, MC, and V.

Ever since 1923, **Preno's,** 601 Lackawanna Ave. (tel. 346-2091), has been one of the leading restaurants for Italian food. Over the years, three generations of the Preno family have operated this spot just one block from the Hilton Hotel at Lackawanna Station. Lunch items, which include pastas, sandwiches, and salads, are priced from $2.95 to $5.95. Dinner entrees, in the $6.95 to $13.95 bracket, focus on homemade pastas, prime ribs, Italian sausage and peppers, veal T-bones, and assorted seafoods such as Pocono Mt. brook trout. All main courses come with salad, potato, or vegetable. Open Monday through Friday from 11 a.m. to midnight; Saturday from 4:30 p.m. to midnight; and Sunday from 4:30 to 10 p.m. All major CC's accepted.

Panoramic views of Scranton come with the meals at the **Castaway,** Route 6, Dickson City (tel. 489-8683), set on a hillside a mile north of downtown. This relatively new (1985) restaurant combines a modern décor of light wood, skylights, and plants with an old stone fireplace, rounded colored-glass windows, and homey furniture. Lunch, priced from $3.95 to $6.95, features salads, sandwiches, burgers, and light dishes (such as teriyaki chicken breast, scampi linguine or a bucket of steamed clams). Cajun cooking and traditional American fare top the menu at dinnertime, with selections ranging from blackened grouper to prime rib, steaks, lobster, shrimp, and scallops. Entrees are priced from $8.95 to $18.95 and come with a choice of salad or soup, potato or rice. Open Monday through Saturday for lunch from 11 a.m. to 3 p.m. and for dinner from 5 to 10 p.m.; and Sunday for brunch from 10:30 a.m. to 2:30 p.m. and for dinner from 5 to 10 p.m. Major CC's accepted.

A Choice for Budget Meals

Another Scranton landmark is **Charl-Mont,** 119 Wyoming Ave. (tel. 344-7270), a 1920s-era restaurant on the ground level of the Globe Department Store, offering both counter and table service. Sandwiches and salads are on the menu for lunch, priced from $1.95 to $3.95. Dinner entrees, priced from $4.95 to $8.95, range from steaks and seafood to liver, and include two vegetables, salad, dessert, and coffee or tea. There is also a bountiful Sunday buffet, which costs $7.95 for adults and $2.95 for children under 12. Open Monday and Thursday from 8:30 a.m. to 9 p.m.; Tuesday through Saturday (except Thursday) from 8:30 a.m. to 5:30 p.m.; and Sunday from 9 a.m. to 5 p.m. Entrance is on the Pennsylvania Avenue side of the Globe Store. CC's accepted: AE, MC, and V.

THE TOP ATTRACTIONS: With its coal-mining and railroading traditions, it is not surprising that Scranton's main sights focus on these two early industries.

The city's pride and joy is **Steamtown USA,** located at the Lackawanna Station, 700 Lackawanna Ave. (tel. 969-1984), behind the Hilton Hotel. Recognized as a National Historic Site in 1986, this outdoor museum contains one of the nation's largest collections of steam-era locomotives including the *Union Pacific Big Boy,* the world's largest steam locomotive, the 1877 *Prince of Liege* from Belgium; the *Rutland,* an oldtime wooden caboose; a rolling railway post office; and the former *Boston & Maine Movie Car.* Visitors are invited to step on board these vintage trains and travel through the surrounding countryside. The basic tour is a two-hour, 26-mile, scenic round-trip excursion from Scranton to Moscow, through the Nay Aug Tunnel and Roaring Brook Gorge. The train operates at 11 a.m. and 1:30 p.m., with an extra 3:45 p.m. excursion on weekends. Admission prices are $8.50 for adults and $5.50 for children under 12. Starting this year, longer rides are also available as far as Pocono Summit, increasing the round-trip to 64 miles, at a total cost of $19.95 for adults and $14.95 for children. Passengers can also board at Pocono Summit for one-way or round-trip rides into Scranton or Moscow. Recently placed under the jurisdiction of the National Park Service, this attraction is open Wednesday through Sunday during May and October; Thursday through Sunday in June and September; and Tuesday through Sunday in July and August.

A visit to this part of Pennsylvania is not complete without taking a few hours to do the **Lackawanna Coal Mine Tour,** 200 Adams Ave. in McDade Park (tel. 963-MINE). This is an authentic underground excursion into the actual abandoned workings of the Slope 190 Mine, a hard-coal, deep-mine at McDade Park. Open weekends from May through October plus Thursdays and Fridays from July 4th to Labor Day. Trips are hourly from 11 a.m. to 5 p.m. Admission fee is $4.50 for adults and $2.50 for children.

If you'd like an in-depth look at the life of a coal miner, step into the adjacent **Pennsylvania Anthracite Heritage Museum,** Bald Mountain Road, McDade Park (tel. 963-4804). This facility not only focuses on the mining community of Northeastern Pennsylvania but also portrays the various aspects of the region's railroads, canals, and silk industries. Open year round, Tuesday through Saturday, from 9 a.m. to 5 p.m., and on Sunday from noon to 5 p.m. Admission fees are $2 for adults and $1 for children.

You can also visit the landmark **Scranton Iron Furnaces,** at 291 Cedar Ave., between Lackawanna Avenue and Moosic Street (tel. 963-4804). These four stone-blast furnaces, with their huge smokestacks, are the remnants of the industry that helped make Scranton the second-largest producer of iron in the nation in the 1860s. The furnaces are open to visitors from 8 a.m. to dusk, year round, free of charge; a parking area is adjacent.

On the cultural side, northeastern Pennsylvania's major showcase of fine arts and natural history is the **Everhart Museum,** Mulberry Street, Nay Aug Park, East Scranton (tel. 346-7186). Outstanding sections include displays of American folk art, Dorflinger glass, primitive and Oriental arts, birds, minerals, and ecology. Open Tuesday through Saturday from 10 a.m. to 5 p.m., and Sunday from 2 to 5 p.m. Admission is free.

The **Scranton Marketplace**, 710 Capouse Ave. (tel. 346-8777), is a 20th-century indoor flea market, housed in the city's historic market building, on the city's northeast side. Opened in 1985, this is a gathering of craftspeople and food vendors with wares ranging from pottery, jewelery, cut glass, imports, and Christmas ornaments to home-baked goods, candy, and seafood. There are also displays of antique dolls, a circus, miniature trains, and a scale model of Scranton. Hours are Thursday, Friday, and Saturday from 10 a.m. to 8 p.m. and Sunday from 10 a.m. to 5 p.m.

To round off your picture of Scranton, don't miss **The Scranton Times "Newseum,"** 145 Penn Ave. This is an outdoor display of printing tools, machinery, artifacts, headlines, and stories illustrating the history of Scranton and its newspaper. Open daily during daylight hours, no admission fee.

NIGHTLIFE: Scranton is the stage for the Broadway Theatre League, the Northeast Pennsylvania Philharmonic and the Community Concerts Association. Most performances are held at the city's unofficial arts center at the **Masonic Temple and Scottish Rite Cathedral,** 420 N. Washington Ave. (tel. 346-7369), a complex that houses two theaters, one with 1,800 seats and the other with 750 seats, and a box office. The building itself may be toured, free of charge, Monday through Friday from 8 a.m. to 5 p.m. For information on what is playing when you are in town, contact the box office (tel. 346-7369) or the Chamber of Commerce. Ticket prices range from $5 to $10 for most events.

Music and dancing are featured at a number of hotels in the area including the **Last Stop** at the Hilton at Lackawanna Station, 700 Lackawanna Ave. (tel. 342-8300), and the **Best Western University Inn,** Franklin and Mulberry Streets (tel. 346-7061). There is also a **Video Disco** at Bentley's Lounge at the Contempri Inn, 1175 Kane St. (tel. 348-1000), and live entertainment nightly at **Jim Dandy's,** Route 11, Clarks Summit (tel. 586-6000).

SPORTS AND ACTIVITIES: Summer sports are centered around Nay Aug Park, 982 Providence Rd., East Scranton (tel. 348-4186). Scrantonians and visitors alike enjoy the various walking trails, Olympic-size swimming pool, and two picnic areas. The pool is open June through September from noon to 7 p.m. Admission is $1.25 for adults and 75¢ for children. The park itself is open daily during daylight hours.

The big news in winter sports is **Montage Mountain,** 1000 Montage Mountain Rd., Scranton (tel. 717/969-7669 for general information; toll-free 800/847-7669 for ski reports). The newest ski resort in Pennsylvania, Montage is located seven miles southeast of downtown, off exit 51 of I-81. With a season that runs from early December through March, it has a 1,000-foot vertical drop, trails that are 150 to 300 feet wide, 400 acres of scenic mountainside with 100 acres of wide-open trails, and triple and double chair lifts that can move 6,300 skiers in an hour. There are facilities for snowmaking, and night-skiing can be enjoyed seven days a week. Other amenities include a lounge, an outside fireplace and barbecue, a rental shop, and adult and children's ski schools. Hours of operation are Monday through Friday from 9 a.m. to 5 p.m.; and weekends and holidays from 8:30 a.m. to 5 p.m.; plus night-skiing seven days a week from 5 to 10 p.m. Ski-lift rates run from $18 midweek and $25 on weekends to $12 at night.

After the snows melt, from Memorial Day through Labor Day, Montage summer activities range from alpine slide rides to chair-lift rides. Summer hours are from 11 a.m. to 6 p.m. every day from June 21 through Labor Day and weekends only from Memorial Day to mid-June. All-day tickets are priced at $7.50; single tickets are $2 for the alpine slide and $1 for chair-lift rides.

CHILDREN'S CORNER: Rocky Glen Park, Rocky Glen Road, exit 50 off I-81, Avoca (tel. 457-7401), is an amusement park with more than 30 rides and attractions, including a water slide, lake swimming, an arcade of games, and live entertainment. Open Tuesday through Sunday, June through August, from noon to 9 p.m., and weekends during May and September. There is a $2 per person gate fee to enter the park. Individual ride tickets are sold, but you can also purchase inclusive passes that entitle you to unlimited rides ($7.50 for adults and $6.50 for children).

3. Wilkes-Barre

Connecticut Yankees were the original settlers of the area known today as Wilkes-Barre. In 1770, following New England custom, these early settlers laid out the town around a central square. Over the years, the square was variously dominated by a fort, a church, a school, a courthouse, and a jail. As the city grew, the area around the square developed into a commercial center, and in 1909 the square became a public park which thrives to this day as an urban focal point.

The name of the city comes from yet another direction, across the Atlantic. It seems that two members of the British Parliament, John Wilkes and Issac Barre were particularly vocal in their support of the American Colonial quest for independence. In recognition of their support, Wilkes-Barre (pronounced Wilks-berry) was named in honor of these two men.

Wilkes-Barre's growth in the 19th century can largely be attributed to the discovery of coal in the region. When mining reached its peak in the early 1900s, Wilkes-Barre was considered the anthracite capital of the world. The city was also a hub for banking, transportation, manufacturing, and other coal-related industries. When the mines closed down in the late 1950s, Wilkes-Barre was undaunted and reached out for new service-oriented industries.

All was going well until a hurricane flood caused a major setback in 1972. The entire core of the city had to be rebuilt, but, in many ways, this has led to the current well-polished look of the city center. The Public Square is now a showcase of greenery with fountains, sculptures, and an ampitheater, as well as a monument to the two men who gave the city its double-barreled name.

Nestled along the banks of the Susquehanna River, Wilkes-Barre today (pop.: 52,000) is the seat of Luzerne County and home to Nabisco and the Planters Nut and Chocolate Company, as well as a variety of health-care and computer-related services. It also boasts a district of 215 buildings listed in the National Register of Historic Places.

GETTING AROUND WILKES-BARRE: Wilkes-Barre is an easy city to master on foot. Most of the hotels, restaurants, and shops are within walking distance of Public Square, as is the city's historic riverfront district. If you prefer to use public transport, however, there is regular **bus service** via the Luzerne County Transportation Authority. The flat fare is 60¢; for further information call 287-8463 (BUS-TIME). Taxis are also readily available at the leading hotels or by calling **American Cab** (tel. 823-3186) or **Airport Taxi** (tel. 654-8545).

VISITOR INFORMATION: Brochures on Wilkes-Barre's accommodations, restaurants, and sightseeing attractions can be obtained from the **Luzerne County Tourist Promotion Agency,** 35 Denison St., Forty Fort, PA 18704 (tel. 717/288-6784 or 717/288-7038); and from the **Greater Wilkes-Barre Chamber of Commerce,** 92 S. Franklin St., Wilkes-Barre, PA 18701 (tel. 717/823-2101).

WHERE TO STAY: Although Wilkes-Barre does not have a large number of hotels, it does have a delightful diversity—from modern high rises to renovated rail cars. All of the downtown hotels fall into the mostly moderate price category.

The **Sheraton-Crossgates**, 20 Public Square, Wilkes Barre, PA 18701 (tel. 717/824-7100 or toll-free 800/325-3535), is right in the heart of the city overlooking the central park-like plaza. Contemporary in design with a brick and concrete façade, this eight-story hotel has 186 rooms and suites, each with king or double beds, color cable TV, air conditioning, and a direct-dial phone. Doubles run from $70 to $80 and suites from $80 to $150. Guest facilities include an indoor swimming pool, a hot tub, enclosed parking, a coffeeshop, a lounge with evening entertainment, and a full-service restaurant called Wanda's on the Park. As its name implies, this dining room overlooks the grassy square outside; its trendy décor includes a 20-foot square stained-glass skylight ceiling and multi-level seating. The menu at lunch, which is priced from $2.95 to $5.95, focuses on salads, sandwiches, burgers, omelets, quiches, and diet delights. Seafood and international dishes are featured at dinner, with such choices as chicken lyonnaise; veal parmigiana; beef Stroganoff; and duckling à l'orange. Entrees are priced from $9.95 to $19.95, with most choices under $15, and come with home-baked breads, salad, and potato or rice. Lunch is served from 11:30 a.m. to 2:30 p.m. and dinner from 5:30 to 10 p.m. All major CC's are accepted.

Just a block from the Public Square is the **Best Western Genetti Motor Inn**, 77 E. Market St., Wilkes-Barre, PA 18701 (tel. 717/823-6152 or toll-free 800/528-1234). A favorite meeting and eating place with the locals, this seven-story brick building stretches for a whole block and cleverly incorporates some of Wilkes-Barre's old town homes in its structure. The 72 bedrooms are all modern in design, with king or double beds, color cable TV, free movies, AM/FM stereo music, air conditioning, and a direct-dial phone. Rates for a standard double are $55 to $70; and $85 to $95 for king units with living rooms. Guest facilities include an outdoor swimming pool, non-smoking rooms, and courtesy transportation to the airport. There is also a conservatory-style restaurant, Della Fox, which features Italian and French cuisines. Dinner entrees range from veal francese and seafood marinara to lobster tails or steaks. Main courses are priced from $7.95 to $19.95, with most dishes around $10, and are accompanied by Italian breads, salad-bar selections, vegetable, and potato or pasta. The restaurant is open for breakfast and light lunches from 7 a.m. each day and for dinner from 5:30 until 9 p.m. on weeknights and until 10 p.m. on Friday and Saturday. All major CC's accepted.

The most unusual lodging experience is at the **Choo Choo Inn**, 33 Wilkes-Barre Blvd., Wilkes-Barre, PA 18701 (tel. 717/829-0000 or toll-free 800/441-1354), located beside the old railroad tracks three blocks from Public Square. Formerly a working passenger railroad depot (built in 1868 and now a national landmark), this "motel" consists of 60 attached railcars totally renovated and refitted as spacious bedrooms. The lobby, where complimentary continental breakfast is served, is a showcase of antique lamps, claw-foot tables, brass trim, and authentic nickelodeons. The bedrooms are similarly furnished with Victorian chairs and sofas, brass beds, and mirrored walls, plus the 20th-century comforts of a private bath, air conditioning, color cable TV, and a direct-dial phone. Doubles range from $50 to $70. The original station building has similarly been converted into a restaurant with railcar-style dining and nightly entertainment. The luncheon menu consists mainly of sandwiches, burgers, and other light dishes, in the $2.95 to $6.95 bracket. Dinner entrees, priced from $11.95 to $15.95, feature primarily Italian cuisine such as veal scaloppine, steak pizzaiola, and shrimp scampi. All main courses are accompanied by salad, vegetable, and potato. Lunch is served Monday through Saturday from 11:30 a.m. to 3 p.m.;

and dinner Monday through Saturday from 5:30 to 10 p.m., and from 1 to 9 p.m. on Sunday. All major CC's accepted.

In the Budget Range

Besides the downtown hotels, a number of major chains have motels and motor inns in the surrounding suburbs, along Routes 315 and 115. One of the loveliest views of downtown can be enjoyed at the **Red Roof Inn,** 1700 East End Blvd. (Route 315), Wilkes-Barre, PA 18702 (tel. 717/829-6422 or toll-free 800/848-7878). Situated in an elevated wooded area about two miles from the city, this newly built (1986) three-story motel has 115 rooms, each with one or two double beds, air conditioning, color cable TV, and a direct dial phone. Doubles range from $30.95 to $32.95. CC's accepted: AE, D, MC, and V.

WHERE TO DINE: In addition to the fine selection of hotel dining rooms, the Wilkes-Barre area has a number of good restaurants, all of which fall into the moderate price range. Here is a sampling of old and new favorites:

One of Wilkes-Barre's great dining traditions is **Hottle's,** 243 S. Main St. (tel. 825-7989), in midtown, just a couple of blocks south of Public Square. Founded by the Hottle family in 1937, this small restaurant has a sports-club atmosphere, with walls full of paintings of local and legendary baseball and football figures. Lunch, priced from $1.95 to $5.95, features hot platters, hearty sandwiches, and salads. Seafood is the focus at dinner, with such entrees as lobster Newburg, pink salmon, freshwater trout and sautéed frogs' legs, as well as a wide selection of steaks, chicken, veal, and pork dishes. Main courses are priced from $6.95 to $16.95 with most choices under $10, and include salad and potato or vegetable. Hours for lunch are Monday through Friday from 11:30 a.m. to 2 p.m.; and for dinner Monday through Thursday from 4:30 to 11 p.m.; and Friday and Saturday from 4:30 to midnight. All major CC's accepted.

Ask the locals where to dine and they will most likely recommend the **Peking Chef,** 15 Public Square (tel. 825-0977), a restaurant that adds a touch of the exotic to the heart of Wilkes-Barre. A lot of effort has been put into the décor with colorful hand-painted screens and pagodas on view at every turn. With entrees ranging from $4.95 to $11.95, all the standard Chinese dishes are featured here, as well as some unusual choices, such as a Polynesian kebab (of steak, pork, and vegetables); Buddha's Delight, an all-vegetarian mélange; and a tasty mixture of chicken and scallops. A house salad is also available for $1.50 (water chestnuts, snow peas, mushrooms, carrots, lettuce, and pineapple). Open daily from noon for lunch and dinner; on Monday through Thursday and on Sunday until 10 p.m.; and on Friday and Saturday until midnight. All major CC's accepted.

If you are looking for good seafood and a panoramic overview of the city, the best choice is the **Lobster Trap,** Route 315 (tel. 825-6909), situated about a mile north of downtown on a hillside. Relatively new to the Wilkes-Barre scene (since 1986), this modern nautical-style restaurant offers both indoor dining and outside deck service. Lunch items, priced from $2.95 to $4.95, include sandwiches, burgers, salads, and light seafood platters. Dinner entrees, in the $6.95 to $12.95 price bracket, feature broiled seafood of all kinds, with emphasis on lobsters, which you can select yourself from the tanks. All main courses include unlimited helpings from the bountiful salad bar. Open Monday through Saturday for lunch from 11 a.m. to 4 p.m. Dinner is served Monday through Thursday from 4 to 10 p.m., and on Friday and Saturday until 11 p.m.; Sunday hours are noon to 8 p.m. CC's accepted: AE, MC, and V.

TOP ATTRACTIONS: Although Public Square is the central point of Wilkes-Barre's downtown today, years ago the focus was along the Susquehanna River, an area now classified as the River Street Historic District. This section of the city, which was placed in the National Register of Historic Places in 1985, begins just west of Public Square, and contains 215 buildings dating back to the 1800s and early 1900s. You'll see a mix of grand old private homes, public buildings, churches, schools, early taverns, and shops. Among the highlights is the **Luzerne County Court House,** North River Street (tel. 825-1500), a 1909 cruciform structure that is the symbol of Wilkes-Barre's heydays. The interior walls and ceilings of this building reflect the history of the area portrayed in mosaics and murals. The best way to see this district is to obtain a copy of the self-guided walking tour folder/map, available free of charge from the Luzerne County Tourist Promotion Agency or from the Greater Wilkes-Barre Chamber of Commerce. Over 30 major historic sights are outlined and described in this handy guide.

For an inside view of what life was like in this part of Pennsylvania during the 19th century, don't miss the **Swetland Homestead,** 885 Wyoming Ave., Wyoming (tel. 823-6244). Located about seven miles northwest of Wilkes-Barre via Route 11, this house was built as a simple settler's cottage by Luke Swetland in 1797. Over the years, additions were made as the family grew and the house came to reflect the changing way of life and architectural styles during the period from 1797 to 1865. Now on the National Register of Historic Places, the homestead includes family furnishings, utensils and memorabilia and a physical structure that embraces a formal staircase, high ceilings, chair rails, and fan windows. Open to the public during June, July, and August, on Thursday through Sunday from noon to 4 p.m. Admission charge is $1 for adults and 50¢ for children.

In contrast, **The Nathan Denison House,** 35 Denison St., Forty Fort (tel. 288-6784), is a blend of Pennsylvania and New England architectures. Located about five miles north of Wilkes-Barre on the other side of the Susquehanna River, this home was the principal dwelling in a town named for the original forty settlers who came to this area from Connecticut in the mid-1700s. Built in 1790, it was fashioned after a Denison home at Mystic, Connecticut, and, with its great central chimney, is more typical of a New England structure than a Pennsylvania residence of its day. The house has been totally restored and is full of furnishings that reflect life in this area during the 18th century. Open to the public from May through October, weekdays from 10 a.m. to 4 p.m. During July and August, it is also open on Saturday and Sunday from 1 to 4:30 p.m.; and in May, June, September, and October, it is open on Sunday from 1 to 4:30 p.m. Admission charge is $2 for adults and students over 12 years of age. The Luzerne County Tourist Promotion Agency maintains its offices on the grounds of this site.

Wilkes-Barre's all-purpose Public Square is the scene of a colorful farmers' market every Thursday from the end of June until the end of November. Although local vegetables, fruits, and home-baked goods are the focus of attention, there is also a program of open-air entertainment and a festival atmosphere throughout the day (from 10 a.m. to 5 p.m.).

NIGHTLIFE: Wilkes-Barre's **Paramount Theatre** on Public Square, an art deco treasure (1937) on the National Register of Historic Places, has been restored recently and is now known as the **Kirby Center for the Performing Arts.** Broadway shows and musical concerts (recently featuring such stars as Tom Jones, Anthony Newley, and Crystal Gayle) are regularly scheduled here on a year-round basis. Tickets are usually priced from $5 to $20, depending on the event.

For full information on the schedule at the time of your visit, call the box office (tel. 826-1100). CC's accepted: MC and V.

Music and dancing are featured most nights at the hotels in the downtown area, including the **Gandy Dancer Room** at the Station Restaurant, 33 Wilkes-Barre Blvd. (tel. 829-0000); the **Club Lounge of the Genetti Best Western** at 77 E. Market St. (tel. 823-6152); and at **Hugs Disco** in the Sheraton Crossgates, 20 Public Square (tel. 824-7100).

SPORTS AND ACTIVITIES: Wilkes-Barre is the home of the **Pocono Downs Racetrack,** Route 315 (tel. 825-6681). Located five miles north of the city, this raceway is reputed to be the fastest five-eighths harness track in the world. Racing is scheduled from mid-March through mid-November (except Wednesdays and most Mondays), with post time at 7 p.m. on Sundays and at 7:30 p.m. on other nights. General admission charge is $2.

Golf: Visitors are welcome at the **Wilkes-Barre Municipal Golf Course,** Laurel Run Road (tel. 472-3590), an 18-hole par-72 facility, seven miles east of the city, off Route 115. Greens fees are usually $8 on weekdays and $10 on weekends and holidays, and motorized carts can be rented for $14. This club also offers a special rate on Mondays ($21 for two golfers and a cart); amenities include a club house, a driving range, and a pro shop.

Chapter VIII

PENNSYLVANIA DUTCH COUNTRY

1. Lancaster
2. Reading

TWO ENGLISH COUNTY SEATS gave their names to Lancaster and Reading in the 18th century, but over the years these southeastern Pennsylvania cities have evolved into the core of "Pennsylvania Dutch" country.

Contrary to popular belief, this collective name does not mean that hoards of Dutch people have settled the land. "Pennsylvania Dutch," in fact, refers to German settlers, primarily immigrants of the Amish and Mennonite sects who came to this new state to find religious freedom. In the German language, the word "Deutsch" actually means "German," and since these people called themselves and their language "Deutsch," the English-speaking settlers in the area misinterpreted the word and labeled them the "Pennsylvania Dutch."

Rather than adapting to American ways, the original Pennsylvania Dutch people clung to their traditions and style of life, and their 20th-century ancestors carry on in the same manner, using horse-drawn buggies for transport and mule-powered machinery to farm the land. Today the simple lifestyles and beliefs of these people are a source of curiosity for visitors. Perhaps that is why tourism generates almost $300 million in revenues annually for Lancaster County alone.

For its part, Reading not only relies on the Pennsylvania Dutch culture, but also is known for the dozens of shoppers' outlet stores that draw busloads of bargain-seekers every day.

1. Lancaster

The name Lancaster refers to a city and a county, both synonymous with the heartland of Pennsylvania Dutch territory. Lancaster the city (pop.: 57,000), originally known as Hickory Towne, was basically an English settlement and is laid out according to a grid plan, with Penn Square at its center. It was the largest inland city in Colonial days, serving as the nation's capital for one day in September 1777.

When most people speak of Lancaster, however, they are usually referring to all of Lancaster County, the city plus its surrounding countryside. Mention Lancaster and distinctive images come to mind: abundant and rich foods, fertile farms, stretches of land without an electric wire, colorful hex signs, barn-raisings, and horse-drawn buggies clip-clopping on peaceful country roads.

Most of all, we think of a group of gentle people who live in a world set apart, the Amish (pronounced "Ah-mish").

The Amish first came to Pennsylvania in the late 1720s and to Lancaster County in the 1760s. Historically, the Amish are part of the Anabaptist family, tracing their origin to Zurich, Switzerland, in 1525. Many of these people were first called Mennonites after Menno Simons, who was an influencial leader and writer who joined the Anabaptists in 1536. In the 1600s, a man named Jacob Ammann differed with the Mennonites on some issues and formed a separate group of worshippers. Thereafter, these people became known as the Amish.

Both the Amish and the Mennonites suffered much persecution in their homelands of Switzerland, Germany, and France, and were happy to accept William Penn's invitation to come to a mecca of religious freedom. Lancaster County's streams and fertile soils closely resembled their native Rhineland and these immigrants easily adapted to their new home.

Today there are several branches of Amish and Mennonite sects within the county. But it is the strictest group, the Old Order Amish, that arouses the greatest curiosity for visitors. These people can be identified by a number of observable features. They drive gray horse-drawn carriages, use mules or horses to pull farm equipment in the fields, opt for diesel or gasoline for power rather than electricity, hold worship services in their homes, have their own one-room schools, and speak the Pennsylvania Dutch dialect. Amish men wear suits of dark-colored fabric, straight-cut coats with no lapels, black footwear, and black or straw broad-brimmed hats. Adult men let their beards grow but do not wear mustaches. Amish women wear modest dresses of solid-colored fabric, with cape and apron, full skirt, and long sleeves. They have long hair and wear a head covering or bonnet.

Lancaster County's Amish population is approximately 16,000 and ever-growing. Large numbers of children are considered desirable, and the average family is seven, but ten or more offspring are not uncommon. Most of the Amish farms are located in the eastern part of Lancaster County, and, as you drive along the country roads, you can see the farmers at work in their fields or the women displaying their quilts for sale. If you have a camera, you'll be tempted to take a photograph, but that is the one thing that the Amish ask that you refrain from doing. They follow the Biblical command that exhorts against "graven images," so please bear this in mind.

In addition to the Amish, Lancaster county has many other claims to fame. It was the home of our fifteenth U.S. president, James Buchanan, and of Robert Fulton. The Conestoga wagon originated here as did the first pretzel. You'll find the Moravian influence at Lititz; a Protestant cloister at Ephrata; the Scots-Irish legacy at Donegal Springs; and railroading relics at Strasburg. You can visit wineries, breweries, and hundreds of antique dealers.

Bordered on the west by the Susquehanna River, Lancaster County is relatively small in size (averaging 30 miles from east to west and 40 miles north to south). Within minutes of Lancaster city, you can enjoy charming country villages with names like Mt. Joy, Paradise, Bird-in-Hand, White Horse, Peach Bottom, Smoketown, Spring Garden, and Intercourse. This latter town, once known as Cross Keys, is said to have been named for one of two reasons: it was an entrance to a horse-racing track and became known as "Entercourse," or because two major throughways intersected here and an "Intercourse" sprang up.

VISITOR INFORMATION: For all types of information on this area, contact the **Pennsylvania Dutch Visitors Bureau,** 501 Greenfield Rd., Lancaster, PA 17601 (tel. 717/299-8901). If you are visiting in person, it is located off Route 30 (the

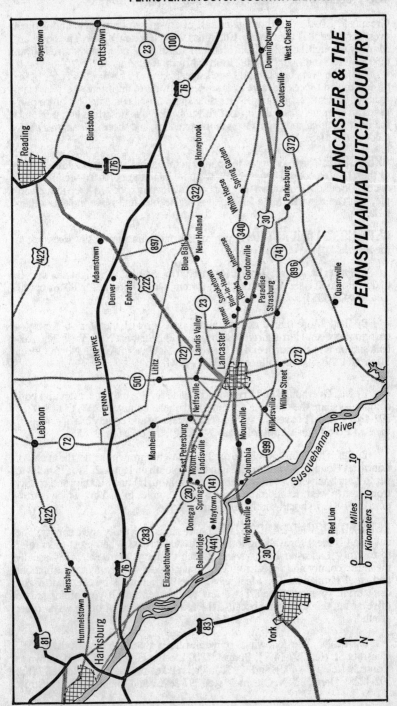

LANCASTER & THE
PENNSYLVANIA DUTCH COUNTRY

Greenfield Road exit), three miles east of downtown Lancaster, and is open every day except Thanksgiving, Christmas, and New Year's Day. The hours are Monday through Thursday from 8:30 a.m. to 7 p.m.; Friday and Saturday from 8:30 a.m. to 8 p.m.; and Sunday from 8:30 a.m. to 6 p.m.

Staffed by very helpful and knowledgeable travel advisors, this is one of the busiest tourist offices we have ever seen, with walls of informative displays and racks of brochures, and ample browsing space for all comers. This office publishes an extremely useful map and visitor's guide that describes and pinpoints major attractions, lodgings, restaurants, activities, and shops. It's an invaluable guide and it's free.

AREA CODE: The majority of telephone numbers in Lancaster County belong to the 717 area code. However, a few numbers in the northern section of the county (around Adamstown) are part of the 215 area code. To keep things simple, you can assume that a 717 code is applicable, unless we indicate otherwise.

GETTING TO LANCASTER: Lancaster city and county are easily accessible to the traveler.

By Plane: Lancaster Airport, Route 501 (tel. 569-1221), is eight miles north of downtown. It is served by **Allegheny Commuter Airlines** (tel. 569-0461 or toll-free 800/428-4253).

By Train: More than a dozen trains a day stop at Lancaster on Amtrak's corridor between Harrisburg/Pittsburgh and Philadelphia/New York. The **Amtrak** station is at the north end of the city, 53 McGovern Ave. at North Queen Street (tel. 291-5000 or toll-free 800/USA-RAIL).

By Bus: Greyhound and **Trailways** provide service into Lancaster and both companies share the same bus terminal and phone number, 22 W. Clay St. (tel. 397-4861). Local bus services within Lancaster city and county are operated by the **Red Rose Transit Authority** (tel. 397-4246); the base fare is 70¢.

By Car: The Pennsylvania Turnpike cuts right through the northern end of Lancaster County; get off at exit 21 and drive south on Route 222 for 15 miles to get to Lancaster City. Route 30 also crosses through Lancaster city and county from east to west. In addition, Lancaster is 30 miles from York which is traversed by I-83 in a north-south direction.

GETTING AROUND LANCASTER: Lancaster is both a city and a county. The city itself is ideal for walking tours and casual strolls. When most folks refer to touring "Lancaster Pennsylvania Dutch Country," however, they usually mean the county and the surrounding countryside with its myriad attractions and rural farmlands. The ideal way to see the county is by car, and, if you can't bring your own, we'll list a few rental agencies. If you prefer not to drive at all, don't despair, because there are a number of other ways to get around.

Car Rental: The following companies have autos for rent: **Avis,** 825 E. Chestnut St. (tel. 397-1497); **Budget,** 2300 Lincoln Highway E., also known as Route 30 (tel. 295-1400), and 1208 Manheim Pike, also known as Route 72 (tel. 392-4228); **Hertz,** 229 N. Queen St. (tel. 397-2896); and **National,** Liberty Street and Lititz Pike (tel. 394-2158). Desks are also maintained at Lancaster Airport by Avis (tel. 569-4345) and Hertz (tel. 569-2331).

Taxis: If you need a taxi, call **Friendly Cab** (tel. 393-9222); **Yellow Cab** (tel. 397-8108), or **Neff Taxi** (tel. 392-7327).

Bus Tours: A good way to get your bearings is to take a guided tour. Four-hour tours of the Amish country are offered throughout the year by **Grayline of Lancaster,** 825 E. Chestnut St., Lancaster (tel. 299-6666). Available Monday through Saturday, this trip includes a visit to the Amish Homestead and sightseeing in downtown Lancaster. The price is $13.50 for adults and $8.50 for children (aged 6 to 11), and departures start at 8:30 a.m. and 12:30 p.m. from the Grayline office, with subsequent pick-ups at all major hotels and motels. If you happen to be in town on a Sunday, Grayline has a special five-hour excursion through Amish territory plus a visit to the railroading center of Strasburg. This tour goes once a day, starting from the Grayline office at 9:30 a.m. with further departures at major lodging points.

Dutchland Tours, Farmer's Market, Route 340, Bird-in-Hand (tel. 392-8622), also offers escorted four-hour bus tours of the Amish farmland, with departures at 9 a.m. and 2 p.m. on Monday through Thursday and at 11 a.m. only on Sunday. The price is $13.75 for adults and $7 for children aged 4 to 14. A shorter two-hour itinerary is also available, departing at 9:30 a.m., noon, and 2:30 p.m. every day but Sunday, priced at $7.50 and $4 respectively. In addition, this company features a tasting tour of Pennsylvania Dutch foods and wines. Commencing at 9 a.m. on Monday through Saturday, this excursion lasts three hours and costs $10 for adults and $7 for children. All tours depart from the Dutchland office, with additional pick-ups at hotels and motels.

Walking Tours: If you are primarily interested in the downtown area, then you can avail of a 90-minute **Historic Lancaster Walking Tour.** Led by Colonially attired guides, these jaunts begin at the **Historic Lancaster office** at 15 W. King St. (tel. 392-1776) and explore courtyards, churches, the farmers' market, the nation's oldest tobacco shop, and other restored buildings. Tours depart daily, April through October, Monday through Saturday at 10 a.m. and 1:30 p.m.; Sunday and holidays at 1:30 p.m. During July and August, there is also a 6:30 p.m. twilight tour on Monday. The cost is $3 per person.

Horse and Buggy Rides: If you'd like to be driven around the countryside via the local Amish mode of transport, then you'll enjoy **Ed's Buggy Rides,** Route 896, Strasburg (tel. 687-0360). Based 1½ miles south of Route 30, Ed and his crew will show you three miles of Amish farmlands from a horse-drawn open wagon or a traditional closed carriage. The cost is $5 for adults and $2.50 for children; rides are available all year from 9 a.m. to 5 p.m.; in the winter months, sleighs are often substituted for wagons. If you are in the area of Route 340, there is also **Abe's Buggy Rides,** 2596 Old Philadelphia Pike (no phone listed). Situated two miles west of Bird-in-Hand, Abe offers a two-mile tour through Amish country in an Amish family carriage, priced at $8 for adults and $4 for children. This facility is also open all year, from 8 a.m. to dusk, except Sunday. No reservations are required for either Ed's or Abe's rides.

Airplane Tours: See the Lancaster countryside from the cockpit of a small plane via **Aerial Tours,** Smoketown Airport, Mable Avenue, Smoketown (tel. 394-6476). Located off Route 340, between Bird-in-Hand and Lancaster, this company will fly you over 20 miles of the Pennsylvania Dutch countryside from

June through October, daily from 9 a.m. to 6 p.m., at a cost of $12.50 for adults and $6.25 for children aged 8 and under. There is a minimum booking of two persons, and cameras are welcome. CC's accepted: MC and V.

LEARNING ABOUT LANCASTER: When you arrive and look over the huge map-guide produced by the tourist office, you might feel a little overwhelmed by all there is to see and do. "Where to start?" is a good question.

Perhaps you should drive along Route 30 east of Lancaster (also known locally as Lincoln Highway East) and be dazzled by scores of man-made interpretations of Pennsylvania Dutch lifestyle, or you can head south on Route 896 to the railroad enclave of Strasburg . . . or east on Route 340 to the farmlands of Bird-in-Hand and Intercourse . . . or maybe west on Route 283 to Mount Joy . . . or north to Lititz and Ephrata. . . .

You could spend a month or two here and still not see everything. In many ways, seeing everything is really not as important as gaining some understanding of the gentle people who reside in this fertile farmland county along the Susquehanna. Happily, there are a number of ways in which visitors can gain an insight into the Amish and Mennonite way of life. No one source will make you an instant expert, but each of the centers described below makes a valuable contribution toward enriching your trip.

The **People's Place,** Main Street (Route 340), Intercourse (tel. 768-7171) is a people-to-people interpretation center, specializing in the story of Amish, Mennonite, and Hutterite people. The focal point is a lifestyle museum called "Amish World," which offers insight into the aspects of the Amish culture so different from the experiences of most visitors: their modes of transportation, dress, energy, schools, sense of time, growing old, peace, and mutual aid. The admission charge is $2.25 for adults and $1.10 for children, including a magnificent display of Pennsylvania Dutch art. For those who prefer audio-visual impact, there is a three-screen 25-minute documentary, *Who Are the Amish?*, which illustrates the Amish way of life from birth to barn-raising. This program is shown continuously from 9:30 a.m. to 5 p.m. daily except Sundays. Admission price is $2.25 for adults and $1.10 for children, and reduced-rate combination packages are available if you wish to explore the museum and see the audio-visual. In addition, from April through October, the center also shows the full-length feature film *Hazel's People,* set in a Mennonite community and starring Geraldine Page and Pat Hingel. The movie is scheduled for each evening, Monday through Saturday, at 6 and 8 p.m. and costs $3.50 for adults and $1.75 for children. Other facilities in this building include a courtyard gallery with art exhibits and a book and craft shop featuring Amish and Mennonite literature and work. The helpful staff will also answer individual questions. The People's Place is open daily year round except Sunday, from 9:30 a.m. to 9:30 p.m. during April through October, and from 9:30 a.m. to 4:30 p.m. the rest of the year. CC's accepted: MC and V.

A similar service is provided by the **Mennonite Information Center,** 2209 Millstream Rd., Lancaster (tel. 299-0954), located off Route 30 about four miles east of downtown. This simple brick building is a welcome center staffed by Mennonite volunteers who provide general brochures on the Pennsylvania Dutch country, sightseeing guidance, assistance in locating accommodations, and explanations as to the similarities and differences between the Amish and Mennonites. There are also displays on the beliefs and lifestyles of the Mennonite people and a film, *A Morning Song,* shown every half hour (no charge but donation welcome). If you wish, you can also tour the adjacent religious museum which houses a reproduction of the Hebrew Tabernacle (admission charge is $2 for adults and $1.25 for children aged 7 to 12). One of the best services provided by this center is a guided tour whereby one of the staff will go in your car and guide you through the area, with relevant explanations of local lifestyles. The tours require a minimum booking of two hours and cost from $12 per car. The center is open Monday through Saturday, from 9 a.m. to 4 p.m. (except Thanksgiving, Christmas, and New Year's Day).

The Lancaster Experience is a 36-minute orientation film shown continuously at the information center of the **Pennsylvania Dutch Visitors Bureau,** 501 Greenfield Rd., Lancaster (tel. 299-8901). The aim of the movie is not so much to explain the Amish or Mennonite lifestyles in any depth, but to provide an overview of the attractions and scope of Lancaster County. It will help you to decide where to go and what to see during your visit. Particularly well suited to children, the film includes footage of a buggy ride with an Amish family, a dramatic barn fire, and a community-spirited barn-raising. Shown daily, on the hour, from April through November; on Saturdays in December; and in January and February by request. Admission charge is $2 for adults and $1 for children (open daily except Thanksgiving, Christmas, and New Year's Day).

WHERE TO STAY: Lancaster County has hundreds of hotels, motels, and country inns, in all price ranges. We shall describe a blend of new and old properties, starting with those easily accessible to the downtown Lancaster area. The prices quoted are summer rates, so bear in mind that you can save up to 30% to 50% by traveling at off-peak times of the year.

Downtown Lancaster and Environs

If you want to be right in the center of town, then the **Brunswick Motor Inn,** Chestnut and Queen Streets, P.O. Box 749, Lancaster, PA 17604 (tel. 717/397-4801 or toll-free 800/233-0182), is the best choice. Built on a site that has been home to seven different hotels or inns since 1776, the current ten-story property is less than 20 years old and is a modern contemporary structure, formerly a Hilton. There are 225 rooms, each with one or two double beds, air conditioning, a direct-dial phone, and color TV. Doubles range from $62 to $72. There are two restaurants, The Copper Kettle for breakfast and lunch, and Bernhardt's, named after Sarah Bernhardt who performed in the Fulton Opera House in 1911. Dinner entrees are priced from $11.95 to $15.95, and include steaks, seafood, and chicken, with vegetable and potato, plus groaning-board selections of salads, appetizers, and desserts. Open for dinner from 5 to 9 p.m. daily; there is also entertainment nightly in the hotel lounge across the corridor. Free parking is provided for guests. All major CC's accepted.

Five miles west of the downtown area is the **Quality Inn Sherwood Knoll,** 500 Centerville Rd., Lancaster, PA 17601 (tel. 717/898-2431 or toll-free 800/228-5151), off Route 30 West. Set on a grassy and wooded hillside, this three-story modern Colonial-style hotel has 167 rooms which were refurbished in 1985. You'll have a choice of a king, queen, or two double beds, along with cable TV, an FM radio, a direct-dial phone, and air conditioning. Doubles range from $54 to $74. There is also an outdoor swimming pool and a cocktail lounge with entertainment six nights a week and jazz on Sundays. A full-service restaurant features American and Pennsylvania Dutch specialties. Lunch is priced from $2.95 to $4.95, and dinner entrees go from $7 to $18 with most choices under $15. The hours are 7 to 10 a.m. for breakfast; 11:30 a.m. to 5 p.m. for lunch; and 5 to 10 p.m. for dinner (except Sunday until 8 p.m.). All major CC's accepted.

The Best Western Olde Hickory Inn, 2363 Oregon Pike, Lancaster, PA 17601 (tel. 717/569-0477), is located three miles north of the downtown area on

Route 272. Under new ownership in 1986 and fully renovated and refurbished, this one-story inn is situated on 116 acres, surrounded by Amish farmsteads and directly across from the Landis Valley Museum. There are 75 rooms and suites, decorated with Amish farm prints, country-quilt bedspreads, and muted floral tones. Each unit has two double beds or one king, color cable TV, a direct-dial phone, and air conditioning. Some rooms surround the inner courtyard, others feature front and back window doors, and many have balconies. Doubles range from $50 to $66 for a standard room and from $60 to $80 for courtyard rooms and suites. Guest facilities include a lounge bar/patio with weekend entertainment, an outdoor swimming pool, and use of the Olde Hickory Racquet Club (with eight indoor tennis courts, four racquetball courts, an exercise/weight room, a sauna, a suntan room, and a pro shop), a nine-hole executive golf course, and an adjacent complex of shops called The Village Square. There is also a Colonial-style restaurant, The Tack Room, serving breakfast, lunch, and dinner, from 7 a.m. to 2 p.m. and from 5 to 10 p.m. Major CC's are accepted.

The **Treadway Resort Inn**, 222 Eden Rd., Lancaster, PA 17601 (tel. 717/569-6444 or toll-free 800/631-0182), is situated a mile north of downtown on Routes 30 and 272. This three-story hotel has 230 rooms and suites, designed in a modernized Tudor-motif. Each unit has a choice of bed sizes, a direct-dial phone, color TV, and air conditioning; and many rooms have steam baths or balconies, and others overlook an outdoor courtyard and exotic tropical pool area. Doubles range from $75 to $95 and suites from $120. The guest facilities include both indoor and outdoor pools, saunas, a health club, twin movie theaters, a game room, a gift shop, two restaurants, and a nightclub. All major CC's accepted.

The largest lodging facility in the region, the **Americana Host Farm Resort,** 2300 Lincoln Highway E. (Route 30), Lancaster, PA 17602 (tel. 717/299-5500), is located five miles east of downtown. This property is composed of two hotels totaling 510 rooms in a setting with two golf courses, 12 tennis courts, four swimming pools, a jogging track, and many other recreational facilities including a dinner-theater and a mini-farm. As we go to press, however, it has just been announced that the entire complex has been sold to the Inn America Corporation. While operations will continue for the moment under the Host name, negotiations are now under way to announce a new franchise agreement and to undertake some changes. If you are interested in staying here, it would be wise to check with the Pennsylvania Dutch Visitors Bureau for rates and an update with regard to any change of name. We'll have a full report in the next edition of this book.

Accommodations Throughout the County

West and North: A narrow country road will lead you to the **Cameron Estate Inn,** Donegal Springs Road, R.D. 1, Box 305, Mount Joy, PA 17552 (tel. 717/653-1773), a three-story Federal house located about 15 miles west of Lancaster city in a secluded farming area. Built in 1805, this palatial building was once the home of Simon Cameron, President Lincoln's first Secretary of War, a four-time senator, and ambassador to Russia. Now listed in the National Register of Historic Places, this rural manor has been graciously restored and transformed into an elegant inn by Abe and Betty Groff, who have also earned a reputation in the area for their Groff's Farm Restaurant (see "Where to Dine"). There are 18 air-conditioned guest rooms, including three ground-floor rooms, and all but two have private bathrooms. Each room is named after an historical figure and furnished in a distinctive style, with antiques, stencil wallwork, brass beds, four-posters, Amish quilts, and plants; seven rooms have fireplaces. A double is priced from $60 to $95 and includes continental breakfast. The grounds include 15 acres of lawns and hiking trails, a trout-stocked stream, and ancient trees. The restaurant, which is open to the general public, offers lunch items such as salads, hot sandwiches, quiches, croissantwiches, omelets, and pasta, in the $4.95 to $7.95 range. Dinner entrees, priced from $14.95 to $17.95, include rainbow trout; seafood cassoulet (shrimp, scallops, flounder, crab, and lobster, simmered in white wine and herbs); roast duckling with brandied peach sauce and wild rice pilaf; and tournedos of beef with green peppercorns and cognac. All main courses are accompanied by salad and potato. Lunch is served from 11:30 a.m. to 2 p.m. daily, and dinner Monday through Thursday from 6 to 8:30 p.m., and Friday and Saturday from 5:30 to 9:30 p.m. CC's accepted: AE, D, MC, and V.

The **Guesthouse at Doneckers,** 322-324 N. State St., Ephrata, PA 17522 (tel. 717/733-8696), is actually three Victorian homes renovated and joined together as one inn on the main throughfare of the town. Opened in 1984, this facility has 12 rooms, all decorated differently in pastel mint, rose, blue, or violet color schemes, and with hand-stenciled walls. If you like the décor of your room, you'll find that many of the country furnishings can be purchased at the Donecker's family store across the street. Eight rooms have private bath and four rooms share baths. The price for a double ranges from $59 to $99; and rooms with queen, double, or twin beds sizes are available, as are ground-floor accommodations. Some units have porches, kitchenettes, or private off-street entrances. For guests' enjoyment, there is a common porch, an upstairs deck, and a parlor with a TV set, books, and games. The room rates include a hearty breakfast of coffee, freshly squeezed juices, fruits, yogurt, sausage, croissants, cereals, and, in the winter months, baked apples. CC's accepted: AE, MC, and V.

Originally known as "The Sign of the Anchor," **The General Sutter Inn,** 14 E. Main St., Lititz, PA 17543 (tel. 717/626-2115), has been a lodging facility known by various names on the square of this Moravian town since 1764. For a time it was called the Springs Hotel because of the natural springs in Lititz. It takes its current name in honor of Gen. John Augustus Sutter, the famous California pioneer and founder of Sacramento on whose land gold was discovered in 1848. The general retired to Lititz, stayed first at the inn, and then built a home on the other side of the square. Furnished with an eclectic medley of Victorian and antique country pieces, the inn now has 11 rooms, all with private tiled baths, air conditioning, and color TV. Doubles range from $55 to $75. Guest facilities include an outdoor tree-lined brick patio overlooking the town square, a coffeeshop, a cocktail bar, and the Zum Anker Dining Room, a festive enclave of cranberry walls, gaslights, and antique accessories. Lunch, priced at $2.50 to $5, focuses on sandwiches, quiches, and salads. The dinner menu features steaks; various seafood including bluefish amandine; chicken breast topped with asparagus soufflé; and roast duckling. The entree price of $9.95 to $14.95 includes a kettle of homemade soup, salad, potato, and vegetable. Lunch is served Monday through Friday from 11 a.m. to 2 p.m.; and dinner Monday through Saturday from 5 to 9 p.m., and on Sunday from 11 a.m. to 7 p.m. As you step inside, you'll be greeted by the birdsong of caged canaries or the cheery voices of innkeepers Joan and Richard Vetter. CC's accepted: AE, MC, and V.

East and South: The **Greystone Motor Lodge,** 2658 Old Philadelphia Pike (Route 340), Bird-in-Hand, PA 17505 (tel. 717/393-4233), sounds like a roadside motel, but it is actually a restored French Victorian mansion and carriage house, dating back to 1883. Perched on high ground on two acres of lawns and trees amid farmlands, this stately old house offers 12 renovated rooms, all with private bath, air conditioning, color TV, and each with an individual décor. Highlights include stained-glass windows, cut-crystal doors, original woodwork, and antique bath fixtures. The lobby is a showcase of Victorian leaded and beveled glass doors and plaster-cast wall and ceiling sculptures; the carriage house was originally a barn and was converted into three sleeping rooms in 1970. Rates for a double range from $44 to $50, and multi-room family suites start at $60 including complimentary coffee and donuts for breakfast. Ground-floor accommodations are available and there is a quilt shop on the premises. Jim and Phyllis Reed are the cordial innkeepers. CC accepted: AE, MC, and V.

The **Historic Strasburg Inn,** Route 896, Strasburg, PA 17579 (tel. 717/687-7691), is actually a new development (1973) built as a replica of the area as it looked in 1793. Located just outside the town on a 58-acre site surrounded by farmlands, it is ideal for people who like the aura and charm of the past without sacrificing any 20th-century comforts. The inn is laid out like an 18th-century village, with its 103 rooms located in ten separate two-story buildings and houses, all clustered around a central courtyard. You might be assigned a room in the carpenter's house, or bishop's house, and so on, with the décor depending on the theme of the house. Rooms are all air-conditioned and feature every modern convenience, at a price ranging from $75 to $115 for a double. The complex also includes quaint country shops, a swimming pool, bicycle rentals, and the Washington House Restaurant, designed to duplicate the original village tavern. Lunch, priced from $3.95 to $6.95, offers light fare, salads, sandwiches, "Strasburgers," pastas, and seafood stews. Dinner, served by candlelight, focuses on such entrees as Cornish hen, beef Wellington, duck à l'orange, rainbow trout, and lobster tails. The prices range from $9.95 to $24.95, with most under $15. Lunch is available Monday through Saturday from 11:30 a.m. to 2 p.m.; dinner Monday through Saturday from 4:30 to 9 p.m.; Sunday brunch from 10 a.m. to 2 p.m.; and Sunday dinner from 3 to 7 p.m. Major CC's accepted.

In contrast, the **Strasburg Village Inn,** 1 W. Main St., Strasburg, PA 17579 (tel. 717/687-0900), is a restored two-story brick building, originally known as the Thomas Crawford Tavern, and an adjacent warehouse, dating back to 1788. Situated on the main thoroughfare of Strasburg, it is now a fully renovated B&B with 11 Colonially decorated rooms, all of varying sizes and décors. With air conditioning and private baths throughout, the units feature one or two double beds, or a queen-size bed; some have canopies or four-posters, private porches, or individual Jacuzzis. Rates for a double range from $59 to $89. Open all year, the inn is next to the Strasburg Country Store and Creamery where overnight guests may avail of a complimentary continental breakfast in the deli-bakeshop. CC's accepted: AE, MC, and V.

The **Hershey Farm Motor Inn,** Route 896, P.O. Box 89, Strasburg, PA 17579 (tel. 717/299-6877), is not connected to the famous chocolate resort or enterprises, but is the private endeavor of local resident Ed Hershey. Laid out in the format of a converted house and barn on a 17-acre farm, with cows, chickens, and a pond, this motel has 27 rooms, each offering two double beds, color TV, and air conditioning. Rates for a double are $38 to $48, and include breakfast. Facilities here include the Meadow Dining Room, a unique restaurant that features three types of cuisine (family-style, Pennsylvania Dutch smorgasbord, and full à la carte menu), with full dinners in every category priced at under $10. There is also an on-premises bakeshop, where you can watch cakes and pies in-the-making and buy everything from 15 kinds of fudge to cookies, candies, and cookbooks. CC's accepted: MC and V.

Children of all ages love the **Red Caboose Motel,** Paradise Lane, P.O. Box 102, Strasburg, PA 17579 (tel. 717/687-6646), a lodging facility made entirely of converted train cabooses. This inn sits among cornfields and horse farms, by the tracks of the Old Strasburg Railroad, so you can often hear the whistles toot or watch the trains chug by in the surrounding countryside. Each of the 39 units has been refitted to include private baths, double beds, and air conditioning, not to mention the TVs built into the pot-bellied stoves. Doubles start at $45; and family units with one double bed and four bunk beds start at $59 for four people. For $15 extra a night, you can also rent an "efficiency caboose" with stove and refrigerator. The complex includes a dining car serving food all day (in the budget bracket), an old-fashioned ice-cream parlor car, and bikes for rent ($1 an hour). CC's accepted: MC and V.

WHERE TO DINE: Nowhere in the Mid-Atlantic states is there such a variety of restaurants as you will find in Lancaster county. From haute cuisine to hearty home-cooked helpings, the food here is an attraction in itself.

The Pennsylvania Dutch cooking is world famous—from heaping trays of fried chicken, sausage, beef, and hickory-smoked ham and garden vegetables to shoofly pie, raspberry tarts, and homemade ice cream. One meal will practically keep you fueled for a whole day. Most restaurants serving this food operate on the "family-style" format, which means you sit at large tables with other guests and share huge platters of food, constantly replenished by gracious local staff. The "all-you-can-eat" principle reigns supreme. Many of these places do not serve liquor, beer, or wine, although some allow you to bring your own. These restaurants are geared to families and often close by 8 or 9 p.m. Above all, they are great value—entire dinners from soup or salad to desserts for an average of $10 to $12 per person for adults and half-price for children. In this genre, you will also find some "buffet"-style restaurants that allow you to select whatever you wish—be it one, two, or 22 items, and then sit at individual tables.

Lancaster is also home to a host of very fine à la carte restaurants and country inns that can hold their own among top gourmet spots of the world. In addition, some kitchens offer a blend of Pennsylvania Dutch dishes and other all-American entrees. You'll probably want to sample a few different types of restaurants, so we'll give you a selection, starting with what we consider one of the best restaurants in all of the U.S.

The Top Choice
If we could give a five-star rating, **Windows on Steinman Park,** 16–18 W. King St., Lancaster (tel. 295-1316), would rate six. In this land of Pennsylvania Dutch cooking, this is a decidedly American dining spot, with a chef from Paris. Located in the heart of downtown, Windows reflects the best of Lancaster and is a joy to all the senses. A tasteful blend of gleaming crystal chandeliers, hand-painted murals, wall mirrors, huge bouquets of fresh flowers, and brass trim, the interior is laid out on three levels, edged by massive windows that are three stories tall. These angled bay windows overlook the cascading waterfalls, fountains, and brick courtyard of Steinman Park, a public plaza named for the founder of the city's newspaper and the father of the restaurant's owner, Peggy Steinman. The views are particularly romantic in the evening when candles flicker on the linen-covered tables and the park is artistically floodlit. No matter where you sit, the panorama is dramatic and the ambience is enhanced by the music of a well-versed pianist. The tuxedoed waiters add to the magic by providing service that is enthusiastic and sparked with panache. Lunch, priced from $4.95 to $9.95, primarily features light entrees and omelets, sandwiches, pastas, and salads, but dinner is the time to splurge and sample the expertise of chef Denis Saunier. You may wish to start with some imported Irish smoked salmon or perhaps escargot, brie in pastry, duck pâté, or caviar. Appetizers run from $5.95 to

$38. Entrees are priced from $13.95 to $24.95 and include impeccably prepared and presented Dover sole; baby frogs' legs; chicken with strawberry sauce; sweetbreads with morrels; roast baby pheasant with cognac truffles and goose liver; rack of lamb; and Chateaubriand. Vegetables or a green salad average $4.

Lunch is served Monday through Saturday from 11:30 a.m. to 2:30 p.m.; dinner Sunday through Thursday from 6 to 10 p.m., and Friday and Saturday from 6 to 11 p.m.; and Sunday brunch from 11:30 a.m. to 3 p.m. Complimentary parking is provided at the Central Parking Garage, West Vine Street, for patrons. All major CC's accepted.

Other Lancaster City Area Moderately Priced Restaurants

Directly across from the Central Market is the appropriately named **Market Fare,** 25 W. King St., Lancaster (tel. 299-7090). Housed in a restored 1910 building, this restaurant conveys much of the flavor of old Lancaster with its décor of exposed brick walls, 19th-century oil paintings, and cushioned armchairs. There are two levels, with a café upstairs for a light breakfast or quick lunch and the main dining room on the ground level. Dinner entrees, priced from $8.95 to $15.95, include marinated and charbroiled sirloin of beef; shrimp, roast duck, and spinach in puff pastry; rock Cornish game hen; and Eastern shore fish stew. All main courses come with salad, vegetable, potato, or rice. Lunch is available Monday through Saturday from 11:30 a.m. to 2:30 p.m.; dinner on Sunday and Monday from 5:30 to 9 p.m., and Tuesday through Saturday from 5:30 to 10 p.m. CC's accepted: AE, Ch, MC, and V.

You can dine in an 1820 farm atmosphere and still enjoy innovative 20th-century cuisine at the **Olde Greenfield Inn,** 595 Greenfield Rd., Lancaster (tel. 393-0668), on Route 30, about three miles east of downtown. Located adjacent to the visitors' information bureau, this restaurant was established in 1979 and features a décor of country-cupboard-style furnishings amid the original stone walls and beams of an authentic farmhouse. Lunch, priced from $4.95 to $8.95, includes seafood omelets, chicken and cashew salad, angel hair neptune salad, and savory sandwiches. Entrees at dinner, priced in the $10.95 to $15.95 bracket, feature such dishes as sweet and sour walnut shrimp; veal sesame; chicken and scallops à l'orange; roast duckling; vegetable and seafood pastas; and steaks. All main courses are accompanied by salad, potato, and vegetable, and there is an extensive vintage wine list. Hours are 7 a.m. to 11:30 a.m. for breakfast daily; lunch, Monday through Friday from 11:30 a.m. to 2 p.m.; dinner, Tuesday through Saturday from 5:30 to 10 p.m.; and Sunday brunch from 11:30 a.m. to 2 p.m. Major CC's accepted.

Full-Service Dining Around the County

Classic French country cooking is featured at **The Restaurant at Doneckers,** 333 N. State St., Ephrata (tel. 738-2421), northeast of Lancaster off Route 272. Part of a complex that also includes fashionable clothing shops and a first-rate guest house, this restaurant is owned by the Donecker family. There are two dining rooms, each with a distinctive décor and ambience. The ground floor features a country flavor with antique furnishings, Bavarian porcelain, and an open-hearth fireplace, while the upper level is a bright and airy garden setting with skylights, plants, and patio furniture. Lunch, in the $4.95 to $7.95 range, features puff pastry sandwiches, as well as burgers and salads. Dinner is more a celebration of chef Jean Maurice Juge's French flair with such dishes as brook trout stuffed with salmon mousse; a trio of lamb, pork, and veal filets with three different sauces; breast of duck with black currant sauce garnished with lingonberry mousse; filet of Black Angus beef with crushed green, white, black, and pink peppercorns sautéed with a sauce of veal glaze, imported mustard, and aged cognac; and roasted Cornish hen with wild-mushroom purée. Main courses are priced from $14.95 to $24.95 and include a spinach, green, or orange and almond salad, and assorted fresh vegetables. There is also an extensive wine cellar. Open from 11 a.m. to 10 p.m. daily, except Wednesday and Sunday. All major CC's accepted.

Nine miles east of Lancaster on Route 30 is one of the area's oldest establishments, **The Revere Tavern,** 3063 Lincoln Highway E., Paradise (tel. 687-8601), a two-story stone house with authentic hitching posts and brick pathways outside. Dating back to 1740, this sturdy building started as a stagecoach tavern known as "The Sign of the Spread Eagle." In 1841 it was converted into a pastoral residence for the Rev. Edward Buchanan and his wife Eliza, sister of Stephen Foster who also visited and penned some of his music here. The house was purchased in 1854 by the pastor's brother, James Buchanan, fifteenth President of the U.S., and, thanks to a careful restoration, it returned in more recent years to its original use as a tavern. During the day it serves as a lunchtime theater venue that draws visitors in busloads from as far away as California. A professional production is staged Monday through Friday by the Rainbow Players (admission is $18.50 per person for show and full meal). In the evening, the restaurant concentrates on candlelit dinners in a relaxed Colonial setting. Entrees, which range in price from $7.95 to $19.95 with most dishes under $15, include steaks; lobster tails; yellow-tailed flounder; Pennsylvania rainbow trout; crab au gratin; country-fried chicken; and hickory-cured ham. All main courses are accompanied by two vegetables. Dinner is served Monday through Thursday from 5 to 10 p.m.; on Friday and Saturday until 11 p.m.; and on Sunday from 4 to 9 p.m. All major CC's accepted.

Afficionados of prime beef sing the praises of Ed Stoudt's **Black Angus Steak House,** Route 272, Adamstown (tel. 215/484-4385), about 20 miles north of Lancaster city. Ever since 1962, this restaurant has concentrated on serving the best of beef in a Victorian setting, enhanced by a mix of chandeliers, antiques, fine art, and conversation pieces such as a 1928 Packard in the foyer. Open for dinner only, the menu features various cuts of steaks served with locally grown mushrooms, and prime ribs cut to order, as well as a selection of seafood and German-Austrian dishes. The entree prices range from $9.95 to $23.95 and include cheese and crackers, salad, and potato. There is also a good raw bar (mixed plates $3.50 to $4.95) and a wine cellar featuring over 70 domestic and imported wines with many Pennsylvania vintages. The hours are 5 to 11 p.m., Monday through Saturday, and from noon to 9 p.m. on Sunday. All major CC's accepted.

There are three restaurants at **Bube's Brewery,** 102 N. Market St., Mount Joy, 12 miles northeast of Lancaster off Route 230. Built to brew beer by German immigrant Alois Bube, this spot flourished in the 19th century during Lancaster County's heyday as the "Munich of the New World" before prohibition. Now a National Historic Landmark, Bube's claims to be the only surviving U.S. brewery still intact. It is a wonderland of old casks, bottles, stone walls, and brewing implements, and from Memorial Day to Labor Day you can take a tour of the premises for $2.50. But any time of year, you can also dine here in the **Catacombs** (tel. 653-2056), an area that includes the aging cellars of the brewery, 43 feet underground. The waiting staff, dressed like serfs in medieval costume, give you a mini-tour en route to your table in the stone-lined vaults of the catacombs. The menu includes seafood, steaks, duckling, sherried chicken, and veal al limone, in the $10.95 to $17.95 price bracket. Dinner is served seven nights a week, until 9 p.m. on weekdays and 10 p.m. on Fridays and Saturdays. If you prefer to dine above ground, there is also a Victorian-style restaurant called **Alois** (tel. 653-2057), and a tavern with outdoor patio known as **The**

Bottleworks (tel. 653-2160). The former features nouvelle American cuisine in the moderate-expensive range and the latter is more of a snackery in the moderate-budget category; both serve lunch and dinner. CC's accepted: AE, D, MC, V.

Pennsylvania Dutch Dining Around the County

With praises from everyone from the late James Beard to Craig Claiborne, the leader of the home-style restaurants is **Groff's Farm,** Pinkerton Road, Mount Joy (tel. 653-2048), a 1756 farmhouse and the home of Abe and Betty Groff. Surrounded by fertile fields and a pond with graceful swans, this charming setting started as an outgrowth of the Groffs' Mennonite hospitality to visitors and grew with the years. Guests so loved Betty's dishes that they often flooded her with requests for recipes; after answering hundreds of letters, she finally decided to please everyone and has written two cookbooks, *Country Goodness* and *Good Earth and Country Cooking.* In recent years, son Charles, trained at the Culinary Institute of America, has added his talents to the family enterprise. Dinner here is served at individual tables, either family-style or on an à la carte basis. If served family-style, you select one entree or a combination of entrees per table; these range in price from $12.50 for a single dish to $21.50 for four meats and seafoods. Featured dishes include chicken Stoltzfus (chunks of white meat in a rich cream sauce with flaky diamonds of butter pastry); hickory-smoked ham; prime ribs; or seafood. The entree price covers soup, fruit salad, vegetables, potatoes, homemade sweet and sour relishes, cracker pudding, homemade pies, and other goodies. The à la carte menu, priced from $12 to $18.95, features individual portions of many of the family-style items or such entrees as crab-stuffed flounder, lobster tails, and steaks, also served with vegetables and relishes. Lunch features a similar à la carte menu, priced from $5 to $8 per person. No alcohol is served, but guests are welcome to bring wine. Reservations are required for dinner only. Open Tuesday through Saturday, with lunch from 11:30 a.m. to 1:30 p.m. and dinner at two seatings, 5 and 7:30 p.m. CC's accepted: MC and V.

A classic example of Pennsylvania Dutch–style service on a large scale is **Good and Plenty,** East Brook Road, Route 896, Smoketown, (tel. 394-7111), originally an Amish house built in 1871, and now a restaurant that can seat up to 650 people. As you enter, you pay the fixed price and then are seated with other guests at tables set for ten or more. It's a nice way to get to know other folks from many states and countries and to share travel experiences. The waiting staff, usually local women who also do much of the cooking, then start with soup or salad and continue to bring large trays of food throughout the meal. Never worry that a platter will be empty when it gets to you, as another round will always be close behind. You can try some of everything or just pick and choose your favorites; the assortment usually includes pork and sauerkraut, baked country sausage, ham, roast beef, crispy fried chicken, rich creamed chicken, mashed potatoes, noodles, homemade breads, apple butter, shoofly pie, raspberry pie, ice creams, and much more, depending on what's in season. All this for $10.50 for adults and $4.50 for children. Open from 11:30 a.m. to 8 p.m. daily, except Sunday and mid-December through January. No CC's accepted.

A similar arrangement prevails at the **Plain and Fancy Farm,** Route 340, Bird-in-Hand (tel. 768-8281), seven miles east of Lancaster. In a setting of village shops and other amusements, this barn-like dining room serves family-style meals, priced at $9.95 for adults and $3.95 for children. Hours are 11:30 a.m. to 8 p.m. daily except Sunday. CC's accepted: MC and V.

Four and a half miles east of downtown is the cottage and garden setting of **Family Style,** 2323 Lincoln Highway E. (Route 30), Lancaster (tel. 393-2323), providing several unique features including family-style breakfasts. In addition, children aged 2 to 12 are charged by their individual weights (5 cents a pound) at dinner, while adults pay $10.95. Beer and wine are also available here. Breakfast costs $4.50 for adults and $2.25 for children. Open daily April through November from 8 a.m. to 8 p.m. CC's accepted: AE, MC, and V.

Spicy meats are the feature at the **The Stoltzfus Farm Restaurant,** Route 772, Intercourse (tel. 768-8156), which has its own butcher shop on the premises. The menu here is likely to include smoked sausage, scrapple, liver pudding, and kielbasa, as well as broasted chicken, chow chow, pepper cabbage, shoofly and cherry crumb pies, and homemade ice cream. The price is $8.95 for adults and from $2.95 to $6.95 for children, depending on age. Open Monday through Saturday, except in winter, from 11 a.m. to 8 p.m. No CC's accepted.

If you prefer to get up and select your own food, then **Miller's Smorgasbord,** 2811 Lincoln Highway East (Route 30), Ronks (tel. 687-6621), is designed for you. Located seven miles east of Lancaster, this Colonial-style restaurant has an open hearth, and a tiered layout with private-table seating. The assortment on the Pennsylvania Dutch buffet table usually includes steamed shrimp, roast beef, honey-glazed ham, salads, vegetables, and desserts ranging from shoofly pie to almond meringue cake and cheesecakes. Dinner costs $12.95 for adults and from $3.95 to $7.95 for children, depending on age. Breakfast is $6.95 for adults and $2.95 for children. This restaurant is open for breakfast from 8 a.m. seven days a week, June through October, and on Saturday and Sunday year round; dinner is served from noon, seven days a week, year round (except Christmas Eve and Christmas Day). CC's accepted: AE, MC, and V.

In the upper section of the county near the Pennsylvania Turnpike is **Zinn's Country Diner,** Route 272, Denver (tel. 215/267-2210), 19 miles north of Lancaster. Operated by the Zinn family since 1950, this busy restaurant is open 24 hours a day for breakfast, lunch, and dinner, with individualized table service. The dinner menu is served from 10:30 a.m. to 9 p.m., with entrees priced from $4.95 to $9.95 including an appetizer and two vegetables. The choices range from Pennsylvania Dutch specialties to seafood, steaks, turkey, veal, and vegetarian platters. The 32-acre Zinn complex also features an arcade of shops, a candy outlet, a snack bar, miniature golf, a picnic area, and recreational fields. No CC's accepted.

THE TOP ATTRACTIONS: As you drive along Lincoln Highway (Route 30) east of Lancaster you will see a parade of billboards announcing an array of man-made attractions, each clamoring for your patronage. All of these sites are designed to show the workings of Amish life—from prototype Amish homesteads, villages, farms, and one-room schools to a wax museum portrayal of Lancaster County heritage. Although each one claims to be authentic and unique, you'll find that there is a lot of duplication and one or two of these attractions will be more than enough. Better still, get off Route 30 and drive the back roads and farm roads, such as Routes 772 and 340. Get into the towns like Intercourse, Bird-in-Hand, and Paradise, to see the real Amish people at work and traveling in their distinctive gray buggies.

A good place to start a tour of the Lancaster area is the **Hans Herr House,** 1849 Hans Herr Dr., Willow Street (tel. 464-4438), off Route 222, about three miles south of downtown Lancaster. Built by the Herr family in 1719, this is the oldest structure in Lancaster County, restored to its original medieval Germanic façade and full of authentic furnishings and farm implements. Listed in the National Register of Historic Places, it is also one of the oldest Mennonite meeting houses in America, constructed when the Lancaster area was still considered a wilderness. Other sights on the grounds include a blacksmith shop, a garden, an orchard, and a visitor's center. Open Monday through Saturday from 9 a.m. to 4 p.m., April through December (except Thanksgiving and Christmas). Admission charge is $2 for adults and $1 for children aged 7 to 12.

Wheatland, 1120 Marietta Ave. (Route 23), Lancaster (tel. 392-8721), is the home of the only man from Pennsylvania to become a U.S. President, James Buchanan. Built in 1828, it was purchased by our fifteenth chief executive in 1848 and used as a country estate and campaign headquarters. Federal in style, the house is listed in the National Register of Historic Places, and is a showcase of Empire and Victorian furnishings, grained woodwork, marble and slate mantels, columned front and rear porticoes. The house, which sits on a four-acre estate, also contains many of Buchanan's unique personal belongings including a huge, porcelain Japanese goldfish bowl and a zinc-lined tub. Open for tours from April through November (except Thanksgiving) from 10 a.m. to 5 p.m., with the last tour at 4:15 p.m. The admission charge is $3 for adults, $2 for students aged 12 to 17, and $1 for children aged 6 to 11.

Landis Valley Museum, 2451 Kissel Hill Rd., Lancaster (tel. 569-0401), off Route 272, is an outdoor museum of Pennsylvania's rural heritage from Colonial times until the end of the 19th century. There are 22 life-size exhibit structures, including a steam engine building, a firehouse, a country store, a blacksmith shop, a seamstress house, a pottery shop, a print shop, a harness shop, spinning and weaving centers, and a tavern, as well as farmsteads. A Conestoga wagon, with its bonnet-like canopy, also sits on the grounds, as a tribute to Lancaster county craftsmen who originated this form of transportation. Throughout the complex, there are demonstrations of crafts, skills, and occupations, reflecting rural life and folk culture. Open Tuesday through Saturday from 9 a.m. to 5 p.m. and Sunday from noon to 5 p.m. Admission is $3 for adults and $1 for children 6 to 17.

The **Ephrata Cloister**, 632 W. Main St., Ephrata (tel. 733-6600), is an 18th-century German Protestant monastic settlement, known for its original religious choral music, and for its printing and publishing achievements. Visitors can tour ten of the original buildings which have been restored and interpreted to re-create the aura of this communal village. On many summer evenings, there is also a 9 p.m. performance of *Vorspiel*, a musical drama depicting the way of life practiced here in the 18th century. Open for touring, April through November, Monday through Saturday from 9 a.m. to 5 p.m. and Sunday from noon to 5 p.m. Admission is $2.50 for adults and $1 for youths (aged 6 to 17). The *Vorspiel* performances are held every Saturday from July through Labor Day Weekend at 9 p.m.; tickets are priced at $4 for adults and $1.50 for children aged 6 through 17.

Lancaster's Scots-Irish influence is the cornerstone of the **Donegal Mills Plantation**, Trout Run Road, off Route 772, Mount Joy, (tel. 653-2168). This is an authentic historic landmark listed in the National Register and deeded by Thomas Penn in 1736. The property includes an original gristmill dating back to 1830, a working bake house, a miller's house and a stately 1870s mansion. There is also a German four-square garden and an herbal garden used for medicine and dyeing from earliest days. Tours are conducted on weekends from noon to 6 p.m., as baking, spinning, and weaving demonstrations are given; the fee is $1.50 per person.

The history and technology of trains is the focus of **The Railroad Museum of Pennsylvania**, Route 741, Strasburg (tel. 687-8628). From the earliest steam engines to 20th-century innovations, you'll see a collection of locomotives, cars, artifacts, and related railroad memorabilia. This museum also provides the opportunity for visitors to enter the cab of a steam locomotive, view the state room of a private car, or examine the interior of a Pullman sleeper. Hours are Monday through Saturday from 10 a.m. to 5 p.m.; Sunday from 11 a.m. to 5 p.m., except holidays. Admission is $2 for adults and $1 for youths aged 6 to 17.

After you have seen all the train workings, it's "All aboard!" for the **Strasburg Rail Road,** Route 741, Strasburg (tel. 687-7522), America's oldest short-line railroad operating since 1832. This 45-minute round-trip will take you through the scenic Pennsylvania Dutch country, from Lancaster to Paradise, via a coal-burning steam locomotive. You'll have a choice of an enclosed car or open-air observation deck seating, ideal for picture-taking. Trains operate from 10 a.m. to 7 p.m. daily from late June through Labor Day, with reduced schedules at other times (except mid-December through mid-March). Adults pay $4.25 and children $2.25; seats in the observation cars are 25¢ extra in every case.

Lancaster County is also the home of America's oldest pretzel bakery, the **Julius Sturgis Pretzel House,** 219 E. Main St., Lititz (tel. 626-4354). This bakery dates back to 1784, although the first pretzels weren't made here until 1861. Visitors can tour the 200-year-old bakery and the modern plant, watch the pretzel dough taking shape, and lend a hand at twisting these handmade soft pretzels. The tour also includes a few samples and an outlet store. Open Monday through Saturday from 9 a.m. to 5 p.m. Admission is 75¢ per person.

This area is also a productive wine-growing region. One of the leading vintners to offer visitor tours is J. Richard Nissley, who heads the **Nissley Winery,** Wickersham Road, Bainbridge (tel. 426-3514). Established in 1976, this family-run winery is set on a 300-acre farm with 52 acres of vineyards in the western part of the county, near the banks of the Susquehanna River. The winery itself is located in a restored 18th-century stone mill and produces over 50,000 bottles a year, many of which have won major awards. Besides touring the winery and enjoying samples, visitors can use picnic tables on the farm grounds. Tours last a half hour and cost $1.50 for adults and children over 12 years of age. Open year round, Monday through Saturday from noon to 6 p.m. (except Easter, Thanksgiving, Christmas, and New Year's Day). Also open on Sundays (April through December only) from 1 to 4 p.m., for sampling and sales only. In addition, on Saturday evenings in the summer, open-air music events are staged on the grounds ($4 admission charge), and in September a harvest festival is held. CC's accepted for wine sales: MC and V.

If you visit the **The Winery at Mt. Hope,** Route 72, Manheim (tel. 665-7021), you won't actually see the workings of the winery but you can sample the products and take a tour of the 1800 mansion of Henry Bates Grubb, one of America's wealthiest ironmasters. Listed in the National Register of Historic Places, this 32-room sandstone house resembles a feudal English manor with castle walls and turrets, but it is furnished in a Victorian theme. The interior includes a winding walnut staircase, hand-painted 18-foot ceilings, Egyptian marble fireplaces, imported crystal chandeliers, and a greenhouse with a solarium. The tour concludes in the billiard room with a formal wine tasting of Mt. Hope estate products. Admission price is $3.50 for adults and $1.50 for children over age 6. Open Monday through Saturday from 10 a.m. to 6 p.m., and Sunday from noon to 6 p.m. (closes at 5 p.m. in the winter months). Located 16 miles northwest of Lancaster, Mt. Hope is also the home of the Pennsylvania Renaissance Faire (see "Events"). CC's accepted for wine purchases: MC and V.

NIGHTLIFE: True to the Pennsylvania Dutch family farming traditions, activities in this area start early and finish fairly early in the evening. You'll find that many of the restaurants, particularly the family-style places, close at 8 p.m. The haute cuisine restaurants, however, like Windows on Steinman Park or

Doneckers, stay open later and often feature live music. The larger hotels and motor inns, such as the Quality Sherwood Knoll, Treadway, Olde Hickory, or Brunswick, also maintain late dining hours (until 9 p.m. on weekdays and 10 or 11 p.m. on weekends) and offer nightly music or entertainment.

In addition, Lancaster is home to one of our nation's oldest theaters in continuous operation (since 1852), the **Fulton Opera House,** 12 N. Prince St., Lancaster (tel. 397-7425). Named for inventor Robert Fulton, who was born in this county, over the years this theater has hosted such greats as Mark Twain, the Barrymores, Sarah Bernhardt, and George M. Cohan. Beautifully restored, it is an attraction in itself with its elaborate Victorian façade, gilt and scarlet décor, and intricately detailed baroque boxes. Today it is a showcase for drama, music, opera, dance, and special events, including the Lancaster Symphony Orchestra. The box office is open Monday through Saturday from 11 a.m. to 6 p.m., and on Sundays from one hour before a performance. Tickets are priced from $7 to $25, depending on the event. The curtain is usually at 8 p.m., Tuesday through Sunday. CC's accepted: AE, Ch, MC, and V.

The newest addition to the area's year-round entertainment scene is the **Dutch Apple Dinner Theatre,** 510 Centerville Rd., Lancaster (tel. 898-1900), five miles west of the city center, off Route 30 and next to the Quality Inn Sherwood Knoll. This is a professional company presenting musicals and comedies, ranging from *Cats* to *A Chorus Line, Oklahoma,* and *42nd Street.* Admission charges range from $17.50 to $22.50 for adults and $13.50 for children under 12, and all shows are preceded by a complete buffet dinner. The meal starts at 6 p.m. for evening performances, Tuesday through Saturday, and at 11:45 a.m. for afternoon matinees on Wednesday, Thursday, Saturday, and Sunday. CC's accepted: MC and V.

SHOPPING: One of the shopping landmarks of the downtown area is the **Lancaster Central Market,** Penn Square, Lancaster (tel. 291-4739). Continuously operating since the mid-1700s and fully restored in 1976, this is one of the oldest covered markets in the U.S. and an ideal venue to see the people and the products of this fertile county. Local Amish and Mennonite farmers bring their vegetables and fruits to this emporium; stroll the aisles and you'll see (and smell) everything from fudge to fish, sausage to spices, preserves to pretzels, and candies to cheese. This is also a good spot for handmade quilts, and homemade pies and cakes. Open Tuesday, Friday, and Saturday from 6 a.m. to 5 p.m.

You can see jams and relishes in-the-making at the **Kitchen Kettle Village,** Newport Road, Route 772, Intercourse (tel. 768-8261), seven miles east of Lancaster. This complex of workshops started in 1954 when Bob and Pat Burnley started making jams in their own kitchen and it has grown into a cluster of 20 small enterprises in a brick-lined courtyard. You can watch not only jam-making, but also see baking, fudge-making, woodworking, and many other crafts, and then buy the products to take home. Many of the foods produced in the village are also served at the adjacent Kling House Restaurant. Surrounded by trees and facing a quiet street, this old house is located opposite a local blacksmith shop, where the Amish bring their carriages and horses throughout the day. Open daily (except Sunday), the shops can be visited from 9 a.m. to 5 p.m. and the restaurant hours are 11 a.m. to 7 p.m. CC's accepted: MC and V.

Also in Intercourse is the **The Old Country Store,** Main Street (tel. 768-7101), an enterprise affiliated with "The People's Place." It is stocked with the work of more than 300 local craftspeople, ranging from quilts, afghans, and patchwork pillows to stuffed animals, dolls, tablecloths, potholders, sunbonnets, and wooden toys. Open daily from 9 a.m. to 5 p.m. and on Thursday and Friday until 9 p.m. CC's accepted: MC and V.

For a 19th-century shopping experience, stop into the **Strasburg Country Store and Creamery,** 1 W. Main St., Center Square, Strasburg (tel. 687-0766). This is the oldest store in continuous operation in this area and it features an 1890s marble soda fountain, an oldtime cigar-store Indian, a potbelly stove, and walls of antique shelves loaded with handcrafts, folk art, stenciling supplies, kitchen utensils, and herbal products. You'll find tasty treats from yesteryear, ranging from penny candy and fire balls to spice drops and cinnamon hearts. All the ice cream is made on the premises and scooped into handmade waffle cones. A real taste of the past! CC's accepted: MC and V.

The hand-painted hex signs that decorate the barns and buildings of this area are a colorful symbol of the Pennsylvania Dutch countryside. They also make ideal souvenirs, and one of the best sources is the **Jacob Zook Shop,** Route 30, Paradise (tel. 687-6333), nine miles east of Lancaster. The author of the book *Hexology,* Jacob began making these signs in 1942 and is recognized as one of the leading designers and craftsmen. Over the years, his signs have been requested by people from all 50 states, presidents, a king, a major league baseball team, and the U.S. Navy. His good-luck designs are most popular, but Jacob stocks at least 28 original designs and other traditional symbols, as well as various local crafts. Open Monday through Saturday from 9 a.m. to 5 p.m. and on Sunday from noon to 5 p.m. CC's accepted: MC and V.

Antique hunters flock to northern Lancaster County and Adamstown, known as the "antiques capital of the U.S.A." More than 1,500 dealers gather to sell their wares here every Sunday along Route 272. Two of the leading markets are **Renninger's No. 1** (tel. 215/267-2177), open year round and the largest with 450 to 1,000 dealers, indoors and outside; and the **Black Angus Antiques Mall,** (tel. 215/484-4385), with over 200 dealers, and which stages an annual Christkindlesmarkt in December. All dealers are open from 7:30 a.m. or 8 a.m. to 5 p.m.

EVENTS: One of the leading annual gatherings in this area is the **Pennsylvania Renaissance Faire,** held on seven successive weekends from late August through mid-October at the **Mt. Hope Estate and Winery,** Route 72 at exit 20 of the Pennsylvania Turnpike, 16 miles northeast of Lancaster. This is a re-creation of a 16th-century English village festival, with costumed lords and ladies; jesters and jugglers; magicians, minstrels, mongers, and merchants; and actors and artisans, not to mention craft demonstrations, medieval jousting tournaments, a human chess match, continuous street theater, and food vendors. Hours are 11 a.m. to 6 p.m., and the admission charge is $7 for adults and $2 for children. For further information, contact the **Mount Hope Estate and Winery,** P.O. Box 685, Cornwall, PA 17016 (717/665-7021).

CHILDREN'S CORNER: Although all of Lancaster County is appealing to children, youthful visitors are particularly drawn to the fairy-tale-castle façade of **Dutch Wonderland,** 2249 Lincoln Highway East, Lancaster (tel. 291-1888), located about four miles east of downtown on Route 30. Set on 44 landscaped acres, this is a family fun park with rides, a monorail, a water slide, a miniature railroad, a riverboat, bumper cars, and shows. Open from Easter weekend through Labor Day from 10 a.m. to 6 p.m. Monday through Saturday, and from noon to 6 p.m. on Sunday (with slightly longer hours in June, July, and August); also open on weekends during September and October. Admission charge ranges from $7.59 to $10.89, depending on if you select a package with five rides or unlimited rides. Children under age 3 enter at no charge. All major CC's are accepted.

2. Reading

Much of the Pennsylvania Dutch influence that permeates Lancaster County is shared by neighboring Berks County and its chief city of Reading (pronounced "Red-ing"). But, as most Reading-bound travelers will tell you, the colorful hex signs and farming traditions of yesteryear take a back seat to a strictly 20th-century lure—outlet shopping. Yes, mention "Reading" to almost anyone in the Mid-Atlantic region and their eyes light up and say "bargains."

Reading is a mecca of more than 250 outlet stores, from fashions to furniture, cosmetics to china, linens to leather, shoes to silver, and toys to tableware (and that's just for starters!).

The outlet method of merchandising began in the factories and mills of Reading in the 1960s when manufacturers sold overruns and seconds to employees. In time, friends and neighbors of employees wanted to be included in the rock-bottom prices. Small stores sprang up inside the factories, and thus a new type of shopping was born and Reading became the "outlet capital of the world."

There is, of course, more to Reading than outlets. Rimmed by the Blue Mountains and nestled along the banks of the Schuylkill River, Reading has a proud history, starting with the fact that Daniel Boone was born here.

Reading is directly associated with William Penn. Two of Penn's sons, Thomas and Richard, settled here in 1748 and laid out the city, naming it after their ancestral home in England. The area that they designated as the center of the town or Market Square is still the focal point of the city, although it is now known as Penn Square. In the 19th and early 20th centuries, Reading was a railroading and industrial center; the products manufactured here ranged from pretzels and cigars to pipe organs and bicycles.

Today, in addition to the outlets, Reading (pop.: 79,000) is also synonymous with mushrooms. The surrounding Berks county countryside is a prime mushroom-growing land, so you'll find that mushroom dishes feature prominently on restaurant menus of the region.

GETTING TO AND AROUND READING: Here's what you'll need to know to get to and around Reading.

By Car: Located 32 miles northeast of Lancaster City and 57 miles northwest of Philadelphia or 57 miles east of Harrisburg, Reading is reached by many roads. It is 12 miles north of the Pennsylvania Turnpike, using exit 21 from the west and then via Route 222 north into Reading; or using exit 22 from the east and then north via Route 176. The city can also be reached via I-78 to exit 10 and then south for 15 miles via Route 61. Route 222 also traverses Reading in a north-south direction and Route 422 crosses through the city from east to west.

The downtown area, which is centered at Penn Square, is easily explored on foot and some of the major outlets are within ten blocks of the main thoroughfare, Penn Avenue. Other groups of outlets are clustered north of the downtown area (around Heister's Lane) and just west of downtown and over the Schuylkill River in an area known as Wyomissing. A good number of hotels and restaurants and the tourist information office are also located on the western side of the river. To see them all, you'll need a car or taxi transport.

By Plane: Two miles northwest of the downtown area on Route 183 is **Reading Municipal Airport** (tel. 372-4666), which handles regularly scheduled flights from Philadelphia, Pittsburgh, and Newark via **Allegheny Commuter Airlines** (tel. 375-4553 or toll-free 800/428-4253).

By Bus: Bus service into Reading is operated by **Capitol Trailways** which maintains a depot at 3rd and Court Streets. (tel. 374-3182). Local transport within the city and county is provided by the Berks Area Transportation Authority, otherwise known as BARTA (tel. 921-0601); the base fare is 75¢.

Car Rental: Three companies have rental desks at the airport: **Avis** (tel. 372-6636); **Hertz** (tel. 374-1448); and **National** (tel. 376-3235). In addition, **Budget** offers three rental bases in the area, at 815 Lancaster Ave. (tel. 775-4888); 3728 Pottsville Pike (tel. 921-1444); and 601 Penn Square Center (tel. 372-2888). **Dollar** is located at 2526 Centre Ave. (tel. 921-9121).

Taxis: If you need a cab, call **Reading Metro Taxi** (tel. 374-5111 or 374-3113).

VISITOR INFORMATION: For maps and travel data about Reading, outlet shopping, and other attractions of the area, contact the **Berks County Pennsylvania Dutch Travel Association,** Sheraton Berkshire Inn, Route 422 West, Paper Mill Road Exit, Wyomissing, PA 19610 (tel. 215/375-4085). Open mid-March to mid-December from 8 a.m. to 8 p.m. Monday through Friday; from 8 a.m. to 6 p.m. on Saturday; and from 10 a.m. to 2 p.m. on Sunday. During the rest of the year, the office is open from 8 a.m. to 5 p.m. Monday through Friday, and from 8 a.m. to 1 p.m. on Saturday.

AREA CODE: All telephone numbers in the Reading and Berks County area are part of the 215 area code.

WHERE TO STAY: Most of Reading's hotels are outside of the downtown area and the majority are on or near Route 422. The Wyomissing area, west of the city center on the other side of the Schuylkill River, is the prime "hotel row." This is because Wyomissing is home to the VF Factory outlet, the Berkshire Mall, and the tourist information office; it also offers quick access to downtown and the other outlets in all directions.

The **Reading Motor Inn,** 1040 Park Rd. and Warren Street Bypass, Wyomissing, PA 19610 (tel. 215/372-7811 or toll-free 800/345-4023), has been "the place" to stay ever since it opened in 1962. Recently renovated (1986) and expanded to 250 rooms, this one- and two-story full-service hotel is laid out in a sprawling ranch-style configuration in a grassy setting just off Route 422 and 1½ miles from the downtown area. A homey early American décor is featured in both the public rooms and in the guest rooms. Each bedroom has a king or two double beds, a vanity area with an extra sink, cable TV with free HBO, a direct-dial phone, and air conditioning. Doubles range from $69 to $75; rooms with a whirlpool are $10 more. Amenities include a lounge with weekend entertainment, a guest launderette, an outdoor swimming pool, a gift shop with a visitor brochure center, and a full-service restaurant, The Publick House. A warm Colonial atmosphere prevails here, with dark Colonial woods, brick walls, and crystal candle lanterns. At lunchtime a buffet is featured for $4.95 including salad and soup bar, hot entrees, and desserts; individual items, such as sandwiches, salads, burgers, and light entrees are also available, in the $2.95 to $6.95 bracket. Dinner entrees, priced from $9.95 to $18.95, with most choices under $15, include crab-stuffed lobster tail; seafood paella; butterflied filet mignon topped with crab imperial and jumbo shrimp; prime ribs; veal piccante; chicken

Cordon Bleu; and Peking duck. All main courses are accompanied by cheese and crackers, salad, potato, or vegetable. On Friday nights, there is also a "Seafood Feast" that costs $16.95 for a complete buffet dinner from appetizers to desserts. This restaurant has its own bakery and is well known for its pumpkin bread and sticky buns which can also be purchased "to go" (from $1).

Hours are Monday through Saturday from 11 a.m. to 2:30 p.m. for lunch, and from 5 to 10 p.m. for dinner. On Sunday, there is a "family hunt brunch" from 10 a.m. to 2 p.m., and dinner from 5 to 9 p.m. All major CC's accepted.

Another top choice in this busy area is the **Sheraton Berkshire Inn,** Route 422, Paper Mill Road Exit, Wyomissing, PA 19610 (tel. 215/376-3811 or toll-free 800/325-3535), set on a hillside with mountain views in the distance. This 15-year-old five-story property was also recently renovated and refurbished (1986), and now sports an art-deco look from its marble-tiled lobby to its rounded furniture and brass rails. Each of the 260 rooms has a contemporary pastel décor, a king, queen, or two double beds, color cable TV, a radio, air conditioning, and a direct-dial phone. Doubles range from $78 to $93. Guest facilities include an indoor heated pool, saunas, an exercise room, the Good Nites entertainment lounge, and the Green Parrot, a moderately priced restaurant serving food all day. There is also a gourmet dining room, City Limits, open only in the evening. The art-deco theme prevails here with light tones of pink, blue, mauve, and turquoise. The walls are lined with modern prints and racks of international wines, and a central swan-motif table is also an eye-catcher. Entrees are priced in the $11.95 to $21.95 bracket for such selections as ballontine of duck with veal and duck stuffing; sea bass roulade with scallop mousse; pear-shaped chicken; Chateaubriand; or steak Athenee (topped with lobster meat, tomatoes, asparagus, and green peppercorn sauce). All main courses are accompanied by potato and vegetable. Hours for City Limits are Monday to Thursday from 6 to 10 p.m., and Friday and Saturday from 6 to 11 p.m.; reservations are a must. All major CC's accepted.

Five miles east of the downtown area is the **Dutch Colony Motor Inn,** 4635 Perkiomen Ave. (Route 422), Reading, PA 19606 (tel. 215/779-2345), in a wooded country setting. Also recently renovated, this is a two- and three-story motel with a Colonial motif. Now approaching its 25th anniversary, the inn is run by the Breithaupt family who have owned this corner of Reading since 1925. Each of the 77 rooms has two double beds, a direct-dial phone, color TV, and air conditioning. A double costs from $42 to $45. Guest amenities include an outdoor swimming pool, a picnic area, a cozy lounge bar, and a unique theme restaurant, the Antique Airplane Room. As its name implies, the décor includes remnants and pictures from a bygone aviation era, such as the 1927 model Monocoupe that hangs from the ceiling. Lunch, priced from $1.95 to $4.95, features sandwiches, burgers, and platters. The dinner entrees, priced from $6.95 to $12.95, focus on prime steaks and seafood such as shrimp and scallops en casserole, or flounder stuffed with crab. Lunch is available from 11:30 a.m. to 3 p.m. and dinner from 5 to 10 p.m.; breakfast is also available from 7 a.m. to 11:30 a.m. daily, except January and February. All major CC's accepted.

WHERE TO DINE: From regional classics to budget choices, you'll enjoy sampling the offerings in Reading-area establishments.

The Top Choices

Mushrooms are the magic ingredient at **Joe's Restaurant,** 450 S. 7th St. (tel. 373-6794), at the corner of Laurel, five blocks south of Penn Avenue in the heart of downtown. This venerable restaurant was started as a tavern in the early 1900s by Jozef and Magdalena Czarnecki from Poland. In 1947 the tavern evolved into a restaurant, and it is now in the hands of the third generation of the same family, chefs Jack and Heidi Czarnecki. Open just for dinner, this elegant old-world dining room seats only 50 and is very popular with Reading residents. The menu offers a variety of beef, veal, fowl, and seafood choices, but the pièce de résistance is the hand-picked local mushroom enhancements. All kinds of the delicate fungi are used in sauces, marinades, or accompaniments: cèpes, morels, slippery jacks, woodblewits, boletus, both domestic and wild. Specialties include wild-mushroom soup; morels Marie stuffed with pheasant mousse; Prince Street duck in burgundy pepper sauce with fresh mushrooms; and wild mushrooms Cracow style, in a creamy sauce and heaped in a vol au vent. Entrees are priced from $16.50 to $24, and the service charge is 18%. Hours are Tuesday through Friday, 5:30 to 9 p.m., and Saturday from 4:30 to 9:30 p.m. All major CC's accepted.

The atmosphere of Colonial Reading permeates the **Widow Finney's,** 30 S. 4th St. at Cherry St. (tel. 378-1776), a midcity landmark that is in the National Register of Historic Places. Named for one of Reading's first residents, this gracious inn is actually three adjoining buildings: the original pine log homestead of Joseph and Sarah Finney, built around 1760; a 2½-story brick residence known as the "Heister House," circa 1810; and the West Reading Market Annex built in 1895. The four dining rooms are a showcase of brass hurricane lamps, beam ceilings, all-wood floors, and brick walls. In the summer months, guests can also dine in a paved-brick courtyard behind the log house. Lunch, priced from $3.95 to $5.95, focuses primarily on salads, omelets, sandwiches, and casseroles. Dinner entrees feature Colonial cuisine and the menu changes often, but most choices are usually in the $15.50 to $18.50 price bracket. Favorites include scallops baked in wine; salmon in leek sauce; chicken breast stuffed with crab; chicken and ham with sherried cream sauce; and veal sautéed with cream, cognac, and walnuts. The wine list offers an extensive array of Pennsylvania vintages. Lunch is served Monday through Friday from 11 a.m. to 2 p.m.; and dinner Wednesday through Saturday from 5:30 to 8 p.m. CC's accepted: AE, MC, and V.

Moderately Priced Dining

Two miles south of the city on Route 222 is **Ye Olde Ironmaster,** 1319 Lancaster Ave. (tel. 777-1886), an 18th-century farmhouse tastefully restored and turned into a tavern and restaurant. The décor is decidedly Colonial and the cuisine is traditional American. Open only for dinner, the menu features generous portions of quality meats and seafood. Entrees, priced from $7.95 to $14.95, include prime ribs, steaks, triple lamb chops, seafood platters, and chicken in puff pastry. All main courses are served with salad, potato, two vegetables, and a basket of homemade corn fritters and sticky buns. Local mushrooms, sautéed or stuffed, are also a focus here ($1.95 to $2.95), as appetizers or accompaniments. Dinner is served from 4:30 to 9:30 p.m. Tuesday through Thursday; until 10 p.m. on Friday and Saturday; and from noon to 8 p.m. on Sunday. CC's accepted: AE, MC and V.

High on Penn Hill overlooking Reading is **Stokesay Castle,** Hill Road and Spook Lane (tel. 375-4588), a replica of a 13th-century English castle. Built in 1932 as a private home by local entrepreneur George Heister, this regal edifice has been a restaurant since 1956. The building is a blend of Norman stucco turrets, Tudor wings, and stone archways on the outside, with an interior of suits of armor, crossed swords, massive oak doors, hand-carved beams, bas-relief figures on plaster ceilings, leaded windows, and electric candle chandeliers. The choice of dining rooms ranges from the splendor of the "Great Hall" to the charm of the Library or Keep Tavern. In the summer months, you can dine on a tree-shaded and canopied flagstone patio with a 20-mile view of the Reading horizon. Lunch is priced from $4.95 to $8.95 for sandwiches, burgers, quiches, crêpes, casseroles, and light entrees. Signature dishes at dinner include shrimp Sebastian (stuffed with crab imperial); frogs' legs sautéed in white wine and garlic; steak Diane; boneless breast of capon; beef Stroganoff; and kingly or queenly portions of prime ribs. Entrees are priced from $10.95 to $17.95 with most under $15, and include potato and vegetable. The restaurant is located in a posh residential section east of downtown on a well-signposted route. Hours are Monday through Saturday, noon to 3:30 p.m. for lunch; and 4 to 9:30 p.m. for dinner. On Sunday it is open from noon to 8 p.m. All major CC's accepted.

Budget Meals

Ever since 1924, **Jimmie Kramer's Peanut Bar,** 332 Penn St. (tel. 376-7373), has been a tradition in downtown Reading. Located between 3rd and 4th Streets, this friendly tavern has been in the same family for three generations. The décor is reminiscent of the 1930s with an old-time long bar, globe wall lights, and wood walls. Dishes of peanuts in their shells are on every table and patrons are encouraged to enjoy the complimentary nuts, discarding the shells like sawdust on the floor. Luncheon fare includes salads, burgers, and hot dishes, in the $2.95 to $4.95 price bracket. Dinner entrees are priced from $6.95 to $17.95, with most under $10; featured items range from seafood platters to mesquite-grilled chicken; veal chops Dijonnaise; steaks; and racks of ribs. All main courses are served with vegetable and potato. Open for lunch from 11 a.m. to 2 p.m. Monday through Thursday, and from 11 a.m. to 5 p.m. on Friday and Saturday. Dinner is available from 5 to 11 p.m. Monday through Thursday; and from 5 p.m. to midnight Friday and Saturday (open all year except for two weeks around Labor Day). CC's accepted: AE, MC, and V.

If you are looking for a good spot to eat while shopping at the downtown Reading Outlet Center, try **The Cafe,** 901 N. 8th St. (tel. 376-4022). Housed in a former shoe-factory building, this restaurant has a bright and airy décor of hanging plants, high ceilings, and brick walls lined with a collage of framed clippings and pictures that tell the history of wine-making in the area. The self-service menu offers heaping salads, overstuffed sandwiches, Oriental dishes, quiches, pastas, and cheese platters, in a $2 to $6 price range. Beer and wine are also available. Open Monday through Wednesday from 9 a.m. to 6 p.m.; Thursday through Saturday from 9 a.m. to 8 p.m.; and Sunday from noon to 5 p.m. CC's accepted: MC and V.

A favorite with families is the **Hitching Post,** 3337 Penn Ave., West Lawn (tel. 678-2495). Located about two miles west of downtown, this restaurant/cocktail lounge features authentic Greek dishes as part of its menu. Lunch, in the $1.95 to $3.95 price bracket, offers sandwiches, salads, burgers, omelets, and moussaka. Dinner entrees cost $5.95 to $10.95 for such dishes as Colorado brook trout amandine; roast turkey; Yankee pot roast; beef Stroganoff; honey-dipped chicken; Greek lamb stew in casserole; prime ribs; and steaks. All selections include two vegetables plus access to the 25-item soup-and-salad bar. Open for lunch and dinner from 11 a.m. to 10 p.m. CC's accepted: MC and V.

TOP ATTRACTIONS: The downtown core of Reading is Penn Square, originally named Market Square, the area laid out by William Penn's sons in 1748. Reading's first courthouse was located here, as were the city's original farmers' markets and commercial buildings. It was later a setting for Victorian storefronts, many of which remain today. The square is now the center of Reading's historic district, which extends along 5th Street (originally named "Callowhill" after Penn's second wife) from Buttonwood Street south to Laurel Street. A self-guided walking-tour folder of this entire district is available free from the Berks County Travel Association.

Panoramic views of Reading and the entire Schuylkill Valley can be seen from the **The Pagoda,** Duryea Drive and Skyline Boulevard (tel. 372-6060), a seven-story Japanese-style tower located on top of Mt. Penn. Listed in the National Register of Historic Places, this 610-ft. pagoda was built of red brick and tile in 1908 by local businessman William Witman and is reputed to be the only Japanese pagoda east of California. The interior includes a 1739 temple bell from Obama, Japan, and an observation deck, while the grounds boast a collection of Japanese cherry trees, a bonsai island, an Oriental bridge, and a gazebo. Open in the summer from 11 a.m. to 9 p.m. and at other times from noon to 9 p.m. Admission is 25¢ per person.

The ideal way to see the Berks County countryside north of Reading is via the **Blue Mountain and Reading Railroad,** 425 Tuckerton Rd., Temple (tel. 921-1442), two miles north of downtown. Dating back to 1885, this steam passenger railway travels a scenic route along the Schuylkill canal, through Pennsylvania Dutch farmland, from Temple station to Hamburg. The trains operate year round daily (except Monday) from Memorial Day to Labor Day, and on weekends during the rest of the year (except January). The summer schedule calls for departures from Temple at 10 a.m., noon, 2, and 4 p.m.; with runs at noon, 2 and 4 p.m. during most other times of the year. The round trip takes approximately two hours and costs $6 for adults and $4 for children.

Nine miles east of downtown Reading is the **Daniel Boone Homestead,** Daniel Boone Road, Birdsboro (tel. 582-4900), off Route 422. Dating back to 1730, this two-story stone house is the spot where the famous frontiersman was born on November 2, 1734, and lived until 1750. A collection of 18th-century farm furniture is displayed in the building, as are many items and memorabilia relating to Daniel Boone. The well-signposted grounds also include a blacksmith shop, a sawmill, barn, picnic areas, nature trails, and a winding wooded road. Open Tuesday through Saturday from 9 a.m. to 5 p.m., and Sunday from noon to 5 p.m. Admission to the grounds is free but if you wish a guided tour through the house, the fee is $1.50 for adults and 50¢ for children aged 6 to 17.

SHOPPING: Reading's outlet shopping centers are located throughout the city, in the Wyomissing area, and in other more suburban points. The merchandise can range from irregulars to first-quality, with discounts of up to 80%. Brand names run rampant across the walls, windows, and doors of every shop.

To sweeten your savings, there is no tax on clothing in Pennsylvania. The shopping season is at its height from mid-July to Thanksgiving weekend, although busy buying times really run from April right through December.

Here are some of the highlights:

The **Reading Outlet Center,** 801 N. 9th St. (tel. 373-5495), is the largest downtown outlet with four floors and 60 individual stores housed in a restored factory-mill building. You'll find such brand names as Jaeger, Pierre Cardin, London Fog, Calvin Klein, Members Only, Jonathan Logan, Polo/Ralph Lauren, Carter's, Manhattan, Munsingwear, Ship-n-Shore, Van Heusen, Fisher Price Toys, Corning Designs, and L'Eggs, Hanes, and Bali Hosiery. Open Monday through Wednesday from 9 a.m. to 6 p.m.; Thursday through Saturday from 9 a.m. to 8 p.m.; and Sunday from noon to 5 p.m. (closed major holidays and early 3 p.m. closings on Memorial Day, Labor Day, Christmas Eve, and New Year's Eve). CC's accepted: AE, MC, and V.

Nearby is the **The Big Mill,** 730 N. 8th St., at Oley Street (tel. 378-9100), a 20-outlet former shoe-factory building with three levels and two open courtyards in its center. Featured products include Adolfo Sport Collectibles, Bass shoes, Nike athletic sneakers, the Shirt Factory (Fruit of the Loom, Botany 500, B.V.D., Christian Dior), Playtex, Toy Warehouse (Mattel, Kenner, Ideal, Coleco, Milton Bradley, Hasbro, and others), pet-supply products, candy, and cookies. Open Monday through Saturday from 9:30 a.m. to 5:30 p.m. and Sunday from 11 a.m. to 4 p.m., with some late evenings. CC's accepted by most units: MC and V.

On the northern edge of the city is the **Heisters Lane Complex,** 800 Heisters Lane at Kutztown Road (tel. 921-9394). This is a 10-outlet, three-building blend of the Flemington Fashion Outlet, Designers (Gloria Vanderbilt, Christian Dior, Saville, Jones of New York), Burlington Coat, Izod, and All-in-One Linen (Fieldcrest, Cannon, Wamsutta, Martex, Springmaid, Bill Blass, Laura Ashley, and others). Open Monday through Saturday from 9:30 a.m. until 5 p.m., on Sunday from noon to 5 p.m.; some units are also open on Friday until 9 p.m. and on Saturday until 8 p.m. in the fall season and at other selected times. Some sections like Burlington Coat are open late every night except Sunday. Closed Easter, Thanksgiving, and Christmas. All vendors accept MC and V and Burlington accepts AE as well.

Among the oldest of this genre is the **VF Factory Outlet Complex,** Hill Avenue and Park Road, Wyomissing (tel. 378-0408), which opened in 1970 to sell surplus hosiery, sleepwear, and Vanity Fair lingerie. There are now 40 outlet stores housed in eight buildings. Vanity Fair is still one of the leading products, along with Lee Jeans and L. L. Bean. These three accept cash or personal checks only. Other companies featured in this complex include Masland Carpets, Windsor Shirts, Adidas footwear, Freeman Shoes, Jonathan Logan, Totes, Oneida stainless flatware, Reading China and Glass, Black and Decker, and an assortment of electronic, candy, pretzel, and toy companies, many of which accept major credit cards, such as AE, MC, and V. Open Monday through Friday from 9 a.m. to 9 p.m.; Saturday from 9 a.m. to 6 p.m.; and Sunday from noon to 5 p.m., with extended hours in the fall months.

All of the major city outlet complexes are well signposted with color-coded directional signs; they also have ample parking lots and many offer shuttle transport from your car to the outlet doors. In addition, there are a number of individual outlets and two suburban outlet complexes: the 50-unit **Manufacturers' Outlet Mall (MOM)** at Morgantown, 12 miles south of Reading on Route 176; and the new **Robesonia Outlet Center,** ten miles west of the city on Route 422. The Berks County Information Center publishes a handy (and free) map/guide to all of the major outlets.

EVENTS: Ever since 1949, one of the leading gatherings in this area has been the **Kutztown Folk Festival,** held in late June-early July at the Kutztown Fairgrounds, about 15 miles northeast of Reading on Route 222. Each year more than 100,000 people come to share in this nine-day celebration of the Pennsylvania Dutch traditions, lore, and folkways. Activities include square dancing, sheep-shearing, glassblowing, hex sign–painting, coppersmithing, ox-roasting, soap-making, kite-making, and quilting. In addition, there are demonstrations of "fraktur," the Pennsylvania Dutch style of artful writing; herb and dried flower work, and portrait painting. Sights include an Amish wedding enactment, antique shows, and crafts galore. A daylight gathering, hours are 9 a.m. to 5 p.m., with activities until 7 p.m. each day. Admission charge is $7 for adults and $3 for children under 12; parking is $2 per car. For further information, contact the **Kutztown Folk Festival,** 461 Vine Lane, Kutztown, PA 19530 (tel. 215/683-8707).

Chapter IX

HARRISBURG AND HERSHEY

1. Getting There
2. Harrisburg
3. Hershey

IN THE HEART OF SOUTH CENTRAL PENNSYLVANIA, Harrisburg and Hershey are known as capitals for different reasons. Harrisburg is, of course, the state capital, but, in many ways, Hershey is better known because it is the world capital of chocolate-making.

Just ten miles apart, Harrisburg and Hershey can easily be visited together, providing an enjoyable blend of historic and sweet experiences.

AREA CODE: Both Harrisburg and Hershey are located in the 717 telephone area code.

1. Getting There

BY PLANE: Both destinations are served by the **Harrisburg International Airport,** located at Middletown, about 15 minutes from downtown Harrisburg and 20 minutes southwest of Hershey. This airport, originally opened in 1945, now has a new $14 million terminal with all-weather jetways and expanded parking facilities. Airlines serving this facility include: **Allegheny Commuter** (tel. 238-9426 and toll-free 800/428-4253); **American** (tel. 233-5500 and toll-free 800/433-7300); **Delta** (tel. 238-1745 and toll-free 800/336-4940); **Eastern** (tel. 236-5013 and toll-free 800/327-8376); **TWA** (tel. 238-0861 and toll-free 800/221-2000); **USAir** (tel. 238-9426 and toll-free 800/428-4322); **PA Airlines** (tel. 717/944-2781); and **Henson-Piedmont** (tel. toll-free 800/368-5425).

Car rental firms with local desks at Harrisburg International include: **Avis** (tel. 944-4401); **Budget** (tel. 944-4016); **Hertz** (tel. 944-4088); and **National** (tel. 944-7671). Taxi service from the airport to Harrisburg and Hershey is provided by **Airport Limo** (tel. 944-4019); **Diamond Cab** (tel. 944-2516); **Penn Harris Taxi** (tel. 238-7377); **West Shore** (tel. 737-8294); and **Yellow Cab** (tel. 238-7252).

BY TRAIN: Amtrak operates regular daily service to Harrisburg from Philadelphia and the Northeast Corridor and via the New York-Chicago route. All trains come into the **Pennsylvania Railroad Station,** 4th and Chestnut Streets (tel. 232-3916), a recently restored facility just two blocks from the State Capitol buildings. There is a taxi stand outside for the ten-mile transfer to Hershey.

(*Note:* If you are staying at the Hershey Hotel or Lodge, complimentary transport will be provided to and from the airport or train station).

BY BUS: Harrisburg is served by **Greyhound** at 1303 N. 7th St. (tel. 232-8601), and **Capitol Trailways,** 411 Market St. (232-4251).

BY CAR: Harrisburg and Hershey are located in the middle of Pennsylvania, about 150 miles northwest of Philadelphia and 250 miles east of Pittsburgh. From east and west, Harrisburg can be reached via the Pennsylvania Turnpike; from the north and south via I-81. An approach from the south can also be made via I-83. In addition, Route 15 also runs from north to south through Harrisburg. In every case, Hershey is ten miles east of Harrisburg via Routes 322 and 422. If you are traveling from the east, it is best to get off the Pennsylvania Turnpike at exit 20 and then take Route 72 north to Route 322 which will bring you into Hershey.

2. Harrisburg

The capital of Pennsylvania since 1810, Harrisburg (pop.: 53,000) is situated in the middle of the state, almost equidistant between the two major metropolitan areas of Philadelphia and Pittsburgh.

Nestled on the shores of the Susquehanna River, this area was originally known as Louisborg, for Louis XVI. Credit for the first settlement goes to John Harris who established a trading post here in 1710; in 1733 he obtained a grant of 800 acres of land. Twenty years later, his son, John Jr., began operating a ferry across the river and he eventually laid out the town in 1785 and asked for the name change to Harrisburg. Visitors to this city today not only enjoy the results of John Harris Jr.'s efforts as a city planner, but they can also visit his house on Front St.

Although the main attraction of this city is understandably the State Capitol Complex, there are many other historic buildings of interest to visitors. From the brick-lined district of Shipoke to the original Market Square, you'll see an 18th-, 19th-, and early-20th-century blend of residential neighborhoods, townhouse streetscapes, and riverfront mansions. In addition, four historic bridges, built between 1890 and 1926, span the Susquehanna River with both pedestrian and motorway crossings.

VISITOR INFORMATION: Brochures, maps and other helpful data can be obtained from the **Harrisburg Area Chamber of Commerce,** 114 Walnut St., P.O. Box 969, Harrisburg, PA 17108 (tel. 717/232-1377). This office can also supply information about Hershey and other surrounding attractions. In addition, the headquarters for the tourism authority for the whole state of Pennsylvania is located here. You can obtain brochures about this city and everywhere else in the state by contacting or visiting the **Bureau of Travel Development,** Pennsylvania Department of Commerce, 416 Forum Building, Harrisburg, PA 17120 (tel. 717/787-5453).

GETTING AROUND HARRISBURG: Since so many of the city's hotels are located on the outskirts of the city, you will probably want to drive your car to the center of the city and park. There are three large parking garages (on Chestnut, Walnut, and Market), all within walking distance to the State Capitol and other major sights. Parking averages $2 an hour or $6 a day.

If you prefer to get around by **taxi**, call **Yellow Cab** (tel. 238-7252); **Penn-Harris Taxi** (tel. 238-7377), or **West Shore Taxi** (tel. 737-8294).

In addition, **Gray Line of Harrisburg**, 1061 S. Cameron St., (tel. 233-7673) operates a six-hour orientation bus tour from early-June through early-September, departing on Tuesdays and Thursdays at 9 a.m. The itinerary takes in the main sights of Harrisburg including a tour of the Capitol, as well as the highlights of Hershey. The price is $18 for adults and $13 for children aged 6 to 11.

WHERE TO STAY: Although many hotels and motor inns claim a Harrisburg address, the majority of properties lie outside the downtown area. Harrisburg is well served by a network of roadways, however, so that no distance is really very far. In general, Harrisburg hotels follow a pattern true of many capital cities—being heavily booked with business traffic during weekdays. Consequently, you'll find most of the normal rates quoted below to be in the expensive range. If you come here on a Friday or Saturday night, however, you'll probably be eligible for weekend packages that could mean a more moderate price level and savings of 35% to 40%. Be sure to check at the time you are booking a room.

In general, the hotels listed below are popular eating places and the focal points for nighttime entertainment. Unless otherwise indicated, the hours for lunch are 11:30 a.m. to 2 p.m. and 5 to 10 p.m. for dinner, with a slightly shorter schedule on Sundays.

The Top Choices

The **Holiday Inn Center City**, 23 S. 2nd St., Harrisburg, PA 17101 (tel. 717/234-5021 or toll-free 800/238-8000), is situated in the heart of the city at the corner of Chestnut and 2nd Streets, two blocks from the rail/bus terminal and three blocks from the capitol complex. This ten-story modern tower offers 261 rooms, recently renovated (1986) and decorated in contemporary style, offering a choice of king, queen, or double beds, as well as smoking or non-smoking rooms. Each unit has air conditioning, color TV, a radio, and a telephone. Doubles range from $85 to $105. Other facilities include an indoor pool, valet parking, an open lobby bar, and a bright and brassy restaurant called Syd's. Moderately priced American cuisine is featured, with pasta, poultry, beef, and seafood dishes priced from $9.95 to $16.95. All major CC's accepted.

Just three miles east of the City Center is the **Sheraton Harrisburg East**, 800 E. Park Dr., Harrisburg, PA 17111 (tel. 717/561-2900 or toll-free 800/325-3535). Located off I-83, exit 29, at Union Deposit Road, this is an ideal place to stay if you'll be dividing your time between Harrisburg and Hershey (nine miles farther east). Surrounded by a country-garden setting, this three-story hotel is designed around a spacious brick-lined courtyard with a skylit atrium. There are 172 modern bedrooms, each with air conditioning, a direct-dial phone, color cable TV, and a choice of double, queen, or king beds. Doubles range from $80 to $93 and suites from $125 to $150. Guest amenities include courtesy shuttle service to and from the airport, an indoor swimming pool, and a complete health club with sauna, whirlpool, and exercise program. In addition, there is the Bourbon Street Lounge with nightly entertainment and music, as well as the French Quarter Restaurant. A "southern plantation" salad buffet is featured at lunchtime as well as assorted sandwiches and light entrees in the $3.95 to $6.95 bracket. Dinner entrees focus on American cuisine with an accent on Créole cooking. Selections, priced from $6.95 to $14.95, include blackened redfish,

Cajun-fried chicken, baked Gulf shrimp, turf and bay (filet mignon and crab cake), as well as prime ribs and stir-fry dishes. All main courses are accompanied by unlimited servings at a 32-item salad bar, plus potato or vegetable. If you prefer to stay on the city's other side, there is a 197-unit sister hotel, the **Sheraton Harrisburg West** at the crossroads of I-83 and the Pennsylvania Turnpike, P.O. Box A, New Cumberland, PA 17070 (tel. 717/774-2721). All major CC's accepted.

Four miles south of downtown is the **Marriott,** 4650 Lindle Rd., Harrisburg, PA 17111 (tel. 717/564-5511 or toll-free 800/228-9290). This modern ten-story hotel is situated at the intersection of I-283 at Route 441. There are 300 rooms, each with oversized beds, air conditioning, color TV, an AM/FM radio, a push-button phone, and heat lamps. Doubles range from $95 to $105. Guest facilities include an indoor/outdoor pool, an exercise room, a sauna, a whirlpool, tennis courts, a jogging track, a game room, valet service, a gift shop, a newsstand, free parking, and a "pets allowed" policy. The Cahoots lounge provides nightly entertainment and dancing and the Penn Square Restaurant offers fine dining in a setting of miniatures and murals that depict old Harrisburg. Lunch, priced from $4.95 to $7.95, includes the usual burgers, salads, and sandwiches plus some creative choices like oysters Benedict, scallops casino, and chicken almond fettuccine. American cuisine is the focus at dinner with selections ranging from rainbow trout with cashew tarragon butter; veal and shrimp scampi; rack of lamb with Dijon crumb dressing; and baked crab in phyllo pastry with lobster sauce to steak Diane. The entree prices, $13.95 to $19.95, also bring salad, potato, and vegetable. All major CC's accepted.

A good lodging choice on the western shore of the Susquehanna is the **Penn Harris Inn,** Routes 11 and 15, P.O. Box 2653, Harrisburg, PA 17105 (tel. 717/763-7117 or toll-free 800/345-7366), located in an area known as Camp Hill. This 260-room Colonial-style motor inn is 1½ miles from the City Center, in a wooded grassy setting. The modern bedrooms have air conditioning, a direct-dial phone, color cable TV, and one or two double beds; and some rooms have mini-refrigerators. Rates for a double range from $75 to $85. Guest amenities include valet and room service, an outdoor pool, a nightclub called Sensations, a coffeeshop, and a dining room called the Harris Ferry, which serves lunch in the $2.95 to $4.95 range and dinner entrees from $8.95 to $16.95. All major CC's accepted.

Nearby is the **Quality Inn Villa Leo,** Limekiln Road and Leo Boulevard, New Cumberland, PA 17070 (tel. 717/774-1100 or toll-free 800/228-5151), five miles southwest of downtown at the juncture of I-83 and exit 18 of the Pennsylvania Turnpike. This rambling Colonial-style hotel has 106 rooms, each with two double beds, air conditioning, color cable TV, and a phone. Doubles range from $55 to $60. Other facilities include an outdoor pool, tennis courts, and a garden-style restaurant serving Italian-American cuisine. Lunch, priced from $2.95 to $5.95, includes salads, sandwiches, burgers, and pizzas. Dinner entrees range from pastas and such Italian specialties as veal parmigiana, chicken cacciatore, mussels marinara, shrimp and scallop scampi, and sausage and peppers to American favorites like steak, seafood, and Chateaubriand. The price bracket is $7.95 to $17.95 with most choices under $15; live entertainment and music are also featured on weekends. Major CC's accepted.

Budget

Midway between the City Center and the airport is the **Red Roof Inn,** 950 Eisenhower Blvd., East Harrisburg, PA 17111 (tel. 717/939-1331 or toll-free 800/848-7878). Situated on I-283 at Route 441, this two-story facility has 111 rooms, with extra-long double- or king-size beds, color TV with free movies, a telephone, and air conditioning. Some non-smoking rooms are also available and free morning coffee is provided in the lobby. Doubles range from $34.95 to $36.95. CC's accepted: AE, D, MC, and V.

As we go to press, a major hotel in this region is in the process of changing hands. For 15 years it was the **AmericanHost Inn,** at I-283 and Route 441 (tel. 717/939-7841), but it is now being transformed into a full-service Days Inn. The facilities include 300 guest rooms on three levels, indoor and outdoor pools, tennis courts, a five-hole golf course, volleyball courts, an ice-skating rink, and a dinner-theater. Check with Days Inns or the Harrisburg Chamber of Commerce for rates and an update at the time of your visit.

WHERE TO DINE: Harrisburg's restaurants, like its lodgings, are situated both downtown and in various suburbs of the city.

The Top Choices

In the heart of Harrisburg, opposite the capitol, is **Hope Station,** 606 N. Second St. (tel. 257-4480), a converted firehouse and a landmark dating back to 1871. The restaurant itself is quite new (1985) but all of the old building's charms remain—arch-headed windows, pressed tin ceilings, plaster flourishes, and a spiral staircase, plus the added touches of crisp linens, fresh flowers, and a very personable staff. Lunch, priced from $3.95 to $7.95, focuses mainly on salads, burgers, sandwiches, quiches, and omelets. A continental menu is featured at dinner with such choices as filet mignon with foie gras; frogs' legs provençal; coquilles St-Jacques; shrimp Romano; veal Oscar; and chicken florentine. The entree prices, $7.95 to $18.95, include salad, potato, and vegetable. With 48-hours' notice, a special order of beef Wellington or bouillabaisse for two can also be prepared ($19.95 a person). Lunch is served from 11 a.m. to 2:30 p.m. Monday through Friday; dinner Monday through Saturday from 5:30 to 10 p.m. A festive brunch, priced from $6.95 to $10.95, is available Sundays from 11 a.m. to 3 p.m.; the menu presents a fruit-and-cheese bar as well as such entrees as quiche, cheese soufflé, boeuf bourguignon, seafood crêpes, and eggs Benedict or "eggs Bernadette" (with filet mignon instead of ham). There is mellow jazz piano music on many nights. All major CC's accepted.

A French menu and décor prevails at **Au Jour Le Jour,** Race and Conoy Streets (tel. 236-2048), a little restaurant on the ground level of a small brick townhouse in Shipoke near the river. This is an older section of the city that is currently undergoing extensive restoration and renovation of private Federal-style homes. Brick walls, burgundy tones, and pictures of Paris dominate the inside décor of this intimate bistro. Lunch, priced from $5 to $9, concentrates on light French dishes like coq au vin, légumes au gratin, and seafood pasta salad. Dinner, in the $12.95 to $17.95 bracket, features such creations as center-cut pork loin filled with sausage, prunes, and herbs; filet of fish poached in white wine; beef au poivre; and lump crab in puff pastry. Open for lunch Monday through Friday from 11:30 a.m. to 1:30 p.m., and for dinner from 5:30 to 9 p.m.; dinner only on Saturday from 5:30 to 9 p.m. The Harrisburgers love this spot, so reservations are always imperative. Most major CC's accepted.

Moderately Priced Dining

In the center of town, near the Strawberry Square shopping complex, is the **Harris House Tavern,** 14–16 N. 3rd St. (tel. 233-0861), a favorite with government employees for the last 25 years. The décor conveys the ambience of Old Harrisburg with lots of city memorabilia mounted on the walls, plus an eclectic blend of old lampposts, stained glass, theatrical lights, dark carved wood, and oil paintings by local artists. Sandwiches, burgers, and salads are available for lunch, priced from $2 to $5. Dinner primarily features charcoal and rotisserie cooking of steaks, chicken, and seafood, in the $5.95 to $15.95 range with most items under $10, and accompanied by coleslaw or salad, apple sauce, vegetable, and potatoes. Open Monday through Saturday from 11 a.m. to 10:30 p.m. All CC's accepted.

On the western side of the river is **Casa Rillo,** 451 N. 21st St., Camp Hill (tel. 761-8617), the domain of the Rillo brothers. Located in a mostly residential neighborhood, this restaurant is surrounded by colorful gardens. The interior décor of the two dining rooms features rich ruby-red walls, baskets of flowers, and knotty-pine trim. Lunch, in the $3.95 to $7.95 bracket, focuses mostly on sandwiches, pastas, and salads (such as a huge "tuna godfather"). Dinner offers a wide array of Italian specialties such as veal with artichokes and prosciutto in cream sauce; crab and pasta; beef pizzaiola; eggplant parmigiana; and "grandma's favorite" (linguine with shrimp and marinara sauce). The entree price range is $8.95 to $17.95 and includes salad and vegetable. Lunch is served Monday through Friday from 11:30 a.m. to 4:30 p.m.; dinner on Sunday through Thursday from 5 to 10 p.m., and Friday and Saturday from 5 to 11 p.m. All major CC's accepted.

For the best view of downtown Harrisburg, take the Market Street Bridge across the Susquehanna to **Catalano's,** 461 S. Front St., Wormleysburg, (tel. 763-7905). Situated right on the water, this restaurant presents wide vistas of the city and the river from its screened-in Venetian terrace and wide-windowed dining room. Sandwiches, salads, and light entrees are served at lunchtime, priced from $2.95 to $8.95. Dinner entrees, in the $7.95 to $18.95 range, include a wide variety of fresh seafood and steaks, plus such Italian dishes as veal saltimbocca, chicken cacciatore, and lobster and chicken Alfredo. Prime rib is also featured on Thursday, Friday, and Saturday nights. All main courses are served with salad and vegetable or pasta. Open Monday through Friday for lunch and dinner from 11:30 a.m. to 10 p.m., and on Saturday from noon to 10 p.m. CC's accepted: AE, MC, and V.

Budget Meals

The music and menus of the 1950s and '60s are the focus at **Rod's Road House Café,** 1031 Eisenhower Blvd. (tel. 939-9915), a casual art-deco restaurant about five miles south of the city (near the Red Roof Inn). Classic cars are incorporated into the daily workings of this huge high-ceiling eatery. You'll see everything from a Chevrolet Impala used as a serving sideboard to a Plymouth Belvedere, as well as tableside jukeboxes. Burgers, sandwiches, and salads are on the lunch menu, priced from $3 to $5, while dinner items range from old-fashioned baked meatloaf and chicken pot pie to honey-dipped chicken and steaks ($6 to $9.50). Open from 11 a.m. to 3 p.m. for lunch and from 5 to 10 p.m. for dinner. The music plays on till 2 a.m. Major CC's accepted.

THE TOP ATTRACTIONS: As the capital of Pennsylvania, Harrisburg naturally revolves around the **State Capitol Complex,** a 65-acre area in the heart of the city, including executive, legislative, and judicial government buildings, as well as archives, a museum, a library, and a concert hall. The focal point is the **Main Capitol Building,** 3rd and State Streets (tel. 787-6810). Constructed in 1906, this is a grand Italian Renaissance edifice with a dome styled after St. Peter's Basilica in Rome and the staircase after the Paris Grand Opera House. It is open to the public for tours Monday through Saturday from 9 a.m. to 4 p.m. (hourly except noon), free of charge.

Also part of this complex is **The State Museum of Pennsylvania,** 3rd and North Streets (tel. 787-4978). Established in 1905 and also known as the William Penn Memorial Museum, this is the official museum of the Commonwealth of Pennsylvania. Moved to its present location in 1965, this six-story circular building is the home of the original charter granted to William Penn by King Charles II in 1681 as well as exhibits on the state's archaeology, decorative arts, fine arts, geology, military history, natural science, science, industry, and technology. There is also a planetarium, a café, and a very intriguing museum shop. Open Tuesday through Saturday from 9 a.m. to 5 p.m. and Sunday from noon to 5 p.m. Admission is free, except for a 50¢ charge to planetarium shows on Saturday and Sunday at 1:30 p.m. and 3 p.m.

A short drive away is the **Governor's Home,** 2035 N. Front St., at Maclay Street (tel. 787-1192). Completed in 1968, this Georgian Revival residence is the third official executive mansion to have been located in Harrisburg. Exhibits include displays of Pennsylvania crafts, local art, and an outside garden planted with trees and shrubs native to the state. Tours are given April through October, on Tuesday and Thursday from 10 a.m. to 2 p.m. Admission is free.

Another house worth seeing is the **John Harris Mansion,** 219 S. Front St. between Mary and Washington Streets (tel. 233-3462), built in 1766 by Harrisburg's founder, John Harris Jr. Listed in the National Register of Historic Places, this riverfront building contains a museum that reflects Harrisburg's early days, plus a reference library and the offices of the local county historical society. Tours are given Monday through Thursday from noon to 4 p.m. and the library is open on the same days from 1 to 4 p.m. No admission is charged but donations are accepted.

Harrisburg is also home to the **Museum of Scientific Discovery,** 3rd and Walnut Streets (tel. 233-7969), a unique "hands-on" museum designed for the scientifically curious of all ages. Located on the third floor of the Strawberry Square shopping complex, there are more than 50 exhibits which encourage visitors to send a whisper, freeze a shadow, feel a calorie, shoot a laser, and many other feats. Open Tuesday through Saturday from 10 a.m. to 5 p.m., and on Sunday from noon to 5 p.m. Admission is $2.50 for adults and $1.75 for students aged 4 to 18.

Harrisburg through the centuries is reflected at the **Ft. Hunter Mansion,** 5300 N. Front St. (tel. 599-5751 or 255-1369). Located six miles north of the city overlooking the Susquehanna River, this spot was originally settled in 1725, and, through the years, took on a number of functions, from a prosperous milling center, military fort, dairy farm, frontier village, and distillery to a private estate. The central house, listed in the National Register of Historic Places, is a testament to two centuries of Pennsylvania living with furnishings of early-American, Empire, and Victorian styles. The grounds, dotted with buttonwood trees dating back to William Penn's time and herb gardens, also include two historic barns, an icehouse, a tavern, a springhouse, and a blacksmith shop. Open from May through December, Monday through Saturday from 10 a.m. to 4:30 p.m. and on Sunday from noon to 4:30 p.m. Admission fees, which include tours by trained guides, are $2 for adults and $1 for children over 6.

NIGHTLIFE: Harrisburg's performing arts are centered at **The Forum,** 5th and Walnut Streets (tel. 787-6196), part of the capitol complex. Housed in the Forum Building, this 1,800-seat theater is an attraction in itself, with marble walls and columns, maps of nations and a remarkable astrological ceiling. It is the home of the Harrisburg Symphony Orchestra and the venue for a varied year-round program of concerts, opera, ballet, jazz, and other musical recitals. Most tickets average $12 to $20, and performances are usually at 8 p.m. CC's accepted: MC and V.

Tickets to the Forum and to all types of other cultural and sporting events in the Harrisburg-Hershey region can be purchased at **Ticketplace,** on the first floor of Strawberry Square, 3rd and Walnut Streets (tel. 236-0483), a one-stop central box office. Open Monday through Wednesday from 11 a.m. to 4 p.m.; Thursday and Friday from 11 a.m. to 6 p.m.; and Saturday from 1 to 4 p.m. All CC's accepted.

SHOPPING: Much of Harrisburg's shopping activity is now focused on Strawberry Square, 3rd and Walnut Streets, a block of renovated buildings transformed into a three-story midtown mall. Housing more than 50 specialty shops and ethnic food nooks, this trendy enclave was built in 1977, and was the first phase of a major downtown revitalization project. Currently being enlarged to include an adjacent block of 11 more historic structures (and more new shops and restaurants), this complex is located across the street from the State Capitol. Open Monday through Friday from 10 a.m. to 6 p.m., and on Saturday from 10 a.m. to 5 p.m.

Harrisburg also boasts one of the oldest continuously operating (since 1860) farmers' market houses in Pennsylvania, the Broad Street Market, at 3rd and Verbeke Streets. Restored in 1976 with new landscaping and a central brick plaza, this market is a great source for fresh farm produce, snacks, home-baked goods, gifts, and local crafts. Open Thursday and Friday from 7 a.m. to 6 p.m. and on Saturday from 7 a.m. to 4 p.m.

SPORTS AND ACTIVITIES: If you're looking for a good place to jog, walk, or bike, try a sojourn to Riverfront Park, which runs along the city's eastern edge at Front Street. Developed from 1902 to 1930, this open park is the focus of Harrisburg's "City Beautiful" movement. It contains trails and pathways extending for five miles along the Susquehanna River, from the historic district of Shipoke on the south side to the city line in the north.

From Riverfront Park it is just a walk (via Walnut St. Bridge) or a drive (via Market Street Bridge) over the Susquehanna to City Island. This floating midriver island contains 64 acres of parkland with a public beach, picnic sites, and an excellent view of the Harrisburg skyline.

Six miles north of downtown is **Fort Hunter Park,** 5300 N. Front St. (tel. 255-2711), a 37-acre grassy knoll along the Susquehanna River with picnic tables, riverside walking trails, a comfort station, and lighted walkways. All facilities are available free of charge, on a first-come basis.

Horse Racing: Fifteen miles northeast of Harrisburg is the **Penn National Race Course,** exit 28 off I-81, Grantville (tel. 469-2211). A setting for thoroughbred horse racing, this track is about five miles from Hershey. Racing is scheduled daily from mid-February to mid-December (except Tuesday and Thursday). Post time is 7:30 p.m. on weekdays and 1:30 p.m. on Sundays and holidays. Admission is $1.50 to the grandstand and $2.50 for the clubhouse reserved seating. Parking is $1.

3. Hershey

It is not hard to tell you've arrived in Hershey—the sweet aroma of chocolate is in the air, street lights are in the shape of candy kisses, and thoroughfares are named "Chocolate Avenue" and "Cocoa Avenue." At every turn, you are welcomed to the "Chocolate Crossroads of the World"; even huge bayberry bushes are meticulously shaped to spell out the words "Hershey Cocoa." Yes, it helps if you have a sweet tooth, but, even if you don't, a visit to Hershey is bound to please vacationers of every age and taste.

Although this area was originally settled in the early 1700s, Hershey today owes both its name and its success as a "chocolate capital" to Milton S. Hershey. He not only started a chocolate factory here in 1903, but he also planned and built the surrounding community and resort.

Located 12 miles east of Harrisburg, Hershey (pop: 18,000) is still widely recognized for the production of chocolate (the huge silos at the chocolate factory in the center of town hold more than 90 million pounds of cocoa beans)—but, thanks to Milton Hershey, it is also a major complex of visitor attractions—from Hersheypark and Hershey Gardens to the Hershey Theatre, the Hershey Arena, and the Hershey Museum of American Life. You can even learn how candy is made at "Chocolate World," a see-and-smell museum that illustrates the whole process, in various stages, from the cocoa bean to the chocolate bar.

GETTING AROUND: When we first looked at Hershey on the map, we thought it would be easy to walk from attraction to attraction and hotel to hotel. But, in reality, that's not quite so. Hershey is spread out over several miles, with the grand old Hotel Hershey and the Hershey Gardens set high on a hilltop overlooking the rest of the town, and the Hershey Lodge is on lower ground at the west edge of town. Most of the other motels are concentrated on **Chocolate Avenue** (Route 422), east or west of the downtown area. The Hersheypark attractions, however, are all grouped together and are adjacent to the Visitors Center, the arena, the stadium, and Chocolate World. Founders Hall, the Hershey Theatre, the Country Club and Parkview golf courses, and the main downtown area are all a short drive away from the hotels or the main entrance to Hersheypark.

In the summer months, a free Hershey Shuttle bus stops at the following locations: Hotel Hershey, the Hershey Lodge, Hershey Highmeadow Camp, Zoo America, Hershey Gardens, and Tram Circle at Hersheypark. The bus runs on the hour between 9 a.m. and 10 p.m. When Hersheypark is closed during the off-season months, the Hersheypark monorail serves as a swift and scenic link between the park attractions and downtown (the fare is $1.50 round-trip or 75¢ one-way). The monorail runs every 15 minutes. If you prefer a **taxi,** local service is provided by **Diamond S. Cabs** (tel. 939-7805) and **Penn Harris Cabs** (tel. 238-7377).

VISITOR INFORMATION: The best place to contact before or during your stay is the **Hershey Visitors Center,** 400 West Hersheypark Drive, Hershey, PA 17033 (tel. 717/534-3005). Staffed by helpful Hershey representatives, this office is located at the main entrance to the amusement park and is well stocked with brochures, maps, and lists of events. To assist you in driving around the area, you can also purchase cassette tape auto tours at this office ($5.95).

WHERE TO STAY: A Hershey chocolate bar to greet you at check-in or chocolate candy kisses on your pillow at night—these are just two of the special touches that sweeten an overnight visit in Hershey. Of course, most people who come to Hershey want to stay at either the old world Hotel Hershey or the modern Hershey Lodge. The hotel is a traditional resort in the grandest style and is most suitable for couples or families with older children. The sprawling lodge, with its movie theater and trio of restaurants, is ideal for families with younger children (room service will even deliver pizza). The rates quoted below are for the peak summer months. If you can travel in the spring, fall, or winter, you'll find that prices are lower and at many times of the year special reduced-rate packages are also in effect. Be sure to check what the best deal will be during the time of year you wish to visit—you could save yourself up to 50%.

Ever since 1933, "the place" to stay in this town has been **The Hotel Her-**

shey, P.O. Box BB, Hershey, PA 17033 (tel. 717/533-2171 or toll-free 800/533-3131), a complete year-round resort set on a 90-acre hilltop wooded estate. Styled after the 19th-century grand villas of the Mediterranean, this palatial five-story property is a showcase of splendid fountains, lavish interiors, exotic sculpture, and magnificent greenery; plus an award-winning circular dining room with tile floors and stained-glass windows overlooking the gardens. The 250 guest rooms have either double-, twin-, or queen-size beds, color cable TV, a direct-dial phone, air conditioning, and a tiled bathroom that feature bars of cocoa-butter soap; the décors range from old world elegance to contemporary designer styles, depending if you are in the old section or the new wings. Non-smoking rooms are available and guest activities include indoor and outdoor pools, saunas, whirlpools, shuffleboard, table tennis, croquet, tennis courts, golf, horseback riding, lawn bowling, hiking, and bicycling. Rates are based on full American plan (three meals a day) and start at $105 per person per day; modified American plan (breakfast and dinner) starts at $98 per person.

Because the hotel is operated on a resort basis, the dining room caters mainly to hotel guests, although you can dine here if you are not registered, providing there is space. Lunch consists of a very attractive buffet or a choice of salads and sandwiches; if purchased separately, the price range is $3.95 to $6.95. The dinner menu changes each day, but usually includes such items as shrimp, scallop and lobster sauté; steamed breast of chicken nouvelle cuisine; sirloin of beef, or leg of lamb. Soup, appetizer, salad, two vegetables, and dessert all come with the main course. If you are not on the meal plan, the basic price is $24, although some choices require a slight supplement. Meal hours are from 7 to 9:30 a.m. for breakfast, from noon to 2 p.m. for lunch, and from 6 to 8:30 p.m. for dinner (two seatings). Jackets are required for men and similar dressy attire for women. The hotel also offers a sandwich shop and an Iberian-style lounge for drinks and evening entertainment. All major CC's accepted.

A relative newcomer, **The Hershey Lodge and Convention Center,** West Chocolate Avenue and University Drive, P.O. Box V, Hershey, PA 17033 (tel. 717/533-3311 or toll-free 800/533-3131), is just 20 years old. It is a large (460 rooms) and sprawling complex, with a combination of Colonial and ranch-style design, built over 30 acres. The bedrooms are modern with a choice of double-, queen-, or king-size beds, smoking or non-smoking interiors, and the usual color cable TV, direct-dial phone, and air conditioning. Guest facilities include indoor and outdoor pools, a sauna, a whirlpool, lighted tennis courts, platform tennis, golf, and two lounges with evening entertainment. Doubles, without meals, range from $98 to $105.

The lodge also offers three restaurants in various price categories. An ideal choice for families is the Copper Kettle, open from 7 a.m. to 10 p.m. daily. Sandwiches and burgers in the $1.95 to $4.95 bracket are featured at lunchtime. Hot entrees for dinner range from $6.95 to $10.95 for such choices as honey-dipped fried chicken, broiled flounder, steak, or a Pennsylvania Dutch dinner (chicken pot pie or ham and green beans). All entrees include soup, salad bar, and potato. The moderately priced Hearth Restaurant offers lunchtime fare and fitness cuisine in the $2.95 to $5.95 price range. The dinner menu, which features "all the steamed shrimp you can eat" and a sumptuous soup-and-salad bar with each entree, is priced in the $12.95 to $17.95 range. The choices include such international dishes as Wiener schnitzel, chicken parmigiana, and Swiss steak. The main course price also includes two vegetables, a beverage, and dessert. Meal hours are 7 a.m. to 11 a.m. for breakfast, 11:30 a.m. to 2 p.m. for lunch, and 5 to 9 p.m. for dinner.

The posh Tack Room, decorated in an equestrian motif with racing silks, saddles, and harnesses, serves lunch in the $4.95 to $9.95 bracket. Choices include seafood platters, salads, and unique sandwiches (the bacon, oyster, and asparagus is a tasty treat). Dinner entrees, from $10.95 to $27.95, focus primarily on steaks and seafood, and such dishes as "surf-and-turf" or "rack-and-tack" (lamb chop and petit filet) and mesquite-broiled chicken. A featured cold dish is "harvest of the sea" (crab Louis, Gulf shrimp, and brook trout with caviar). All entrees are accompanied by salad, potato, or rice. This is also the ideal place to try Hershey creamy cocoa pudding or chocolate cream pie, layer cake, or ice cream ($1 to $3). Lunch is served from 11:30 a.m. to 2 p.m. and dinner from 5:30 to 10 p.m., with service until 11 p.m. on Friday and Saturday nights. A brunch buffet, priced at $9.95, is also served from 10:30 a.m. to 1:30 p.m. on Sunday. All major CC's accepted throughout the lodge and all of its restaurants.

In addition to the main hotel and lodge, Hershey also has a number of good motor inns and motels, located mostly along Route 422 (also known locally as Chocolate Avenue), on the east and west sides of the town of Hershey. The rates quoted below are for the peak summer period; bear in mind that prices can be as much as 25% to 50% less in the spring, fall, and winter months.

The **Best Western Inn,** Route 422 and Sipe Avenue, P.O. Box 364, Hershey, PA 17033 (tel. 717/533-5665 or toll-free 800/528-1234), is located just off Chocolate Avenue and is close to both Hersheypark and the center of town. It's a modern two-story brick facility with 122 rooms, each with two double beds or a king bed, color cable TV, a direct-dial phone, and air conditioning; some non-smoking rooms are also available. Guests here can also enjoy free movies, a complimentary continental breakfast, and adult and children's outdoor swimming pools. Doubles range from $70 to $100. All major CC's accepted.

About 1½ miles east of the town center is the **White Rose Motel,** 1060 E. Chocolate Ave., Hershey, PA 17033 (tel. 717/533-9876). Surrounded by flower gardens and lots of plants, this extremely well-kept family-run facility started small in 1962 and was expanded in 1972 and 1986; it now has 24 units with a Colonial décor including stencil-design on the walls and cocoa-bark accessories. The rooms all have two double beds, color cable TV, air conditioning, and free in-room coffee and tea; many of the upper-level rooms have balconies. Guest facilities include an outdoor heated pool and patio and an American country crafts shop. Rates for doubles range from $60 to $75. CC's accepted: AE, MC, and V.

Just across the street is **The Fairway,** 1043 E. Chocolate Ave., Hershey, PA 17033 (tel. 717/533-5179), a modern motel overlooking the greens of the Hershey Country Club. This two-story brick building has also been recently expanded (1986) and now offers 26 units, many with balconies and neatly kept flowerboxes under the windows. Each room has two double beds, color cable TV, a direct-dial phone, and air conditioning; non-smoking rooms are available. Other guest facilities include complimentary coffee and hot chocolate, a heated outdoor swimming pool and patio, and well-landscaped gardens. Doubles range from $65 to $75. CC's accepted: AE, MC, and V.

About a mile farther east of town is the **Milton Motel,** 1733 E. Chocolate Ave., Hershey, PA 17033 (tel. 717/533-4533). Open 15 years ago, this modern two-story building has 30 units, each with one or two double beds, air conditioning, color cable TV, and a phone. There are some non-smoking rooms and upper-level units have balconies. Guest amenities include a heated swimming pool, a picnic and play area, and a game room. Doubles range from $65 to $78. CC's accepted: AE, MC, and V.

Directly across the street is the **Chocolatetown Motel,** 1806 E. Chocolate Ave., Hershey, PA 17033 (tel. 717/533-2330), in a rural setting beside a cornfield. This two-story property has a Colonial brick façade with chocolate-colored doors. Open from March through October only, the 24 units are each equipped with one or two double beds, air conditioning, and color cable TV. There is also a heated outdoor pool. Doubles range from $60 to $75. CC's accepted: MC and V.

WHERE TO DINE: In addition to the Hotel Hershey and the Hershey Lodge, this area has two very fine restaurants, both located east of town along Route 422 (Chocolate Avenue).

The Top Choices

For over 50 years, **Hobart's,** 814 E. Chocolate Ave. (tel. 533-7450) has been a dining tradition in the Hershey area. Guests are welcomed to this country home setting by vivacious Patricia Umberger while her chef-husband Hobart supervises the kitchen. The elegant décor includes bouquets of fresh flowers and walls lined with original oil paintings. Opened for dinner only, Hobart's is a place for a relaxing evening. With all entrees individually prepared, the menu concentrates on a limited number of top-quality choices, such as West Coast salmon; Maryland blue crab; baby flounder with lump crabmeat; veal medallions Oscar; tournedos of beef, and double-cut lamb chops. The price of each main course, from $13.95 to $19.95, includes appropriate fresh vegetables and salad. Proper attire is required and reservations are a must; it is not really suitable for young children. Open from 5:30 to 11 p.m. (except Sundays, the first week in January, and the first week in July). CC's accepted: AE, MC, and V.

Another longtime favorite in this area is **Spinners Inn Restaurant,** 845 E. Chocolate Ave. (tel. 533-9050), opened in 1947 by Zurich-born William Spinner, who had previously been the head chef at the Hotel Hershey. Today this Colonial-style restaurant is in the hands of son Joe who carries on the tradition of fine continental cuisine. Open only for dinner, the menu features such dishes as crab-stuffed flounder; sweetbreads sautéed on ham; roast leg of lamb; calves' liver sauté; a variety of veal and steak selections; and daily specials of seafood and chicken. The prices range from $9.95 to $18.95 and include salad and vegetables. The hours are Tuesday through Saturday from 5 to 10 p.m. Although it is known primarily for its gourmet restaurant, Spinners also has a first-rate 52-unit **motel** on its grounds (direct line: 717/533-9157). Rates for a double range from $50 to $70. All major CC's accepted at the restaurant and the inn.

For Light Meals

No visit to Hershey is really complete without an ice-cream sundae topped with chocolate kisses and chocolate sauce at the soda fountain of the landmark **Hershey Drug Store,** One Chocolate Ave. (tel. 534-3255), right in the heart of town. Ice-cream sundaes of all types are the specialty here but you can also get a variety of freshly made salads and sandwiches, all in the $1.50 to $2.95 price bracket. Open from 9 a.m. to 9 p.m. in the summer, with shorter hours in the off-season.

THE TOP ATTRACTIONS: The center of attention is **Hersheypark** (tel. 534-3900), an amusement and theme park situated on 81 landscaped and tree-filled acres in the heart of Hershey. Originally established in 1907 (the same year that candy kisses were first manufactured), it started as a picnic and pleasure ground for Hershey employees and gradually evolved into a giant wonderland for people from all parts of the world. Often called America's "cleanest and greenest" theme park, Hersheypark has more than three dozen rides, a monorail, five theaters, eight theme areas, six restaurants, and more than 50 fast-food and snack locations. Visitors can get a sky-high overview of the park by entering a 330-foot tower with candy-kiss-shaped windows that serves as an observation-style ride. An all-inclusive one-price admission ($15.75 for adults and $12.75 for children aged 4 to 8) entitles you to all attractions and rides (except paddleboats and miniature golf), live performances, and ZooAmerica. Open daily from late May through August and then weekends until early October, from 10:30 a.m. to 10 p.m. (except certain evenings when the park closes at 6 or 8 p.m.). Most major CC's accepted.

Hershey Museum of American Life (tel. 534-3439) is an entertaining and educational look at America, including exhibits on Pennsylvania German life in the early 1800s, Indian and Eskimo galleries, and the story of Milton Hershey, "The Man Behind the Chocolate Bar." You'll also see a unique animated Apostolic clock, and collections of early photographs, musical instruments, and music boxes. Open year round from 10 a.m. to 5 p.m. and until 6 p.m. from Memorial Day through Labor Day (except Thanksgiving, Christmas, and New Year's Day). Admission charges are $3 for adults $1.25 for children aged 4 to 18, and free for children 3 and under.

Hershey Gardens (tel. 534-3492) established in 1936, started out as a three-acre rose garden and has grown today into a 23-acre botanical oasis including 15,000 roses, 50,000 tulips, 12,000 annuals, and hundreds of rare trees, vines, and shrubs. To help you appreciate just what you are seeing, all the trees and plants are identified with small plaques. The award-winning collection of roses is particularly fascinating because many species are named after famous people or places (from John F. Kennedy and Dolly Parton to the Blue Nile and Las Vegas). Open daily April through December from 9 a.m. to 5 p.m. and until 7 p.m. from Memorial Day through Labor Day. Garden highlights tours are conducted throughout the summer season at 10 a.m., 11 a.m., 1:30, and 2:30 p.m., and musical concerts are featured during summer evenings. Admission charges are $3 for adults, $1 for children from 4 to 18, and free for children 3 and under.

ZooAmerica, North American Wildlife Park (tel. 534-3860), is a ten-acre educational walk-through zoo. Opened in 1978, this park is home to more than 200 animals, ranging from bison and bears to elk and eagles. The animals thrive in natural settings, created to duplicate their own habitat from all parts of North America. Open daily year round from 10 a.m. to dusk (except on Thanksgiving, Christmas, and New Year's Day). Admission charges are $3 for adults, $1.75 for children aged 4 to 8, and free for 3 and under.

Since visitors are no longer permitted at the Hershey Chocolate factory, the next best thing is **Hershey's Chocolate World** (tel. 534-4927). This Disney-style visitor's center of the Hershey Food Corporation presents the story of chocolate via an automated ride through various settings ranging from tropical plantations to the manufacturing and candy-wrapping processes. More than 16 million people have savored this sweet tour since the facility opened in 1973. Chocolate souvenirs and chocolate-related crafts are also for sale at the end of the tour. Open daily from 9 a.m. to 4:45 p.m., except closed on Sunday mornings, Thanksgiving, Christmas, and New Year's Day. Admission is free.

Founders Hall, with its impressive dome (the largest unsupported dome in the Western Hemisphere and second in the world only to St. Peter's in Rome), is the visitor's center and the hub of the Milton Hershey School, founded by the entrepreneur of the chocolate world to provide a home and tuition-free education for 1,200 children. A short film and walk-through displays tell the story of the legendary school that had its beginnings in its founder's home. Open Monday through Friday from 9 a.m. to 4 p.m. and Saturday and Sunday from 10 a.m. to 3 p.m. Admission is free.

NIGHTLIFE: Top-name entertainers and attractions such as the Ice Capades appear regularly at the Hershey Arena, a 10,000-seat facility at Hersheypark. Opened in 1936, this hall is also home to the Hershey Bears hockey team. The adjacent Hersheypark Stadium, with a capacity for 17,000 spectators, is the setting for professional wrestling; high school, college, and all-star football; drum and bugle competitions; and outdoor concerts. Tickets to all such events are available at **The Hersheypark Arena and Stadium Box Office,** 100 W. Hersheypark Drive (tel. 534-3911). Box office hours: Monday through Friday from 9 a.m. to 6 p.m. and Saturday from 9 a.m. to 5 p.m. Shows and games are usually at 7:30 p.m. and tickets are priced from $8 to $16 depending on the event. CC's accepted: MC and V.

The **Hershey Theatre,** East Caracas Avenue (tel. 534-3405), is a magnificent old-world theater of arched ceilings and gilded trim, located in the downtown Hershey area. The program here features a wide range of entertainment from classic films to Broadway Shows, the Vienna Boys Choir, and the Sistine Chapel Choir. The *Nutcracker* is a tradition in mid-December. The box office is open Monday through Friday from 10 a.m. to 5 p.m. and immediately before showtimes. Film prices are $3.50 for adults and $2 for children; tickets to live performances average from $10 to $20, depending on the event. Most major CC's accepted.

The **Hershey Lodge Cinema** (tel. 533-5610) features an ever-changing program of current family-oriented movies, with shows each evening at 7 and 9 p.m. and matinees on many Sunday afternoons at 2 p.m. The charge is $3.50 for adults and $2.50 for children 12 and under.

SPORTS AND ACTIVITIES: Hershey is known as the "golf capital" of Pennsylvania, with 72 holes of golf all in a small radius. Here is a run-down of the facilities and applicable charges:
- **Hershey Country Club** (tel. 533-2464), two nationally acclaimed 18-hole courses, with greens fees ranging from $20 to $25 on weekdays and $22 to $30 on weekends; electric cart fees are $21 at both courses and club rental is $8.
- The **Hotel Hershey**'s nine-hole course (tel. 533-2171, ext. 2223) charges $9 for greens fees on weekdays and $10 on weekends; with a cart fee of $8 per nine holes; club rental is also $8.
- The 18-hole **Parkview Course** (tel. 534-3450) has a greens fee price of $11 on weekdays and $13 on weekends; cart fees are $16 for 18 holes or $8 for nine holes; clubs are $8 per day.
- **Spring Creek** is a nine-hole course (tel. 533-2847) that charges $6 for greens fees on weekdays and $7 on weekends; cart fees are $10 for 18 holes or $5 for nine holes.

Horseback Riding: The **Hotel Hershey Riding Stables** (tel. 534-1928) provide public horseback-riding facilities amid miles of wooded trails surrounding the Hotel Hershey. Riding fees are $10 per half-hour and $15 per hour; lessons are also available from $15 for group instruction or $20 for private tutorage. Horse-drawn carriage rides can also be arranged around the Hotel Hershey grounds, at $8 per adult and $6 for children. Open from 8 a.m. to 1 p.m. and from 3 to 8 p.m. from Memorial Day through Labor Day; and from 10 a.m. to 5 p.m. in the fall, winter, and spring months. CC's accepted: Ch, MC, and V.

Camping: Hershey **Highmeadow Camp,** 300 Park Blvd., P.O. Box 860, Hershey, PA 17033 (tel. 566-0902), welcomes year-round campers to 260 sites on 55 acres of open and shaded rolling terrain, two miles from Hersheypark. Facilities are provided for tents, campers, trailers, and motor homes, plus cabin rentals, two swimming pools, a game room, a laundromat, a grocery and supply store, and a free shuttle to Hershey attractions. Rates with hook-up, electric, water, and sewer start at about $20 a day or $115 per week. Cabin rentals are available from $24 a day (for four persons).

EVENTS: Without a doubt, Hershey is the ideal venue for the annual **Great American Chocolate Festival.** Ever since 1983, this "one sweet weekend" has been held in mid-February, a delight to chocolate enthusiasts of all ages. Chocolate events include "the ultimate chocolate meal," a "chocolate blast-from-the-past" '50s hop, a chocolate fashion show, and chocolate trivia. Both the Hotel Hershey and the Hershey Lodge have special packages for this festival; for further information write to the individual hotels or call toll free 800/533-3311.

HersheyArts is a fine arts-and-crafts festival that takes place on the third weekend in September in the horticultural haven known as Hershey Gardens. The festival program, which runs from 9 a.m. to dusk on Saturday and until 5 p.m. on Sunday, includes traditional instrumentalists, wandering street entertainers, puppeteers, folk and jazz performers, and exhibits of one-of-a-kind originals in ceramics, textiles, metals, sculpture, glass, photography, painting, prints, and drawings. Admission charge is $3 for adults and $1 for children aged 4 to 18. For more information and a complete program, call 717/534-3492.

Christmas at Hershey, which extends from late November through December, is a winter wonderland setting of madrigal dinners, choral concerts, breakfasts with Santa Claus, magic shows, traditional carriage rides, caroling, ice-carving demonstrations, Christmas light tours, puppet shows, flute music, animated holiday characters performing in village shop windows, old-time toy trains chugging through winter scenes, candlelight ceremonies, and all the usual Hersheypark attractions, many opened with extended hours. For a brochure and more information call toll-free 800/533-3131.

CHILDREN'S CORNER: In addition to the many attractions for all ages at Hershey, this area is also the home of **Indian Echo Caverns,** off U.S. Route 322 at Hummelstown, (tel. 566-8131). Situated just three miles west of Hersheypark, this underground wonder is full of massive pillars, pipes, and cascades of stone. Once the preserve of the Susquehannock Indians, these caves have been opened to visitors since 1783, but it is only in the last century that the natural paths have been enhanced with electric lights and walkways for visitor safety. Facilities include a Trading Post shop, playgrounds, and picnic areas. Open from April through October, the hours are daily from 10 a.m. to 4 p.m. (except from Memorial Day to Labor Day when the schedule is 9 a.m. to 6 p.m.). Admission price is $4 for visitors over 12 years of age, $2 for children aged 5 to 11, and free for younger children.

Chapter X

GETTYSBURG AND YORK

1. Gettysburg
2. York

THE FOCUS OF HISTORY makes Gettysburg and York two of Pennsylvania's most significant attractions. Located in the middle of the state, near the southern edge, these relatively small places both played major roles in Pennsylvania and U.S. history.

Gettysburg, the scene of the mightiest battle of the Civil War, was also the setting of President Abraham Lincoln's long-lived and oft-quoted Gettysburg Address. A century earlier, York had its heyday as our nation's capital during the days when the United States of America was first taking shape as a legal entity.

Today these two destinations have built thriving tourist industries around the events of the past. A visit to both of them will not only give you an insight into the 18th and 19th centuries, but will also offer a medley of fine lodging, dining, and sightseeing experiences.

AREA CODE: The area code for all telephone numbers in the Gettysburg and York regions is 717.

1. Gettysburg

Everyone who has ever recited "Four score and seven years ago . . ." knows of Gettysburg. Each year hundreds of thousands of Americans flock here to see the spot that inspired the speech.

They come to see the place where President Lincoln stood as he delivered his history-making "Gettysburg Address" on November 19, 1863. Thanks to a well-organized tourist industry, they can also see a draft of the speech in the president's own handwriting, visit the room where he stayed as he penned the final words, hear his voice reciting the words. . . .

But Abraham Lincoln's speech is only half of the Gettysburg story. Why Lincoln ever came here at all, and the reason there ever was a need for a Gettysburg address, is because of the major Civil War encounter that took place on the soil here in July of 1863. The bloodiest battle of the war and one of the most decisive in history, this encounter claimed 51,000 casualties. Five months after it was over, Lincoln arrived here to dedicate the cemetery and to offer some words of consolation and hope for the future.

Today's visitors to Gettysburg can tour the historic battlefield and walk the hollowed ground. They can also see the Battle of Gettysburg re-enacted through a variety of media, from wax figures and dioramas to films, revolving artwork, and sound-and-light shows. No one can come away without a better understanding of what happened here. History lives at Gettysburg.

A small town (pop.: 7,000) surrounded by apple orchards on the Pennsylvania-Maryland border, Gettysburg has indeed been thrust into the tourism industry by history's events. Although the late 1800s are the focus of much of Gettysburg's lore, the town itself dates back to the early 1700s, when Samuel Gettys acquired 381 acres of land from the descendents of William Penn and opened a tavern. It was his son, James, who eventually had the town lots drawn up and named the area Gettysburg.

In this century, the town's most famous resident has been former President Eisenhower who chose a peaceful corner of Gettysburg farmland as his retirement home.

VISITOR INFORMATION: Brochures, hotel and restaurant guides, schedules of festivals, walking tour leaflets, and other information are available from the **Gettysburg Travel Council,** 35 Carlisle St., Gettysburg, PA 17325 (tel. 717/334-6274). This office is housed in the former Western Maryland Railway Station, built in 1858 and the depot where President Lincoln arrived in town prior to his historic Gettysburg address.

The ideal starting point for most Gettysburg sightseeing activities is either this office or the visitor center of the Gettysburg National Military Park, on Route 134 just south of the downtown area.

GETTING TO GETTYSBURG: Situated in the central part of the state, Gettysburg is on the southern rim, less than ten miles from the Maryland border. From the east or west, Route 30 will lead you right into the heart of Gettysburg; from the north or south, Route 15 crosses the town. The nearest airport is **Harrisburg International,** about 45 miles northwest of Gettysburg. Bus service into the town is provided by Greyhound and Trailways, which both pull into the town's **bus depot** on North Stratton Street (tel. 334-7064). If you need a taxi to get to your hotel or motel, call **Gettysburg Cab** (tel. 334-1177).

GETTING AROUND GETTYSBURG: You'll want to know about tours to see the Gettysburg sights—bus tours, car tours, walking tours, train tours, and helicopter tours.

Bus Tours: Two-hour narrated sightseeing trips around the area are conducted by **Battlefield Bus Tours,** from the Gettysburg Tour Center, 778 Baltimore St. (tel. 334-6296), open every day except Christmas. Using either open-air double-decker buses or conventional equipment, these tours depart every half-hour and take in all the major battlefield areas and town sights, with a choice of a recorded narration by Raymond Massey with a cast of Hollywood actors or a commentary by a registered guide. The prices are $8.95 for adults and $5.95 for children under 12. A free trolley-like shuttle service is operated from most major hotels to the tour depot. This company also operates several package plans involving a bus tour plus admission to many of the town's attractions at a reduced cost. If you purchase a package, you can also avail of free trolley shuttle transport between the attractions. CC's accepted: MC and V.

Car Tours: The best way to see the **Gettysburg National Military Park** in your own car is to engage the services of a licensed National Park guide ($14 for two hours). You can arrange for such a tour at the **National Park Visitor Center,** Route 15 (tel. 334-1124, ext. 31), or at the guide station on Route 30 (tel. 334-9876), one mile west of Gettysburg. If you wish to drive yourself around, you can also rent a 90-minute auto tape and player ($9.50) from the **National Civil War Wax Museum,** Route 297, Steinwehr Avenue (tel. 334-6245).

Walking Tours: Self-guided strolls are made easy, thanks to an eight-page walking-tour folder of the downtown area including a very detailed map, available free of charge from the Gettysburg Travel Council Inc. The walk covers 14 blocks and is 1½ miles in length, taking about two hours at a leisurely pace. You'll notice small plaques on certain buildings, indicating that they were constructed prior to the Civil War; a total of 118 buildings have these bronze plaques.

Train Tours: The steam passenger trains of the **Gettysburg Railroad,** North Washington St. (tel. 334-6932), provide a way of seeing the sights of the surrounding countryside. These trains offer a 16-mile round-trip between Gettysburg and Biglerville, operating every day during July and August (11 a.m. and 1 p.m.) and on weekends from June through October (1 and 3 p.m.). The fare is $4.50 for adults and $3 for children. In addition, a 50-mile round-trip itinerary is also available between Gettysburg and Mt. Holly Springs on some weekends at 10 a.m. (by reservation only). That fare is $12 for adults and $8 for children.

Helicopter Tours: You can arrange to see the sights from on high via a helicopter by contacting the **Battlefield Heliport,** Route 15 (tel. 334-6777), three miles south of downtown. These panoramic tours are operated daily from 8 a.m. to 5 p.m. at a cost of $15 per person for 5 minutes; $55 for two people for 10 minutes; or $75 for two people for 15 minutes. Reservations are necessary.

WHERE TO STAY: There are dozens of hotels, motels, and motor inns lining the streets in and around Gettysburg. In general, you'll find that rates are at their highest levels from June to September, although, even then, they can still be classified in the mostly moderate category.

If you can travel in the spring or fall, expect to save up to 35% or 40% off summer room rates. On the other hand, you'll also find that room prices can be subject to surcharges on holiday weekends or at festival times, so it is always best to check in advance.

For something different and in keeping with the 1800s aura of the town, consider staying in one of Gettysburg's very fine bed-and-breakfast inns.

The Top Hotels

You can't get a better location than the **Holiday Inn,** 516 Baltimore St., Gettysburg, PA 17325 (tel. 717/334-6211 or toll-free 800 HOL-IDAY), right in the heart of all the attractions, between the downtown area and the Gettysburg Battlefield. Just park your car in the hotel's free parking lot and you can walk to just about everything during your stay. Recently renovated, this five-story hotel has a Colonial façade and décor, with a fountain and rock garden in its lobby area. There are 100 modern bedrooms, each with two double beds or a king bed, color cable TV, air conditioning, and a direct-dial phone. Many rooms also have balconies that overlook the outdoor pool or the town. Doubles range from $55 to $70, and king-leisure rooms are priced from $60 to $75. The Plantation Room restaurant offers breakfast, lunch, and dinner, mostly in buffet style, although individual service is also available. In the summer months, the hotel organizes outdoor barbecue buffet dinners beside the pool. Breakfast buffets are $3.95 and dinners are $9.95. The standard lunch choices, priced from $2.95 to $4.95, offer sandwiches, salads, and burgers. The regular dinner menu features such dishes as chicken Cordon Bleu and charbroiled ham, as well as steaks, seafood, and nightly specials, in the $9.95 to $14.95 price bracket. Breakfast is served from 7 a.m. to 10 a.m.; lunch from 11:30 a.m. to 2:30 p.m.; and dinner from 6 to 10 p.m. All major CC's accepted.

The largest hotel in the area is the **Sheraton Inn,** 2634 Emmitsburg Rd., Gettysburg, PA 17325 (tel. 717/334-8121 or toll-free 800/325-3535), situated five miles south of downtown in a quiet country setting on Business Route 15 near the Eisenhower farm. This modern 203-room property is designed in a Tudor motif with early American–style furnishings. Each unit has double or oversized beds, color cable TV, air conditioning, and a phone; and many rooms have private patios or balconies. Doubles range from $70 to $80. Guest amenities include an outdoor/indoor swimming pool, a sauna, a tropical courtyard, tennis and racquetball courts, an exercise center, and a jogging trail. There is also a full-service restaurant, The Old Wharf, which specializes in seafood, steaks, and prime ribs, and features a large salad bar. Lunch prices range from $2.95 to $6.95 and dinner from $9.95 to $21.95, with most choices under $15. Lunch is served from 11 a.m. to 2 p.m. and dinner from 5:30 to 9:30 p.m. All major CC's accepted.

Motors Inns and Motels

The **Heritage Motor Inn,** 64 Steinwehr Ave., Gettysburg, PA 17325 (tel. 717/334-9281), is at the intersection of Steinwehr Avenue and Baltimore Street, between downtown and the battlefield area, right in the midst of a cluster of sightseeing attractions. This one-story Colonial-style motel has 28 rooms, each with two double beds, air conditioning, color TV, and a phone. Doubles range from $40 to $50 and some two-room family units are available from $56. All major CC's are accepted.

One mile west of downtown is **Larson's Quality Inn,** 401 Buford Ave., Gettysburg, PA 17325 (tel. 717/334-3141 or toll-free 800/228-5151), situated in a well-landscaped area next to General Lee's headquarters on Route 30. There are 41 rooms, each with one or two double beds, Colonial-style motif, color TV, a phone, and air conditioning. Guest amenities include a heated outdoor pool and a putting green; the General Lee Family Restaurant is adjacent. Doubles range from $50 to $60. Major CC's are accepted.

One block north of the town's Center Square is the **Colonial Motel,** 157 Carlisle St., Gettysburg, PA 17325 (tel. 717/334-3126), in a mostly residential section opposite Gettysburg College. This well-kept two-story property has 30 modern units, each with color cable TV, air conditioning, a phone, and one king or two double beds. Some rooms also have balconies. Doubles start at $49. CC's accepted: AE, Disc, MC and V.

Five miles south of downtown is the **Perfect Rest Motel,** 2450 Emmitsburg Rd., Gettysburg, PA 17325 (tel. 717/334-1345), in a quiet garden setting on Business Route 15, south of the battlefield and the Eisenhower homestead. There are 25 rooms, each with color TV and air conditioning; some with king-size beds and others with extra-long beds. Rates for doubles range from $48 to $54; two-room family units are also available from $75. All of the rooms are clustered around a well-landscaped outdoor pool and patio area. Open mid-May to through October. CC's accepted: MC and V.

In the other direction, four miles north of the town, is the **Blue Sky Motel,** 2585 Biglerville Rd., Gettysburg, PA 17325 (tel. 717/677-7736), adjacent to farm lands on Route 34. This modern one-story motel has 16 units, each with one or two double beds, color cable TV, and air conditioning. Guest facilities include an outdoor swimming pool and a picnic area. Doubles range frm $36 to $40. CC's accepted: MC and V.

Bed-and-Breakfast Inns

The **Brafferton Inn,** 44–46 York Ave., Gettysburg, PA 17325 (tel. 717/337-3423), is situated right in the heart of town on the main street, one block west of the square. This is actually two houses, a two-story 1786 stone Federal home and a pre–Civil War clapboard addition. Originally the property of Nicholas Codori, the larger structure is the earliest deeded house in the town plan designed by James Gettys and is listed in the National Register of Historic Places. Opened as a B&B in 1986 by Mimi and Jim Agard, this beautifully restored building has seven guest rooms, three with private bath and four with shared facilities. Each room is decorated individually, but all have furniture reflecting the Colonial period, from canopy, four-poster, or brass beds to primitive antiques, samplers, oil paintings, and copies of 18th-century stencilwork on whitewashed walls. Guests can also enjoy a sunlit glass-covered atrium filled with plants and flowers from the garden. The dining room, where a sumptuous breakfast is served each morning, has a fascinating hand-painted primitive wall mural depicting 18 of Gettysburg's most famous buildings. Doubles, including breakfast, range from $50 to $65. Open all year, this inn has its own parking facilities. CC's accepted: MC and V.

Two blocks north of the town square is **The Old Appleford Inn,** 218 Carlisle St., Gettysburg, PA 17325 (tel. 717/337-1711), a Federal-style mansion dating back to 1867 and once the home of a local judge. Opened as a B&B in 1984 by Del and Nancie Gudmestad, this gracious house has nine air-conditioned guest rooms, one with private bath and the rest with shared facilities. The bedrooms feature hand-stenciled artwork and furnishings dating back to the 1850–1890 period, including brass and canopy beds. Guests can also enjoy the house's parlor with a 1912 baby grand piano, an upstairs sun room with a balcony, and the well-stocked library that also displays menus from local restaurants, a great help in deciding where to dine. Behind the house there is a craft shop that specializes in the work of local artisans. Doubles range from $45 to $68 including a country gourmet breakfast that is served in the dining room. Open all year except the last three weeks of January. CC's accepted: MC and V.

South of downtown on the road to the battlefield is the **Gettystown Inn,** 89 Steinwehr Ave., Gettysburg, PA 17325 (tel. 717/334-4930), a two-story Civil War–era stone house. Fully renovated and restored to convey an 1863 atmosphere, this building overlooks the spot where Lincoln gave his Gettysburg address. It is furnished with brass, trundle, and canopy beds, hooked and braided rugs, and antique oak, cherry, and walnut chests and nightstands. All seven rooms are fully air-conditioned, and three have private baths and four have shared facilities. This inn is associated with the Dobbin House restaurant next door and overnight guests enjoy a hearty country breakfast in the sun parlor of the restaurant, with a menu usually consisting of freshly squeezed juices, fruit, cereal, eggs, country ham, pancakes or crêpes, and home-style breads and jams. Rates for a double range from $50 to $60. No smoking is permitted in the inn. CC's accepted: AE, MC, and V.

WHERE TO DINE: Tourist attractions in themselves, many of Gettysburg's restaurants are historic landmarks or sites that are featured in the town's history. Because Gettysburg is a great favorite with young visitors and students, many dining spots are also geared to families. You'll find the prices to be in the moderate range or even lower.

The top choice is the **Dobbin House Tavern,** 89 Steinwehr Ave., (tel. 334-2100), listed in the National Register of Historic Places. Built in 1776 by Rev. Alexander Dobbin, a minister from Ireland, this sturdy structure started as his family home and a classical school and was then used as a hospital during the Civil War. Today it still has its original two-foot thick stone walls, walk-in hearth, hand-carved woodwork, and seven fireplaces. Three natural springs, which were a source of water and a refrigerating facility, are still located in the basement which now serves as the Springhouse Tavern. Lunch items, such as sandwiches and salads, priced from $3.95 to $4.95, are served in the tavern all day from 11:30 a.m. The upstairs Alexander Dobbin Dining Rooms offer a choice of nine different settings for dinner, including a library, a parlor, a study, a spinning room, and four bedrooms (yes, you can even dine in bed!). All rooms are furnished in typical early-American style with candlelight, hurricane lamps, Colonial crockery, costumed wait-persons, and background music from the 1800s hit parade. Dinner entrees range from $10.95 to $22.95, with most dishes priced under $15. The selections are an eclectic blend of pork and sauerkraut; Cumberland chicken (with mushroom and blue cheese sauce); prime ribs, veal Madeira with Pennsylvania mushrooms; a trio of lamb chops; roast duck with cider sauce and citrus herbs; rainbow trout with crabmeat; and a seafarer's platter (flounder, shrimp, scallops, crab, and lobster tail). All main courses are accompanied by a basket of nutty breads and muffins, salad, and potato, but save room for the homemade desserts ($2), such as warm gingerbread with lemon sauce. Open for dinner every day from 5:30 to 10 p.m. CC's accepted: AE, MC, and V.

More than 100 bullet holes are visible in the walls of the **Farnsworth House,** 401 Baltimore St. (tel. 334-8838), an 1810 stone structure in the center of town which once belonged to Union Brigadier General Elon John Farnsworth who was killed on the third day of the battle of Gettysburg. The original walls, flooring, and rafters of the building have stood the test of time well and today a Civil War décor serves as a setting for lunch and dinner. In the summer months, you can also dine al fresco under ancient trees on an outside garden deck beside a freshwater stream, waterfall, and rock garden. Lunch focuses primarily on sandwiches and salads, in the $1.95 to $4.95 price bracket. At dinner the Colonially costumed staff starts your meal off with several house specialties, including hot spoon bread, corn relish, and apple butter. The menu features early-American cuisine, with such dishes as game pie (pheasant, duck, and turkey blended with mushrooms, bacon, red currant jelly, long-grained and wild rice); and Virginia chipped ham with grape sauce; as well as a variety of seafood and steaks. Entrees are priced from $8.95 to $15.95, and include salad, vegetable, and potato or rice. Desserts average $2.50 for such old-time treats as rum cream pie or walnut apple cake. Lunch is served from 11:30 a.m. to 3 p.m. and dinner from 5 to 10 p.m. CC's accepted: AE, MC, and V.

A casual atmosphere prevails at the **Herr Tavern,** 900 Chambersburg Rd. (tel. 334-6022), situated two miles west of town on Route 30. Dating back to 1828, this stone building has had a checkered life as a stagecoach stop, a tavern, a counterfeiters den, a Civil War hospital, and a private residence. Now modernized and expanded, but still retaining its original stone walls, wood floors, gas lamps, fireplaces, and beamed ceilings, this restaurant offers an extensive lunch menu of hearty tavern sandwiches, vegetable plates, cheese steaks, quiches, and homemade soups with cornbread muffins, in the $2.95 to $4.95 price bracket. Dinner entrees, priced at $7.95 to $16.95, include fried chicken; Kansas City-cut steaks; prime ribs; jambalaya (chicken, shrimp, and Cajun sausage); veal alla marsala; flounder Anatole (with cheese soufflé); and pan-fried trout. Lunch is served from 11 a.m. to 5 p.m. daily; and dinner Monday through Thursday from 5 to 9 p.m., Friday and Saturday until 10 p.m., and Sunday until 8 p.m. CC's accepted: AE, MC, and V.

Three blocks north of the town square is the **Lamp Post Restaurant,** 301 Carlisle St. (tel. 334-3315), a two-story Federal-style house in a residential neighborhood, surrounded by a white picket fence and gardens. Inside there are four dining rooms with a homey early-American décor. Lunch offers mainly sandwiches, salads, burgers, and hot platters, in the $1.95 to $7.95 price range. Dinner entrees are priced in the $5.95 to $10.95 range, with such choices as prime ribs, leg of lamb, baked ham, roast turkey, steaks, and seafood. All main courses come with a relish tray, salad, and two vegetables. On the side of the house there is also an all-day coffeeshop featuring moderate-to-budget priced meals. Lunch is available in the restaurant from 11 a.m. to 2 p.m. and dinner from 5 to 8:30 p.m. (with a 7:30 p.m. closing in winter). No liquor is served, but you can bring your own wine. No CC's accepted.

Pennsylvania Dutch cooking is on the menu at the **Dutch Cupboard,** 523 Baltimore St., (tel. 334-6227), conveniently located between downtown and the battlefield and an ideal restaurant for the whole family. The décor conveys a farmhouse atmosphere, with walls displaying Pennsylvania Dutch sayings as well as an array of kitchen implements, ladles, scoopers, muffin pans, and dinner bells. Breakfast, in the $2 to $4 range, features hearty egg-and-meat combinations as well as Dutch fried bread topped with powdered sugar and maple syrup. Choices at lunch, in the $2.95 to $6.95 bracket, focus on salads and sandwiches, plus such dishes as knockwurst or turkey with waffles. Dinner entrees, priced from $6.95 to $11.95, include chicken and dumplings; beef and noodles; fried country ham; pan-fried chicken; sauerbraten; roast turkey; meatloaf; and seafood. All main courses are accompanied by two vegetables, homemade bread, and apple butter. Breakfast is served from 8 to 11 a.m., lunch from 11 a.m. to 3 p.m., and dinner from 4 to 9 p.m. Beer and wine are available. CC's accepted: MC and V.

Another favorite with visitors of all ages is **General Lee's Family Restaurant,** 401 Buford Ave. (tel. 334-2200), situated a mile west of town on Route 30 next to General Lee's historic headquarters. There are three dining rooms, with an authentic décor of beamed ceilings, whitewashed walls, old stone fireplaces, and pictures of early Gettysburg. Breakfast, priced from $2.95 to $3.95, features such dishes as country omelets, corned-beef hash, scrapple, creamed chipped beef, and apple fritters, while lunch offers mainly sandwiches and burgers in the $1.95 to $3.95 bracket. Down-home country cuisine is also on the menu at night, with such selections as meatloaf, cabbage rolls, chicken pot pie, ham steak, and roast turkey, as well as steaks and seafood. All main courses, priced from $4.95 to $10.95, come with salad and vegetables. Cocktails are available. Open daily, continuously from 7 a.m. to 9 p.m. CC's accepted: AE, MC, and V.

TOP ATTRACTIONS: Plan to devote at least a day to seeing the **Gettysburg National Military Park,** Route 134 (tel. 334-1124), the historic site commemorating the July 1863 Battle of Gettysburg. The bloodiest battle of the Civil War with 51,000 casualties, this event became a turning point in the action as Union forces drove back the troops of Gen. Robert E. Lee. Under the auspices of the National Park Service, this 3,500-acre park is open daily from 6 a.m. to 10 p.m. Start your tour at the Visitors Center where you'll find orientation displays, Civil War exhibits, and a schedule of ranger-conducted programs, talks, walks, and tours. You can also obtain a free pamphlet detailing a self-conducted auto tour of the battlefield (two to three hours in duration). Various trails have also been marked off for walking tours of the area; students will find walks to be particularly educational as all sites are marked with plaques and trees are similarly identified. The visitor center is open from 8 a.m. to 6 p.m. In addition, there are a number of man-made attractions within the park that are well worth seeing to help understand the scope and aura of the battle:

● **The Electric Map:** This is an orientation program within the Visitor Center that explains the movements of the Battle of Gettysburg by means of a large relief map with colored lights and narration, in a theater setting. The 30-minute program is shown every 45 minutes, from 8 a.m. to 6 p.m. daily. Admission is $1.50 for adults; children under 15 are free.

● **The Cyclorama Center:** Housed in a specially built structure adjacent to the visitor center, this is a giant circular oil painting of the Battle of Gettysburg. The work of artist Paul Philippoteaux, it is 356 feet in circumference and 26 feet high. You feel like you are right in the midst of the battlefield as you step onto a platform in the center of the painting. A 20 minute sound-and-light narration helps you to focus on the various scenes of the painting as you are moved in a circular direction. Open from 9 a.m. to 5 p.m., the admission charge is $1 for adults; children under 15 are free. The Cyclorama building also contains other exhibits of interest including a copy of the second draft of the Gettysburg Address (courtesy of the Library of Congress).

● **The National Tower:** This attraction provides the best overall views of the battlefield and the surrounding Gettysburg countryside. Elevators whisk you to the 300-foot high observation decks, including a glass-enclosed level that provides a 12-minute audio program and an upper open-air platform with telescopes, ideal for picture-taking. Open from April through November, from 9 a.m. to 7:30 p.m. in summer, and from 9 a.m. to 6 p.m. in spring and fall. Admission charge is $2.95 for adults; $1.55 for children between the ages of 6 and 14; and children under 6 are free.

Just outside the battlefield is one of Gettysburg's most popular attractions, the **National Civil War Wax Museum,** 297 Steinwehr Ave. (tel. 334-6245). This display tells the story of the Civil War in 30 different scenes with life-like wax figures, backed by narration. An animated figure of President Lincoln delivering his Gettysburg address is also on view. Open daily from 9 a.m. to 9 p.m. Admission is $3.50 for adults; $2.50 for children aged 13 to 17; and $1.50 for children 6 to 12. Auto tape tours of the entire Gettysburg area are also on sale at this facility (see "Getting Around" above).

A fine collection of Civil War memorabilia is housed in **General Lee's Headquarters,** Bulford Avenue and Route 30 (tel. 334-3141), built in the 1700s and one of the few original Gettysburg houses open to the public. General Lee established his personal headquarters here on July 1, 1863, and planned his battle-line strategy. The house was ideal because of its 20-inch stone walls, which remain today. Exhibits include Union and Confederate military equipment, rifles and sabers, uniforms, buttons, belt buckles, saddles, and cavalry equipment, plus original kitchen and Civil War period furnishings. Open daily from 9 a.m. to 5 p.m. from mid-March to mid-April and mid-October through November; and from 9 a.m. to 9 p.m. from mid-April through mid-October. No admission charge.

Lincoln Room Museum, 12 Lincoln Square (tel. 334-8188), is a showcase of the room where our sixteenth president prepared the final draft of his Gettysburg Address. Located on the second floor of the David I. Wills House, the room has been preserved with many original furnishings. Visitors can also view a tableau with a life-like figure of Lincoln reciting the speech. Open daily in the summer months from 9 a.m. to 7 p.m. and Friday and Saturday until 9 p.m.; and until 5 p.m. in the spring and fall. Admission charge is $2.95 for adults and $1.50 for children.

Next to the Holiday Inn is the **Jennie Wade House and Olde Town Square,**

Baltimore Street (tel. 334-4100), an attraction that commemorates the story of the Civil War's only civilian casualty, Mary Virginia Wade. As this young girl was baking in the kitchen, a stray shot from a sharpshooter's gun pierced through the wall and killed her instantly. Today you can tour the house, see the bullet holes and hear the saga. Behind the house is an olde village courtyard, re-created to look the way it did in Jenny's time. You'll see a barbershop, a general store, a blacksmith, and a printer, all part of a self-guided walking tour with recorded narration. Open daily in the summer from 9 a.m. to 10 p.m., and in the spring and fall until 5 p.m. Admission is $2.95 for adults and $1.50 for children.

Each day 1,100 visitors can tour the **Eisenhower National Historic Site,** Business Route 15, once the farm home of President and Mrs. Dwight D. Eisenhower. This 495-acre estate includes a 15-room Georgian-style house, an 1887 bank-style barn, and lots of memorabilia relating to Ike and Mamie. Tickets for the 1½-hour tours are $1 per person and are sold on a first-come first-served basis at the **National Park Visitor Center** (Electric Map building) from 8 a.m. to 4:15 p.m. Participants are also required to avail of shuttle bus transportation to the homestead ($1.25 for adults and 70¢ for children aged 15 and under). Advance reservations are available only for groups of ten or more (by phoning 334-1124, ext. 61).

For a change of pace, you might like to visit the **Adams County Winery,** 251 Peach Tree Rd., Orrtanna (tel. 334-4631), seven miles west of Gettysburg, in the midst of Adams County fruit orchards. Originally planted in 1974, this vineyard produces a range of white wines from its grapes, plus a line of more unusual wines such as strawberry, sour cherry, and apple. The vineyards and winery are open for tours and tastings from 12:30 p.m. to 6 p.m. Thursday through Monday, free of charge.

SHOPPING: Shopping, especially for Civil War–related souvenirs, is a big business in Gettysburg. Almost every major attraction maintains a souvenir shop on its premises and there are independent shops lining all of the streets. Here are some of the more interesting specimens:

The **Old Gettysburg Village,** 777 Baltimore St., is a complex of a dozen old-world shops designed to re-create an 1863 atmosphere, with cobblestone streets and all sorts of wares ranging from fudge and ice cream to Civil War relics, dolls, hand-carvings, and moccasins. Most stores are open from 10 a.m. to 9 p.m. daily and the majority accept MC and V credit cards.

The **Centennial General Store,** 237 Steinwehr Ave. (tel. 334-9712), is housed in a gray stone dwelling that served as a hospital during the Civil War. Appropriately enough, it specializes in Union and Confederate war uniforms and officers' hats, clay pottery, jewelry, and early-American products. Open daily from 8:30 a.m. to 9 p.m. in summer, with shorter hours at other times. CC's accepted: MC and V.

The **Civil War Art Gallery,** 219 Steinwehr Ave. (tel. 334-6188) features military limited-edition prints, autographs of Civil War generals, military note cards, oil paintings, and bronzes. Open Monday through Saturday from 9 a.m. to 5 p.m. and Sunday from 10 a.m. to 4 p.m. CC's accepted: AE, MC, and V.

One of the most fascinating places is **Codori's Bavarian Gift Shop,** 19 Barlow St. (tel. 334-5019), situated in a residential setting off North Stratton Street on the north side of town. This chalet-style store sells German and Scandinavian gifts, Black Forest cuckoo clocks, toy soldiers including Civil War figures, wooden nutcrackers, hand puppets, teddy bears from around the world, collector dolls from Europe, hundreds of types of music boxes, and Victorian Christmas ornaments. Hours are Monday through Saturday from 10 a.m. to 7 p.m. and on Sunday from noon to 6 p.m. CC's accepted: AE, MC, and V.

Seven miles north of Gettysburg is the **Thomas Bros. Country Store and Museum,** Route 34 at Biglerville (tel. 677-7447). An historic landmark, this building consists of three floors and more than 50,000 products—from china and calicoes to lamps, long johns, penny candy, handmade quilts, top hats, and wedding gowns. Open year round, Monday through Wednesday from 9:30 to 5 p.m.; Thursday and Friday until 8:30 p.m.; and Saturday from 9:30 a.m. to 6 p.m. CC's accepted: MC and V.

SPORTS AND ACTIVITIES: Gettysburg is ideal territory for bikers, so bring your own if you have one. If not, you can rent a three-speed model from **Lawver's Bicycle Shop,** 280 Barlow St. (tel. 334-3295). Open March through September, Monday through Friday from 9 a.m. to 7 p.m. and Saturday from 9 a.m. to 4 p.m. The charge is $4 an hour, or $9 a day.

Horseback Riding: You can go riding at the **Manor Stables,** Route 116 (tel. 334-7230), situated on a 150-acre estate of fields and woods. Both western and English saddles are available, and the rental charge is $8 per hour. Reservations are advisable.

Golf: Visitors are welcome at the **Piney Apple Golf Course,** R.D. 1, Biglerville (tel. 677-9264). Greens fees for nine holes are $5 on weekends and $4 on weekdays; for 18 holes, it is $9 on weekends and $7 on weekdays. Motorized carts can be rented at $7 for nine holes and $13 for 18 holes. Clubs are also available from $3 a set.

EVENTS: One of the best times of year to plan to be in Gettysburg is late June/early July when the **Civil War Heritage Days** are scheduled. This annual observance commemorates the Battle of Gettysburg with activities that include a "living history" encampment, battle re-enactments, concerts, lectures by some of America's foremost historians, and a fireman's festival. In addition, there is a **Civil War collectors show** that features rare collections of antique arms, uniforms, accoutrements, documents, books, photographs, and personal effects. Admission to the show is $3 for anyone over 16 years of age. For a detailed program of all events, contact the **Gettysburg Travel Council,** 35 Carlisle St., Gettysburg, PA 17325 (tel. 717/334-6274).

A highlight every fall in the Gettysburg area is the **Apple Harvest Festival,** traditionally held on the first two weekends of October at the South Mountain Fairgrounds on Route 234, Arendtsville, ten miles northwest of downtown. The program includes continuous free entertainment, tours of the orchards, peanut roastings, arts and crafts shows, antique gas engine displays, apple bobbing, and pie-eating contests. Among the foods on sale are apple jellies, apple syrups, candied apples, hot spiced cider, apple butter boil, apple pancakes, apple sauce, apple desserts, and fresh-picked apples. Admission is $3 for adults; children under 12 are free. Parking is $1 per car. Festival hours are from 9 a.m. to 6 p.m. For a complete schedule of events, contact the Gettysburg Travel Council.

CHILDREN'S CORNER: Some of the world's smallest horses are on view at the **Land of Little Horses,** located at 125 Glenwood Drive, Gettysburg, off Route 30 (tel. 334-7259). Children of all ages are fascinated by the miniature pintos, appaloosas, draft horses, and thoroughbreds. Open daily from Memorial Day through Labor Day from 10 a.m. to 6 p.m. with indoor arena shows scheduled at 11 a.m., 1, 3, and 5 p.m.; also open from April 1 to Memorial Day and from Labor Day to November from 10 a.m. to 5 p.m. and with all daily shows except the 5 p.m. performance. Other attractions include rides, a picnic area, a gift shop, and a snack bar. Admission for adults is $4.40 and $2.75 for children.

2. York

Thirty miles east of Gettysburg is York, an area first settled in 1736. Named for York, England, this city had its greatest moments of glory between September 30, 1777, and June 28, 1778, when the Colonial capital was moved here from Philadelphia. The Continental Congress met at the York Courthouse during that period and adopted the Articles of Confederation. Since this was the first document to describe the colonies as the United States of America, York lays claim to being our nation's first legal capital.

In addition, while serving as capital, York was the site of the first proclamation establishing Thanksgiving as a national holiday.

Today York (pop.: 50,000) is a city that has preserved or restored much of its original architecture. The midtown historic district is the largest in Pennsylvania outside of Philadelphia. With landmark Continental Square as its heart, this city still retains many of its Colonial street names like King, Queen, Princess, and Duke. The restored York County Colonial Courthouse stands across from a 1741 tavern and near a parade of Federal and Victorian buildings, many with brick walkways, carved doors, stained-glass windows, or cast-iron trim.

But York's charm is not all from the past. A prosperous industrial city situated on the banks of the Codorus Creek, modern York is famous as a candymaking center and for its nearby orchards and wineries. York is home to a trio of farmers' markets and a variety of other attractions ranging from the Harley-Davidson Motorcycle Museum to the Bob Hoffman Weightlifting Hall of Fame.

Located 25 miles south of Harrisburg, 50 miles north of Baltimore, and 90 miles west of Philadelphia, York is also a convenient vacation hub for visits to nearby Gettysburg and Lancaster.

VISITOR INFORMATION: For self-guided walking tour brochures and complete information about York, contact the **York County Convention and Visitors Bureau,** One Marketway East, P.O. Box 1229, York, PA 17405 (tel. 717/848-4000). When in York, there is also a walk-in **Visitors Information Center** located at the Colonial Courthouse, 205 W. Market St., York, PA 17405 (tel. 717/856-1977).

GETTING TO AND AROUND YORK: Located 30 miles east of Gettysburg, York is traversed in a north-south direction by I-83 and Route 30 cuts through York from east to west. There is also good access to York via I-81 (30 miles north) and the Pennsylvania Turnpike (17 miles north).

By Plane: The closest full service airports to York are **Harrisburg International** (a half-nour drive), and **Baltimore International Airport** (95 minutes away).

By Bus: Service into York is operated by **Capitol Trailways,** 53 E. North St. (tel. 845-9611), and **Greyhound,** 315 N. George St. (tel. 843-0095). Local bus transport within the city (except Sunday) is provided by **YATA (York Area Transportation Authority),** 401 Yale St. (tel. 846-9282); an exact fare of 70¢ is required.

Taxis: If you require a cab, call **McCarthy's Flowered Cabs,** 53 E. King St. (tel. 843-8811).

Car Rental: The following companies maintain depots in York: **Avis,** 1439 Mt. Rose Ave. (tel. 843-1147); **Budget,** 12088 Manheim Pl. (tel. 392-4228); **Hertz,** 1509 Whiteford Rd. (tel. 848-2839); and **National,** 1000 S. George St. (tel. 854-1730).

WHERE TO STAY: Although you'll find York's best hotel, the Yorktowne Inn, located in the heart of downtown, most all of the other lodging choices are situated on major access routes outside the city. In general, rates at York's hotels and motels can be classified as moderate and some properties also offer cost-saving weekend packages. Be sure to check for the best rate when you reserve a room.

The "grand dame" of lodgings in this area is the **Yorktowne Inn,** 48 E. Market St., P.O. Box 1106, York, PA 17405 (tel. 717/848-1111 and toll-free 800/233-9323), in the center of the historic district. Originally opened in 1925, this National Register landmark was completely and graciously renovated in 1983. An old-world aura still prevails in the public rooms with dark paneled walls, electric candles, crystal chandeliers, and high ceilings of ornate plaster work. The 160 bedrooms have been handsomely refurbished with modern private bathrooms and Colonial-style furniture. Each room has either two double beds, a queen, or a king bed; color cable TV with movies; a direct-dial phone; and air conditioning. Doubles range from $51 to $61. Other guest amenities include free parking, a barber shop, a trendy art deco café-lounge called Autographs (for breakfast, lunch, snacks, or late-night jazz), and a full-service restaurant, The Wedgwood Room. Open for dinner only, this Colonial-style dining room offers an eclectic menu, with entrees priced in the $10.95 to $16.95 bracket. Choices include the house specialty, prime ribs with corn pudding, as well as a pleasingly piquant "chicken Elizabeth" (chicken breast in sour cream and blue cheese sauce); lemon-braised veal; stuffed breast of capon; rack of lamb; steak Diane; and a wide array of seafood. All main courses are accompanied by a relish tray, salad, vegetable, and potato or pasta. Hours are Monday through Thursday from 5:30 to 9:30 p.m.; Friday and Saturday from 5 until 10 p.m.; and Sunday from 5 until 9 p.m. All major CC's accepted.

Situated slightly northwest of downtown is the **Sheraton Inn,** Routes 30 and 74, York, PA 17404 (tel. 717/846-9500 or toll-free 800/325-3535), adjacent to the West Manchester Mall, a 100-unit shopping complex. A cheery blend of art deco and contemporary design, this two-story hotel offers 181 rooms, with rates ranging from $53 to $90 for two people. Each room has two double beds or a king bed, color cable TV, a direct-dial phone, and air conditioning. Guest facilities include indoor and outdoor swimming pools, saunas and fitness equipment, a game room, and a miniature golf course. There is also a multi-level restaurant, Harrigan's, specializing in seafood, steaks, veal, and prime ribs, with dinner entrees from $10 to $20; ethnic buffets are featured on Friday evenings. Hours are from 11 a.m. to 2 p.m. for light lunch fare and from 5 to 10 p.m. for dinner. All major CC's accepted.

Two blocks from the Sheraton is the **Best Western Westgate Inn,** 1415 Kenneth Rd., P.O. Box 1348, York, PA 17404 (tel. 717/767-6931 or toll-free 800/528-1234), in a rural setting just off Route 30. This modern three-story hotel has 101 spacious rooms, each with two queen beds plus two vanities, remote control color cable TV, a direct-dial phone, an AM/FM clock radio, and air conditioning. Guest amenities include a café, a lounge, and a game room. Doubles range from $50 to $60; kitchenette suites are also available from $65. All major CC's accepted.

East of the downtown area is the **Quality Inn York Valley,** 3883 E. Market St. (Route 462), York, PA 17402 (tel. 717/755-2881 or toll-free 800/228-5151), in a sylvan countryside setting. This Colonial-style property offers 162 rooms in a rambling one-story layout. The units are newly decorated and contain double or king beds, color cable TV, air conditioning, and a phone. Guest facilities include an indoor and an outdoor pool, two saunas, a Jacuzzi, a fitness center, a sun-tanning room, and an all-day restaurant featuring regional cooking in the moderate price range. Non-smoking rooms are available. Doubles range from $50 to $62. All major CC's accepted.

Budget Range

A homey atmosphere prevails at the **Barnhart's Motel,** 3021 E. Market St. (Route 462), York, PA 17402 (tel. 717/755-2806), located near the Eastern Farmers' Market. Surrounded by blue spruce trees, this one-story motel has 40 units in a garden setting. Each room has one or two double beds, color cable TV, an AM-FM radio, a phone, air conditioning, and wall-to-wall carpet. Doubles range from $28 to $34. All major CC's accepted.

WHERE TO DINE: Like its hotels, **York's restaurants** are spread throughout the city and generally fall into the mostly moderate price range.

On the edge of the city's historic district is **Chez John,** 243 W. Market St. (tel. 846-5514), housed in a renovated brick townhouse, with its front entrance actually on Grant Street. With a Parisian bistro décor and paintings by local artists on the walls, this restaurant features French nouvelle and haute cuisine. Lunch items, priced from $3.95 to $7.95, include hot dishes (such as veal and sweetbreads in truffle sauce) and quiche as well as gourmet sandwiches, burgers, and salads. The menu at dinner features stuffed lobster; rack of lamb; roast loin of pork; and "poulet honfleur" (chicken grilled with Calvados and mushroom sauce). Entrees fall into the $10 to $18 bracket, with most choices under $15, and are accompanied by salad and vegetable. Lunch is served Monday through Saturday from 11 a.m. to 2 p.m., and dinner from 5:30 to 10 p.m. CC's accepted: AE, MC, and V.

The Hill, 1839 S. Queen St. (tel. 846-5265), is located in a suburban area south of the historic district, and, as its name implies, at the top of Queen Street Hill. This Tudor-style, lantern-lit restaurant has a cavalier atmosphere with rich red tones, boxed windows, colored glass, and lots of brass. A favorite with the locals, this place has an ample parking lot. Lunch, priced from $2.95 to $6.95, concentrates on steakburgers, omelets, salads, sandwiches, and light entrees (such as chicken tempura or crab cakes). The dinner menu falls into the $9.95 to $19.95 price bracket, with most entrees under $15. Selections include seafood such as flounder oregano, frogs' legs, haddock Mornay, and shrimp parmigiana; as well as a wide choice of beef and veal dishes. All main courses come with salad and baked potato or vegetable. Open daily for lunch from 11 a.m. to 2:30 p.m. and dinner from 5 to 11 p.m. All CC's are accepted.

A turn-of-the-century carriage house is the setting of **Wickey's at the Woods,** 2510 E. Market St. (tel. 757-5605), located east of downtown on Route 462. Run by two chefs who also operate a catering business in an adjacent former tack shop, this restaurant is decorated in the style of a formal English dining room. Lunch, priced from $4.25 to $6.95, features burgers, salads, sandwiches, and light entrees, such as brie in pastry, pasta primavera, and shrimp rémoulade. The dinner menu is a medley of such choices as salmon scaloppine; julienne of beef tenderloin and shrimp; cheddar-stuffed flounder; seafood crêpes; and grilled medallions of lamb. The prices run from $8.95 to $21.95, with most under $15, including salad, potato, rice pilaf, and pasta or vegetable. If you are just passing through, you can also get an "express box" or "brown-bag gourmet" lunch from $3.95 to $8.95. Open from 11:30 a.m. to 11 p.m. Monday through Saturday; and on Sunday from 11:30 a.m. to 3 p.m. for brunch and from 4 to 10 p.m. for dinner. Jazz piano music is featured on Friday and Saturday from 9:30 p.m. to 1:30 a.m. CC's accepted: AE, MC, and V.

A British pub atmosphere prevails at **Granfelloons,** 41 E. Princess St. (tel. 843-2541), two streets south of the Yorktowne Inn in downtown. Two old brick town houses have been converted into this trendy two-story meeting and eating place. Lunch items include sandwiches, salads, quiches, crêpes, and omelets, priced from $2.95 to $4.95. A blackboard of dinner specials changes daily but steaks and burgers are always available. The price range averages $9.95 to $14.95, and includes a salad and appropriate garnishes. Open for lunch and dinner, Monday and Tuesday from 11 a.m. to 10 p.m., and Wednesday to Saturday from 11 a.m. to 11 p.m. CC's accepted: MC and V.

York's 100-year-old **Foundry Building,** listed on the National Register of Historic Places, is the setting for the **Gingerbread Man,** Foundry Plaza, 200 W. Philadelphia St. (tel. 854-1555). Situated on the east bank of the Codorus Creek, this building offers two indoor dining areas plus an outdoor deck overlooking the water. Brick walls, brass rails, colored tiles, and ceiling fans dominate the décor. Lunch focuses on sandwiches, hoagies, burgers, omelets, croissantwiches, salads, pizzas, and Mexican tacos, burritos and nachos, all in the $3 to $5 price range. Dinner entrees, priced from $5.95 to $9.95, include steaks, fried shrimp, honey-dipped chicken, and veal parmigiana, all served with french fries and cole slaw. Open daily from 11 a.m. to 2 a.m. All CC's accepted.

Homemade soups, salads, quiches, casseroles, and baked goods are featured at **Café Intermezzo,** 361 W. Market St. (tel. 854-2233), a converted Federal townhouse, located almost opposite the city's Farmers' Market West. The interior dining room, which seats 25, is decorated with an eclectic collection of antique furnishings and pictures; in the summer there is also seating in an outdoor courtyard. The menu changes daily but the average price for a hearty lunch is $3.95 to $4.95. Open for breakfast and lunch, Monday through Friday from 7 a.m. to 3 p.m. and on Saturday from 8 a.m. to 3 p.m. No CC's are accepted.

TOP ATTRACTIONS: A good place to start a tour of this historic city is at the **York County Colonial Courthouse,** an authentic reconstruction of the building where the Continental Congress adopted the Articles of Confederation in 1777. Located at 205 West Market St. (tel. 846-1977), this landmark houses 200-year-old artifacts and memorabilia as well as a multimedia presentation on York's epic year as our nation's capital. Admission charge is $1.50 for adults and 50¢ for students. Hours are Monday through Friday from 1:30 to 4 p.m.; Saturday from 10 a.m. to 4 p.m.; and Sunday from noon to 4 p.m.

Across the street from the courthouse is the **The Golden Plough Tavern,** 157 W. Market St. (845-2951), a Germanic half-timber building dating back to 1741. Thought to be the oldest surviving structure in York, this tavern contains a fine collection of furnishings dating back to the early 18th century. It is also the centerpiece in a cluster of three historic buildings on this corner. Adjacent to it is the **General Gates House,** once the Colonial residence of Horatio Gates and the place where Lafayette gave an historic toast to General Washington that insured his continued command of the continental forces. The third building is the **Bobb Log House,** an 1811 dwelling typifying life in York in the early 19th century. One price covers admission to these three attractions; $2.00 for adults, and $1.25 for children aged 6 through 13. Hours are 10 a.m. to 4 p.m. Monday through Saturday, and from 1 to 4 p.m. on Sunday.

Another highlight of the historic district is the **York County Museum,** at 250 East Market St. (tel. 848-1587), a restored brick townhouse with exhibits on early settlers and their crafts and customs; models of local architecture and industry; early automobiles, and life-size village square. You'll also see drawings by Lewis Miller, York's folk artist of the 1800s and old newspapers on display. Open Monday through Saturday from 9 a.m. to 5 p.m. and Sunday from 1 to 4 p.m. Admission charge is $1.50 for adults and 75¢ for children aged 6 through 13.

York is also the home of the **Currier and Ives Antique Gallery** at 43 West King St. (tel. 854-7851), housed in an 1870 Victorian mansion that is under the auspices of the Kling Brothers Insurance Co. This collection includes more than 400 original lithographs and antiques of this genre. Open by appointment, Monday through Friday from 9 a.m. to 4 p.m. Admission is $2 for adults and free for children under 12 years of age.

Two miles east of downtown on Route 30 is the **Harley-Davidson Motorcycle Museum,** 1425 Eden Rd. (tel. 848-1177), headquarters of the only American motorcycle manufacturer. This museum includes exhibits of vintage models of motorcycles from 1903 to present; half-hour guided museum tours are conducted Monday through Saturday at 10 a.m., 12:30 p.m., and 2 p.m. On weekdays, it is also possible to tour the plant and see motorcycles-in-the-making; the hours of these tours vary, so it is best to check in advance (children under 12 are not permitted in the plant). No admission charge.

The **Bob Hoffman Weightlifting and Softball Hall of Fame** (tel. 767-6481) is located just north of downtown York on I-83, exit 11. This attraction honors Olympic weight lifters, power lifters, body builders, and strongmen. There is also a display spotlighting the history of softball. Open Monday through Saturday, except holidays, from 10 a.m. to 4 p.m., with guided tours at 1 p.m. Admission is free.

Farmers' Markets

As a rich agricultural area, York is well known for its farmers' markets which started years ago when local farmers would gather in the square on market days and sell their produce from their wagons. Today, York's markets are housed in all-weather buildings, but the wares remain essentially the same—homemade cakes, cookies, pies, and soups, as well as fruits, vegetables, candy, flowers, meat, poultry, eggs, jellies, preserves, and hand-crafted items.

York's three main markets operate year round as follows:

Central Market House, 34 West Philadelphia Street (tel. 848-2243), open Tuesday, Thursday (7:30 a.m. to 4:30 p.m.) and Saturday (6:30 a.m. to 4:30 p.m.).

Farmers' Market West, 380 West Market Street (tel. 848-1402); open Tuesday, Friday, and Saturday (7 a.m. to 4 p.m.).

New Eastern Market, 201 Memory Lane (tel. 755-5811); open Friday (1 to 10 p.m.).

About 15 miles southeast of downtown York is the home of **Naylor Wines,** R.D. 3, Ebaugh Road, Stewartstown (tel. 993-2431), an area that was one of the original grape-growing and wine-making regions in America. This particular winery dates back to 1975, with its first wine production in 1978. Visitors can tour the 27-acre vineyards as well as the extensive indoor award-winning winery operations. There is no charge for touring or for sampling. Open daily 11 a.m. to 6 p.m. and Sunday from noon to 5 p.m. CC's accepted for wine purchases: MC and V.

NIGHTLIFE: For professional live entertainment, plan an evening at the **Strand-Capitol Performing Arts Center,** 50 North George St. (tel. 846-1111). A former vaudeville hall and a 1920s movie palace, this 1,214-seat theater, restored in 1980, is the venue for a varied program of Broadway shows, symphony concerts, ballet, opera, and big bands; on weekends, there is also a selection of classical movies. The box office is open Monday through Friday from 11:30 a.m. to 5 p.m. and on Saturday from 10 a.m. to 1 p.m. Tickets to most live performances range from $9 to $20, and films are $2.50 for adults and $1 for children under 12. CC's accepted: AE, Ch, MC, and V.

In contrast, the **York Little Theater,** 27 South Belmont St. (tel. 854-3894), is a community playhouse showcasing amateur actors with professional directors. The repertoire includes six main stage productions a year (musical, drama, and comedy), plus several children's productions and innovative "Studio Five" dramas. Box-office hours are weekdays from 9 a.m. to 5 p.m.; tickets are priced from $8 for musical and comedies and $9 for dramas. CC's accepted: MC and V.

EVENTS: Since 1973, the **Olde York Street Fair** has been a highlight among the yearly festivals in southern Pennsylvania. Held on Mother's Day, this outdoor gathering is centered in a five-block stretch of Market Street in the historic district. The attractions include more than 35 performing groups and ethnic folk dancers, plus 300 craftspeople displaying their handmade jewelry, weavings, artwork, and homemade foods. There is no admission charge; hours are 1 to 7 p.m. Complete details are available from the York County Tourist Convention and Visitors Bureau.

Chapter XI

CENTRAL PENNSYLVANIA

1. Columbia and Montour Counties
2. Williamsport
3. Altoona
4. Johnstown

A COLLAGE OF FERTILE FARMS, verdant valleys, and mighty mountains, central Pennsylvania is an expansive area covering hundreds of miles. Much of this land, from north to south, is also influenced by the gentle waters of the Susquehanna River.

Some of the more popular parts of this region, such as Harrisburg, Hershey, Gettysburg, and York, are already covered in other sections of this book. This chapter focuses on some of the lesser known highlights of central Pennsylvania.

And what a territory this is—almost 200 miles in width and length, with Interstate 80 traversing its center.

We'll look at four areas that illustrate the diversity of this vast chunk of Pennsylvania, starting with the covered bridges, historic sights, and farmlands of Columbia and Montour Counties. Our next stop is Williamsport, a city of great lumbering traditions and the home of Little League baseball. Farther westward, we'll explore the railroading center of Altoona, and finally, on to Johnstown, the indomitable city that has built a tourism industry around its flood history.

1. Columbia and Montour Counties

Located about 50 miles west of the Poconos, Columbia and Montour counties are best known as "the nation's covered-bridge capital." This area is home to more than 30 such structures, including a twin covered bridge, believed to be the only one of its kind left in the U.S.

Bisected in the middle by Interstate 80 (I-80), Columbia and Montour comprise a relatively small destination, approximately 30 miles wide and 35 miles from the most northerly to southerly points. The region's two principal towns, Bloomsburg and Danville, are both well known for different reasons. Bloomsburg (pop.: 11,700) is the home of a university considered to be one of the top learning institutions in central Pennsylvania, and Danville (pop.: 5,200), just ten miles west, is the headquarters of the internationally acclaimed Geisinger Medical Center.

Historically, Columbia County, which was part of Northumberland County until March 1813, is often associated with the origin of the song, "Hail, Columbia." Montour County, in turn, was formed from Columbia County in 1850 and named in honor of Madame Montour, a woman of considerable education, who was conversant in English, French, and a variety of Indian tongues. It is said that she was frequently present at Indian conferences and treaties in the early formation days of the county.

In addition to the covered bridges and other landmarks of days gone by, some of Pennsylvania's most productive and scenic farmlands are located in Columbia and Montour counties. Happily for visitors, these natural attributes are supplemented by a blend of top-notch culinary experiences, classic country inns, and craft shops.

VISITOR INFORMATION: Information on all visitor attractions, activities, accommodations, and events can be obtained from the **Columbia-Montour Tourist Promotion Agency,** R.D. 2, at exit 35 of I-80, Bloomsburg, PA 17815 (tel. 717/784-8279).

AREA CODE: All telephone numbers in the Columbia and Montour counties are part of the 717 area code.

GETTING TO AND AROUND COLUMBIA AND MONTOUR: The best way to get to Columbia and Montour counties is by car, whether your own or rented. Interstate 80 runs through the county from east to west, with exits 34 and 35 at Bloomsburg and exit 33 at Danville. The counties can also be approached from the north or south via Routes 15 and 11 or, slightly to the east, via I-81. The nearest airports are **Williamsport** (45 miles), **Wilkes-Barre** (65 miles) or **Harrisburg Airport** (80 miles). **Greyhound** and **Trailways** buses stop in both Danville and Bloomsburg.

WHERE TO STAY: Country inns and classic old-world hotels dominate the scene in Columbia and Montour, although there are also modern motels here. With the exception of suites, most accommodations are in the moderate price range.

Bloomsburg Area

The Inn at Turkey Hill, I-80 at exit 35, Bloomsburg, PA 17815 (tel. 717/387-1500), may be one of the newest lodging choices in the Bloomsburg area (opened in 1984) but it imparts the history and ambience of a family home dating back to 1839. Although it is located just south of the major interstate highway, the inn is secluded in a peaceful setting of rolling farmlands with a beautifully landscaped courtyard, a lily pond, and a sturdy old barn. A family enterprise with an enthusiastic and well-trained young staff, the inn is open all year and offers 18 guest rooms (two in the original house and the rest in new cottage-style buildings). All rooms have a private bath, air conditioning, color cable TV, a phone, and are individually furnished and decorated; there are two suites, each with a working fireplace and Jacuzzi bath. Complimentary continental breakfast is included in the room price (from $50 for a double and $120 for a suite). For lunch or dinner, there is a choice of two different atmospheres— The Greenhouse, a glass-enclosed conservatory overlooking the gardens and lily pond, or two early American dining rooms in the main house that feature wall murals depicting Turkey Hill as it was 150 years ago. The menu, which is the same in all rooms, features salads, casseroles, and sandwiches at lunchtime ($2.95 to $7.95). Dinner entrees are priced from $9 to $18, with most choices

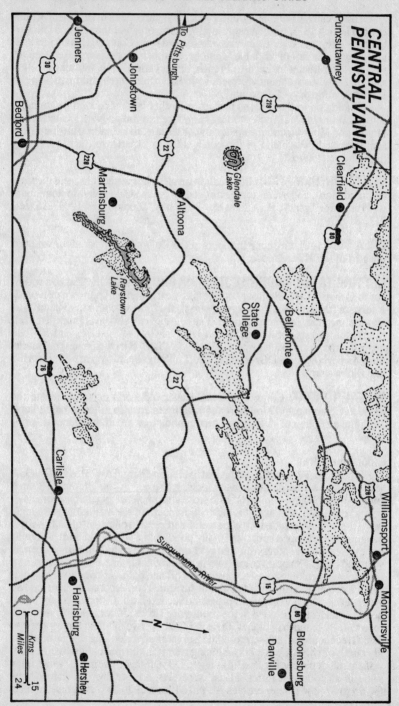

under $15. Specialties include rolled duck with wild-cherry sauce; fresh salmon in puff pastry; orange roughy and shrimp in champagne sauce; and, appropriately, country turkey en croûte. Appetizers, which are priced from $3.50 to $5, include baked brie, spinach manicotti, and smoked turkey with fresh fruit. All main courses are accompanied by salad, sorbet, potato, and vegetable. Restaurant hours are from 11 a.m. to 2 p.m. and from 5:30 to 10 p.m., Monday through Saturday; on Sunday from 11 a.m. to 2 p.m. for brunch and from 4 to 8 p.m. for dinner. All major CC's are accepted.

Ever since 1855, the **Hotel Magee and Publick House,** 20 W. Main St., Box 149, Bloomsburg, PA 17815 (tel. 717/784-3200), have upheld a tradition of fine lodgings and bountiful food. A sturdy brick inn located in the heart of the town, the Magee has recently been renovated; all of its 55 units have handsome reproduction furnishings, modern private baths, air conditioning, color cable TV, and a phone. The rooms offer a choice of one or two double beds or a king-size bed; and room rates for two people range from $35 to $60. Once you have settled into the Magee, however, the main attraction is in the Publick House Restaurant which calls its dinner menu "an American Heritage Festival." Entrees (priced from $15.95 to $25.95) include Hawaiian steak teriyaki; roast duckling with California brandy sauce; chicken Stoltzfus (Pennsylvania Dutch–style); mesquite-grilled pork chops; Maryland crab cakes; and lobster tails. If the prices seem high, it's because you also get unlimited trips to the "groaning board" of appetizers and desserts which range from shrimp in the shell and seafood salad to liver pâté, chicken corn chowder, herring in wine, and all sorts of salads and sweets. Open for dinner from 4:30 to 9:30 p.m. Monday through Thursday; until 10 p.m. on Friday and Saturday; and on Sunday from 2:15 to 8 p.m. The Publick House also features Saturday night seafood smörgåsbords ($11.95) and other seasonal feasts. All major CC's accepted.

Danville Area

A 19th-century barn has formed the cornerstone for the lodging and restaurant complex known as the **Pine Barn Inn,** 1 Pine Barn Place, Danville, PA 17821 (tel. 717/275-2071). With various additions and extensions over the last 40 years, the inn now has 45 bedrooms of varying sizes and shapes, with one or two double beds. All units have private bath, color cable TV, telephone, air conditioning, and are furnished with quality Colonial-style furniture (doubles are priced from $37 to $41). Located off Bloom Street in a quiet corner of Danville, away from all the highways, the Pine Barn is adjacent to the famous Geisinger Medical Center. The restaurant, which is open from 7 a.m. to 10 p.m. daily except Sunday (until 8 p.m. only), features light and inexpensive fare throughout the day and goes gourmet in the evenings (entrees priced from $9.95 to $17.95). Some of the dishes include rock Cornish game hen; veal cutlet sautéed with mushrooms, onions, cream, and apple brandy; and baked scallops. In keeping with its Americana theme, the Pine Barn often features Yankee pot roast, Virginia ham, and various turkey dishes. With each main course comes potato, vegetable, and unlimited visits to a tempting salad bar. Paintings by area artists (which are often for sale) add a touch of class to the homey décor. After dinner, you may wish to stroll in the Pine Barn's Swallow Gift Shop to see the mixed array of local crafts. All major CC's accepted.

The **Sheraton Danville Inn,** R.D. 2, Box 100, Danville, PA 17821 (tel. 717/275-5510 or toll-free 800/325-3535), is situated just off exit 33 on I-80, three miles north of Danville. Modern in design, many of the rooms of this two-story property surround a central courtyard with a heated indoor pool, an open-air café, and rows of hanging plants and palms. The 146 bedrooms are spacious with two double beds and country-style furnishings including rocking chairs, autumn-toned bedspreads and drapes, and pictures of farm scenes. Doubles range from $51 to $65; bi-level suites are also available with a terrace, from $110. Facilities also include a sauna, a whirlpool, miniature golf, a gift shop, and a lounge with evening entertainment. The main three-tiered restaurant, The Glenwood, also faces the inner courtyard and enjoys a tropical ambience, even in the snowy winter months. Dinner entrees, priced from $7.95 to $15.95, range from chicken teriyaki and filet mignon to seafood dishes, all accompanied by salad, vegetable, and potato. All major CC's accepted.

Budget Range

Established in 1983, the **Pine Barn Guest House,** 641 Bloom Street, Danville, PA 17821 (tel. 717/275-2071), is a three-story residence adjacent to the 40-year old inn of the same name. With six cheerily decorated bedrooms and two shared bathrooms, this Colonial-style house offers simple lodgings, priced from $18.95 for two people. All major CC's accepted.

WHERE TO DINE: In addition to the fine dining rooms of the above inns, the Columbia/Montour area has a variety of good restaurants of both contemporary and country inn types, all mostly in the moderate price category.

Bloomsburg Area

Two miles north of Bloomsburg is the little town of **Lightstreet,** (exit 35N off I-80). Although it's worth a visit here just to see the rows of immaculately kept Federal-style houses, most people head in this direction to feast at the **Lightstreet Hotel,** Main Street, (tel. 784-1070). Founded in 1856, the inn has been in the hands of the Milroy family since 1985 and is now exclusively a restaurant, with a choice of three dining rooms and a convivial lounge bar. The early American décor includes hand-crochet placemats and miniature streetlamp candle holders on the tables. Light snacks are featured at lunch, but the restaurant is busiest at dinnertime when the menu features steaks from Montfort of Colorado; chicken breast with mushrooms; and various seafood dishes such as boneless rainbow trout, and crab au gratin. Main courses, priced from $8.95 to $16.95, are accompanied by salad, vegetable, and potato. Open Monday through Saturday from 11 a.m. to 10 p.m. and Sunday from 11:00 a.m. to 7 p.m. (but closed on major holidays). All major CC's are accepted.

Established in 1981, **Russell's,** 117 W. Main St. (tel. 387-1332), is a trendy restaurant conveniently situated right in the center of Bloomsburg. Lemon, peach, olive, and cream tones dominate the décor which is also enhanced by watercolor and oil paintings and a wealth of hanging plants and flowers. Lunch and Sunday brunch items include salads, sandwiches, omelets, burgers, and mini- and maxi-salads (all under $5). This restaurant is particularly popular for dinner when the menu ranges from chicken with champagne and cashews and prime ribs of beef to eight different veal creations and a dozen seafood choices, such as haddock hollandaise, Cajun shrimp, and scallops scampi. The entrees, priced from $9.95 to $17.95, come with salad, potato, and vegetable. The service is extremely attentive and eager. Open Monday through Saturday from 10 a.m. to 2 a.m. and Sunday from 8 a.m. to 2 a.m. CC's accepted: MC and V.

A country setting surrounds **Ridgway's,** 801 Central Road, Bloomsburg (tel. 784-8354), situated south of exit 35 of I-80 and just down the road from the Inn at Turkey Hill. The building is rustic inside and out with old sidebarn décor and fixtures. In addition to a cozy bar and a main dining room, there is a shaded deck outside for cocktails or snacks. During the day, the menu features light meals, such as sandwiches, salads, chilis, and burgers, priced from $1.95 to $4.95. Dinner entrees, in the $9.95 to $17.95 bracket, include chicken Kiev, charbroiled filet mignon, crab legs, and combination dishes (pairing steak with chicken or seafood). Open Monday through Saturday from 11:30 a.m. until midnight, and on Sunday from 4 to 10 p.m. All major CC's accepted.

North of Bloomsburg and Lightstreet, you'll find good value and a country-inn atmosphere at the **Heritage House,** Route 487, Orangeville (tel. 784-5581). Breakfast, lunch, snacks, and dinner are served here, with evening entrees ranging from roast beef and seafood to turkey and smoked ham, priced from $6 to $11. A salad bar and homemade ice creams are also featured. A 115-year-old reconstructed covered bridge adds a welcoming touch to the outside of the restaurant and the interior décor, which changes seasonally, features Columbia County antiques. Open Monday through Saturday from 10 a.m. to 10 p.m. and Sunday from 11:30 a.m. to 10 p.m. No CC's accepted.

Danville Area

An early 1800s hardware store is the setting for a reliable restaurant right in the middle of Danville at 336 Mill St. (tel. 275-6615). Appropriately called **The Old Hardware Store,** this spacious high-ceiling structure consists of several dining sections, all with a bright and airy atmosphere enhanced by potted and hanging plants and a collection of seasoned hardware implements hung along the spotlessly white walls. As you munch on burgers, sandwiches, or pasta dishes, you can glance up at the classic old farm tools, rug-beaters, and washboards. Most lunch choices average $2 to $4 and evening meals run about $4 to $6; there is no liquor license but a wide choice of sodas, fruit juices, coffees, and teas. Open Monday through Thursday from 11 a.m. to 8 p.m.; Friday and Saturday from 11 a.m. to 9 p.m.; and Sunday from 11:30 a.m. to 2 p.m. CC's accepted: MC and V.

TOP ATTRACTIONS: It is not surprising that a covered bridge is the joint emblem of Columbia and Montour counties. Within a small radius, you can tour 30 **covered bridges,** including the only twin-covered bridges in the U.S., named East and West Paden at Forks (on Route 487). With the earliest specimen dating back to 1844, almost all of the bridges are well over 100 years old. To help you plot a route to take in as many bridges as possible, you can obtain a free guide/map of all the bridges from the Columbia-Montour Tourism Agency.

Bloomsburg Historic District

Pennsylvania's only incorporated town, Bloomsburg has more than 650 homes which are designated as part of a National Historic District. Mostly private dwellings or commercial enterprises, these buildings span a 150-year period and include a diversity of styles—from Georgian, Federal, and Italianate to Gothic Revival, Victorian, Colonial Revival, Queen Anne, and art deco. The historic district encompasses all of Main Street, and East Market Street to Fifth Street. A good starting point is the **Columbia County Court House** (1891) in the center of town. Largely Romanesque, this building is admired for its flowing arches, columns, and chiming clock. Other contrasting structures include the **Greek Revival post office** and the **art deco fire station.** Self-guided walking tour pamphlets are available from the Columbia-Montour Tourist Office or at the various hotels and restaurants in the town. During the months of June through October, Bloomsburg's Market Square is also the scene of a colorful **farmers' curb market,** every Tuesday, Thursday, and Saturday from 7 a.m. to 1 p.m. Local farmers pull in their vans along the tree-shaded curb to sell a variety of fresh-picked vegetables and fruits as well as flowers and baked goods.

No matter where you wander around downtown Bloomsburg, one sight dominates the horizon—**Carver Hall** (1867), at the entrance to Bloomsburg

University, College Hill (tel. 389-3900). With an ornately carved dome-shaped Colonial tower, this landmark has become a symbol of the town and the nucleus of the school's sprawling 173-acre campus. Visitors are welcome to walk around the grounds and visit the library and other public exhibits.

In addition to Bloomsburg, other towns in this dual-county area (especially Danville, Lightstreet, and Orangeville) are also worth a walk or a drive to see the neat rows of Federal-style buildings and the gaily painted Victorian houses with turrets, gazebos, and gingerbread trim. Plan to spend a few hours a day driving the back roads, particularly Route 487, both north and south of I-80. This meandering country route provides ever-changing vistas of tree-lined mountains and expansive valleys with horse, dairy, and vegetable farms. If you are looking to take some fresh produce home, the Catawissa area, eight miles south of Bloomsburg, is home to a variety of roadside stands along Route 487, such as Rohrbach's and Krum's.

Although technically in neighboring Schuylkill County, the **Pioneer Tunnel,** Route 61, Ashland (tel. 875-3850), is so close to Columbia that you shouldn't miss it. Located in the heart of Pennsylvania's anthracite coal region, this is a genuine horizontal drift mine, running 1,800 feet straight into the side of Mahanoy Mountain. Visitors can tour the mine (adults, $3.50 and children, $1.50) and take a steam-locomotive (lokie) ride around mine country (adults, $1.50 and children, 75¢). Open weekends only in May and daily from May 30 through Labor Day weekend from 10 a.m. to 6 p.m. Picnic and playground facilities are available in the park adjoining Pioneer Tunnel, and 200 yards away is the state-sponsored **Museum of Anthracite Mining** (tel. 875-4708), an exhibit devoted to mining technology and geology. Maintaining the same opening hours as the **Pioneer Tunnel** (except only from noon to 6 p.m. on Sunday), the museum charges $2 for adults and $1 for children.

NIGHTLIFE: The region's only resident professional company, the **Bloomsburg Theatre Ensemble** performs throughout the year at the refurbished art deco–style **Alvina Krause Theatre,** 226 Center St., Bloomsburg (tel. 784-8181), about a block away from the Hotel Magee. Recent plays have ranged from classics like *The School for Scandal* to contemporary Neil Simon Broadway hits. Performances are staged on Thursdays, Fridays, and Saturdays at 8 p.m. (tickets are $11, with reductions for seniors and children) and occasional matinees on Saturdays at 2 p.m. ($8.50). The box office is open from 10 a.m. to 5 p.m. Monday through Friday; from noon to 2 p.m. on Saturday; and one hour before each performance. Credit cards: MC and V.

SHOPPING: With so many Victorian- and Federal-style homes lining the streets of Bloomsburg, Danville, Berwick, Lightstreet and Orangeville, you'll find frequent yard, barn, and porch sales along the major and minor roads. Among the permanent shops worth a stop is **Red Mill Antiques,** 44 Red Mill Road, Bloomsburg (tel. 784-7146). This is a three-story converted gristmill loaded with antique and country furniture, brass fixtures, baskets, candlesticks, lamps, and the like. Open Monday through Saturday from 9 a.m. to 5 p.m., and on Sundays from 1 to 4 p.m. CC's accepted: MC and V.

For smaller collectibles like old glass bottles, china, and stoneware, try **Liberty Antiques** at 2615 Old Berwick Rd., Bloomsburg (tel. 683-5419). During the summer months, it's open Wednesday through Saturday from noon to 4:30 p.m., and at other times by appointment. No CC's accepted.

For locally made country crafts, from pottery, candles, and vine wreaths to chimes and dried floral arrangements, drive north from Bloomsburg to **The Pottery Barn,** Route 487, Orangeville (tel. 683-5965). Open Wednesday through

Saturday from 10 a.m. to 5 p.m. (until 8 p.m. on Fridays), and on Sundays from 1 to 5 p.m. CC's accepted: MC and V.

Another shop worth a visit for its sightseeing value as well as its wares is **The Village Sampler,** Route 54, Riverside (tel. 275-0690), just across the river from Danville. Actually a pair of shops, this dual enterprise is housed in the buildings which were once the local railroad depot and Susquehanna Hotel. The former is chock full of gift items from folk art to cross-stitch supplies and the latter is an emporium of early American and Colonial furnishings. Open Monday through Saturday from 9:30 a.m. to 5:30 p.m. (Friday until 9 p.m.). CC's accepted: MC and V.

This area is also a mecca for doll collectors, with at least two shops specializing in nothing but dolls and stuffed animals of all kinds and vintages: **Carol & Janet's Doll House,** 260 West Main St., Bloomsburg (tel. 784-1787) and **Simple Country Treasures,** 119 Mill St., Danville (tel. 275-4580). Both shops are open Monday through Saturday from 9 a.m. to 5 p.m. and both accept MC and V credit cards; the latter also accepts AE.

There is always a holiday spirit at **The Christmas Shoppe,** Route 642 West, Danville (tel. 275-7785), located just south of I-80 exit 33. A newly restored 18th-century bank barn, this is a yuletide treasure-trove at any time of year and the ideal spot to stock up on gaily decorated holiday wrappings, boxes, and bags. Ornaments are arranged in aisles—from angels, bears, and baubles to santas, sports cars, or farm animals. Nutcracker figurines, music boxes, puppets, and heirloom dolls also line the walls. Open from February through December, this festive emporium operates daily from 10 a.m. to 4 p.m. Monday through Saturday and from 1 to 4 p.m. on Sunday. No CC's accepted.

SPORTS AND ACTIVITIES: With facilities that include a fitness track, tennis courts, a municipal swimming pool with a sunbathing area, picnic tables, and outdoor grills, **Bloomsburg Town Park** (tel. 387-0443) is a playground for residents and visitors alike. In a sylvan setting along the banks of the Susquehanna River, the park is located at the juncture of Market Street and Fort McClure Boulevard on the southern edge of the town; no admission charge.

A variety of nature trails (including a multi-sensory Braille Trail) draws many visitors to the **Montour Preserve,** Route 54, Washingtonville (tel. 437-3131), north of exit 33 on I-80. Open year round, the preserve also includes areas for picnicking (with tables, benches, and outdoor grills) and a lake for fishing and bird watching. Admission is free; opening times for the grounds vary with the seasons and times of darkness, but a **Visitors Center** is open Monday through Friday from 9 a.m. until 4 p.m. all year and from 2 until 5 p.m. on Saturday and Sunday, from the second weekend of April to the second weekend of September.

Although just about any spot along a country road is ideal for a picnic, one special venue to keep in mind is the park at the **Twin Bridges** at Forks, Route 487, north of exit 35 off I-80. Picnic tables are provided both under and beside the bridges in a sheltered brookside setting. No admission charge.

Golf: Visiting golfers are warmly received at the **Mill Race Golf Resort,** Route 487, Benton (tel. 925-2040), an 18-hole complex north of I-80. Greens fees average $8 for 18 holes on weekdays and $10 on weekends. Motorized carts are available for rent from $12 to $14 a round.

EVENTS: Ever since 1854, the **Bloomsburg Fair** has drawn people to Columbia County. Always scheduled to start on the third Monday after Labor Day, this event has become the largest six-day fair in the U.S., spread over permanent fairgrounds of 236 acres and 50 spacious buildings. Highlights of the fair include big-name entertainment, an all-weather racetrack, a demolition derby, marching bands, arts and crafts, and all types of agricultural exhibits. General admission is $2. For full information, contact the **Columbia-Montour Tourist Promotion Agency** or call the festival committee (tel. 784-4949).

CHILDREN'S CORNER: Described as Pennsylvania's "No. 1 family fun park," **Knoebels Amusement Park,** Route 487, Elysburg (tel. 672-2572), is in a secluded forest setting, just south of Columbia County. This complex is a children's haven with all sorts of outdoor games and rides such as bumper boats and cars, water slides, and a classic wooden roller coaster (rides range in price from 40¢ to $1). Parking, general admission, and picnic facilities are free. The park also offers 400 camp sites, swimming pools, gift shops, restaurants, and cafeterias. Open daily, mid-June to Labor Day, from 11 a.m. to 10 p.m.; and weekends only from late-May to mid-June and early September from 10 a.m. to 6 p.m.

2. Williamsport

The largest city in north-central Pennsylvania, Williamsport (pop.: 33,000) is bisected by the Susquehanna River in a sylvan setting of woodland and mountain vistas.

In the second half of the 19th century, this well-forested area boomed as one of the largest lumbering centers in the world. Local timber tycoons prospered and built grand homes in the town. It is said that Williamsport had more millionaires per capita than any other city in the U.S. To this day, West Fourth Street, lined with Gothic and Victorian mansions, is still called "Millionaires' Row." Small wonder that other streets in midtown still bear appropriate names like Spruce, Walnut, Birch, Locust, Laurel, Cherry, Willow, Maple, Pine, and Lumber.

In this century, Williamsport also became the birthplace of Little League baseball (1939). Ever since then, thousands of young fans come here each year to see the Little League Museum and the annual World Series.

The forests that surround Williamsport today are primarily used for recreation, offering an abundance of hiking and hunting trails, fishing and boating sports. Williamsport is also the home base for the "Hiawatha" paddleboat cruises along the Susquehanna River.

VISITOR INFORMATION: Brochures and maps about Williamsport and the surrounding county can be obtained by contacting the **Lycoming County Tourist and Convention Bureau,** 454 Pine St., Williamsport, PA 17701 (tel. 717/326-1971).

AREA CODE: The telephone area code for Williamsport and the surrounding region is 717.

GETTING TO AND AROUND WILLIAMSPORT: The best way to reach Williamsport is by car; the city is located 15 miles north of exit 30 (Route 15) on the east-west I-80. From a north-south direction, Route 15 passes through the city.

By Plane: Allegheny Commuter (tel. toll-free 800/428-4253) operates regular small craft air service into **Williamsport/Lycoming County Airport,** at Montoursville (tel. 368-2444), four miles east of downtown Williamsport.

By Bus: A daily schedule of services from other cities in Pennsylvania, New York, and beyond is operated by **Susquehanna Trailways,** 56 E. Third St. (tel.

322-5361 or toll-free 800/692-6314). Local transport is provided by **City Bus,** 1500 W. Third St. (tel. 326-2500).

Car Rental: Two firms have desks at the airport, **Avis** (tel. 368-2683) and **National** (tel. 368-8151); **Hertz** maintains a rental station in the city of Williamsport at 152 E. Church St. (tel. 323-6169).

Taxis: Local service is provided by **McCarthy Flowered Cabs** (tel. 322-2222).

WHERE TO STAY: Whether you prefer a hotel, motel, or bed-and-breakfast inn, Williamsport offers a fine range of accommodations. In general, the rates can be considered in the moderate bracket.

In the central part of the city, near the main Market Street Bridge, is the **Sheraton Inn,** 100 Pine St., Williamsport, PA 17701 (tel. 717/327-8231 or toll-free 800/325-3535). Fairly new to the area (1983), this modern brick structure enjoys an ideal location two blocks from the banks of the Susquehanna and with distant mountain views. The 148 rooms each have contemporary décor, double or oversized beds, air conditioning, a direct-dial phone, and color cable TV. Doubles range from $52 to $54. Other amenities include an indoor heated pool, free parking, a lounge with entertainment nightly, and a full-service restaurant called Seasons. Hot and cold sandwiches and salads are featured at lunchtime, in the $2.95 to $4.95 bracket. Dinner entrees, priced from $8.95 to $15.95, focus on prime rib, surf-and-turf, steaks, seafood, and international favorites such as veal parmigiana and chicken Cordon Bleu. All main courses come with a chilled relish tray, soup or salad, potato, and vegetable. Lunch is available from 11:30 a.m. to 2 p.m., and dinner from 5 to 10 p.m. All major CC's accepted.

In the heart of the business district is the **Genetti-Lycoming Hotel and Motor Lodge,** West Fourth and William Streets, Williamsport, PA 17701 (tel. 717/326-5181), a combination of traditional hotel and modern motel units. With a total of 200 rooms, this property offers a blend of old-world and contemporary décors, featuring brass beds and Queen Anne chairs in some rooms and modern light wood furnishings in others. Doubles start at $50. Guest facilities include an outdoor swimming pool, a patio, sunbrellas, a TV lounge, a barber, and a beauty shop. There is also an early English restaurant, Rhonabwy's, with a King Arthur–style décor. Lunch, priced from $1.95 to $3.95, features sandwiches, burgers, salads, and omelets. Dinner entrees are in the $6.95 to $18.95 price bracket, with most dishes under $12. Choices include steaks and seafood, such as mako shark, swordfish, tuna, and haddock, all served with salad and rice or potato. Lunch is available from 11:30 a.m. to 2:30 p.m. daily; dinner from 5 to 10 p.m. on Monday through Saturday, and until 8 p.m. on Sunday. CC's accepted: AE, MC, and V.

If you'd like to experience the glamour and style of the city's lumbering era, the top choice is **Reighard House,** 1323 East Third St., Williamsport, PA 17701 (tel. 717/326-3593). Located a mile east of midtown, this grand old Victorian mansion was built in 1905 on a hillside overlooking the Susquehanna. It served variously as a private residence, a county barracks, a boarding house, and a nursing home before it was purchased, lovingly restored, and turned into a B&B by Susie and Bill Reighard in 1986. All six bedrooms, each decorated individually with four posters, canopy, or brass beds, now have spacious private bathrooms and are air-conditioned. Guests can also enjoy the rest of the house, including a front porch overlooking the river, a formal parlor, a music room with a grand piano, a library, a TV room, and an oak-paneled dining room (where a country/gourmet breakfast is served each morning). Doubles range from $45 to $50 per night and that includes breakfast, afternoon refreshments, use of bikes, off-street parking, and, if you arrive by plane, airport pick-up and delivery. The personable and obliging Reighards will also suggest local sightseeing itineraries and go to great lengths to make sure your stay in Williamsport is a happy one. No smoking is permitted in the bedrooms or eating areas. CC's accepted: AE, MC, and V.

On the south side of the Susquehanna near the Little League Museum is the **Quality Inn,** 234 Montgomery Pike (Route 15), South Williamsport, PA 17701 (tel. 717/323-9801 or toll-free 800/228-5151). This modern 115-room property is nestled in a forest setting with views of both the mountains and the city. Each bedroom has a choice of double, twin, or king size beds, with air conditioning, color TV, free movies, and a direct-dial phone. Doubles range from $44 to $64. Guest facilities include an outdoor pool, a sauna, a restaurant, and an adjoining lounge with nightly musical entertainment. Major CC's accepted.

Budget

The hillside directly opposite the Little League complex is the location of the **Kings Inn Motel,** 590 Montgomery Pike (Route 15), South Williamsport, PA 17701 (tel. 717/322-4707). This 48-unit motel was started in 1954 by John King and today it is run by the Rosato family. The modern bedrooms each have two double beds, a direct-dial phone, color TV, and air conditioning. Doubles range from $35 to $45 and include complimentary coffee, juice, and donuts. The adjacent St. Regis Room restaurant, run by the same family, is opened for dinner daily from 5 to 10 p.m., and features prime ribs, steaks, and seafood, mostly in the moderate price range. All CC's accepted.

A favorite with families is the **City View,** Route 15, R.D. 4, Box 550, South Williamsport, PA 17701 (tel. 717/326-2601), a one-story motel overlooking both the downtown area and the Little League Park. There are 42 units, each with two double beds, color cable TV, air conditioning, and a phone; some rooms also have radios and balconies. Doubles range from $40 to $44. This is also the home of the Country House Restaurant, which features a lumbering era décor and 100-year-old photographs of Williamsport on the walls. Open daily for breakfast from 6:45 to 10 a.m. (in the $1.95 to $3.95 price range), and for dinner from 4:30 to 8:30 p.m., offering such entrees as steaks, seafood, country baked ham, and chicken dishes, in the $5.95 to $7.95 bracket, including a soup-and-salad bar. CC's accepted: MC and V.

WHERE TO DINE: Like the city's hotel dining rooms, the top restaurant choices in the Williamsport area fall mostly into the moderate price range.

The best restaurant in the city is the **Peter Herdic House,** 407 West Fourth St. (tel. 322-0165), a restored Italian-style villa on the street known as "Millionaire's Row." Built by the city's most famous lumbering baron in 1854–1855, this beautifully restored home was opened as a restaurant in 1984 by two local sisters, Marcia and Gloria Miele. Painted in tones of pink both outside and within, the décor is a mix of furnishings from Williamsport's earlier days, including a bar that was once a witness stand in the courthouse, a double crystal chandelier, stained-glass-trimmed mirrors, floral frescoes, hurricane candle lamps, lace table coverings, plush velour Victorian chairs, and spotlit paintings of the Herdic House during its heydays. Lunch, priced from $3.50 to $5.95, focuses primarily on sandwiches, salads, pastas, omelets, and light entrees (such as tenderloin tips, barbecued seafood, or parmesan chicken). The gourmet choices at dinner range from chicken with champagne cream sauce; salmon in puff pastry; and rolled veal alla marsala to pork with roasted peppers; filet mignon with Dijon cream sauce; tournedos of beef Oscar; blackened Cajun-style fish; and rack of lamb. The entrees, priced from $9.95 to $15.95, are accompanied by vegetables and potato or rice. Lunch is served Monday through Friday from 11 a.m. to 2 p.m., and dinner Monday through Saturday from 5 to 10 p.m. CC's accepted: AE, MC, and V.

Panoramic views of Williamsport are part of the dining experience at the **The Hillside Restaurant,** 2701 Four Mile Drive, Montoursville (tel. 326-6779), about 6 miles to the northeast. Lunch, priced from $2.95 to $4.95, includes salads, quiches, pastas, omelets, burgers, and sandwiches. Dinner entrees, priced from $8.85 to $14.95, are a creative blend of American cuisine (such as sweet apple pork or charbroiled veal chop); international dishes (cashew chicken, veal Romano, and pork Oriental); steaks, and seafood (from king crab, red snapper, salmon and halibut to catfish amandine). Lunch is served from 11 a.m. to 4:30 p.m. Monday through Friday; and dinner from 4:30 to 10 p.m. Monday through Saturday. All major CC's accepted.

Budget Meals

The Miele sisters, the same capable duo who have transformed the Peter Herdic House into a gourmet gem, are the proprietors of the **Court and Willow Café,** 326 Court St. (tel. 322-0135), and they are ably assisted by two other generations of their family. Started ten years ago, this bistro-style restaurant offers light menus with fresh ingredients and lots of homebaked breads and desserts. Lunch items, priced from $1.95 to $3.95, focus on salads, hot and cold sandwiches, and pitawiches. Dinner entrees, in the $4.95 to $6.95 range, include quiches, pastas, pan-fried seafood, chicken Diane, and freshly roasted turkey. All main courses are served with salad, potato, and vegetable. There is no bar, but soft drinks, juices, and beer are available. Open Monday through Friday from 11 a.m. to 3 p.m. for lunch and from 5 to 9 p.m. for dinner; on Saturday for lunch from 11 a.m. to 2 p.m.; and on Sunday for brunch from 10 a.m. to 2 p.m. No CC's accepted.

TOP ATTRACTIONS: Nearly three million youngsters in 25 countries of the world will be quick to tell you that 1989 is the fiftieth anniversary of Little League. Perhaps you were once on the mound yourself or maybe you have a Little Leaguer in the family, or even if you just enjoy watching the game, then you're sure to relish a trip to Williamsport, the home of the **Peter J. McGovern Little League Baseball Museum,** Route 15 (tel. 326-3607). This "hands-on" baseball showcase for all ages invites visitors to participate in the batting and pitching cages, watch instant replay on video monitors, relive the highlights of past world series, and see films and exhibits that tell the story of Little League's growth to over 7,000 leagues. Open Monday through Saturday from 10 a.m. to 5 p.m. (until 8 p.m. from Memorial Day through Labor Day), and on Sunday from 1 to 5 p.m. (Closed Thanksgiving, Christmas, and New Year's Day). Admission charges are $3 for adults; $1.50 for seniors; $1 for children (5 to 13); or an inclusive family charge of $8 for parents and dependent children.

You don't have to be a baseball fan to enjoy Williamsport. Many travelers come here just to take an old-fashioned paddle-wheeled **riverboat cruise** along the Susquehanna River on board *The Hiawatha,* docked at Susquehanna Park, about two miles west of the city center. From May 1 through June 14, 1½-hour sightseeing excursions are scheduled on Wednesday at 2 p.m., and on Saturday and Sunday at 2 and 4 p.m. From June 15 through August 31st, there are 2 p.m. cruises every day except Monday and additional 4 p.m. sailings on Wednesday, Saturday, and Sunday. An expanded schedule also is in effect for holiday weekends and Little League World Series Week. The admission price for adults is $4, and $2 for children 12 and under. Weekly dinner cruises are also scheduled on Thursday evenings from mid-June to early September at 6 and 8 p.m., priced at $16 per person; and from June 1 through mid-October, brunch cruises are operated at 11:30 a.m. and 1 p.m. at $10 per adult and $6 for children under 10. The dinner and brunch cruises must be booked in advance. For reservations and full information, contact the **Williamsport Chamber of Commerce,** 454 Pine St., Williamsport, PA 17701 (tel. 717/326-1971).

Lycoming County Historical Museum, 858 West Fourth St. (tel. 326-3326) is a modern structure but with a host of memorabilia garnered from the area, including the components of a Colonial kitchen, a one-room school, an 1870 "Millionaires' Row" Victorian parlor, and an 1896 bedroom. In addition, there are dioramas of an Indian village and an early lumbering community, as well as the $400,000 Shempp Toy Train Collection, one of the finest of its kind in the U.S. with 337 complete trains and 100 individual locomotives of which 12 are one-of-a-kind. There is also an "operate-it-yourself" train set that delights visitors of all ages. Open Tuesday through Saturday from 9:30 a.m. to 4 p.m., and on Sunday from 1:30 to 4 p.m.; admission is $2 for adults and $1 for children.

The **Fin, Fur, and Feather Wildlife Museum,** Route 44, Lock Haven (tel. 769-6620), is a unique collection dedicated to animals, birds, and fish from around the world. Located about 20 miles northwest of Williamsport, this rural outpost explores the roles of the hunter, trapper, fisherman, and conservationist in a panorama of life-size wildlife exhibits. The **National Taxidermists Hall of Fame** is also located here, as is a "trading post," featuring clothing, books, and gifts designed for the outdoor life. The museum is open from mid-April to mid-December from 9 a.m. to 5 p.m. daily; and from late December to mid-April on weekends from 9 a.m. to 5 p.m. Admission charge is $4 for adults and $2 for children. The shop is open daily year round.

SHOPPING: Baseball card collectors flock to the **Dixie Baseball Card Shop,** Route 15, South Williamsport (tel. 326-1297). More than four million baseball cards and posters from 1900 to the present are stocked here. Open seven days a week from noon to 5 p.m. No CC's accepted.

All kinds of memorabilia from yesteryear are on sale at the **Sterner's General Store,** Route 405, Dewart (tel. 538-5280), about 12 miles southeast of Williamsport. Family-owned since 1873, this old-fashioned country shop and post office are chock full of everything from coffee grinders to spools of thread, Christmas ornaments, nutcrackers, jumping jacks, singing tops, salt-glazed pottery, hand-stenciled stoneware, rag dolls, teddy bears, handwoven rugs, tinware, and baskets of all kinds. Food items include penny candy, cheese wheels, and barrel molasses. If you prefer to browse, there's lots to catch your eye: original brass fixtures, a butter churn, a wicker sleigh, and a brass cash register. Open Monday through Saturday from 8:30 a.m. to 5:30 p.m., and until 8 p.m. on Fridays. CC's accepted: MC and V.

For country crafts of top quality, **The Lambert House,** 1429 W. Southern Ave., South Williamsport (tel. 322-7939) is in a class by itself. A two-story Federal town house, this eight-room shop is so cleverly decorated that all of the items for sale combine to reflect the aura of a Colonial home. The crafts, which represent the efforts of more than 100 local artisans, include Amish quilts, home furnishings, candles, crockery, wreaths, wood carvings, baskets, dolls, needlepoint, watercolors, crochet, and pewter. Open Monday through Saturday from 10 a.m. to 5 p.m. CC's accepted: MC and V.

SPORTS AND ACTIVITIES: The **Susquehanna State Park,** on the western edge of the city, is an ideal spot for walking, jogging, picnicking, and water sports. From May through October, **Delaware Canoe Rentals** maintain a stand near the *Hiawatha* dock, offering canoes for $3.50 an hour or $20 per day. For a more extensive selection, you can also try **Deliverance Lifetime Sports,** 2 W. Southern Ave., South Williamsport (tel. 322-8066).

About a half-hour north and west of Williamsport is Pine Creek Valley, a haven for canoeing, fishing, hiking, hunting, camping, skiing, and snowmobiling. Named for Little Pine Creek, which was originally one of the main streams used to raft logs during the great lumber years, this area is known locally as Pennsylvania's "Grand Canyon Country." It is a natural woodland expanse of twisting mountain roads, rambling brooks and creeks, giant pines, mountain trails, and free-roaming wildlife. The focal point for sports enthusiasts is **Little Pine State Park,** Route 44, P.O. Box 100, Waterville, PA 17776 (tel. 717/753-8209). Open year round, this park is the best overall source for canoe and rowboat rentals ($5 an hour or $25 a day); paddleboats ($5 an hour); camping ($5 a night); and fishing (seven-day licenses from $15).

Golf: About five miles south of Williamsport is the **White Deer Golf Course,** Route 15, Montgomery (tel. 547-2186). This 18-hole public course welcomes visitors; greens fees are $8 on weekdays and $10 on weekends; electric carts can be rented for $13. Facilities include a pro shop and a cafeteria-style restaurant.

EVENTS: Two of Williamsport's top happenings take place in the last weeks of summer. The **Susquehanna Boom Festival,** held in mid-August, is named for the lumber era that spurred Williamsport from a small village into the "lumber capital of the world." This nine-day celebration includes a parade, a hot-air-balloon rally, a water carnival, a professional horse show, drum and bugle corps competition, a professional woodsman's rally, and top-name entertainment nightly. Tickets to various events range from $2 to $10. For more information and a program, contact the tourist bureau or the Susquehanna Boom Festival, P.O. Box 34, Williamsport, PA 17703 (tel. 717/322-2435 or 327/BOOM).

The most famous event of the year is the **Little League World Series.** Held in late August, this is an international celebration, with top Little League players from around the world competing in an elimination tournament before thousands of fans, proud families, stars from the major leagues, and leading sports broadcasters. There is no admission charge for the games; all tickets for the 9,000-seat Lamade Stadium are complimentary. For further information, contact the Little League Baseball Series, P.O. Box 3485, Williamsport, PA 17701 (tel. 717/326-1921).

CHILDREN'S CORNER: From the Little League Museum to the *Hiawatha*, almost all of this area holds fascination for youngsters. An added nearby attraction is **Clyde Peeling's Reptileland** on Route 15, Allenwood (tel. 538-1869), about ten miles southeast of Williamsport. Described as a natural-history safari, this unique zoo is home to cobras, giant pythons, boa constrictors, rattlesnakes, crocodiles, alligators, lizards, tortoises, and 50 other specimens. Open daily May 15 through September 15 from 9 a.m. to 8 p.m., plus weekends in spring and fall from 10 a.m. to 5 p.m. (closed January, February, and March). Admission charges are $4 for adults, $2 for children aged 4 to 11, and free for youngsters under 4.

3. Altoona

Deep in the Allegheny Mountains of south-central Pennsylvania, Altoona (pop. 57,100) is approximately 225 miles west of Philadelphia and 100 miles east of Pittsburgh. The name Altoona is said to come from a Cherokee word signifying "highlands of great worth." Through the centuries, the name has proved very fitting.

The height of Altoona's prominence came in the 1840s as the Pennsylvania Railroad pushed westward. It was not easy to cut through the mountains to lay new tracks, but it was from Altoona that the task was done. The most famous achievement was the "Horseshoe Curve," an engineering feat just west of Altoona which allowed locomotives to travel around the bend of a mountain, and which is still considered a panoramic marvel.

Over the years, the railroad was considered to be "the river" of Altoona, and the city literally developed as the tracks were laid. At one time, 40 trains a day passed through, although current schedules bring only half a dozen. Today Altoona is still known for its railroad connections and is the home of the Railroader Memorial Museum. It is also the base for dozens of local industries and the setting for a wide variety of visitor attractions from the landmark Baker Mansion and historic Fort Roberdeau to the modern "Boyertown" theme park.

VISITOR INFORMATION: Brochures and maps describing the attractions of Altoona are available from **The Convention and Visitors Bureau of Blair County,** 1212 Twelfth Avenue, Altoona, PA 16601 (tel. 814/943-8151).

AREA CODE: The telephone area code for Altoona and the surrounding area is 814.

GETTING TO AND AROUND ALTOONA: The most direct way to reach Altoona by car is via the Pennsylvania Turnpike to the Bedford exit (11), and then travel north on Route 220 for 20 miles. Altoona can also be approached via I-80 from the west, to exit 20, and then south on Routes 970, 322, 350, and 220, for 27 miles. From the east via I-80, get off at exit 23, and then go south on Route 220 for 35 miles. Route 220, which becomes Pleasant Valley Boulevard within Altoona, is the main business and commercial road of the city. If you require a rented car, **Hertz** maintains a station downtown at 829 24th St. (tel. 944-3591) and at the local airport at Martinsburg (tel. 793-3983).

By Plane: Allegheny Commuter flights (tel. toll-free 800/428-4253) are operated between Altoona and Pittsburgh, from the **Altoona Airport,** Route 866, Martinsburg (tel. 695-9813), south of the city.

By Train: Altoona is served by **Amtrak** (Conrail), on the main east-west corridor between New York and Pittsburgh, Chicago, and beyond. The Amtrak station is located at 10th Avenue and 12th Street (tel. 946-1110) in the heart of downtown; **taxis** are readily available outside the station, but, if you need to call one, try **Altoona Cabs** (tel. 944-9349) or **Yellow Cabs** (tel. 944-6105).

By Bus: The **Altoona Transit Center,** 1213 11th Ave., is the depot for both **Greyhound** (tel. 944-8911) and **Fullington Trailways** (tel. toll-free 800/252-3893). Local services are provided by **Altoona Metro Transit** (tel. 944-4074); the flat fare is 75¢ to all parts of the city.

WHERE TO STAY: Route 220, known within Altoona as Pleasant Valley Boulevard, is the heart of the city's prime business district. This two-mile stretch is also the setting for the major hotels and motels. In general, Altoona's lodging choices all fall into the moderate category.

The top choice for overnighting and for dining is the **Sheraton Altoona,** R.D. 2, Box 704, Altoona, PA 16601 (tel. 814/946-1631 or toll-free 800/325-3535), located about a mile south of the city, off the Plank Road exit of Route 220. This modern and recently renovated (1986) hotel has 227 rooms and suites in a country setting opposite a golf course. Each room has two double beds or a king bed, air conditioning, color TV, and a direct-dial phone. Some non-smoking rooms are available. Doubles range from $59 to $68, with suites from $120. Visitor facilities include an indoor swimming pool with a Jacuzzi, a complete health center with a fitness track, a courtyard café (which serves breakfast and lunch), and a lounge with live music and entertainment nightly (except Sunday). The hotel's restaurant, The Laurel Room, is the best in the city, with a chef trained at the Culinary Institute of America. It's very popular with the locals; and reservations are a must. The dinner menu features flambé dishes such as steak Diane, shrimp piccante, and veal Oscar, as well as such varied selections as veal and lobster in port wine; Cajun meat pie; and beef Stroganoff. Entrees are priced from $9.95 to $17.95, with most dishes under $15, and are accompanied by a relish tray, salad, and potato or vegetable. Save some room for the flambé desserts, also very noteworthy here, including baked Alaska, cherries jubilee, and bananas foster (from $4.95). The décor is equally rich, with cascading fountains, copper wall hangings, and candlelight. Open for dinner only, from 5 to 10 p.m. Monday through Friday, and from 5 to 11 p.m. on Saturday. All major CC's accepted.

Five miles north of the city on Route 220 is the **Minuet Manor Motel,** R.D. 3, Box 592, Altoona, PA 16602 (tel. 814/742-8441), situated on a quiet grassy hillside. A tradition for over 30 years, this Colonial-style property offers 45 units on one level, each with one or two double beds, a coffee maker, air conditioning, color cable TV, and a phone. Doubles range from $39.50 to $45.50; some rooms feature waterbeds and others have canopy or brass beds. Guest facilities include a large pool in a spacious lawn setting with a gazebo and an early-American theme restaurant called the Manor House. It is open daily for breakfast from 7 to 10 a.m., and for dinner daily from 5 to 9 p.m. (except Sunday), with a moderately priced menu. All major CC's accepted.

Another modern lodging is the **Holiday Inn,** 2915 Pleasant Valley Blvd., Altoona, PA 16602 (tel. 814/944-4581 or toll-free 800/HOL-IDAY). This two-story property has 142 rooms, each with two double or one king bed, air conditioning, cable TV, and a phone. Doubles range from $49 to $60. Facilities include a landscaped courtyard with an outdoor pool and a trendy full-service restaurant called Gullifty's, with a turn-of-the-century décor of etched glass, tiled floors, and lots of brass. Lunch focuses on sandwiches (made with croissants and pita bread), salads, omelets, quiche, and burgers, in the $2.95 to $5.95 bracket. Dinner entrees, priced from $7.95 to $11.95, include pasta, steaks, ribs, seafood, and chicken. Lunch is served daily from 11 a.m. to 2 p.m., and dinner from 4 to 10 p.m. All major CC's are accepted.

The newest motel in the area is the **Days Inn,** 3306 Pleasant Valley Blvd., Altoona, PA 16602 (tel. 814/944-9661 or toll-free 800/325-2525), which opened in 1986 in the heart of the business strip. There are 111 modern rooms, with double or oversized beds, remote-control color cable TV, air conditioning, a phone, and computer-card room keys. Some non-smoking rooms are available. Doubles range from $40 to $48. All major CC's accepted.

WHERE TO DINE: It is no coincidence that some of the best restaurants in the Altoona area are Italian. In the 19th century, many of the people who came to work on the railroads were of Italian heritage and most of them liked the area so much that they stayed permanently. Their descendants are today's chefs, and, in a culinary sense, Altoona can be considered the "Little Italy" of western Pennsylvania. All restaurants listed below fall into the mostly moderate price bracket.

The top choice is **Erculiani's Restaurant,** 600 Tunnel Hill, Gallitzin (tel. 886-8832), about seven miles southwest of Altoona off Route 22. A tradition in this area since 1935, this restaurant has an eclectic décor of plants and flowers, statues, wine casks, and porcelain plates. Open for dinner only, the menu offers complete dinner feasts from $12.50 to $22. You choose the entree and the Erculiani family does the rest. House favorites include steaks, lobster, osso buco, veal scaloppine, stuffed leg of lamb, brook trout, and red snapper. All are accompanied by a parade of courses, starting with your choice of antipasto, and then an olive and relish assortment, salad, pasta, vegetables, and dessert. Open from April through November, Tuesday through Saturday from 4 to 9 p.m. and on Sunday from noon to 7 p.m. No CC's accepted.

On the eastern side of the city is **Olivo's,** 101 E. Second Ave. (tel. 942-8854), a restaurant that has been pleasing palates in Altoona since 1956. The décor is a blend of wrought iron and statuary as well as an open kitchen that invites you to watch the pastas and sauces in-the-making. Lunch, priced from $1.95 to $5.95, features sandwiches, salads, and light entrees. Complete dinners, which include appetizer, salad, vegetable, potato, dessert, and beverage, cost from $9.95 to $20.95, with most under the $15 mark. Platters with only salad and potato can be ordered for $3 less. The menu includes seafood, veal, pasta, steaks, and an appealing list of weight watchers' entrees. Open daily for lunch from 11:30 a.m. to 2 p.m., and for dinner from 5:30 to 10 p.m. CC's accepted: D, MC, and V.

Veal is the house specialty at **Allegro,** 3926 Broad Ave. (tel. 946-5216) on the south side of the city. Whether you order veal as a main course or not, you'll be treated to a plate of veal meatballs, compliments of the chef. Other entrees range from steaks, surf-and-turf, chops, and pastas to seafood, including a bountiful cioppino (seafood stew). Prices are $8.95 to $16.95 for main course and soup or juice, salad, potato, and vegetable or spaghetti. Open for dinner only, Monday through Friday from 4 to 9:30 p.m. and until 10 p.m. on Saturdays. All major CC's accepted.

Budget Meals
Deli sandwiches and light snacks are featured at **Cross's Ice Cream,** 100 E. Fifth Ave. (tel. 942-3683), a city landmark since 1935. This is also the place to come for freshly made ice cream in hand-rolled waffle cones. Two hundred ice cream recipes are used but the flavors are rotated each week, depending on which fruits or ingredients are in season. Favorites include black raspberry, fresh peach, teaberry, and coconut cream. Ice-cream cones are usually under $1 and sandwiches run from $1 to $2. Open from 11 a.m. to 11 p.m. Monday through Saturday, and from 9 a.m. to 11 p.m. on Sunday.

THE TOP ATTRACTIONS: One of Altoona's grandest historic buildings is the **Baker Mansion Museum,** 3500 Baker Blvd., off Oak Lane (tel. 942-3916), dating back to 1848. A fine example of Greek revival architecture, it was built as a home for Elias Baker, an ironmaster whose furnaces helped spur the industrial development of Altoona. The 35 rooms contain an array of hand-carved oak period furniture, Indian and railroad artifacts, and 19th-century memorabilia. Open daily from May 15th to September 15th, except Mondays and holidays, from 1 to 4:30 p.m., and on weekends through October. Admission is $2 for adults, $1 for students, and 50¢ for children 12 and under.

Altoona's railroad heritage is the keystone of the **Railroader's Memorial Museum,** 1300 9th Ave. (tel. 946-0834), built as a community project and dedicated to American railroaders through the centuries. In particular, the exhibits trace the growth of the Altoona rail works with artifacts, artwork, photographs, scale models, and an operating model railroad. There is also an exterior display yard with passenger rolling stock, a restored dining car, and steam and electric locomotives. Open year round, Tuesday through Saturday from 10 a.m. to 5 p.m., and Sunday from 12:30 p.m. to 5 p.m. From June through August, it is also open on Monday from 10 a.m. to 5 p.m. Admission is $2.50 for adults and $1 for children.

One of railroading's greatest engineering feats can be seen at **The Horseshoe Curve,** five miles west of Altoona, built in 1854 to carry the main line of the Pennsylvania Railroad over the Allegheny Mountains. Now a National Historic Landmark, this semi-circle of track is still used by all passenger and freight trains as they pass through the mountains. The site includes a viewing area (a 118-step climb); the most spectacular panorama is usually to be seen in early October during fall foliage season. Open mid-April through October from 9 a.m. to dusk; no admission charge. For further information, call 943-5150.

Six miles northeast of Altoona is **Fort Roberdeau,** Kettle Street off Route 220 (tel. 695-5541). Erected by Brig. Gen. Daniel Roberdeau in 1778, this fort was used to protect lead miners whose product was vital to Revolutionary War efforts. The present site is a reconstruction of the original seven buildings and a smelter, using stockade logs that are horizontal rather than vertical. A 21-acre nature park and picnic area are also part of the complex. Open, free of charge, May 15 through early October, Tuesday through Saturday from 11 a.m. to 5 p.m. and on Sunday from 1 to 5 p.m.

Another long-time attraction is the **Bentzel Bretzel Factory,** 5200 6th Ave. (tel. 942-5062), established in 1911. Three generations of the Bentzel family have worked here to produce "bretzels" (pretzels), potato chips, and snack items. Visitors are welcome to watch the complete baking process, from the giant automatic mixers kneading mounds of dough, the shaping and baking, to sampling the finished product. Open Monday through Friday from 9 a.m. to 5 p.m. Self-guided tours are free of charge.

SPORTS AND ACTIVITIES: About 20 miles northwest of Altoona is the **Prince Gallitzin State Park,** at Patton, off Route 53 (tel. 674-3691), a 6,249-acre expanse of forest and lakelands. Most facilities are free of charge, and include scenic look-outs, self-guided walking paths, picnic areas, hiking trails, beach areas, and a nature center. Rental charges for canoes, rowboats, and paddleboats are $3.50 an hour or $15 to $20 a day; sailboats and motorboats are $7 an hour and $30 to $35 a day; pontoons are $12 an hour and $60 a day. Access to the park is by Routes 36, 53, and 219.

Golf: The **Park Hills Country Club,** Route 220 (tel. 944-2631) welcomes visitors to play its 18-hole course, situated opposite the Sheraton Hotel. Greens fees are $14 and cart fee is $7 per person.

Winter sports: Good skiing is available 25 miles south of Altoona at **Blue Knob Ski Resort,** Claysburg (tel. 239-5111). Blue Knob is the second highest point in Pennsylvania, with an elevation of 3,152 feet. Facilities include 18 trails and slopes, two triple chair lifts, two double chairs, and two platter pulls; skiing lessons can also be arranged, on a group or individual basis. Slope fees for adults range from $16 on weekdays to $22 on weekends and holidays; reduced half-day and night rates are also available. Skis, boots, and poles can be rented from $12 a day. CC's accepted: MC and V.

CHILDREN'S CORNER: For over 50 years, **Boyer's Candies** (famous for such treats as "Mallo Cup," "Peanut Butter Cup," and "Smoothie"), have been manufactured in Altoona, and so it was a natural for the company to open a giant theme park here in 1986. **Boyertown** is located off the Frankstown exit of Route 220 (tel. 944-4404) and is a playground for the whole family. The complex includes more than 40 rides and the "skyliner," one of largest wooden roller coasters in the U.S.A. There is also a 13-acre lake, a swimming pool, three water slides, row and skeeter boats, a working candy factory, and an entertainment center featuring professional shows and big-name bands. Open Memorial Day through Labor Day from 10 a.m. to 10 p.m. Admission price is $12.95 for adults, $10.95 for children aged 4 to 8, and free for youngsters under 4.

The **Forest Zoo and Fantasy Forest,** Horse Shoe Curve Road, Gallitzin (tel. 944-4811), is eight miles west of Altoona, between Routes 22 and 36. This is home to hundreds of wild and exotic animals from around the world as well as storybook characters and exhibits. Hours are daily early May through Labor Day from 10 a.m. to dusk, plus weekends to mid-November. Admission charge of $3 for adults and $2 for children (under 60 inches). CC's accepted: MC and V.

A VISIT TO BEDFORD: About 30 miles south of Altoona is Bedford, once considered the western frontier of America, and now a resort known for its historic buildings and its healing mineral springs. The downtown area contains more than 50 structures dating back to the early 1800s, still in use and many listed in the National Register of Historic Places.

For information including walking tour brochures, contact the **Bedford Tourist and Resort Bureau,** 137 E. Pitt St., P.O. Box 1771, Bedford, PA 15522 (tel. 814/623-1771).

The main attractions are the **Fort Bedford Museum,** Fort Bedford Drive (tel. 623-8891), the first British outpost captured by American rebels in 1769. This blockhouse structure houses a collection of antiques, Indian artifacts, tools, old rifles, and household articles. Open May through October from 9 a.m. to 5 p.m. daily, with an admission charge of $2 for adults and $1 for children aged 6 to 12.

On the banks of the Juniata River amid groves of sycamore trees is **Old Bedford Village,** Route 220 (tel. 623-1156), an authentic reconstruction of a pioneer settlement of the 1790s. The flavor of early America prevails at this "living-history" museum, as craftsmen and women demonstrate the lifestyle of long ago in the setting of 40 authentic log homes and buildings. You'll see costumed cobblers, quilters, carpenters, printers, bakers, toy-makers, candle-makers, leather-workers, blacksmiths, wheelwrights, potters, weavers, and tinsmiths, to name a few. Open mid-April to October from 9 a.m. to 5 p.m., and also on weekends until mid-December. Admission charge is $5 for adults and $3.50 for children aged 6 to 18.

WHERE TO STAY AND DINE: With so much to see, it won't be surprising if you want to stay longer than a few hours. Here are two special places where you'll find an especially warm welcome:

Dating back more than 150 years, the **Bedford Springs Hotel,** Box 639, Bedford, PA 15522 (tel. 814/623-6121 or toll-free 800/233-0308), was built around the natural magnesia springs which were discovered here in 1790. A sprawling old-world resort of five buildings set in 2,800 acres of hillside and mountains, this idyllic setting once served as a summer White House (during the James Buchanan presidency). Today you'll feel like a president or first lady as you enjoy the stylish accommodations and activities such as indoor and outdoor pools, golf, tennis, and stream fishing. Furnished with antiques and reproductions, the 242 bedrooms have all the modern conveniences including a private bath; twin, double, or king beds; and air conditioning. Doubles range from $50 to $80 per person and are based on the modified American plan and include breakfast and dinner. Open May through October. CC's accepted: AE, MC, and V.

If you prefer a bed-and-breakfast atmosphere, you'll enjoy the **Jean Bonnet Tavern,** Routes 30 and 31, P.O. Box 724, Bedford, PA 15522 (tel. 814/623-2250), three miles west of downtown. Built circa 1762 and named for its 18th-century owner, this three-story native-stone building is listed in the National Register of Historic Places. Opened as a B&B in 1985 by the Baer family, the house has double porches front and back, tilted floors, huge chestnut beams, and Colonial-style furnishings. The inn offers six bedrooms, two with private bath and four with shared baths. Double occupancy rates start at $39.95 including breakfast. The tavern downstairs is also open to the public for meals; lunch, priced from $1.95 to $4.95, focuses on sandwiches, salads, burgers, and omelets. Dinner entrees are priced from $6.95 to $16.95, with most under $10. Selections include steaks, seafood, and specialty dishes like beef Stroganoff, chicken alla marsala, and burgundy ham steak. Lunch is served from 11 a.m. to 2 p.m. daily; dinner from 5 to 9 p.m. Monday through Thursday, until 10 p.m. Friday and Saturday, and until 8 p.m. on Sunday. CC's accepted: AE, Disc, MC, and V.

4. Johnstown

About 60 miles east of Pittsburgh, Johnstown is situated in the Conemaugh River Valley, surrounded by the Allegheny Mountains. Originally known as "Conemaugh Old Town," this area was settled in 1793 by Joseph Johns, an immigrant from Switzerland who eventually bestowed his name on the city.

No doubt Johnstown's pleasant mountain and river landscapes reminded Joseph Johns of his native land. Unfortunately, this idyllic setting has also led to Johnstown's tragic history as America's "Flood City."

Since 1808 Johnstown has been flooded 22 times, but the one most remembered was in 1889 as a result of the collapse of the South Fork Dam, about ten miles to the east of the city. This tragic flood claimed over 2,200 lives in less than ten minutes. Other floods in this century, most notably in 1936 and 1977, also took their toll on the city. Today you can see the "high-water marks" etched on many buildings, including the sturdy stone-faced City Hall.

But Johnstown today (pop. 35,500) is a city of great spunk and spirit and has managed to recover and prosper. Some leading sites, like the inclined plane and the museum, were built as the result of flood waters, but have become prime tourist attractions.

On May 31, 1989, Johnstown will mark the centennial of the "great flood," and the local citizens plan on using the occasion to attract new interest and enthusiasm for their lovely city.

VISITOR INFORMATION: Brochures and maps covering Johnstown are available from the **Cambria County Tourist Council, Inc.,** 711 Edgehill Drive, Johnstown, PA 15905 (tel. 814/536-1816). If you wish to visit the office, it's at the top end of the inclined plane route, a spot where you'll enjoy the best overall view of the city.

AREA CODE: All telephone numbers in Johnstown and the surrounding area belong to the 814 area code.

GETTING TO AND AROUND JOHNSTOWN: From the Pennsylvania Turnpike, Johnstown is a 40-minute drive north from exit 10 (Somerset) on Route 219 or exit 11 (Bedford) on Route 56. Approaching from a northerly direction, Johnstown can be reached via Routes 53, 56, and 219. From Pittsburgh, take Route 22 via the Conemaugh Gap and Routes 56 and 403.

By Plane: **Allegheny-Commuter** airlines (tel. toll-free 800/428-4253) provides regular service into **Johnstown-Cambria County Airport,** Route 56 (tel. 536-0002), five miles northeast of downtown.

By Train: Johnstown is on **Amtrak**'s main East-Midwest route between New York/Philadelphia and Chicago. The train station is on the north side of town at 47 Walnut St. (tel. 535-3313).

By Bus: Regular bus service to and from other cities around the U.S. is provided by **Greyhound,** 47 Walnut St. (tel. 536-4714). Local bus services are provided by the **Cambria County Transit Authority,** Transit Center, Main Street East (tel. 535-7831); the base fare for trips within the city is 60¢.

Car Rental: The following firms have stations in Johnstown: **Avis,** 1530 Scalp Ave. (tel. 266-6068); **Hertz,** 307 Bedford St. (tel. 536-8755); and **Rent-a-Wreck,** 1500 Scalp Ave. (tel. 266-6682).

Taxis: If you require a taxi, call **Yellow Cab** (tel. 535-7737) or **Friendly Cab** (tel. 467-5587).

WHERE TO STAY: Johnstown does not have a great variety of lodging choices. The Holiday Inn dominates the downtown area and several motels are located on the outskirts. All choices fall into the moderate price category.

Right in the heart of downtown is the **Holiday Inn,** 250 Market St., Johnstown, PA 15907 (tel. 814/535-7777 or toll-free 800/HOL-IDAY). The social and business hub of the city, this modern six-story hotel has 167 rooms, each with double or king beds, air conditioning, color cable TV, and a phone. Doubles range from $68 to $80. Guest facilities include an indoor heated pool, a sauna, a whirlpool and fitness equipment, a lounge with evening musical entertainment, and a greenhouse-style restaurant, Harrigan's, which looks out onto Market Street. This multi-level dining room is furnished in contemporary style with pink, rose, and salmon tones, rattan furniture, and lots of hanging plants. Lunch items, priced from $3.95 to $8.95, range from salads and sandwiches to burgers and croissantwiches. Dinner entrees, priced in the $9.95 to $15.95 bracket, focus on Cajun dishes, steaks, seafood, chicken, and pasta. All main courses come with salad, vegetable, and pasta or potato. Lunch is served from 11 a.m. to 5 p.m., and dinner from 5 to 10 p.m. daily. Breakfast is also available from 7 a.m. to 11 a.m.; and from 2 to 4 p.m. on Saturday, a traditional afternoon tea is served (an array of pastries, preserves, canapés, and finger sandwiches at $4.95 per person). There are non-smoking bedrooms as well as a non-smoking section of the restaurant. All major CC's accepted.

The Cottage, Route 22, Ebensburg, PA 15931 (tel. 814/472-8002), is a modern family-run two-story motel situated 20 miles north of Johnstown. There are 52 units, each with one or two double beds, color cable TV, air conditioning, and a phone. Doubles range from $39 to $45. Guest facilities include an outdoor pool and a game room. There is also a full-service cottage-style restaurant which features Italian-American cuisine. Sandwiches, salads, and burgers are the focus at lunch, in the $1.95 to $3.95 price bracket. Entrees at dinner cost from $6.95 to $19.95, with most under $10. The menu includes steaks, fried chicken, veal parmigiana, seafood, and "combination specialties" such as beef and bird (Delmonico steak and fried chicken); fish and fowl (stuffed shrimp and chicken); and sea and shore (steak and shrimp). All choices come with salad or cole slaw, potato, vegetable, and home-baked cottage bread. Lunch is served Monday through Saturday from 11 a.m. to 2 p.m.; dinner Monday to Thursday from 3 to 11 p.m., Friday and Saturday from 3 p.m. to midnight, and Sunday from 11:30 a.m. to 10:30 p.m. CC's accepted: AE, MC, and V.

Eight miles east of the city is the **Quality Inn,** 1540 Scalp Ave., Johnstown, PA 15904 (tel. 814/266-5851 or toll-free 800/228-5151), located on Route 56 and surrounded by sylvan valley views. This modern two- and three-story property has 115 rooms, each with one or two double beds, color cable TV, air conditioning, and a phone. Doubles range from $39 to $51. Some non-smoking rooms are available, and other amenities include a café, a lounge with dancing and nightly entertainment, a heated indoor pool, saunas, a whirlpool, an exercise room, a game room, and barber and beauty shops. All major CC's accepted.

WHERE TO DINE: The top choice is the **Surf and Turf Inn,** 100 Valley Pike (tel. 536-9250), a country house located on the city's southern edge as Route 403 enters the midtown area. Surrounded by huge old trees and rambling gardens, this restaurant is furnished in a Colonial style with natural stone walls, dark woods, and candlelight. Open for dinner only, it is presided over by chef-owner James Loveridge. As you might guess, surf-and-turf heads the menu, and the emphasis is on steaks and broiled seafood. Other dishes include surf and sea (shrimp and crab cake); steak'n'sea (steak, shrimp, crab, and scallops); as well as honey-dipped chicken, veal parmigiana, and pastas. Entrees are priced from $7.95 to $19.95, with most under $15, and that includes a bountiful salad-and-soup bar, potato, and vegetable. Hours are 4 to 10 p.m. Monday through Saturday, and from 11:30 a.m. to 8 p.m. on Sunday. All major CC's are accepted.

When you are in this area, you really should not miss the **Green Gables Restaurant,** Jennerstown (tel. 629-9412), 20 miles southeast of Johnstown in a forest setting on Route 985. Started as a wayside stand in 1927, this Stoughton family enterprise has grown over the years into a Pennsylvania landmark with a choice of two Colonial-style dining rooms and an outdoor terrace overlooking the Beaver Creek Dam. Lunch, priced from $3.95 to $5.95, features open-face sandwiches from the broiler, salads, and hot platters (such as chicken à la king or shrimp rarebit). Traditional and contemporary American cuisine is the focus at dinner with selections such as tenderloin of pork, roast turkey, Cajun chicken, shrimp Créole, rainbow trout, scallops au gratin, and steaks. Entrees are priced from $8.95 to $19.95 and include salad, potato or rice, and vegetable. The Mountain Playhouse Theatre is adjacent (see "Nightlife"). Open on Tuesday for dinner from 4 to 9 p.m.; and for lunch and dinner on Wednesday through Saturday from noon to 9 p.m., and Sunday from noon to 7 p.m. In the winter months, it is open on weekends only. All CC's are accepted.

THE TOP ATTRACTIONS: The **Inclined Plane Railway,** Vine Street and Roosevelt Boulevard (tel. 536-1816), is to Johnstown what the cable car is to San Francisco. No visit to this city is complete without a ride on this unique conveyance. It's located on the west edge of town by the Stoney Creek River, with its base at Routes 56 and 403, and connects the downtown area with Westmont, a residential section 500 feet above. Constructed as a direct result of the 1889 flood, the inclined plane was built as a "lifesaver" to prevent people from becoming stranded on low ground if more floods followed. Today it serves as a commuter run for people who live on the hill and it is also the city's prime tourist attraction. The original cars, motorworks, and gear drives are still used, although the steam has been replaced by 400 horse-power electric current. Listed in the National Register, this inclined plane has carried more than 40 million people and is the world's steepest passenger funicular railway, often described as a "trip to the stars." Reaching the top also rewards passengers with a panoramic view of Johnstown and the surrounding mountain valleys. The Cambria Council Tourist Office has very cleverly chosen to have its office at the top of the hill. Two equally balanced cars run every 15 minutes for the 45-second ride; the fare for adults is $1.25 one-way and $2 round-trip, and for children 75¢ one-way and $1.25 round-trip. Cars are also permitted ($1.50). Operating hours are Monday through Friday from 6:30 a.m. to 9 p.m.; Saturday from 7:30 a.m. to 9 p.m.; and Sunday from 9 a.m. to 9 p.m.

The best place to learn about the city's dramatic history is the **Johnstown Flood Museum,** 304 Washington St. (tel. 539-1889). This beautiful French Gothic building was built in 1891, after the disastrous flood of 1889, as a library and a gift to the city from Andrew Carnegie. The displays, which chronicle 175 years of life in Johnstown, include photographs, newspaper stories, and a 25-minute narrated slide show on the flood, presented every half-hour; there is also a comprehensive coal-mining exhibit on the second floor. Open all year, Tuesday through Saturday from 10:30 a.m. to 4:30 p.m. and on Sunday from 12:30 to 4:30 p.m. Admission is $1.25 for adults and 75¢ for children aged 6 to 18. The museum shop also sells a "Walking Tour of Johnstown" brochure, which is well worth the 60¢ price.

For a different perspective, you should visit the **Johnstown Flood National Memorial,** ten miles northeast of the city, on Routes 219 and 869, near the town of St. Michael. This is the spot where the South Fork Dam broke in 1889, causing the most disastrous of Johnstown's floods. The site includes a **visitor center** (tel. 493-5718 and 886-8176), walking trails, picnic areas, and interpretative exhibits. Open daily, free of charge, from 9:30 a.m. to 6 p.m. from June through September; and from 8:30 a.m. to 4 p.m. during the rest of the year (except Thanksgiving, Christmas, and New Year's). It is expected that a new visitor center and more extensive displays will be built in 1989 to coincide with the centennial of the 1889 flood.

For a look at the arts and crafts of the area, plan a visit to the **Community Arts Center of Cambria County,** 1217 Menoher Blvd. (tel. 255-6515), a two-story log house originally built in 1834. In addition to displaying the works of local artisans, this organization features exhibits on Johnstown's pioneer days and hosts free outdoor musical concerts on Wednesday evenings in the summer months. Open Monday through Friday from 10 a.m. to 4 p.m.; Monday and Thursday evenings from 7 to 9 p.m.; Saturday from 10 a.m. to 3 p.m.; and Sunday from 2 to 5 p.m. No admission charge.

NIGHTLIFE: Broadway musicals and comedies are presented by a resident professional company at **The Mountain Playhouse,** Stoughton Lake, Jennerstown (tel. 629-9201), 20 miles southeast of Johnstown. Located just north of the intersection of Routes 985 and 30, this country theater was started

50 years ago on the site of a restored log gristmill that had been in use from 1805 until 1918 by the Stoughton family who are still involved in the daily operations. A plaque on the wall states that ticket prices here were 66¢ to $1.10 in 1939, but today they are slightly higher (from $5 for matinees to $14 for evening performances). The playhouse is associated with the adjacent Green Gables Restaurant, and, in fact, offers dinner/theater combinations if desired (from $18.75 per person). Open mid-May to mid-October, with curtain at 8:45 p.m. weeknights (except Monday); 9 p.m. on Saturday; 2 p.m. for Friday and Wednesday matinees; and 3 p.m. on Sunday. CC's accepted: AE, MC, and V.

In downtown Johnstown, you can also see indoor sporting events and concerts at the **Cambria County War Memorial Arena,** 326–350 Napolean St. (tel. 536-5156). This building was erected in 1950 as a tribute to local citizens who had served in the armed forces, and was totally funded by voluntary contributions from 24,000 people. Tickets average $5 to $10, depending on the event; the box office is open weekdays from 10 a.m. to 5 p.m. Check with the Cambria County Tourist Council to find out what will be scheduled when you plan to be in town.

Chapter XII

WESTERN PENNSYLVANIA

1. Pittsburgh
2. Erie

REACHING ALL THE WAY to the Ohio border is the western edge of this vast state of Pennsylvania. Encompassing the major cities of Pittsburgh and Erie, the 180-mile stretch of land takes in the Allegheny Mountains, various rivers, and the southern shores of Lake Erie.

To the south, western Pennsylvania is also bordered by West Virginia and Maryland, and, to the north, it is edged by New York State.

We acknowledge that this is a huge chunk of territory and we are only scratching the surface by highlighting the attractions of Pittsburgh and Erie, Pennsylvania's second- and third-largest cities. But, hopefully, this survey will whet your appetite and encourage you to explore the area more fully for yourself.

1. Pittsburgh

Pittsburgh's past and present have been shaped by its unique location embracing the confluence of three rivers, at the point where the Allegheny and Monongahela rivers form the Ohio. A natural fortress, the area was first surveyed by George Washington (then a 21-year-old major in the Virginia militia), and it was quickly recognized as a strategic gateway to the west. In 1758 it was named Fort Pitt and then Pittsborough, in honor of the elder British statesman, William Pitt.

Pittsburgh's early years after the Revolution were marked by great commercial prosperity. Coal, glass, iron, and steel made Pittsburgh a giant in the industrial age, but they also covered the metropolis with billows of polluted air, earning it the image of "Smoky City."

By the end of World War II, however, things began to change and the smoke has been cleared in more ways than one. Thanks to enlightened urban planning, a $5 billion renewal program, and spirited community efforts, Pittsburgh has been reborn and refashioned into a smoke-free urban center. The horizon is now a vista of aesthetically impressive skyscrapers in an open milieu of parklets, pedestrian walkways, trees, fountains, waterfalls, and flowers.

Still a leader in commerce, this "Renaissance city" has attracted many of the top Fortune 500 companies, and is the third largest corporate headquarters city in the nation. Westinghouse, Rockwell, Heinz, and U.S. Steel are just some

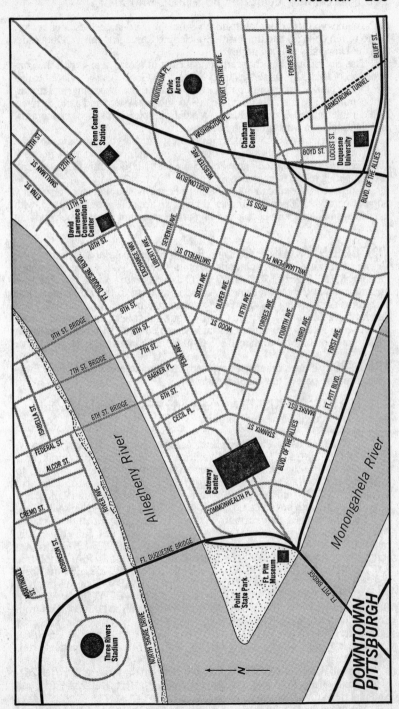

DOWNTOWN
PITTSBURGH

Monongahela River

Allegheny River

Three Rivers Stadium

Point State Park

Ft. Pitt. Museum

Gateway Center

Penn Central Station

David Lawrence Convention Center

Civic Arena

Chatham Center

Duquesne University

N

NORTH SHORE DRIVE

FT. DUQUESNE BRIDGE

RIVER AVE.

FT. PITT BRIDGE

MARTINDALE ST.

ROBINSON ST.

CREMO ST.

ALCOR ST.

FEDERAL ST.

ISABELLA ST.

9TH ST. BRIDGE

7TH ST. BRIDGE

6TH ST. BRIDGE

9TH ST.

8TH ST.

7TH ST.

BARKER PL.

6TH ST.

CECIL PL.

COMMONWEALTH PL.

PENN AVE.

EXCHANGE WAY

LIBERTY AVE.

SEVENTH AVE.

SIXTH AVE.

FT. DUQUESNE BLVD.

10TH ST.

11TH ST.

12TH ST.

13TH ST.

SMALLMAN ST.

ETNA ST.

WOOD ST.

SMITHFIELD ST.

OLIVER AVE.

FIFTH AVE.

FORBES AVE.

FOURTH AVE.

THIRD AVE.

FIRST AVE.

MARKET ST.

STANWIX ST.

FT. PITT BLVD.

BLVD. OF THE ALLIES

WILLIAM PENN PL.

WEBSTER AVE.

BIGELOW BLVD.

ROSS ST.

WASHINGTON PL.

AUDITORIUM PL.

COURT CENTRE AVE.

FORBES AVE.

BLUFF ST.

ARMSTRONG TUNNEL

BOYD ST.

LOCUST ST.

BLVD. OF THE ALLIES

of the names you'll find here. Pittsburgh is also the third-largest research center, home to ten colleges and universities, including Carnegie-Mellon, Duquesne, and the University of Pittsburgh.

The city skyline has changed dramatically in recent years, with the construction of such skyscrapers as the $200 million Gothic glass "palace" called PPG Place, and with Oxford Centre, a fashionable office, shopping, and restaurant complex. There is a swift and clean new subway system and a trendy riverside complex called Station Square—a delightful blend of shops, restaurants, and sightseeing in a restored railroad depot.

As a mark of its ecological achievements, Pittsburgh also claims to have more trees within its limits than any other city in America. Clusters of greenery abound here including the 36-acre Point State Park, the downtown tip of the city at the meeting of the three rivers.

Truly the metropolitan hub of western Pennsylvania, Pittsburgh has a city population of 423,000 in its compact downtown area (1½ square miles), with almost two million more people residing in the sprawling greater metropolitan area.

VISITOR INFORMATION: For maps, brochures, and helpful data, contact the **Greater Pittsburgh Convention and Visitors Bureau,** Four Gateway Center, Pittsburgh, PA 15222 (tel. 412/281-7711). Once you get to town, stop by the **Visitor Information Center** on Liberty Avenue, adjacent to the Equitable Plaza. The hours are Monday through Friday from 9:30 a.m. to 5 p.m.; Saturday and Sunday from 9:30 a.m. to 3 p.m. (April through October); and Saturday from 9:30 a.m. to 3 p.m. (November through March). For daily information about what's going on in Pittsburgh, call 391-6840 for a recorded message.

AREA CODE: Unless otherwise specified, all telephone numbers in the Pittsburgh area are part of the 412 area code.

GETTING TO PITTSBURGH: Whether you prefer wings or wheels, Pittsburgh is easily reached via plane, bus, or train.

By Plane: Greater Pittsburgh International Airport, Airport Parkway, Route 60 (tel. 778-2504), is located 14 miles west of downtown Pittsburgh, near Corapolis. Currently the thirteenth busiest terminal in the U.S., with up to 1,000 flights a day, this airport is planning to add a new air terminal on a 556-acre site at a cost of $325 million. The new terminal will combine a funnel, hub, and spoke concept, with an increased capacity of 90 to 100 gates by the 1990s.

Leading airlines that currently fly into Pittsburgh International include **American** (tel. 771-4437 or toll-free 800/433-7300); **Delta** (tel. 566-2100 or toll-free 800/336-4940), **Eastern** (tel. 471-7100 or toll-free 800/327-8376), **Pan Am** (tel. 391-6907 or toll-free 800/424-3220); **Piedmont** (tel. 561-1610 or toll-free 800/251-5720); **Northwest** (tel. 391-8484 or toll-free 800/225-2525); **Trans World** (tel. 391-3600 or toll-free 800/221-2000); **United** (tel. 288-9900 or toll-free 800/241-6522); and **USAir** (tel. 922-7500 or toll-free 800/428-4322). Three years ago, **British Airways** (tel. toll-free 800/221-7150) also established direct flights from London to Pittsburgh. Regional airlines using this airport include **Allegheny Commuter** (tel. toll-free 800/428-4253); **Colgan** (tel. toll-free 800/336-5016); **Cumberland** (tel. toll-free 800/624-0070); and **Jet Stream International** (tel. 573-3100).

The following **car rental** firms maintain desks at the airport: **Avis** (tel. 262-5160); **Budget** (tel. 262-1500); **Dollar** (tel. 566-2288); **Hertz** (tel. 262-1705); and **National** (tel. 262-2312).

Motorcoach and mini-bus service between the airport and downtown is operated by **Airlines Transportation Co.** (tel. 471-8900). The fare is $8 each way. Taxi service is $24 each way.

By Train: Amtrak provides regular daily service between Pittsburgh and Philadelphia/New York, Chicago, and other onward and intermediate points. All trains arrive and depart from the Amtrak Station, Liberty and Grant Streets (tel. 471-8752 or toll-free 800/USA-RAIL). The station is situated downtown, one block from the David Lawrence Convention Center and close to all major hotels and attractions.

By Bus: The two major bus lines, Greyhound and Trailways, operate regular services into Pittsburgh. The **Greyhound** terminal is located at 11th Street and Liberty Avenue (tel. 391-2300); and the **Trailways** station is at 10th Street and Penn Avenue (tel. 261-5400). Both depots are within a block of the Convention Center and close to major hotels.

By Car: Pittsburgh is surrounded by major highways, facilitating easy access from any direction. If you are coming from the north or south, I-79 is the best route, and then onto I-279, taking the Fort Pitt tunnel into the heart of downtown. The best approach from the east or west is via the Pennsylvania Turnpike (I-76), and then via I-376 to the Grant Street exit for the center of the city.

OVERVIEW OF THE CITY: The heart of Pittsburgh's downtown area is concentrated in a 1½-square-mile tip of land known as the Golden Triangle. The name is derived from the triangular shape of the area, thanks to the three rivers (Allegheny, Monogahela, and Ohio) that surround it. In this section, you will find Point State Park, where the city had its early beginnings, and the major buildings that have signaled the "Renaissance" of the Pittsburgh skyline. The Golden Triangle is also the location of the city's major downtown hotels, restaurants, theaters, and shops. In addition, the town's original Market Square, now a modern plaza, is here, as are the rail and bus stations.

The streets and avenues are a hodge-podge of diagonal and perpendicular shapes. Most of the avenues, which go in an east-west pattern, are numbered (that is, First, Third, Fourth, and Fifth), but Second Avenue is also called the Boulevard of the Allies. Other avenues have names, like Forbes and Oliver, and still other avenues, like the main thoroughfares of Penn and Liberty, go in a diagonal direction. Likewise, some streets have names and some have numbers, so it is really best to follow a good street map.

Thanks to the development of the former Pittsburgh and Lake Erie Railroad Terminal into a bustling mecca of shops and restaurants called Station Square, the South Side is fast becoming the alter ego of the Golden Triangle, especially for visitors. Located on the other side of the Monongahela River, the South Side can be reached in less than five minutes by car (over the Smithfield, Ft. Pitt, or Liberty bridges) or via the sleek new subway. The Station Square development has also spurred the rejuvenation of this entire strip (Carson Street) and has encouraged a flock of artists, antique dealers, and craftsmen to set up shop.

In addition, the South Side is the base of Pittsburgh's two inclines, the Monongahela and the Duquesne, which climb the steep hill to Mt. Washington, a fashionable residential enclave that overlooks the Golden Triangle. This hilltop area is also home to a dozen fine restaurants that specialize in haute cuisine and "haut pas" views.

In the opposite direction, beyond the Allegheny River, is the city's North Side, home of the Three Rivers Stadium and the new North Shore Center, a four-building commercial complex with its own restaurants featuring views of the city from yet another angle.

The other prime section of Pittsburgh that draws visitors is the Oakland district, east of the Golden Triangle. The headquarters of many of the city's cultural, educational, and medical landmarks, Oakland is the home of the University of Pennsylvania and the Carnegie Institute.

GETTING AROUND PITTSBURGH: The options are many, so read our roundup, which follows.

Buses: Port Authority Transit, 514 Wood St. (tel. 231-5707), operates daily bus and trolley service throughout the city and the surrounding areas. The minimum fare is $1 and exact change is required. Fares are based on the zone system, with most destinations used by visitors, such as Oakland, within the minimum fare. If you should be traveling farther, each additional zone costs 25¢ more.

Subway: Pittsburgh Area Transit (PAT) also operates a light rail transit service called the "T." Inaugurated in 1985, this system currently travels between three downtown points, Gateway Center, Wood Street, and Steel Plaza. It then crosses the Monongahela River by bridge, stopping at Station Square, before continuing on to suburban locations south of the city. The unique feature of the "T" is that the fare is free between downtown stations until 7 p.m. each day. The fare after 7 p.m. is 60¢. At any time of day or night, it also costs 60¢ to ride from any point downtown to Station Square. Fares are paid at exit points, and exact change is required. Trains operate daily from 5:22 a.m. to 12:52 a.m. during weekdays, with slightly curtailed service on weekends. Plans call for further stops within the downtown area including Penn Station. For more information, call PAT (tel. 231-5705).

The Inclines: Pittsburgh has two inclines, better known as hill-climbing trolleys, that connect the city's South Side to the Mt. Washington area. Originated in the 1870s and both National Historic Landmarks, these hillside cable cars are a sightseeing attraction as well as being the quickest source of transport between the two points. The Duquesne incline travels from 1197 W. Carson Street up to the section of Grandview Avenue where a number of leading restaurants are located. It operates from 5:30 a.m. to 12:50 a.m. Monday through Saturday, and from 7 a.m. to 12:50 a.m. on Sunday and holidays. The Monongahela incline climbs from Station Square to a residential section of Grandview Avenue, where there is a scenic overlook. It operates from 5:30 a.m. to 12:45 a.m. Monday through Saturday, and from 8:45 a.m. to midnight on Sunday and holidays. The one-way fare on both inclines is 60¢ for adults and 30¢ for children aged 6 to 12. There is ample parking on ground levels. For further information, call 381-1665.

V.I.P. Pass: PAT has designed a V.I.P. Pass for visitors who are going to be in Pittsburgh for a short time. For a one-time fee of $4.50, this pass entitles you to unlimited travel on the buses, trolleys, subways, and inclines. It is valid for the day purchased plus the following day until 2 a.m. You can buy the pass at the Pittsburgh Visitor Information Center, major hotels, and the PAT Downtown Service Center, 514 Wood St. (tel. 231-5707).

Taxis: Cabs line up at the city's downtown hotels and outside of midtown attractions, theaters, hospitals, and such. Taxis can also be hailed as they cruise the streets or, to be sure, phone in advance to such companies as **People's Cabs** (tel. 681-3131) or **Yellow Cabs** (tel. 665-8100).

Car Rental: If you haven't brought your own car to Pittsburgh, you really don't need one to see the major downtown sights. If you require a car to get out to the suburban areas or for onward travel, however, you can rent one at these downtown locations: **Avis,** 625 Stanwix St. (tel. 261-0540); **Budget,** 700 Fifth Ave. (tel. 261-3320); **Dollar,** 412 Stanwix St. (tel. 566-2288); **Hertz,** One Chatham Center (tel. 262-1705); and **National,** 434 Blvd. of the Allies (tel. 261-5500). Parking on the streets of the downtown area is extremely limited, but public parking garages and lots are plentiful. Rates can range from 50¢ an hour in open lots to $7 to $8 a day in underground or covered facilities.

Sightseeing Bus Tours: Gray Line of Pittsburgh operates several escorted bus tours during the period from Memorial Day through Labor Day, all departing from downtown hotels. The choice includes a 2½-hour basic tour, priced at $12 for adults and $6 for children aged from 6 to 11; and a 5½ hour trip that includes all of the basic sightseeing of the previous tour plus a river cruise and a visit to Station Square, priced at $18.50 and $10, respectively. Both of these tours depart at 10 a.m. daily. In addition, there is also a 3½-hour evening tour that takes in several rooftop views, available Tuesday and Thursday at 6 p.m., at a fare of $16 and $8. For complete information, check at hotels or call 761-7000.

Sightseeing Cruises: The **Gateway Clipper Fleet,** Station Square Dock, (tel. 355-7979), operates a variety of different paddlewheel riverboat cruises, scheduled from early June through Labor Day, including the following:
• **"Good Ship Lollipop Cruises":** one-hour narrated cruises of the harbor, departing hourly from noon through 4 p.m. and at 6 p.m. Monday through Friday, with an extra 7 p.m. departure on Monday, Wednesday, and Friday; plus hourly departures noon through 7 p.m. on weekends. The charge is $4 for adults and $3 for children, aged 12 and under.
• **"Three Rivers Cruises":** two-hour narrated riverline tours of the city, on Monday through Saturday at 11 a.m., and Sunday at 1:30 and 3 p.m. The fare is $6 for adults and $4 for children aged 12 and under. In addition, there are 2½-hour cruises of Pittsburgh's locks and dams, daily at 1:30 p.m.; and two-hour twilight fountain cruises on Tuesday and Thursday at 7:30 p.m., for the same price as the basic two-hour tours.
• **"Dinner-Dance Cruises":** three-hour cruises, including a buffet dinner, live music, and dancing. Operates Friday, Saturday, and Sunday evenings, with boarding at 6 p.m. and cruise from 7 to 10 p.m. Cocktail and beverage service available. These cruises commence in mid-April and continue through Labor Day. The price is $17.95 on Friday and Sunday and $19.95 on Saturday. Some weekday cruises are also available.

WHERE TO STAY: Downtown Pittsburgh does not offer a great choice of hotels; in fact, only 2,000 rooms (spread among seven hotels) are available for visitors and most all of these fall in the upper price brackets and all but one are affiliated with national chains.

An additional 5,000 rooms of hotel capacity are available in the outlying regions. Such clusters of suburban hotels, located primarily in areas near hospitals, universities, shopping malls, and major industries, are ideal for business traffic, although a bit remote for the average tourist who seeks to explore midtown Pittsburgh.

If you bring your own car to Pittsburgh, however, you'll find that areas like Greentree and Monroeville can provide convenient and economical bases, especially if you are traveling with children. On the other hand, if you fly or train into town with only a couple of days to sample the highlights of Pittsburgh, then it's worth the big splurge to check into one of the City Center luxury properties. One point worth noting: like most major cities, Pittsburgh hotels are at their busiest from Monday through Thursday nights, and usually offer greatly reduced rates on weekends. Many properties also have weekend packages that can save you up to 50% off regular rates, with lots of other goodies thrown in. Be sure to ask if special rates or packages apply at the time you are planning to be there.

The Top Choices

The "grande dame" in the center of the city is the **Westin William Penn,** 530 William Penn Way, Mellon Square, Pittsburgh, PA 15230 (tel. 412/281-7100 or toll-free 800/228-3000), at the corner of Sixth and Grant Streets, opposite Steel Plaza. Originally built as a 1,600-room hotel in 1916 by industrialist William Clay Frick, this property is designed in an E-shape with three 23-story towers. Thanks to a recent $30 million renovation and restoration program (1984–1986), this national historic landmark now has a total of 595 spacious guest rooms, including 47 elaborate suites. The focal point of the public areas is a Georgian lobby with a Fontainebleau-style ceiling, crystal chandeliers, and a palm court that serves as an old-world setting for afternoon tea or cocktails. The bedrooms are furnished in Colonial Williamsburg, French Provincial, or Italianate décors, and all have solid wood floors, plush carpeting, brass hardware, and marble baths, as well as air conditioning, a direct-dial phone, color cable TV, and a choice of king, queen, or two double beds. Doubles range from $130 to $260 per night. The main restaurant, The Terrace Room (direct line: 553-5235), is a showcase of rich walnut paneling, crystal chandeliers, soaring windows, and a mural depiction of George Washington at Ft. Pitt. Lunch, priced from $4.95 to $12.95, features salads, sandwiches, and light entrees (such as Oriental stir-frys, seafoods, and petit filet mignon). The menu at dinner focuses on such entrees as prime ribs; mignonettes of lamb with pistachio nuts and cognac; veal medallions with apple slices and Calvados cream sauce; and filet of Coho salmon with artichoke hearts and chives in Pernod sauce. The prices range from $9.95 to $19.95. If you bring your car, there is an underground public parking garage at Mellon Square, across from the hotel. Open weekdays for lunch from 11 a.m. to 2:30 p.m., and for dinner daily from 6 to 10 p.m. All major CC's accepted.

Opened at the end of 1986, the **Vista International,** 1000 Penn Ave., Pittsburgh, PA 15222-3873 (tel. 412/281-3700 or toll-free 800/HILTONS), is the city's newest downtown hotel. Located between 10th and 11th Streets and Liberty and Penn Avenues, this $69.8 million mega-property is connected by a pedestrian bridge walkway to the David L. Lawrence Convention Center. The dramatic façade consists of a four-story glass atrium lobby with a 21-story guest-room tower of 616 rooms, including 45 suites. The expansive lobby area, with its transparent glass roof, is a panorama of imported marble, cherry wood paneling, bronze fixtures, and original pottery, paintings, and ceramics created by Pittsburgh area craftsmen. With views of the city or the Allegheny River, guest rooms offer a choice of bed sizes, plus a contemporary décor with mahogany furniture, pastel-tone fabrics, and prints by local artists. Each unit has a computer-card keyless lock; two direct-dial phones, color TV with 36-channel cable service; an AM/FM radio; a work desk, an armchair, and a sofa, plus air conditioning and a mini-bar. The entire fourteenth floor is reserved for nonsmokers, as is part of the twenty-fourth floor executive wing. The hotel also offers "no-stop video check-out," allowing guests who pay by credit card to view their charges on the TV set in their rooms and close their account by following instructions on the screen, making a stop at the front desk unnecessary. Doubles range from $115 to $150; from $170 for executive rooms; and from $150 for suites. The guest facilities include a fitness center with an indoor swimming pool, exercise equipment, a whirlpool, a sauna, an aerobics room, and a two-level, 600-car garage. For dining and entertainment, there is the Orchard Café, serving moderately priced meals from 6:30 a.m. to 9:30 p.m.; Juliana's, an entertainment lounge and disco; and a gourmet dining room, American Harvest. This restaurant features a menu that changes seasonally, but the choices usually include prime ribs, rack of lamb, veal loin steak, Atlantic salmon, lobster, and blackened redfish. The dinner entrees range from $11.95 to $19.95, and are accompanied by vegetables and potato. The American Harvest hours are lunch, Monday through Friday from 11:45 a.m. to 2:30 p.m., and dinner from 6 to 10:30 p.m.; also Saturday dinner from 5:30 to 10:30 p.m. Major CC's accepted.

Other Downtown Luxury Lodgings

In an area known as Chatham Center, near Duquesne University and the Civic Arena is **The Hyatt,** 112 Washington Place, Pittsburgh, PA 15219 (tel. 412/471-1234 or toll-free 800/228-9000), a modern 21-story brick and glass structure. There are 404 guest rooms, featuring two double, queen, king, or oversized beds, with a blend of contemporary furnishings. Each unit is outfitted with cable color TV, air conditioning, and a direct-dial phone. Doubles range from $115 to $145. Facilities include an indoor heated swimming pool, a sauna, health club privileges, and a pay garage. In addition, there is QQ's Café for all-day light meals, and a full-service restaurant, Hugo's Rotisserie, for gourmet fare. Featuring a turn-of-the-century décor, this restaurant is known for its sumptuous salad bar and duckling, veal, and seafood entrees, in the $10.95 to $22.95 price range. Hours are 11:30 a.m. to 2:30 p.m. for lunch, and from 5:30 to 11 p.m. for dinner (except 10 p.m. closing on Sunday). All major CC's accepted.

Located near the tip of the Golden Triangle with Point State Park at its doorstep, is the **Pittsburgh Hilton and Towers,** Gateway Center, Pittsburgh, PA 15222 (tel. 412/391-4600 or toll-free 800/445-8667). This modern 24-story tower has 800 rooms, recently refurbished and renovated; many with views of the harbor or the Three Rivers Stadium. Rooms are outfitted with two double, queen, or king size beds, plus color cable TV, a radio, air conditioning, and a direct-dial phone. Doubles range from $115 to $135. Amenities include an indoor pool, a health club, barber and beauty salons, and a valet parking garage. Moderately priced meals are served throughout the day at the indoor-outdoor Promenade Café. The main dining room, Sterling's, has a clubby theme with polished brass, leather chairs, wall tapestries, and an autographed picture gallery of sporting, political, and entertainment figures who have dined there. Dinner entrees, priced from $14.95 to $19.95, include such dishes as sole with caviar, poached shrimp, chicken Dijon, osso buco, prime ribs, and steaks. Lunch is served Monday through Saturday from 11:30 a.m. to 2:30 p.m., and dinner from 5:30 to 10 p.m. There is also nightly jazz in the lobby lounge. All major CC's accepted.

On the city's South Side is the 293-room **Sheraton Hotel,** 7 Station Square Drive, Pittsburgh, PA 15219 (tel. 412/261-2000 or toll-free 800/325-3535), right on the banks of the Monongahela River. This modern 15-story hotel is adjacent to the Station Square shopping and restaurant complex, and across the street from the Monongahela Incline. The skylit lobby features a seven-story atrium, with fountains, plants, and a waterfall. Many guest rooms face this indoor courtyard and others look out onto the river and the cityscape. Each room features double, queen, or king beds, color cable TV, air conditioning, and a direct-dial phone. Doubles range from $114 to $135. Among the guest facilities are a lounge with nightly dancing and entertainment, a heated indoor pool, a whirlpool, a sauna, a health center, free parking, a beauty salon, and a barber shop. Restaurants include the Waterfall Terrace in the center of the atrium, an outdoor Fountainview Patio, and Reflections, a dining room featuring American and continental cuisine, with views of the Pittsburgh skyline. Entrees at dinner, priced from $13.95 to $19.95, focus on such dishes as chicken Cordon Bleu, crab-stuffed flounder, and veal alla marsala. Lunch is served from 11:30 a.m. to 2:30 p.m., and dinner from 5:30 to 10:30 p.m. All major CC's accepted.

The only independent property in downtown Pittsburgh, the **Bigelow,** Bigelow Square, Pittsburgh, PA 15219 (tel. 412/281-5800 or toll-free 800/225-5858), features the all-suite concept. Located across from the Hyatt near the Civic Arena and the subway, this property has 450 suites, with configurations as studios, one-, two-, or three-bedroom apartments. Each unit has a fully equipped kitchen, color TV, an AM/FM radio, and air conditioning. Rates for a studio for two people start at $80 and a one-bedroom apartment from $100; monthly rates are also available. The guest facilities include a barber shop, a beauty salon, a coin-operated laundry, valet parking, and complimentary breakfast on weekdays. There is also a restaurant, the Ruddy Duck, which is open Monday through Friday for breakfast, lunch, and cocktails. Lunch choices, priced from $5.95 to $7.95, offer salads, sandwiches, burgers, and light entrees such as fowl quiche (with chicken, duck, and turkey); Cajun chicken and scallop kebab; double roasted duck leg in smoky sauce; and filet mignon Wellington. Open from 7 a.m. to 7 p.m. All major CC's accepted.

Suburban Choices

There are no fewer than eight **Holiday Inns** in the greater Pittsburgh area, literally covering points north, south, east, and west. One of the closest to the city center and the most distinctive of the group is the **Holiday Inn—Green Tree,** 401 Holiday Drive, Pittsburgh, PA 15220 (tel. 412/922-8100 or toll-free 800/HOL-IDAY), located in a park-like setting three miles from downtown. It is a modern four-story property, with 205 units, including 50 king-leisure rooms, each with color cable TV, radio, a direct-dial phone, and air conditioning. Doubles range from $97 to $107. Guest facilities include an outdoor swimming pool, a sauna, indoor tennis courts, racquetball, exercise facilities, free parking, and courtesy transport to and from the airport. In addition, there is a lounge featuring the top 40 hits nightly, and the Greenery Restaurant, a moderately priced dining room with a bountiful salad bar, serving food from 7 a.m. to 10 p.m. daily. All major CC's accepted.

Nearby is one of the region's most outstanding suburban resorts, the **Pittsburgh Green Tree Marriott,** 101 Marriott Dr., Pittsburgh, PA 15205 (tel. 412/922-8400 or toll-free 800/228-9290), three miles south of downtown in a wooded setting. This seven-story property has 500 rooms, each with a contemporary décor, color cable TV with free HBO, an AM/FM radio, air conditioning, a direct-dial phone, a heat lamp, and "his and her" bath accessories. Doubles range from $109 to $129. Guest facilities include two outdoor pools, an indoor pool, tennis courts, a sauna, a Jacuzzi, an exercise room, and free parking. In addition, there are two restaurants, Ashley's, featuring fine American cuisine, and Market Square for moderate all-day meals; a piano bar lounge, and a disco with live entertainment and video dancing. In the summer months, a giant tent on the grounds becomes a dinner theater, featuring a top-notch show and buffet for $25 per person on Thursday, Friday, and Saturday nights. All major CC's accepted.

If you want to be near the major schools, museums, or hospitals, a good choice is the **University Inn,** Forbes Avenue at McKee Place, Pittsburgh, PA 15213 (tel. 412/683-6000 or toll-free 800/245-6675), in the Oakland district of the city. This modern property currently has 130 rooms, and is building 70 more, to make a total of 200 by 1988. Each room is contemporary in décor, with air conditioning, a direct-dial phone, an AM/FM radio, and color TV. The double-occupancy rate ranges from $85 to $100. Guest facilities include valet indoor parking and a lower-level brick-walled restaurant called Rebecca's Place, which serves lunch and dinner in the moderate price range. All major CC's accepted.

Also in this university and museum district of Oakland is the **Howard Johnson,** 3401 Boulevard of the Allies, Pittsburgh, PA 15213 (tel. 412/683-6100 or toll-free 800/654-2000). This eight-story modern hotel has 119 rooms, with all standard facilities including color TV, air conditioning, and a direct-dial phone. Doubles range from $65 to $70. There is also a 24-hour restaurant, an outdoor swimming pool, and ample free parking. All major CC's are accepted.

Six miles southeast of the downtown is the **Holiday House,** 3755 William Penn Highway, Monroeville, PA 15146 (tel. 412/856-1500 or toll-free 800/322-8029), a modern four-story hotel in an area known for its malls and business marts. Each of the 150 rooms offers color cable TV, a direct-dial telephone, air conditioning, and a modern functional décor. Doubles range from $48 to $56. Amenities include an outdoor swimming pool, free parking, a restaurant, a coffeeshop, and two nightclubs, one featuring the hits of the '80s, and the other swinging with the live band sounds of the '40s and '50s. This is also the home of The Main Room, a supper club featuring big-name entertainment, and a dinner theater presenting Broadway shows, from May through December. All major CC's accepted.

WHERE TO DINE: In addition to downtown near the major hotels, the restaurants of Pittsburgh are spread throughout the surrounding areas, with the major clusters in Station Square and the South Side; Mt. Washington overlooking the city; Oakland near the university and medical centers; and, to a lesser degree, the North Side. Here is an overview by area:

The Golden Triangle—Downtown Pittsburgh

The Top Choices: If there is one restaurant that proves that outward appearances are deceiving, it is **The Common Plea,** 308 Ross St. (tel. 281-5140), situated a block from the City-County Building and the Courthouse. Established over 15 years ago in two old buildings, one of which was a dairy barn, this establishment still looks like a diner from the exterior, but the minute you push back the heavy oak door, you know you have made a real find. The plush furnishings, dark paneled walls, and antique prints in the bar area provide a fitting prelude for the elegant dining room. The dinner menu, which is written on legal-size yellow ruled paper attached to a clip-board, ranges from $14.50 to $23.50 for classic beef, veal, and seafood dishes. The surprising part is that the price also includes a variety of house appetizers from marinated mushrooms to stuffed baked clams, homemade soup, salad, fruit, and dessert, all enhanced with extremely attentive service. At lunch time, prices range from $4.95 to $10.95 and include salads, sandwiches, steaks, and light entrees. Reservations are taken for lunch, but in the evening only parties of five or more can reserve a table in advance. Open for lunch from 11:30 a.m. to 2:30 p.m. on weekdays; and for dinner from 5 to 10:30 p.m. Monday through Saturday year round, and from 4 to 9 p.m. on Sunday (September through mid-May only). CC's accepted: AE, MC, V.

The **Top of the Triangle,** 600 Grant St. (tel. 471-4100), is Pittsburgh's skyscraper rooftop restaurant, 62 stories above the city's hustle and bustle. If you choose to view the city in the noonday sun, you'll have a choice of dishes like chicken and fruit plate; pasta and shrimp marinara; beef stir-fry; or prime-rib sandwich ($8 to $12). Watching the sunset brings a more elaborate menu, with such entrees as lobster-stuffed sole, tournedos Rossini, or roast duckling (in the $12 to $20 bracket). Lunch is served Monday through Friday from 11:30 a.m. to 3 p.m., and Saturday from noon to 3 p.m.; dinner hours are Monday through Friday from 5 to 10 p.m., and on Saturday from 5:30 p.m. to midnight. Cocktails are available until 2 a.m. each evening (except Sunday) in the Triangle Lounge which also offers great city views for the price of a drink (from $2.75). Major CC's are accepted.

Established in 1900, **Klein's,** 330 Fourth Ave. (232-3311), is one of the city's best seafood houses. Framed pictures of Pittsburgh's waterfront, fish tanks, ships' lanterns, captain's chairs, steering wheels, and driftwood dominate the décor. The menu is priced from $3.95 to $9.95 at lunch for most choices except lobster, which is usually $15 or more. Dinner entrees, priced from $10.95 to $25, include bouillabaisse; shrimp jambalaya; filet of red king salmon; mahi mahi; red snapper; simmered smoked finnan haddie; Florida stone crabs; sea squabs; boned mountain trout; walleyed pike; mesquite-smoked tuna; mako shark; cornmeal-breaded catfish; and lobster, as well as prime ribs and other limited meat selections. Klein's is also noted for its Caesar salad ($4.50) and its trademark garlic puffs which are served with all meals. Open Monday through Friday from 11 a.m. to 10 p.m., and for dinner only on Saturday from 4:30 to 10 p.m. All major CC's accepted.

The **Warner Premiere,** Warner Centre, 332 Fifth Avenue (tel. 471-7200), is housed in the old Warner Theatre. This $25 million restoration is pure Hollywood and conveys all the excitement of an opening night at every meal. The spectacular setting embraces a theatrical décor, a sweeping staircase, brass fixtures, tuxedo-clad waiters, and one of the largest private collections of movie costumes and memorabilia in the country, from Vivian Leigh's *Gone With the Wind* honeymoon hat to John Wayne's tunic for *The Conquerer.* Happily, the food is also star quality here, with extensive luncheon and dinner menus. Lunch items ($4 to $12) can be as light as a vegetarian sandwich or as elaborate as osso buco alla Milanese. Dinner entrees, priced from $8 to $20 with an average of $15, range from sesame-breaded chicken breast to Chateaubriand. Open for lunch, Monday through Saturday from 11:30 a.m. to 3 p.m.; and for dinner, Monday through Thursday from 5 to 10 p.m., and Friday and Saturday from 5 to 11 p.m. All major CC's are accepted.

Moderately Priced Dining: The **1902 Tavern,** 24 Market Square (tel. 471-1902), is as authentic as its name implies. Just look at the pictures on the walls, the vintage map of Pittsburgh, the tin ceiling, the etched glass, the brass beer pumps, the tile walls, and the old crank-handle phone, to experience the turn-of-the-century ambience. If you come for lunch, don't miss the oyster bar entrees ($6.95 to $9.95) or the hearty 1902-style sandwiches ($3.95 to $5.95). Dinnertime choices, priced from $7.95 to $16.95, include beef, veal, chicken, and pasta dishes as well as an array of fresh fish. Most regulars select the house specialty, seafood Nicole (priced at $22.95 for two people), which is a bounty of shrimp, clams, scallops, mussels, oysters, and baby whitefish served in marinara sauce over imported linguine. Open Monday through Saturday from 11:30 a.m. to 2 a.m. All major CC's accepted.

City Hall, 428 Forbes Ave. (tel. 391-8873), a clubby and dark-paneled restaurant, located in the basement of the Lawyers Building, is a handy and appropriate favorite with local politicians and attorneys. Lunch can be anything from salads, sandwiches, and pastas to sole jardiniere and tenderloin of beef, with prices ranging from $5.50 to $8.50. Dinner, with entrees from $9.95 to $14.95, focuses on steaks and chops as well as the house's four specialties of prime rib, chicken Dijon, veal saltimbocca, and pork au poivre. All dinners include salad, fresh vegetable, rice, and potato or pasta. Open for lunch and dinner, Monday through Friday from 11 a.m. to 10 p.m., and for dinner only on Saturday from 5 to 10 p.m. All major CC's accepted.

On the plaza level of the Oxford Centre building, **Dingbats**, 301 Grant St. (tel. 392-0350), is an informal and contemporary oyster bar-style restaurant, with multi-level seating, tiled floors, and lots of oversized plants and greenery, plus outdoor-café seating in the summer months. The emphasis is on "fun foods" like nachos, peel-'n'-eat shrimp, potato skins, chicken fingers, burgers, sandwiches, pizza, and exotic salads (all priced from $1.75 to $4.95 throughout the day). Dinner entrees feature charbroiled seafoods and meats ($5.95 to $12.95). Open for breakfast, lunch, and dinner Monday through Friday from 7 a.m. to 2 a.m.; and Saturday from 11:30 a.m. to 2 a.m., with music and dancing on Friday evenings. Credit cards accepted: AE, MC, V.

Another plaza-level restaurant of the Oxford Centre is **Harpers,** Grant Street and Fourth Avenue (tel. 391-1494), noted equally for its nightly jazz as well as its new American cuisine. Subtle art-deco tones are highlighted in a private club atmosphere. The lunch menu offers sandwiches named for jazz greats like the George Benson Club or Chuck Mangione Reuben ($4.75 to $6) or creative quiches and hearty salads ($4.50 to $7.95). Similar fare is available in the evening as well as steak, fish, and pasta entrees ($8.95 to $17.95). Open from 11 a.m. to 2 a.m. Monday through Saturday. All major CC's accepted.

Upstairs on level three of the Oxford Centre, you'll find a quiet ambience at **The Wine Restaurant,** 301 Grant St. (tel. 288-WINE). You'll be surrounded by floor-to-ceiling wine racks and a modern cubist décor of oak furniture, indirect lighting, parquet floors, and stainless steel and chrome trim. At lunchtime, you'll find the Regional American Express Food Bar ($3.50 to $5) or entrees like seafood stew, spaghetti Mediterranean, or smoked trout salad (average tab $6). Complete dinners at night are priced from $10 to $16 including soup or salad and dessert, with entrees like Cajun étouffée; swordfish steak; duckling with black currant sauce; or calves' liver with sage and parsnips. In addition, wines of the world (more than 60) are served by the taste, glass, or bottle. Open from 11:30 a.m. until 10 p.m. Monday through Thursday, and until midnight on Friday and Saturday. All major CC's are accepted.

The Convention Center is surrounded by a number of trendy eating spots, such as the **British Bicycle Club (BBC)** at 923 Penn Ave. (tel. 391-9623). Formerly a warehouse, this tastefully converted two-level restaurant exudes an old-English-pub charm with its brick walls, brass lamp fixtures, rugby photos, and bicycle prints, not to mention its long clubby bar. Luncheon fare consists mostly of sandwiches and burgers ($3.50 to $4.95) while dinner favorites ($10.95 to $15.95) are handcut steaks and seafood dishes like whole baked trout or crab imperial. Particularly popular with the young professional crowd who enjoy sampling the 18 or more imported beers, BBC is open from 11 a.m. to 10 p.m. Monday through Thursday and until 11 p.m. on Friday and Saturday. All major CC's are accepted.

Etched glass, ceiling fans, and climbing plants predominate at **Bernard's Place,** 711 Penn Ave. (tel. 261-3808), a modern and congenial restaurant located two blocks from the Convention Center. There is booth and table seating on the ground floor beside the long wooden bar and tables also fill the spacious upstairs gallery. Lunchtime selections, priced from $3.50 to $7.95, include seafood salads, croissant sandwiches, and garden omelets. The emphasis at dinner is on charbroiled meats and shrimp as well as Italian-American favorites like veal alla Romano, fettuccine Alfredo and scallops Siciliano. Entrees are priced from $7.95 to $15.95 and include salad, potato, and vegetable. Open for lunch and dinner, Monday through Saturday from 11 a.m. to 11 p.m. All major CC's are accepted.

The Convention Center area is also known for its excellent Italian restaurants, such as **F. Tambellini,** 139 Seventh St. (tel. 391-1091), which has been here for over 15 years. At lunchtime, the menu focuses on seafood, steaks, and salads with daily pasta specials ($3.95 to $8.95). In the evening, all entrees are cooked to order with emphasis on Northern Italian veal dishes and homemade pastas, priced from $8.95 to $19.95, with most under the $15 mark. Open for lunch Monday through Saturday from 11:30 a.m. to 4 p.m., and for dinner from 4 to 11 p.m. Credit cards accepted: AE, MC, V.

Budget Meals: A good choice near the Convention Center is **Mahoney's,** 949 Liberty Ave. (tel. 471-4243), an area favorite since 1968. Although its exterior is dark and ordinary, the inside of this restaurant is a delight, with its whitewashed brick walls, batik hangings, and cane furniture. The various alcoves and hutches also serve to house a mini-museum of local memorabilia, from kitchen implements and farm tools to handcrafts. Salads, sandwiches, and omelets are available at lunchtime ($3 to $4.95). The international dinner selections, priced from $4.95 to $7.95, range from moussaka and shish kebab to chicken alla marsala and Irish stew. Open for lunch and dinner Monday through Friday from 11 a.m. to 8 p.m. Most major CC's accepted.

If you are looking for a tasty meal near Heinz Hall, don't miss **Richest,** 140 Sixth St. (tel. 471-7799). Established in 1936, this is the oldest kosher-style deli in western Pennsylvania. All the usual deli goodies are featured plus a full bar and a low-cost dinner menu in a casual and relaxed atmosphere. Prices range from $2.95 to $7.95 for most dishes. Open Monday through Saturday from 7 a.m. to 11 p.m. All major CC's accepted.

For a hearty Irish beef stew at lunch, try **Gallagher's Pub,** 2 S. Market Place, Market Square (tel. 261-5554). A variety of sandwiches, salads, burgers, and hoagies are also on the menu, all priced from $3 to $4.95. Lunch is served Monday through Friday from 11 a.m. to 2:30 p.m. and on Saturday from noon to 3 p.m. Gallagher's also has a sing-along piano bar at night, from 9 p.m. to 1:30 a.m. on Monday and Saturday, and from 5 to 7 p.m. Wednesday through Friday. You might want to wet your whistle with some Irish coffee, $2.75, or a Harp beer, $2.50. All major CC's honored.

The South Side and Station Square

The Top Choices: It's worth the trip to Station Square just to see **The Grand Concourse,** One Station Square (tel. 261-1717), a palatial Beaux-Arts landmark built in 1901 as the terminal of the Pittsburgh and Lake Erie Railroad. Recently restored to the tune of over $2 million, the Grand Concourse is set on the banks of the Monongahela River with expansive views of the downtown skyline. The décor abounds in stained glass, decorative marble, gilt, and mosaics. Seafood is featured here, although meat and chicken dishes are also excellent. The menu at lunch, priced from $6.95 to $11.95, ranges from shrimp pastas and salads to baby halibut, red snapper, lemon sole, and yellow pike, as well as burgers and crêpes. Dinner entrees feature such dishes as scallops primavera; paella; bouillabaisse; Norwegian salmon in parchment paper; Idaho rainbow trout; Louisiana redfish; yellow-fin tuna; and Cape bluefish, as well as chicken Dijon; rack of lamb, and steaks. All main courses, priced from $11 to $19, are accompanied by vegetables and potatoes. Lunch is served Monday through Friday from 11:30 a.m. to 2:30 p.m.; dinner Monday through Thursday from 5 to 10 p.m.; until 11 p.m. on Friday and Saturday; and until 9 p.m. on Sunday. Brunch is also available on Sunday from 10:30 a.m. to 2:30 p.m. Most major CC's accepted.

If you prefer a lighter meal and a more casual atmosphere, step into the adjacent **Gandy Dancer Saloon and Oyster Bar,** adjoining the main restaurant. Emphasis is on raw-bar platters, homemade pastas, and light dishes, in a milieu of live entertainment. An all-day menu prevails, with such choices as Florida rock shrimp, fish and chips, fried smelts, oysters, clams, and shrimp-in-the-rough, as well as burgers, sandwiches, and salads. The price range is $2.95 to $9.95. Open Monday through Saturday from 11:30 a.m. to 2 a.m., and on Sunday from 2:30 p.m. to midnight. Most major CC's accepted.

Le Pommier, 2104 E. Carson St., South Side (tel. 431-1901). The apple-tree-shaped sign over the door of this two-story building beckons you to enjoy dinner in the rustic atmosphere of a French country inn. The one-page menu, which changes nightly, offers anything from quail or braised sweetbreads to salmon en papillote or Roquefort-glazed sirloin. Entrees range from $10 to $18, with salads, soups, or house pâtés $2 to $4 extra. The 14-page wine list begins at $10 and goes to $85 a bottle. Open for dinner only, Tuesday through Saturday from 6 to 10 p.m.; reservations a must. Credit cards accepted: AE, MC, and V.

Moderately Priced Dining: Little Bavaria, 1924 E. Carson St., South Side, near Station Square (tel. 381-2443), is as close to a German village inn as you'll get in Pittsburgh, with its brick walls, beam ceilings, stained-glass, coats of arms, and waitresses dressed in the traditional "dirndl" costume. Specialties, which include sauerbraten, rouladen, wiener schnitzel, and smoked sausage, range from $3.95 to $5.95 at lunch, and average from $8.95 to $14.95 for dinner-size servings with all the trimmings. Open for lunch, Tuesday through Friday from 11:30 a.m. to 2:30 p.m.; and for dinner, Tuesday through Thursday from 4:30 to 10 p.m., and Friday and Saturday from 4:30 to 11 p.m. There's piano music on Friday and Saturday nights and German oompah bands play once a month. All major CC's accepted.

Brady Street Bridge Café, 2228 E. Carson St., South Side, near the Birmingham Bridge (tel. 488-1818), is a restored old riverside tavern. With two dining areas, there is a choice of seating in a homey Victorian-style dining parlor with textured wallpaper and an old oak fireplace, or a bright and leafy conservatory-style room. In the summer there is also an outdoor garden patio. The menu, which emphasizes American regional cuisine, offers salads, burgers, and sandwiches at lunchtime, mostly under $5 (try the chicken and fruit salad with peanuts or the turkey Devonshire). Dinner entrees, priced from $8.50 to $14.50, include Créole/Cajun specialties; pastas; seafoods; and duck breast with orange sauce and white grapes. Live entertainment on Saturday nights. Major CC's accepted.

If you are longing for Hunan pork or Peking duck, an ideal choice is **Dynasty,** Station Square (tel. 642-6688). Located on the upper level of the Station Square complex, this restaurant is a little oasis amidst the bustle of the shops and eateries on the main level. Open for lunch and dinner every day, with brunch on Sunday as well and Chinese music on Saturday nights. Dinnertime entrees range from $8 to $20, with most in the $10 to $12 bracket; lunchtime prices are about half the evening's prices. CC's accepted: AE, MC, and V.

Budget Meals: The ambience and décor of a European wine cellar prevails at the **Cheese Cellar,** Station Square (tel. 471-3355). The eclectic menu ranges from cheese fondues to chili, pizza, croissant sandwiches, and burgers, all priced around $5 or less for lunch. Dinners, mostly all priced at $10 and under, feature stir-fry dishes, char-grilled seafood and meats, and a half-dozen pastas. Open Monday through Saturday from 11 a.m. to 1 a.m. for lunch and dinner, and from 10:30 a.m. to 3 p.m. for Sunday brunch. All major CC's accepted.

Mt. Washington—you can reach most of these restaurants by taking the Dusquesne Incline from West Carson Street in the South Side section of the city. The majority of these dining spots serve dinner only and fall into a fairly expensive price bracket, but then, the views are the best in town.

In an area known for its spectacular views of Pittsburgh, **Christopher's,** 1411 Grandview Ave., Mt. Washington (tel. 381-4500), has towered over all for the last 15 years. An exterior glass elevator brings you up to the twelfth floor and this panoramic tri-level restaurant. Three walls of windows, said to be the tallest glass walls in the country, emphasize the view. The setting also includes a 60-foot-long wall made entirely of coal; four central columns and platforms signifying Pittsburgh's four major industries of coal, steel, iron, and glass; hanging theater lights; a mélange of plants; and a collection of original rod sculptures. There is also a mini-museum of artifacts and mementos of the city's past, from old telephones and presidential campaign buttons to baseball equipment.

The emphasis at Christopher's is on tableside entrees such as steak Diane and tournedos Rossini, as well as a wide selection of seafood dishes including Idaho rainbow trout; flounder with crabmeat; and a combination platter of petit lobster, sole, crab imperial, oysters Rockefeller, and shrimp. Entrees are priced from $14 to $27 and are accompanied by soup or juice, rice, and vegetable of the day. Open for dinner only, Monday through Thursday from 5 to 11 p.m., and until midnight on Friday and Saturday. Reservations are a must and jackets are required for men. All major CC's are accepted.

LeMont, 1114 Grandview Ave., Mt. Washington (tel. 431-3100), is open for dinner only when the sunset and evening views of Pittsburgh are the most spectacular. Decorated in a "classic contemporary" style, with the emphasis on Italian and French cuisine. Entrees, priced from $12.95 to $24.95, include salad, vegetable, and pasta. Some of the specialty dishes include tournedos of veal and lobster; roast duck in raspberry sauce; medallions of beef topped with lump crabmeat in béarnaise sauce; seasoned rack of lamb; and seafood au gratin in an eggplant boat. In the summer months, a selection of light dishes such as veal scaloppine, trout francese, or chicken romano is featured every night but Saturday. Priced from $7.95 to $9.95, these entrees come with salad and vegetable or pasta. Desserts, which include tempting fresh pastries, white chocolate mousse pie, baked Alaska, and crêpes Suzette, range from $1.50 to $8 (for two). Reservations necessary; jackets required for men. Most major CC's accepted.

Established in 1957, **The Tin Angel,** 1200 Grandview Ave., Mt. Washington (tel. 381-1919), was one of the first of the area's restaurants overlooking Pittsburgh's Golden Triangle. Known for its romantic candlelight dining on three levels, this spot offers a complete meal from appetizer to dessert, from $19.95 to $29.95, depending on choice of one of six entrees of the evening. The selections usually include filet mignon, lobster, surf-and-turf, filet of sole, and steak. Open Monday through Saturday from 5:30 to 9:30 p.m. Jackets are required for men; reservations are essential. All CC's are accepted.

If you'd like to view and possibly buy some art works while you dine, you'll enjoy **Cliffside,** 1208 Grandview Ave., Mt. Washington (tel. 431-6996), where customers enjoy a new show and artist on display every two months. Entrees here, which include salad or soup, breads, and a vegetable or side dish, range from $14 to $22 and include some creative veal and chicken entrees as well as shrimp Cordon Bleu, surf-and-turf, and strip steak stuffed with crabmeat. Open Monday through Thursday from 5 to 10:30 p.m., and until 11 p.m. on Friday and Saturday, with cocktails served until 2 a.m.; piano music nightly. All major CC's are accepted.

In contrast to all the others, **The Shiloh Inn,** 123 Shiloh St., Mt. Washington (tel. 431-4000), is reached via the Monongehela Incline, a half-block from its door. This restaurant is an old-world oasis amid the modern residences of the area. As you enter under the brown canopy, you'll be charmed by the warm décor, from the open fireplace to the stained-glass windows and pictures that reflect another era. The menu showcases Italian cuisine with at least six veal dishes from picatta and parmigiana to romano and marsala. Beef and seafood choices are basically American in style. Entrees range from $14 to $20 and come with salad and vegetable or potato. For $2 extra, you can have a complete dinner that includes the above plus pasta, dessert, and coffee. Open every night except Sunday from 5:30 to 11:30 p.m., and on weekends till midnight. Piano music nightly. All major CC's accepted.

A Moderately Priced Place for Lunch and Dinner: One of the few restaurants in this area that serves lunch, the **Georgetowne Inn,** 1230 Grandview Ave., Mt. Washington (tel. 481-4424), blends a rustic décor with 20th-century wraparound windows. Ideal for families, the emphasis here is on good value with dinner entrees ranging from $11 to $22. Most choices are below $15, and that includes cheeseboard, soup or juice, salad, potatoes or pasta, vegetable, coffee, and dessert. The typically American menu offers everything from steak or prime ribs to sole or crab legs. At lunchtime, the prices for full meals range from $5.50 to $8.95 and there is also a wide variety of salads and overstuffed sandwiches from $3.25 to $7.50. Lunch hours are Monday through Saturday from 11 a.m. to 3 p.m.; dinner Monday through Thursday from 5 p.m. to midnight, Friday and Saturday from 5 p.m. to 1 a.m., and Sunday from 4 to 10 p.m. All major CC's accepted.

The Oakland Area

The Top Choice: Angel's Corner, 405 Atwood St. at Bates Street, Oakland (tel. 682-1879), is convenient to Pittsburgh's medical and university centers. A $5 taxi ride from downtown, this restaurant is housed in a converted corner church, complete with stained-glass windows and a classical guitarist playing in the choir loft. The "divine dishes" on the menu include Coho salmon jardinière; sole St-Jacques stuffed with scallop mousse and garnished with King crab and caviar; beef en brochette; casmaron chicken (with jumbo crabmeat served over fettuccine); and medallions of pork with a creamy Dijon sauce. Entrees range from $11.95 to $18.95, with most choices under $15, and include salad and vegetables. Open for dinner only, Monday through Saturday from 5 to 10 p.m. CC's accepted: AE, MC, and V.

Other Moderate Suggestions: For thirty years, **The Black Angus,** 114 Atwood St., Oakland (tel. 621-5844), has been known for its beef, as its name and western-style décor indicate. In addition to hearty cuts of sirloin and prime rib, the menu features Greek and Italian dishes and seafood. All entrees are priced from $8.95 to $16.95, and come with salad, potato, and pasta or vegetable. Lunchtime prices average about half of the evening's tab. Open from 11 a.m. weekdays to 10:30 p.m. Monday through Thursday, and until 11 p.m. on Friday. On Saturday, only dinner is served, from 4 to 11 p.m. and there is also Greek music and belly-dancing entertainment. Early-bird dinners, priced from

$6.95, are also featured most nights from 4 to 6 p.m. Patrons enjoy free car parking. All major CC's accepted.

If you are visiting the Carnegie Museum and would like a change of pace, try the pub atmosphere of **Great Scot,** 413 S. Craig St., Oakland (tel. 683-1450). The menu, which changes bi-weekly to reflect regional American recipes, averages about $5 at lunchtime for burgers, salads, and vegetable quiches, and runs from $8.95 to $12.95 in the evening for such dishes as lemon catfish or calves' liver. Soups (try the chilled blueberry at $1.95) are both tasty and creative. Open daily for lunch from 11 a.m. to 3 p.m., and dinner from 5 to 10 p.m. CC's accepted: AE, MC, and V.

For a lunch with an arty ambience, don't miss **The Museum Café,** at the Carnegie Institute, 4400 Forbes Ave. (tel. 622-3144), featuring a décor of contemporary prints, fine linen, silver, and fresh flowers. Salads and hot entrees average $4.50 to $7.95, and there is full-bar service. Open Tuesday through Friday from 11:30 a.m. to 3:30 p.m. In the lower level of the Museum of Natural History, you can also enjoy budget-stretching cafeteria-style meals (entrees from $2 to $4) from 9 a.m. to 4 p.m. Tuesday through Friday. CC's accepted in the Café: AE, MC, and V, but no CC's in the cafeteria.

The North Side

Figgins, Two North Shore Center (tel. 321-9000), is drawing Pittsburghers and visitors alike to the city's north side. Situated next to the Seventh Street Bridge and near the Three Rivers Stadium, this ground-level restaurant is on the edge of the Allegheny River with sweeping views of the downtown area. Décor is modern with emphasis on glass, brass, and brick, in a multilevel seating combination inside and an outdoor patio next to a sculpture park for warm days. To encourage more traffic from downtown at lunchtime, the restaurant also operates a free mini-bus shuttle for four or more customers. Menu at lunch features an oyster bar as well as salads, sandwiches, and finger foods, such as pizza, chicken wings, and nachos, with prices ranging from $3.50 to $11.95. Figgins also operates a popular lunch buffet, priced from $3.95 to $6.95 for soups, salads, and/or sandwiches. The dinner menu, priced from $8.95 to $18.95, focuses on more than a dozen seafood entrees, ranging from crab imperial and scallops Szechuan, to sole and salmon lattice, as well as a variety of beef, veal, chicken, duckling, and lamb dishes. All main courses include salad, vegetable, potato, or rice.

Open for lunch Monday through Saturday from 11 a.m. to 4 p.m.; and for dinner Monday through Thursday from 4 to 10 p.m., Friday and Saturday until 11 p.m., and Sunday until 10 p.m. Live jazz entertainment can be enjoyed Thursday through Sunday evenings and "late-night city bites" are also available until 1 a.m. on Friday and Saturday, and until midnight on Monday through Thursday. Free parking. Major CC's accepted.

THE TOP ATTRACTIONS: Pittsburgh's earliest years are depicted at the **Fort Pitt Museum,** Point State Park (tel. 281-9284), located at the point of the Golden Triangle, where the Allegheny and Monongahela Rivers meet to form the Ohio. The city itself first began here, as French and British forces fought for control of this outpost which served as a gateway to the west. At one time, this was the most elaborate British fortress in the colonies, and it also served as a place for trade and negotiation with the Indians. After the British left in 1772, Ft. Pitt remained a key spot in the development of early Pittsburgh, as the city literally grew up around it. The present fort museum is a reconstruction, built to duplicate the look of the original bastions. Displays include dioramas, exhibits of original objects, models, and reconstructed rooms. Open Wednesday through Saturday from 9 a.m. to 5 p.m., and Sunday from noon to 5 p.m. Admission is $1.50 for adults and 50¢ for children aged 6 through 17. While you are here, take time to enjoy the surrounding park, riverwalks, and the sights across the waters, such as the Three Rivers Stadium to the north and the hills of Mt. Washington to the south.

Pittsburgh's skyline is an impressive tableau of multi-story **skyscrapers** of modern concrete and glass. Most of these buildings are surrounded by grassy plazas with fountains, trees, plants, and benches that beckon the pedestrian to sit down and be a part of the scene. You'll get a good feel for the city if you start at Point State Park and stroll eastward into the heart of the city. Take special note of such hallmarks as the **Gateway Center,** a cluster of skyscrapers with a two-acre pedestrian garden walkway; the **PPG Tower,** a 40-story Gothic-style "cathedral" of glass between Third and Fourth Avenues; the **Alcoa Building,** 425 Sixth Ave., 30 stories of aluminium; the **Mellon Bank Building,** Fifth Avenue and William Penn Place, finished in stainless steel panels; and the **U.S. Steel Building,** 600 Grant St., the tallest skyscraper (62 stories) between New York and Chicago.

The **Cathedral of Learning,** Fifth Avenue at Bigelow Boulevard (tel. 624-6000), is the focal point on the University of Pittsburgh campus in the Oakland section of the city. Designed to be a "meeting of modern skyscraper and medieval cathedral," this 42-story building was begun in 1926 and the first classes were held in 1935. A National Historic Landmark, it is considered to be the last great monument of Gothic revival in the U.S., with 165,000 blocks of Indiana limestone on its exterior walls. Among the highlights are the Nationality Classrooms, 19 different exhibit rooms displaying the cultures of many lands, including China, Russia, Greece, Syria-Lebanon, most of Europe, and an early-American room. These enclaves were created primarily in the 1930s and 1940s, with the most recent addition being the Irish Classroom (1957). Each was a gift to the university from the specific ethnic group depicted, and all were designed by artists and architects from the nations represented. Used for teaching the arts and sciences, these rooms can also be enjoyed year round by visitors. Guided tours are scheduled daily from 9 a.m. to 4 p.m. Monday through Friday; from 9:30 a.m. to 3:30 p.m. on Saturday; and from 11 a.m. to 3:30 p.m. on Sunday. Reservations are required; nominal fees ($1 for adults and 50¢ for children over 8) are usually requested.

The **Museums of the Carnegie Institute,** 4400 Forbes Ave. (tel. 622-3127), are also located in the Oakland section of the city, about a ten-minute cab or bus ride from downtown. This complex consists of the Museum of Art, with a permanent collection of European painting, sculpture, and graphic arts from the Renaissance to the 20th century; and the Museum of Natural History, which is known as the "home of the dinosaurs." In addition to the much-heralded Dinosaur Hall, there is also Botany Hall, Polar World, Geology Hall, and the Hillman Hall of Minerals and Gems. The latter is a display of 2,500 dazzling specimens from around the world, such as a 197-carat opal, a 500-pound section of amethyst geode, and a "touchable" meteorite. Hours are Tuesday through Saturday from 10 a.m. to 5 p.m., and Sunday from 1 to 5 p.m. Suggested donations are $2 for adults and $1 for children.

Two miles farther east of the downtown area is the **Point Breeze section** of the city and the **Frick Art Museum,** 7227 Reynolds St. (tel. 371-7766), located in a grassy setting across from Frick Park. Established in 1970, this Italian Renaissance–style building houses a permanent collection of Italian, Flemish, and French paintings and tapestries from the 15th through 18th centuries. Other treasured objects on display include an 18th-century marble urn from the gardens at Versailles; a 15th-century Florentine stone fireplace; a glazed terra-cotta plaque from the atelier of Andrea della Robbia; two chairs made for Marie Antoinette and the palace at St. Cloud; imperial Russian parcel-gilt silver pieces; and ancient Chinese porcelains. Open Wednesday through Saturday from 10 a.m. to 5:30 p.m., and Sunday from noon to 6 p.m. There is no admission charge.

In the city's North Side is the **Pittsburgh Aviary,** Ridge Avenue and Arch Street (tel. 322-7855), situated in the West Park section of the Allegheny Commons. Claiming to be the only indoor facility in the country totally devoted to birds, this walk-through museum displays over 250 species of birds in free flight. With exhibits and rooms planted with tropical foliage and trees, this unique feathered zoo illustrates the color and song of birds from around the world. Open from 9 a.m. to 4:30 p.m. daily. Admission is $1.50 for adults and 50¢ for children.

Also on the North Side is the **Three Rivers Stadium,** 400 Stadium Circle (tel. 321-0650), home of the Pittsburgh Pirates baseball and Steelers football teams. During days when no events are scheduled, the staff conducts one-hour walking tours of the stadium, designed to show a cross-section of behind-the-scenes activity. For those who want to spend another hour here, there is also a one-hour tour of the Hall of Fame Museum and Theatre featuring sports highlights and blooper films. Tours are given between 8 a.m. and 5 p.m., and reservations are required. The stadium tour is $1.50 for adults and $1 for children (16 and under); the stadium tour plus the Hall of Fame Theatre is $3 for adults and $2 for children.

NIGHTLIFE: You'll find many ways to fill your nights while you're in Pittsburgh. Our choices follow.

Theaters and Performing Arts

Pittsburgh's premier stage is the **Heinz Hall for the Performing Arts,** 600 Penn Ave. (tel. 281-5000), a restored 1926 movie theater, situated downtown between Sixth and Seventh Streets. This is the home of the Pittsburgh Symphony Orchestra, The Pittsburgh Dance Council, and the Pittsburgh Ballet Theatre. A varied program of concerts and Broadway shows is also featured here throughout the year. Performances are usually Tuesday through Saturday, with curtain at 8 p.m., and matinees on Saturday and Sunday at 2 p.m. Ticket prices vary from $10 to $25, depending on the event. *(Note:* this splendid theater itself can be toured on Monday, Wednesday, and Friday, at 12:30 p.m., by appointment only; call 392-4844). CC's accepted: AE, MC, and V.

As we go to press, the **Benedum Center for the Performing Arts,** 207 Seventh St. (tel. 261-2800), is scheduled to open in late 1987 with some limited shows and its first full season in 1988. Formerly the Stanley Theatre, this facility will be the new home of the Civic Light Opera (tel. 281-3973) and the Pittsburgh Opera (tel. 281-0912), both of which have previously been headquartered at the Heinz Hall. Check with the Greater Pittsburgh Visitors and Information Bureau for an update at the time of your visit.

Pittsburgh's modern **Civic Arena,** Washington Place (tel. 642-2062), is also a frequent setting for major concerts, circuses, and ice shows, as well as professional hockey and soccer. This $22 million structure is an attraction in itself, with a stainless-steel retractable dome roof three times the size of that of St. Peter's in Rome. Ticket prices range from $9 to $19, depending on the attraction. CC's accepted: AE, Disc, MC, and V.

Dinner Theaters

Year-round productions are staged at the **Holiday House Hotel**

and Entertainment Complex, 3755 William Penn Hwy., Monroeville (tel. 856-1500), six miles southeast of the city. The program here focuses on Broadway plays with a buffet dinner commencing at 6 p.m. followed by an 8 p.m. curtain on Friday and Saturday nights. The cost is $17.50 per person; all major CC's are accepted.

During the summer months, you can enjoy an outdoor stage show under a tent at the **Marriott Green Tree Theatre-on-the-Green,** 101 Marriott Dr. (tel. 922-8400), three miles south of downtown. Scheduled on Thursday, Friday, and Saturday evenings, buffet dinner starts at 7 p.m. with showtime at 9 p.m. Cost for dinner and show is $25. Major CC's accepted.

Music Lounges

In the downtown area, **Harper's,** One Oxford Centre (tel. 391-1494) is the place to go for jazz Tuesday through Sunday nights.

Other good spots to enjoy nightly contemporary music and dancing are **Chauncy's,** Station Square (tel. 232-0601); the **Gandy Dancer,** at the Grand Concourse, One Station Square (tel. 261-1717); and **Figgins,** Two North Shore Center (tel. 321-9000).

SHOPPING: In downtown Pittsburgh, **Kaufmann's,** 400 Fifth Ave. (tel. 232-2000) is a tradition. In business since 1898, this is a grand emporium with 12 fashion shops, a budget store, beauty salons, a dental clinic, and a post office. Open Monday and Thursday from 10 a.m. to 9 p.m.; and every other day (except Sunday) from 10 a.m. to 5:45 p.m.

Just two blocks away, you'll find one of the newest midcity shopping complexes, **One Oxford Centre,** Grant Street and Fourth Avenue. This is a 46-story office tower with a glass atrium filled with shops such as Valentino, Bill Blass, Ferragamo, Ralph Lauren, and Gucci. It's open weekdays from 10 a.m. to 5:30 p.m. with late opening until 9 p.m. on Monday and Thursday, and Saturday from 10 a.m. to 5:30 p.m.

Sunday shopping is never a problem at the **The Shops at Station Square,** Smithfield Street Bridge and Carson Street (tel. 261-9911), open daily from 10 a.m. to 9 p.m. and Sunday from noon to 5 p.m. A tourist attraction as well as a shopping complex, this is a restored turn-of-the-century railroad center with 70 shops and restaurants, much like San Francisco's Ghirardelli Square or New York's South Street Seaport. The merchandise here ranges from imported fashions and vintage Pennsylvania wines to Laura Ashley and Crabtree and Evelyn products, as well as candies and crafts, teddy bears, and tobaccos.

If you are in the Oakland area to see the museums and university buildings, don't miss South Craig Street, a four-block area that is a treasure-trove for shoppers in search of distinctive quality crafts. The shops here include the **Carnegie Mellon University Art Gallery,** 407 S. Craig St. (tel. 268-3110); **Made by Hand** (tel. 681-8346) and the **Irish Design Center** (tel. 682-6125), both at 303 S. Craig St.; the **Marcus/Gordon Poster Gallery,** 418 S. Craig St. (tel. 682-2841); **Over the Rainbow Handcrafted Gifts,** 214 S. Craig St. (tel. 683-4351); **Papyrus Designs,** 319 S. Craig St. (tel. 682-3237); and the **Yarn Connection,** 406 S. Craig St. (tel. 681-3830).

EVENTS: The **Three Rivers Arts Festival** is a 17-day gala of visual arts, music, and food, held annually in mid-June (1988 will be its 29th year). This open-air event happens throughout the downtown area on the grounds of such places as the Gateway Center, Point State Park, PPG Place, and several Grant Street locations. The exhibits include painting and craft demonstrations, children's activities, and live music and dance performances, plus films, videos, and an artists' market. The schedule goes from noon to 10 p.m. and is free. For a complete program, contact the Greater Pittsburgh Visitors Bureau.

The major summer event is the **Three Rivers Regatta,** Point State Park, held in late July-early August. This is a free, family-oriented weekend of water, land, and air exhibitions highlighting the city's three rivers. The activities include a water festival featuring ski shows, turn-of-the-century sternwheeler and "anything that floats" races, and a Formula One Grand Prix, plus parades of decorated boats, and hot-air-balloon competitions. The hours are 8 a.m. to dusk. Full details can be obtained from the Greater Pittsburgh Visitors Bureau.

CHILDREN'S CORNER: The **Pittsburgh Children's Museum,** One Landmarks Square, Allegheny Center, (tel. 322-5058), is a unique youth-oriented complex housed in the city's Old Post Office Building on the North Side. There are six exhibit areas designed just for children, including an international puppet collection; an audio and video communication center where children can "appear" on TV; a playpath for toddlers, and a summertime circus. Open Monday through Saturday from 10 a.m. to 5 p.m. and Sunday from 1 to 5 p.m. Admission is $2.50 per person.

DAY-TRIPS FROM PITTSBURGH: Just a few miles from the heart of Pittsburgh you'll come to an exuberant area known as the **Laurel Highlands.** Often overlooked as an "adjunct" to Pittsburgh, the Laurel Highlands are indeed a full-fledged destination in their own right, affording a sampling of fresh country air and outdoor living to visitors from near and far.

Encompassing a region that begins at New Kensington north of Pittsburgh and stretches 60 miles eastward and 45 miles as far south as the Maryland and West Virginia borders, the Laurel Highlands take in the counties of Westmoreland, Fayette, Somerset, and Cambria. This area embraces Pennsylvania's tallest mountain range, the Alleghenies, and Mt. Davis, the highest point in the state. As its name implies, the land is also rich in mountain laurel, the official flower of Pennsylvania.

Historically, this was the western frontier, the wilderness on the edge of the Revolutionary War battlefields, and today's visitor will find old forts and military strongholds, a frontier courthouse site, restored stagecoach inns, and log taverns. Most of all, the Laurel Highlands draw people to lush forest and mountain scenery and a wealth of year-round outdoor sports.

VISITOR INFORMATION: For a helpful packet of brochures, advice, and up-to-date data, contact the **Laurel Highlands, Inc.,** Town Hall, 120 E. Main St., Ligonier, PA 15658 (tel. 412/238-5661).

TOP ATTRACTIONS: Among the most heralded spots of this area is the architectural panorama known as **Fallingwater,** Route 381, Mill Run (tel. 329-8501). Designed by Frank Lloyd Wright in 1936, this unusual house, which is perched over a waterfall, was created as a mountain retreat for a Pittsburgh department store owner, Edgar J. Kaufmann. Opened to the public in 1964, the site can be toured daily (except Monday) April through mid-November from 10 a.m. to 4 p.m. Admission is $5 and reservations are advised; the drive from Pittsburgh is approximately two hours. From May through October, free **natural history walks** on the Fallingwater grounds are led on Saturdays and Sundays at 11:15 a.m., 1:15, 2:15, and 3:15 p.m.

In contrast, **Linden Hall,** off Route 51, Dawson (tel. 529-7543), is an opulent turn-of-the-century mountaintop mansion dating back to 1913. The estate originally belonged to Phillip J. Cochran, who amassed an enormous fortune by operating the first profitable beehive coke ovens in this part of the state. Sixty stonemasons were brought from Italy to complete the mansion, which is fueled by three natural gas wells and also displays glass from the Tiffany studios, an Aeolian pipe organ, and Chippendale furniture. It is currently operated as the Walter J. Burke Labor Education Center by the United Steelworkers of America. Tours are conducted every hour, starting at 1 p.m. until 5 p.m. daily from March through October and on weekends from November through mid-December; the cost is $4.50.

The aura of Colonial America is preserved at the **Compass Inn Museum,** Route 30, Laughlintown (tel. 238-4983). Built in 1799, this log house was originally a drovers' and traders' tavern, an ideal stopping place at the foot of the mountain. A fine stone addition was added in 1820, making this inn an attractive lodging for wealthy cross-country travelers on the Philadelphia-Pittsburgh Turnpike. Completely restored today, it is furnished with documented pieces and implements, and includes a cookhouse, a blacksmith shop, a barn, and an authentic Conestoga wagon. From May through October, costumed guides lead 90-minute tours, Tuesday through Saturday from noon to 4:30 p.m., and on Sunday from 1 to 4:30 p.m., with extended hours during the summer months. Candlelight tours are also scheduled on weekends (from 1:30 to 4:30 p.m.) in November and December. The cost is $2.50 for adults and $1 for children.

In this area, you can also visit the largest natural cave in Pennsylvania and north of the Mason-Dixon line, the **Laurel Caverns,** off Route 40, Farmington, PA 15437 (tel. 329-5968). This natural wonder has 4½ acres of floor space and 2.3 miles of passages. Qualified guides lead hourly explorations, with narrations on the cave's history and geology. A trackless train also provides a 35-minute ride to the top of the westernmost ridge of the Appalachian Mountains, affording spectacular 180° views over 4,000 square miles of land (don't forget your camera!). Open daily from 9 a.m. to 5 p.m. May through October. Admission is $6 for adults and $4 for children; the train trip is $2 extra per person.

The Great Outdoors

Of all the reasons to go to the Laurel Highlands, **whitewater rafting** tops many a list. Ohiopyle and Confluence, two towns about 70 miles southeast of Pittsburgh, are leading centers for whitewater rafting and canoeing. Rates vary from about $25 to $50 a person, depending on the day (highest rates on weekends) and the length of the raft trip. The season runs from March through October on some rivers and March through June on others; two-day packages are also available. For reservations and further information, contact any of the following: **Laurel Highlands River Tours,** Box 107, Ohiopyle, PA 15470 (tel. 329-8531); **Mountain Streams and Trails Outfitters,** Box 106, Ohiopyle, PA 15470 (tel. 329-8810); **Ohiopyle Raft Rental,** Box 4, Ohiopyle, PA 15470 (tel. 329-4730); **Riversport, Inc.,** 213 Yough St., Confluence, PA 15424 (tel. 814/395-5744); **White Water Adventures,** Box 31, Ohiopyle, PA 15470 (tel. 329-8850) and **Wilderness Voyageurs Inc.,** Box 97, Ohiopyle, PA 15470 (tel. 329-4752).

The Laurel Highlands are equally popular in the winter with facilities for both downhill and cross-country skiing in several locations. There are 11 slopes and trails with the east coast's only dual/triple chairlift at the **Hidden Valley Resort,** R.D. 4, Somerset, PA 15501 (tel. 814/443-6454 or toll-free 800/458-0174). Two other large and challenging complexes are the **Laurel Mountain Ski Slopes,** R.D. 2, Box 328A, Boswell, PA 15531 (tel. 814/238-6688), and the **Seven Springs Resort** at Champion, PA 15622 (tel. 814/352-7777).

WHERE TO STAY: It is hard to pass through the Laurel Highlands without wanting to stay a while. One of the best places to soak up the ambience of the area is the **Mountain View Inn,** 1001 Village Dr., Greensburg, PA 15601 (tel. 412/834-5300). Located 30 miles east of Pittsburgh on Route 30, this hotel offers sweeping views of Chestnut Ridge and the foothills of the Alleghenies. An early-American atmosphere prevails in the public rooms, with a prototype Colonial parlor re-created near the lobby. The corridors and halls are lined with cherrywood benches, rolltop desks, candle lamps, kerosene lanterns, hutches, and cupboards full of china and porcelain including a display of Royal Copenhagen Christmas plates dating back to 1908. In addition, there are timeworn prints of early Greensburg and the first days at the hotel in 1925. The 34 bedrooms are also furnished with antiques and touches of Americana; you might even find a spinning wheel in your room. Each unit, outfitted with one or two double beds or a king bed, has also been updated with such modern comforts as a private bath/shower, color TV, a direct-dial phone, and air conditioning. Doubles range from $35 to $48; suites are also available from $48 to $70. Guest facilities include the 1776 Tavern for cocktails and light fare, and a Colonial-style restaurant, **The Candlelight Room,** which features regional and traditional cuisine. Lunch prices average $2.95 to $6.95. Entrees at dinner, priced from $9.95 to $19.95, offer an extensive range of seafood as well as prime ribs, steaks, grilled Cornish game hen, baked ham, veal alla marsala, and chicken Wellington. Meals are served from 7 a.m. to 9 p.m., with slightly later hours on weekends. All major CC's accepted.

If you prefer a modern resort, then nearby is the **Sheraton Greensburg,** 100 Sheraton Dr., Route 30, Greensburg, PA 15601 (tel. 412/836-6060 or toll-free 800/325-3535). This modern two-story hotel was built in 1978, in a verdant hillside setting near the Westmoreland Mall, a major shopping complex. The 146 rooms are furnished in a contemporary décor with spring and autumn tones. Each unit has two double or oversized beds, air conditioning, color cable TV, a radio, and a direct-dial phone; and some rooms have refrigerators. The price for a double ranges from $65 to $69. Guest amenities include an indoor pool, a sauna, a cocktail lounge with live entertainment, and a full-service restaurant, The Vista Plateau. Offering panoramic countryside views, this dining room features light lunch, priced from $3.95 to $7.95. The dinner menu offers entrees in the $8.95 to $19.95 bracket, with selections such as shrimp and scallops au bleu; stuffed duckling; veal Dijon; broiled catfish; and Danish lobster tails. Meals are served from 7 a.m. until 10 p.m. All major CC's accepted.

A top choice in the bed-and-breakfast category is the **Ligonier Country Inn,** Route 30, Laughlintown, PA 15655 (tel. 412/238-3651), right at the base of Laurel Mountain. Dating back to 1927, this three-story house has been handsomely restored and furnished in a Colonial motif. The 16 bedrooms are individually decorated in soft pastels, many with brass beds and stenciled walls. Each room has a private bath, wall-to-wall carpeting, air conditioning, a telephone, and a color TV. Rates for a double start at $60 including continental breakfasts. Guest amenities include an activity/sitting room, a fireside lounge, a patio, and an outdoor pool. In addition, there is a full-service restaurant on the premises which features American cuisine. Dinner entrees, priced from $9.95 to $15.95, include pan-fried mountain trout with almonds and a touch of Amaretto; linguine with shrimp, crab, and salmon in a casserole of cream, wine, and cheese; roast raspberry duck; and brochette of beef with garden vegetables. Dinner is served daily from 6 to 9 p.m. (except Christmas Eve and Day). CC's accepted: AE, MC, and V.

2. Erie

A little over 100 miles north of the Pittsburgh area is Erie, Pennsylvania's only port on the Great Lakes and the state's third largest city.

Named for the Eriez Indians who first inhabited this area, Erie was subsequently ruled by the French and the British in the 17th century. Erie's great moment in history came during the War of 1812 when Commodore Oliver Hazard Perry, commanding the *Flagship Niagara,* forced the British squadron to surrender. It was Perry who proclaimed the famous words: "We have met the enemy, and they are ours."

Today's Erie (pop. 118,000) is significant as a major industrial area and inland port, situated midway between New York and Chicago. The downtown area, laid out in a grid with State Street as its central thoroughfare dividing east and west, is currently undergoing a significant revitalization.

The recreational focus of Erie is Presque Isle State Park, situated three miles from midtown. This thin peninsula stretches like an arm out into the lake and then curves back toward the city. It is said that the Indians used the word "Presque," meaning "arm of God," to describe this beautiful natural expanse of beach and parkland. Obviously the Indians knew a good thing when they saw it, because Presque Isle is still the pride of Erie, drawing millions of visitors every year.

VISITOR INFORMATION: Brochures on accommodations, restaurants, attractions, and activities can be obtained from the **Greater Erie Area Chamber of Commerce,** 1006 State Street, Erie, PA 16501 (tel. 814/454-7191).

AREA CODE: All telephone numbers in the Erie area belong to the 814 area code.

GETTING TO ERIE: By Car: Situated directly north of Pittsburgh, Erie is a 2½-hour drive via I-79. The northern leg of this highway terminates in downtown Erie. From an east-west direction, Erie is best approached by I-90, or Routes 20 or 5. Route 5 runs through the city and becomes 12th Street, and Route 20 also crosses through the heart of Erie as 26th Street.

By Plane: Erie International Airport, Route 5 (tel. 833-4258), is located four miles west of downtown. It is served by **USAir** (tel. 452-6951 or toll-free 800/428-4322); **Republic/Northwest** (tel. 453-6649 or toll-free 800/225-2525); and **Jet Stream International** (tel. 838-1322 or toll-free 800/442-8357).

By Train: Daily service into Erie is provided by **Amtrak** via the corridor between Boston/New York and Cleveland/Chicago. For further information and schedules, contact Amtrak, Union Station, 14th and Peach Streets (tel. 452-2177 or toll-free 800/USA-RAIL).

By Bus: Erie is also served by **Greyhound Bus Lines,** which pulls into the bus depot at 28 N. Perry Square (tel. 452-3387).

GETTING AROUND ERIE: Public Transport: The **Erie Metropolitan Transit Authority (EMTA),** 127 E. 14th St. provides local bus services throughout the city (tel. 452-3515); the exact fare (75¢) is required.

Sightseeing Tours: During the month of August, EMTA also operates a series of narrated sightseeing tours each Tuesday and Thursday, departing from Perry Square at 6th and State Streets at 1:10 p.m. These tours last 2½ hours, and visit the main city highlights plus Presque Isle Park. The cost is $3 for adults and $1.50 for students aged 5 to 18; exact fare is required. For further information, contact EMTA (tel. 452-3515).

Another locally based company, **Erie Tours and Convention Services (ETCS)**, 707 Aline Dr. (tel. 866-0900), also conducts escorted individual and group tours. Itineraries include a "heritage trail" within the city or sightseeing in the surrounding countryside. Operating throughout the year, ETCS trips require advance reservation and will depart according to request. A flat rate of $35 per day (or $25 per half-day) is charged for one or two individuals or an entire family.

Car Rental: If you need to rent a car, the following firms maintain stations at the airport: **Avis** (tel. 833-9879); **Hertz** (tel. 838-9691); and **National** (tel. 838-7739). In addition, **Budget** is located at 4656 W. 12th St. at Asbury Road (tel. 838-4502).

Taxis: For local taxi service, call **Area Taxi** (tel. 725-3677), **Erie Cab** (tel. 455-4441), or **Erie Independent Cab** (tel. 899-4566).

Ferry Service: In the summer months, May through September, daily ferry service is operated between the Erie Public Dock, at the foot of State Street, and Presque Isle State Park. The service is scheduled continuously, from 10:30 a.m. to 6:30 p.m., and the fare is $1.50 each way. No reservations required; for more information, call 455-5892.

WHERE TO STAY: Here are our favorite lodgings in the Erie area.

The Top Choice
In the middle of the revitalized downtown area is **The Erie Hilton,** 16 W. 10th St., Erie, PA 16501 (tel. 814/459-2220), between Peach and State Streets. This modern eight-story hotel is ideal if you want to be in the heart of the city, near the major theaters and historic sights. It is also just a ten-block walk from the lakefront. Each of the 191 rooms has been recently refurbished in a contemporary style and contains color cable TV, a radio, a direct-dial telephone, air conditioning, and either a king-size or two double beds. Doubles range from $70 to $90. Facilities include an indoor heated pool, saunas, an exercise room, and free indoor parking. There is also a lounge with evening entertainment called Billy's Saloon, a garden-style café, and a full-service restaurant, The Hunt Room. Lunch, available from $3.95 to $8.95, features sandwiches, salads, and light entrees. Dinner specialties include prime ribs, steaks, veal alla marsala, chicken Cordon Bleu, and seafood. Entrees are priced in the $10.95 to $15.95 bracket and include salad and potato or vegetable. Lunch is served daily from 11:30 a.m. to 2 p.m., and dinner from 5:30 to 10:30 p.m. in the Hunt Room; breakfast and lunch are also available in the café. Special reduced-rate weekend packages are often available. All major CC's accepted.

Mostly Moderate Lodgings
Three miles west of downtown and a block from the entrance to Presque Isle Park is the **Bel Aire Hotel,** 2800 W. 8th St., Erie, PA 16505-4084 (tel. 814/833-1116). This modern two-story resort is set on its own tree-lined grounds off Route 5A. The 143 guest rooms vary in size and style, but each offers a distinctive décor, color cable TV, air conditioning, and a direct-dial phone; a choice of double, queen, or king beds is available. Doubles range from $49 to $89. Guest amenities include a California garden-style indoor swimming pool, an outdoor pool, saunas, a Jacuzzi, an exercise room, and a moderately priced café that serves meals throughout the day. There is also a gourmet restaurant called Victor's, noted for its Cajun entrees, mesquite-grilled meats, and seafoods, priced

in the $13.95 to $19.95 bracket. Victor's is open for dinner from 5:30 to 9 p.m. on weekdays, and until 10 p.m. on weekends. All major CC's accepted.

Nearby is **Scott's Motel**, 2930 W. 6th St. and Peninsula Drive, Erie, PA 16505 (tel. 814/838-1961), located at the entrance to Presque Isle Park and opposite the Wild Waters Water Park. Ideal for families, this tree-lined lodging has 58 units clustered in various one-story wings around a large outdoor swimming pool. Each well-kept room has color TV and air conditioning; doubles are priced from $55 to $65, with lower rates in the off-season. CC's accepted: AE, MC, and V.

The **Downtowner,** 205 W. 10th St., Erie, PA 16501 (tel. 814/456-6251), is a handy and homey motel in the midcity area. Located at the junction of 10th and Sassafras Streets, opposite the city's Cathedral of St. Peter, this two-story property has 75 rooms, each with air conditioning, a direct-dial phone, color TV, and one or two double beds. Facilities include a parking lot, an outdoor pool, a coffeeshop, and a cocktail lounge. Doubles start at $42. CC's accepted: AE, MC, and V.

If you'd like a room with a view of the water, the ideal choice is the **Lakeview on the Lake Motel,** 8696 East Lake Rd., Erie, PA 16511 (tel. 814/899-6948), ten miles east of Erie on Route 5. This lovely property is situated on high ground overlooking Lake Erie on a ten-acre site with dozens of old shady trees, picnic tables, grills, bicycles, a playground, and an outdoor swimming pool. Accommodations include a choice of modern cottages or motel units, each with one or two double beds, color TV, carpeting, and a knotty-pine décor. The units are not air-conditioned, but there is a constant breeze off the lake. Motel rooms are priced from $35 to $42, and the cottages range from $33 for one room to $60 for two large connecting rooms. The rates include continental breakfast. CC's accepted: MC and V.

WHERE TO DINE: Erie's restaurants are located both downtown and by the water along the public dock. In general, they all fall into the moderate price range.

The best of the city's lakefront restaurants is **The Buoy,** 4 State St. (tel. 459-0617), a nautical spot with wide windows and a décor of authentic harpoons, anchors, solid brass buoy lamps, captain's chairs, and spotlit oil paintings of historic sea scenes. The walls are said to be made of wood harvested in 1890 and first used as a dairy barn. Seating is tiered on two levels, allowing most of the 35 tables to enjoy views of Lake Erie including splendid sunsets. Lunch, priced from $1.95 to $5.95, includes salads, light fish entrees, seafood crêpes, omelets, and sandwiches. The menu at dinner is priced in the $8.95 to $21.95 bracket, with most choices under $15. The selection ranges from Lake Erie perch and Great Lakes yellow pike to bouillabaisse, cioppino, rock shrimp, and lobster, as well as steaks, chicken, and lamb. All main courses are accompanied by salad and potato. Hours for lunch are from 11 a.m. to 3 p.m. Monday through Saturday; for dinner from 5 to 10 p.m. Monday through Thursday, until 11 p.m. on Friday and Saturday, and until 9 p.m. on Sunday. CC's accepted: AE, MC, and V.

The ambience of a Roman villa is the keynote of **Michaeleno's,** 17 E. 8th St. (tel. 454-6988), a midtown dining creation of the Victor family. You'll dine on French-Italian cuisine as strolling musicians play your requests; the décor is a rich array of tapestries, statues, brick walls, flickering candelabras, and fresh flowers. Lunch, priced from $2.95 to $11.95, features seafood, pastas, steaks, open-faced sandwiches, and creative croissantwiches. The dinner entrees fall

into the $8.95 to $16.95 range, for gourmet pastas (such as angel's hair with garlic and broccoli or linguine with basil, pine nuts and parmesan); shrimp and scallops in white wine and Swiss Cheddar sauce; veal pizzaiola; filet mignon
prepared tableside; and chicken breast with chopped tomatoes, rosemary, and
mushrooms. All main courses are accompanied by salad and vegetables. Lunch
is served Monday through Friday from 11:30 a.m. to 2 p.m., and dinner Tuesday
through Saturday from 5 to 10 p.m. CC's accepted: AE, MC, and V.

As its name implies, the **Pufferbelly Restaurant,** 414 French St. (tel. 454-
1557), recalls the era a hundred years ago when steam pumpers were used in
firefighting. Housed in a restored 1907 firehouse in the downtown area, this
eatery is decorated with artifacts and memorabilia of the Erie Fire Department
dating back to 1816. As you dine on eclectic American cuisine, you'll be surrounded with vintage fire hats, fire hoses, ladders, and photographs. Lunch, in
the $1.95 to $4.95 price bracket, features salads, chili, quiches, pizzas, omelets,
vegetable griddle cakes, burgers, and sandwiches. The menu at dinner, priced
from $8.95 to $13.95, includes orange roughy with shrimp; teriyaki steak; barbecued ribs; and veal Dijon florentine. All entrees come with salad and appropriate vegetables. Open for lunch and dinner, Monday through Thursday from
11 a.m. to 10 p.m.; Friday and Saturday from 11 a.m. to midnight; Sunday from
11 a.m. to 7 p.m. CC's accepted: AE, MC, and V.

In the same historic downtown neighborhood is one of the city's newest
restaurants, **Rachel's,** 4th and State Streets (tel. 455-7272). This trendy
Victorian-themed bistro is part of Modern Tool Square, an historic building and
former tool factory that has been transformed into a fashionable complex of
shops, offices, and apartments. Lunch items, priced from $2.95 to $7.95, include
seafood salads, croissantwiches, stuffed potato skins, and burritos. Dinner entrees, in the $7.95 to $13.95 price range, feature Cajun-blackened redfish;
steaks; seafood combinations; chicken francese; and veal Oscar. Hours are
daily from 11 a.m. to 11 p.m. CC's accepted: AE, MC, and V.

TOP ATTRACTIONS: The *Flagship Niagara* is docked at the foot of State
Street (tel. 871-4596), on the lakefront. Originally constructed in Erie, this famous brig served as Commodore Oliver Hazard Perry's flagship in the victori-
ous battle of Lake Erie against the British fleet on September 10, 1813. Listed in
the National Register, this vessel is one of only three surviving American war-
ships. It was fully restored in 1913, and has been opened to the public. However,
in preparation for the 175th anniversary of its victory (September 10, 1988), it is
currently being refurbished and may not follow its normal opening times until
then. It would be best to check what hours apply if you are visiting before then.
The usual times are Tuesday through Saturday from 9 a.m. to 5 p.m., and on
Sunday from noon to 5 p.m., during May to September; during other months
from 10 a.m. to 4:30 p.m. Tuesday through Saturday and from noon to 4:30
p.m. on Sunday. Admission is $2 for adults and $1 for youth, aged 6 to 17.

In the heart of downtown is the **Old Customs House,** 411 State St. (tel. 459-
5477), an impressive Greek Revival edifice built in 1839 as a branch of the U.S.
Bank of Pennsylvania. The front steps and columns of the building are made
from Vermont marble, brought from the quarry to the Erie Canal by ox cart,
thence to Buffalo, and via Lake Erie to the city. Listed in the National Register,
this was one of the first major buildings in the country to use native marble.
Today it serves as a home for the permanent and ever-changing collections of
the Erie Art Museum. Open Tuesday through Saturday from 11 a.m. to 5 p.m.
and on Sunday from 1 to 5 p.m. Admission is $1 per person and free on Wednes-
days.

Also in the National Register is the **Cashier's House,** 417 State St. (tel. 454-

1813), a Greek Revival townhouse built in 1839 as a residence for the cashier from the adjacent United States Bank. Notable features include the keyhole door and window frames with scroll decoration and coffer ceilings, along with furnishings that reflect both the American Empire and Victorian periods. Housing an excellent library, this three-story structure is the headquarters of the Erie County Historical Society and the Erie Society for Genealogical Research. Open Tuesday through Saturday from 1 to 4 p.m. Admission is $1 per person.

In the residential area west of downtown is the **Erie Historical Museum,** 356 W. 6th St. (tel. 453-5811), a Victorian mansion built in 1889–1891. The interior is a showcase of elaborate woodwork, paneled walls, marble and tile fireplaces, glass and marble mosaics, wall and ceiling friezes, and restored Tiffany windows. This house also offers a number of exhibits including a multi-media presentation on the Battle of Lake Erie, a regional history, and an extensive bug collection. Open September through May, from 1 to 5 p.m. on Sunday; June through August from 10 a.m. to 5 p.m. Tuesday through Friday, and from 1 to 5 p.m. on Saturday and Sunday. Admission is $1 for adults and children over 16 on all days, except Tuesday when it is free. In addition, the adjacent 19th-century carriage house is a planetarium under a 20-foot dome, with weekend shows scheduled throughout the year. There is an additional admission charge of $1 for adults and 50¢ for children.

Also on the western side of the city, four blocks from State Street, is the **Firefighters Historical Museum,** 428 Chestnut St. (tel. 456-5969). Housed in the Old Station House Number Four, this museum contains over 1,000 articles, including a large collection of antique fire extinguishers, early nozzles, helmets, and badges, as well as an 1830 hand-pumper, an 1886 hand-pulled hose cart, and a 1927 American La-France. Open from May through August, on Saturday from 10 a.m. to 5 p.m. and on Sunday from 1 to 5 p.m.; and during September and October, on Saturday and Sunday from 1 to 5 p.m. Admission is $1.50 for adults and 50¢ for children aged 10 to 18.

NIGHTLIFE: Concerts and national touring shows are featured at **The Warner Theatre,** 811 State St. (tel. 452-4857), a 2,500-seat art-deco landmark dating back to 1931. Originally commissioned by the Warner Brothers as a movie theater, this building has recently been restored as part of the Erie Civic Center complex. Now the home of the Erie Philharmonic, it is considered the city's chief performing arts center. Tickets are usually priced from $10 to $20, depending on the event. Check with the box office or the Chamber of Commerce for an up-to-date schedule. If you visit during the summer months, there is an annual film classic series, at 7:30 p.m. on Tuesday, Wednesday, and Thursday evenings, and a Wednesday matinee at 1:30 p.m. All seats are $2.50. Tickets are also available at the Civic Center Box Office, 809 French St. (tel. 825-4444). CC's accepted: MC and V.

One of the oldest community theaters in the U.S. is the **Erie Playhouse,** 13 W. 10th St. (tel. 454-2851), founded over 70 years ago. This local troup performs in a 550-seat building that was the old Strand movie theater and subsequently renovated by local volunteer efforts in 1983. The ever-changing year-round repertoire ranges from *Flower Drum Song,* and *Can Can,* to *The Odd Couple* and other Broadway favorites. Shows are scheduled for Thursday, Friday, and Saturday nights at 8 p.m., with some Sunday matinees at 3 p.m. The Playhouse Box Office is open weekdays from 10 a.m. to 4:30 p.m. and on Saturday from 10 a.m. to 2 p.m. or prior to shows. Ticket prices average $10. CC's accepted: MC and V.

SPORTS: A host of outdoor sporting activities is available year-round at the

3,200-acre **Presque State Park,** off Route 832 and Route 5 (tel. 871-4251). Situated on the shores of Lake Erie, this facility includes 11 sandy beaches, waterways, hiking trails, bike paths, picnicking areas, and a nature center. In addition, there are lagoons, a bird-watching sanctuary, and an ecological preserve for ferns and marshes. Admission is free, and the park is open from dawn to sunset all year.

Boat Rental: Presque Isle boating activities are also available at the following rates: motorboats, two hours for $15 or $45 a day; rowboats, $6 an hour or $31 a day; canoes, $4 an hour or $17 a day; and paddleboats, $7 an hour or $38 a day. The rental station is located at the East Boat Livery, between Thompson Drive and Fisher Road on the bay side of the park. Open daily April through October, 6 a.m. to 8 p.m. In addition, pontoon boats leave the East Boat Livery every day at 1, 2, and 3 p.m. The pontoon rides are free, on a first-come basis.

Bike Rental: Presque Isle is ideal for cycling. If you haven't brought your own, you can rent from **Sara's Bike Rental,** Presque Isle State Park entrance, off Route 832 (tel. 833-3442). Rates start at $2.50 an hour and $12 a day; tandems from $3.50 an hour or $15 a day. Open daily 8 a.m. to dusk, from April through October.

Boat Cruises: Narrated sightseeing cruises around the Lake Erie harbor are operated daily, from May through September, by **Rugare's Boats,** Public Dock (tel. 455-5892). Departures begin at 10:30 a.m. and continue until 9 p.m. The fare is $4 for adults and $2 for children. **Dinner cruises** are also available, in conjunction with the Buoy Restaurant, for $14.95 per person. Reservations are required for dinner cruises. CC's accepted: MC and V.

Fishing: From May through October, fishing boats leave the Public Dock, according to demand and advance reservations. Species caught include Coho salmon, bass, perch and walleyed pike. Half-day charters cost $275 for six people. For full information, contact **Rugare's Fishing Boats,** Public Dock (tel. 455-5892). CC's accepted: MC and V.

Horse Racing: Thoroughbred racing is scheduled from late May through September at **Erie Downs,** 7501 Anonia Rd., Fairview (tel. 474-5584), about eight miles west of downtown Erie (exit 4 off I-90). Post times are 7:15 p.m. on Monday, Thursday, Friday, and Saturday; 4 p.m. on Sunday and holidays. General admission is $1 and clubhouse entrance is $2.

WINERY TOURS: According to latest statistics, Erie is the third-largest grape-growing area in the U.S. Four wineries are situated about ten miles northeast of downtown Erie at a town appropriately named North East. Located within a few miles of each other and all open daily, these four wineries make a pleasant afternoon's tour. Here are the particulars: (1) Heritage Wine Cellars, 12162 E. Main Rd. (tel. 725-8015) offers free tours and tastings, and is located on Route 20; (2) also on Route 20 is Presque Isle Wine Cellars, 9440 Buffalo Rd. (tel. 725-1314), which gives tastings but no formal tours; (3) Mazza Vineyards and Winery, 11815 East Lake Rd. (tel. 725-8695), offers wine tastings and conducted tours for $1 charge, and is located on Route 5; and (4) Penn Shore Vineyards, 10225 East Lake Rd., also on Route 5, which has free self-guided tours and tastings (tel. 725-8688).

EVENTS: Scheduled for the third week of June each year, the **Erie Summer**

Festival of the Arts is a week-long music fest that features big bands, local rock groups, the Erie Philharmonic, the Erie Chamber Orchestra, and the Pennsylvania Dance Theatre. Admission is free and it is held on the campus of Villa Maria College. For further information, contact the Summer Festival of the Arts Committee, Room 106, Villa Maria College, 2551 W. Lake Rd., (tel. 833-5690).

"We Love Erie Days" Festival is an annual event held on the lakefront in mid-August. The program includes a 10-kilometer race, stage performances, sailboat races, waterskiing shows, parachute shows, food fests, and fireworks. Admission is free to most events. For full details, contact the Chamber of Commerce (tel. 454-7191).

CHILDREN'S CORNER: Erie Zoo, 423 W. 38th St. (tel. 864-4901) is a 15-acre park with over 300 animals, but the highlight is Pixieland, a section where children can see and feed baby animals. Open year round from 10 a.m. to 5 p.m., and until 7 p.m. on Sunday and holidays during the summer. Admission is $2.50 for adults and $1.50 for children aged 3 to 11; children under 2 enter free. In addition, there is a 75¢ charge for a train ride to "Safariland" where wild deer and bison wander.

Waldameer Park, Route 832, (tel. 838-3591), located near the entrance of Presque Isle, offers 24 amusement rides and picnic facilities. Individual ride tickets are 35¢ or you can purchase all-day ride-a-rama tickets for $6.50 per person. Open mid-May through Labor Day except Monday and holidays.

Splashing and smiles are the keynotes at **Wild Waters Water Park,** 611 Peninsula Dr. (tel. 838-4818), which contains a "wild wave" pool with seven different shapes of continuous waves. There is also a five-story water slide, a sun deck, a game arcade, a picnic pavilion, and a pollywog pond for small youngsters. Admission for adults is $6.95 on weekdays and $7.95 on weekends; for children aged 4 to 8, it is $4.95 and $5.95 respectively, and free for children under 4. Go-kart rides are $2.50 extra. Open daily Memorial Day to Labor Day from 11 a.m. to 11 p.m. CC's accepted: MC and V.

Chapter XIII

INTRODUCTION TO NEW JERSEY

1. Welcome to the Garden State
2. Getting to New Jersey
3. Getting Around New Jersey
4. Useful Facts

WITH 127 MILES OF ATLANTIC COASTLINE, New Jersey is a natural vacation destination. Places like Atlantic City, Cape May, the Wildwoods, Ocean City, and Long Beach Island draw millions of people year after year.

But New Jersey is more than sun, surf, and sand. It is the home of the "Miss America" Pageant, the trend-setting Meadowlands Sports Complex, and Liberty State Park, a riverside grassland that offers the best views of the famous statue. A visit to New Jersey also means historic towns like Wheaton, Bridgeton, Smithville, Princeton, and Morristown, site of our nation's first historic national park; and Newark, the fastest growing airport in the U.S.A. Some of our nation's leading educational institutions—Princeton, Drew, Fairleigh Dickinson, Rutgers, and Seton Hall, are headquartered in New Jersey.

With over 800 lakes and ponds, 11 state forests, and 40 state parks, 15 wineries, and 8,000 farms, New Jersey also embodies natural countryside at its best. New Jersey is among the top five producers in the nation of blueberries, cranberries, tomatoes, asparagus, and summer potatoes. No wonder New Jersey is called the "garden state."

1. Welcome to the Garden State

Settled by the Dutch in the early 1600s and later by the English, New Jersey played a leading role in our nation's early history. More than 100 battles of the Revolutionary War were fought on the rich soil of the "garden state." The third of the original 13 colonies to ratify the U.S. Constitution, New Jersey was the seat of our national government for a brief period in 1783 when the Continental Congress met in Princeton.

Of all the Mid-Atlantic states, New Jersey is the most densely populated, with 7,515,000 people living in an area 166 miles long and 32 miles wide. New Jersey is a leader in industry, with more than 13,000 manufacturing establishments located within its borders.

The state's major roadway, the New Jersey Turnpike, is a non-stop flow of trucking traffic, lined with industrial sights ranging from smoke stacks and oil tanks to gray-colored factories and multiwire power lines. Stretching 133 miles

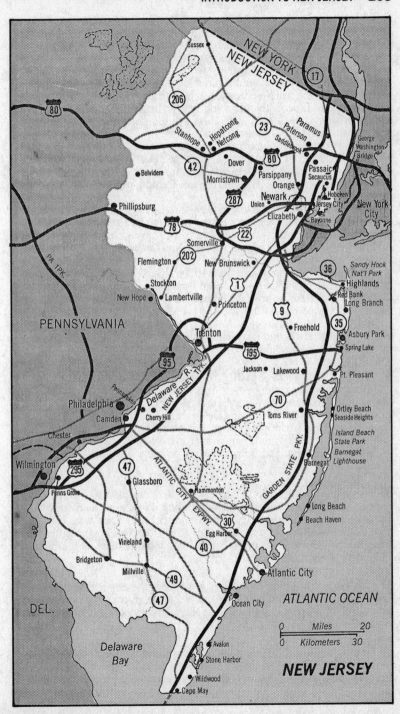

NEW JERSEY

from the George Washington Bridge to the Delaware Memorial Bridge, it is not a pretty or scenic sight, and, to make matters worse, you have to pay (from 70¢ to $2.10) for the privilege of stop-and-go driving on this charmless corridor. Unfortunately, for many people on the move the New Jersey Turnpike is all they ever see of New Jersey. What a pity!

Obviously, the "garden state" has a lot more to offer than this multilane roadway. To see the real New Jersey, you have to get off and explore the towns and cities, follow the country routes and byways. In the north-south direction, a good alternate is the Garden State Parkway, a roadway lined with tall trees, grassy knolls, and fertile farmlands.

In addition to its verdant vistas, New Jersey is almost entirely surrounded by water. Bordered by the Atlantic Ocean, the Hudson and Passaic Rivers on the east, it is rimmed by the Delaware River for its entire western expanse and most of its southern shore. The state capital, Trenton, overlooks the meandering waters of the Delaware.

Most of all, New Jersey is known for its beach towns, more than 50 communities of all sizes and shapes, from barrier islands to bird sanctuaries, from dry towns to dazzling boardwalk amusement strips. The most famous, of course, is Atlantic City, a showplace of glitz, glamour, and gambling, and the destination that is not only number one in the state but for the entire nation.

In contrast, less than 50 miles away, there is Cape May, a fanciful Victorian town that thrives on its turn-of-the-century ambience and, in another direction, the pristine Pine Barrens, an uninhabited marshy woodland that is natural habitat for birds, animals, and wildflowers.

So, like the high rollers of Atlantic City, take a gamble on New Jersey. With so many diverse sights and experiences, chances are you'll have a winner of a vacation.

2. Getting to New Jersey

Bounded on the north by New York State, New Jersey is surrounded by water on all of its other sides—on the east, by the Atlantic Ocean, Hudson, and Passaic Rivers; on the west, by the Delaware River; and on the south, by the Delaware and the Atlantic. However, the state is easily accessible from New York City on the east or from Pennsylvania on the west by a variety of interstate bridges and highways, and from Delaware on the south via the Cape May-Lewes Ferry.

BY CAR: New Jersey is traversed in a north-south direction by I-95, the main east-coast highway between Maine and Florida. From a northerly direction, I-87 also crosses into New Jersey from New York State. Travelers heading for New Jersey from the west can take I-80 or I-78. Most New Yorkers enter New Jersey via the George Washington Bridge, the Lincoln Tunnel, or the Holland Tunnel, all of which connect with I-95.

BY PLANE: You can fly to New Jersey, via most of the country's domestic airlines, into **Newark International Airport,** a major east-coast gateway and the fastest-growing airport in the U.S. A profile of the services at this airport follows in Chapter XIV.

BY TRAIN: Newark and Trenton are main destinations on **Amtrak's** northeast corridor route between Washington, D.C., and New York/Boston. Amtrak offers convenient daily services to both of these cities, linking them to all parts of the U.S.

BY BUS: Two major national bus companies, **Greyhound** and **Trailways,** operate daily services into both Newark and Trenton, and into Atlantic City, as well as smaller towns and cities along the Jersey shore.

BY FERRY: The **Cape May–Lewes Ferry** travels daily between the lower Delaware coast and southern New Jersey. This 70-minute crossing is operated on a drive-on, drive-off basis and can accommodate up to 800 passengers and 100 cars. Full details are given under Cape May (Chapter XVII).

3. Getting Around New Jersey

BY CAR: In addition to the primary interstate highways, New Jersey is well served by hundreds of local roads. The Garden State Parkway is New Jersey's "road to the shore," winding its way from the New York Thruway to the southern tip of the state at Cape May. Running inland parallel to the beaches, the Parkway is the best way to reach Sandy Hook, Asbury Park, Atlantic City, Ocean City, the Wildwoods, and Cape May. A 25¢ toll is required an average of every 20 miles along the route.

Travelers coming from Philadelphia and points west should use the Atlantic City Expressway, which cuts across the state in an east-west direction between Atlantic City and the Delaware River area. One of the most scenic roads is Route 29 which hugs the Delaware River shoreline from Trenton northward to Frenchtown. Interstate-195 connects Trenton to the Jersey shore in an east-west direction.

Note: On all major roads in New Jersey, a left-hand turn is made from the right-hand lane. The turnoff laneways are well signposted.

BY TRAIN: **Amtrak** services along the northeast corridor can be used as local links between Newark and Trenton/Princeton. In addition, **New Jersey Transit** operates an extensive rail system within the state. Full details are given in Chapter XIV.

BY BUS: **New Jersey Transit** maintains a diverse network of bus transport covering all of the state's large and small cities and towns. In particular, regular service is provided from the northern and central part of the state to the shore communities. Details follow in Chapters XIV through XVII.

4. Useful Facts

VISITOR INFORMATION: For general brochures and other data to help you plan a trip, contact the **New Jersey Division of Travel and Tourism,** 1 West State St., No. 600, Trenton, NJ 08625-0826 (tel. 609/292-2470). In the chapters that follow, we'll also list the individual tourist offices for the various New Jersey cities or regions we are describing.

CLIMATE: Like the rest of the Mid-Atlantic states, New Jersey has relatively warm summers and cold winters, with moderate temperatures in the fall and spring. In the June through August period, it is common for temperatures to reach the 90° level during the day in all parts of the state. Thanks to the offshore sea breezes, it can get quite cool in the evenings, particularly along the coast. The average temperature at Atlantic City in the summer is 73°, while it hovers around 74° in the Newark or Trenton areas.

In the cold winter months, New Jersey gets its share of snowstorms, particularly in the higher elevations of the northwestern part of the state, close to the

Pocono Mountains of Pennsylvania. The average temperature in Newark or Trenton in the winter is 33° while it is 35° in Atlantic City.

NEW JERSEY OUTDOORS: With hundreds of miles of river shores and ocean coastline, dozens of state forests and parks, and many lakes and creeks, New Jersey is prime turf for outdoor camping vacations. There are more than 130 modern and well-equipped campgrounds throughout the state. To assist vacationers in planning camping vacations, New Jersey has published a handy booklet, "Your N.J. Campsite Guide." Be sure to ask for it when you contact the **N.J. State Tourist Office,** 1 West State St., No. 600, Trenton, NJ 08625-0826 (tel. 609/292-2470).

AREA CODES: New Jersey has two area codes within its borders: (201) covers Newark and all of the northern part of the state, down to the middle of the Jersey shore; and (609) is used throughout the southern half of the state including Trenton, Princeton, Atlantic City, and Cape May. To avoid confusion, we remind you of the applicable area code at the beginning of each chapter or section.

SALES TAX: All hotel room charges, meals, and purchases within the state of New Jersey are subject to a 6% sales tax; some other local or county taxes often apply. It is best to check in the course of your travels to see what tax will be added to your bill.

Chapter XIV

NEW JERSEY'S MAIN CITIES

1. Introduction
2. Traveling to the Cities
3. Getting Around
4. The Newark Gateway
5. Trenton and Princeton

THE MOST DENSELY POPULATED of the Mid-Atlantic states, New Jersey is known for its dozens of cities and towns with memorable names, like Hoboken and Hackensack, Paramus and Parsippany, Secaucus and Saddle Brook.

Many of the state's major cities, such as Jersey City, Elizabeth, Paterson, Bayonne, and Union, are concentrated in the state's northern half, near the Hudson or Passaic Rivers. These are the hubs of commerce and industry, and are not generally considered as vacation destinations.

The two cities that are best known are Newark, the largest metropolitan area, and Trenton, the capital of the state.

1. Introduction

Centrally located in the heart of New Jersey's most populated corridor, Newark is the focal point of an area that has long been known as a "gateway." Hugging the shores of the Hudson River, this was the arrival point for generations of immigrants who came to begin their lives anew in America. With the Statue of Liberty dominating the harbor, the Jersey shores, like the New York skyline, conveyed the first images of the new world. It is also interesting to note that the great statue and Ellis Island are both technically located in New Jersey waters.

Today Newark retains its role of gateway, thanks to its airport, which serves 30 million travelers a year. Newark Airport is one of the fastest growing airline facilities in the country.

The city of Newark is also a hub of urban transit, for buses and trains, and for road traffic, including the New Jersey Turnpike and the Garden State Parkway.

For vacationers, Newark is the natural gateway to all of New Jersey's many attractions, from the skyscrapers to the shores.

In contrast, Trenton is tucked away on the Delaware River in the western center of the state, closer to Philadelphia than to Newark. With its impressive capitol buildings, Trenton is the governmental hub of the state. It is also a center of commerce, and, like Newark, a gateway to many attractions in the surrounding region including the ivy-league town of Princeton.

2. Traveling to the Cities

BY PLANE: **Newark International Airport,** exit 13A or exit 14, New Jersey Turnpike, Newark (tel. 201/961-2000), is the fastest-growing airport in the U.S., and is currently adding a new $300 million terminal. Situated on a 2,300-acre tract less than five miles from Newark's central business district, it serves over two dozen major and commuter airlines. Some of the leading carriers that fly into Newark include: **American** (tel. 201/433-7300); **Continental** (tel. 201/596-6000); **Delta** (tel. 201/622-2111); **Eastern** (tel. 201/622-2121); **Northwest** (tel. 201/643-8555); **Pan American** (tel. 201/624-1300); **Piedmont** (tel. 201/624-8311); **Trans World Airlines** (tel. 201/643-3339); **United** (tel. 201/624-1500); and **USAir** (tel. 201/622-3201).

Taxi stands, located on the lower (arrivals) level of all the terminals, are attended during peak hours by a taxi dispatcher who assists arriving passengers to get the best taxi for a particular destination. For bus travel to downtown Newark, look for the **"Airlink"** minicoaches (tel. 201/762-5100). This company runs a continuous schedule 20 hours a day, at a cost of $3 one-way.

If you are flying into Newark but staying in New York City, **New Jersey Transit** operates express buses to/from Port Authority Bus Terminal in Manhattan (tel. toll-free 800/772-2222); the fare is $5 one-way. **Olympic Trails Buses** also offers express service to/from New York City's downtown (World Trade Center) or midtown (41st Street and Park Avenue); this fare is also $5 each way.

In addition, the following car-rental firms maintain counters at Newark Airport: **Avis** (tel. 201/961-4300); **Budget** (tel. 201/961-2990); **Dollar** (tel. 201/824-2002); **Hertz** (tel. 201/621-2000); and **National** (tel. 201/622-1270).

BY TRAIN: Both Newark and Trenton are part of **Amtrak's** east coast corridor of daily service. **Newark's Penn Station,** Raymond Plaza West (tel. 201/643-1770), has recently undergone a $20 million restoration and is now connected by enclosed overhead walkways to the Gateway Center. The **Amtrak Station** in Trenton is located at South Clinton and Fairview Avenues (tel. 609/394-2604).

Many trains on this corridor also stop at **Princeton Junction,** Wallace Road, three miles outside of Princeton, with shuttle service on some trains to **Princeton Borough Station,** University Place, in the heart of Princeton (tel. 609/921-8527). For full information on all Amtrak services to New Jersey, call toll-free 800/USA-RAIL.

In addition, **New Jersey Transit** (tel. 201/762-5100) operates regular commuter rail services between Trenton/Princeton and northern New Jersey or New York City.

BY BUS: Bus service into Newark from major cities across the U.S. is provided by **Greyhound** into Penn Station at Market Street (tel. 201/642-8205); and by **Trailways** into West Penn Station, at Raymond Plaza (tel. 201/642-0505).

Bus service to/from all parts of New Jersey into Newark or Trenton is operated by **New Jersey Transit** (tel. 201/762-5100).

BY CAR: Newark and Trenton are both accessible via I-95, the major north-south artery of the east coast. From the west, New Jersey can be approached via

I-78 or I-80. From New York City, take the George Washington Bridge (which leads to I-95 and I-80), the Lincoln Tunnel (which leads to I-95), or the Holland Tunnel, which also feeds into I-95. From upper New York state, New Jersey can also be reached via I-87.

3. Getting Around

BY CAR: The best way to get around the Newark or Trenton areas is by car and the aid of a good map. With all of the roads that converge on Newark, it can be quite confusing to find your way at times. In general, the New Jersey Turnpike is the fastest link to most major points and attractions including the Meadowlands, but, you'll find that the secondary routes are far more scenic.

The east-west I-280 and I-80 are good roads to bring you west of Newark to such areas as Montclair or Morristown. Route 24 will take you to Millburn, Madison, and Morristown, and a collection of other communities along the way. The New Jersey Turnpike is the most direct connection between Newark and Trenton.

BY BUS AND RAIL: New Jersey Transit (tel. 201/762-5100) provides regular service from Newark or Trenton/Princeton to all major points throughout the state. If you plan to do a lot of travel by public transport, send for a copy of the **N.J. Transit Guide,** from New Jersey Transit, Dept. C 005, P.O. Box 6047, Elizabeth, NJ 07206.

4. The Newark Gateway

Newark is not only New Jersey's largest metropolis (pop.: 329,000), but it is also one of the oldest cities in the U.S.

Founded as a Puritan settlement in 1666 and chartered as a city in 1836, Newark started as a simple agrarian community, but very quickly grew into a major commercial center, especially for the leather industry (patent leather was invented in Newark in 1819). Thanks to its position 12 miles west of New York City and at the port of entry for so many immigrants, Newark continued to thrive in the industrial age.

The 20th century, however, has not been so kind to Newark. The 1950s and 1960s, which brought the inevitable development of the suburbs, drew many people to move to the surrounding communities outside of Newark. Many of its fine old buildings were neglected or disappeared.

Happily, the 1980s have brought a turnaround. Multistory riverfront developments, such as the Gateway Center, are adding new life and new hope to the city. Proud old landmarks, such as Penn Station, have been restored and rejuvenated. The growth of Newark Airport and the addition of the **Meadowlands Sports Complex** to the area have likewise injected a spirit of renaissance into this city.

To appreciate Newark at its best, it has to be understood not just as a city destination, but as the gateway it has always been. From Newark, you can easily tour many of the attractions of northern and central New Jersey. Some of the most notable sights include nearby Morristown, site of the first national historic park in the United States, and Liberty State Park, which boasts the best views of the magnificently restored Statue of Liberty, as well as the Thomas Alva Edison laboratory at West Orange, and the award-winning Paper Mill Playhouse, New Jersey's official state theater, at Millburn.

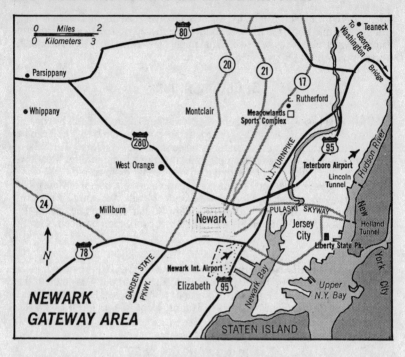

NEWARK GATEWAY AREA

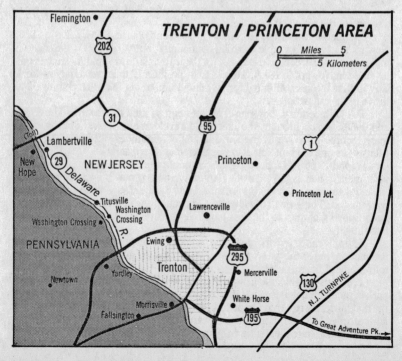

TRENTON / PRINCETON AREA

This part of northern New Jersey is also home to some of America's finest educational institutions, including Drew University, Fairleigh Dickinson University, Rutgers University, St. Peter's College, and Seton Hall University.

VISITOR INFORMATION: For travel brochures on Newark and its environs, contact **The Gateway Regional Tourism Council,** c/o Montclair State College, Legge House No. 860, Upper Montclair, NJ 07043 (tel. 201/893-4429).

AREA CODE: The area code for all telephone numbers listed in this section is 201.

WHERE TO STAY: The hotels in the area in and around Newark are generally geared to the corporate traveler, which means that the facilities are top notch and quite expensive. In addition, the main restaurants of these hotels are attractions in themselves and draw a large local following. Most rooms average $100 a night or more throughout the year. Happily for the vacation traveler, however, this also means that weekends are relatively quiet, enabling most of these hotels to offer very attractive weekend rates or packages. If you come here on a Friday, Saturday, or Sunday, you can usually save at least 50% off normal tariffs, so steer away from midweek visits and be sure to ask what is the best weekend rate available.

Newark City and Airport Hotels

The major downtown hotel is the **Hilton Gateway,** McCarter Highway and Raymond Boulevard, Newark, NJ 07102 (tel. 201/622-5000 or toll-free 800/HIL-TONS), a modern ten-story hotel, located across the street from Penn Station and within the Gateway Center, the upscale commercial complex that has brought a renaissance to the city's riverfront area. Enclosed and elevated passageways conveniently link the hotel to the station and the other buildings and shops of the Gateway Center. Thanks to a $15 million renovation in 1986–1987, this hotel now offers 254 refurbished guest rooms, each equipped with color cable TV, an AM/FM radio, free HBO movies, air conditioning, and a direct-dial telephone. Doubles start at $109. In addition, guests enjoy a rooftop swimming pool, free parking, and shuttle service to Newark Airport. There is also a lounge with evening entertainment, a coffeeshop, and a restaurant, The Trader, which features international cuisine. Lunch items, priced from $3.95 to $10.95, include hefty sandwiches, salads, burgers, pastas, and light entrees. The menu at dinner, priced from $11.95 to $15.95 for most main courses, ranges from blackened swordfish and steak Diane, to prime ribs, chicken Dijon, and crab-stuffed shrimp wrapped in bacon. Open Monday through Friday only, the hours are 11:30 a.m. to 3:30 p.m. for lunch, and 5 to 9:45 p.m. for dinner. All major CC's are accepted.

One of the top airport hotels in the U.S. is the **Sheraton Newark Airport,** 901 Spring St., Elizabeth, NJ 07201 (tel. 201/527-1600 or toll-free 800/325-3535), just a mile south of the terminal, at exit 13A of the New Jersey Turnpike. Completely refurbished in 1986, this modern 11-story property has 260 contemporary-style rooms, furnished with light woods and pastel tones, and equipped with the usual amenities of air conditioning, a direct-dial phone, and color cable TV. Doubles range from $70 to $125. Facilities include free parking, an indoor/outdoor heated swimming pool, tropically landscaped gardens and patio, and courtesy car service to the airport. But the biggest draw to this hotel is its unique art-nouveau restaurant, Daphne's. Stained-glass windows, brick alcoves, and fashion-magazine posters serve as the perfect backdrop for the waitresses who are the real stars here. With individually styled dresses, hats, gloves, and accessories, these waitresses look more like high-fashion models than serving staff. The food can be equally glamorous and surprising. Lunch items, priced from $3.95 to $9.95, focus mainly on exotic salads, sandwiches, pastas, pizza, omelets, and light entrees. The dinner entrees, priced from $8.95 to $17.95, include lemon chicken, baby back ribs, prime ribs, lobster tails, veal francese, veal Oscar, and steaks. All main courses come with salad and vegetables. Hours for the restaurant are 7 a.m. to 11 p.m. daily, and all major CC's are accepted.

Hotels in the Newark Environs

Just 20 minutes north of the airport is **Loews Glenpointe Hotel,** 100 Frank W. Burr Boulevard, Teaneck, NJ 07666 (tel. 201/836-0600 or toll-free 800/223-0888), conveniently located at the intersection of I-80 and I-95, local lanes exit 70/70B. Ever since this $40 million hotel opened in 1983, it has been drawing people to the northern New Jersey suburbs. New Yorkers often cross the George Washington Bridge just to dine at the hotel's award-winning Italian restaurant, and other travelers choose to base themselves here because of the ready access to major highways and the proximity (10 minutes) to the Meadowlands. This modern 14-story tower has 350 colorful art-deco-style guest rooms that offer expansive views of the New York skyline or the New Jersey meadows. Each unit is equipped with color cable TV, air conditioning, a direct-dial telephone, a marble bathroom, and amenities that range from terry robes to toiletries. Doubles start at $139. Guest facilities include a spa with health club, an oversized heated indoor swimming pool, a sundeck, a sauna, and a health food bar; there is also free enclosed or open parking, an adjacent complex of shops and cafés, a grillroom serving moderately priced meals all day, and a classy atrium lounge with nightly entertainment. In addition, a focal point here is Bronzini's, a palazzo-style restaurant, named for Il Bronzini, a 16th-century Florentine painter. Reproductions of the artist's work hang on the opulent fabric-lined walls and adorn the menu covers. Open for dinner only, the menu changes often but usually features such dishes as sole oreganata; breast of duck with lime sauce; puff pastry tarts of lobster, salmon, and scallops; filet of young rabbit with apples; or shrimp and pasta with wild mushrooms in champagne sauce. Entrees run from $20 to $27, and everything else is extra, so figure at least $100 for two, but it's worth the big splurge. Hours are Monday through Saturday from 6 to 11 p.m. All major CC's are accepted.

A relatively new hotel (1986), the **Sheraton Meadowlands,** Sheraton Plaza Drive, Two Meadowlands Plaza, East Rutherford, NJ 07073 (tel. 201/896-0500 or toll-free 800/325-3535), is situated directly across from the giant sports complex, at the intersection of Route 3 and exit 16W of the New Jersey Turnpike, 12 miles north of the airport. It is a 20-story tower, with 428 modern rooms, outfitted with the standard amenities of air conditioning, a direct-dial phone, and color cable TV; many units also offer views of the New York skyline. Doubles range from $120 to $148. Guest facilities include an indoor pool and health club, a sauna, a whirlpool, an outdoor patio, a sundeck, free parking, shuttle service to Newark Airport, a lounge with evening entertainment, and a garden-style café serving moderately priced meals all day. In addition, there is a gourmet restaurant, Roses, which has a horsey décor including oil paintings of the recent winners in the Hambletonian Classics run at the Meadowlands. Dinner entrees, priced from $13.50 to $19.95, feature loin of veal, breast of pheasant, twin quails, escalopes of salmon, lobster and shrimp sauté, and steaks. Hours are 6 to 11 p.m. daily. All major CC's are accepted.

A country-estate setting is the main attraction of **The Marlboro Inn,** 334 Grove Street at Watchung Avenue, Montclair, NJ 07042 (tel. 201/783-5300), about 15 miles northwest of Newark at exit 151 of the Garden State Parkway.

Built in the 1850s as a private home, this property was converted into an inn in 1903 and was recently updated and refurbished, although many of the house's original furnishings remain. Surrounded by 3½ acres of residential property, it is a four-story Tudor-style building, with a central turn-of-the-century living room and a large stone fireplace where you'll often see guests roasting chestnuts. Each of the 44 rooms offers standard modern amenities such as a private bath and air conditioning. Doubles range from $90 to $95 with continental breakfast included. The old-world dining room serves lunch items such as sandwiches, quiches, pastas, crêpes, and light entrees, in the $3.25 to $10 price range. Dinner entrees cost from $10 to $19, and include steaks, duck à l'orange, veal piccata, filet of sole, bay scallops, and salmon steak. No liquor is served, but you are welcome to bring your own wine for dinner. Hours for lunch are Monday through Friday from noon to 2:30 p.m.; dinner Monday through Friday from 6 to 9 p.m., Saturday until 9:30 p.m.; and brunch on Sunday from 11 a.m. to 3 p.m. All major CC's are accepted.

One of the best places to stay in the countryside is **The Madison,** One Convent Rd., Morristown, NJ 07960 (tel. 201/285-1800 or toll-free 800/526-0729), about 20 miles west of Newark on Route 24, and opposite the grounds of the College of St. Elizabeth. Designed by famed architect Walter C. Pfeiffer, this is a classic Georgian Revival–style hotel, with a dramatic entrance colonnade and a classic clock tower atop its four-story façade. There are 192 rooms, with a turn-of-the-century décor, reproduction furnishings, and a choice of double or king beds. Each unit has color cable TV, air conditioning, a direct-dial telephone, and a sitting area. Doubles start at $123 and include complimentary continental breakfast. Guests can also enjoy the use of an indoor/outdoor swimming pool, a Jacuzzi, and a health center with an exercise room and sauna. The Madison is also home to a landmark eatery, **Rod's 1890s Restaurant,** famed for its classic Victorian gilded décor and dining rooms which include two restored private railroad cars, once the property of busines moguls John Wanamaker and Jay Gould. Lunch, priced from $5.95 to $10.95, focuses mainly on sandwiches, burgers, seafood, crêpes, omelets, pastas, and salads. The dinner menu is more elaborate, with entrees in the $9.95 to $24.95 bracket, but mostly around the $15 mark. Featured dishes include breast of capon, veal steak, prime ribs, baby back ribs, frogs' legs, native bluefish, sole amandine, beer-batter shrimp, rack of lamb, and steaks. All main courses come with salad bar, and potato or vegetable. Open daily for lunch from 11:30 a.m. to 4:30 p.m., and for dinner from 4:30 to 11 p.m. All major CC's are accepted.

The **Headquarters Plaza,** Three Headquarters Plaza, Speedwell Avenue, Morristown, NJ 07960 (tel. 201/898-9100 or toll-free 800/225-1942), is 23 miles west of Newark in the heart of the historic town that George Washington chose as his base for two winters. This modern hotel is the centerpiece in a trendy new downtown complex of shops and offices. Although you might expect a Federal or Victorian motif to match many of the other buildings in this area, you'll find an art-deco theme here, with imported marble floors, silver-gray and peach furnishings, and floor-to-ceiling mirrors. The 260 rooms are similarly outfitted with an art-deco flair and all the modern conveniences. Doubles start at $125. Guest facilities include a fitness center, a disco lounge, underground parking, a moderately priced café that is open all day, and a French restaurant, the Black Orchid. Entrees average from $16 to $24, with such dishes as Norwegian salmon with caviar, grilled swordfish, braised lobster, sliced breast of duck, and veal tenderloin with artichoke in puff pastry. Dinner is served from 5:30 to 11 p.m. Monday through Saturday. All major CC's are accepted.

Castle turrets and towers will greet you when you arrive at the **Sheraton Tara Hotel,** 199 Smith Road, Troy Hills, Parsippany, NJ 07054 (tel. 201/515-

2000 or toll-free 800/325-3535), a newly opened (1987) lodging extravaganza about 20 miles northwest of Newark, off Route 287 and I-80, at Route 46. Nestled on its own wooded grounds with a private pond, this $53 million hotel is named after the Hill of Tara, the seat of Ireland's ancient high kings, and hence the regal façade and interior. Arched windows, carved wood trim, a large open fireplace, and costumed staff add to the old-world castle-like ambience. There are 389 rooms, with reproduction furnishings and every modern amenity. Doubles range from $130 to $150. There are no jousting fields, but modern-day kingly and queenly guests can avail of indoor and outdoor pools, an exercise room, racquetball courts, tennis courts, saunas, steam rooms, and a whirlpool. Other facilities include a moderately priced all-day café, an Irish pub, a lounge with evening entertainment, and an upscale restaurant appropriately dubbed The Upper Crust. The dinner menu, with entrees priced from $13.95 to $23, ranges from such royal treats as rack of lamb or Chateaubriand to quail with baby corn and leeks, veal with white zinfandel sauce, prime ribs, rosettes of salmon and sole, and cioppino with lobster, clams, mussels, swordfish, scrod, and scallops. Dinner is served from 6 to 11 p.m. daily. All major CC's are accepted.

WHERE TO DINE: In addition to fine hotel restaurants, this section of New Jersey has many fine local dining spots. Here are two you should not miss, one in the upper price bracket, and the other in the moderate category.

A pink-and-blue Victorian house is the setting for **Le Delice**, 302 Whippany Rd., Whippany (tel. 884-2727), an award-winning restaurant about 20 miles northwest of Newark and three miles north of Morristown on a quiet country road (Route 511). Owner/chef John Foy started this restaurant about ten years ago after working at the 21 Club in New York, and accolades have followed ever since. Designed with the corporate customer in mind, prices are not cheap, but the food is hard to beat, and where else in this area can you choose from a wine list representing over 250 vineyards? Menus change four times a year, but lunch selections are usually in the $9.50 to $20 range and include fish tartare; warm salad with salmon; calves' liver; roulade of chicken; and tournedos of beef. The dinner entrees cost from $17.50 to $26 for such dishes as duck Dijonnaise, Hawaiian blue prawns, rack of lamb with eggplant soufflé, Dover sole with artichoke purée, salmon en croûte, partridge with truffle sauce, buffalo steak au poivre, and sautéed sweetbreads. Open for lunch, Tuesday through Friday from 11:30 a.m. to 2 p.m.; and for dinner, from 6 to 9:30 p.m. Monday through Thursday, and until 10 p.m. on Friday; there are two seatings on Saturday, from 6 to 7 p.m. and from 9 to 10 p.m. CC's accepted: AE and D.

The **Polo Club**, 142 South St., Morristown (tel. 267-8466), is on the main throughfare of this historic town, 23 miles west of Newark. Housed in a 1910 building, this restaurant features an eclectic décor with a skylit front room and a rear dining area crowned by a tin ceiling. Local art, leafy plants and ferns, and classical music fill both rooms. Lunch items, priced from $4.95 to $8.95, focus on salads, burgers, quiches, omelets, and an out-of-the-ordinary list of sandwiches, ranging from chicken Cordon Bleu to beef and spinach béarnaise. Entrees at dinner, priced from $9.75 to $16.75, with most under the $15 mark, include a savory house specialty of chicken Beethoven, which consists of breast of chicken with white wine, cream, ham, and parmesan cheese; other selections are trout amandine, shrimp stir-fry, veal Dijon, beef Stroganoff crêpes, vegetarian platter, and filet of beef Madeira. Open Tuesday through Thursday from 11:30 a.m. to 10 p.m., Friday until 11:30 p.m., Saturday from 10 a.m. to midnight, and Sunday from 10 a.m. to 10 p.m. All major CC's are accepted.

THE TOP ATTRACTIONS: The **Newark Museum**, 49 Washington St., Newark (tel. 733-6600), is the largest museum in the state. This seven-building complex houses the most important Tibetan art collection in the western hemisphere, as well as a planetarium, exhibits of industry and science, a fire fighters' museum, and a sculpture garden. Of particular interest is the adjacent Ballantine House, a beautifully restored Victorian home that is entered via the museum. Once the residence of brewer John Ballantine, it is a landmark that reflects the elegant life of prosperous Newarkers of the 1890s. Open Tuesday through Sunday from noon to 5 p.m. No admission is charged, but contributions are welcomed.

The number-one draw in this area is The Meadowlands, a 750-acre sports complex located on Route 3 at exit 16W of the New Jersey Turnpike. Once an area of mosquito-infested marsh and wetlands, this $500 million development represents the greatest story of reclamation and rejuvenation in the entire east coast. Now home to the New Jersey Giants and Jets football teams, the Nets basketball squad, and the Devils hockey team, the Meadowlands boasts a 76,900-seat football stadium, a 20,000-seat arena, and a racetrack that can accommodate 35,000 people, all within sight of the N.Y.C. skyline.

The focal point of the complex is the **Brendan Byrne Arena,** which houses the box office (201/935-3900) for all events except racing. The arena is used for boxing and wrestling matches, basketball, indoor soccer, ice hockey, tennis, track and field, ice shows, concerts, and arts and crafts shows. Tickets range in price from $6 to $20 for most sports events. The box office is open from 10 a.m. to 6 p.m. Monday through Saturday, and on Sunday from noon to 5 p.m. Tickets can also be ordered by phone using a credit card (tel. toll-free 800/682-8080). All major CC's are accepted at the box office and by phone.

The **Meadowlands Racetrack** (tel. 201/935-8500) is the scene of both thoroughbred and harness racing, live and simulcast, throughout the year. Admission is $2 to the grandstand and $3 to the clubhouse; general parking is $3.

Less than five miles north of the Meadowlands is the **Aviation Hall of Fame and Museum of New Jersey, Teterboro Airport,** Teterboro (tel. 288-6344), located off Routes 17 and 36. Although it is now overshadowed by Newark Airport, Teterboro was one of the most important airports in the early days of flight. The museum consists of two sites, an Aviation Educational Center on the east side of the airport, and a Hall of Fame on the west side. Attractions include a 28-minute film on the history of aviation, hands-on exhibits, models, photographs, aeronautical memorabilia, and a control tower. The entire tour takes about 1½ hours. Open daily from 10 a.m. to 4 p.m. Admission is $2.50 for adults and $1.50 for children under 12 years of age.

Nearby is the **Liberty State Park,** Morris Pesin Drive, Jersey City (tel. 915-3400), off exit 14B of the New Jersey Turnpike. This is an open waterfront park and recreation area overlooking the Hudson River. Located less than 2,000 feet from the Statue of Liberty, this park is closer to the statue than any other point except on water. Besides providing spectacular views, the park also contains an historic railroad terminal, a plaza, and a ferry service to Liberty Island. Boats operate between 10 a.m. and 4 p.m. daily; the round-trip fare is $3.25. The park is open year round from 6 a.m. to 10 p.m., and there is no admission charge.

Less than ten miles west of Newark is the **Edison National Historic Site,** Main Street and Lakeside Avenue, West Orange (tel. 736-5050), off I-280, or exit 145 of the Garden State Parkway. Housing the preserved laboratory complex of inventor Thomas Alva Edison, this museum represents 44 years of inventing and includes the first lightbulb and a replica of the first motion-picture studio, "Black Maria," a tar-papered room. The museum lobby display is open daily from 9 a.m. to 5 p.m., but admission to the lab complex is by tour only. Tours operate from 9:30 a.m. to 3 p.m. continuously on Saturday and Sunday, and every hour on the half-hour Wednesday through Friday. The tour includes a screening of *The Great Train Robbery*, the first motion picture ever made. The tour fee is $2 per person for those over age 12. In addition, Thomas Edison's home, Glenmont, is located a mile away in Llewellyn Park. The house is currently closed and undergoing major restoration, but it will shortly be available for tours by the public; check at the museum to see if the house is open at the time of your visit.

Our nation's first national historical park was created at Morristown in 1933, to commemorate the site of Gen. George Washington's Revolutionary War encampment during the winters of 1777 and 1779. Today more than 800,000 visitors a year come to the **Morristown National Historical Park,** 230 Morris St., Washington Place (tel. 539-2017 or 539-2085), about 23 miles northwest of Newark. The park encompasses three main sites, which are spread out in and around Morristown. The prime attraction is **Washington's headquarters,** the home of Jacob Ford and commonly known as the **Ford Mansion,** built between 1772 and 1774 in the Georgian style. Filled with furnishings and utensils of the time, the house also has a visitors center, staffed by park rangers, and a series of exhibits depicting Washington's occupancy. A 20-minute film is also shown at intervals throughout the day. Other components of this historic area include Fort Nonsense, a hilltop site overlooking the town, off Route 24; and Jockey Hollow, six miles south of town on Route 202, the site of the soldiers' encampment. You can see reconstructions of the soldier's log-cabin huts, made of oak, walnut, and chestnut, as well as a wildlife santuary and nature trails. Open daily from 9 a.m. to 5 p.m. (except Thanksgiving, Christmas, and New Year's Day). Admission to Washington's Headquarters at the Ford Mansion is $1 per person; Jockey Hollow and Fort Nonsense are free.

NIGHTLIFE: Less than ten miles west of Newark is the **Paper Mill Playhouse,** Brookside Drive, Millburn (tel. 376-4343), off Route 24 and exit 142 of the Garden State Parkway. Located on the site of a 1790 red-brick papermill that was destroyed by fire in 1980, this is New Jersey's official state theater. Classics and full-scale Broadway productions are performed by professional casts at this 1,192-seat proscenium-style facility. The main season runs from September to June with a summer festival during June through August. The year-round program also includes regular appearances by the New Jersey Ballet and the New Jersey Symphony. Ticket prices vary from $7 to $23 for summer events to $11 to $29 for prime attractions. Children's shows are also held throughout the year, priced from $3 to $5. The box office is open on Monday and Tuesday from 10 a.m. to 7 p.m., Wednesday through Saturday from 10 a.m. to 9 p.m., and Sunday from noon to 9 p.m. CC's accepted: MC and V. Parking is $3.

Newark Symphony Hall, 1020 Broad St., Newark (tel. 643-4550), is a restored 1925 landmark theater in the heart of the city. It is the home of the New Jersey State Opera, the Theatre of Universal Images, and the New Jersey Symphony Orchestra. Evening performances also include visiting artists, concerts, dance groups, and plays. Ticket prices vary, according to event, but usually average between $16 and $20. The box office is open daily from 11 a.m. to 6 p.m. All major CC's are accepted.

5. Trenton and Princeton

As the capital of New Jersey, Trenton (pop.: 92,000) is the chief city in the state, but, like Newark, it is not currently a major visitor destination on its own. Other than the state capitol complex itself, there are few sights to interest visitors in Trenton, and the city's only downtown hotel, the Capitol Plaza, closed in 1986.

However, when grouped with its neighbor ten miles away, prosperous Princeton (pop.: 12,000), the Trenton area takes on a different dimension. If we add the nearby antiques-rich community of Lambertville and the shopping mecca of Flemington, the package becomes irresistible.

Both Trenton and Princeton were settled in the 1680s. Of the two, Trenton was blessed with the better location, right on the Delaware River, and grew accordingly.

The two cities played important parts during our country's struggle for independence and its early days. The Battle of Trenton represented a key victory for General Washington's troops, and Princeton's Nassau Hall was used by the Continental Congress for some of its sessions in 1783.

Trenton became the state capital in 1790 and went on to build a reputation in industry, particularly as a producer of pottery and porcelain.

In contrast, inland Princeton followed more cerebral pursuits, gaining worldwide recognition through its famous school, established as the College of New Jersey at Nassau Hall in 1756 and renamed Princeton University in 1896.

With the university as its hub, Princeton today is a leader in research and high-tech industries. It has also managed to maintain an old-world ambience, with tree-lined streets and ivy-covered buildings of Greek Revival, Federal, and Tudor styles. Chic shops and trendy cafés make this the quintessential ivy-league college town, and ideal for a walking tour.

To round out the picture, we add Lambertville, a pleasant little town of 4,000, situated on the banks of the Delaware, about ten miles north of Trenton on Route 29. It is also across the bridge from hectic New Hope in Bucks County, Pennsylvania. Known for its Victorian homes, antique shops, fine country inns, and restaurants, Lambertville is an ideal place to stay or dine if you are visiting Trenton.

Once you are in this area, you really should not miss Flemington, a rural town dating back to 1756 when Samuel Fleming built a home on 105 acres deeded to him by William Penn. It is located ten miles northeast of Lambertville, or 17 miles directly north of Trenton, off Route 202. Flemington today is a town of 4,000, with many of its Federal and Victorian buildings in the National Register, but it is best known as a mecca for factory-outlet shopping, especially fur coats and glassware.

VISITOR INFORMATION: The tourism office for the whole state of New Jersey is located in Trenton, and brochures on local sights are also available. Contact the **New Jersey Division of Travel and Tourism,** 1 West State St., No. 600, Trenton, NJ 08625-0826 (tel. 609/292-2470). Other good sources of local information are the **Chamber of Commerce of the Princeton Area,** 32 Nassau Street, 2nd floor, P.O. Box 431, Princeton, NJ 08542, (tel. 609/921-7676); the **Lambertville Area Chamber of Commerce,** 4 S. Union St., Lambertville, NJ 08530 (tel. 609/397-0055); and the **Hunterdon County Chamber of Commerce,** 119 Main St., Flemington, NJ 08822 (tel. 201/782-5955).

AREA CODE: All telephone numbers listed in this section belong to the 609 or 201 area codes. To avoid confusion, we shall specify the area code with every telephone number given below.

WHERE TO STAY: The best places to stay in this area are Princeton, Lambertville, or Flemington, using one town as a base, and traveling around to the others including Trenton. Thanks to its high-tech and corporate corridor along Route 1, Princeton is blessed with many top-class hotels, appealing to business travelers. Consequently, the highest rates prevail during midweek periods, and the best deals can be enjoyed by vacationers on weekends. Be sure to inquire about the weekend packages offered by Princeton's hotels—you can save up to 50% off normal Monday through Thursday rates. As for Lambertville and Flemington, rates tend to be pretty much the same all week.

Princeton

The only hotel right in the center of town is the **Omni Nassau Inn,** Palmer Square, Princeton, NJ 08542 (tel. 609/921-7500 or toll-free 800/THE-OMNI). Dating back to 1757, it is built on the site of an old tavern that was called At The Sign of New Jersey College, one block from Princeton University. Located on a grassy square with brick-lined courtyards and streets, the inn today is a blend of old and new, with Colonial-style public rooms and a new wing of bedrooms that opened in 1985. In all, there are 220 guest rooms with reproduction furnishings conveying an 18th-century ambience while still providing all the standard modern amenities of air conditioning, color cable TV, and direct-dial telephones. Doubles start at $98, and weekend packages are considerably less. Guest facilities include a health club, an indoor swimming pool, and valet parking. There are two restaurants, each with an individual personality; Palmer's is the more formal and pricey dining room where dinner only is served Tuesday through Sunday from 6:30 to 10:30 p.m., and The Greenhouse is a contemporary bright and airy room overlooking Palmer Square, open from 7 a.m. to 10 p.m. daily. The Greenhouse offers dinners in the $9.95 to $15.95 range, including such items as almond fried shrimp, prime ribs, lamb steak au poivre, steamed filet of salmon, and breast of chicken with pineapple and pecans. In addition, all-American meals, from burgers and ribs to steaks and seafood, are also served in the Yankee Doodle Tap Room, a pièce de résistance with wooden tables, a vintage fireplace, pictures of Princeton sports heroes, and an original Norman Rockwell mural. Lunch and dinner are available here, in the moderate price range, from 11:30 a.m. to 10:30 p.m. daily. All major CC's are accepted.

The **Hyatt Regency Princeton,** 102 Carnegie Center, Princeton, NJ 08540 (tel. 609/987-1234 or toll-free 800/228-9000), is located slightly south of the town center on Route 1, the corporate corridor. A modern five-story property, this hotel is built around a central atrium with landscaped terraces, cascading waterfalls, marble fountains, and brick paths. There are 348 guest rooms, many of which look out onto the atrium or face the gardens. Each of the guest rooms has a contemporary décor and all the modern amenities such as air conditioning, color cable TV, and a direct-dial phone. Double-occupancy rates are $142 during midweek and $75 on weekends. Facilities include tennis courts, a health club, a swimming pool, a whirlpool, a sauna, a lounge with live entertainment six nights a week, a by-the-glass wine bar, and a full-service restaurant, The Crystal Garden. Dinner entrees, which range in price from $17 to $24, feature such dishes as beef Cordon Rouge, rack of lamb Dijon, tournedos of veal nouvelle, scaloppine of salmon, prime ribs, and duckling in Calvados sauce. The restaurant is open daily from 6:30 a.m. to 11 p.m. All major CC's are accepted.

A unique property in this area is the **Scanticon-Princeton,** Princeton Forrestal Center, 100 College Road East, Princeton, NJ 08540 (tel. 609/452-7800 or toll-free 800/222-1131), located southeast of town off Route 1, in a wooded setting on 25 acres. As its name implies, a Scandinavian theme prevails throughout this modern hotel, with sleek Danish architecture and a décor of natural woods, copper, and tinted glass. Primarily an executive conference center during the week, this hotel seeks to attract vacation travelers on weekends. There are 300 guest rooms with contemporary Scandinavian furnishings and every modern convenience including air conditioning, color cable TVs, refrigerators, and direct-dial phones. Doubles start at $130 per night during the week, and weekend packages are available from $44 per person a day. Facilities include an indoor solarium with a swimming pool, saunas, and a whirlpool; four lighted tennis courts; a fitness room; jogging trails; and a game room. Danish cooking is the specialty of the three restaurants. The gourmet dining room, The Black Swan, is open Monday through Saturday for dinner only from 6 to 10 p.m.; it features such entrees as lobsters, poached salmon, red snapper, roasted quail, duckling Danish-style, rabbit braised in burgundy sauce, filet of beef Diane, and medallions of venison with cognac cream, in the $18.50 to $26 price bracket. For more moderate meals, try the delightful Tivoli Gardens, which is open for three meals a day from 7 a.m. to 11 p.m. It offers luncheon buffets for $11.95 on weekdays, and seafood buffets on Friday and Saturday nights for $22.95. There is also a "Tivoli at Twilight" complete dinner menu served from 4 to 6 p.m. from Sunday through Thursday at a cost of $30 per couple. On Sundays, you can enjoy a sumptuous brunch in the Copenhagen Room for $16.95. Entertainment is available each evening at the Scanticon, with a varied program of piano, guitar, or harp music. All major CC's are accepted.

Lambertville

The **Inn at Lambertville Station,** 11 Bridge St., Lambertville, NJ 08530 (tel. 609/397-4400 or toll-free 800/524-1091), is a modern four-story inn built on the banks of the Delaware. The interior reflects an old-world charm, with 45 antique-filled guest rooms. No two rooms are exactly alike, with some furnishings from as far away as Hong Kong, Paris, London, and New Orleans. Each unit has a view of the river, as well as a private bath and standard modern amenities. Many of the suites also have a fireplace or whirlpool bath. Double-occupancy rates, which include continental breakfast, range from $65 to $100, and suites from $125 to $150, with a two-day minimum on weekends. Non-smoking rooms are available. This complex also includes a restored Victorian train station (1867) which has been converted into a restaurant (direct line: 609/397-8300). A showcase of etched glass, oak woodwork, gilded mirrors, and brass light fixtures, this restaurant offers creative American cuisine in a relaxed setting. Lunch, priced from $4.95 to $7.95, focuses on sandwiches, salads, quiches, omelets, pastas, seafood, and light entrees. Entrees at dinner are priced from $9.95 to $18.95, with most under the $15 mark. The selection includes jambalaya, trout amandine, seafood fettuccine, sesame chicken, veal Cordon Rouge, grilled shrimp, lobster tails, and steaks. All main courses come with salad and vegetables. Lunch is served, Monday through Saturday from 11:30 a.m. to 3 p.m.; and dinner, Monday through Thursday from 4 to 10 p.m., and Friday and Saturday from 4 to 11 p.m. In addition, early bird "sunset on the Delaware" three-course dinners are available Monday through Thursday from 4 to 6:30 p.m., from $8.95 including a choice of ten entrees. A dance club operates on the lower level. Reservations are taken only for parties of eight or more, or for any number on holidays. All major CC's are accepted.

Flemington

The **Bel-Air Motel,** Routes 202 and 31, Flemington, NJ 08822 (tel. 201/782-7472), is located on spacious landscaped grounds south of Flemington Circle and close to all the major outlets. It is a modern two-story property with a Colonial façade. There are 103 units, with double or king beds, color TV, AM/FM radios, air conditioning, and direct-dial phones; some rooms also have thermasol steam baths. Doubles range from $45 to $60. Guest facilities include an outdoor swimming pool and a full-service restaurant called **Voyager's** (direct line: 215/788-5228). Burgers, sandwiches, pizzas, and salads are the focus at lunch, in the $2.95 to $6.95 price range. Dinner entrees, which cost from $8.95 to $15.95, include seafood Wellington; shrimp and lobster scampi, sherried sea scallops, blackened fish, prime ribs, Cajun chicken, veal Oscar, and steaks. Open Monday through Saturday from 6:30 a.m. to 11 p.m., and Sunday from 11 a.m. to 11 p.m. CC's accepted: AE, MC, and V.

A good bed-and-breakfast choice in this area is **Jerica Hill,** 96 Broad St., Flemington, NJ 08822 (tel. 201/782-8234), a restored 1901 Victorian home with a striking cranberry-and-gray façade. Located two blocks from historic Main Street and within walking distance of most of the major outlets, this lovely house has five antique-filled guest rooms, two with private bath and the rest with shared facilities. Doubles range from $45 to $65 and include a continental breakfast of fresh fruits, homemade breads, and pastries. Guests can enjoy the use of a wicker-filled screened porch and a living room with an open fireplace, TV, and well-stocked bookcases. No smoking is allowed in the house and young guests must be at least 12 years of age. For something a little different, innkeeper Judith Studer also offers "Bed, Breakfast, and Balloon Weekends," which provide accommodations plus a hot-air-balloon ride over the rolling hills of Hunterdon county, for $130 per person. CC's accepted: MC and V.

WHERE TO DINE: Our favorites in the Princeton and Lambertville areas follow. Let us know if you discover others.

Princeton

Alchemist and Barrister, 28 Witherspoon St., Princeton (tel. 609/924-5555), is an old-world restaurant housed in a 100-year-old building in the heart of town next to Palmer Square. Known locally as the A and B, it offers a main dining area with a Colonial motif plus an outdoor deck overlooking a brick courtyard. Lunch items, which cost $3.95 to $6.95, range from fruit and cheese boards to soups, salads, burgers, steaks, and seafood. Dinner entrees, priced from $12.95 to $18.95, with most dishes under the $15 mark, include coquilles St-Jacques; monkfish au gratin; baked stuffed pork chops; chicken florentine; spinach fettuccine with fresh vegetables; and steaks. All main courses come with salad and potato. Lunch is served Monday through Saturday from 11:30 a.m. to 2:30 p.m.; and dinner Monday through Thursday from 5:30 to 10 p.m., Friday and Saturday until 10:30 p.m., and Sunday from 4:30 to 8:30 p.m. Sunday brunch is also available from noon to 3 p.m. All major CC's are accepted.

Lambertville

Some of the best views of the countryside can be seen from the **Yellow Brick Toad,** 225 Highway 179, Lambertville (tel. 609/397-3100), a modern restaurant set on a bluff with 12 acres of grounds, one mile northeast of town. Designed to show off the panoramic views to the best advantage, the main restaurant is on the upper floor of this two-story building, with wide windows, a cathedral ceiling, and dozens of leafy plants. On warm summer days, brunch is also served on a garden terrace outside. Lunch items, priced from $3.95 to $6.95, include sandwiches, burgers, casseroles, pastas, crêpes, omelets, eggs Benedict, and light dishes. The menu at dinner features such dishes as chicken champagne; vegetarian platter; beef Wellington with a pocket of lobster, shrimp and scallops, pan fried sirloin Cajun-style; prime ribs (Saturday only); surf-and-turf; lobster and shrimp sauté; and flounder francese. Entrees are priced from $11.75 to $18.95, and come with a salad, vegetable, and potato or pasta. In addition, for those who wish to avoid salt, refined sugars, and saturated fats, an alternative "wellness menu" is offered at every meal. Lunch is served from 11:30

a.m. to 2:30 p.m. Tuesday through Saturday; and dinner from 5 to 10 p.m. Tuesday through Saturday. On Sunday, brunch is on tap from noon to 3 p.m., as well as dinner from noon to 8 p.m. All major CC's are accepted.

Two blocks from the Delaware River is **The Bridgestreet House,** 67 Bridge Street, Lambertville (tel. 609/397-2503), a two-story Victorian building surrounded by antique shops and country stores. Opened as a restaurant in 1983 by Michael and Eileen Heaton, it has four small dining areas including a bright and airy conservatory room. Open for dinner only, entrees are priced from $11.95 to $17.95, and include such dishes as Cornish game hen; Coho Salmon; sea scallops with kiwi and grapes in champagne sauce; broiled loin of lamb; and veal medallions and sliced shrimp in sherry butter. Main courses are accompanied by vegetables, potato, and freshly baked breads. Open Monday through Saturday from 6 to 10 p.m., and on Sunday for brunch and dinner from noon to 8 p.m. The Heatons also have four guest rooms on the second floor which they make available on a B&B basis; one room has a private bath and the rest are shared. Overnight guests can also use the outdoor garden area which includes a hot tub. Doubles start at $55 including breakfast. CC's accepted: MC and V.

Along the banks of the Delaware-Raritan Canal is **Gerard's,** 8½ Coryell Street in The Porkyard, Lambertville (tel. 609/397-8035), a cozy restaurant with two small dining rooms just large enough for 40 guests. In the 1920s, this corner of Lambertville was used as a pig-slaughter and sausage-making area, and thus the name Porkyard. Today, however, it is the setting for antique shops, an art gallery, and fine dining at Gerard's, which overlooks the canal. Dinner entrees are priced in the $14 to $25 bracket, and include selections such as rack of lamb, Chateaubriand, sautéed sweetbreads, Dover sole, baked rock shrimp, and sautéed frogs' legs. Each main course is accompanied by a salad and two vegetables. Open daily, except Tuesday, for dinner from 5:30 to 10 p.m.; noon to 8 p.m. on Sunday for brunch and dinner. No alcoholic beverages are served, but you are welcome to bring your own; a liquor shop is also located in the Porkyard. CC's accepted: AE, MC, and V.

THE TOP ATTRACTIONS: The center of attention in Trenton is the **State Capitol,** 121 W. State St. (tel. 609/292-6347), America's second-oldest capitol building in continuous use. Constructed in 1792, this gold-domed seat of the New Jersey government is open to the public, free of charge, Tuesday through Friday from 9 a.m. to 4 p.m.

The State House is the highlight of State Street, the city's wide main thoroughfare, lined with wonderful old specimens of Federal, Greek Revival, and Victorian architecture, many of which are being restored.

Adjacent to the capitol is the three-building **New Jersey State Museum complex,** 205 W. State St. (tel. 609/292-6308), which has a variety of exhibits on fine arts, decorative crafts, state history, archeology/ethnology, natural sciences, and space science, including a planetarium. The museum is open Tuesday to Saturday from 9 a.m. to 4:45 p.m. and on Sunday from 1 to 5 p.m.; no admission charge.

Nearby is New Jersey's oldest home, the **William Trent House,** 15 Market Street, at Route 29 (tel. 609/989-3027), a brick Queen Anne–style residence situated along the shores of the Delaware River. It was built in 1719 by Justice William Trent who planned the surrounding community, which soon became known as Trent Town or Trenton. The interior includes many original furnishings and the judge's personal inventory. The gardens outside illustrate the Colonial style of landscaping and are meticuously maintained by the Trenton Garden Club. Open Monday through Saturday from 10 a.m. to 4 p.m., and on Sunday from 1 to 4 p.m. Admission is 50¢ for adults and 25¢ for children.

Eight miles northwest of Trenton is the **Washington Crossing State Park,** Route 29, Titusville (tel. 609/737-9304), an 840-acre site along the Delaware. It was here that General Washington and his troops pulled in their boats after their historic Christmas 1776 crossing of the Delaware. In other words, this side of the river is the other half of the park that originates in Bucks County (Chapter IV). The attractions here include the Ferry House (a restored Colonial inn), an arboretum, an open-air amphitheater, nature trails, and bird-watching areas. In addition, there is a visitor center that houses a unique collection of Revolutionary period items (1758 to 1783), ranging from weapons and uniforms to coins, documents, eating utensils, medical equipment, and games. The center is open daily from 8:30 a.m. to 5 p.m. during the summer; and from 9 a.m. to 4:30 p.m. Wednesday through Sunday at other times. The park is open daily from 8 a.m. to 8 p.m. Memorial Day to Labor Day, and from 8 a.m. to 4:30 p.m. during the rest of the year. Admission is free to the park and the exhibits, but parking is $1 per car in the summer.

All visits to Princeton revolve around **Princeton University,** Nassau Street (tel. 609/452-3000), a medley of many fine buildings spread over 2,500 acres, and the home of scholars from around the world. Originally known as the College of New Jersey, this school had its beginnings in 1746 when it was founded in Elizabeth, New Jersey. Ten years later, it was moved to Princeton, but it was not officially named Princeton University until 1896.

The centerpiece of the Princeton campus is **Nassau Hall,** dating back to 1756, and once the largest academic structure in the 13 colonies. Used as a barracks during the Revolutionary War, it also served as the capitol of the United States for six months in 1783. The building is open to the public, Monday through Friday from 2 to 5 p.m., Saturday from 9 a.m. to 5 p.m., and Sunday from 1 to 5 p.m. No admission charge.

Other buildings that are open free to the public include the **Art Museum,** in McCormack Hall, which contains a permanent collection of American folk art, as well as art and artifacts from the Orient, Africa, South America, Greece, and Europe. Open Tuesday to Saturday from 10 a.m. to 4 p.m., and on Sunday from 1 p.m. to 5 p.m.

To get the most out of a visit to Princeton, it is wise to arrange for a one-hour escorted tour, conducted free of charge by members of the **Orange Key Guide Service,** MacLean House, 73 Nassau Street (tel. 609/452-3603). Tours are usually scheduled Monday through Saturday at 10 a.m., 11 a.m., 1:30 p.m., and 3:30 p.m.; and on Sunday at 1:30 and 3:30 p.m. Reservations are necessary.

One of the oldest homes in Princeton is **Morven,** 55 Stockton St., (tel. 609/683-1755), originally built between 1701 and 1709 by Richard Stockton on land purchased from William Penn. Stockton's namesake grandson also lived in the house and was a signer of the Declaration of Independence. A national historic landmark, Morven was the official residence for five of New Jersey's recent governors, and it is now the headquarters of the New Jersey Historical Commission. The house contains portraits of New Jersey governors and a gallery of changing exhibits, as well as many furnishings reflecting its centuries of history. Open April through September, on Wednesday and Saturday from 10 a.m. to 4 p.m., and on Sunday from 1 to 4 p.m. Admission is $1.50 for adults and 75¢ for students.

NIGHTLIFE: The **McCarter Theatre,** 91 University Place, Princeton (tel. 609/683-8000), is the performing-arts center of Princeton University. Recently renovated, the theater is the home of a professional resident company, the Triangle Club, that stages everything from the classics to contemporary plays. Open year round, prices average $10 to $26. CC's accepted: AE, MC, and V.

SHOPPING: Although Princeton offers many trendy designer boutiques, the chief shopping mecca in this area is Flemington, home to a variety of outlet stores. To get around, it is best to park your car in one of the many designated areas and walk, taking an opportunity to enjoy this historic town along the way. In addition, you can ride from point to point on the **The Flemington Trolley** (tel. 201/782-7740), a motorized bus that connects over 100 stores and attractions in the town, on a 40-minute signposted loop route. The trolley operates Tuesday through Sunday from 10 a.m. to 5:30 p.m., and the $1 fare allows on-off privileges all day.

Unless otherwise specified, all of the shops in Flemington are open daily from 10 a.m. to 5:30 p.m. (except Easter, Thanksgiving, Christmas, and New Year's Day). Here are a few highlights:

Liberty Village and Turntable Junction, One Church St. (tel. 201/782-0500), is made up of over 80 outlets, shops, and cafés, clustered in an 18th-century village setting around a restored railroad depot. Opened in 1965, this complex is home to outlets for such names as Adidas, Butcher Block, Corning, Fieldcrest, Hamilton Clock, Anne Klein, Calvin Klein, Royal Doulton, and Van Heusen. CC's accepted by most shops: MC and V.

The **Flemington Fur Company,** 8 Spring St. (tel. 201/782-2212), opened in 1921 and now the largest fur outlet in the United States. In addition to full-length fur coats, you'll find fur hats and accessories, as well as a "fur exchange" for used garments. This company also maintains the **Flemington Fur Company's Coat World** at Liberty Village (tel. 201/782-3414), which sells leathers, suedes, woolens, cashmeres, and fake furs, as well as real furs. CC's accepted: MC and V.

The grand-daddy of these shops is the **Flemington Cut Glass Factory,** 156 Main St. (tel. 782-3017), established in 1908, and a leading source for glassware, pottery, and bone china. You can also visit the cutting department and observe glass-cutters at work, custom decorating and monogramming. In addition to the factory's own production, glassware from around the world is on sale here. CC's accepted: AE, MC, and V.

The **Dansk Factory Outlet,** Routes 202 and 31, at Flemington Circle (tel. 201/782-7077), sells dinnerware, teakwood serving pieces, flatware, glassware, cookware, and gifts at substantial savings. CC's accepted: MC and V.

Wedgwood, Flemington Tabletop Village, 110 Broad St. (tel. 201/782-1511), is a direct outlet for Wedgwood, Adams, and Coalport brands, among others. Products stocked include bone china, earthenware, ironstone dinnerware, giftware, and crystal. CC's accepted: AE, MC, and V.

The **Flemington Gem Center,** 80-82 Main St. (tel. 201/788-9662), is an international outlet for gems, jewelry, pearls, ivory, cloisonné, amber, and semi-precious stones. All major CC's are accepted.

For a change of pace, Lambertville is an antique-lovers enclave. Most shops here are open daily from 10 a.m. or 11 a.m. to 5 p.m. in the summer, with reduced schedules in the off-season months.

A good place to start browsing is at the Porkyard Antique Dealers (609/397-2088), where you'll find eight different shops in a small courtyard, off Coryell Street, between North Union Street and the canal. Other interesting shops include **Joseph Sulzberg Stained Glass Shop and Studio,** 28 N. Union St., 2nd floor (tel. 609/397-8478); **Artfull Eye,** 12 N. Union St. (tel. 609/397-8115); **Bridge Street Antiques,** 15 Bridge St. (tel. 397-9890); and the half-dozen shops along Church Street, collectively known as "Antique Alley."

CHILDREN'S CORNER: The **Six Flags Great Adventure Park,** Jackson (tel. 201/928-3500), is located about 30 miles southeast of Trenton. It is about equally distant from the Spring Lake area of the Jersey shore, so it is hard to choose exactly where it should be listed in this book. Since you may read this chapter first, we have decided to put it here. The best way to reach the park from Trenton is via I-195 east to Route 537. Situated in a 1,700-acre woodland setting, Great Adventure is a giant theme park with more than 100 rides, plus concerts, flumes, and water shows featuring trained dolphins and sea lions. In addition, there is a 350-acre drive-through safari park, with over 2,000 wild and unusual animals. Open mid-April through mid-October, the amusement park hours are 10 a.m. to 10 p.m. Sunday through Thursday and until midnight on Friday and Saturday. The safari is open daily from 9 a.m. to 5 p.m. The admission charge is $16.95 for a combination ticket to the theme park and safari; the park alone is $15.95; and the safari alone is $5.95. Parking is $2. CC's accepted: AE, MC, and V.

Chapter XV

THE JERSEY SHORE

1. Getting to the Shore
2. Sandy Hook to Asbury Park
3. Spring Lake to Long Beach Island
4. Ocean City to the Wildwoods

MORE THAN FIFTY BEACHSIDE COMMUNITIES make up the 127-mile strip along the Atlantic Ocean collectively known as "The Jersey Shore."

These back-to-back beach towns stretch from Sandy Hook in the north to Cape May at the southern tip of the state, and include such well-known resorts as Atlantic City, Asbury Park, Spring Lake, Long Beach Island, Ocean City, and the Wildwoods. Because of the interest in Atlantic City's gambling casinos and Cape May's Victorian architecture, we have devoted separate chapters to each of them (see Chapter XVI for Atlantic City and Chapter XVII for Cape May).

The rest of the Jersey shore territory, however, will be compressed in this chapter. We know we can't possibly do justice to all of these resorts, but, at least, we'll give you some of the highlights, and, hopefully, interest you to see more for yourself.

Whether you seek quiet beaches or busy beaches, you are bound to find something of interest along the Jersey shore. Many of the resorts are famed for their boardwalk and amusement strips like Seaside Heights, Point Pleasant, or the Wildwoods. A family atmosphere prevails at Ocean City, while Victorian architecture draws folks to Ocean Grove or Spring Lake, and a bird sanctuary is the claim to fame of Stone Harbor. And the list goes on . . .

No matter what destination you choose, you'll usually have to pay for the privilege of swimming on the beach. Daily beach passes range from $2 to $8, although some beaches, like the Wildwoods, are free. The good news is that these fees are generally only charged from Memorial Day through Labor Day, so, if you plan a spring or autumn visit, you can enjoy the beaches for free. You can also save substantially on accommodations in the off-season months.

A note on shore restaurants: Most eating places are open seven days a week, throughout the day and evening during the summer season. More limited hours are in effect in the spring and fall. Although we have tried to note hours of operation, these times are often subject to change, depending on the weather and the flow of business. We suggest you always call in advance to check the days and the times that restaurants are open, especially in the off-season.

1. Getting to the Shore

BY CAR: The best way to get to the Jersey Shore, and to tour around, is by car. From points north, take the New Jersey Turnpike south to exit 11, and then get on the Garden State Parkway. The beach resorts start at exit 117 (for the Sandy Hook area) and continue southward, running parallel to the coastline, to exit 0 (Cape May). From the west, take the Atlantic City Expressway to the Garden State Parkway, and then go either north or south, depending on which resort is your destination. From the south, you can travel via Delaware and the Cape May/Lewes Ferry (for full description, see Chapter XVII on Cape May or Chapter XX covering Lewes).

BY PUBLIC TRANSPORT: New Jersey Transit provides daily bus service from New York, Philadelphia, and Newark to most points along the Jersey shore. Rail service is also available to major northern shore towns such as Red Bank and Asbury Park. For complete information on schedules and fares, call 215/569-3752 or toll-free (in northern New Jersey) 800/772-2222 and (southern New Jersey) 800/582-5946.

2. Sandy Hook to Asbury Park

The northernmost tip of the Jersey shore is Sandy Hook, part of the Gateway National Park which also includes parts of New York (Staten Island and Long Island). Besides the Sandy Hook coast, the beaches in this area include Sea Bright, Monmouth, and Long Branch (primarily on Route 36).

In addition to the beaches, this area extends inland along the Navesink River (via Route 35) and includes the historic town of Red Bank, known as the "hub" of the northern shore. Nearby is Eatontown, famed for its thoroughbred racetrack. The final town we'll cover in this section is Asbury Park, a once-glorious resort that has seen hard times in recent years, but is now in the midst of a $500 million rejuvenation.

VISITOR INFORMATION: For travel information in advance of your visit, contact the **Shore Region Tourism Council,** P.O. Box 788, Toms River, NJ 08753 (tel. 201/671-2670).

AREA CODE: All telephone numbers for this part of the Jersey shore fall into the 201 area code.

THE SANDY HOOK REGION: The highlight of this section of the shore is the Sandy Hook unit of the **Gateway National Recreation Area,** Route 36, Highlands (tel. 872-0115), within viewing distance of the World Trade Center and the rest of the New York City skyline. Administered by the National Park Service, this spit of beachland which juts upward into the Atlantic is 6½ miles long and three-quarters of a mile at its widest point. There are 11 different parking areas and beach sections. Besides the free beaches, highlights of the island include the Sandy Hook Lighthouse, built in 1764 and one of the oldest in the nation. Go first to the **Visitor Center,** Spermaceti Cove, next to parking lot E, open daily from 9 a.m. to 5 p.m. Here you can pick up self-guiding tour leaflets of the area and see exhibits and a 14-minute slide program. In addition, rangers conduct regular walks departing from the museum. Although the beaches are technically free, there is a $2 parking fee on weekdays and $3 on weekends, from Memorial weekend through Labor Day.

About five miles east of Sandy Hook along the coast is **The Spy House Museum,** 119 Port Monmouth Rd., Port Monmouth (tel. 787-1807). Overlooking lower New York Bay, this is a plantation house built in 1663 by Thomas Whitlock. It is said that this site was the earliest land claim in the area and that Whitlock was the first permanent resident of New Jersey. The house was subsequently used as a base for Revolutionary soldiers who "spied" on the arriving British and often sank their ships. Now on the National Register, this folk museum is full of artifacts and furnishings from New Jersey's earliest days. Open Monday through Friday from 9:30 a.m. to 3:30 p.m.; Saturday from 1 to 3:30 p.m.; and Sunday from 2:30 to 5 p.m. Admission is free, but donations are welcomed.

Where to Dine

Less than a mile south of Sandy Hook is the **Riverhouse On the Quay,** 280 Ocean Avenue (Route 36), Sea Bright (tel. 842-1994), situated on the Navesink River, with the ocean across the street. It is a modern, bright, and airy restaurant, with wide windows that overlook the marina on three sides, a bright pastel décor, framed scenes from the nearby beaches and boardwalks, and rattan and cane furnishings. Besides the views, on cooler days, you can also enjoy an open fireplace in the bar area. Lunch items, priced in the $5 to $10 range, include sandwiches, quiches, fruit plates, seafood, and "spa" selections such as grilled paillard of chicken. Dinner entrees, in the $15 to $25 price bracket, change daily, but usually offer whole lobsters, local seafoods, and steaks, as well as international recipes, especially from Greece, France, and the Caribbean. Open year round, for lunch Monday through Saturday from 11:30 a.m. to 3 p.m.; and for dinner Monday through Friday from 5 to 10 p.m., Saturday until 11, and Sunday from 3 to 10 p.m. All major CC's are accepted.

THE RED BANK AREA: Dating back to Colonial times, Red Bank is not a beach town but a river town, situated on the Navesink River which flows into the Atlantic. It was a thriving shipping center in the early 19th century and a regular stopping point for stately masted schooners and paddlewheel steamers which plied the waters of the east coast.

Incorporated as a town in 1870 and a borough in 1908, Red Bank has grown into a commercial and social hub for the beach towns and other neighboring communities. Situated at exit 109 of the Garden State Parkway, Red Bank is also the gateway to a variety of attractions, as well as some of the shore's best hotels and restaurants, which, surprisingly, are not along the beach, but inland.

Among the area highlights are the **Monmouth Battlefield State Park,** Route 33, Freehold (tel. 462-9616), off Route 9, about 20 miles west of Red Bank. The scene of one of the longest battles of the Revolutionary War (1778), this is where the legendary Mary Ludwig Hays (more commonly known as "Molly Pitcher") became a heroine by bringing pitchers of water to men in the field, and by taking up arms against the British when her own husband fell in battle. To learn the whole story, stop into the **visitors center,** open daily from 10 a.m. to 6 p.m. in the summer and from 10 a.m. to 4 p.m. the rest of the year. There is also a nature center and picnic facilities on the grounds. No admission charge.

If you visit from mid-June through September, plan to spend at least one evening at the **Garden State Arts Center,** Telegraph Hill, Holmdel (tel. 442-8600), about ten miles west of Red Bank and exit 116 of the Garden State Parkway. Set on a hillside on a 400-acre park, this 5,100-seat amphitheater offers a summertime program of evening open-air pop and classical concerts, musicals, ballets, and ethnic heritage festivals. Prices vary with events, but usually average between $10 and $15. For a schedule of upcoming events, write to the center at P.O. Box 116, Holmdel, NJ 07733.

For sports fans, there is **Monmouth Park,** Oceanport Avenue, Oceanport (tel. 222-5100), about five miles south of Red Bank, off Route 36 or exit 105 of the Garden State Parkway. Ever since 1946, this has been a prime New Jersey venue for thoroughbred flat and turf racing. The season extends from the end of May through the first week in September, with racing Monday through Saturday; post time is 1:30 p.m. General admission is $2.50 and $4.50 for the clubhouse.

Visitor Information

For specific data on Red Bank and its environs, contact or visit the **Chamber of Commerce of Red Bank,** 5 Broad Street, Red Bank, NJ 07701 (tel. 201/741-0055). The office is open Monday through Friday, year round, from 9 a.m. to noon and from 1 to 5 p.m.

Where to Stay

One of the Jersey shore's newest (opened in 1986) and most deluxe properties is the **Oyster Point Hotel,** Bodman Place, Red Bank, NJ 07701 (tel. 201/530-8200 or toll-free 800/354-3484). This six-story $6 million hotel takes its name from the fact that it is built on a marina site overlooking the Navesink River which was once known as Oyster Shell Point, famous for its oyster beds. It is a grand hotel in the European style, complete with marble lobby, atrium, and lots of glass, brass, and potted foliage. There are 52 double-occupancy rooms and six suites, all with king or double beds, river views, private balconies, and standard amenities, plus two telephones in each room, a sitting area, and an extra mini-TV in each bathroom. Doubles range from $125 to $140. Guest facilities include a spa with Jacuzzi, an exercise room, and a gourmet restaurant, La Rive. Lunches, priced from $7 to $19, feature imported John Dory sole, lobster club sandwiches, corn fritters with golden caviar, and stir-fried squab. The dinner menu is equally upscale, in price and choice, with entrees including ragout of rabbit, navarin of lamb, maple-glazed roast pheasant, free-range chicken, and pasta with oysters. The prices run from $17 to $29. Lunch is served from 11:30 a.m. to 2:30 p.m. and dinner from 5:30 to 10:30 p.m. daily. All major CC's are accepted.

The Navesink River marina is also home to the **Molly Pitcher Inn,** 88 Riverside Ave., Red Bank, NJ 07701 (tel. 201/747-2500 or toll-free 800/221-1372), on Route 35. Named for the local heroine Molly Pitcher, this is a three-story brick Colonial hotel that dates back to 1928. There are 65 rooms in the old (and refurbished) inn and 40 in an adjoining motel-style wing. Each unit has all the modern amenities including air conditioning, color TV, and a telephone. Doubles range from $60 in the motel section and from $65 in the main building. Facilities include a tavern and a moderately priced restaurant, both overlooking the river, and an outdoor heated swimming pool. All major CC's are accepted.

Racing fans favor the **Crystal Motor Lodge,** Route 35, Eatontown, NJ 07724 (tel. 201/542-4900), just a mile from the Monmouth Park Racetrack, and three miles from the beach. There are 77 modern rooms, which surround an outdoor pool, in a secluded wooded setting. Each unit is decorated in contemporary style, with two double beds, wall-to-wall carpeting, color TV, a telephone, air conditioning, and a refrigerator. Doubles range from $55 to $65 in the summer season, with reduced rates during the rest of the year. All major CC's are accepted.

Where to Dine

The **Shadowbrook,** Route 35, Shrewsbury (tel. 747-0200), has been a favorite in this area for almost 40 years. Owned and operated by the

Zweben family, this is a two-story Georgian mansion, situated on 20 secluded acres of woods and rose gardens, about two miles south of Red Bank. The posh décor includes antiques, dark wood paneling, crystal chandeliers, gilt-edge mirrors, and stone fireplaces. Lunch is usually an "English Hunt Buffet," priced at $10, while dinner is strictly à la carte. Entrees, priced from $15.95 to $25.95, feature such dishes as Dover sole, Chateaubriand, rack of lamb, flaming duckling à l'orange, caponette Kiev, heart of sirloin steaks, prime ribs, veal Oscar, and "seafood trifecta" (king crab, Gulf shrimp, and scallops on pasta). All main courses are accompanied by salad, vegetable, and potato or rice. Lunch is served Tuesday through Saturday from 11:30 a.m. to 2 p.m.; and dinner from 5:30 to 9:30 p.m. on Tuesday through Friday, and until 11 p.m. on Saturday. On Sunday, an expanded version of the luncheon Hunt Buffet (including prime ribs) is available from 3 to 9 p.m. and is priced at $24.95. All major CC's are accepted.

A country-club atmosphere prevails at the **Old Orchard Inn,** 74 Monmouth Road (Route 71), Eatontown (tel. 542-9300), situated on the grounds of the Old Orchard 18-hole public golf course. Incidentally, the greens fees range from $12 to $16, if you want to take in a game before or after a meal (tel. 542-7666). There are two dining rooms, one a fairly new and modern enclosed veranda overlooking the course, and the other an older clubby room with hunt scenes, tapestries, and a fireplace, along with piano music most nights. Sandwiches, burgers, crêpes, omelets, light dishes, and cold platters are the focus at lunch, in the $3.95 to $8.95 range. Dinner entrees, priced from $11.95 to $19.95, with most under $15, include steaks, seafood, pork medallions, calves' liver, double-cut lamb chops, veal dishes, and "chicken Old Orchard" (a tasty blend of sautéed breast meat with tomatoes, onions, and prosciutto). Lunch is served daily from 11:30 a.m. to 2 p.m.; and dinner from 5 to 9 p.m. Sunday through Thursday, and until 11 p.m. on Friday and Saturday. CC's accepted: AE, MC, and V.

Nestled on the banks of the Navesink River is the **The Olde Union House,** 11 Wharf Ave., Red Bank (tel. 842-7575), which started in 1791 as a Colonial tavern and inn. Restored and enlarged 25 years ago, this restaurant offers a cozy old tavern room with gas lights, antiques, a timbered ceiling, and stained glass, and a modern section with a New Orleans atmosphere and wide windows overlooking the river. Lunch items, priced in the $3.95 to $11.95 bracket, include sandwiches, salads, burgers, seafood, pastas, diet dishes, and omelets. Entrees at dinner are priced from $9.95 to $18.95 for such selections as veal Cordon Bleu, London broil, steaks, pastas, and a variety of seafood including bouillabaisse. Lunch is available, Monday through Saturday from 11:30 a.m. to 5 p.m.; and dinner, Monday through Thursday from 5 to 10 p.m., on Friday and Saturday until 11 p.m., and on Sunday from 3 to 10 p.m. Sunday brunch is also served from noon to 3 p.m. All major CC's are accepted.

ASBURY PARK: Founded in 1871, Asbury Park was once the pride of the northern Jersey shore, a favorite with honeymooners and families alike. With its mile-long boardwalk and beaches, Asbury Park was also known for its amusement area, arcades of games, and the grand 1928 Convention Hall that drew the top names in big-band music from Glenn Miller to Harry James.

Alas, competition from other emerging shore destinations brought hard times by the 1960s, and Asbury Park gradually went into a period of deep decline and neglect. That was the case, at least, until a local talent named Bruce Springsteen got his start in an Asbury Park rock and roll bar called The Stone Pony. In no time at all, Springsteen and his "Born in the U.S.A." were propelled into worldwide fame, and Asbury Park was back on the map.

The sudden notoriety gave local citizens the impetus to try and bring Asbury Park back to its former glory. The first evidence of a rejuvenation has been the restoration of the Berkeley Carteret Hotel, a landmark property in the heart of the city. The successful re-opening of the hotel has, in turn, inspired the start of a $500 million waterfront redevelopment that promises great things for Asbury Park's future.

One of the attractions in coming to Asbury Park is to see the unique contrast of its next-door neighbor, Ocean Grove. Founded in 1869 as a Methodist camp meeting, this orderly little resort has changed little in the intervening years. Still a "dry" town and untouched by the progress or decline of its larger neighbor, Ocean Grove is the setting for beautiful old Victorian structures and a Great Auditorium where religious gatherings are still held.

Visitor Information

For brochures and specific travel data about the Asbury Park area, contact the **The Greater Asbury Park Chamber of Commerce,** 100 Asbury Avenue, P.O. Box 649, Asbury Park, NJ 07712 (tel. 215/775-7676). Beach passes at Asbury Park cost $3 for a weekday and $5 on Saturday or Sunday.

Where to Stay

The focal point of the city's restoration is the eight-story **Berkeley Carteret Hotel,** Ocean Avenue, Asbury Park, NJ 07712 (tel. 201/776-6700 or toll-free 800/524-1423), re-opened in 1985 after an $18 million restoration by the Vaccaro family. The impressive lobby décor now includes marble floors, hand-painted Chinese screens, crystal chandeliers, restored moldings, huge columns, and potted ficus trees. Originally built in 1925 with 425 small rooms, this "new" hotel has 257 spacious rooms, most of which face the mile-long beach and boardwalk; each unit has deluxe contemporary furnishings, color cable TV, a radio, a telephone, and air conditioning. Doubles range from $100 to $130. Guest facilities include valet parking, an outdoor swimming pool, a sun deck, beach privileges, a lounge, and a first-rate restaurant, Olivia's. An international menu is featured, with dinner entrees in the $8.95 to $19.95 price range for such dishes as Dover sole, rack of lamb, steaks, veal, and pastas. Restaurant hours are 7 to 10 a.m. for breakfast; 11:30 a.m. to 2:30 p.m. for lunch; and 5 to 10 p.m. for dinner. All major CC's are accepted.

For good value and convenience, the best choice in this area is the **Howard Johnson Motor Lodge,** Route 35, Asbury Park Circle, Neptune, NJ 07753 (tel. 201/776-9000), just a mile from the beach, in a wooded setting along the main road. This two-story building was completely refurbished in 1985, using contemporary furnishings of autumn and forest tones. Each room has a color cable TV, a telephone, air conditioning, and most units overlook an outdoor swimming pool or the gardens. At present there are 60 rooms, but 40 more are being added, along with a new health spa. Doubles range from $65 to $75. All major CC's are accepted.

3. Spring Lake to Long Beach Island

The stretch of Jersey shore from Spring Lake southward to the bottom of Long Beach Island takes in over 50 miles. South of Spring Lake, these resorts are primarily barrier island beaches, with the Atlantic on one side and intracoastal waterways on the other. They are grouped together on two slender land masses, the Barnegat Peninsula and Long Beach Island, and are connected to the mainland by bridges and causeways.

The best single source for travel information in advance of your visit is the **Shore Region Tourism Council,** P.O. Box 788, Toms River, NJ 08753 (tel. 201/671-2670).

SPRING LAKE: Of all the resorts along the Jersey shore, Spring Lake is in a class by itself. Yes, it has a lovely beach and a two-mile boardwalk, like many of the other resorts, and it boasts fine mansions and Victorian bed-and-breakfast inns like Cape May. But, as a unique feature, this tidy community also has the ambience of a lakefront enclave, with its namesake, Spring Lake, at its heart, surrounded by parklands, footbridges, and ancient shady trees.

Thanks to its natural endowments, Spring Lake is one of the most unspoiled and under-commercialized of the Jersey resorts, with a regular clientele that comes back year after year. There are no noisy amusements or arcades, no fast-food strips, and no nightclubs. Chic shops line its main throroughfare, Third Avenue, and a motorized San Francisco–like trolley takes vacationers from shop to shop, and from inn to boardwalk or lakefront. (The trolley runs from May to September and costs 50¢).

As you ride around, you may wonder why so many Irish flags fly side-by-side with the Stars and Stripes. That brings us to Spring Lake's other claim to fame. Over the years, thanks to an influx of devotees with Irish roots, Spring Lake has become known as "The Irish Riviera." A focal point of the town is the **Irish Centre,** 1120 Third Avenue (tel. 449-6650), one of the Mid-Atlantic's classiest import stores and a showcase of Irish crystal, linens, tweeds, knitwear, fashions, paintings, and gifts. One of the most popular items for sale here is a map of Ireland showing the origins of more than 1,000 Irish family names.

Spring Lake also takes the prize for the highest rates for beach usage, $7 for a weekday and $8 for a Saturday or Sunday (if you plan to stay for a while, it costs $45 for the season). However, many of the hotels and bed-and-breakfast inns do supply beach tags to their guests, as part of the overnight rate. Be sure to check in advance.

For specific data about Spring Lake in advance of your trip, contact the **Greater Spring Lake Chamber of Commerce,** P.O. Box 694, Spring Lake, NJ 07762 (tel. 201/449-0577). There is no full-time tourist office.

The telephone **area code** for all numbers in the Spring Lake region is 201.

Where to Stay

If you'd like a room overlooking the beach, the best choice is **The Breakers,** 1507 Ocean Ave., Spring Lake, NJ 07762 (tel. 201/449-7700), a four-story Victorian landmark in this area. A large wrap-around porch beckons guests to sit on a rocker and enjoy the sea breezes, and a turn-of-the-century aura prevails in the congenial public rooms with their high ceilings, polished wood floors, antiques, and royal-blue-and-white tones. The 70 guest rooms, each with a private bath, have all been modernized, and feature up-to-date amenities such as air conditioning, color TV, a refrigerator, and a telephone. Open from mid-May to mid-October, doubles range from $100 to $140, with two- or three-night minimum stays required in the summer season. Lower rates apply in the spring and fall months. Breakfast and lunch are available daily in a traditional dining room from 8 a.m. to 3 p.m., but dinner is served in a new Ristorante, which offers a menu of Italian specialties such as veal saltimbocca, shrimp parmigiana, chicken with sausage and peppers, and pastas, as well as charbroiled steaks and lobster tails. Entrees are priced from $12.95 to $19.95; and the hours are from 5 to 10 p.m. Tuesday through Saturday, and from 2 to 9 p.m. on Sunday. No liquor is served, but you are welcome to bring your own. Guest facilities include beach passes, an outdoor swimming pool, and a whirlpool. All major CC's are accepted.

The best of both worlds can be enjoyed at the **The Chateau,** 500 Warren Avenue at Fifth Avenue, Spring Lake, NJ 07762 (tel. 201/974-2000), a charming country inn overlooking the lake and five blocks from the beach. Originally built in 1888, this property has been renovated and updated by its current owners, Scott and Karen Smith. The décor is bright and summery, with lots of wicker furniture, leafy plants, and pastel furnishings. Over the years, the guest list has included a number of celebrities, from Buster Keaton to Basil Rathbone, and many of the rooms are named and decorated in the style of the stars who stayed within. Open from April to early November, this 40-unit inn is a combination of hotel suites and ground-floor motel rooms; many units have private porches, patios, or sundecks. Each room is fully air-conditioned with a modern bath, plus color cable TV, a refrigerator, and a direct-dial phone. Doubles range from $59 to $89, and suites begin at $98, with a three-night minimum required on summer weekends. Prices include beach and tennis privileges; reduced rates are in effect before mid-June and after early September. All major CC's are accepted.

The **Comfort Inn,** 1909 Route 35 South, P.O. Box 14, Spring Lake, NJ 07762 (tel. 201/449-6146 or toll-free 800/228-5150), is conveniently situated in a garden setting on the main shore road and a mile from the center of town. A modern two-story structure, this 70-unit property has a contemporary décor, with all the standard amenities including color cable TV, a direct-dial phone, and air conditioning. Non-smoking rooms are available, and free continental breakfast is provided to guests. Facilities include an Olympic-size outdoor swimming pool and a complete fitness center. From May through September, doubles range from $70 to $105, with a $10 surcharge on holiday weekends; a two-night minimum applies on weekends, and a three-night minimum for holiday weekends. Rates at other times are $40 to $50. All major CC's are accepted.

The **Carriage House,** 208 Jersey Avenue, Spring Lake, NJ 07762 (tel. 201/ 449-1332), is a three-story Victorian bed-and-breakfast inn on a quiet tree-lined street, situated two blocks from the ocean. Owned by Marie and Tom Bradley, this grand old house has eight rooms, six with private bath and two with shared bath. Furnished with family antiques and heirlooms, it has a shady front porch with rockers for relaxing, gardens, and on-site parking. Each bedroom is air-conditioned, although, with three to five windows in most rooms, there is a lovely natural cross-ventilation. Open all year, doubles run from $55 to $70 with private bath, and $45 with shared bath. The price includes complimentary morning coffee and there is a guest refrigerator on each floor. No CC's accepted.

Note: The Carriage House is one of about two dozen restored Victorian-style bed-and-breakfast inns in the Spring Lake area. For a free brochure describing all of these properties, write to the Spring Lake Hotel and Guest House Association, P.O. Box 134, Spring Lake, NJ 07762.

Where to Dine

One of the newest (opened in 1986) restaurants in Spring Lake is **Cosmo's,** 500 Morris Avenue, Spring Lake (tel. 449-9000), a Colonial-style house at the corner of Fifth Avenue, in a quiet tree-shaded residential neighborhood, one block from the lake. With a surprisingly modern décor of red, black, and gray tones, tinted mirrors, and textured wallpaper, this spot is a favorite with the locals, not only for its food, but also for its live music and dancing most evenings. Open for dinner only, the entrees range in price from $10.95 to $21.95. Selections include charbroiled steaks, Chateaubriand, rack of lamb, veal chops, flounder francese, lobster tails, and pastas. "Early-bird" patrons who dine between 5 and 7 p.m. can also order a complete dinner, from $9.95. Open daily (except Sunday and Tuesday) from 5 to 10 p.m., with plenty of off-street parking. All major CC's are accepted.

Victorian towers and gables are the keynote of **The Beach House,** 901 Ocean Avenue (tel. 449-9646), at Mercer Avenue, opposite the Spring Lake oceanfront. You have a choice of dining on a screened-in wrap-around porch or in one of three clubby old-world rooms lined with oak-framed prints depicting Spring Lake of yesteryear. The setting is casual, the menus are simple, and the food straightforward, but the views and ambience are the best in town. Lunch runs from $2.95 to $5.95 for burgers, sandwiches, quiches, and salads. Entrees at dinner, priced from $12.50 to $14.95, include steaks, lamb chops, and seafoods such as flounder and scampi. All main courses come with salad, and potato or rice. In the summer, lunch and dinner are served daily from noon to 10 p.m., and on weekends only during the rest of the year. All CC's are accepted.

Two miles south of Spring Lake is the **Yankee Clipper,** 1 Chicago Blvd., Sea Girt (tel. 449-7200), a modern and elegant dining room with floor-to-ceiling windows overlooking the Atlantic. This spot is particularly popular in the evening as the birds gather on the waters when the sun goes down. The focus at lunch is primarily on sandwiches, salads, seafood, omelets, and crêpes, priced in the $3.95 to $6.95 range. Dinner entrees, which run from $10.95 to $18.95 with most under the $15 mark, include a variety of daily seafood specials such as shrimp with lobster stuffing, or "fruits of the sea" with fettuccine, plus steaks, prime ribs, veal, and poultry dishes. All main courses are accompanied by vegetable and potato or rice. Open from Monday through Saturday, for lunch from 11:30 a.m. to 2:30 p.m., and for dinner from 6 to 10 p.m. A champagne brunch is also featured on Sunday from 11:30 a.m. to 2:30 p.m., priced at $15.95. All major CC's are accepted.

POINT PLEASANT BEACH AREA: If you follow Route 35 southward from Spring Lake, you'll cross over the Manasquan Inlet into Point Pleasant Beach. This is the start of a 22-mile island known as the Barnegat Peninsula. You can also enter the island from the more southerly points via Routes 88 and 37.

Point Pleasant is best known for its fine sandy beaches, family-oriented boardwalk, seafood restaurants, and beachside bungalows. The communities that lie to the south are lined primarily with residential or rental properties, from the mansions of well-to-do Bay Head to the back-to-back cottages of Normandy, Chadwick, and Lavallette.

For specific brochures about this area, contact the **Greater Point Pleasant Chamber of Commerce,** 517 Arnold Avenue, Point Pleasant, NJ 08742 (tel. 201/899-2424).

The telephone **area code** for all numbers in the Point Pleasant region is 201.

Where to Stay

The **White Sands Motel,** 1106 Ocean Avenue, Point Pleasant, NJ 08742 (tel. 201/899-3370), is a modern 40-unit two-story property located on the beachfront in a quiet section of the shoreline. Totally refurbished in 1986, each unit has one or two double beds, air conditioning, color cable TV, and a direct-dial phone, and most have ocean views and terraces. Guest amenities include an outdoor pool and a snack bar; ten efficiency units are being added at the moment. Open year round, doubles from $90 to $115 in the summer, with off-season prices in the $45 to $65 bracket. CC's accepted: MC and V.

Mariner's Cove Motor Lodge, 50 Broadway, Point Pleasant Beach, NJ 08742 (tel. 201/899-0060), is one block from the ocean, overlooking the marina.

This two-story property has 24 units, each with two double beds, color cable TV, air conditioning, and wall-to-wall carpeting; many rooms also have balconies. Outdoor facilities include a swimming pool and a sundeck. Open all year. Doubles start at $78, with lower rates in the off-season. CC's accepted: AE, MC, and V.

Where to Dine

Since 1950, good seafood has been synonymous with the **Lobster Shanty,** 83 Channel Drive, Point Pleasant Beach (tel. 201/899-6700). Overlooking the Manasquan Inlet, the décor of this restaurant is understandably nautical. Open for dinner only, the menu includes a variety of sizes and styles of lobster, Atlantic flounder, crab cakes, Cajun/Créole scampi, seafood samplers, chicken and shrimp stir-fry, and steaks. Entree prices range from $7.95 to $16.95, except for lobster which is priced according to size. All main courses entitle you to unlimited helpings at the salad bar. Open from 5 to 9:30 p.m. daily in the summer; from 5 to 9:30 p.m. Wednesday through Saturday; and from 1 to 9 p.m. on Sunday during the rest of the year. All major CC's are accepted.

SEASIDE BEACH AREA: The lower half of the Barnegat Peninsula (south of the Route 37 causeway) consists of the beach communities of Seaside Heights, Seaside Park, and South Seaside Park, as well as the 12-mile strip known as **Island Beach State Park.**

Often called the captain of the boardwalk towns, Seaside Heights has a mile-long boardwalk, with rides at both ends, and lots of games and fast food in between. You'll be dazzled by wheels of chance, water slides, music bars, and playlands of all sizes and descriptions. This is the type of resort that draws the same families year after year. Consequently, accommodation choices are rather limited; most of the area is covered with small cottages, bungalows, and mobile homes.

Where to Stay

At the south end of the island, in a quiet area, just before you get to the Island State Park, is **Island Beach Motor Lodge,** 24th and Central Avenues, South Seaside Park, NJ 08752 (tel. 201/793-5400). Situated right on the ocean, this is a modern two-story property with 60 rooms, most with balconies or small patios. Each unit has double or oversized beds, air conditioning, a refrigerator, color cable TV, and wall-to-wall carpeting. Doubles start at $90 from late June to September, with a three-night minimum; in the spring and fall, rooms run from $35 to $55, with some two-night minimums. In addition, there are some efficiencies and penthouse suites available. Outdoor facilities include a heated pool and a sundeck. No CC's are accepted.

Where to Dine

The **Top o' the Mast,** 23rd Avenue on the Ocean, South Seaside Park (tel. 201/793-2444), is a modern restaurant on the second floor of a rustic building right on the beach. Wrap-around windows provide panoramic sea views, and the décor is appropriately nautical, with captain's chairs, fish nets, lanterns, and paintings of ocean scenes. Lunch items, priced from $4.95 to $6.95, include seafood samplers, brochettes, and casseroles, as well as salads, sandwiches, and omelets. The menu at dinner has an international flair, with such dishes as scallops Polynesian; shrimp niçoise; bouillabaisse; and flounder francese; as well as lobster tails; crab legs and claws; and beef (steaks, Chateaubriand, beef Wellington, and prime ribs). Dinner entrees are priced from $10.95 to $18.95, with most under $15, and are accompanied by salad and vegetable. If you get there between 4 and 6 p.m., ask about the "early-bird" four-course dinner specials from $9.95. Open daily year round, for lunch, Monday through Friday from 11:30 a.m. to 2:30 p.m.; and for dinner daily from 4 to 10 p.m., with entertainment on Friday and Saturday evenings. All major CC's are accepted.

LONG BEACH ISLAND: Long Beach Island is an 18-mile stretch of sand, quite different from its somewhat noisy neighbors to the north and to the south (Atlantic City). With only one connection to the mainland (the Route 72 causeway), Long Beach Island is the most remote of the Jersey shore resorts.

This slender isle, which is no more than three blocks wide in some places, was discovered by the Dutch in the 17th century and was a major whaling station in the years that followed. Officially named Long Beach Island in 1890, it grew into a fashionable resort at the turn of the century, particularly because it is said to be pollen-free, a big inducement for hay fever sufferers to this day.

Long Beach Island's main claim to fame, however, is the 172-foot Barnegat Lighthouse at the northern tip of the island. Known variously as the "Grand Old Champion of the Tides" and "Old Barney," it was built in 1857–1858, and played a key role on the Jersey coast in alerting approaching vessels to the dangers of the Barnegat shoals.

Today the Barnegat Lighthouse is the central fixture in a small 36-acre park. Visitors are welcome to climb the 217 steps to the top and enjoy a panoramic view and picture-taking location. It's open from 9 a.m. to 5 p.m. Memorial Day to Labor Day, and on weekends in May, September, and October. Admission is 50¢ for everyone over 12; free under 12.

Long Beach Island consists of more than 20 separate towns and communities, with evocative and diverse names like Loveladies, Ship Bottom, Holly Lagoons, Harvey Cedars, Spray Beach, The Dunes, Beach Haven, and Surf City. One main artery, Long Beach Boulevard, extends the length of the island (although it sometimes changes its name simply to The Boulevard), and there is no boardwalk. In general, the northern communities of the island are primarily geared to residential or rental housing, and the majority of motels are concentrated on the southern stretch, below the causeway.

Swimming and sunning are undoubtedly the most popular pastimes (beach badges vary in price among the different towns, but are usually around $2 per day), but fishing is also a favorite sport. If you'd like to join in, head for the **Beach Haven Fishing Center,** Centre Street and the Bay, Beach Haven (tel. 492-0333). From June through September, half-day fishing trips are available on the *Black Whale,* departing at 8 a.m. or 1 p.m.; the cost is $14 for adults and $10 for children, with a $3 rod rental. This same company also operates 1½-hour evening sightseeing cruises at 6:30 and 8 p.m., with live entertainment, priced at $5 for adults and $3 for children under 12.

Another focal point on this strip is the **Fantasy Island Amusement Park,** 320 W. 7th St., Beach Haven (tel. 492-4000), a Victorian-style amusement center, with rides and video games for children and a casino arcade with "gambling" machines for adults. It's a pleasant setting, with brick walkways, oak benches, ornate lampposts, and colored-glass fixtures. Admission is free, but rides are 75¢ to $1.50 each; on Friday, there is an all-inclusive price of $5 for unlimited rides.

For complete information on this area, contact the **Long Beach Island/ Southern Ocean County Chamber of Commerce,** 265 W. Ninth St., Ship Bottom, NJ 08008 (tel. 609/494-7211), open from 10 a.m. to 4 p.m. Monday through Saturday, from March through October; and from 10 a.m. to 4 p.m. Tuesday through Saturday during the rest of the year.

Long Beach Island marks the point on the shore where New Jersey **area codes** change from 201 to 609, so all telephone numbers listed below belong to the 609 area code.

Where to Stay

The **Spray Beach Motor Inn,** 24th Street at Ocean Boulevard, Spray Beach, NJ 08008 (tel. 609/492-1501), is located on the beach overlooking the Atlantic. It is a three-story property with 88 rooms, of which about one-third directly face the ocean. Each room has one or two double beds, color cable TV, a telephone, a refrigerator, and air conditioning; most rooms have private balconies or a deck. Doubles start at $96 from July 4 to September 1; and three- or four-night minimum stays apply. Rates range from $45 to $80 during the rest of the year (closed in January). Guest facilities include a heated outdoor pool, a café, and a lounge. CC's accepted: MC and V.

Engleside on the Ocean, 30 Engleside Avenue, Beach Haven, NJ 08008 (tel. 609/492-1251), is a modern three-story motel with 69 units, right on the beach. Each guest room has two double beds, air conditioning, color cable TV, a telephone, a refrigerator, an in-room coffee maker, a balcony, and wall-to-wall carpeting. Rates start at $96 in the mid-June through September 1 period; and range from $45 to $75 during the rest of the year. Facilities include a heated pool, a Jacuzzi, a health club, and a small dining room, the Leeward, which serves meals in the moderately priced bracket. Dinner entrees, priced from $7.95 to $14.95, include flounder florentine with spinach soufflé, chicken alla marsala, and crêpes Newburg. CC's accepted: AE, MC, and V.

The **Harborside Motel,** 31st Street and Long Beach Boulevard, Beach Haven Gardens, NJ 08008 (tel. 609/492-2233), is a small 10-unit property on the bay side of the island, one block from the beach. It is a one-story motel with a semi-Colonial motif, and has been welcoming guests to the shore for over 35 years. Each room has one or two double beds, air conditioning, color TV, and a small refrigerator. Open all year, rates range from $85 in the summer to $35 in the off-season. CC's accepted: MC and V.

Where to Dine

Flowers and plants dominate the décor at **Charles' Seafood Garden,** 8611 Long Beach Boulevard, Beach Haven Crest (tel. 492-8340), a modern conservatory-style restaurant at 87th Street, set back on the island's main road. Open for dinner only, the menu includes vegetarian specials and an imaginative blend of seafoods and pastas, such as clam tortellini, seafood pasta, fettuccine of the sea (with king crab), seafood florentine, as well as veal and lobster, seafood gumbo, steaks, and mushroom-rolled veal zinfandel. Entrees, priced from $9.95 to $18.95 with most under $15, are accompanied by house dip, salad, vegetable, and potato or pasta. Hours are daily from 5 to 10 p.m. May to October; and weekends only in the spring and fall. No liquor, but you can bring your own. CC's accepted: AE, MC, and V.

The elegant **Bayberry Inn,** 13th Street and Long Beach Boulevard, Ship Bottom (tel. 494-8848), has been a restaurant since 1975, but it has a 1795 décor and ambience. Colonial-style furnishings and red, white, and blue table linens add to the atmosphere. Sandwiches, salads, and light entrees are featured at lunch, in the $3.95 to $7.95 price bracket. The menu at dinner, with most items priced from $7.95 to $14.95, includes Chesapeake oysters stuffed with crab; rock Cornish hen; red snapper; seafood crêpes; veal alla marsala; chicken Cordon Bleu; Grand Marnier duckling; daily local seafood specials; and steaks. All entrees come with salads, corn pudding, and potato. Open year round for lunch, Monday through Saturday from 11:30 a.m. to 3 p.m.; for dinner daily from 4:30

to 10 p.m.; also for Sunday brunch from 10 a.m. to 1:30 p.m. All major CC's are accepted.

Port O' Call, Engleside Avenue at the Bay, Beach Haven (tel. 492-0715), is a contemporary restaurant that overlooks the bay side of the island. Lunch items, priced in the $2.95 to $6.95 range, include salads, sandwiches, platters, quiches, and burgers. The menu at dinner is heavily slanted to creative seafood dishes, such as seafood burrito, fish brochettes, or coconut shrimp. Other selections range from Jersey flounder and cioppino, to surf-and-turf, lobster, steaks, and prime ribs. Entree prices run from $9.95 to $24.95, with most under the $15 mark, and include a 20-item salad bar that is laid out on a miniature ship, plus vegetable and potato. Open daily year round, lunch is served from 11:30 a.m. to 4:30 p.m., and dinner from 5 to 9:30 p.m. In addition, "early-bird" dinners, priced from $6.95, are available to those who dine from 5 to 6 p.m. All major CC's accepted.

4. Ocean City to The Wildwoods

The remainder of the Jersey shore takes in the strip from Atlantic City to Cape May, both of which are covered in separate chapters. The purpose of this section will be to look at the major resorts in between, and, in particular, Ocean City, Stone Harbor, Avalon, and the Wildwoods—an area of about 35 miles and at least 150 small islands and four substantial barrier islands.

VISITOR INFORMATION: All of the resorts covered in this chapter are promoted by the **Cape May County Chamber of Commerce,** P.O. Box 74, Garden State Parkway (exit 11), Cape May Court House, NJ 08210 (tel. 609/465-7181). This office is open year round, daily from 9 a.m. to 5 p.m. from mid-April to mid-October; and Monday through Friday from 9 a.m. to 4:30 p.m. during the rest of the year.

AREA CODE: All of the telephone numbers in this section belong to the 609 area code.

OCEAN CITY: Of all the Jersey shore resorts, Ocean City prides itself as being the most family-oriented. Year after year, many of the same families come back, most often renting cottages and bungalows by the sea. Unlike its famous neighbor to the north, Atlantic City, this resort has no gambling, no nightclubs, and no liquor. It is a dry town and always has been, dating back to its founding as a Methodist retreat in 1879.

Ocean City's main claims to fame are its eight-mile stretch of beach, 2½-mile boardwalk, and its unique turn-of-the-century Music Pier, at 8th Street and Boardwalk, which is the scene of summertime open-air events. The premier attraction is the Ocean City Pops Orchestra, conducted for over 50 years by New York musical virtuoso Frank Ruggieri. These Pops concerts are held Sunday through Wednesday (admission is $1, except Sunday when it is free).

Visitors to Ocean City also come for the fishing, particularly bluefish, sea trout (weakfish), flounder, fluke, and black sea bass. If this is your sport, head for the **Ocean City Marina and Fishing Center,** 3rd Street and Bay Avenue (tel. 399-5011 or 399-5586). From late May through September you can take a four-hour fishing trip for $12 for adults or $7 for children, with $2 rod rental. Trips leave the dock daily at 8 a.m. and 1 p.m.

In addition, this company offers six-hour night bluefishing trips from $22 on Friday and Saturday nights. If the lures of Atlantic City tempt you instead, there are also nightly trips to the gaming capital, from June through September, and on weekends in spring and fall; departure times vary, so it is best to call in advance. The round-trip fare is $20, and reservations are required. For those who prefer a sightseeing cruise, this is also the place to come. Boats go out from mid-June through mid-September, Monday through Thursday, at 7 p.m. for 1½-hour narrated cruises; the cost is $5 for adults and $2.50 for children.

For specific information about this resort, contact **Ocean City Vacations,** 1300 Ocean Ave., Ocean City, NJ 08226 (tel. toll-free 800/225-0252). Walk-in information centers are also maintained at the Causeway Entrance to Ocean City, Route 52 (year round), and at the Music Pier, 8th Street and Boardwalk, in the summer months. The cost of a pass for Ocean City beaches is $2 a day or $5 a week.

Where to Stay

Dominating the scene along the beach is the **Flanders, On the Boardwalk** at 11th Street, Ocean City, NJ 08226 (tel. 609/399-1000), a red tile-roofed old-world hotel. Built in 1923, this grande dame was recently refurbished and updated, but it is still a favorite with Ocean City regulars. The 220 guest rooms are outfitted with all the standard amenities including color TV and air conditioning, and offer a choice of twin, double, or king size beds. In the summer season (late June through August), doubles start at $75 per person and that includes dinner and breakfast. At other times of the year, a room-only charge is available from $45 for a double. Guest amenities include a dining room, a full social program, a heated pool, two tennis courts, a shuffleboard, miniature golf, entertainment, a shopping arcade, and barber and beauty salons. Parking is extra, at $3 a day. CC's accepted: AE, MC, and V.

The **Port-O-Call Hotel and Motor Inn,** 1510 Boardwalk, Ocean City, NJ 08226 (tel. 609/399-8812), is a modern nine-story beachfront property, between 15th and 16th Streets. There are 98 guest rooms, some with ocean views and others facing the bay. Each unit has a contemporary décor, a private balcony, air conditioning, color cable TV, a phone, a refrigerator, and complimentary in-room coffee. Doubles start at $105, with bay views, and $125 a day with ocean views. Off-season rates average $60 to $75 per day. Facilities include free parking, an outdoor beachfront pool, a terrace, and a sauna. There is also a moderately priced restaurant overlooking the beach, the Portsider, which specializes in seafood and steaks at dinnertime, with most entrees in the $11.95 to $16.95 range. All major CC's are accepted.

The **Harbor House Motor Inn,** 200 Bay Avenue at 2nd Street, Box 582, Ocean City, NJ 08226 (tel. 609/399-8585), is not on the beach, but on the edge of Egg Harbor Bay, and is the only motel/marina on the bayfront. Open from early April through mid-October, it is a three-story property, and a particularly good location if you want to be near the fishing fleets and boat rides. There are 68 modern rooms, each with air conditioning, color TV, a phone, wall-to-wall carpeting, two double beds, and a balcony or terrace overlooking the marina. Doubles from mid-July to the end of August start at $78, with a three-day minimum, and range from $42 to $72 at other times. Guest facilities include a coffeeshop, a heated pool, a sundeck, and free parking. CC's accepted: AE, Disc, MC, and V.

Where to Dine

Ever since 1917, the **Plymouth Inn,** 717 Plymouth Place and Atlantic Avenue (tel. 399-3730), has been an Ocean City favorite. Located a block from the boardwalk, this restaurant has a Colonial-style décor with antiques and memorabilia from Ocean City's early days. Homemade chowders, sandwiches, salads, quiches, and pastas are featured at lunch, in the $2.95 to $5.95 price range. The menu at dinner includes flounder stuffed with crab, shore scallops, crab au gratin, lobster tails, chicken Cordon Bleu, pasta Alfredo, steaks, and prime ribs (on Friday and Saturday). The entrees, priced from $7.95 to $18.95, with most under the $15 mark, come with salad and two vegetables. This restaurant also serves hearty shore breakfasts, mostly in the $2 to $4 bracket. Open all year, the hours are from 7:30 a.m. to 2 p.m. for breakfast and lunch, and from 4:30 to 8:30 p.m. for dinner. CC's accepted: MC and V.

Booker's New England Seafood House, 9th Street and Wesley Avenue, (tel. 339-4672), is one of the city's newest restaurants. Designed with a fishing-inn motif, this busy eatery is two blocks from the boardwalk. Open for dinner only, the entrees are priced in the $6.99 to $14.99 range, with many dishes under $10. The menu blends fresh daily seafood specials with southern cooking, and includes such choices as stuffed flounder, lobster, deviled crab, Salisbury steak, Virginia baked ham, and fried chicken. Each entree comes with two vegetables; and for 99¢ extra, you can also have unlimited helpings from the salad and hot appetizer bar. Open daily from 4:30 to 9:30 p.m.; reservations are taken for parties of five or more only. There is free parking and a seafood take-out, in case you prefer a picnic by the sea. CC's accepted: AE, MC, and V.

STONE HARBOR AND AVALON: These two resorts share an island called Seven Mile Beach.

On the north end, Avalon is a relatively quiet town, appropriately named after the mythical resting place of Greek heroes. Strong zoning ordinances have protected the beach and the high dunes from overdevelopment; and consequently, there are relatively few motels or commercial enterprises. Avalon is further preserved by the fact that the World Wildlife Fund owns 1,000 acres of meadowland and has left it in its natural state.

On the southern end of Seven Mile Beach is Stone Harbor, a lagoon development of the Intracoastal Waterway and a haven for pleasure boaters. Dating back to 1892, Stone Harbor consists mainly of family homes and rental properties.

The community is best known as the home of **The Stone Harbor Bird Sanctuary,** Ocean Drive (tel. 368-6101), a National Landmark and a prime nesting place for herons. Located at the southern end of Stone Harbor, between 111th and 116th Streets, this 21-acre facility is the only one of its kind in the U.S. that is sponsored by and located within a municipality. Established in 1947, it is home to more than 6,000 birds, including the American (common) egret, snowy egret, Louisiana heron, green heron, yellow crowned and black crowned night herons, cattle egrets, and glossy ibises. Visitors cannot enter the heronry, but can park in a special observation area and watch the birds flying in and out of this natural nesting site, generally in the March through October period. No charge.

While in Stone Harbor, you should also visit the **Wetlands Institute,** Stone Harbor Boulevard (tel. 368-1211), a research facility located on the edge of a 6,000-acre salt marsh. Founded in 1969 to promote an understanding of the coastal and wetlands ecosystem, this attraction includes a visitor center with a wetlands "touch museum," exhibits, a saltwater aquarium, and an observation tower. Hours are 10 a.m. to 4:30 p.m. Tuesday through Saturday, from mid-May to September; and 10 a.m. to 4:30 p.m. Tuesday, Thursday, and Saturday, during the rest of the year. Admission charge is $1 for anyone over 12; free under 12.

For specific data and travel literature about this area, contact the **Chamber of Commerce of Stone Harbor,** 212 96th St., P.O. Box 422, Stone Harbor, NJ 08247 (tel. 609/368-6101).

Where to Stay

An outstanding facility in this area is the **Golden Inn,** 78th Street and Dune Drive, Avalon, NJ 08202 (tel. 609/368-5155), located on the oceanfront in the middle of Seven Mile Beach, two blocks from the city line between Avalon and Stone Harbor. Open year round, this three-story property has 153 units, most of which have balconies. The guest rooms are furnished in a contemporary style, each with a direct-dial telephone, color cable TV, a refrigerator, and air conditioning. Doubles range from $97 to $130 in July and August; from $60 to $95 at other times; and reduced-rate package plans are also available in the off-season. Besides the views of the ocean, the facilities include a well-landscaped setting with a rock garden, an outdoor swimming pool, and parking. There is also an oceanfront restaurant that features sandwiches, salads, calorie-counter dishes, croissantwiches, quiches, and mixed seafood grills, for lunch at $2.95 to $8.95. Dinner entrees are priced at the $12.95 to $24.95 level, with most choices between $15 and $20, and include lobster tails, filet of flounder, veal Oscar, char-grilled steakfish, bouillabaisse, roast duck, and steak au poivre. Breakfast and lunch are available daily from 8 a.m. to 2:30 p.m., and dinner from 5:30 to 10 p.m. CC's accepted: AE, MC, and V.

The **Seaward Motel,** 9720 Second Avenue, Stone Harbor, NJ 08247 (tel. 609/368-5900), is in the heart of Stone Harbor, one block from the beach in a residential neighborhood. Open from April through October, this three-story property has 20 units, each with two double beds, picture windows, color cable TV, a radio, and air conditioning. Doubles range from $65 to $75 in the July–August period; and from $39 to $50 at other times. Two-room efficiency units with kitchenettes are also available, from $78 to $98 in the summer, and from $45 to $60 at other times. Outdoor facilities include a heated swimming pool, a sundeck, a patio, and off-street parking. No CC's are accepted.

Where to Dine

For fine seafood, **Henny's,** 97th Street and 3rd Avenue (tel. 368-2929), is a tradition in the heart of Stone Harbor. There are no ocean views, but the décor is mostly nautical, with an elegant touch including linen tablecloths and a Steinway grand piano. Open for dinner only, the entrees range from $8.95 to $15.95 in price and include seafood platters, filet of baby flounder, deviled crab, local sea scallops, Delaware Bay oysters with pepper hash, and stuffed soft-shell crabs, as well as prime ribs, veal scalloppine, and steaks. Nightly entertainment adds to the atmosphere, and the Ship's Wheel lounge is a favorite with local boat owners. Dinner is served daily from 5 to 10 p.m. from June through September, and on Friday, Saturday, and Sunday during the rest of the year (except closed in December). CC's accepted: AE, MC, and V.

The **Whitebrier Inn,** 260 20th Street, Avalon (tel. 967-5225), is a new contemporary-style restaurant between Ocean and Dune Drives. The décor features light pastel sea tones, pine woods, and skylights. Sandwiches, salads, and light lunch items are available in the $5 to $8 range. The extensive dinner menu features such dishes as lobster scampi, surf-and-turf, prime ribs, veal piccante, and at least four different local flounder choices. Entrees are priced from $9.95 to $22.95 with most under $15, and come with salad and two vegetables. There is live music on Friday and Saturday evenings. Lunch is served Monday through Saturday from 11:30 a.m. to 2:30 p.m.; and dinner from 5 to 9 p.m. Monday through Thursday, and until 10 p.m. on Friday and Saturday. Sunday hours are from 10 a.m. to 2 p.m. for brunch, and from 5 to 10 p.m. for dinner. There is a reduced schedule from mid-September to mid-May. CC's accepted: AE, MC, and V.

THE WILDWOODS: An island known as **Five Mile Beach** is home to the Wildwood area of the Jersey shore. Wildwood is actually not one town but five. Known primarily as a place to party, the Greater Wildwoods attract a predominantly young crowd, although many families also return year after year. The beaches are clean, wide, and free of charge, and the 2½-mile-long boardwalk is lined with fast-food stands, amusements, and rides. Many of the bars are open until 5 a.m. and the horizon is crammed with back-to-back motels, at least 400 of them, offering more than 25,000 rooms.

The focal point of this island is Wildwood, three miles long with a 1,000-foot wide beach, and the home of most of the boardwalk entertainment, arcades, and nightclubs. The other sections are designated as North Wildwood, West Wildwood, Wildwoods-by-the-Sea, and Wildwood Crest. The latter and southernmost portion of the Wildwoods is unique because it features two equally picturesque coasts, with the Atlantic to the east and Sunset Lake on the west.

The Wildwoods are also famous for water sports. If sightseeing on the water is your sport, try the *Delta Lady*, a Mississippi riverboat. It sails daily, June through August, from the **Wildwood Yacht Basin,** 508 W. Rio Grande Avenue (tel. 522-1919), at 10:30 a.m., 2, 7, and 10 p.m. (a banjo cruise). The two-hour boat trip takes in the inland waterway, the bird sanctuary, and other harbor sights. The cost for adults is $5.19, and $3.30 for children.

If you'd like to go fishing or crabbing in the bay, boats are available for rent from **B. and B. Boats,** 560 W. Rio Grande Ave., Wildwood Yacht Basin (tel. 729-6065). All boats are U.S. Coast Guard–certified, and come with fishing and crabbing instructions, a waterway map, nets, and so on. The rental office is open daily from 7 a.m., and the prices start at $41.25 for an eight-hour day or $30.75 for four hours.

Deep-sea-fishing parties also go out each day, April through October, from the Wildwood Yacht Basin, for all-day trips from 8 a.m. on board *The Rainbow* (tel. 522-0881). The catch ranges from mackerel and weakfish to blues, fluke, and drum. The price is $23 for adults and $15 for children. In addition, night fishing trips are available on Friday, Saturday, and Sunday, departing at 7 p.m. The cost is $30 for adults and $18 for children.

Specific travel data about the Wildwoods can be obtained from the **North Wildwood Tourism Commission,** P.O. Box 814, North Wildwood, NJ 08260 (tel. 609/522-4520 or toll-free 800/223-0317); **Wildwood Publicity Bureau,** Box 609, Wildwood, NJ 08260 (tel. 609/522-4546 or toll-free 800/221-1532); **Wildwood Crest Bureau of Tourism,** Nesbitt Center, Rambler Road and Beach Avenue, Wildwood Crest, NJ 08260 (tel. toll-free 800/524-2776).

Where to Stay

Lush tropical gardens surround the **Thunderbird Inn,** Surf Avenue at 24th Street, North Wildwood, NJ 08260 (tel. 609/522-6901), situated one block from the beach. This modern two-story property has a driftwood motif and a Polynesian village atmosphere. There are 76 rooms, each with one or two double beds, air conditioning, color TV, a refrigerator, a telephone, wall-to-wall carpeting, and a coffee-maker. Doubles range from $73 to $85 in the mid-June to early-September period; at other times of the year, rates average $51 to $65. Guest facilities include an outdoor swimming pool, a sun patio, a café, and a lounge. All major CC's are accepted.

The **Beach Terrace,** 3400 Atlantic Avenue, Wildwood, NJ 08260 (tel. 609/522-8100), is located at the corner of Oak Street, one block from the beach. This modern six-story property has 68 units, each with two double beds, color cable TV, air conditioning, wall-to-wall carpeting, a telephone, a small parlor, and a balcony. Open from April 1 through early October, the double-occupancy rate in July and August starts at $91; and ranges from $34 to $68 at other times. Guest facilities include an Olympic-size pool, a patio, and the Rusty Rudder restaurant, which features nightly 40-item all-you-can-eat buffets from $12.95. CC's accepted: MC and V.

The **Newport Motel,** 4900 Ocean Avenue, Wildwood, NJ 08260 (tel. 609/522-4911), is a five-story property at Rio Grande Avenue on the ocean-front. There are 32 modern units, each with color cable TV, air conditioning, FM music, wall-to-wall carpeting, a refrigerator, and a private balcony. Open mid-April to mid-October, the basic motel rate in July and August is $75, and in the off-season it ranges from $35 to $65. In addition, deluxe rooms and two-room efficiencies are available from $86 to $96 in the summer, and from $40 to $85 at other times. Three-night minimums apply for all rooms in the peak season. Facilities include a swimming pool, a guest laundry, and free parking. CC's accepted: MC and V.

The **Adventurer Motor Inn,** 5401 Ocean Avenue, Wildwood Crest, NJ 08260 (tel. 619/729-1200), is located at Morning Glory Road on the beach and beside the boardwalk. Open from April through October, this modern six-story property has 104 rooms, all with ocean views and most with a private balcony. Each unit has air conditioning, color cable TV, a telephone, and a refrigerator. Double-occupancy rooms with ocean views are priced from $99 in July and August, and from $37 to $62 at other times; two-room efficiency units are also available from $100 a day in the summer and from $47 in the off-season. A three-day minimum applies for all rooms in the peak season. Guest facilities include a parking garage under the building, a heated outdoor pool, a beachfront sundeck, a grill room, a guest laundry, and a game room. CC's accepted: AE, MC, and V.

The **Singapore Motel,** 515 E. Orchid Rd., Wildwood Crest, NJ 08260 (tel. 609/522-6961), is a modern 56-room property on the beachfront. As its name implies, it is designed with a pagoda-style façade, surrounded by Japanese gardens, pine trees, and fountains. The décor of the guest rooms also has a Far Eastern motif. The room styles range from basic motel to efficiency, with varying views, some oceanfront and others overlooking the pool, street, and gardens. Each unit has air conditioning, a telephone, color TV, and a refrigerator. From late June through September, doubles range from $60 to $120; in the spring and fall, the prices run from $30 to $75. Facilities include a café, an outdoor swimming pool, a game room, a guest laundry room, an enclosed rooftop shuffleboard, and table tennis. CC's accepted: MC and V.

Where to Dine

A classic dining spot in this area is **Ed Zaberer's,** 400 Spruce Avenue, North Wildwood (tel. 522-1423). Started in 1955 with a dozen tables, this popular spot has grown into a 1,000-seat restaurant, with eight dining rooms, four lounges and bars, and its own bakery and butcher shop. The décor is an attraction in itself, with more than 300 authentic Tiffany lamps, antique stained-glass wall panels, art works from around the world, French tapestries, theatrical posters, animated animals, and toys. Open for dinner only, from mid-May to mid-September, the menu offers a blend of seafood including lobster Newburg, soft-shell crabs, rock lobsters, and king crab legs, as well as meat dishes from "down south," such as ribs and barbecue chicken. Other selections range from vegetable platters to baked capon, duckling, and prime ribs. Entrees, priced from $8.95 to $21.95, with most under the $15 mark, come with a relish tray, salad, potato, and vegetable. Hours for dinner are from 4 to 10 p.m. daily. CC's accepted: AE, D, MC, and V.

Bay views are part of the attraction at **Urie's Fish Fry Restaurant,** 588 W.

Rio Grande Avenue, Wildwood (tel. 522-4947), a shore favorite for more than 30 years. Located over the bridge, at the Wildwood Yacht Basin, this dockside restaurant offers a lot more than a "fish fry." Dinner entrees include baked bluefish, broiled stuffed shrimp, steamed snow-crab legs, baked stuffed lobster tail, shrimp tempura, lobster Thermidor, scrod Oscar, and cioppino. Steaks and prime ribs are also available. Main courses range in price from $9.95 to $23.95, with most choices under $15; a salad and two vegetables accompany all orders. Lunch items focus mainly on salads, sandwiches, and light entrees, in the $5 to $10 bracket. Open daily from Mother's Day through September, from 11 a.m. to 2 a.m. Urie's also provides complimentary docking facilities if you arrive by boat. All major CC's are accepted.

The success of Urie's Fish Fry led to the recent opening of **Urie's Reef and Beef,** 448 W. Rio Grande Avenue, Wildwood (tel. 522-7761). This restaurant, open year round, is more formal, with a tropical garden atmosphere. Lunch items, which are priced mostly in the $5 to $10 bracket, focus on sandwiches, salads, and light dishes. Dinner entrees cost between $11.95 and $23.95, with most under $15. The menu includes the namesake dish "reef and beef" (stuffed lobster tail and filet mignon), as well as lobster and shrimp marinara; jumbo shrimp and scallops mornay; crab au gratin; filet of flounder au gratin; filet of sea trout; lobster tails; fishermen's platters; prime ribs, steaks, chicken, and veal. All main courses come with salad, potato, and vegetable. Open daily all year, from noon to 10 p.m. in the summer, and from 4 to 9 p.m. for dinner in the off-season. All major CC's are accepted.

Cajun and Italian cuisines are featured at **Seasons,** 222 E. Schellenger Avenue, Wildwood (tel. 522-4400), a restaurant in midcity without a view, but with a décor that conveys a yachty ambience. Salads, burgers, omelets, and sandwiches are the focus at lunch, in the $2.95 to $5.95 price range. The versatile menu at dinner, priced from $7.95 to $22.95, emphasizes Cajun blackened seafood and steaks, as well as such Italian specialties as flounder francese, scampi, lobster fra diavolo, and eight different veal dishes. All entrees come with salad, vegetable, and potato or pasta. Open daily (except Monday), lunch is served from noon to 3 p.m.; and dinner from 4:30 to 9:30 p.m., except Sunday, when hours are 3 to 9:30 p.m. All major CC's are accepted.

The best place to see the sun go down on Sunset Lake is the **Mariner Inn,** 8100 Bayview Drive, Wildwood Crest (tel. 522-1287), off St. Paul Avenue in an idyllic setting overlooking the lakefront. Open for dinner only, entrees are priced from $7.95 to $25.95 with most items between $10 and $15. The selections include farm-fresh turkey, spring chicken, prime ribs, surf and turf, steaks, and a wide variety of seafood, such as Jersey flounder, swordfish, scampi, and jumbo lobster tails. If you dine between 4:30 and 6 p.m., you can catch the early-bird specials, offering complete dinners from $5.95 to $10.95. Open daily, from 4:30 to 9:30 p.m., with a reduced schedule in the spring and fall. Major CC's are accepted.

Nightlife

Among the hundreds of Wildwood clubs and bars that vie for attention during the summer months, you may wish to start with **Cozy Morley's Famous Club Avalon,** Spruce and New Jersey Avenues, North Wildwood (tel. 729-2210), known for its music and name entertainment. Nearby is the **Red Garter,** Spruce and New Jersey Avenues, North Wildwood (tel. 522-7414), a haven for ragtime banjo playing.

Entertainment and dancing are on tap nightly at **Urie's Porthole Lounge,** 588 W. Rio Grande Avenue (tel. 522-4947), and **The Pegleg Parrot Lounge,** 448 W. Rio Grande Avenue (tel. 522-7761).

Chapter XVI

ATLANTIC CITY

AS THE NATION'S MOST VISITED DESTINATION, Atlantic City welcomes approximately 30 million people a year. Although this beachfront resort has been a leading Jersey Shore vacation spot for well over a hundred years, the credit for the most recent growth in tourism goes beyond beautiful beaches and a landmark boardwalk.

Atlantic City's official rebirth came on Election Day, November of 1976, with the passage of the casino-gambling referendum. Since then, 12 high-rise casino hotels have sprouted up, over 1,300 gaming tables have been rolled in, more than 18,000 slot machines are in use, and 42,000 jobs have been created in the area. Now a city that never sleeps, Atlantic City is working hard to be the "nation's playground."

1. Introduction

Located on Absecon Island, in a sheltered strip of land warmed by the Gulf Stream, Atlantic City is not the most accessible mecca for travelers. It is totally offshore, separated from the mainland by bays, inlets, and marshes, and connected only by man-made bridges and roadways. To this day, the best way to reach the island is by car or bus. Rail service, which was suspended in 1982, is currently being reactivated, but regularly scheduled air service by major carriers is still surprisingly absent. No doubt, some enterprising airline will shortly seize the opportunity and then others will be quick to follow, perhaps by the time you read this.

In spite of its location, Atlantic City has been attracting visitors to its white and wide sandy beaches since 1854 when it became an incorporated village. It

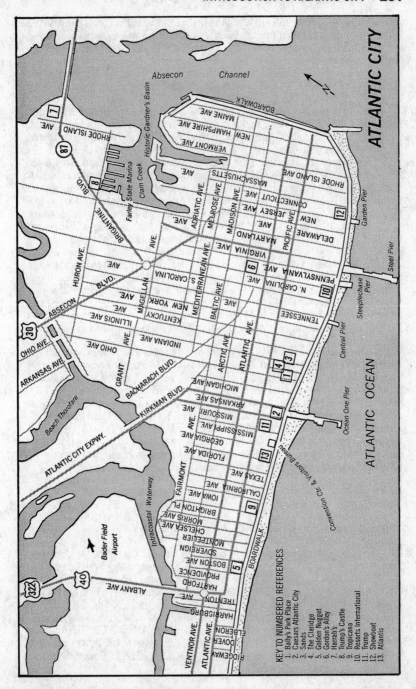

ATLANTIC CITY

Absecon Channel

N

BOARDWALK

MAINE AVE.
NEW HAMPSHIRE AVE.
VERMONT AVE.
RHODE ISLAND AVE.
MASSACHUSETTS
ADRIATIC AVE.
MELROSE AVE.
CONNECTICUT AVE.
NEW JERSEY AVE.
MADISON AVE.
MARYLAND AVE.
DELAWARE AVE.
PACIFIC AVE.
VIRGINIA AVE.
PENNSYLVANIA AVE.
N. CAROLINA AVE.
S. CAROLINA AVE.
MEDITERRANEAN AVE.
TENNESSEE AVE.
BALTIC AVE.
NEW YORK AVE.
KENTUCKY AVE.
ARCTIC AVE.
ATLANTIC AVE.
INDIANA AVE.
ILLINOIS AVE.
MICHIGAN AVE.
ARKANSAS AVE.
MISSOURI AVE.
MISSISSIPPI AVE.
GEORGIA AVE.
FLORIDA AVE.
TEXAS AVE.
CALIFORNIA AVE.
IOWA AVE.
BRIGHTON Pl.
MORRIS AVE.
CHELSEA AVE.
MONTPELIER AVE.
SOVEREIGN AVE.
BOSTON AVE.
PROVIDENCE AVE.
HARTFORD AVE.
TRENTON AVE.
HARRISBURG
RIDGEWAY
DOVER AVE.
ELBERON
VENTNOR AVE.
ATLANTIC AVE.
ALBANY AVE.
FAIRMONT AVE.
GRANT AVE.
BACHARACH BLVD.
KIRKMAN BLVD.
MAGELLAN AVE.
HURON AVE.
ABSECON BLVD.
BRIGANTINE BLVD.
RHODE ISLAND AVE.
OHIO AVE.
ARKANSAS AVE.
BEACH Thorofare
ATLANTIC CITY EXPWY.
Intracoastal Waterway
Bader Field Airport
ALBANY AVE.

BOARDWALK

Historic Gardner's Basin
Farley State Marina
Clam Creek

Steel Pier
Garden Pier
Steeplechase Pier
Central Pier
Ocean One Pier
Convention Ctr. & Visitors Bureau

ATLANTIC OCEAN

30
40
322
187

1 2 3 4 5 6 7 8 9 10 11 12 13

KEY TO NUMBERED REFERENCES
1. Bally's Park Place
2. Caesars Atlantic City
3. Sands
4. The Claridge
5. Golden Nugget
6. Gordon's Alley
7. Harrah's
8. Trump's Castle
9. Tropicana
10. Resorts International
11. Trump
12. Showboat
13. Atlantis

gained worldwide fame in 1870 when the first ocean boardwalk was constructed here, and ever since then, this has been a city of firsts and foremosts.

The first salt-water taffy was introduced here in 1883, quickly followed by the first color picture postcards (1893). Other claims to fame include the world's first ferris wheel (1869), the first amusement pier over water (1882), and the first Easter Parade (1876). The Miss America Pageant, synonymous with Atlantic City, took place here for the first time in 1921.

But life in this city-by-the-bay has not always been a celebration. The area began to decline in the 1930s and remained so until the casino law was passed. Consequently, not all of Atlantic City has been revived to unprecedented heights of glitter and glamour.

The Boardwalk, lined with the opulent casino hotels, may be a showplace, but just a few blocks away, you will find many neglected or abandoned buildings. Gradually, new housing is being built, as the profits from the casinos are being poured back into the municipal coffers. All casinos are required to pay 8% of gross gaming revenues to a Casino Revenue Fund, used exclusively for transportation, health, and housing for seniors and the disabled. Since 1978, more than $750 million has been paid to this fund and nine social-service programs are in operation.

On the whole, Atlantic City (pop.: 40,000) is making great strides toward a total renaissance. The casino hotels are expanding and reinvesting in their properties, and new non-casino hotels and motor inns are springing up within and near the city. The world's top stars appear here regularly in the showrooms and theaters; and cars and buses roll in by the thousands each day. Everywhere you look, people are placing their bets in favor of this magical city and its future.

VISITOR INFORMATION: When planning your visit to this area, contact the **Atlantic City Convention and Visitors Bureau,** 2314 Pacific Avenue, Atlantic City, NJ 08401 (tel. 609/348-7100). This office can supply you with maps and brochures on lodgings, restaurants, and activities. When you arrive in the city, you can also visit the office to collect the latest data on shows and events scheduled during your stay. It's located at the corner of Mississippi and Pacific Avenues, and the hours are on Monday through Friday from 9 a.m. to 5 p.m. If you happen to be in town on a weekend, there is an unmanned visitor center with racks of brochures on the first floor of the Convention Hall, 2300 Boardwalk (between Mississippi and Georgia Avenues).

AREA CODE: The area code for all telephone numbers in the Atlantic City area is 609.

2. Getting To Atlantic City

BY CAR: From the north, the best approach to Atlantic City is the Garden State Parkway to exit 38 and then via the Atlantic City Expressway into the heart of the city near the Convention Center (Missouri Avenue). You can also get off the Garden State at exit 40N (the White Horse Pike, Route 30), which brings you into the north end of the city (Absecon Boulevard), or exit 36 (the Black Horse Pike, Route 40), which comes into town at Albany Avenue, on the city's southern edge. From the west, via Philadelphia, take the Atlantic City Expressway directly into the heart of Atlantic City. From points south, the best route is via I-95 and Route 40 from Washington, D.C. (or Routes 13 and 9 from the Norfolk area via the Cape May–Lewes Ferry).

BY BUS: Every day more than 1,200 buses travel into the **Atlantic City Munici-**

pal Bus Terminal, at Arkansas and Arctic Avenues. The buses come from both the big cities and the small towns on the east coast, and are operated primarily by New Jersey Transit (tel. 344-8181), Greyhound (tel. 345-5403), and Capitol Trailways (tel. 344-4449), although many other charter bus companies also run buses to Atlantic City. Many of the casino hotels also sponsor daily bus trips from New York, Philadelphia, Washington, D.C., and other cities.

BY PLANE: Strange as it may seem, Atlantic City does not enjoy full-scale regularly scheduled airline service. At the moment, the best way to reach this destination from far points is to fly into Philadelphia International Airport. You can then connect with Allegheny Commuter (tel. 344-7104 or toll-free 800/351-0033) into Bader Field Airport, Albany Avenue, a mile south of the city. Similar commuter flights are available from Washington, D.C. and New York.

If you prefer ground transfer, the following companies provide mini-bus or car service between Philadelphia International Airport and Atlantic City: AA Limousine Service (tel. 344-2444); Blue and White Airport Limousine Service (tel. 848-0770); Casino Limousine Service (tel. 646-5555); May's Call-a-Cab (tel. 646-7600); and Rapid Rover Airport Shuttle (tel. 344-0100).

In addition, charter flights operate into Atlantic City International Air Terminal, Tilton Road, at Pomona, ten miles from Atlantic City. At the moment, a new terminal and runway apron are currently under construction to the tune of over $2 million, and it is hoped that a major airline will shortly inaugurate regularly scheduled service into this facility. Check with your travel agent when you are planning your trip.

If you are heading to Atlantic City from the New York area, you can use the helicopter flights offered by Resorts International Air (RIA), Steeplechase Pier (tel. 344-0833). This service operates between Atlantic City and midtown Manhattan's West 30th Street Heliport or Teterboro Airport, NJ. Flights are approximately 50 minutes in duration, on 24-passenger aircraft, and are priced from $89 to $99 per person one-way.

BY TRAIN: Although there is no rail service into Atlantic City at the moment, plans call for Amtrak passenger service by mid-1989. Amtrak is currently laying track for an Atlantic City–Philadelphia line that will interface with the railroad's Northeast corridor route between Boston and Washington. Under the planned rail service, New Jersey Transit and Amtrak will cooperate on daily commuter and express runs between Atlantic City and Philadelphia and on a New York–Atlantic City daily run. The rail service is expected to add 2.2 million visitors annually.

3. Getting Around Atlantic City

If you ever played the board game "Monopoly," you may feel a sense of déjà vu as you stroll around Atlantic City. This is because the famous board game layout was designed by using the street names of this seaside city. You'll see Boardwalk, Park Place, Mediterranean Avenue, and Baltic Avenue, but this time you'll be rolling the dice on the gaming tables, and not using play money!

As in the board game, all of Atlantic City's main streets are called avenues, all named for bodies of water—Mediterranean, Baltic, Arctic, Atlantic, and Pacific. These main thoroughfares run parallel to the ocean. The cross streets running to and from the ocean are also called avenues and, for the most part, are named for states. However, they are not in alphabetical (or logical geographic order), although Maine is in the northeast and California and Texas are in the city's southwest. Just to add to the confusion, not every state is represented and some state capitals are used in the lower part of the city. All streets are logically numbered, however, in blocks of hundreds. The best way to get around initially is to refer to the handy map supplied by the Atlantic City Convention and Visitors Bureau. To get from place to place, here is a summary of Atlantic City's main means of transportation:

Buses: Municipal service is operated by the **Atlantic City Transportation Company (ACTA),** 19-21 S. New York Ave. (tel. 344-8181) covering the length of Absecon Island. You can board a bus at any corner along Atlantic Avenue. The fare depends on the distance traveled, but the minimum is 85¢, and exact change is required. Most bus routes operate seven days a week, and some run 24 hours.

Taxis: Like most major cities, taxis line up at major hotels; they also cruise the streets, allowing people to hail a ride from curbside within Atlantic City. The local meter rate is $1.35 for the first one-fifth mile, plus 20¢ for each additional one-fifth mile, and 20¢ for each additional passenger. The average cab ride is $3 to $4 within the city. If you wish to order a cab, call: **Mutual Taxi Service** (tel. 345-6111); **Red Top** (tel. 344-4101); and **Yellow Cab** (tel. 344-1221).

Car Rental: Among the car rental companies based at Atlantic City and its environs are **Avis,** 114 S. New York Ave. (tel. 345-3350); **Budget,** 37 N. Florida Ave. (tel. 345-0600); **Dollar,** 1401 Absecon Blvd. (tel. 344-4919); **Hertz,** 1400 Albany Ave., West Atlantic City (tel. 646-1212); **National,** Boston and Atlantic Avenues (tel. 344-0441); and **Thrifty,** 2100 E. Verona Blvd., West Atlantic City (tel. 645-1901).

Parking: If you bring your own car or rent one, you'll find that parking can be expensive, so you may wish to stay at a hotel that provides free parking. There are parking lots in various locations throughout the city, with day-long rates that range from $3 to $6 on weekdays and $4 to $12 on weekends. You'll find that rates are at the highest closer to the Boardwalk.

Jitneys: One of the best ways to get from casino to casino or among the restaurants is via the Atlantic City jitneys. These mini-buses provide 24-hour service up and down Pacific Avenue, for the length of the city, in a north-south direction. They also travel from Park Place to Harrah's Marina and Trump's Castle, both located on the bay. Jitneys with a red sign in the windshield remain on Pacific Avenue only, and vehicles with a blue sign travel across to the bay. The one-way fare in either case is 75¢. For further information, call 344-8642.

Boardwalk Trams: For an oceanfront ride, there is a fleet of motorized trams that run along the Boardwalk from Garden Pier (New Jersey Avenue) to Albany Avenue, and return. You can board or disembark at any point along the route, or just stay on and enjoy the trip as a sightseeing experience. Trams run continually from 9 a.m. to midnight (and until 2 a.m. on weekends) in the summer months, and from 10 a.m. to 8 p.m. (and until 10 p.m. on weekends) during the rest of the year. The fare for adults is $1 one-way and 75¢ for children aged 3 to 12. For further information, call 340-6972.

Rolling Chairs: Of all the forms of transport in this city, however, the most famous is the "rolling chair." Ever since 1887, these unique wicker chairs on wheels have been synonymous with the Atlantic City Boardwalk. Often topped by a surrey-style canopy, these mini-carriages are leisurely pushed along by attendants in 19th-century style. Rolling chairs are available for set tours or as a link between casinos. Tour rates for two passengers are $15 per half hour or $25 per hour; the hourly rate for three persons is $30. Casino transfers (up to ten blocks) cost $5 for two people and $7.50 for three people. During the summer season you can hire a chair (and pusher) between 9 a.m. to 4 a.m. daily; winter hours are 11 a.m. to 2 a.m. You can board a rolling chair outside any of the casino hotels along the Boardwalk, from the Golden Nugget at the south end to the Showboat on the north tip, a distance of 30 blocks. No reservations are necessary, but, if you wish further information, call 347-7148.

Bus Tours: In the summer months, **Gray Line Tours,** 9 N. Arkansas Ave. (tel. 344-0965), operates three-hour sightseeing tours of Atlantic City including stops at Margate, historic Smithville, and the Renault Winery at Egg Harbor. The price is $9 per person. In addition, other trips are available on selected days to such attractions as the Great Adventure Theme Park, or Cape May and additional points along the Jersey Shore. These all-day excursions run from $14 to $20; all trips depart from the Gray Line terminal and reservations are necessary.

Boat Sightseeing: The *Basin Queen,* Harrah's Marina, 1725 Brigantine Blvd. (tel. 441-5315), offers one-hour sightseeing cruises of the Atlantic City coastline, with daily sailings at noon, 1:30, 3, 4:30 and 6 p.m. The price is $6 per person.

4. Playing the Games

Whether your favorite game is blackjack, big six, or baccarat, you'll find plenty of opportunities to play in Atlantic City. There are also ample tables for craps and roulette, not to mention over 18,000 slot machines of all shapes, varieties, and payouts.

Each casino has pamphlets or booklets to acquaint you with the "rules of the game." Be sure to ask for a copy when you arrive and study it before you try your luck at the tables.

Atlantic City's casinos are open from 10 a.m. to 4 a.m. on weekdays and from 10 a.m. to 6 a.m. on weekends and legal holidays. The legal age for entrance into a casino is 21. During daylight hours, attire should be casual and tasteful, but no shorts or T-shirts are allowed at any time. After 6 p.m., men are requested to wear jackets and women are expected to dress accordingly.

Here is a breakdown of the facilities available:

Casino Games

Hotel	Total Tables	Blackjack	Craps	Roulette	Big Six	Baccarat	Slot Machines
Atlantis	92	61	16	9	3	3	1,411
Bally's	117	77	22	12	4	2	1,596
Caesar's	114	72	24	11	4	3	1,598
Claridge	85	60	14	8	2	1	1,284
Golden Nugget	93	57	20	10	4	2	1,230
Harrah's Marina	121	80	24	12	3	2	1,717
Resorts Int'l	123	82	20	14	4	3	1,750
Sands	96	62	18	12	2	2	1,439
Showboat	114	75	22	12	4	2	1,628
Tropicana	114	76	20	11	4	3	1,471
Trump Plaza	126	84	24	11	4	3	1,655
Trump's Castle	117	74	24	12	4	3	1,684
TOTALS:	**1,312**	**860**	**248**	**134**	**42**	**29**	**18,463**

5. Where to Stay

THE CASINO HOTELS: Atlantic City currently has 12 casino hotels, with at least another one in the building stage. All of these grand hotels are located in the prime scenic spots of the city; ten of the existing hotels line the Boardwalk (with one more to come) and two are located on the bay side. All of these casino properties opened their doors in the last decade, ever since gambling was approved in 1976.

In addition to a casino, each hotel has at least 500 rooms, a variety of restaurants in various price categories, swimming pools, health facilities, and entertainment centers. With all of these amenities, it is not surprising that rooms are usually at least $100 a night. Furthermore, all hotels in Atlantic City quote one-price rates, whether a room is used for single or double occupancy, and minimum stays of two or three nights sometimes apply on weekends.

However, that does not mean you have to be a big winner to stay in Atlantic City. There are bargains to be found, especially if you are willing to come during midweek in the October through March period. Most hotels offer special package plans, as low as $29 to $49 per person a night, which often include welcome cocktails, some meals, discounts, car parking, and special extras. So, if you request a hotel brochure, be sure to ask for any package rates that may apply at the time you plan to visit.

To avoid repetition, we'll point out only what is different in the casino hotels described below. You can assume that they are all equipped with the standard amenities of a private bath, air conditioning, color TV, and direct-dial telephone, and, in most cases, very plush furnishings. Each property also has one, two, or more cocktail lounges, often with live evening entertainment. All of the casino resorts and their restaurants accept major credit cards. The gambling facilities have been outlined in the "Playing the Games" section.

With regard to meals, the casino hotels usually offer several coffeeshop/deli/fast-food facilities which remain open for breakfast and lunch and sometimes 24 hours a day. Buffet-style restaurants are also popular, and these are normally available for lunch and dinner, from 11 a.m. to 11 p.m. The majority of these eateries fall into the mostly moderate category.

Each casino also has at least one "gourmet" restaurant which is ordinarily open for dinner only (6 to 11 p.m. or midnight). Some hotels have two or three of these top-class restaurants, usually with a theme décor and menu, offering either classically American, continental, French, Italian, or Oriental cuisines. The prices in these top restaurants can be classified as very expensive, with most entrees in the $20 to $30 bracket.

The following summary lists these casino hotels in the order in which they were opened, starting with the trailblazer, Resorts International, which premiered on May 26, 1978.

Resorts International Casino Hotel, Boardwalk at North Carolina Avenue, Atlantic City, NJ 08401 (tel. 609/344-6000 or toll-free GET-RICH), is at the north end of the Boardwalk by the Steeplechase Pier. This 15-story property incorporates the façade of the former Chalfonte-Haddon Hall, a Victorian hotel, and has 686 rooms (518 in the main wing and 168 in an adjoining north tower). The guest rooms feature a modern décor and most have expansive views of the ocean or Boardwalk. Room rates are $95 to $150 a night. With a total of eight restaurants, the top spots open for dinner only are Le Palais, for French haute and nouvelle cuisine; Camelot, which serves English specialties in a setting like a medieval baronial manor; and Capriccio, a gourmet enclave for northern Italian fare. For lunch and dinner, there is the House of Kyoto, an authentic Japanese eatery featuring everything from tempura to teriyaki. More moderate meals can be enjoyed throughout the day at the Pavilion Buffet, the Oyster Bar, the Celebrity Deli, and at a coffeeshop and ice-cream parlor. Other facilities include 15 shops, a swimming pool, a health club, separate men's and women's spas and saunas, whirlpools, squash courts, a video arcade, and valet and free parking for 4,000 cars. In the evening, top stars (such as Dolly Parton, Tom Jones, Julio Iglesias, and Johnny Mathis) perform regularly in the Superstar Theatre and a Las Vegas-style revue is presented in the Carousel Cabaret.

Caesars Hotel/Casino, Missouri to Arkansas Avenues, and Boardwalk, Atlantic City, NJ 08401 (tel. 609/348-4411 or toll-free 800/257-8555), has a Roman flair with a décor of statues, fountains, and white columns, a showroom called Circus Maximus, and a shopping mall known as The Appian Way. The 645 modern rooms, spread out over 19 stories, offer views of the city, pool, or ocean. Rates range from $115 to $155. There are nine restaurants; the upscale dinner venues are the Oriental Palace, for gourmet Chinese cuisine; Le Posh, a tableside continental dining room; Primavera, for the specialties of northern and southern Italy; Hyakumi Japanese, featuring seven-course teppanyaki meals; and the Imperial Steakhouse for classically American steaks and seafood. More moderate meals throughout the day are on tap at the Boardwalk Café, which serves an all-day buffet; Milt and Sonny's Deli; Ambrosia, a garden-style café; and Señor Pedro's, an ideal stop for Mexican platters and snacks. Other facilities include two swimming pools, a health spa, an amusement arcade, a beach club with canopied cabanas, volleyball courts, rooftop tennis and paddleball, free use of bicycles, and valet and self-parking for over 1,000 cars. In addition, the ship-shaped Ocean One shopping and restaurant complex is at the Boardwalk doorstep of Caesar's.

A touch of yesteryear can still be seen at **Bally's Park Place,** Park Place and Boardwalk, Atlantic City, NJ 08401 (tel. 609/340-2000 or toll-free 800/BALLYS-7). Located on 8½ acres of oceanfront property, this modern property occupies the site of three historic hotels, the Dennis (built in 1860 and incorporated into the current structure), the Marlborough (1902), and the Blenheim (1906). Although the latter two had to be torn down, many of their original ornaments and gargoyles were salvaged and blended into the current modern décor of raspberry and grape tones, brass columns, and mirrors. There are 510 guest rooms furnished in contemporary style, some with round beds and mirrored ceilings. The rates are $115 to $145 from July through mid-September and $105 to $135 during rest of year, and include free valet parking. Of the eight restaurants, the two top dinner spots are By The Sea, an elegant seafood dining room which offers panoramic views of Atlantic City by candlelight; and Prime Place, a steakhouse also known for its wide-windowed views of the city and ocean. More moderate all-day meals can be enjoyed at Pickles—More than A Deli, plus an oyster bar, a coffeeshop, a Tex-Mex snackbar, and an ice-cream parlor. Facilities include indoor and outdoor pools, a new $24 million health spa, a beauty salon, two video game rooms, a garage, and open parking for over 1,000 cars. This is also the home of Atlantic City's longest-running show, *An Evening at La Cage,* a female impersonation revue. Bally's is currently adding a 30-story tower of 800 more rooms, due for completion in mid-1988.

The **Sands Hotel/Casino,** South Indiana Avenue and Brighton Park, Atlantic City, NJ 08401 (tel. 609/441-4000 or toll-free 800/257-8580), was known as the Brighton when it opened originally in 1980. A 21-story property, it has 501 rooms, decorated in one of four motifs—traditional, modern, French traditional, and Italian contemporary. The rates range from $95 to $155 from April through October, and $70 to $120 at other times. Dining facilities include a French haute cuisine restaurant, Mes Amis. More moderate meals are offered at Rossi's Italian Buffet ($19.95 for a complete dinner); and for lunch and dinner, try the Brighton Steak House, known not only for beef but also for its Turkish and Weight Watchers specials and Chinese dishes. In addition, there is a Food Court that is comprised of a dozen fast-food eateries from Boston Pizza, Nathan's Famous (hot dogs), and Pat's Steaks to Bookbinder's Seafood and David's Cookies. Amenities include an indoor/outdoor swimming pool, tennis, racquetball, a health club, boutiques, and valet parking for 450 cars. Registered guests also enjoy the use of the 18-hole championship golf course at the Sands Country Club in Somers Point. In the evening, you can see top-name entertainment (from Rodney Dangerfield to Racquel Welch) at the Sands' Copa Room, an 850-seat theater.

If you prefer the quiet of the bay side of town, you'll enjoy **Harrah's Marina,** 1725 Brigantine Blvd., Atlantic City, NJ 08401 (tel. 609/441-5000 or toll-free 800/2-HARRAH). This is a 750-room property, with a 15-story and 16-story tower on a 14-acre site. All guest rooms have bay views, and two floors are set aside as non-smoking rooms. Rates are $90 to $115. The top dinner spots include The Meadows, a gourmet French restaurant overlooking the harbor; Andreotti's for northern Italian specialties; and The Steak House. More moderate meals are available at Marina Garden (open 24 hours), The Buffet (lunch, dinner, and Sunday brunch), The Deli, and The Holiday Food Bazaar for light snacks all day. Facilities here include free parking for 2,400 cars, a boardwalk along the bay, a beauty salon, an enclosed swimming pool, an exercise room, deck tennis, and shuffleboard. A unique indoor sight here is a display of antique slot machines and antique cars. For younger guests, there is a fun center arcade for teens and a supervised nursery for children aged 2 to 8. This is also the only U.S. gaming resort with a 107-slip marina (docking facilities are priced from $20 to $50 a day). In the evening, Harrah's offers the Broadway-by-the-Bay Theatre, featuring such stars as Sammy Davis Jr., Wayne Newton, Andy Williams, and Crystal Gayle. For a change of pace, you can also board a jitney and travel over to the Boardwalk at any time of the day or night.

The most southerly resort on the Boardwalk is the **Golden Nugget Hotel/Casino,** Boston and Pacific Avenues, Atlantic City, NJ 08401 (tel. 609/347-7111 or toll-free 800/257-8677). Opened in 1980, this 22-story property is a glittering Victorian-style palace with gilt columns, gold-foiled walls, gold filigree ceilings, crystal chandeliers, and a white marble lobby. The 522 rooms offer ocean views and varying décors, from summer garden motifs to art-deco or reproduction styles, some with semi-canopies over the beds. Rates are $140 to $175 from mid-May to the end of September, and $110 to $150 during the rest of the year, and include valet parking. The upper-bracket restaurants for dinner include Victoria's for continental cuisine, overlooking the ocean in a Victorian setting; and Lillie Langtry's for gourmet Cantonese dining. More moderate prices prevail at Charlie's Steak House (for lunch and dinner); Stefanos, an Italian restaurant for dinner only. In addition, there is the Cornucopia Café (open 24 hours) and Cornucopia Buffet (for lunch and dinner); and the Sweetheart Café and The Creamery for fast food and exotic desserts. Guest amenities include a health club with an indoor swimming pool, a sundeck, and valet and self-parking for more than 1,900 cars. There is also a 540-seat cabaret theater, The Opera House, which features musical and comedy revues and top-name entertainment.

The **Atlantis Casino Hotel,** 2500 Boardwalk, at Florida Avenue, Atlantic City, NJ 08401 (tel. 609/344-4000 or toll-free 800/257-8672), opened in 1981 as the Playboy's Hotel and Casino, and was renamed Elsinore's Atlantis in 1984. With a décor of brass and glass, this hotel is adjacent to the convention hall, in the middle of the casino hotel strip. There are 500 modern bedrooms, with rates from $95 to $105 on weekdays and from $115 to $125 on weekends. The top restaurants for dinner include Jeanne's, an elegant enclave serving continental and American cuisines; the Empress, serving Cantonese, Mandarin, Szechuan, and Hunan cooking in a setting of traditional Chinese architecture; and The Golden Steer, a steak and lobster house. All-day eating spots include the 24-hour Garden State Cafe overlooking the Boardwalk, the cafeteria-style Galley, and Le Club, for gourmet snacks. Facilities include a swimming pool, a health club, saunas, steam rooms, racquetball courts, free parking (valet or self) for 1,400 cars, and a cabaret theater which presents musical variety shows and headliner entertainment.

Del Webb's Claridge Casino Hotel, Indiana Avenue at Boardwalk, Atlantic City, NJ 08401 (tel. 609/340-3400 or toll-free 800/257-8585), is an expanded and updated version of an earlier hotel built in 1930. While offering every modern amenity, the current version retains much of the original appearance and character, with a décor dominated by dark woods, rich reds, and crystal chandeliers. Set back slightly from the Boardwalk, this 24-story hotel overlooks the gardens of Park Place while still enjoying unobstructed ocean views. There are 504 rooms, modernized with designer draperies, spreads, and sleek new furniture. Rates range from $95 to $105 on weekdays and $115 to $125 on weekends. The top restaurant is Le Pavilion, a gracious French Provincial setting with a menu featuring French/new American cuisine. In addition, there is the Twenties Supper Club for mesquite-grilled food; Garden Room for 24-hour service; the Stadium Deli; Wally's, a coffeeshop open for lunch and dinner; and the Great American Buffet, offering regional specialties from 11 a.m. to 11 p.m. at moderate prices. Facilities include an enclosed swimming pool, a sundeck, a health club, men's and women's spas, a hair salon, and free valet parking for 831 cars. At night, the Palace Theatre stages productions of hit Broadway shows, and the Celebrity Cabaret Room features new stars in a nightclub setting.

The **Tropicana,** Boardwalk at Iowa Avenue, Atlantic City, NJ 08401 (tel. 609/340-4000 or toll-free 800/THE-TROP), is in the process of changing and expanding. At the moment, there are 513 modern rooms, priced from $100 to $135 a night. However, thanks to a $200 million development (expected to be complete in late 1988), "The Trop" is adding 508 more rooms, a two-acre Disney-like indoor theme park, to be called Tropworld, four new restaurants, two cocktail lounges, a shopping arcade, and an expanded casino. The current restaurant line-up includes Les Paris, for classic French cuisine; Il Verdi, a gourmet Italian dining room in an art deco setting; and the Regent Court, serving prime steaks in a country-manor atmosphere. In addition, there is Summerfields, a buffet eatery open for lunch and dinner; the 24-hour Brasserie coffeeshop; and the Backstage Deli, open from 11:30 a.m. to midnight. Guest facilities include two lighted tennis courts, an outdoor swimming pool, a fully equipped health club, and free valet and self parking for 2,000 cars. The Trop is a member of the Ramada Renaissance group of hotels.

Adjoining the Convention Center in the middle of the strip is the **Trump Plaza,** Boardwalk and Mississippi Avenues, Atlantic City, NJ 08401 (tel. 609/441-6000 or toll-free 800/441-0909), a 39-story tower, also in the process of an expansion. A total of $50 million is currently being spent to add a new 10-story transportation center called "Central Park" with 2,700 parking spaces and 13 bus lanes, plus new boutiques, and restaurants, all due for completion by mid-1988. At present, this hotel offers 614 rooms, all with ocean views, priced from $100 to $135 on weekdays and $120 to $155 on weekends. Of the seven restaurants, Ivana's is the premier spot, offering East Coast continental cuisine amid plush velvet furnishings, piano music, and orchids. Other upper-bracket dinner choices are Maximillian's, for prime rib and lobster in a mahogany and marble setting; also expensive is the New Yorker, which is also open for lunch and breakfast. More moderate prices prevail for lunch and dinner at Le Grand Buffet, Harvey's Deli, and the Casino Snack Bar. Guest facilities include two tennis courts, a swimming pool, a health spa, a beauty salon, a teen center video arcade and nursery, racquetball, and a current underground valet parking facility for 1,300 cars (free with casino validation). In addition, there is a 750-seat theater which presents top name entertainment.

Trump's Castle Hotel and Casino, Huron Avenue and Brigantine Boulevard, Atlantic City, NJ 08401 (tel. 609/441-2000 or toll-free 800/441-5551), is a 26-story property on 14 acres overlooking the Senator Frank S. Farley State Marina on the bay. Opened in 1985, it is well known for its distinctive 85-foot-long rainbow, a $350,000 multi-hued sign of good luck which caps the hotel tower 400 feet above the guest arrival area, and is visible for miles. The 605 rooms, which offer panoramic views of the city skyline, ocean shoreline, or the marina, are decorated in an art-deco theme, with shades of brown, beige, and green, blondwood furnishings, and marble vanities. The rates are $95 to $165 from mid-March to the end of November and $85 to $135 during the rest of the year. The top dinner restaurant is Delfino's, for continental cuisine in a Mediterranean villa style. For lunch and dinner, there is the Beef Baron, a first-rate steakhouse in the upper price bracket; and the Food Fantasy Buffet for more moderate fixed-price eating. All-day dining is available at the 4th Floor Deli, The Coffee Shop, and the Poolside Snack Bar (May to September only). Guest facilities include a health spa, a swimming pool, five tennis courts, a jogging track, a pro shop, shuffleboard courts, and free parking for more than 3,000 cars. In addition, the King's Court Showroom features a permanent skating rink, surrounded by a 462-seat theater. The current production, *City Lites,* is a 90-minute ice dancing and musical extravaganza.

The newest addition to the scene is the **Showboat Hotel,** Casino and Bowling Center, 801 Boardwalk at Delaware Avenue, P.O. Box 840, Atlantic City, NJ 08804 (tel. 609/343-4000 or toll-free 800/621-0200), now the northernmost property on the oceanfront strip. Launched in April of 1987, this 24-story hotel has 516 modern rooms, with rates that range from $125 to $160 in the July through mid-September period, and from $105 to $130 during the rest of the year. With a striking façade shaped like a cruise ship, this hotel is designed with a Victorian riverboat interior, but the most unique attraction here is a state-of-the-art computerized 60-lane bowling center, which is open 24 hours a day. The main restaurant in the upper price bracket is Mr. Kelley's, an American gourmet spot; other fine-food dining spots include the Ocean Inn for seafood; Casa di Napoli for Italian cuisine; and the Outrigger for Polynesian dishes. For all-day dining in a more moderate bracket, there is a deli, an oyster bar, a snack bar, a buffet room, a coffeeshop, and a Swiss pastry and ice-cream bar. Guest amenities include an outdoor swimming pool, a sundeck, two Jacuzzi pools, a family/youth care center and video game center, self and valet parking for 2,500 cars, and the Mardi Gras Lounge, which showcases New Orleans-style entertainment.

In addition to this current dozen, a thirteenth casino hotel, the $525 million **Taj Mahal** is currently under construction, with a projected opening date of mid-1988. Originally conceived by Resorts International and purchased in 1987 by Donald Trump, this project is reportedly the largest casino hotel in the U.S., with 1,270 rooms, a 5,000-seat theater, nine restaurants, and a huge 120,000-square-foot casino, more than twice the size of any of the existing casinos. The décor owes its inspiration to a maharajah's palace, with a Far Eastern motif. More than 40 minarets and onion-shaped domes, with fiberoptics lighting, illuminate the complex. The overall site covers 18 acres, or approximately the size of three football fields, extending out into the ocean on the Steel Pier. The hotel tower, at 42 stories, is the tallest building in New Jersey.

NON-CASINO HOTELS: Besides the casino hotels, Atlantic City has recently welcomed an array of new hotels and motor inns, located both in the city and on the many access roads. Usually providing shuttle transport to the casinos, these properties offer more moderate rates and packages, and generally have ample free parking. Each of the hotels described below is also equipped with the standard amenities of private bathrooms, air conditioning, a direct-dial telephone, and color television.

A top midcity choice, just a block from the Boardwalk, is the new **Quality Inn,** South Carolina and Pacific Avenues, Atlantic City, NJ 08401 (tel. 609/345-7070 or toll-free 800/228-5151). Opened in July 1986, this 16-story lodging is the first full-service new non-casino hotel to be built in the city since 1963. Erected on the site of the historic Quaker Friends School and Meeting House, this hotel has preserved much of the original 1927 structure and masterfully turned it into portions of the ground-floor public rooms, the multi-level Friends Restaurant, and the cozy Assembly Lounge. The 203 spacious guest rooms offer sweeping views of the ocean and the bay; furnishings are modern, featuring light woods and color schemes of dusty rose, mint green, soft beige, or misty aqua tones, with framed sea-scene prints on the walls. Doubles range from $93 to $105 from July through early September and $80 to $90 during the rest of the year. The old-world Friends Restaurant is open for a breakfast buffet ($4.95) from 7 a.m. to 11 a.m.; lunch specials, averaging $5.95, are available from noon to 3 p.m.; and dinner, with entrees mostly in the $12.95 to $15.95 range, is served from 5 to 10 p.m. In addition, there is an all-day coffeeshop and a game room, and non-smoking rooms are available. With ample free parking for guests, this hotel is located near the north end of the Boardwalk, two blocks from the casinos of Resorts International and the new Showboat and four blocks from the Sands. All major CC's are accepted.

An old-world charm prevails at the **Madison House,** 123 S. Illinois Ave., P. O. Box 179, Atlantic City, NJ 08404 (tel. 609/345-1400 or toll-free 800/4-LUXURY), a 12-story hotel with a Georgian-style façade that dates back to the 1920s. Located a half block from the Boardwalk and opposite the Sands Hotel, this property was completely restored and refurbished in 1986. The 209 rooms, of varying sizes, are outfitted with reproduction furniture, and some have views of the ocean. Doubles range from $95 to $145 in July and August and $60 to $130 at other times of the year. Facilities include a lounge with live evening entertainment, free valet parking, and a mostly moderate restaurant, The Palladian, open for breakfast from 7 a.m. to 11:30 a.m., and for dinner from 6 to 10 p.m. (except Monday). Entrees at dinner fall into the $12 to $20 range. All major CC's are accepted.

Outside of the city, a prime choice is the new **Comfort Inn,** 405 E. Absecon Blvd., (Route 30), Absecon, NJ 08201 (tel. 609/646-5000 or toll-free 800/228-5150), situated three miles from the Boardwalk, in a northeasterly direction. In an ideal setting overlooking the Atlantic City skyline on Absecon Bay, this six-story hotel opened in 1986. There are 200 modern rooms, furnished in pastel tones and blond woods; and non-smoking units are available. Doubles range from $75 to $85 from July through early September, and from $69 to $82 during the rest of the year. Guest amenities include free parking, a shuttle service to the casinos, an outdoor swimming pool, and an all-day coffeeshop. In addition, another new 200-room Comfort Inn, which charges the same rates and offers similar facilities, is located on the southwest of the city. It is the **Comfort Inn,** Black Horse Pike (Route 40), at Dover Place, West Atlantic City, NJ 08232 (tel. 609/645-1818 or toll-free 800/228-5150). The latter inn is three stories and overlooks Lakes Bay three miles outside of Atlantic City. All major CC's are accepted at both inns.

The summer of 1986 also brought the debut of an upscale **Howard Johnson Hotel,** 539 Absecon Blvd., Absecon, NJ 08201 (tel. 609/641-7272 or toll-free 800/654-2677), located about three miles from downtown. It is a modern seven-story tower with 218 modern rooms, many with views of Absecon Bay. Doubles range from $75 to $95 from July to mid-September and $55 to $70 during rest of year. Guest amenities include a free shuttle service to the casinos, free parking, a sundeck, a mini-spa with an exercise room, and a Jacuzzi. In addition, there is an all-day garden-style restaurant with budget to moderate prices and picturesque views of the bay. All major CC's are accepted.

A quiet wooded setting surrounds the **Whittier Inn,** Black Horse Pike, Pleasantville, NJ 08232 (tel. 609/484-1500 or toll-free 800/237-9682), located eight miles from the Boardwalk and near the Garden State Parkway (exit 37). This four-story Georgian-style lodging offers 198 rooms decorated with pastel colors and furnishings reflecting a Queen Anne motif; and non-smoking units are available. Doubles range from $70 to $80 during the late May to mid-September period, and from $50 to $80 at other times of the year. Guest amenities include complimentary continental breakfast, a free shuttle bus, free parking, an all-day coffeeshop/snackbar, and an outdoor swimming pool. All major CC's are accepted.

6. Where to Dine

RESTAURANTS WITHIN ATLANTIC CITY: Atlantic City is rich in fine restaurants, both within the city and in the environs. We have tried to give you a cross-section, spotlighting some of the seasoned traditional places as well as the trendy new spots, with various price ranges and cuisines. Many of the in-town restaurants are either near a jitney stop or provide free parking at dinnertime for their patrons; be sure to check when you phone for a reservation.

The Top Choices

At the southern end of the city, where two main thoroughfares meet, is the **Knife and Fork Inn,** Atlantic and Pacific Avenues (tel. 344-1133). Built in 1912 and run by the Latz family since 1927, this landmark restaurant has a striking Tudor façade with a copper roof and an interior with a clubby and nautical style. The décor includes dark beam ceilings, fish nets, duck decoys, and fish mobiles, as well as a vintage fireplace and lots of leafy plants. Open for dinner only, this popular eatery accepts reservations for parties of four or more only. The menu, known for its outstanding seafood, offers such choices as lobsters, shore platters, bouillabaisse, whole baby flounder, swordfish, and meat entrees including prime steaks and five-ribbed lamb chops. Main courses cost between $11.50 and $20, with most over $15. Even if you're a first-time visitor, don't be surprised if owner Mack Latz comes over to your table to check on how you like the food.

Open from 5:30 to 10:30 p.m. daily; the jitney stops outside the door. CC's accepted: AE only.

Just a few blocks west is **Johan's Zelande,** corner of Sovereign and Fairmount Avenues (tel. 344-5733), a restaurant in a small turn-of-the-century home tucked in a residential neighborhood, just a block from the bay. This is the domain of a top-rated, Dutch-born master chef, trained in Lausanne, and practitioner of his own style of "spontaneous classical" cuisine. The restaurant seats just 34 guests in three rooms amid a Victorian décor of flowered wallpaper and brass candle chandeliers. Open for dinner only, Johan's offers a seven-course fixed-price meal, priced at $47.50 per person. The menu changes each evening, but there is normally an entree choice of filet mignon, veal, duck, lamb, pheasant, or seafood; the other six courses include appetizer, soup, salad, fish, cheese, and dessert. Reservations are a must; open year round, Monday through Saturday from 6 to 10 p.m., and every night from Memorial Day through Labor Day. CC's accepted: AE, MC, and V.

The oldest continuously operating seafood restaurant in Atlantic City is **Dock's Oyster House,** 2405 Atlantic Ave. (tel. 345-0092) between Florida and Georgia Avenues. Owned and operated by the Dougherty family since 1897, this old-world eatery is a showcase of dark woods, etched and colored glass, brass chandeliers, and seafaring symbols such as lobster tanks. Entrees are priced from $12 to $21, with most under $15, for such selections as crab imperial in puff pastry; shrimp scampi; scallops sauté; fried oysters; and lobster tails. Charbroiled steaks are also a specialty, and all baking is done on the premises. Main courses come with a selection of breads and pepper hash. Open Tuesday through Sunday from 5 p.m. to closing; the jitney stops outside. CC's accepted: AE, MC, and V

Another long-time favorite in this city is **Culmone's,** 2437 Atlantic Avenue (tel. 348-5170), at Florida Avenue. Established in 1964, this elegant old-world style restaurant blends Italian, French, and American cuisines with style. The tuxedo-clad waiters are particularly attentive and helpful. Open for dinner only, the entrees are priced from $12 to $23, and include such choices as chicken cacciatore; coquilles St-Jacques; sole Veronique; lobster francese; crab au gratin; rack of lamb; veal Oscar; and a unique surf-and-turf à la Giovanni (veal francese and shrimp scampi). All main courses are accompanied by vegetable and potato or linguine. Open from 4 to 11 p.m., daily during mid-June to mid-September, and six days a week (closed Tuesday) during the rest of the year. The jitney stops outside. CC's accepted: AE, D, and V.

Moderately Priced Dining

Ever since 1930, **McGee's,** 1615 Pacific Ave. (tel. 344-7521), has been an Atlantic City favorite for lunch or dinner. Located between Kentucky and Illinois, this restaurant has preserved its original décor of brick and stucco walls, hurricane lamps, brick arches, and wall lanterns. Lunch, priced from $3.45 to $10.95, offers salads, sandwiches, burgers, seafood, sandwiches, and steaks. Dinner entrees, priced from $9.75 to $17.75, include prime ribs, shrimp and crab Newburg, frogs' legs, filet mignon and crab, deviled crab cakes, and double-thick pork chops. Main courses come with salad or cole slaw and potato or rice. Open Monday through Friday from 11 a.m. to 4 p.m. for lunch, and for dinner from 4 p.m. until closing; Saturday for dinner only from 4 p.m. All major CC's are accepted.

Angeloni's II, 2400 Arctic Avenue (tel. 344-7875), at Georgia Avenue, is known for its Italian menu and extensive wine list (more than 85 vintages). The décor is dominated by a winery theme, with wine racks and cabinets, stone walls, and alcoves. The dinner menu offers pastas from $5.95 to $8.95 (the choices include spinach ravioli, linguine, and lasagne). Main courses, priced from $8.95 to $18.85, range from veal sorrentino (with eggplant, ham, and mozzarella in red sauce), chicken francese, charbroiled steaks, pork chops pizzaiola, surf-and-turf, steak-and-tail, zuppa di pesce, and seafood Angeloni (mussels, shrimp, clams, and scallops over linguine). All entrees are accompanied by salad, with two vegetables, or a side order of pasta. Dinner is served Sunday through Thursday from 5 p.m. to 5 a.m., and Friday and Saturday from 5 to 8 a.m. CC's accepted: CB, D, MC, and V.

Ocean views enhance the ambience at **Duke Mack's,** 2641 Boardwalk at California Avenue (tel. 345-2719), a modern and trendy restaurant that turns into a disco after midnight. Dinner entrees, priced from $11.95 to $20.95, with most under $15, include prime ribs, steak au poivre, lobster tails, veal Cordon Bleu, shrimp fra diavolo, scallops fettuccine, and king-crab legs. All dishes are accompanied by a salad and pasta. Dinner is served from 5 to 11 p.m. daily; light lunches are also available from noon to 3 p.m. The jitney stops a half block away. CC's accepted: AE, MC, and V.

A wall mural map of Italy dominates the décor at **Scannicchio's,** 119 S. California Ave. (tel. 348-6378), just half a block from the Boardwalk. This small and newly renovated restaurant offers a varied menu of Italian specialties including a wide range of pasta dishes, such as cheese ravioli, ziti with asparagus, fettuccine, and gnocchi, priced from $5.95 to $12.95. Entrees cost $9.95 to $22.95, with most under $15, and include stuffed calamari, shrimp parmigiana, flounder florentine, lobster francese, chicken with sausage and peppers, steaks, and at least nine veal choices. There is a jitney stop half a block away. Open Monday through Saturday from 4 to 11 p.m., and on Sunday from 3 to 11 p.m. CC's accepted: AE, D, MC, and V.

Another favorite Italian restaurant is **Mama Mott's,** 151 S. New York Ave. (tel. 345-8218), a fixture for more than 15 years, in an area that is slowly feeling the prosperous effects of the nearby Boardwalk development. This small family-run dining room has a Victorian aura with period furniture and floral wallpaper. The pasta courses, priced from $5.25 to $11.50, include white or green ravioli; cheese or potato gnocchi; and manicotti stuffiti. The entrees range from $9.95 to $22.50, with most under $15. Specialties are veal saltimbocca; steak pizzaiola; chicken florentine; flounder marinara; zuppa di pesce; lobster fra diavola; and scampi cacciatore. The jitney stops at the corner of the street. Open from 4 to 10 p.m. on weekdays, and 4 p.m. to midnight on weekends. All major CC's are accepted.

A patio garden is the setting for **Aubrey's,** 2024 Pacific Ave. (tel. 344-1632), between Michigan and Arkansas Avenues. This modern glass-enclosed bistro offers light dishes as well as traditional American entrees at dinnertime. If you are not too hungry, you can choose croissantwiches, burgers, salads, omelets, and quiches, in the $3.95 to $5.95 price bracket. Regular entrees, priced from $9.95 to $24.95, with most under $15, include steaks, southern fried chicken, lobster tails, poached salmon, and stuffed flounder. Open from 4 to 7 a.m. The jitney stops outside. CC's accepted: AE, D, MC, and V.

Budget Meals and Lunch Suggestions

The **Delegate Café,** 2301 Boardwalk (tel. 344-5511), is located in the Convention Center, and is an ideal place for light meals. Continental breakfast and lunch are served, with emphasis on bake shop items and deli-style sandwiches, as well as salads, quiches, soups, and diet platters. Lunch items are priced in the $3.95 to $5.95 range. Open from 8:30 a.m. to 4:30 p.m. Monday through Saturday. No CC's are accepted.

To paraphrase an old ad slogan, you don't have to be Irish to love **The Irish Pub,** 164 St. James Place and The Boardwalk (tel. 345-9613). It's a special Atlantic City landmark that no one should miss. The décor reflects a turn-of-the-century atmosphere with dark paneled ceilings, stained-glass windows, bentwood chairs, mounted newspaper front pages, framed old posters, and business cards from previous patrons tacked up at every turn. There is even a Jack Dempsey Corner, filled with sporting memorabilia, and an old jukebox that most often plays "Danny Boy." Lunch items, priced from $1.95 to $3.95, include hearty sandwiches, burgers, and salads. You can also have dinner here, with such choices as Dublin beef stew, corned beef and cabbage, New England flounder, crab cakes, honey-dipped chicken, chili, and sandwiches, in the $3.95 to $5.95 price bracket. Lunch is served Monday through Friday from 11:30 a.m. to 2 p.m.; dinner Monday through Friday from 2 to 6 a.m., and on Saturday and Sunday from 11:30 a.m. to 6 a.m. The jitney stops half a block away. No CC's are accepted.

Ever since 1946, visitors and locals alike have flocked to the **White House Sub Shop,** 2301 Arctic Avenue (tel. 345-8599), the ideal place to try one of the famous Atlantic City submarine-shaped overstuffed sandwiches. Located at the corner of Mississippi Avenue, this busy restaurant claims to have sold over 12 million of its gigantic specialties in the past four decades, and, when you try one, you'll know why. Besides subs stuffed with everything from meatballs and ham cappacolla to provolone and salad, you can also order cheese steaks and burgers. Prices are in the $2 to $6 bracket. Open from 10 a.m. to midnight daily. No CC's are accepted.

RESTAURANTS NEAR ATLANTIC CITY: The out-of-town choices all offer ample free parking (and are well worth the trip).

A Special Experience

If you are going to be in Atlantic City on a weekend, plan ahead by reserving a table at **Restaurant Atop the Winery,** Renault Winery, 72 N. Bremen Ave., Egg Harbor City (tel. 609/965-2111), located about 16 miles west of Atlantic City, off Route 30. This is indeed one of New Jersey's best restaurants on all counts, from ambience and atmosphere to food and service. Located on the grounds of a 120-year-old working winery, this gourmet enclave is open only for dinner. As you enter, a unique ramped entryway takes you through a pathway enclosed by three redwood wine casks that date back a century, via thick oak doors and beveled glass-paneled windows, into the dining area, or "Methode Champenoise" Room, where champagne was once made. Much of the original room has been preserved and restored, including 100-year-old oaken casks which have been fashioned into seating booths. Other furnishings include Oriental rugs and tapestries, Tiffany lamps, rattan fanback chairs, open wine racks on walls, a wine arbor, and a gazebo. You'll be greeted by host and winery owner, Joe Milza, who will show you to your table and present a hand-scripted and picture-framed menu. The meal is composed of six courses, with a choice of five entrees that change each week. The price of the dinner is determined by the cost of the entree you choose, usually in the $19.50 to $25.50 range.

On our most recent trip, the main course choices were ocean perch with bay scallops in a sorrel sauce; lobster tail in pastry with orange butter and Grande Marnier sauce; sautéed veal and beef filets with burgundy mushroom sauce; charbroiled Black Angus sirloin with hollandaise sauce; and prime ribs of beef. Your meal is served by a team of two wait-persons who introduce and describe the makings of each dish. The other courses, which also change weekly, include an appetizer, soup, pasta, sorbet, salad, and desserts (which range from passion fruit cake to pistachio cheesecake). The pre- and post-entree portions are delicate and artfully presented, so that you will not be overwhelmed by too much good food. Best of all, the price of dinner includes red and white wine tastings with appropriate courses from the Renault cellars plus a sampling of the winery's signature product, blueberry champagne (yes, it has a blue tint). You can also order a full bottle of the wine of your choice to sip throughout the meal, at winery prices (from $5 to $9.50). Exotic and standard cocktails, all made with a wine base, are also available at extra cost. A family operation, this marvelous restaurant is presided over by Executive Chef Cynthia Milza, who was recently named Chef des Grillardin by the prestigious Chaine des Rotisseurs. Open Friday and Saturday from 5 to 9:30 p.m., and Sunday from 3 to 7:30 p.m. CC's accepted: AE, MC, and V.

Other Fine Dining Spots

A favorite with the stars who perform on the Atlantic City stages is **The Ram's Head Inn,** 9 W. White Horse Pike, Absecon (tel. 652-1700), located in a grassy setting at the intersection of the Garden State Parkway and Route 30, about eight miles from the Boardwalk. This is a beautiful Colonial-style restaurant with a choice of dining areas ranging from a cozy early-American room with a piano accompanist to a skylit garden-style conservatory and an outdoor brick courtyard. The décor includes a gallery of original paintings by modern American artists, many of which are for sale. Lunch items, priced from $6 to $13, include sandwiches, salads, omelets, quiches, and light entrees such as boned breast of capon or seafood crêpes. The menu at dinner, priced from $11.95 to $23.95, focuses on seafood and traditional dishes such as baked New Bedford scrod, crab imperial in pastry crust, lobster tails, chicken pot pie, crisp roasted duckling, stuffed pork loin, prime ribs, beef Wellington, and rack of lamb. All main courses are accompanied by vegetable and potato. In addition, if you can dine early in the evening, you'll find great value with the "Sunset Dinner" menu on weekdays (from 5 to 7 p.m.). Complete four-course meals are available for a fixed price of $18. Open for lunch, Monday through Friday from 11:30 a.m. to 2:30 p.m.; and for dinner, Monday through Friday from 5 to 10 p.m., on Saturday from 5 to 11 p.m., and on Sunday for dinner from 3:30 to 9:30 p.m. All major CC's are accepted.

A Colonial theme also prevails at the **Smithville Inn,** Route 9, Smithville (tel. 652-7777), situated in a reconstructed village 12 miles north of Atlantic City. Established in 1787, and named for first owner John Smith, this much-expanded restaurant now has eight rooms, with all the trappings of early Americana, and a menu that focuses on authentic South Jersey cuisine. Lunch items, which cost $4.95 to $8.95, include chicken shortcake, crab quiche, and salads. The entrees at dinner are in the $10.50 to $22.95 price bracket, with most under $15. The selections usually comprise oyster pie, chicken pot pie, Absecon duckling, coconut shrimp, stuffed pork chops, rack of lamb, and surf-and-turf. All main courses come with a crudite tray, traditional popovers and breads, preserves and relishes, and potato and vegetable. Open Monday through Saturday from 11:30 a.m. to 3 p.m. for lunch, and from 4 to 9 p.m. for dinner. On Sunday, brunch is served from 10 a.m. to 2 p.m., and dinner from 2 to 9 p.m. All major CC's are accepted.

7. The Top Attractions

Although the medley of gambling casinos, high-rise resorts, star-studded shows, and white sandy beaches would probably be enough to make Atlantic City the nation's number-one destination, this ever-growing city has other notable attractions, not the least of which is the famous **Boardwalk.**

Built in 1870 as an eight-foot wide line of planks on the sand, the Atlantic City Boardwalk was the world's first oceanside walkway of its kind. It was built to allow the Atlantic City vacationers to enjoy a stroll by the sea without tracking sand into the grand hotels of that era. Today it is a much-expanded (now 60 feet wide) structure, built of herringbone-pattern wood, raised well above the sand and supported by steel and concrete. It is now the doorway to major casinos, hotels, amusements, shops, and snackeries. Take a stroll, breathe the sea air, and listen to the voices from all over the world. We think you'll agree that it is truly the benchmark of all boardwalks.

Although the main Atlantic City casino strip covers about three miles of the total boardwalk distance, the complete structure stretches for five miles along the ocean and takes in the neighboring communities of Ventnor, Margate, and Longport. The best way to enjoy the sights, sounds, and smells of this oceanfront path is to walk, meandering at your leisure, dropping into a casino or two, shopping along the way, and perhaps sampling the saltwater taffy and other tempting foods on display.

If you prefer to see the sights on wheels, you can board a motorized tram, or be pushed around via a "rolling chair," this city's unique form of transport, which dates back to 1887.

The Boardwalk also includes a series of piers, which extend out into the ocean and enhance the festive atmosphere. The **Garden Pier,** on the northern end at New Jersey Avenue, is the home of the Atlantic City Art Center, with new exhibitions each month, while the **Steeplechase Pier,** at Pennsylvania Avenue, is a children's amusement area with games, rides, and shops. The **Central Pier,** at Tennessee Avenue, also offers a large electronic game center and a 380-foot observation tower. The former Million Dollar Pier, at Arkansas Avenue, is now a ship-shaped shopping mall called **Ocean One.**

Two blocks south of Ocean One is the **Convention Hall,** 2300 Boardwalk (tel. 348-7044), home of the **Miss America Pageant.** Built in 1929, this recently restored building which seats 70,000 (and is set on seven acres of land), is also a meeting place for many businesses and conventions each year, and the venue for auto races, boat and flower shows, boxing matches, and other sports. In addition, the world's largest pipe organ is housed here.

Moving a block away from the Boardwalk is the **Absecon Lighthouse,** Pacific and Rhode Island Avenues (tel. 345-6328), an imposing 167-foot-tall structure which was first lit in 1857. Now the center of a small park, it once sat at the water's edge, using its beacon to warn sailors away from dangerous shoals nearby. In time, jetties were built to divert the flow of water in the Absecon Inlet, and land was created between the lighthouse and the water. Consequently, the lighthouse itself has been unused since 1933, but the restored tower contains a marine environmental museum, well worth a look. Open Thursday through Tuesday from 10 a.m. to 5 p.m., June through October; and Friday through Monday from 10 a.m. to 5 p.m. during the rest of the year. The museum is free, but admission charge to enter the lighthouse is 50¢ for adults and 25¢ for children.

One of the most famous sights along the beach is **Lucy, the Margate Elephant,** 9200 Atlantic Ave., Margate (tel. 823-6473), about three miles south of

Atlantic City. Originally built of wood and tin in 1881, this giant elephant-shaped building has been used over the years to house a bazaar, a tavern, and as a gimmick by a real-estate developer to draw prospective buyers. Now fully restored, Lucy is a National Historic Landmark. Guided tours of the elephant allow visitors to walk inside and see various exhibits illustrating the giant animal's history. Open weekends, Memorial Day to the end of June, from 10 a.m. to 4:30 p.m.; and from late June through Labor Day, daily, from 10 a.m. to 4:30 p.m.; and until 9 p.m. during July and August weekends. Also open on weekends Labor Day through October from 10 a.m. to 4:30 p.m. Admission is $1.50 for adults and $1 for children aged 6 to 12.

The **Historic Towne of Smithville,** Old New York Road, Route 9, Smithville (tel. 652-7775), 12 miles north of Atlantic City, is a reconstructed 1800s village, now comprised of more than 30 specialty shops, cobblestone paths, a lake, and various Colonial buildings, including a gristmill and smokehouse. There is no admission charge into the village, but you'll probably be tempted to spend a few bucks in some of the craft shops or restaurants. Open daily from 11 a.m. to 9 p.m. in the summer months, with slightly shorter hours during the rest of the year.

America's heritage thrives in a remote part of the nearby Pine Barrens, about 25 miles northwest of Atlantic City, at **Batso Village,** Route 542, Hammonton (tel. 561-3262), dating back to 1766. Once the site of the Batso Furnace and Iron Works, this restored Colonial settlement was the principal source of cannons and cannonballs during the Revolutionary War. It was also the home of the first American glass factory (1846), which produced flat glass for windowpanes and gas lamps. Today you can tour the original furnace site as well as the ironmaster's mansion, gristmill, sawmill, and glassworks. Stroll around and watch craftspeople demonstrating early occupations, such as chair caning, potting, weaving, spinning, woodcarving, and candlemaking. Open from 10 a.m. to 4 p.m., Memorial Day to Labor Day; with slightly shorter hours during the rest of the year. There is no admission charge to the grounds, but guided tours of the mansion cost $1.50 for adults and 75¢ for children aged 6 to 11. During the summer months, you can also traverse the grounds via stagecoach (75¢ per person). From Memorial Day through Labor Day, there is a $2 parking fee.

A landmark of another sort is the **Renault Winery,** Berman Avenue, Egg Harbor City (tel. 965-2111), founded in 1864 by Louis Renault, from Reims, France. Now in the hands of the Joseph P. Milza family, this 1,400-acre vineyard has enjoyed more than 120 years of uninterrupted grape-growing and has blossomed into a leading winery with its own gourmet restaurant (see "Where to Dine"). Visitors are welcome to tour the facilities, including a look at the old and new methods of making wines and champagne. You'll also see a unique glass museum that houses antique champagne and wine glasses dating back to the 13th century. The tour concludes with tastings of award-winning Renault wines, which are red, white, and blue (a blueberry champagne). Hours are Monday through Saturday from 10 a.m. to 5 p.m., and Sunday from noon to 5 p.m. The charge is $1 per person.

8. Nightlife

While it's true that much of the Atlantic City nightlife is centered around the casinos, you don't have to gamble to enjoy this town after dark.

Most of the casino hotels have large theaters and showrooms that offer a regular program of top-name entertainers, Broadway-style plays, or musical revues. The smaller lounges of these hotels also vie for attention with comedy acts and individual up-and-coming performers.

Shows and stars can change weekly, so if you are interested in top-name entertainment, it is best to check with the Atlantic City Convention and Visitors Bureau in advance to see what will be scheduled during your visit.

Here are a few suggestions:

Bally's Park Place, Boardwalk and Park Place (tel. 340-2000), is the home of *An Evening at La Cage,* the longest-running show along the strip (at the moment). It's a female impersonation revue, staged in the hotel's Park Cabaret Theatre. Depending on the day of the week, the show goes on two or three times nightly; ticket prices range from $14 to $17, with a one-drink minimum.

Another long-running revue is the *City Lites* show at the **King's Court Showroom of Trump's Castle,** Huron Avenue and Brigantine Boulevard (tel. 442-2000). This lavish Las Vegas–style production features chorus-line entertainment, magic, acrobats, jugglers, and ice skaters, with two shows a night, except Wednesday. Tickets are $12.50 per person with a one-drink minimum.

Top-name stars and Broadway shows are featured at **Claridge's Palace Theatre,** Boardwalk and Indiana Avenue (tel. 340-3400). Performances are twice nightly and tickets range from $12.50 to $19.50. The **Showroom at the Tropicana,** Boardwalk and Iowa Avenue (tel. 340-4000) also presents headliners, with tickets usually in the $12.50 to $15 price range. Big names also appear regularly at the **Trump Theatre** at the Trump Plaza Hotel, Boardwalk and Mississippi Avenue (tel. 441-6000). Tickets are priced from $22.50 to $27.50.

In addition, **Harrah's Marina,** 1725 Brigantine Blvd. (tel. 441-5000) is the setting for Broadway-by-the-Bay, where recent shows have included such names as Sammy Davis, Jr., Andy Williams, and Crystal Gayle. Tickets are generally in the $20 to $22.50 bracket.

For a change of pace, you can dance to the disco beat at **Duke Macks,** California Avenue and Boardwalk (tel. 345-2719), a restaurant that is open 24 hours a day, with music from midnight to early morning.

Another 24-hour spot is the **Irish Pub,** St. James Place and Boardwalk (tel. 345-9613), where Irish balladeer Peter McDonald entertains every night during the summer and on weekends during the rest of the year. A guitarist plays on Friday and Saturday nights at **McGettigan's Saloon,** 440 N. Albany Avenue (tel. 344-3030), also open around the clock.

9. Shopping

The most famous product on sale in Atlantic City is undoubtedly **Fralinger's Salt Water Taffy,** On the Boardwalk at Ocean One (tel. 344-0442), Kentucky Avenue (tel. 344-1603), and Tennessee Avenue (tel. 344-0758). Established in 1885, this is the oldest name on the Boardwalk. Step inside any one of the shops and you'll find the fourth generation of Fralingers now serving 15 flavors of saltwater taffy, as well as almond macaroons, chocolates, and seafoam fudge. CC's accepted: MC and V.

New Jersey's first pedestrian mall is located at **Gordon's Alley,** Gordon's Alley and Atlantic Avenue (tel. 344-5000). A cluster of 40 shops in a two-block-square area, between Atlantic, Pacific, Virginia, and Pennsylvania Avenues, this is Atlantic City's version of San Francisco's Ghirardelli Square or Boston's Faneuil Hall. You'll find everything from books and antiques to the latest designer fashions and fine arts.

The city's most unique shopping complex is **Ocean One,** The Boardwalk at Arkansas Avenue (tel. 347-8082). Shaped like an oceanliner on a pier that extends 900 feet over the sea, this is a complex of more than 125 boutiques, shops, and restaurants. There is also a video-game emporium, and facilities for shuffleboard, horseshoes, and boccie, as well as lounge chairs on the Top Deck.

10. Sports and Activities

With its location between the ocean and the bay, Atlantic City is ideal for swimming and water sports. All of the large casino hotels have indoor and outdoor swimming pools, sundecks, health centers, fitness tracks, tennis courts, and other sports facilities. The smaller inns and motor hotels usually also have outdoor swimming pools. Best of all, the three-mile-long Atlantic City beach is free and open to everyone.

The Boardwalk is also available for walking, strolling, and jogging at all times. In addition, bicycling is permitted on the boardwalk from 6 to 10 a.m. If you haven't brought your own, you can rent a bike from **H. Longo and Sons and Daughter,** 1133 Boardwalk (tel. 344-8288), or from **Bikeworld,** Michigan and Atlantic Avenues (tel. 345-0077). The rates average $4 an hour and both shops are open daily from 8 a.m. to 5 p.m.

Boating: If you arrive in Atlantic City via your own craft, you can dock at the **Sen. Frank S. Farley State Marina,** 600 Huron Ave. (tel. 441-3600). Rates range from $15 to $80 a night for dockage.

Fishing: The waters off Atlantic City are known for good catches of striped bass, flounder, kingfish, snapper blues, and tautog. Deep-sea fishing also yields marlin, tuna, bonito, and albacore. A fleet of fishing boats that welcome visitors go out daily from the Farley State Marina. A good choice is **Capt. Applegate,** South Carolina and Brigantine Boulevards (tel. 345-4077), who will set up all-day excursions from 8 a.m. to 4 p.m., priced at $18 for adults and $12 for children under 12. Night blue-fishing trips can also be arranged from 7:30 p.m. to 2 or 3 a.m.

Bowling: You can bowl 24 hours a day at the state-of-the-art 60-lane bowling center in the **Showboat Hotel,** Delaware Avenue and Boardwalk (tel. 343-4000). This new bowling center features Brunswick automatic scoring with colorvision, a spectator area, a pro shop, an arcade, and a beverage-snack bar. The bowling fee is $1.80 per game; shoe rental is $1.

Horse Racing: If you tire of the tables or slots, you can always put your money on the horses. The thoroughbreds race at the **Atlantic City Race Course,** Black Horse Pike (Route 40), McKee City (tel. 641-2190), at Route 322, 14 miles from Atlantic City. Open daily from early June to early September (except Tuesday and Sunday), this track charges $2.00 for admission to the grandstand and $3.00 to the clubhouse. Post time is 8 p.m. There is year-round simulcasting from other tracks, and admission to this telebetting is free. Check with the track for details about what tracks are being simulcast.

11. Events

"There she is! Miss America!" If you have heard that tune over the years and wished that someday you could see the **Miss America Pageant** for yourself, why not plan a visit to Atlantic City for the week after Labor Day. Started in

1921, and held without interruption since 1935, this glamorous annual event includes a host of varied activities, such as a powerboat show and a Boardwalk parade, as well as the televised competitions, finals, and crowning of the new Miss America. Ticket prices range from $6 to $16 for most events. For ticket information and a full program, contact the Miss America Pageant, 1325 Boardwalk, Atlantic City, NJ 08401 (tel. 609/344-5278).

CAPE MAY

AT THE SOUTHERN TIP OF NEW JERSEY, Cape May claims to be the nation's oldest (since 1761) seashore resort. Like the dozens of other Jersey shore destinations, Cape May has expansive sandy beaches, a boardwalk, and a string of oceanfront motels. But Cape May is a lot more than sea, sun, and surf.

Thanks to its preservation-minded citizens, Cape May is a mecca of Victoriana. With more than 600 beautifully restored buildings, the entire city of Cape May has been declared a National Landmark.

1. Introduction

Like many points along the east coast, Cape May was first discovered in 1609 by Henry Hudson who claimed it for the Dutch. Credit for the founding of the town, however, goes to Captain Cornelius Jacobson Mey, a Hollander who arrived in 1620, and so enjoyed the area that he bestowed his name on it. ("Mey" was eventually anglicized to "May.")

Captain Mey was the first of many who would sing the praises of this secluded spot. Jutting out into the sea, with the Atlantic Ocean on the east and Delaware Bay on the west, Cape May enjoys relatively cool summers and mild winters. It is one of the few vantage points in the Mid-Atlantic states where both sunrise and sunset are visible over the water.

In the early 1800s, Cape May began to develop as a popular resort, even though it often took two or three days for vacationers from major east-coast cities to journey here by horseback, stagecoach, or sailing vessel. Tourism really flourished by the mid-19th century, with the advent of the steamboat and locomotive. This was also the beginning of the Victorian era, a prosperous time during the reign of Queen Victoria (1837–1901), when a new ornate and showy style of architecture took hold on both sides of the Atlantic.

This Victorian influence brought new buildings with sloping mansard

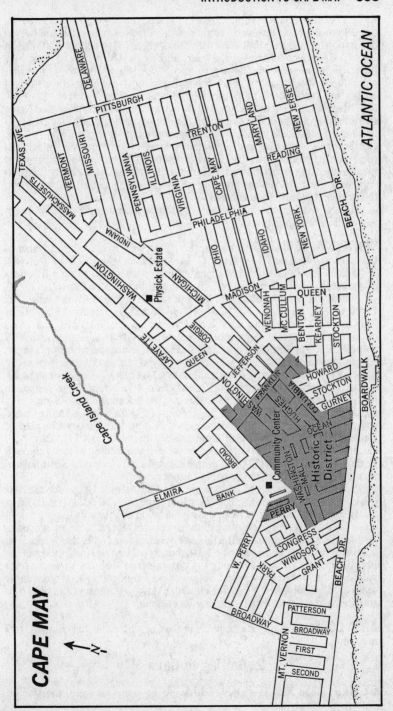

CAPE MAY

roofs, sweeping verandas, bright colors, and intricate flowery carvings that became known as "gingerbread" work because they resembled fanciful baking decorations. Cape May was lined with these whimsical structures, but, alas, a fire in 1878 leveled 30 acres in the heart of the city. The people of Cape May were quick to rebuild, however, and concentrated on the capricious gingerbread-style structures, each one trying to outdo the next. The results, of course, are the hundreds of Victorian buildings that we enjoy today.

Many visitors come to Cape May to walk the tree-lined streets and to see these buildings or perhaps to overnight in one of the dozens of Victorian bed-and-breakfast inns. Thanks to an active preservationist group, the Mid-Atlantic Center for the Arts, visitors can also take guided walks around the historic district, tour the inside of many of these houses, or take a narrated sightseeing trip through the city via a motorized Victorian-style trolley. Other enterprising citizens also offer horse-and-carriage tours or antique-car jaunts, all in keeping with the spirit and style of a gracious era.

It's no wonder that the Cape May population (normally about 5,000) swells to over 50,000 in the summer.

VISITOR INFORMATION: In advance of your visit, contact the **Chamber of Commerce of Greater Cape May,** P.O. Box 109, Cape May, NJ 08204 (tel. 609/884-5508). This office publishes a handy vacation directory, chock full of facts about hotels, motels, bed-and-breakfast inns, restaurants, and activities.

Once you arrive in town, your first stop should be **The Welcome Center,** 405 Lafayette St., Cape May, NJ 08204 (tel. 609/884-3323). During the months of May through October, this is a full-time visitor information office, where you can obtain walking tour maps, brochures, tide tables, ferry schedules, and other helpful data. The staff here also stocks sample menus from restaurants in the city and operates a "hot-line" service to help you find accommodations if you have not reserved a room in advance. The office is open Monday through Saturday from 9 a.m. to 4 p.m., and on Sunday from 1 to 3 p.m. When you are in town, you can also get on-the-spot advice at the **Information Booth** located in the Washington Street Mall, at the corner of Ocean Street. Another good source for walk-in data and brochures is the **Cape May County Chamber of Commerce,** Old Court House, Garden State Parkway (exit 11), Cape May Court House (tel. 465-7181). This office is open year round, Monday through Friday from 9 a.m. to 4:30 p.m., with extended hours including Saturday and Sunday, from mid-April through mid-October.

Last, but by no means least, is the **The Mid-Atlantic Center for the Arts (MAC),** 1048 Washington St., P.O. Box 164, Cape May, NJ 08204 (tel. 609/884-5404). Since its founding in 1970, this organization has played a leading role in Cape May's revival by sponsoring tours and events that promote an interest in Victoriana. MAC administers the Emlen Physick House and Estate, which is an architectural focal point of the city, and conducts walking and trolley tours of the historic district. This not-for-profit organization also sponsors Victorian festivals, and the "theater-by-the-sea" series of performing arts. As a community service, MAC publishes "This Week in Cape May," a summary of all of its own activities and other leading happenings in the area.

AREA CODE: All telephone numbers in the Cape May area belong to the 609 area code.

2. Getting to Cape May

BY CAR: Cape May is at the end (or, to be more accurate, the starting point) of the Garden State Parkway (exit 0). As the parkway finishes, follow the signs into the heart of Cape May (Lafayette Street). If you prefer the local roads, you can also drive southward from any of the Jersey shore points via Route 9. From the west, you can use Routes 47 or 49 and the Atlantic City Expressway, and then southward via the Garden State or Route 9.

BY FERRY: If you are coming from points south, the most direct (and delightful) way to travel is via the Cape May–Lewes Ferry, a 70-minute mini-cruise on Delaware Bay from Lewes, in mid-Delaware, to Cape May.

In operation since 1964, this ferry service maintains a fleet of five vessels, each holding up to 800 passengers and 100 cars. Departures are operated daily year round, from early morning until evening, with almost hourly service in the summer months, starting at 7 a.m. until midnight.

Passenger rates begin at $4 per trip; vehicle fares, calculated by car length, range from $17 to $50, with reduced prices for motorcycle and bicycle passengers. A drive-on, drive-off service is operated, so reservations are not necessary. The Cape May terminal is in West Cape May at the end of Route 9. Further information can be obtained by calling 609/886-2718 (in Cape May) or 302/645-6313 (in Lewes).

Note: This ferry ride can also be enjoyed as a round-trip sightseeing cruise. If you go for the day, plan to spend some time in Lewes on the other side. It's a charming seaport town with a bustling marina and an historic district with houses dating back to the 17th and 18th centuries (see Chapter XX).

BY BUS: Regular service into Cape May, from major cities such as Philadelphia and New York, is operated by the **Cape May Line of New Jersey Transit** (tel. 884-6139). Buses arrive and depart from the corner of Washington and Ocean Streets in the center of the Cape May historic district. Tickets and information can be obtained from the **Village Store,** Victorian Village Plaza (tel. 884-5689). For information in advance of your trip, contact **New Jersey Transit,** McCarter Highway and Market Street, P.O. Box 10009, Newark, NJ 07101 (tel. 215/569-3752 or toll-free in southern New Jersey 800/582-5946).

BY PLANE: The nearest air terminal is **Cape May County Airport,** Route 47, Erma (tel. 886-1500), about five miles northwest of the city. Regular service to this facility is operated by **Allegheny Commuter** (tel. toll-free 800/428-4253) from Bader Field in Atlantic City and Philadelphia International Airport.

3. Getting Around Cape May

The best way to see and savor Cape May is to walk. The streets follow no particular grid or pattern, but, with a small map in hand, you'll find it easy to get to know this charming little city. The beautiful Victorian homes (over 600 of them) are on almost every street, so you'll be delighted at every turn. The oceanfront street, known as Beach Drive, is primarily a 20th-century strip, with a parade of modern motels, restaurants, and shops, although there are still some grand beachfront homes and buildings to be seen.

If you have brought your car, you probably should leave it parked at your guesthouse or motel and do most of your sightseeing on foot. Parking spaces are at a premium in Cape May and meters along the streets and at the beach offer very limited stays (usually 25¢ per half hour) and sometimes even metered parking is restricted to certain non-peak hours. You'll get around a lot faster on foot, and, if you get tired, there are many other ways to see the sights (from trolley rides to horse-drawn carriages and antique roadsters). Cape May is also ideal biking territory, so, if you are so inclined, bring your own or rent one (see "Sports and Activities").

WALKING TOURS: Guided walking tours of the Cape May historic district are conducted by members of the **Mid-Atlantic Center for the Arts (MAC),** 1048 Washington St. (tel. 884-5404). Designed to provide insight into the customs and traditions of the Victorians and their ornate architecture, these tours last about 1½ hours and take in a cross-section of buildings and streets. Departure times vary with the season, but summer tours are usually at 10 a.m. daily, with some additional 7 p.m. tours. The schedule in the spring and fall varies between 10 a.m. or 11 a.m., operating on weekends and some weekdays, so it is best to check with MAC in advance or to consult "This Week in Cape May." The cost is $4 for adults and $1 for children. All tours assemble at the Information Booth of the Washington Street Mall, at the corner of Ocean Street.

MAC also organizes **self-guided tours** of historic Victorian homes, allowing participants to go inside four or five leading Victorian houses, on an individual basis. These tours usually are offered in the evenings, by gaslight, from 8 to 10 p.m. On Monday the tour leaves from the Dr. Henry Hunt House, 209 Congress Place, and on Wednesday from the Emlen Physick House, 1048 Washington Street. Tickets can be purchased prior to each tour at the respective starting-point houses. The cost is $10 per person and $5 for children; and the fare includes admissions to houses and transfers from house to house by continuous trolley bus service. For complete information, contact the **Mid-Atlantic Center for the Arts,** 1048 Washington Street (tel. 884-5404).

TROLLEY TOURS: An informative introduction to Cape May is provided by the open-air trolley-bus tour service. Narrated by knowledgeable driver-guides, these tours depart from the Trolley Station at Beach Drive and Gurney Street during the summer (late-June through August) and from Washington Street, opposite the Washington Street Mall, in the spring and fall months. Three different historic tour routes are offered: the east end featuring Columbia Avenue, Hughes Street, and Ocean Street; the west end around Congress Hall and its environs; and a beach drive, covering shorefront housing, from Victorian cottages to turn-of-the-century mansions. Tours are scheduled daily from 10 a.m. to 7 p.m. in the summer months, with additional "moonlight" rides at 8:30 and 9:30 p.m.; in the spring and fall, the trolleys roll between noon and 4 p.m. only. Each tour lasts a half hour and costs $3.50 per person and $1 for children. Further information is available from the **Mid-Atlantic Center for the Arts,** 1048 Washington St. (tel. 884-5404).

CARRIAGE TOURS: If you'd like to see the sights from a surrey with a fringe on top, contact the **Cape May Carriage Co.,** 677 Dias Creek Rd., Cape May Court House (tel. 465-9854). This firm conducts half-hour horse-drawn carriage tours around the historic district, departing from the Washington Street Mall, at the corner of Ocean Street. Tours operate daily, from mid-June through Labor Day weekend, from 10 a.m. to 10 p.m.; from early to mid-June and in September and October, daily from noon to 4 p.m.; and from mid-April through Memorial Weekend, on weekends only from noon to 4 p.m. The fare is $5 for adults and $2.50 for children, and tickets can be purchased from the driver.

ANTIQUE AUTO TOURS: In 1986, Robert W. Elwell, Jr., a fourth-generation Cape May resident, added something new to the roster of visitor activities in this city—a **"horseless carriage" tour** via his 1928 Model A Ford convertible. Step into this elegant vehicle and roll along the tree-lined streets in roaring '20s style, as Mr. Elwell shows you the highlights of Cape May architecture. This half-hour tour is available continuously from 10 a.m. to 10 p.m., mid-April to mid-May on weekends, and from mid-May through August on a daily basis. All tours leave from the "Horseless Carriage Tours" signpost on Ocean Street (between Washington and Lafayette Streets), on a first-come basis or by prior appointment. The cost is $5 for adults and $2.50 for children. With advance notice, you can also reserve the car/driver for longer trips to Cape May Point, picnic lunches, and sunset/moonlight tours. For further information or reservations for specific times, contact Robert W. Elwell, Jr., Horseless Carriage Tours, 808 Columbia Ave. (tel. 884-7486).

TAXIS: If you need a cab, radio-dispatched service is provided by **Stiles Taxi** (tel. 884-5999).

4. Where to Stay

Accommodations in Cape May primarily fall into two main categories, Victorian bed-and-breakfast inns and modern motels. Inns such as the Mainstay and the Abbey have achieved widespread publicity over the last ten years, and they are usually everyone's first lodging choice, but, between them, they have less than 20 rooms! Needless to say, these two are usually booked out a year in advance, so the Cape May "Welcome Office" is quick to remind visitors that the city has dozens of excellent bed-and-breakfast choices. The office staff is always happy to assist visitors in finding available rooms.

BED-AND-BREAKFAST INNS: Before you race to book a B&B, however, we should warn you that these gingerbread-trimmed and mansard-roofed masterpieces are not for everyone. First of all, with their heirloom antiques and Victorian furnishings, these houses are really not suitable for children. Most inns require young guests to be at least 12 or 13. In general, Victorian B&B's do not have elevators, air conditioning, or in-room televisions and telephones; usually less than half of the rooms in any house have private baths. Rates quoted by innkeepers are for double occupancy; singles are usually $10 less per night. Minimum stays of three or four nights often apply in the summer months. The majority of B&Bs do not accept credit cards, although some do take MasterCard and Visa, and all of them usually require a deposit of at least one night's charges in advance to confirm a reservation. Smoking is generally limited to verandas, and parking is not always provided.

As a rule, Cape May's B&Bs are open from April/May through October/November, although more and more are staying open all year. Rates in the off-season are often substantially less than summer.

The variety of B&Bs in Cape May is a feast for the eyes—all different shapes, sizes, and colors. Each house has its own distinctive personality, but, in the main, they all offer a wonderful opportunity to experience a gracious lifestyle of long ago. Whether you are sipping iced tea on the veranda or enjoying a country breakfast by candlelight, you'll treasure your Victorian vacation days at Cape May. We'll describe a cross section of these inns for you, in alphabetical order.

In addition to the classic B&Bs, Cape May is home to some very fine motels, many located right on the oceanfront. For folks who like a modern décor, air conditioning, in-room TVs, and the privacy of their own bathroom, these properties are ideal. We'll select a few of our favorites for your consideration, and we'll also tell you about a hotel that is in a class by itself, The Chalfonte.

One of the most photographed homes in the city is **The Abbey,** Columbia Avenue and Gurney Street, Cape May, NJ 08204 (tel. 609/884-4506), a Gothic gingerbread three-story inn with a steep mansard roof. Built in 1869 as a summer villa for John McCreary, a coal baron and U.S. Senator, this delightful house was restored by current owners, Jay and Marianne Schatz. It is painted in authentic Victorian colors, both inside and out (even the paint on the fence matches the façade). The name Abbey was chosen because of the building's resemblance to a Gothic church, thanks to its 60-foot tower, which, by the way, offers panoramic views of the town and nearby sea. The typically Victorian décor includes stenciled and ruby-glass windows, gaslights of different styles, Oriental rugs, tufted velvet chairs and sofas, and 12-foot mirrors. The seven guest rooms, three of which have private bath, are furnished with tall walnut bedsteads, carved armoires, and ornate dressers. Open from April through November, the rates are $58 to $88 per night, and that includes a hearty breakfast, on-site parking, and beach passes. Often featured in magazine and newspaper stories, the Abbey is one of the most popular inns in town and is often booked out up to a year or more in advance. For those who are not lucky enough to secure a reservation, the Schatzes conduct tours of the first floor on Thursdays through Sundays, April through October, at 5 p.m. (the cost is $3 per person). CC's accepted: MC and V.

Those who enjoy the sounds of the ocean and the cool offshore breezes enjoy **The Abigail Adams Bed-and-Breakfast By the Sea,** 12 Jackson Street, Cape May, NJ 08204 (tel. 609/884-1371). Located just half a block from the beach, this three-story country inn offers six guest rooms, of which three face the ocean. The architecture is a mixture of Victorian and Federal styles with a flat roof, an open front porch, and a festive front flower garden. With an eclectic all-American décor, this house is full of antiques, chintzes, quilts, and wicker, collected over the years by owners Donna and Ed Misner. Room rates are $60 to $85 per night, with the highest charges for three rooms with private bath. The price includes afternoon tea, beach tags, parking, and a full country breakfast, ranging from scones and soufflés to quiches and cakes, served in the hand-stenciled dining room. Open from April through November.

The **Brass Bed Inn,** 719 Columbia Avenue, Cape May, NJ 08204 (tel. 609/884-8075), is a 2½-story Gothic revival cottage, built in 1872, and used as a guesthouse since 1930. The present owners, John and Donna Dunwoody, bought the building in 1980 and completely restored it, using much of the original furniture, including the 19th-century brass beds that inspired a new name for the inn. Each of the eight bedrooms is individually furnished and named after one of the city's great Victorian hotels of yesteryear; two rooms have private facilities and the rest share bathrooms. The décor includes a medley of lace curtains, Oriental carpets, elaborate brass gas lamps, and Queen Anne chairs; the wide front veranda is a comfortable oasis with large rockers and wicker chairs overlooking the gardens. From mid-June through Labor Day, the rates are $80 for a room with a private bath, and from $50 to $70 for rooms with half or shared baths. The price includes a full breakfast served in the Victorian dining room, beach tags, and the use of a shower/changing area. Rates at other times of the year cost from $5 to $15 less per room. Open all year; two blocks from the beach. CC's accepted: MC and V.

Built in 1890, **Captain Mey's Inn,** 202 Ocean Street, Cape May, NJ 08204 (tel. 609/884-7793 or 884-9637), is named after Captain Cornelius J. Mey, the Dutch explorer who is credited with founding and bestowing his name on Cape May in the 1620s. Strikingly decorated in Victorian purples and browns, this 2½-story structure still conveys the heritage of Holland with its collection of Delft-blue china and Dutch artifacts. Even the breakfasts hark back to the days of Captain Mey—homemade breads, egg dishes, cheeses from Holland, fresh fruits, and jelly made from beach plums, all served by candlelight with classical music in the background. Thanks to the restoration and care of innkeepers, Carin Feddermann and Milly LaCanfora, the inn is a showcase of European antiques, rich oaken woodwork, chestnut-oak Eastlake paneling, leaded-glass windows, and a fireplace with an intricately carved mantle. The ten guest rooms, three of which have private bath, are furnished with marble-topped dressers, walnut high-back beds, carved vanities, handmade quilts, and Dutch lace curtains. Located at the corner of Hughes Street, two blocks from the beach, the inn also boasts a wrap-around sun porch and shaded veranda with wicker furniture, hanging ferns, and Victorian wind curtains. Open all year, the rates are $65 to $90, including full country breakfast, afternoon tea, beach passes, sand chairs, and beach towels. Lower rates in the off-season. CC's accepted: MC and V.

Although there are many motels located right on the ocean, one of the few guesthouses is **Columns by the Sea,** 1513 Beach Drive, Cape May, NJ 08204 (tel. 609/884-2228). Owned by Barry and Cathy Rein, this three-story 1910 Italian palazzo townhouse with Colonial revival accents was originally known as the "great cottage." As its name implies, the façade is dominated by grand fluted columns on its wrap-around porch. The interior décor is equally striking, with 12-foot ceilings, hand-carved woodwork, and coffered ceilings. Best of all, this house commands sweeping views of the Atlantic from most of its rooms and from the rockers on the front porch. There are 20 large and airy guest rooms with tall windows, Victorian antiques, and Chinese ivory carvings; about half have private bath. Rates range from $69 to $89 and include gourmet breakfast, afternoon refreshments, use of bikes, beach badges, and off-street parking. Open May through October, it is at the east end of the beachfront, two blocks east of the landmark Christian Admiral.

Elaborate Victorian woodwork is the keynote of the **Gingerbread House,** 28 Gurney Street, Cape May, NJ 08204 (tel. 609/884-0211), the pride and joy of innkeepers Fred and Joan Echevarria. Dating back to 1869, it was one of eight "cottages" designed by Stephen Decatur Button and built in conjunction with the long-gone Stockton Hotel. In addition to its décor of Victorian antiques, original watercolors, seashells, and leafy plants, this inn is enhanced with many photographs of the east coast taken by owner Fred. There are six guest rooms, three of which have private bath, including a huge master bedroom with its own porch. Rates are $55 to $80 per night, with reductions of 20% to 30% in the off-season. The price includes a continental breakfast featuring homemade baked goods, plus beach tags and the opportunity to sit back and relax on the wicker-filled front porch just a block away from the beach. Open all year.

To many people, there is only one place to stay in town and that is the **Mainstay Inn,** 635 Columbia Avenue, Cape May, NJ 08204 (tel. 609/884-8690). Undoubtedly the best known of Cape May bed-and-breakfasts, the Mainstay has certainly helped to put Cape May on the map as a showcase of Victoriana, and consequently is often booked out a year or more in advance. If you can't get a reservation on your first or second try, don't be too disappointed. You can always visit the inn; tours are conducted at 4 p.m. on Tuesday, Thursday, Saturday, and Sunday. The fee of $4 for adults and $3 for children includes afternoon tea. And just what makes the Mainstay so popular? Built in 1872 as a clubhouse for wealthy gamblers, it is the creation of architect Steven Decatur Button, who was told to "spare no expense." The result is a grand villa of 14-foot high ceilings, ornate plaster moldings, elaborate chandeliers, a sweeping veranda, Italianate windows, and a cupola to top it all off. Now in the hands of devoted preservationists, Tom and Sue Carroll, the Mainstay has been restored to its original grandeur and is furnished with richly ornamented Victorian pieces. There are six guest rooms in the main house, two with private bath, and another six rooms, all with private bath, in an adjacent 1870s summer cottage. Each bedroom is decorated with period antiques, quilted bedcovers, ornate headboards, 12-foot mirrors, and elaborate armoires. To complete the picture, the stately wrap-around porch beckons you to recline on a deep wicker seat or on a vintage chair-swing, while the gardens invite you to walk among their medley of color and fragrance. Open from April through October, the rates are $50 to $90 and include a country breakfast (often featuring strawberry crêpes or quiche Lorraine), afternoon tea, and beach passes.

Nearby you'll find the **The Summer Cottage Inn,** 613 Columbia Ave., Cape May, NJ 08204 (tel. 609/884-4948), an Italianate-style three-story house, owned by Bill March and Nancy Risforth. Another Steven Decatur Button creation, this inn dates back to 1867 and features large first-floor and second-floor wraparound verandas, tall windows, and a cupola on top of the building. Highlights of the interior include a three-story circular staircase, walnut and oak inlaid floors, Victorian furnishings, and lace curtains. There are nine guest rooms, three of which have private bath, which are variously decorated with brass beds, oak chests, ornate floral wallpaper, lacy drapes, quilts, and wicker. Open all year, rates are $55 to $85 and include beach passes, afternoon tea, and creative country breakfasts (with such dishes as marinated melon with blueberry mousse, or sausage cheese crêpe, and savory quiches). CC's accepted: MC and V.

HOTELS AND MOTELS: Cape May has modern hotels, and motels, and, most delightful of all, a restored old Victorian establishment.

A Victorian Charmer

The last of the great Victorian hotels is the **Chalfonte,** 301 Howard St., Cape May, NJ 08204 (tel. 609/884-8409), erected in 1876 and one of the few buildings to survive the great fire of 1878. With its gingerbread arches, verandas, balconies, and pillars, this three-story hotel was the work of Col. Henry Sawyer, a Civil War hero who was released from a Confederate prison in exchange for Robert E. Lee's son, and it hasn't changed very much since. There are 108 rooms, but only 11 have private bath; the Victorian-style guest rooms have neither air conditioning, telephone, nor TV. Located at Sewell Street just two blocks from the beach, this sprawling grande dame of a hotel does welcome children, however, and offers its adult guests lots of activities, such as a classical music series, wine tastings, comedy shows, films, soap-opera theme parties, and other entertainments. Purchased in 1983 by Anne LeDuc and Judy Bartella, the Chalfonte is in a constant process of restoration, and guests are invited to pitch right in. The hotel has gained a lot of attention for its "work weekends" in May and late October when architecture students, specialists, and interested tourists can exchange work for room and board. The Chalfonte's other claim to fame is its restaurant that serves family-style meals, prepared by Helen Dickerson, who has been delighting guests with her down-home southern cooking for 45 years. Helen's country breakfasts include spoonbread, homemade biscuits, fresh fish, bacon, eggs, and kidney stew on Sundays. Dinners feature Virginia ham, roast turkey, fried chicken, deviled crab, and leg of lamb. Open from Memorial Day through mid-September and on weekends until mid-October, doubles range from $96 to $100 with private bath, and from $59 to $98 with shared facilities; breakfast and dinner are included in the prices. There are special reduced rates for youngsters, plus a children's dining room and babysitting services. Breakfast is served Saturday and Sunday, at 8:45 a.m. and 10:15 a.m.; dinner is available Monday through Saturday from 5:30 to 8:30 p.m., and on Sunday from 2:30 to 3:30 p.m. only. Meals are open to people not registered at the hotel, for the additional charges of $6.50 for breakfast and $14.95 for dinner. CC's accepted: MC and V.

Modern Oceanfront Motor Inns

Of the many motels that line the beachfront, one of the best values is **The Montreal Inn,** Beach Drive at Madison Avenue, Cape May, NJ 08204 (tel. 609/884-7011), just three blocks from the heart of the Victorian inn district. This is a modern four-story property across the street from the ocean, open from mid-March through November. There are 70 units, all with private bath, most with two double beds, a telephone, air conditioning, color cable TV, and picture windows. A basic motel-style double without an ocean view costs from $48 to $59 in the mid-June through mid-September period and $23 to $41 at other times. Rooms with ocean views and balconies are $5 to $25 more per night. Efficiency units also available at supplementary charges. In most cases, no minimum stay is required. Facilities include a heated outdoor swimming pool, a sauna, miniature golf, and free parking. The inn also offers a full-service restaurant, The Promenade (direct line: tel. 884-5858), which has a modernized bi-level Victorian décor of aqua and rose tones, gingerbread trim, and views of the water. Breakfasts/brunch choices, priced from $1.95 to $6.95, include omelets, hot apple waffles, French toast, eggs Benedict and florentine, as well as an assortment of salads, pastas, burgers, and croissantwiches. The dinner menu, with entrees priced from $9.95 to $15.95, offers such choices as surf-and-turf, shrimp provençale, crab imperial, shellfish Alfredo, bouillabaisse, chicken Cordon Bleu, veal francese, roast duckling, and steaks. The restaurant is open from Mother's Day to mid-October. Breakfast/brunch is served from 8 a.m. to 4 p.m., and dinner from 5 to 10 p.m. CC's accepted: AE, MC, and V.

Another good choice is **La Mer Motor Inn,** Beach Drive and Pittsburgh Avenue, Cape May, NJ 08204 (tel. 609/884-2200), on the east end, across from the landmark Christian Admiral building in a quiet neighborhood. Open from early May to mid-October, this modern two-story property has 64 units, each with private bath, color TV, one or two double beds, and air conditioning. Doubles range from $74 to $90 in the July through early September period and from $38 to $70 at other times. There is a three-night minimum on summer weekends. Guest facilities include an outdoor swimming pool, a sundeck, a barbecue area, free parking, a guest launderette, bike rentals, and mini-golf. There is also a full-service restaurant, The Water's Edge, with sea views, open for light meals from 8 a.m. to 3 p.m., and for dinner from 5 to 10 p.m. Dinner entrees range from $9.50 to $17.95, with most in the $10 to $15 bracket; featured dishes range from surf-and-turf to chicken Kiev, and crab coquilles. All major CC's are accepted.

One of the best bargains in town is the **Sea Breeze Motel,** Pittsburgh and New York Avenues, Cape May, NJ 08204 (tel. 609/884-3352), two blocks from the beach in a residential neighborhood on the east end. Open from the end of March through October, this is a basic one-story motel with 12 units, each with a tiled bathroom, two double beds, air conditioning, color cable TV, and a mini-refrigerator. There is a small porch area in front of each room with lawn chairs. Parking is on a first-come basis on the street in front of the motel, but there is usually more than ample space for guests in this quiet area. Doubles are $65 in the summer months and from $32 to $55 at other times, with a three-day minimum in the period from July through Labor Day. CC's accepted: MC and V.

The **Blue Amber Motel,** Madison and Virginia Avenues, Cape May, NJ 08204 (tel. 609/884-8266), is a modern two-story property that was completely renovated in 1986. Each of the 40 units has a private bath, two double beds, color TV, air conditioning, and a refrigerator. Guest facilities include an outdoor swimming pool, off-street parking, barbecue grills, and picnic tables. Open from May through September, it is seven blocks from the beach and just one block from the Emlen Physick Estate and other Victorian homes. Doubles are $59 to $69 from mid-July through August and from $28 to $49 at other times; efficiency apartments are available at a $10 additional charge per night. In the summer months, there is usually a weekend minimum stay of three nights, and a per night surcharge of $10 on weekends and $20 on holiday weekends. CC's accepted: MC and V.

5. Where to Dine

Like the lodging choices of Cape May, many restaurants offer the ambience and setting of the Victorian era. In addition, you'll find some very fine seafood houses overlooking the water, and other ethnic specialty eateries.

Because so many people are on the beach or out touring during the day, quite a few Cape May restaurants serve dinner only. Some of the places that we describe below offer lunch. In addition, you'll find a number of cafés, taverns, and fast-food places near the beach and in the Washington Street Mall, the city's main shopping area.

If you enjoy a cocktail or wine with your meal, be advised that some of Cape May's best restaurants do not serve alcoholic beverages, but they usually let you bring your own bottle (BYOB). They'll also supply ice, wine glasses, and whatever set-ups you may need, sometimes at a nominal extra charge of $1 or so. It is always best to check in advance. For a couple of suggestions on where to buy wine, beer, or liquors in town, see "Shopping."

THE TOP CHOICES: The best of European, Asian, and regional American fare can be enjoyed at Cape May's leading restaurants.

Restaurant Maureen, 429 Beach Drive at Decatur Street (tel. 884-3774), is the elegant creation of Maureen and Steve Horn, of Philadelphia culinary fame. Located on the second floor of a 110-year-old Victorian building, this restaurant overlooks the ocean from an enclosed glass veranda. It's a romantic candlelit setting, surpassed only by the innovative new American cuisine that Maureen presents each evening. Entrees are priced from $14.75 to $22, and include such dishes as veal au poivre; farm-raised pheasant in hunter sauce; cassoulet of lobster; filet of fish in parchment; flounder baked with a mixture of lobster, shrimp, and scallops; crab Versailles (with sherry, Dijon mustard, and Gruyère cheese); and filet mignon with a sauce of bourbon and fresh mushrooms. All main courses are accompanied by a salad and seasonal vegetables. Open for dinner from 5 to 10 p.m. daily from Memorial Day through September; weekends from early May until Memorial Day; and Wednesday through Sunday from mid-October to the end of October. CC's accepted: AE, MC, and V.

A fanciful three-story Victorian house complete with cupola is the setting for the **Mad Batter,** 19 Jackson Street (tel. 884-5970). Situated less than one block from the beach, this trendy restaurant offers a choice of dining al fresco on an ocean-view veranda or a shaded garden terrace, as well as indoors in a skylit Victorian dining room. Drawing raves from morning till night, the cooking here is totally eclectic, from Asian and Cajun dishes to eggs Benedict or bouillabaisse. One menu covers breakfast, brunch, and lunch, with prices in the $3.95 to $8.95 bracket for such items as cheese and fruit blini; venezia pizza omelet; seafood frittata; sausage, vegetables, and cheese in phyllo pastry; and crêpes filled with cream cheese and smoked seafood; plus daily specials of quiche, pastas, salads, and seafood. Dinner is equally adventuresome, with most entrees priced from $11.50 to $22.50. The choices include shrimp en brochette with sausage and bell peppers in a Créole mustard sauce; sea scallops baked in parchment with Thai peanut–chili pepper sauce; roasted rack of lamb with goat cheese and Chinese mustard; sugar-dipped chicken with raspberry vinegar, cream, and cracked cranberries; and pan-blackened sirloin of Colorado Black Angus beef. BYOB. Open daily from April through October (except Mondays), for brunch/lunch/dinner, weekdays from 9 a.m. to 2:30 p.m., and weekends from 8 a.m. to 2:30 p.m.; and for dinner from 5:30 to 9:30 p.m. weekdays, and until 10 p.m. on weekends. CC's accepted: MC and V.

You'll dine in true Victorian style at **Alexander's Inn,** 653 Washington Street (tel. 884-2555), a gourmet gem with tuxedoed waiters and a French-influenced menu. The four candlelit dining rooms are the essence of Victoriana with gilt-framed pictures, crystal, lace, antiques, and Oriental rugs. Tables are set in the Victorian manner, with the silverware placed upside down, and coffee is served from a silver pot on a swing. Appetizers, priced from $5.95 to $11.95, include sausage nut strudel; steak tartare; or a sampler of lumpfish caviar, smoked salmon, and brandy-marinated turkey. Entrees, priced from $17.95 to $26.95, with most about $20, usually include veal alla marsala or veal with morels; steak au poivre; Cornish game hen; sweetbreads in puff pastry; and rack of lamb. All main courses are accompanied by salad, intermezzo sorbet, and vegetables. BYOB. Open weekends only from mid-April to Memorial Day and from the end of September until mid-December; and daily (except Tuesday) from Memorial Day to the end of September. Dinner is served from 6 to 10 p.m., and brunch is also available from 9 a.m. to 1 p.m. on Sunday. Overnight accommodations can also be booked here, and afternoon tours of the building, including the kitchen, are conducted at 3:30 and 4 p.m. on Monday, Wednesday, Friday, and Saturday in July and August; Monday, Friday, and Saturday in June and September; and at 2 p.m. and 2:30 p.m. on weekends in October. Major CC's are accepted.

A southern tropical atmosphere prevails at **410 Bank Street,** 410 Bank Street (tel. 884-2127), a restored 1840 drover house, across from the Rotary bandstand. Dinners are served on an outdoor deck and in a garden-style dining room with cane furniture, ceiling fans, and lots of hanging plants. The menu focuses on the cuisines of France, New Orleans, and Cajun country, with most entrees in the $14.95 to $18.95 range. Specialties include mesquite-grilled fish, whole lobsters, and Black Angus strip steaks; as well as Cajun shellfish gumbo; barbecue-glazed chicken; blackened redfish; blackened prime rib; escalopes of veal with fettuccine; and soft-shell crabs with capers, hazelnut butter, and lemon sauce. All entrees come with freshly baked breads and seasonal vegetables. BYOB. Open from mid-April through October, from 5:30 to 10 p.m. Valet parking. CC's accepted: AE, MC, and V.

A restaurant on the water is **A. & J. Blue Claw,** Ocean Drive (tel. 884-5878), north of downtown Cape May overlooking the fishing fleet and docks of the inlet. (In case you are wondering, the initials A. & J. stand for the surnames of the two owners, Axelsson and Johnson). A relatively small dining room with fine linens, hanging plants, ship's wheel chandeliers, hurricane candle lamps, and windows on just one side, this restaurant is more elegant than nautical. Open for dinner only, entrees are priced in the $11.95 to $21.95 range. Specialties include blackened red snapper; seafood kebab (of shrimp, scallops, lobster tail, and vegetables); soft shell crabs; local flounder; Gulf shrimp; and steaks. Main courses come with salad and two vegetables. In the fall, the cuisines of different European countries are featured (from coquilles St-Jacques and cioppino to paella and spanokopita). Free parking. Open for dinner from 5 to 10 p.m. nightly from June through mid-September, and on weekends during the rest of the year (except December and January). CC's accepted: MC and V.

MODERATELY PRICED DINING: The **Washington Inn,** 801 Washington St. (tel. 884-5697), is a restored 1856 plantation house and the restaurant of the Craig family since 1979. Victorian décor prevails in the main dining room as well as in the air-conditioned garden terrace, a newly added and delightful room of seasonal flowers, fountains, fans, wicker furniture, and flickering gaslights. Open for dinner only, the menu blends new American and international cuisines, featuring such dishes as shrimp and scallops fettuccine, crab au gratin, chicken in raspberry cream sauce, surf-and-turf, veal champignon, and veal Betsy (with cheese and wine sauce). Entrees cost between $10.95 to $17.95, with most under $15. Free parking. Open from 5 to 10 p.m. from early March until Mother's Day on weekends only; daily from Mother's Day through September. In the fall, the schedule is Wednesday through Sunday in October, and Friday through Sunday in November and December. All major CC's are accepted.

The **Lobster House,** Fisherman's Wharf (tel. 884-8296), is a top-notch seafood restaurant overlooking Cape May Harbor. The décor is decidedly nautical, and the menu focuses on the freshest of seafood. (You know it has to be good, because the boats pull up right outside the door, and the restaurant also maintains its own seafood store on the premises). Lunch items, priced from $3.95 to $7.95, include chowders, fish stews, seafood salads, and sandwiches. Best of all, you can have your lunch in the main dining room with air-conditioned views of the wharf or on board the *Schooner America,* a tall ship docked beside the restaurant. Entrees at dinner, served in the main restaurant only, are priced from $11.95 to $18.95, with most under $15. The selections range from pan-blackened and herb-crusted red fish to locally caught bluefish, swordfish, and flounder; as well as lobster; crab au gratin; shrimp and scallops en papillote; fisherman's wharf platters (lobster tail, shrimp, scallops, crab cake, filet of local fish, and stuffed clams); and filet mignon. Throughout the day, a dockside take-out service also operates, with outdoor tables along the wharf. Free parking. Open year round. Lunch is served Monday through Saturday from 11:30 a.m. to 3 p.m.; and dinner, Monday through Saturday from 4:30 to 10 p.m., and on Sunday from 4 to 10 p.m. CC's accepted: AE, MC, and V.

Summers, 429 Beach Drive at Decatur Street (tel. 884-3504), is a casual beachside café on the ground-floor level of the same building that houses the more formal Restaurant Maureen. Cape May memorabilia decorates the place, with everything from old pictures to a turn-of-the-century barber's chair and pole, while the cuisine is mostly contemporary American. Sandwiches, salads, eggs Benedict or Rockefeller, pastas, and crab fritters dominate the menu at lunch, in the $4.25 to $6.95 bracket. Dinner entrees, priced from $9.50 to $18.95, with most under $15, include shrimp in coconut with sweet-and-sour sauce; flounder parmigiana; lobster tails; lemon chicken breast; beef ribs; and filet mignon en brochette. All main courses come with potato and vegetable. Open daily, April through October, from 11:30 a.m. to 3 p.m. for lunch and from 5:30 to 10 p.m. for dinner. CC's accepted: AE, MC, and V.

The **Winchester Inn,** 513 Lafayette St. (tel. 884-4358), is a restored Victorian country mansion (1865), with an old-world décor of floral wallpaper, velvet drapes, electric candles, chandeliers, and ceiling fans. Classical music plays in the background and bouquets of red roses are proudly displayed on marble tabletops. A restaurant since 1950, this inn features a homey all-American menu. Lunch, priced from $3.50 to $8.95, includes salads, sandwiches, seafoods, and light dishes. Dinner items cost from $8.95 to $19.95, with most choices under $15. The menu changes daily, but specialties include flounder or monkfish amandine; frogs' legs; shad row with bacon; bluefish filet, chicken fricassee; baby back ribs; and carpetbagger filet mignon (stuffed with oysters and wrapped in bacon). Main courses are served with a relish tray including apple butter, a salad, and two vegetables. Customers who dine between 4:30 and 6 p.m. can take advantage of the early-bird specials, with complete dinners from $8. Reservations are accepted, only if made before 4:30 p.m. Open March through December, for lunch Monday through Saturday from noon to 2:30 p.m., and for dinner daily from 4:30 to 10 p.m. All major CC's are accepted.

In the heart of the Victorian shopping district is **A Ca Mia,** 524 Washington Street Mall (tel. 884-1913), a northern Italian garden-style restaurant in a restored Victorian house. Open for dinner only, entrees are $8.95 to $18.95, with most under $15. Choices include spinach and ricotta ravioli; tortellini with asparagus cream sauce and parmesan cheese; lobster in its shell with a marsala mustard sauce; shrimp in cognac with prosciutto; beef Wellington; Cornish hen with cognac in duck-liver sauce; rack of lamb; and vegetarian dishes such as broccoli and cauliflower in puff pastry topped with cheese. This restaurant also has its own patisserie, which is open separately throughout the day (so save room for dessert). Open from May through October, every day except Tuesday (and Wednesday in May and October), for dinner from 5:30 to 10 p.m.; Sunday brunch is also available from 8:30 a.m. to 2 p.m. CC's accepted: MC and V.

One of the oldest restaurants in town is **Watson's Merion Inn,** 106 Decatur St. (tel. 884-8363), continuously serving the public since 1885. Located one block from the water, this inn has a Victorian atmosphere with candlelit tables, fresh flowers, antique bar, and gilt-framed paintings. The menu is classically American, with entrees such as crab-stuffed flounder; lobster tails; surf-and-turf; honey-glazed ham steak; leg of veal with white wine and mushrooms; steak Dijon; sautéed and brandied chicken breast à l'orange; and Delaware Bay drum fish. The price range is $11.95 to $22.95, with most choices under $15. If you are seated before 6 p.m., you can avail of an "early-bird" complete dinner from $7.95. Valet parking. Open daily from May through October, from 4:30 to 10 p.m. CC's accepted: MC and V.

Pasta lovers are flocking to **Frescos,** 412 Bank St. (tel. 884-0366), a relative newcomer to the Cape May dining scene (1986). Under the same management as the adjacent 410 Bank Street restaurant, Frescos describes its décor and ever-changing menu as "new wave" Italian. Open for dinner only, the entrees are priced from $7.95 to $15.95 for such choices as rigatoni with wild mushrooms, fennel, and sausage; green noodle lasagne with four cheeses; tagliatelle with pesto and sun-dried tomatoes; veal chop with sage; filet mignon marsala; or Norwegian salmon with fresh green herb sauce. BYOB. Open from 5 to 10 p.m., daily during June through August; and Thursday through Monday in April, May, and mid-September to October. CC's accepted: MC and V.

BUDGET MEALS: One of the best values in town is the dinner buffet at the **Huntington House,** 107 Grant St. (tel. 884-5868), a three-story 1878 Victorian house one block from the beach. For $11.95, you can eat your fill of fisherman's chowder, a 30-item salad bar, and at least eight entrees ranging from roast beef and country ham to chicken with Chinese vegetables; Italian sausage and ravioli; fish filets; stuffed peppers; and fried shrimp. The buffet table also offers vegetables, potatoes, corn pudding, macaroni and cheese, and rice, as well as an array of tempting desserts. Soft drinks, lemonade, coffee, and tea are also included in the price. The hours are from 4:30 to 9 p.m. on weekends, mid-May through June and mid-September through October; and daily from July through mid-September. Children under 10 pay $3.95. CC's accepted: MC and V.

Ocean View, Beach Drive and Grant Avenue (tel. 884-3772), is a modern ranch-style restaurant overlooking the beach, particularly suitable for family dining. Lunch items, priced from $2.50 to $6.95, include sandwiches, hoagies, burgers, and salad platters. Dinner entrees cost from $5.95 to $18.95, but the majority of choices are under $10. The menu includes veal parmigiana; honey-dipped fried chicken; roast turkey; Virginia ham steak; filet of blue fish; whole baby flounder; surf-and-turf; and lobster tails. Main courses come with soup or salad, two vegetables or spaghetti. This restaurant also serves breakfast, with most items under $3. Open daily during the summer season, from 7 a.m. to 9 p.m.; check for hours during spring and fall. CC's accepted: AE, MC, and V.

6. The Top Attractions

The benchmark of the restored Victorian homes of Cape May is the **Emlen Physick House,** 1048 Washington St. (tel. 884-5404). Designed by Philadelphia architect Frank Furness and built in 1879, it is a fine example of stick-style architecture, with inverted chimneys and jerkin-head dormers. The interior contains an extensive collection of Victorian furniture, clothing, toys, tools, and artifacts. The house was saved from destruction in the early 1970s by the Mid-Atlantic Center for the Arts (MAC), the Cape May preservationist group. MAC has since opened its headquarters in a small building on the grounds of the estate and conducts tours of the house on a regular basis. From this base, the organization also coordinates trolley tours of Cape May's historic district, gaslight walks to other outstanding homes in the area, Victorian Fairs, Christmas events, and an open-air summer theater series. In the summer months, guided tours of the Physick House are conducted daily, every 45 minutes from 10:30 a.m. to 3 p.m. Admission is $4 for adults and $1 for children. Tours are also conducted on weekends in the spring and fall, but hours vary so it is best to check in advance. (For further information on tours of other Victorian homes, see "Getting Around Cape May").

Two buildings that are historically significant in Cape May are owned and administered as hotels by the Christian Beacon Press and the Cape May Bible Conference. The first of these, **Congress Hall,** Beach Drive and Perry Avenue (tel. 884-8421), was one of the earliest hotels (built in 1812), and was originally called the "Big House." It was changed to its present name when the owner at the time, Tom Hughes, decided to run for Congress in 1828. The current building is actually the third structure built on this site, and it was erected after the disastrous fire of 1878. Declared a national landmark in 1974, Congress Hall is best known because it served as the summer White House for Pres. Benjamin Harrison. Free tours are conducted in the summer months at 4:30 p.m., but you are welcome to walk around at any time and see the magnificent stencil work and restored furnishings.

The **Christian Admiral,** Beach Drive and Pittsburgh Avenue (tel. 884-8471), was originally called the Hotel Cape May when it was built in 1908. This building is significant for its marbled lobby, Tiffany glass dome in the front portico, and stained-glass windows on the staircase. It was used as a hospital by the Navy during World Wars I and II, and purchased in 1962 by the present owners who conduct it as a Bible Conference hotel. Free tours are conducted on Wednesday at 4:30 p.m. in July and August, but you can visit at any time.

The **Cape May County Historical Museum,** Shore Road, Cape May Court House (tel. 465-3535), is 13 miles north of Cape May on Route 9. This bastion of Cape May history is housed in the pre-Revolutionary home of John Holmes, an Irish immigrant who arrived in the area in 1773; the house remained in the

Holmes family until 1935, and is now on the National Register. The exhibits include an 18th-century kitchen, bedroom, dining room, medical room, and collections of china, furniture, and glass. The barn of the house contains a mining exhibit, a decoy collection, whaling instruments, as well as Indian artifacts, a maritime display including some of the famous Cape May "diamonds," and the original flag from the *Merrimac*. This building is also the home of the **Cape May County Historical and Genealogical Society,** founded in 1927. Open from April through December, Tuesday through Saturday from 10 a.m. to 4 p.m. (last tour at 3 p.m.). Also open on Monday from mid-June to mid-September. Admission charge is $2 for adults and 75¢ for students aged 12 to 18.

The area's horticultural heritage is on display at the **Leaming's Run Gardens and Colonial Farm,** 1845 Route 9 North, Swainton (tel. 465-5871), a delightful open-air attraction 17 miles north of Cape May. The grounds encompass 25 separate gardens, each with a different theme, set amid 20 acres of lawns, ponds, and ferneries. In addition, there is a vegetable and herb garden, a cooperage, and a Colonial farm with tobacco and cotton fields growing much as they would have done in 1685. Open daily from mid-May to mid-October, from 9:30 a.m. to 5 p.m. Admission is $3 for adults and $1 for children aged 6 to 12.

A mile north of Cape May is **Historic Cold Spring Village,** 735 Seashore Rd., Cold Spring (tel. 884-1810), on Route 9. Although Cold Spring itself never existed, over a dozen buildings from all over Cape May County have been brought here to depict what a typical south Jersey 19th-century farm village would have been like. Set on 35 acres, this outdoor museum includes a blacksmith shop, a school, a train station, a jail, a nautical museum, an inn, and various shops. In the summer months, there are craft demonstrations, weekend entertainment, antique shows, and military encampments on the grounds. Open early April through early October, from 10 a.m. to 5 p.m. Admission is $1.50 for adults and 75¢ for children aged 6 to 12.

About an hour's drive northwest of Cape May is **Wheaton Village,** 10th and G Streets, Glasstown Road, Millville (tel. 825-6800), an authentic village started in 1790, and the home of the nation's oldest operating glass factory (1806). Here you can watch glass-blowing demonstrations and tour the Museum of American Glass, a building with over 7,000 items on display, ranging from poison bottles to fiber optics. Other attractions include a crafts and trades row, a print works, a tinsmith, a make-your-own paperweight shop, a general store, a potter, lamp workers, decoy carvers, a medicine show, and a train ride. Open daily, April through December, from 10 a.m. to 5 p.m. (except Easter, Thanksgiving, Christmas, and New Year's Day). Admission is $4 for adults and $2 for students.

Another 15 miles will bring you to Bridgeton, a city of 19,000 people on the Cohansey Creek. Founded by Quakers in 1686, this town today comprises New Jersey's largest historic district. It is a mélange of 2,200 houses, taverns, and churches, embracing the Colonial, Federal, and Victorian periods. For self-guided walking-tour leaflets and further information, stop into the tourist information center at 50 E. Broad Street (tel. 451-4802).

7. Nightlife

Compared to the dazzling nightlife of Atlantic City or other neighbors like the Wildwoods, Cape May is relatively quiet after dark. If you are in town in the late June through August period, however, you can enjoy the **Theatre-by-the-Sea,** staged nightly by the Mid-Atlantic Center for the Arts at the Physick Estate, 1048 Washington St. Using an outdoor stage, this is a professionally produced program of plays, with shows ranging from *Deathtrap* and *George M* to *Godspell*. Tickets are $6 for adults and $3 for children and can be purchased at the MAC office behind the Physick house. You are advised to bring your own chairs or blankets to the performance. For further information, call 884-ARTS.

In addition, free music concerts are held throughout the summer at the Rotary Bandstand on Lafayette Street, usually at 8 p.m. Wednesday and Sunday. No tickets required.

The summer months also bring music and entertainment to the **King Edward Bar** of the Chalfonte Hotel, Howard and Sewell Streets (tel. 884-8409). The **Nite Club of The Grand Hotels,** Oceanfront at Philadelphia Avenue (tel. 884-5611), offers music and dancing nightly.

Live jazz can be enjoyed on weekends at the **Old Shire Tavern,** 315 Washington Mall (tel. 884-4700). Another bar that often features live music is the **Ugly Mug,** 426 Washington Mall (tel. 884-3459).

8. Shopping

Shoppers and strollers alike enjoy the pedestrian area known as **Washington Street Mall.** Situated between Ocean and Perry Streets, this three-block span is Cape May's original downtown shopping district, restored and re-created to represent the commercial architecture of the Victorian era with brick walks, benches, and lots of shrubs. Today there are over 60 shops with wares ranging from pottery and prints to pastry, as well as fashions, antiques, stained-glass, estate jewelry, needlepoint work, wicker, brass, nautical gifts, and the unique Cape May "diamonds." If you work up an appetite, you'll also find ice-cream parlors, cafés, fudge kitchens, and fast-food shops. In the summer season, most shops are open daily, from 10 a.m. to 10 p.m.; hours vary at other times of the year.

The other major cluster of shops, called **Washington Square,** is located on a shady block between Ocean and Franklin Streets. These shops are primarily good for crafts, antiques, and Victorian-related items. One of our favorites is the **Baileywicke Leather Shop,** 656 Washington St. (tel. 884-2761), a good source of custom-made cowhide items, vests, hats, leather carvings, bags, wallets, luggage, and sandals, as well as solid brass hardware and antique restoration work. For Victorian furniture, vintage clothing, antiques, and collectibles, try **Midsummer Night's Dream,** 668 Washington St. (tel. 884-1380); while the **Victorian Sampler,** 680 Washington St. (tel. 884-3138), specializes in Victorian needlework kits and patterns.

One of the most elaborately decorated gingerbread-style cottages in Cape May is the **Victorian Pink House,** 33 Perry Street (tel. 884-7345), a photographer's dream (and a painter's challenge). The shop housed inside sells Victorian era collectibles, antiques, cards, and prints.

As mentioned in the "Where to Dine" section, many Cape May restaurants do not serve liquor, wine, or beer, but they welcome you to bring your own, to accompany your dinner. Two centrally located liquor stores are **Collier's,** Jackson and Lafayette Streets (tel. 884-8488), and the **Montreal Liquor Store,** Beach Drive and Madison Avenue (tel. 884-1186).

9. Sports and Activities

SWIMMING: Between Second and Philadelphia Avenues, Cape May has more than a dozen individually named beaches in a row along its Atlantic shoreline. With names like Broadway, Stockton, Grant, and Congress, these beaches usually take their names from the nearby streets which lead to the shore.

One of the city's most popular strands, **Sunset Beach,** is at the end of Sunset

Boulevard, at nearby Cape May Point. At low tide, this beach is a favorite with beachcombers who wade out a quarter mile to search for sand dollars and "Cape May diamonds," semi-precious pebbles and stones of pure quartz. These "diamonds" come in various colors and sizes, and when polished, cut and set, they make most attractive jewelry, and have been popular since early Victorian times.

Like many New Jersey beaches, Cape May requires beach tags, which can be purchased at the entrances to the beaches. The cost is $2 a day for adults and children over 12, or $5 a week. If you prefer not to get the sand in your shoes, most Cape May beaches are rimmed by a boardwalk and promenade.

FISHING: The waters around Cape May yield over 30 kinds of fish, including mackerel, flounder, cod, pollock, tautog, sea bass, fluke, sea trout, porgies, tuna, bluefish, bonito, albacore, and white and blue marlin. Deep-sea fishing trips can be arranged at the **Miss Chris Fishing Center,** 3rd Avenue and Wilson Drive (tel. 884-5445 or 886-8164). Boats go out every day from the end of March to November, and no reservations are required. Eight-hour day-fishing trips depart at 8 a.m. and cost $28 per person, with rod rental $4 extra. Half-day trips, priced at $14, are also available, pushing out at 8 a.m. or 1 p.m.; and night fishing from 7 p.m. to 3 a.m., at $28. The craft used are 70-foot twin diesel boats, with the latest modern electronic fish-finding and safety equipment. CC's accepted: MC and V.

SAILING: You can sail the waters around Cape May on board the 18-passenger *Delta Lady,* an authentic Chesapeake Bay "Bugeye" or oyster schooner, built in 1972, and known for its rose-colored sails. This 65-foot vessel sails from the **Miss Chris Fishing Center,** 3rd Avenue and Wilson Drive (tel. 609/884-1919). On Monday through Saturday, in July and August, three-hour cruises, priced at $22 per person, depart at 10 a.m. and 2 p.m., with a sunset cruise at 6 p.m. In addition, there is a "barefoot cruise," priced at $40, from 10 a.m. to 4 p.m. every Sunday, and includes a buffet lunch. Passengers are invited to lend a hand in hoisting sails and setting anchor. Trips are operated by reservation or by showing up on the dock on a first-come basis. In the spring and fall months, two cruises a day are operated at 11 a.m. and 4 p.m., at the off-season rate of $20 per person. CC's accepted: MC and V.

HORSEBACK RIDING: For travelers who enjoy seeing the sights from the saddle, horseback trail rides can be arranged through **Hidden Valley Ranch,** 4070 Bayshore Rd., Cold Spring, off Routes 641 and 607 (tel. 884-8205). Trails include the Cape May woods, fields, and the beach at low tide, and last from 45 to 90 minutes. The cost ranges from $8.50 to $18, depending on time of day and the duration of the ride; lessons can also be arranged from $8 to $20 an hour. Open Monday through Saturday from 9 a.m. to dusk, and reservations are necessary.

BICYCLING: If you haven't brought your own bicycle, you can hire one at **Let's Rent Bikes, Inc.,** Cape Island Mall, Beach Drive and Howard Street (tel. 884-BIKE). The cost is $3 an hour (or $8 a day) for a one-passenger vehicle or $6 for tandem ($16 a day). Hours are 8 a.m. to 7 p.m. in the summer, with shorter hours during the rest of the year. Other bike-rental shops with similar rates are: **La Mer Bike Rentals,** Beach Drive and Pittsburgh Avenue (tel. 884-2200); **Village Bicycle Shop,** 2 Victorian Village Plaza (tel. 884-8500); and **Buckingham Bike Rental,** 1111 New Jersey Ave. (tel. 884-3760).

BIRD WATCHING: Situated on the Eastern Flyway, Cape May has long been famous for its excellent bird-watching opportunities, especially in the spring and fall months when the great migrations take place. Most of this activity is concentrated in the vicinity of Cape May Point State Park and in the picturesque South Cape May Meadows along Sunset Boulevard, a 1,080-acre wildlife preserve. For further information, contact the **Cape May Bird Observatory,** 707 E. Lake Drive, Cape May Point (tel. 884-2736); there is also a 24-hour bird-sighting hotline (tel. 884-2626).

CAMPING: In the area surrounding Cape May, there are 31 campgrounds, catering to tent, trailer, or motor-home visitors, for weekends, by the week, or monthly. Most of these campgrounds have swimming pools, modern bath facilities, stores, laundromats, video arcades, and full hookups. For a complete listing, contact the **Cape May County Campgrounds Association,** P. O. Box 175, Cape May Court House, NJ 08210.

10. Events

Cape May summers get off to a festive start each year with the **Victorian Fair,** held on the grounds of the **Emlen Physick Estate,** 1048 Washington St. (tel. 884-5404). Scheduled on the third Saturday of June, from 10 a.m. to 4 p.m., this festive open-air gathering features music and entertainment, craftspeople, and games of skill and chance. Admission is free. For complete information, contact the **Mid-Atlantic Center for the Arts,** P.O. Box 164, Cape May, NJ 08204 (tel. 609/884-5404).

The premier event of the year in Cape May is **Victorian Week,** held for ten days in mid-October, including two weekends. The program includes antique shows, guided tours of the Victorian district, concerts, stained-glass tours, Victorian-style vaudeville, lawn parties, teas, craft demonstrations, fashion shows, workshops, and dinners. Tickets for a weekend of activities range from $35 to $42; some events, like dinners and workshops, are extra. For a complete program and ticket information, contact the Mid-Atlantic Center for the Arts (address above).

Christmas is a special time at Cape May. Carolers stroll the streets, gas-lit street lamps are bedecked with wreaths, and the Washington Street Mall merchants organize traditional "hospitality nights" for shoppers, with cider and cookies or wine and cheese. Other activities include a yuletide parade, a community tree-lighting ceremony, gingerbread house displays, and candlelight walks. Visitors can take tours in heated enclosed trolley cars to see Victorian homes bedecked in twinkling lights and holiday finery. For a Christmas calendar of events, write or phone the **Greater Cape May Chamber of Commerce,** P.O. Box 109, Cape May, NJ 08204 (tel. 609/884-5508).

Chapter XVIII

INTRODUCTION TO DELAWARE

1. Welcome to the Nation's First State
2. Getting to Delaware
3. Getting Around Delaware
4. Useful Facts

THE SECOND SMALLEST STATE in the nation, Delaware takes precedence over all others at official functions and carries the title of "First State." This honored position harks back to 1787 when the people of Delaware rushed to ratify the new Constitution and became the first state to enter the Union. History tells us that Delawareans' motives were mixed—many people felt that by endorsing the Constitution they would also guarantee their individual statehood and would never again have to worry about merely being the "three lower counties" of neighboring Pennsylvania. No matter what the reason, Delaware was then and still is the first of our 50 states.

1. Welcome to the Nation's First State

In spite of its small size (96 miles long and from nine to 35 miles wide, with a population of 622,000), Delaware today is a giant in many respects. With due credit to one of its leading families, the du Ponts, Delaware has long been known as the chemical capital of the world, and thanks to its rich agricultural land, this state also produces 180 million broiler chickens per year, as well as bountiful crops of soybeans, corn, tomatoes, strawberries, and asparagus.

In the corporate world, more than half of the Fortune 500 companies are incorporated in the state of Delaware. Novel tax incentives, along with the elimination of ceilings on interest rates, have added over 3,500 new jobs and many new institutions to Delaware's list of banking and financial service firms.

This tiny state is also a most appealing vacation land, as evidenced by the more than $500 million that is tallied annually in tourism-related expenditures. Indeed, Delaware has a lot to offer the visitor besides its premier position in the parade of states. Often referred to as a "small wonder," Delaware is a blend of cosmopolitan cities, historic museums, landmark squares, unspoiled beaches, meandering gardens, artistic treasures, sylvan parks, abundant fishing shores, and fertile farmlands.

You could easily drive from north to south or east to west across this state in less than a day, but that is not the way to see Delaware. You need to allow at least three or four days to explore Wilmington and its historic neighbors, New

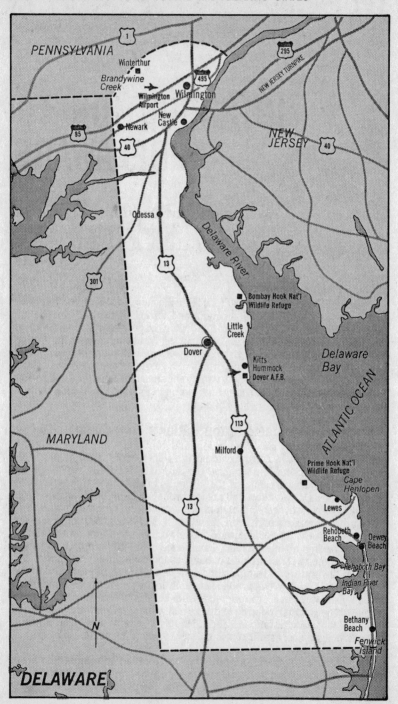

Castle and the Brandywine Valley. A week is never enough to savor the sun and sand at Rehoboth, Lewes, Bethany, or Fenwick. And who can resist a day or two in the capital of Dover to walk the fabled Green and tour the Victorian homes. Best of all, there is the hospitality—from restored country inns to modern motels and seaside resorts, with a "Delmarvelous" cuisine of freshly caught seafood, garden-ripened produce, and locally raised chicken.

No matter how long you stay, it will never be enough. From Cape Henlopen to the banks of the Brandywine, Delaware really does prove that good things come in small packages.

2. Getting to Delaware

Situated on the eastern seaboard of the U.S., Delaware is bordered by the Atlantic Ocean and Delaware Bay as well as by the states of New Jersey, Pennsylvania, and Maryland. The state's location affords easy access from the major metropolitan areas of the Northeast, and Washington, D.C., Philadelphia, and Baltimore are all within a two-hour drive.

BY PLANE: United Airlines and a number of commuter airlines operate scheduled services into the Greater Wilmington Airport. In addition, many travelers to Delaware choose to fly into Philadelphia International Airport, which is only a 30-minute drive from Wilmington. Philadelphia is a gateway for more than 25 national, regional and international airlines including American, Continental, Delta, Eastern, Northwest, TWA, Pan American, and United (see "Chapter III").

BY TRAIN: Amtrak offers convenient daily Metroliner service to Wilmington from New York and Washington, with further passenger links from Boston, Florida, and points west. The beautifully restored Wilmington station is conveniently located downtown on 2nd and French Streets, close to major hotels and with a taxi stand at its entrance.

BY BUS: Both Greyhound and Carolina Trailways serve major points in Delaware such as Wilmington, Dover, and New Castle. Carolina Trailways also provides summer services to the beach resorts of Rehoboth and Bethany.

BY CAR: Interstate 95, the eastern seaboard's major north-south link from Maine to Florida, runs right through Wilmington. The twin-span Delaware Memorial Bridge, peaking to a height of 441 feet over the Delaware River, connects the state to New Jersey. From the south, Route 13 will also bring you to Delaware via Virginia; and from the west, the best access is via Routes 50 and 301 from Maryland.

BY FERRY: The Cape May–Lewes Ferry travels daily between southern New Jersey and the lower Delaware coast. This 70-minute crossing is operated on a drive-on, drive-off basis and can accommodate up to 800 passengers and 100 cars. Full details are given in the Lewes section of Chapter XX.

3. Getting Around Delaware

BY CAR: The best way to see Delaware is by car. The north-south highway known as Route 13 runs the entire length of the state and is the major link between Wilmington and the beaches of Delmarva. This road is also known as du Pont Highway because it was built with $40 million provided by the du Pont family. When it was constructed at the turn of the century, Route 13 was then the most modern four-lane highway in the U.S. Today it also provides a link to many smaller secondary roads, such as Route 1, which connects the beaches of Lewes, Rehoboth, Bethany, and Fenwick to the mainland. With the exception of the Delaware Memorial Bridge and the I-95 turnpike, all roads in Delaware are toll-free. Most car rental companies have stations in Wilmington and Dover (see listings under each city).

BY BUS: Bus connections between Wilmington and Dover are provided by **Dawson Bus Service,** 403 E. Camden-Wyoming Ave., Dover, DE 19901 (tel. 302/697-9501 or toll-free 800/282-8525). In addition, Wilmington has its own transportation network known as DART (Delaware Administration for Regional Transit). This system also connects Wilmington to New Castle, the Brandywine Valley, and the Greater Wilmington Airport. Details follow in Chapter XIX.

4. Useful Facts

VISITOR INFORMATION: For a complete packet of information about Delaware, contact the **Delaware State Travel Service,** Delaware Development Office, 99 Kings Highway, P.O. Box 1401, Dover, DE 19903 (tel. toll-free 800/441-8846 or in Delaware toll-free 800/282-8667). This is an extremely helpful agency, with a wide range of publications covering accommodations, restaurants, sightseeing, and all types of activities from festivals to fishing.

CLIMATE: Delaware's climate is moderate throughout the year. The average mean temperature for the entire state is 39°F in winter, 65° in spring, and 74° in summer. About 57% of the days per year are sunny and the annual precipitation is approximately 45 inches. Temperatures along the Atlantic are about 10° warmer in winter and 10° cooler in summer than the rest of the state.

AREA CODE: All telephone numbers in the state of Delaware belong to the 302 area code.

SALES TAX: Although there is a 6% occupancy tax for lodgings in Delaware, there is no sales tax in the state. This makes Delaware a very attractive place for dining out and shopping.

Chapter XIX

WILMINGTON AND ENVIRONS

1. Wilmington
2. Brandywine Valley
3. Historic New Castle

TUCKED UNDER THE PENNSYLVANIA BORDER, Wilmington and its environs dominate northern Delaware. An area less than 15 miles at its widest or longest, this corridor of Delaware is the busiest part of the state. With the Delaware Memorial Bridge at its eastern shore and Interstate-95 cutting through its middle, Wilmington is the hub of the state's industrial, cultural, and social activity.

For such a compact area, it is amazing how much there is to see and do. On the next few pages, we'll describe the highlights of this cosmopolitan and charming city. We'll also explore two of Wilmington's most well-known suburbs, New Castle and the Brandywine Valley, both of which can stand on their own merits as outstanding travel destinations as well as being vital parts of the overall Wilmington experience.

1. Wilmington

Wilmington, Delaware's largest city, is located in the northeast corner of the state, at the confluence of the Christina, Brandywine and Delaware Rivers.

First settled 350 years ago by the Swedes who planted a permanent settlement at the mouth of the Christina River, this area was initially known as New Sweden until the Dutch conquered the colony and it became part of New Netherland. The English eventually claimed the land and thus it evolved into prominence during Revolutionary times as Wilmington.

The city's ability to generate water power spurred its growth in the 18th century. By 1802 Wilmington also attracted a Frenchman named Eleuthere Irenee du Pont who established a black powder mill on the banks of the Brandywine. This mill, of course, was the foundation of a family empire that was to become the largest chemical company in America and a powerful influence, to this day, on the city and the whole state of Delaware.

Today Wilmington is an industrial, financial, and banking hub with an ever-changing skyline of sleek new buildings. It is also the gateway to the scenic and historic Brandywine Valley, home to some of America's greatest living history museums and art treasures.

WILMINGTON & THE BRANDYWINE VALLEY

N

Pottstown

Schuylkill River

PENNA. TURNPIKE N.E. EXTENSION

202

Norristown

Ft. Washington

276

Valley Forge

King of Prussia

Wayne

76

Saint Davids

Exton

252

Berwyn

Newton Square

Downington

3

320

West Chester

202

1

Philadelphia

52

100

Swarthmore

Lenape

CONCORD PIKE

95

13

82

Longwood Gardens

Brandywine Battlefield

Brandywine Raceway

Chester

Chadds Ford

Kennett Square

KENNETT PIKE

Brandywine

92

Talleys Corner

Delaware River

48

Ashland Nature Center

Winterthur Museum

Talleyville

Nemours

PHILADELPHIA PIKE

PENNSYLVANIA

LANCASTER PIKE

495

295

N.J. TURNPIKE

Wilmington

Penns Grove

DELAWARE

2

95

141

NEW JERSEY

DELAWARE TNPK.

New Castle

Delaware Memorial Bridge

Greater Wilmington Airport

Miles 0 10

Kilometers 0 10

GETTING TO WILMINGTON: By Plane: The city is served by the **Greater Wilmington Airport,** Route 13, New Castle (tel. 323-2680), located seven miles south of Wilmington. Regularly scheduled flights are operated by a number of local commuter airlines as well as **United Airlines** (tel. 328-1311). Taxi service between the downtown area and Greater Wilmington Airport is available via **Diamond Cabs** (tel. 658-4321). The approximate fare from the airport to the city is between $12 and $14.

Most people flying into the northern Delaware area, however, use the **Philadelphia International Airport** as a gateway. It is within a half-hour's ride of downtown Wilmington, and many Wilmington hotels operate courtesy transfer services to or from the Philadelphia Airport. (For more details on Philadelphia Airport, see Chapter III).

In addition, **Airport Shuttle Service Inc.** operates a 24-hour transfer system between Philadelphia International Airport and any address in Delaware. The company has desks at the airport and a downtown location at the Radisson Hotel, 700 King St. at Customs House Plaza (tel. 302/655-8878). Rates per person range from $12.90 to $17.90 depending on pick-up point. Departures are scheduled from Philadelphia Airport every 5 to 20 minutes between 6:30 a.m. and 11:30 p.m. and every 10 to 40 minutes between 11:30 p.m. and 6:30 a.m. CC's accepted: AE.

By Train: Wilmington is a stop on the main East Coast corridor of **Amtrak,** between Philadelphia and Baltimore. The Wilmington Amtrak station is located at Second and French Streets (tel. 658-1575), on the city's southern edge, adjacent to the Christina River. This imposing structure, originally designed and built in 1907, is an attraction in itself—an eclectic blend of terracotta window arches, red-clay tile roofing, and marble steps. Recently restored (1983–1984) to its former glory, it is now on the National Register of Historic Places. There is a taxi stand outside the station.

By Bus: Daily service is provided into the Wilmington Bus Station at 318 N. Market St., by both **Carolina Trailways** (tel. 652-7391) and **Greyhound** (tel. 655-6111).

By Car: The best way to drive to Wilmington is via I-95, which cuts across the city at its center. The Delaware Memorial Bridge also connects Wilmington to the New Jersey Turnpike and points north. From the south, Route 13 will bring you into the city via Virginia and southern Delaware.

VISITOR INFORMATION: A complete selection of literature about Wilmington, the Brandywine Valley, and historic New Castle is available from one source, the **Greater Wilmington Convention and Visitors Bureau,** 1300 Market St., Wilmington, DE 19801 (tel. 302/652-4088). The bureau prints separate folders on accommodations, restaurants, attractions, shopping, and activities for the entire northern Delaware area.

GETTING AROUND WILMINGTON: Whether you prefer to do your own driving or to take public transportation, Wilmington offers a variety of choices.

By Public Transport: Wilmington has no subway but it does have an efficient bus system known as DART (Delaware Administration for Regional Transit). Blue and white signs indicating DART stops are located throughout the city and regular routes can take you to museums, theaters, parks, hotels, and the Greater Wilmington Airport, as well as such popular sights as Winterthur and New

Castle. Exact fares, based on a zone system, are required; the minimum fare for one zone is 60¢ during off-peak periods and the maximum rush hour four-zone fare is $1.50. Complete information on schedules and applicable fares is available at most banks or by calling the DARTLINE (tel. 655-3381).

By Taxi: Taxi stands are located at the du Pont Hotel, the Radisson Hotel, and the train station. If you wish to order a cab, call **Diamond Cab** (tel. 658-4321) or **Yellow Cab** (tel. 654-4100).

Car Rental: Major car rental firms represented in the Wilmington area include **Avis,** Front and Walnut Streets (tel. 656-6696); **Dollar,** 2100 Gov. Printz Blvd. (tel. 655-7117); **Hertz,** 1218 French St. (tel. 658-2461); and **National,** 1212 Washington St. (tel. 655-7555).

Sightseeing Tours: One of the best ways to see the Wilmington skyline is via a harbor cruise on board the *Lady Christina*. This handsome 275-passenger vessel operates narrated sightseeing cruises daily, from May through November. Prices, which include a buffet lunch, dinner or brunch, as well as a musical revue, are priced from $13 to $26, depending on the time of day. For complete details, contact the *Lady Christina* box office, 100 S. King St., near the Pennsylvania Railroad station (tel. 658-4522 for reservations and 658-4688 for 24-hour information). The ticket office is open from 9 a.m. to 7 p.m. each day. CC's accepted: MC and V.

For those who prefer terra firma, the **Wilmington and Western Railroad** offers sightseeing excursions in the neighboring countryside south of the city via vintage steam trains. This tourist railroad is located at Greenbank Park on Route 41, near the junction of Route 2 (tel. 998-1930). The basic itinerary takes passengers on a one-hour, eight-mile ride through the Red Clay Valley to the Mt. Cuba picnic grove. The fare for adults is $4; children, from 2 to 12 years, $2; and free for children under 2. Trains operate on Sunday at noon, 1:15, 2 and 3:45 p.m., May through October; and on Saturday at noon, 1:15, 2:30, and 3:45 p.m. during June and September only. Reservations are not required.

WHERE TO STAY: No matter where you go in Delaware, when the natives refer to "the hotel," you can be sure they mean the du Pont in Wilmington. For the last 75 years, this hotel has dominated the Delaware lodging scene. Consequently, there are relatively few other full-service hotels in downtown Wilmington. In recent years, however, as the Wilmington suburbs have grown, a number of new hotels and motels have sprung up in the surrounding areas. The following summary reflects this trend. One other point should be noted: Wilmington hotels, like other city hotels, charge top dollar during the Sunday-through-Thursday period. The best way to save money is to reserve a one- or two-night (Friday and Saturday) weekend package, which, in most cases, can represent a 50% reduction off normal midweek room rates.

The Luxury Leader

Opened in 1913 and owned by E. I. du Pont de Nemours and Company, the **Hotel du Pont,** 11th and Market Streets, Wilmington, DE 19899 (tel. 302/594-3100 or toll-free 800/441-9019), is the benchmark for all other Delaware hotels. Located right in the heart of the city, this palatial structure is a showcase of polished marble, elegant coffered ceilings, richly carved walnut, oak paneling, original artwork, and genteel services. The 280 bedrooms are decorated with traditional furnishings and antique reproductions as well as the modern comforts of color TV, direct-dial phones, and air conditioning. Doubles are priced from $125, executive rooms from $150, and suites from $250, with weekend packages about half of these rates.

Even if you can't overnight at the du Pont, do try to treat yourself to a meal in the main restaurant, the **Green Room.** The décor is dominated by tall arching windows, 2½ stories high; walls of quartered oak paneling; plush green-toned carpets and furnishings; and a set of six handcrafted golden chandeliers from Spain. Tuxedoed waiters and musicians playing sweet tones from the gallery complete the tableau. Lunch, priced from $9.95 to $13.95, includes an array of salads (such as a crab and pecan combo), open-faced sandwiches, and hot entrees (such as sliced veal in light curry sauce, papaya golden sole, or garlic-lime marinated beef). The selections at dinner, priced from $16.95 to $33, range from rack of lamb; paillard of chicken with fine herbs; salmon and veal in puff pastry; roast sliced venison in green peppercorn sauce; and fillet of beef with béarnaise sauce, to les fruits de mer (a trio of lobster, scampi, and lump crab, with mushrooms, tarragon, and Pernod and flamed with brandy). Lunch is served from 11:30 to 2 p.m. Monday through Saturday; and dinner from 6 to 9:30 p.m. Friday through Sunday. Breakfast is also available from 7 a.m. to 11 a.m. Monday through Saturday; and Sunday brunch from 9:30 a.m. to 2:30 p.m.

The du Pont also has another, more clubby restaurant called the **Brandywine Room,** paneled in rich Italian walnut and decorated with a collection of original art featuring three generations of the Wyeth family. Lunch choices, priced from $4.95 to $12.95, include omelets, sandwiches, quiches, gourmet burgers, and hot entrees from crab cakes to filet mignon. Dinner entrees, priced from $14.95 to $30, range from lobster and Dover sole to veal Oscar, duck à l'orange and Chateaubriand. Lunch is available from 11:30 a.m. to 2:30 p.m. Tuesday through Friday, and dinner from 6 to 11 p.m. Monday through Saturday. Jackets and reservations are required for both restaurants. In addition, the elegant hotel lobby is also the venue for High Tea (light sandwiches, warm scones, and pastries) daily from 2:30 to 4:30 p.m., at $7.50 per person. Within the Hotel du Pont there is also a bank, a brokerage, a barbershop, a beauty salon, and gift shops. All major CC's accepted.

Other Luxury Lodgings

A modern glass-and-concrete façade prevails at the nine-story **Radisson Hotel,** 700 King St. at Customs House Plaza, Wilmington, DE 19801 (tel. 302/655-0400 or toll-free 800/228-9822), just four blocks from the old-world aura of the du Pont. Conveniently located in the heart of Wilmington's business and financial district, this hotel is a half block from the Opera House and the Market Street Mall. The 222 rooms are decorated in a contemporary style, with double or queen-size beds, colorful wall hangings, cable TVs, air conditioning, and phones; many guest rooms also overlook a tropical indoor garden court and patio with a swimming pool and a whirlpool. Other facilities include indoor parking, an arcade of shops and an airport shuttle service. Doubles start at $105 from Sunday through Thursday and from $55 on Friday and Saturday. The Hearth restaurant provides a delightful setting for meals, with its illuminated murals, stained-glass skylights, and rich red décor. Lunch, priced from $6.95 to $14.95, offers a choice of burgers, pastas, crêpes, and hot entrees. Dinner entrees, which range from chicken breast Oscar and shrimp dijonnaise to pasta carbonara, cost from $10.95 to $21.95. Hours for lunch are 11:30 a.m. to 2:30 p.m., and dinner from 6 to 10 p.m. All major CC's accepted.

Just north of downtown Wilmington and a few miles from the major historic museums and gardens is the **Sheraton Brandywine Inn,** 4727 Concord Pike, Route 202, Wilmington, DE 19803 (tel. 302/478-6000 or toll-free 800/325-3535).

A modern seven-story structure, it has 149 rooms, all with double or queen beds, color TVs, phones, and air conditioning. Doubles range from $90 to $96. Guest facilities include an outdoor swimming pool, Avery's lounge with evening entertainment, and a courtesy limousine service to downtown. This hotel is also very well known for its restaurants. The Hunt Room, which serves breakfast and lunch, is decorated in rich green tones and spotlit paintings of hunt scenes. The lunch menu, priced from $3.95 to $8.95, offers a selection of pita or croissantwiches, salads, omelets, burgers, and seafood platters. The adjacent Tapestry Room, decorated with framed tapestries and plush rose- and burgundy-toned furnishings, features such dinner choices as shrimp Diane, crab-stuffed brook trout, sherried scallops, lobster Thermidor, blackened prime rib, chicken raspberry, and veal with Cajun seasonings, all served with salad, fresh vegetables, and potato or rice. Entrees are priced from $10 to $21.50. Hours for lunch are from 11:30 a.m. to 1:30 p.m., and dinner from 5:30 to 9:30 p.m. Major CC's accepted.

Moderate Choices

Another hotel in the heart of the Brandywine Valley is the **Best Western El Capitan,** 1807 Concord Pike (Route 202), Wilmington, DE 19803 (tel. 302/656-9436 or toll-free 800/528-1234). As its name implies, this villa-style hotel is designed in a Spanish motif, with whitewashed walls and black and red trim. The 58 units have two double beds, modern Colonial furniture, wall-to-wall carpeting, color TVs, direct-dial phones, and air conditioning. Many rooms face the pool and gardens, which are artistically floodlit at night. Rates for a double range from $62 to $70. Other advantages of this hotel include a full-time valet/concierge service, proximity to the Brandywine Valley attractions including the racetrack, and a variety of weekend packages. All major CC's accepted.

Business travelers often choose **The Wilmington Hilton,** I-95 and Naamans Road, Wilmington, DE 19703 (tel. 302/792-2700) because of its handy location. Northeast of the city, it is adjacent to exit 11 of the interstate highway and close to the Tri-State industrial complex and the Northtowne Plaza shopping mall; it is also just 12 miles from Philadelphia Airport. There are 194 rooms, in various configurations as bedroom/sitting rooms, queen studios, king rooms, and suites. All are furnished in a contemporary style, with direct-dial phones, color TVs, and air conditioning. Hotel facilities include valet/laundry, an outdoor swimming pool, a complimentary shuttle to and from the airport, and a disco-style lounge called Whispers which features live music Thursday, Friday, and Saturday evenings. Doubles start at $76 and suites at $100. The main restaurant, Evergreens, is a tri-level dining room with a garden atmosphere. The lunch menu, priced from $3.95 to $8.95, offers sandwiches, burgers, salads, quiches, and ethnic dishes such as chili, eggrolls, or pasta. Dinner entrees, priced from $11.95 to $19.95, range from chicken and crab Wilmington, steak and lobster, honey-almond duck, and shrimp and scallops with fettuccine to blackened swordfish. Lunch is served daily from 11:30 a.m. to 2:30 p.m., and dinner from 5:30 to 10 p.m. Breakfast is also available from 6:30 to 11:30 a.m. and Sunday brunch from 10:30 a.m. to 2:30 p.m. All major CC's accepted.

A real find for value-conscious vacationers is **Shoney's Inn,** 900 Churchman's Rd., Newark, DE 19713 (tel. 302/368-2400 or toll-free 800/222-2222). Located off I-95 about 15 minutes south of downtown Wilmington, this modern motel-style facility is less than five miles from the Greater Wilmington Airport and historic New Castle; it is also just a mile from the Delaware Park Racetrack. A three-story structure, Shoney's offers 150 rooms, each with a queen-size or double bed, a direct-dial phone, air conditioning, and color TV. Doubles range from $39 to $52. There is also an outdoor swimming pool and an on-premises restaurant called Gatwicks Inn. The restaurant, decorated in a country theme, serves breakfast from 7 a.m. to 2 p.m. (in the $2.45 to $4.95 price range). Lunch items, in the same price bracket as breakfast, include sandwiches, burgers, pasta, and salads. The dinner menu, priced from $5.95 to $9.95, features broiled beefsteak, petit filet mignon, Delmarva ham steak, fried chicken, Eastern Shore crab cakes, veal, and pasta dishes, all served with potato and vegetable. Lunch hours are from 11 a.m. to 5 p.m. and dinner from 5 to 10 p.m. CC's accepted: AE, MC, and V.

A Motel in the Budget Range

The **Tally Ho Motor Lodge,** 5209 Concord Pike (Route 202), Wilmington, DE 19803 (tel. 302/478-0300) is located 3½ miles north of the city in the Brandywine Valley, next to Brandywine Raceway. This modern two-story brick motel has 100 rooms, each with one or two double beds, air conditioning, color TV, a direct-dial phone, and some have kitchenettes. Other facilities include an outdoor swimming pool and a guest laundromat. Doubles range from $36 to $40, and all major CC's are accepted.

WHERE TO DINE: With so many fine hotel dining rooms, it is not surprising that Wilmington's restaurants are also of a very high standard. As our selections show, many of the best restaurants are not located in the downtown business and financial sections of the city but are clustered in residential areas. In surveying the Wilmington restaurant scene, we remind you that the dining spots listed in the Brandywine and New Castle sections of this chapter are also considered part of the Wilmington gastronomic experience.

The Top Choices

No restaurant conveys Delaware's southern charm better than **Bellevue in the Park,** 911 Philadelphia Pike (tel. 798-7666). Once the home of William du Pont, this mansion is situated right in the heart of the city's Bellevue State Park. You'll feel as pampered as a du Pont in this idyllic setting of Greek Revival architecture with crystal chandeliers, delicate plasterwork, fine linens, and tuxedoed waiters. Lunch, which offers a variety of dishes from salads, sandwiches, omelets, crêpes, and quiches to filet mignon, is priced from $5.95 to $10.95. The dinner menu, which runs from $12.95 to $22.75, features lobster, blackened redfish, breast of chicken framboise, bouillabaisse, veal piccante, roast duckling, and Chateaubriand. Lunch is available Monday through Friday from 11 a.m. to 3 p.m., and dinner Monday through Saturday from 5 to 10 p.m. A sumptuous Sunday brunch buffet is also very popular with Wilmington families; served from 10:30 a.m. to 2:30 p.m., it includes soups, salads, specialty omelets, hot casseroles, and pastries, as well as main courses like fresh salmon and roast beef cut-to-order. The price for adults is $14.50 and $9.50 for children aged 3 to 10. Be sure to save time before or after a meal for a stroll in the gardens. Jackets required. CC's accepted: AE, MC, and V.

For the best steak in town, don't miss **Constantinou's House of Beef,** 1616 Delaware Ave. (tel. 652-0653). You'll also enjoy the Victorian décor, filled with original tankards, prints, and bric-a-brac from around the world. Flags of all nations, lots of American eagles, gold-framed mirrors, touches of brass, and tuxedoed waiters add to the charm. Lunch, priced from $4.95 to $12.95, includes beef entrees such as prime ribs and steak teriyaki, as well as seafood platters, salads, and hearty sandwiches. Aged tender beef takes center stage at night with a variety of cuts of prime Kansas steaks as well as cut-to-order prime ribs. Other dishes that are favorites here include rack of lamb, surf-and-turf, lobster tails, shrimp scampi, and jumbo crab imperial. All selections, priced from $11.95 to $25.95, come with salad, potato, and a loaf of bread; prices are slightly higher on Sunday, Monday, and Thursday, when all entrees include unlimited raw bar selections. Lunch is served from 11:15 a.m. to 4 p.m. Monday through Friday; dinner from 4:30 to 11 p.m. Monday through Saturday, and from 4:30 to 10 p.m. on Sunday. Major CC's accepted.

Tucked away in the heart of this city's Little Italy, you'll find **Sal's Petite Marmite,** 603 N. Lincoln St. (tel. 652-1200), the award-winning Italian/French restaurant of master-chef Sal Buono. With rich leather furnishings and a hint of country-club atmosphere, this restaurant is a blend of French and Italian cuisines. Great care is taken to obtain the freshest and best ingredients daily, and all the tomatoes and herbs are grown in the owner's private garden. Lunch focuses on salads and light entrees such as shrimp scampi, veal piccata, coquilles St-Jacques, and fettuccine Alfredo, priced $6.95 to $12.95. Dinner, more of an event, largely depends on what is in season, but can often include salmon filet, whole Dover sole, frogs' legs, duckling flambé, beef Wellington, rack of veal, or game dishes. The entrees run from $13.95 to $21.95, with most dishes around $18. Lunch is served from 11:30 a.m. to 2 p.m. Monday through Friday, and dinner from 5:30 to 10 p.m. Monday through Saturday. The restaurant has a non-smoking section and a private parking lot; jackets are required. All major CC's are accepted.

One of the most heralded of the city's restaurants is the **Silk Purse,** 1307 North Scott St., corner of Scott and 13th Streets (tel. 654-7666). It's located just off Pennsylvania Avenue (Route 52), on the city's north side, in the middle of a quiet residential block in a private house (an inconspicuous brick building with a small discreet sign). Once inside, you'll find a welcoming contemporary décor of fresh flowers, graceful glass lamps, framed gallery prints, and light rattan furniture. The menu and service are all very personalized here, reflecting the private-home ambience. Dinner entrees, priced from $17.50 to $24.50, include such creations as veal with wild mushrooms; zinfandel-marinated roast duck; venison steak; lamb with tomato béarnaise; sirloin with caramelized shallots and bordelaise sauce; or calves' liver with mustard cognac sauce. The Silk Purse is also known for its inventive greens ($7.50 to $8.50 a portion), such as smoked pheasant and baked goat cheese salad or a sweetbread salad with wild mushrooms. Various fixed-price specials are also available each evening, averaging around $35 for a complete meal. Dinner is served Monday through Saturday from 6 to 9:30 p.m. CC's accepted: MC and V.

Moderately Priced Dining

One of the city's oldest buildings, a stone house dating from 1798, is the setting for the **Columbus Inn,** 2216 Pennsylvania Ave. (tel. 571-1492). Set on a hill on its own grounds, this restaurant overlooks the main route (Route 52) to the Brandywine Valley. The décor is a clubby Colonial blend of old brick walls, brass fixtures, and original oil paintings of the area. This inn is a popular lunch gathering place for Wilmington business people, who enjoy the choice of hot beef and seafood entrees, salads, sandwich board, or burgers, priced from $4.95 to $8.95. The dinner menu, which runs $9.95 to $19.95, with most dishes about $15, includes such items as shore dinner (lobster tail, oyster Rockefeller, jumbo shrimp, clams casino, scallops, and flounder), veal francese, prime rib, roast duck, and breast of capon. A salad, vegetable, and potato accompany each entree. Lunch is served from 11:30 a.m. to 2:30 p.m., and dinner from 5 p.m. to midnight, Monday through Saturday. Jackets are required after 6 p.m. Major CC's are accepted.

The residential area near the Delaware Art Museum is the setting for

Leounes' at the Mansion, 68 Bancroft Estate Rd. (tel. 658-5266). It isn't the easiest place to find, but you'll have no trouble if you follow a map to Rockford Park on Kentmere Parkway, just off Delaware Avenue on the city's north side. This secluded Victorian mansion and its beautiful gardens are well worth the effort at any time of day. At lunchtime, the menu features light fare such as salads, sandwiches, seafood, and meat platters, priced from $4.95 to $7.95. The dinner selections range from double veal porterhouse, breast of capon, roast duckling, or prime ribs to flaming steak au poivre or lobsters. If you are a crab lover, then don't miss the crab imperial or the crab au gratin, both award winners in the annual culinary contest known as the "Crab Olympics." All dinner entrees are priced from $9.95 to $24.95, with most dishes under $16. Accompaniments include a salad, vegetable or potato, and fresh rolls. Open Monday through Saturday, for lunch from 11:30 a.m. to 2 p.m., and for dinner, from 5:30 to 9 p.m. All major CC's accepted.

Crabs are also the pièce de résistance at **DiNardo's,** 405 N. Lincoln St. (tel. 656-3685). This small and casual family-run Little Italy restaurant, a tradition in Delaware since 1938, is just the place to go if you enjoy cracking your own crustaceans. Crabs, flown in daily year round from Louisiana waters, are served steamed or sautéed, from $1.50 to $3 each, depending on size. Of course, other dishes requiring less work are also on the menu. Lunchtime choices, from $3.95 to $6.95, include crab and shellfish platters, salads, and pastas. Dinner entrees, in addition to crabs in the shell, range from crab cakes, crab claws, crab legs, and crab imperial to shrimp, lobster, flounder, scallops, oysters, and steaks as well as combination platters ($7.95 to $14.95). Crabs are also available to go, singly (from $2) or by the bushel ($60). Open Monday through Saturday from 11 a.m. to 10 p.m., and Sunday from 3 to 10 p.m. All major CC's accepted.

Schoonover's, 3858 Kennett Pike (Route 52), Greenville (tel. 571-0561), is named for the Brandywine Valley artist Frank Schoonover, whose paintings decorate this restaurant. Located north of the city in a chic mall known as **Powder Mill Square,** this Colonial-style brick building is full of arches and alcoves, cozy booths and shelves of timeworn books. Lunch, priced from $3.25 to $7.95, features burgers, salads, and creative sandwiches (try the open-faced crab and cheese, or turkey julienne on a croissant). Dinner choices, priced from $9.95 to $18.95, include veal and oysters, rainbow trout, veal scampi, and tenderloin of beef with lobster medallions. Most entrees average under $14 and come with salad, vegetable, and potato or pasta. Lunch is served from 11:15 a.m. to 3 p.m. Monday through Friday; from 12:15 p.m. to 3 p.m. on Saturday; and dinner from 5:30 to 9:30 p.m. Monday through Thursday, until 10 p.m. on Friday, and from 6 to 10 p.m. on Saturday. Sunday brunch is also available from 10 a.m. to 1:30 p.m. Major CC's accepted.

The **Waterworks Café,** 16th and French Streets (tel. 652-6022), is a trendy new midcity restaurant that overlooks the Brandywine. As its name implies, it is housed in the former water-station buildings and makes the most of its location on the banks of the river. The décor is colorful and contemporary with maximum use of glass and brass; there is also an outdoor deck and patio seating in good weather. Lunch, priced from $3.95 to $8.95, includes a variety of fish and meat entrees, omelets, and cold platters (try the Cape May lobster salad or the pasta salad), as well as hot and cold sandwiches and burgers. At dinnertime the selections include roast duckling Brandywine, chicken Oscar, Oriental sautéed filet mignon and scallops, flounder with hollandaise, prime ribs, and surf-and-turf. Each entree, priced from $9.95 to $17.95, is accompanied by a salad and vegetables. Lunch is available Monday through Friday from 11:30 a.m. to 2:30 p.m.; and dinner Monday through Thursday from 5:30 to 9:30 p.m., and Saturday from 5:30 to 10:30 p.m. Most evenings there is music and dancing, from 8:30 p.m. to 1 a.m. All major CC's accepted.

The **Greenery,** 410 Market St. Mall (tel. 652-1404), is located right in the heart of the city close to the historic buildings and on the central pedestrian mall. Tile floors, dark wood paneling, brick and stone walls, and tin ceilings convey the aura of old Wilmington in a relaxed atmosphere. Lots of leafy plants, which give the restaurant its name, add a contemporary touch. Lunch items, priced from $2.95 to $7.95, include salads, croissants, omelets, pastas, burgers, and hot entrees (such as chicken teriyaki or filet mignon). Dinner focuses on a variety of French/Italian dishes, priced from $10.95 to $15.95, such as shrimp parmigiana, lobster au sherry, chicken florentine, veal Oscar, and homemade pasta; all entrees include vegetable and potato. Since the Greenery is almost adjacent to the Grand Opera House, it also caters to a theater crowd and offers complete dinner specials including entree, salad, and dessert from $11.95. In addition, on Friday and Saturday nights, a comedy cabaret is staged on the upper level of the Greenery, with dinner/show packages available, starting at $18.95 per person. Hours for lunch are Monday from 11 a.m. to 2 p.m., Tuesday through Friday from 11 a.m. to 2:30 p.m.; and dinner Tuesday through Thursday from 5 to 9 p.m., and Friday and Saturday from 5 to 10:30 p.m. All major CC's accepted.

Budget Meals

Kid Shelleen's, 14th and Scott Streets (tel. 658-4600), is a lively restaurant tucked in a residential area on the city's north side. Known for its casual atmosphere and open charcoal kitchen, the décor is highlighted by oil paintings of old Wilmington and New Castle on brick and wood walls. Lunch features an array of sandwiches, pastas, and burgers, priced from $2.95 to $6.95. Dinner entrees, which run from $6.75 to $9.95 and come with a huge house salad, include blackened grouper, barbecued chicken, baby back ribs, centercut swordfish, sirloin steak, and seafood or beef brochettes. The bar here is also well known for "kreamie" drinks (made with ice cream and liqueurs), ideal for dessert, priced from $3.25 to $3.95. Hours of business are 11 a.m. to midnight daily. CC's accepted: AE, MC, and V.

If you have a sweet tooth, you'll fall for **Temptations,** 11A Trolley Square, Delaware Avenue (tel. 429-9162). This small ice-cream-parlor-cum-restaurant serves an all-day selection of sandwiches, salads, and burgers, priced from $2.95 to $4.95, as well as an extensive selection of ice creams. The menu includes more than a dozen sundaes such as the appropriately named creation called "Original Sin" (a huge banana split, with fig leaves in season), priced at $3.95. For four to six people, there is a family-sized sundae called "Demolition Derby," a monster dish of ten flavors of ice cream and every topping in the house ($9.95). Open from 10 a.m. to 10 p.m. Monday through Thursday; from 10 a.m. to 11 p.m. on Friday and Saturday; and from noon to 10 p.m. on Sunday. All major CC's accepted.

WHAT TO SEE: Thanks to the restoration of the Wilmington Railroad Station, much of the area around the city's waterfront is taking on a new vitality. An "Avenue of the Arts" has sprung up along the banks of the Christina River and many people see this as a forerunner to a new "inner harbor" development much like Baltimore's. The central downtown area has also been restored into a five-block pedestrian area of shops and restaurants known as **Market Street Mall.** Although many of Wilmington's historic and cultural attractions are still to be found on the outskirts of the city in New Castle or the Brandywine Valley, the downtown area has much to offer in its own right.

In the heart of the city is **Old Town Hall,** 512 Market Street Mall (tel. 655-7161). Now a museum operated by the Historical Society of Delaware, this landmark building features permanent and rotating exhibits that depict life in the state over the centuries. Antique silver, furniture, and related objects of Americana are on display. In addition, restored jail cells in the basement are also open to the public. Open Tuesday to Friday from noon to 4 p.m., and Saturday from 10 a.m. to 4 p.m. There is no admission charge, but donations are welcomed.

Nearby is **Willingtown Square,** 506 Market Street Mall (tel. 655-7161), a beautiful cobblestone and brick courtyard rimmed by four 18th-century houses moved from other parts of the city to this site in 1975–1976. Also owned by the Historical Society, these stately houses are not open to the public at the moment, except for the corner building which contains a museum store, **The Eclectic Depot,** well stocked with gifts and souvenirs reflecting early Delaware, including an excellent selection of pottery, pewter, prints, and books. Open Tuesday to Friday from 11 a.m. to 3 p.m. CC's accepted: MC and V.

Six blocks south you'll find another aspect of Delaware and American history in the **USCG** *Cutter Mohawk* 78, at the Foot of King Street on the Christina River (tel. 656-0400). Built in Wilmington, this ship was first launched on October 23, 1934, and subsequently went into service during World War II on the North Atlantic. It has since been refurbished and dedicated as a living memorial to the men who fought with her on the high seas. Open to the public on Saturdays from 9 a.m. to 3 p.m., or by appointment. Admission charge is $1 for adults and 50¢ for children aged 5 to 12.

The other side of the city, close to the waters of the Brandywine, is the setting of one of the oldest houses of worship in the U.S., **Old Swedes Church,** 606 Church St. (tel. 652-5629). Erected in 1698, this church stands as it was originally built and is still regularly used for religious services. Open Tuesday to Saturday from noon to 4 p.m.; guide service is available and donations are welcomed.

Two of Wilmington's most prestigious museums are located just north of downtown in residential areas of the city. Renowned for its collections of American art (from 1840 to the present) is the **Delaware Art Museum,** 2301 Kentmere Parkway (tel. 571-9590). This is the home of the largest holding of works by Howard Pyle, the father of American illustration and founder of the Brandywine School of painting. Other outstanding examples of American sculpture, photography and crafts, traditional and contemporary, are also on view here, as is the largest display of English pre-Raphaelite art in the U.S. Open, free of charge, Monday to Saturday from 10 a.m. to 5 p.m., and Sunday from 1 to 5 p.m.

One of the largest shell collections in this hemisphere (over 1,550,000 shells) is on display at the **Delaware Museum of Natural History,** Route 52 between Greenville and Centreville (tel. 658-9111). Other highlights of this museum include an African water-hole diorama, a walk over the Great Barrier Reef, the largest bird egg in the world, and a 500-pound clam. Open Monday through Saturday from 9:30 a.m. to 4:30 p.m., and Sunday from noon to 5 p.m. Admission charge is $2.50 for adults and $1.75 for seniors, students, and children over 6; free for children under 6.

NIGHTLIFE: Much of Wilmington's nightlife is centered around the **Grand Opera House,** 818 Market St. Mall (tel. 658-7897 for information; box office tel. 652-5577). Built in 1871 as part of a Masonic Temple, this 1,100-seat showplace is one of the finest examples of cast-iron architecture in America and is listed on the National Register. Known as the "Grand Lady" of Wilmington, this splendidly restored Victorian theater serves as Delaware's Center for the Performing Arts and is home to the Delaware Opera and the Delaware Symphony, as well as an ever-changing program of guest artists in ballet, jazz, chamber music, pop concerts, and theatrical productions. Box office hours are 11 a.m. to 4 p.m. Monday to Friday, and from 11 a.m. to showtime on days of performances. CC's accepted: AE, MC, and V.

The **Delaware Theatre Company,** 200 Water St., at Foot of Orange Street, next to Avenue of the Arts (tel. 532-1100; box office tel. 594-1100), is the state's only resident professional company. This is a modern 300-seat state-of-the-art facility, with no seat more than 12 rows from the stage. An ever-changing program of classic and contemporary plays is produced throughout the year. Performances are Tuesday through Saturday at 8 p.m., with matinees on Wednesday at 12:30 p.m., Saturday at 2 and 4 p.m., and Sunday at 2 p.m. Prices vary with the production and with the day of the week but are usually between $12 to $20 a ticket. CC's accepted: MC and V.

For more than 75 years, big-name Broadway companies have brought their hits to the stage of **The Playhouse,** 10th and Market Streets (tel. 656-4401), the 1,250-seat theater that is housed in the du Pont Building. Over the years, audiences here have applauded for such memorable performers as Rosalind Russell in *Auntie Mame,* Henry Fonda in *On Golden Pond,* Walter Matthau in *The Odd Couple,* and Ben Vereen in *Pippin.* Performances are usually scheduled for Tuesday through Sunday nights, curtain at 8 p.m., and ticket prices from $21 to $40. CC's accepted: AE, MC, and V.

Delaware's first and longest-running dinner theater is the **Candlelight Music Dinner-Theatre,** 2208 Miller Rd., (tel. 475-2313). For almost 20 years, this resident company has staged such productions as *Camelot, Gigi, My Fair Lady, Man of La Mancha* and *Fiddler on the Roof* in a restored red barn. Each performance begins with cocktails at 6 p.m., followed by a buffet dinner at 6:30 p.m. and showtime at 8:15 p.m. Members of the cast and crew double as costumed waiters and waitresses. Performances are scheduled year round, on Thursday, Friday, Saturday, and Sunday; prices range from $16 to $19, plus gratuity. Box office hours are 10 a.m. to 5 p.m. daily, and until 11 p.m. on show nights. The theater, which is located in the Wilmington suburb of Arden near the Hilton Hotel, is signposted off Harvey Road. No CC's are accepted.

The Wilmington dancing-and-disco scene is centered largely on the big hotel lounges such as **Avery's** at the Sheraton Brandywine and **Whispers** at the Hilton. Two other popular spots are the trendy **Primavera** at The Galleria Center, 2006 Pennsylvania Ave. (tel. 575-0300) and the art deco–style **George's Next Door,** 1614 Delaware Ave. (tel. 652-0653).

Note: For most Wilmington performing arts events, you can also call **Chargit** reservations (tel. toll-free 800/223-0120). Tickets are also available at **B & B Tickettown,** 322 W. 9th St. (tel. 656-9797).

SPORTS AND ACTIVITIES: Wilmington's playground is **Bellevue State Park,** 800 Carr Rd. (tel. 571-3390). Located on the northern perimeter of the city, this 270-acre park was once the home of the William du Pont family. Facilities include picnic areas, garden paths for walking, and fitness trails for jogging. Admission is free, but a $2 parking fee is charged between Memorial Day and Labor Day.

Horse Racing: From mid-April to mid-September, racing fans flock to **Delaware Park Race Course,** Route 7, off I-95 exit 4N, Stanton (tel. 994-2521), about five miles south of Wilmington. Daytime thoroughbred racing is scheduled seven days a week in a picturesque setting with a tree-lined picnic grove. Post time is 1:30 p.m., and admission is $2 for adults, children under 12 free. Parking is $1.

On the city's other side, harness racing is the sport at the **Brandywine Raceway,** Route 202, Wilmington (tel. 478-1220). This track features para-mutuel night racing Tuesday through Sunday, during March through mid-August. Post time is 8 p.m. Tuesday through Saturday, and 7:30 p.m. on Sunday. Admission charges are $4 to the clubhouse, $2 for the grandstand, and children under 12 are admitted free.

CHILDREN'S CORNER: Children of all ages take delight in looking at the many exotic species of animals from North and South America on view at the **Brandywine Zoo,** 1001 N. Park Dr., Brandywine Park (tel. 571-7747). Open daily from 10 a.m. to 4 p.m., admission is free from October to March; from April to September, there is a $2 charge for adults and $1 for children aged 3 to 12.

2. Brandywine Valley

The scenic and historic Brandywine Valley is in a unique geographic position, embracing part of Delaware and part of Pennsylvania. Technically, the Brandywine starts as a creek in Philadelphia's western suburbs and ends 35 miles south, a full-scale tributary emptying into the Delaware River at Wilmington. The entire 15-mile-wide valley can be traversed by a number of routes, often crisscrossing and paralleling each other, and intertwining the attractions across state lines.

One of the most difficult choices for us in writing this book was to decide where to put the Brandywine Valley—on these Delaware pages or in a Pennsylvania chapter. We finally chose this part of the book because the most outstanding Brandywine Valley attractions and museums are in Delaware. At the same time, we are quick to point out that the majority of country inns and restaurants are scattered on the Pennsylvania side of the border.

So rich in history is this lovely valley that it might draw you here for a visit on its own merits, not just because you happen to be visiting Wilmington or Philadelphia. If you are coming to either one of these two cities, however, be sure to save some time for the Brandywine Valley—you'll find an incomparable blend of historical museums, art galleries, idyllic gardens, and a parade of welcoming inns and gourmet restaurants.

VISITOR INFORMATION: Since the Brandywine Valley meanders over parts of northern Delaware and southeastern Pennsylvania, there are at least three separate sources of information that are well worth tapping: the **Greater Wilmington Convention and Visitors Bureau,** 1300 Market St., Wilmington, DE 19801 (tel. 302/652-4088); the **Chester County Tourist Bureau,** 117 West Gay St., West Chester, PA 19380 (tel. 215/431-6365); and the **Delaware County Convention and Tourist Bureau,** 602 E. Baltimore Pike, Media, PA 19063 (tel. 215/565-3679).

AREA CODE: Like the rest of Delaware, the Brandywine Valley attractions that are located in the Wilmington area belong to the 302 area code. Many of the neighboring sights, inns, and restaurants of the Brandywine Valley are located on the Pennsylvania side of the border, however, and they belong to the 215 area code. To avoid confusion, we'll specify the area code for every listing.

THE TOP ATTRACTIONS: There are literally dozens of places to see in this valley—from the open countryside of Brandywine Park (where the Revolutionary War's Battle of Brandywine took place in 1777), to the sheltered Phillips Mushroom Museum and the flourishing Chaddsford Winery.

The most famous of all the attractions, however, is **Winterthur Museum and Gardens,** Route 52, Wilmington, DE 19735 (tel. 302/654-1548). Named for a town in Switzerland, this nine-story mansion was once the country home of the late Henry Francis du Pont. A collector of furniture, du Pont himself made the initial acquisitions that laid the foundation for what is ranked today as the world's premier collection of American antiques and decorative arts. All of the objects, displayed in period room settings, were used in this country between 1640 and 1840, including Chippendale furniture, silver tankards by Paul Revere, and a dinner service made for George Washington. Adding to the splendid aura of the house, the Winterthur grounds contain more than 200 acres, meticulously landscaped in the naturalistic tradition of an 18th-century English garden. The museum staff conducts several types of guided tours (in small groups of four to ten persons), about two hours in length and which require advance reservations. The gardens can be explored separately, April to mid-November, or in conjunction with a house tour. The house is open year round, Tuesday through Saturday from 10 a.m. to 4 p.m., and Sunday from noon to 4 p.m. The reserved tours cost $12.50 for adults and $6 for young adults aged 12 to 16. General admission (reservations not required) is $8 for adults and $6.50 for students 12 or over; no charge for children under 12. Since Winterthur requires at least a half day and possibly longer to savor, you may wish to try the glass-enclosed **Pavilion Restaurant,** which serves breakfast, lunch, and snacks (in the $1.50 to $4.95 bracket) from 8 a.m. to 3:30 p.m.; in the spring, summer, and fall months, similar food service is also available at an outdoor café, from 11:30 a.m. to 4 p.m. Winterthur also has a tempting array of shops that sell reproductions and facsimiles of many of the objects on display.

Another du Pont family undertaking is located three miles away at the **Hagley Museum,** Route 141, Wilmington, DE 19807 (tel. 302/658-2400). This peaceful woodland setting directly on the Brandywine River is the place that attracted French émigré Eleuthere Irenee du Pont to establish a black powder mill in 1802. The first of the du Pont family developments in America, the mill was the forerunner of the large chemical companies developed by subsequent generations of du Ponts. Today this 230-acre outdoor museum site re-creates the lifestyle and atmosphere of the original 19th-century mill village through a series of restored buildings, displays, replicas, demonstrations, and working machines. The pièce de résistence of this museum, however, is a building called **Eleutherian Mills,** the first (1803) du Pont home in America, a Georgian-style residence furnished to reflect five generations of the du Ponts. Open from 9:30 a.m. to 4:30 p.m., daily during April to December; and on weekends from January 2nd through March. Admission charge is $5 for adults, $4 for students, $2 for children aged 6 to 14, and free for children under 6.

Yet another du Pont home is the **Nemours Mansion and Gardens,** Rockland Rd., between Routes 141 and 202, P.O. Box 109, Wilmington, DE 19899 (tel. 302/651-6912). This is the 300-acre estate of Alfred I. du Pont, a 77-room Louis XVI–style chateau with landscaped gardens. Built in 1909–1910, Nemours was named after the du Pont ancestral home in north central France. The house contains antique furnishings, Oriental rugs, tapestries, and paintings dating from the 15th century, as well as personal items like vintage automobiles, billiards equipment, and a nine-pin bowling alley. The gardens, which stretch almost a third of a mile along the main vista from the mansion, represent one of the finest examples of formal French-style gardens in America. Like Winterthur, tours of the rooms and gardens are conducted by qualified guides and take a minimum of two hours. Reservations are usually required for these tours, which operate from May through November at 9 a.m., 11 a.m., 1 p.m., and 3 p.m. Tuesday through Saturday, and at 11 a.m., 1 p.m., and 3 p.m. on Sunday. Admission charge is $6; visitors must be over 16 years of age.

One of the world's most celebrated horticultural displays is also nestled in the Brandywine Valley at **Longwood Gardens,** Route 1, Kennett Square, PA 19348 (tel. 215/388-6741). More than 11,000 different types of plants and flowers thrive amid 350 acres of outdoor gardens and woodlands, and indoor conservatories. Longwood's attractions not only include ever-changing seasonal plant displays, but also illuminated fountains and open-air theater programs. Open every day. Admittance to the conservatories is from 10 a.m. to 5 p.m. The outdoor gardens can be explored from 9 a.m. to 6 p.m. April through October, and from 9 a.m. to 5 p.m. November to March. Fountain shows are held June through August at 9:15 p.m. on Tuesday, Thursday, and Saturday. Admission is $5 for adults, $1 for children aged 6 to 14, and free for those under 6.

In a rural setting amid nature trails and wildflower gardens is the **Brandywine River Museum,** Routes 1 and 100, P.O. Box 141, Chadds Ford, PA 19317 (tel. 215/459-1900). Housed in a century-old restored gristmill, this museum is home to a display of paintings that reflect the best of Brandywine area artists including Howard Pyle, Frank Schoonover, and three generations of Wyeths, as well as 100 other American artists and illustrators. Open daily, year round, from 9:30 a.m. to 4:30 p.m. Admission charge is $2.50 for adults and $1.25 for children.

WHERE TO STAY: Most of the Wilmington area hotels are convenient bases from which to tour the Brandywine Valley. In addition, here are a few nearby inns that are on the Pennsylvania side of the border:

One of the most beautifully restored country inns in the area is the **Duling-Kurtz House,** 146 S. Whitford Rd., Exton, PA 19341 (tel. 215/524-1830), a 150-year-old stone home and barn nestled in the quiet countryside, just south of Route 30. Eighteen rooms, all with private bath and modern comforts like air conditioning, wall-to-wall carpeting, telephones, and color TVs with VCRs, are available for guests. Rooms vary in size and style (some are connecting, others are on the ground floor with a private courtyard); each room is individually decorated and named for various historical figures from George Washington and Dolly Madison to Winston Churchill or Susan B. Anthony. Furnishings include canopy, four-poster, and brass beds, claw-foot tubs, fireplaces, and antique writing desks. Doubles range from $65 to $95; suites are also available from $115 to $125. A continental breakfast of fresh fruits and baked goods is delivered in the morning to each room as part of the room rates. For other meals, the adjacent restaurant, open to the public, offers a Williamsburg-type setting overlooking woodlands and gardens. Lunch choices, priced from $3.95 to $8.95, include salads; open-face, pita, or croissant sandwiches; omelets; pasta; seafood; and meat dishes. Dinner entrees, ranging in price from $12.95 to $19.95, are served with potato and vegetable plus house specialties of warm popovers, date-nut muffins, cranberry sauce, relish, and chutney. Featured dishes include brook trout, pheasant, duckling, tenderloin of venison, rack of lamb, prime ribs, veal chops, and medallions of pork. Lunch is served from 11:30 a.m. to 3 p.m. Monday through Friday; dinner from 5:30 to 10 p.m. Monday through Friday, and from 5:30 to 11 p.m. on Saturday. CC's accepted: AE, D, and V.

The **Longwood Inn,** 815 E. Baltimore Pike (Route 1), Kennett Square, PA 19348 (tel. 215/444-3515), is not only one-half mile west of Longwood Gardens, but it is also surrounded by beautifully landscaped flower beds and gardens of its own. The accommodations here are modern, almost motel-style, with a Colonial motif. The 28 bedrooms, all with private bath, are fully air-conditioned and have one or two double beds, color TVs, phones, and garden views. Doubles range from $55 to $60. This inn is probably most famous for its adjoining restaurant, open to the public for lunch and dinner, and well known for its mushroom dishes. Lunch, from $3.95 to $7.95, includes salads, seafood sandwiches, and mushroom specialties (mushroom strudel, mushroom omelets, mushroom burgers). Dinner entrees, priced from $9.95 to $18.95, with an average of $15, include salad, potato, vegetable, and rolls from the restaurant bakery. The selection ranges from prime ribs, steak au poivre, and rack of lamb to shrimp tempura, rainbow trout, lobster and shrimp Newburg, and a "cuisine minceur platter" (saffron rice, sautéed fresh mushrooms, broiled tomato stuffed with shiitaki mushrooms, potato, and two steamed vegetables). A must to start any meal is either the Kennett Square mushrooms, stuffed with crab imperial ($4.95) or the cream of mushroom soup, $2.95. Open daily for lunch from 11 a.m. to 4 p.m., and dinner from 4 to 9 p.m.; breakfast is available each day, and a hearty brunch is offered on Sundays from 11 a.m. to 3 p.m. CC's accepted: AE, MC, and V.

Just on the other side of the Delaware border is the **Mendenhall Inn,** Route 52, Kennett Pike, P.O. Box 208, Mendenhall, PA 19357 (tel. 215/388-1181). This historic site is part of property purchased from the heirs of William Penn by John and Benjamin Mendenhall in 1703. Restored as a country inn almost 15 years ago, it offers 20 modern rooms and one suite, all with double beds, private bath, color TV, phone, and complimentary coffee. Doubles range from $45 to $60, and from $70 to $120 for the suite. The dining room, which is part of an original family house, is dominated by a huge open fireplace, old-wood timbers, area antiques, whitewashed walls, and wide windows overlooking blossoming gardens. Lunch, priced from $4.95 to $10.95, offers a creative menu of cold platters, salads, omelets, crêpes, quiches, and elegant sandwiches (try the open-face Icelandic whitefish caviar with cucumber and cream cheese, or the avocado and lump crabwich). Dinner entrees, priced from $10.95 to $21.95, include boneless brook trout stuffed with crab; baked stuffed oysters; calves' liver sautéed with Canadian bacon; prime ribs; and tenderloin of beef en brochette. A salad and two vegetables accompany all main courses. Lunch is served Tuesday through Saturday from 11:30 a.m. to 2:30 p.m.; and dinner Tuesday through Thursday from 5 to 10 p.m., Friday and Saturday until 11 p.m., and on Sunday from 3 to 9 p.m. CC's accepted: AE, D, MC, and V.

An excellent budget choice in the Brandywine region is **Abbey Green Motor Lodge,** 1036 Wilmington Pike (Route 202), West Chester, PA 19382 (tel. 215/692-3310). Located near the Brandywine Battlefield Park close to scenic Routes 52 and 100, this 18-unit family-run motel is courtyard-style, set back from the road on its own grounds with picnic tables and an outdoor fireplace. All rooms, priced from $32 to $42, have double beds, air conditioning, and color TV. The owners also operate a quality gift shop on the premises. CC's accepted: AE, MC, and V.

WHERE TO DINE: Fine dining is as much a trademark of the Brandywine area as are the historic museums and rambling gardens. With literally dozens of excellent restaurants in all price ranges, the following choices represent just a cross-section of old and new, a partial sampling of expensive to moderate menus.

The **Chadds Ford Inn,** Routes 1 and 100, Chadds Ford, PA (tel. 215/388-7361), dates back to the early 1700s when it was first the home of the Chadsey family and then a tavern and a hotel. Over the years, this sturdy stone building has evolved into a fine restaurant. Recently renovated and with a completely new kitchen, the inn still retains much of its Colonial charm with antique furnishings and century-old memorabilia. The walls also proudly display paintings by local artists like Andrew and Jamie Wyeth. Lunch choices, priced from $5.25 to $8.95, reflect 20th-century tastes (shrimp salad croissants, tortellini Alfredo, sole and spinach roulade, and burgers). Dinner entrees, priced from $11.95 to $15.95, include a range of dishes to please many palates—from grilled duck steak with port, Cornish game hen and braised quail, to veal Oscar, shrimp fra diavolo, and stuffed baby salmon en croûte. All main courses come with salad, vegetable, potato or pasta, and homemade breads. Open for lunch Monday to Saturday from 11:30 a.m. to 2 p.m.; and for dinner Monday through Thursday from 5:30 to 10:30 p.m., on Friday and Saturday from 5 to 10:30 p.m., and on Sunday from 3 to 8 p.m. CC's accepted: AE, MC, and V.

A similar history belongs to the **Dilworthtown Inn,** Old Wilmington Pike and Brinton Bridge Road, Dilworthtown, PA (tel. 215/399-1390). Located on the road that was once the principal connection between Wilmington and West Chester, this establishment was built as a house by James Dilworth in 1758, and, thanks to its strategic position, it also became a tavern within ten years. Restored in 1972 by innkeeper Timothy McCarthy, this restaurant now has seven dining rooms, on two levels, including the house's original kitchen. The décor is a blend of Victorian settees, old wood floors, hand-stenciled walls, 11 fireplaces, gas and candlelight lamps, copper fixtures, and Andrew Wyeth paintings. Open for dinner only, the menu features a gourmet medley of entrees such as filet mignon Beaujolais, breast of capon, shrimp scampi, crab en casserole, coquilles St-Jacques, and a variety of lobster dishes. Priced from $11.95 to $23, the main courses are accompanied by a house salad, potato, and fresh vegetable. The extensive wine cellar offers a choice of 400 different labels. Open Monday through Saturday from 5:30 to 10:30 p.m., and on Sunday from 3 to 9 p.m. All major CC's are accepted.

Expansive views of the Brandywine River and a modern décor are the keynotes of the **Lenape Inn,** Routes 52 and 100, West Chester, PA (tel. 215/793-2005). Although the original structure on this site was built as an inn in 1852, the current multi-level brick-façade restaurant is of much more recent vintage (1985). Lunch, priced from $4.95 to $8.95, presents a choice of salads, sandwiches, quiches, omelets, and a variety of hot meat and seafood dishes. Evening selections, which include salad, potato, and two vegetables, range from salmon in puff pastry, Dover sole, rainbow trout, and lobster medallions in champagne sauce to duckling with cider and apples, breast of capon with ginger, vegetable lasagne, grilled loin of pork, rack of lamb, and prime western sirloin steaks. Entree prices fall into the $9.95 to $19.95 level. Other features here are an extensive boat-shaped appetizer cart of raw bar items and attentive tuxedoed waiters. Open Monday through Saturday, for lunch from 11:30 a.m. to 3 p.m.; and for dinner from 4:30 to 10:30 p.m., and on Sunday from 3 to 9 p.m. CC's accepted: AE, D, MC, and V.

International dining is the theme of **Cuisines Restaurant,** 200 Wilmington-West Chester Pike (Route 202), Chadds Ford, PA (tel. 215/459-3390). Contemporary in style, this 90-seat restaurant is furnished with a relaxing blend of rose-toned fabrics, plush comfortable chairs, light wood trim, and plenty of glass and brass. Lunch focuses on hot and cold entrees, salads, and sandwiches, priced from $3.95 to $7.95. Dinner entrees include recipes from many lands such as paella, sole beurre blanc, sesame chicken, venison chasseur, sirloin steak Créole, shepherd's pie, and veal coquilles. These prices range from $11.95 to $18.95 and include a selection of seasonal vegetables. Classical guitar or piano is featured in the evenings. Open Monday through Saturday, for lunch from 11 a.m. to 2 p.m., and for dinner from 5:30 to 10 p.m. CC's accepted: AE, MC, and V.

A 30-foot soup, salad, and dessert bar is the secret of success at **La Grande Salade-Saloon,** Route 202, Glens Mills, PA (tel. 215/459-9915). Owned and operated by the Mangan family, this busy restaurant is decorated in a contemporary-country style with brass chandeliers, mirrored walls, captain's chairs, and paintings by a local artist. Lunch, priced from $3.95 to $8.95, features sandwiches, burgers, and entrees such as sesame chicken stir-fry, crab imperial, and petite filet mignon. The dinner menu, which ranges from $8.95 to $15.95, with most selections at the $11.95 mark, offers a choice of such dishes as prime ribs, soft-shell crabs, roast duckling, veal piccante, or scallop and red pepper pasta. The soup, salad, and dessert (make your own sundae) bar is part of all lunch and dinner selections. Other features of this restaurant include nonsmoking sections, live music on Saturday evenings, and an extensive wine list of California boutique labels. Lunch is served from 11 a.m. to 3:30 p.m. Tuesday through Friday; dinner from 4 to 10 p.m. Tuesday through Thursday, until 11 p.m. on Friday and Saturday, and from 4 to 9 p.m. on Sunday. Sunday brunch is also available from 10:30 a.m. to 2 p.m. All major CC's are accepted.

3. Historic New Castle

Located seven miles south of Wilmington, New Castle was Delaware's original capital and a major Colonial seaport. First known as Fort Casimir, this area was purchased from the Indians as a Dutch settlement by Peter Stuyvesant in 1651. It is said, in fact, that Stuyvesant designed the town's central Green by "pegging it off" with his wooden leg.

Later conquered by the Swedes and then the English who named it New Castle, this stretch of land along the west bank of the Delaware River is today much the way it was in the 17th and 18th centuries. Original houses and public buildings have been restored and preserved, the sidewalks are made of brick and the streets of cobble stones, and the people subscribe to the "commons" system of government—every property owner is part owner of the city.

THE TOP ATTRACTIONS: Chief among the sights to see in this historic district is the **Old Court House,** Delaware Street (tel. 323-4453). This is the hub of the town, and one of the oldest public buildings still in use in the United States. Originally built in 1732, with modifications and remodeling throughout its history, this landmark was Delaware's Colonial capital and meeting place of the State Assembly until 1777.

One of the court house's other claims to fame occurred in the 1760s when its cupola was used as the center of a 12-mile radius used by Mason and Dixon to devise Delaware's unique curved northern border. Among the contents on view are old maps and surveys, original meeting-room desks, quill pens, brick floors, working fireplaces, and paintings depicting the early days of New Castle. Tours are conducted by costumed volunteers, free of charge, Tuesday through Saturday from 10 a.m. to 4:30 p.m., and on Sunday from 1:30 to 4:30 p.m. (donations are welcome).

Among the restored residences open to the public is the **George Read House,** 42 The Strand (tel. 322-8411). Situated on the banks of the Delaware River, this house was built between 1797 and 1804, and is a fine example of Federal architecture in a garden setting. The man for whom it is named was a prominent lawyer of the town and the son of a signer of the Declaration of Independence. Interior features include elaborately carved woodwork, relief plasterwork, gilded fanlights, and silver door hardware, all reflecting the height of Federal fashion. The house is open year round (except January and February), Tuesday through Saturday from 10 a.m. to 4 p.m., and Sunday from noon to 4 p.m. Admission charge is $3 for adults and $1.50 for children.

These are just two of the more than 50 buildings and sites that can be seen throughout the New Castle district. The ideal way to explore the area is to take a self-guided walking tour called **The New Castle Heritage Trail.** This route is described in a leaflet proudly produced by the "Mayor and Council of New Castle and the Trustees of New Castle Common." To obtain a copy, contact the Mayor and Council, 220 Delaware St., New Castle, DE 19720 (tel. 302/322-9802).

WHERE TO STAY: Even though New Castle is less than ten miles from Wilmington, many visitors choose to stay overnight or longer in this charming corner of Delaware. If you have a car, New Castle can even be a convenient base for touring all of the northern part of the state, including the Brandywine Valley.

The Top Choice in the Center of Town

The best way to enjoy the ambience of this old-world town is to check into the **David Finney Inn,** 216 Delaware St., New Castle, DE 19720 (tel. 302/322-6367). Dating back to the 17th century and originally two separate structures, this building has had a varied life as an inn and private home to such leading citizens as a Delaware chief justice and the 18th-century attorney and militia officer David Finney, whose name is still over the door. It is ideally situated in the middle of town with its front facing The Green and its back overlooking the Delaware River waterfront. With its brick walls, warming fireplaces, and antique furnishings, the inn is much the way it used to be, enhanced by an added measure of modern comforts. The 24 guest rooms, some of which overlook the river and some the town Green, all have private bath; and for those who wish a color television or phone, portables are available. Rates for a queen or twin room run from $45 to $75, and suites are $90 to $120, including a continental breakfast in each case.

Meals are served in the gracious Colonial-style dining room or in the outdoor courtyard which is surrounded by well-tended rose gardens. Many tables also enjoy views of the waterfront. The menu changes daily, but at lunchtime you can expect to find an interesting array of salads, sandwiches, and hot entrees such as sautéed veal liver, ham and mushroom crêpes, monkfish with kiwi, or crab cake platter, priced from $3.95 to $7.95. Dinner entrees, which run from $12.95 to $16.95, usually include such enticing dishes as roast pork tenderloin, sautéed veal au citron, shrimp Provençal, chicken breast with raspberries, sea scallop stir-fry, or twin filet mignons with lump crabmeat. Lunch is served daily from 11 a.m. to 2 p.m.; dinner Monday through Thursday, from 5:30 to 9 p.m., Friday and Saturday until 10 p.m., and on Sunday, from 3:30 to 8 p.m. CC's accepted: AE, MC, and V.

Moderate Lodging on the Main Highway

Just outside of the town on the main north-south road, Route 13, you'll find the **Quality Inn–Dutch Village,** 111 S. du Pont Hwy., New Castle, DE 19720 (tel. 302/328-6246 or toll-free 800/228-5151). As its name implies, this distinctive motel is laid out like a little village of 41 individual cottage units with Amsterdam-style tile roofs and façades and front gardens with picket fences. Set back from the main road, with aged shade trees and an outdoor swimming pool, the motel offers large modern rooms with king beds or two double beds, color TV, individual air conditioning, and direct-dial phones; all rooms are ground-floor level and many are non-smoking. Doubles range from $45 to $55 per night. All major CC's are accepted.

Another convenient choice is the **Ramada Inn–New Castle,** I-295 and Route 13, P.O. Box 647, Manor Branch, New Castle, DE 19720 (tel. 302/658-8511 or toll-free 800/228-2828). Situated three miles from New Castle and close to the Delaware Memorial Bridge, this modern two-story 135-room hotel is designed in a modernized Colonial motif. The bedrooms, which are decorated with watercolors of historic New Castle, have two double beds or a king-size bed, color TV, a direct-dial phone, and air conditioning. Rates for a double run from $55 to $65. Guest facilities include an outdoor swimming pool and a lively pub lounge called Packet Alley with evening entertainment and music. In addition, there is a garden-style coffeeshop and a full-service restaurant, The Rose Room. Lunch items, priced from $3.95 to $8.95, focus on an assortment of sandwiches, salads, and hot dishes. Dinner entrees, priced from $8.95 to $19.95, include chicken alla marsala, duck à l'orange, Japanese beef salad, and "fisherman's wharf" (crab imperial, flounder amandine, shrimp, and baby lobster tail). Lunch is served from 11:30 a.m. to 4 p.m. daily, and dinner from 4 to 10 p.m. All major CC's accepted.

In the Budget Range

Also along Route 13 is the relatively new (1985) **Budget Motor Lodge,** 140 S. du Pont Hwy., New Castle, DE 19720 (tel. 302/322-1800). This 60-unit facility is designed in a U-shaped configuration, all on ground-floor level. The rooms are equipped with one or two double beds, air conditioning, and color cable TV. Rates for a double start at $35 and include complimentary coffee. All major CC's are accepted.

WHERE TO DINE: In addition to being the home of a very historic district, the New Castle area is also the location of the Greater Wilmington Airport and a growing number of commercial industries. Consequently, the majority of restaurants conveniently line the du Pont Highway, otherwise known as Route 13. Price-wise, the three restaurants below fall into the mostly moderate category.

Authentic Air Force memorabilia is the focus of attention at the **Air Transport Command,** 143 N. du Pont Hwy., New Castle (tel. 328-3527). Appropriately located close to the runways of Wilmington Airport, this restaurant commemorates the flying heroes and heroines of the World War II period with a décor of aviation memorabilia including old uniforms, newspaper clippings, pictures, and flying equipment. You can even pick up a set of headphones and listen to the ground-to-air instructions at the nearby control tower. The layout of the restaurant lends itself to browsing with lots of nooks and alcoves and a gentle room-to-room flow of background music from the '40s. Lunch, priced from $4.95 to $8.50, ranges from sandwiches and salads to hot beef and seafood dishes. Dinner entrees, priced from $10.95 to $15.95, include such varied dishes as veal saltimbocca, rack of lamb, prime ribs, shrimp and lobster stir-fry, farmhouse chicken, and roast duckling. All main courses are accompanied by soup, salad, choice of potato or rice, and baked cracked-wheat bread. Lunch is served Monday to Friday from 11 a.m. to 3 p.m., and Saturday from 11 a.m. to 2:30 p.m. The dinner schedule is Monday to Thursday from 5 to 11 p.m.; Friday until midnight; Saturday from 4:30 to midnight; and Sunday from 4 to 10 p.m. There is also a bountiful Sunday brunch from 11 a.m. to 3 p.m., priced at $12.95 for adults and $5.95 for children. All major CC's accepted.

An early American atmosphere prevails at the nearby **Lynnhaven Inn,** 154 N. du Pont Hwy., New Castle (tel. 328-2041). This reliable 30-year-old restaurant, just opposite the airport, has a décor of honey-colored brick walls, Colonial-style furniture and lots of brass fixtures including a huge American eagle over the open fireplace. Lunchtime selections, priced from $3.95 to $9.95, range from sandwiches, omelets, and salads, to hot seafood, beef, and chicken dishes. Dinner entrees, which come with salad and potato or vegetable, include steak Diane; veal medallions with mushrooms; soft-shell crabs au sherry; scallops in wine; crab-stuffed flounder; Chincoteague oysters in season; and broiled petit lobster tails. The prices range from $10.95 to $21.95, with most around $14. Open Monday through Friday from 11:30 a.m. to 9:30 p.m.; Saturday from 4 to 10 p.m.; and Sunday from 1 to 9 p.m. All major CC's are accepted.

Another good choice for seafood lovers is the **Lobster Shanty,** 130 S. du Pont Hwy., New Castle (tel. 322-2411). Lunch selections include fish burgers, lobster rolls, fried chicken, and a variety of sandwiches, priced from $3.50 to $6.95. The dinner menu, which runs from $7.95 to $16.95, offers many lobster entrees as well as surf-and-turf, shrimp and chicken stir-fry, flounder amandine, shrimp Créole, blackened fish, shrimp dijonnaise, and seafood fettuccine. Many main courses are $10 or under, and all include coleslaw, salad bar, and a choice of vegetable. Lunch is served Wednesday through Saturday from 11:30 a.m. to 2:30 p.m.; dinner Monday through Saturday from 4:30 to 10 p.m., and Sunday from noon to 9 p.m. All major CC's are accepted.

EVENTS: For more than 60 years, on the third Saturday of May, the residents of this historic district have opened their doors and staged **A Day in Old New Castle,** an event that can best be described as a grand open-house tour of the whole town. On this one day, New Castle's private homes, public buildings, gardens, churches, and museums are all simultaneously open to the public from 10 a.m. to 5 p.m. In addition, special events, such as a maypole dance, carriage rides, musical programs, and bell ringing are scheduled throughout the day. Tickets, priced at $10 for adults and $8.50 for students, can be purchased at the Old Court House on the day of the tour; advance reservations are not necessary. Proceeds are used for the preservation and continued restoration of the town's historic buildings. For further information, contact the Greater Wilmington Convention and Visitors Bureau, 1300 Market St., Wilmington, DE 19801 (tel. 302/652-4088).

Chapter XX

DOVER AND DELMARVA

1. Dover
2. The Delaware Beaches

SITTING IN THE HEART of the state, Dover is the capital of Delaware, located literally at its geographic center.

More than half of Delaware's total area is located between Dover and the state's southern border with Maryland. This also makes Dover the nearest major city hub to Delaware's 20-mile stretch of Atlantic coastal beaches.

GETTING TO DOVER AND THE BEACHES: Situated slightly inland, Dover is about an hour's drive south of Wilmington, approximately 40 miles away.

By Car: The best way to reach Dover from points north and west is to take I-95 or I-295 to Wilmington and then proceed southward via Route 13 to Dover. Route 13, which runs the entire length of Delaware, is also the best way to approach Dover from the south, via Virginia. From Dover, the most direct way to reach the beaches is to travel southward to Route 113 and then to Route 1 along the shore.

By Bus: Regular service into Dover is provided by **Greyhound,** 1465 S. Governor's Ave. (tel. 302/734-3372) and by **Carolina Trailways,** 650 Bay Court Plaza (tel. 302/734-1417). In addition, during the summer season, Carolina Trailways provides service into the **Rehoboth Bus Center,** Rehoboth and Lake Avenues, Rehoboth Beach (tel. 302/227-7223), and into **Bethany Beach** at Harry's Bait and Tackle Shop, 201 Central Blvd. and Pennsylvania Avenue, Bethany Beach (tel. 302/539-6244).

1. Dover

As Delaware's capital, Dover is the center of state government and home to many historic sites. Plotted in 1717 according to a charter rendered in 1683 by William Penn, Dover was designed as the court house seat for Kent County, a rich grain-farming area.

In 1777, however, this agrarian city's importance was greatly increased. The legislature of Delaware, seeking a safe inland location as an alternative to the old capital of New Castle on Delaware Bay, moved to Dover.

Dover subsequently became the state's permanent capital in 1792. One of the city's greatest claims to fame lies in the fact that a tavern on the Dover Green was the site of the Delaware convention that ratified the Federal Constitution on December 7, 1787. Since it was the first state to ratify, Delaware has ceremonial precedence as "First State" in all national occasions.

Today's Dover, a city of 30,000 people, is also the home for a cross-section of American industry. At least 18 major companies, from International Playtex and Scott Paper to General Foods, are located here. Don't be surprised if you suddenly find the aroma of chocolate pudding in the air!

VISITOR INFORMATION: The best place to begin a visit to Dover is at the **Delaware Visitor Center,** Federal and Court Streets, Dover, DE 19901 (tel. 302/736-4266). Centrally located near Dover's historic Green, this well-stocked office provides a wide range of literature on attractions of the city and state. The obliging staff also operates a free eight-minute audio-visual profiling the major landmarks and historic buildings. Hours are Monday through Saturday from 8:30 a.m. to 4:30 p.m., and Sunday from 1:30 to 4:30 p.m.

GETTING AROUND: Dover is almost two destinations in one. The downtown area is concentrated in a relatively small radius around The Green, an historic area where you'll find brick sidewalks and most of the government buildings and sightseeing attractions. You can park your car and easily explore on foot (with comfortable shoes). Dover's hotels and motels, however, are concentrated just east of the historic district, primarily along Route 13, otherwise known in Dover as du Pont Highway. This strip, which is also home to the Dover Downs Raceway, Delaware Agricultural Museum, Delaware State College, the Dover Shopping Mall, and the Dover Air Force Base, extends for several miles and requires a car to get from place to place.

Car Rental: If you haven't brought your own car to this area, some of the major car-rental agencies that have offices in Dover include **Avis,** 1620 S. du Pont Highway (tel. 734-5550); **Budget,** 1127 S. du Pont Highway (tel. 734-8200); **Dollar,** 324 Martin St. (678-0207); **Hertz,** Route 113 and Lebanon Road (tel. 678-0700); and **National,** Routes 13 and 113 (tel. 734-5774). **Rent-A-Wreck** also has a branch here, on Route 13 and Kings Highway (tel. 674-2077).

Taxis: **City Cab of Dover** (tel. 734-5968), operates a reliable taxi service, with 24-hour radio-dispatched vehicles.

Guided Walking Tours: An ideal way to get your bearings in Dover is to take a two-hour walking tour conducted by the knowledgeable guides of **Dover Heritage Trail,** P.O. Box 1628, Dover, DE 19903 (tel. 678-2040). Two different itineraries are available: (1) the Old Dover historic district, commencing from the Visitor Center; and (2) the streets of Victorian Dover, departing from the Delaware Department of Natural Resources and Environmental Control, 89 Kings Highway. Both walks are scheduled for Thursday at 10 a.m., May through October; no advance reservation is necessary. Tours can also be arranged for other days and times by appointment, year round. Rates are $3.50 for adults and $1 for youths aged 5 to 17 years.

WHERE TO STAY: Dover is not a city for grand or historic hotels, but for modern motels and motor inns, all open year round and set on their own grounds, with ample parking facilities. The major properties are situated along Route 13 (du Pont Highway). This road is basically a commercial strip, full of shopping and fast-food establishments.

In general, the rates for accommodations in Dover are in the moderate category. On some weekends, however, slightly higher prices are in effect, and surcharges as high as $30 a night can be levied during the May and September races at Dover Downs. It is best to check in advance, in case your planned visit coincides with a peak period.

The most complete hotel facility in town is the seven-story **Sheraton Inn-Dover,** 1570 N. du Pont Hwy., Dover, DE 19901 (tel. 302/678-8500 or toll-free 800/325-3535). All 145 rooms are furnished in a bright contemporary motif, with color cable TV, AM/FM radio, phones, and air conditioning. Doubles range from $61 to $64; suites are available from $85 a night. Guest amenities include a swimming pool, a kiddie pool, two tennis courts, a putting green, and babysitting services. Gilligan's, the hotel's tropical-style restaurant overlooking the swimming pools, features lunch items such as burgers, salads, and sandwiches, from $3.50 to $5.95. The dinner menu offers an international selection of dishes from wiener schnitzel, veal parmigiana, and chicken Cordon Bleu to London broil and a Chesapeake Treasure Chest (filet mignon with crab imperial or lobster tail). The entrees, served with salad bar and potato, are priced from $8.95 to $16.95, with the majority at $13 or under. Each evening from 8 p.m. to 1:30 a.m., except Sunday, there is also music and live entertainment in the hotel's Rooftop Lounge. Hours for lunch are 11 a.m. to 2 p.m., and dinner from 5 to 10 p.m. Breakfast is served in the coffeeshop adjacent to Gilligan's, from 7 to 11 a.m. each morning. All major CC's are accepted.

The closest accommodations to the city's historic district are at the **Comfort Inn of Dover,** 222 S. du Pont Hwy., Dover, DE 19901 (tel. 674-3300 or toll-free 800/638-2657). Situated five blocks from downtown, this facility has 94 rooms, laid out in two adjoining bi-level wings. All units are air-conditioned and have color TV; some non-smoking rooms are available. Doubles range from $38 to $50. Facilities include an outdoor heated swimming pool, gardens, and complimentary morning coffee for guests. All major CC's are accepted.

A Colonial country-style décor prevails at the **Best Western Capitol City Lodge,** 246 N. du Pont Highway, P.O. Box 543, Dover, DE 19901 (tel. 302/678-0160 or toll-free 800/528-1234). The 39 rooms, all on ground level in a semicircular layout, are equipped with color TVs, phones, and refrigerators. Doubles range from $38 to $45. Guest facilities include free coffee, an outdoor swimming pool, and a launderette. All major CC's are accepted.

One of the city's newest motels is the **Atlantic Budget Inn,** 1426 N. du Pont Hwy., Dover, DE 19901 (tel. 302/734-4433), opened in 1986 and located opposite the Dover Mall and just north of Delaware State College. This two-story brick facility offers 68 air-conditioned units, all with color cable TV, and many with balconies; non-smoking rooms are also available. Doubles range from $38 to $44 in a room with one double bed, $40 to $45 in a room with two double beds, and $42 to $50 in rooms with a king-size bed. There is also an outdoor swimming pool for guests. All major CC's are accepted.

A Budget Choice

The **PM Dover Motel,** Route 13 (North du Pont Highway), Dover, DE 19901 (tel. 302/734-5993), is located one-half mile south of Dover Downs. The 50 units of this motel are clustered into six building groupings, each with a Colonial-style façade and a cupola on the roof. All rooms are air conditioned and have one or two double beds, phones, and color TVs. Doubles range from $33 to $38, with slightly higher charges on weekends. There is an outdoor swimming pool for guests. CC's accepted: AE, D, MC, and V.

WHERE TO DINE: Dover has many fine restaurants in all price brackets. Here are some of our favorites.

The Top Choices

Located just north of downtown in a garden setting on Silver Lake, the **Blue Coat Inn**, 800 N. State St. (tel. 674-1776), takes its name from the uniform worn by the Delaware Regiment that marched from Dover Green in August of 1766 to join General Washington's army in the struggle for independence. Opened as a restaurant 20 years ago, this lakefront Colonial-style structure was once a private home. Four original stone fireplaces, weathered timbers, and antiques from the area, are all incorporated into the décor. The names of the various dining rooms, from the Independence Room and Liberty Room to George's Tavern, also reflect the early-American theme. Costumed waiters and waitresses add to the ambience. At lunchtime there is an extensive menu of hot and cold entrees, priced from $4.95 to $8.95, including Delmarva chicken, veal parmigiana, crab-stuffed lobster tail, and plantation shortcake (a turkey and ham pie topped with broiled peaches). Dinner entrees, priced from $10.95 to $19.95, range from Southern crab couplet (Maryland blue crab with Virginia Smithfield ham), shrimp Rockefeller, crab Benedict and prime ribs to seafood combination platters, all served with salad, potato, and vegetable. Complete dinner specials are also offered from $14.95, including the main course and accompaniments plus appetizer, dessert, and a glass of wine. Open Tuesday through Friday for lunch, from 11:30 a.m. to 2 p.m., and for dinner from 4:30 to 10 p.m.; on Saturday for dinner from 4:30 to 10:30 p.m., and on Sunday from noon to 9 p.m. CC's accepted: AE, MC, and V. For after-meal browsing, there is an adjacent stable, which once housed thoroughbreds, now converted into a "Gift Shoppe and Countrie Store."

In the heart of Dover's downtown district, you'll also find a Colonial atmosphere at the **Dinner Bell Inn**, 121 S. State St., (tel. 678-1234). A favorite with Dover area business persons, this restaurant does a busy lunch trade, featuring a menu of open-face and stacked sandwiches, create-your-own salads, and hot entrees ranging from chicken-'n'-dumplings to veal à la Gruyère, crab cakes, and petit filet mignon; prices range from $3.95 to $8.95. Dinner choices focus on an extensive seafood list (crab imperial, lobster scampi, shrimp Créole, and Cajun blackened redfish), as well as a variety of beef, veal, and chicken dishes from veal Oscar to Chateaubriand. Prices range from $9.95 to $19.95, with most less than $15, including salad and two vegetables. This is also the place to try flaming tableside desserts—bananas Foster, cherries jubilee or crêpes Suzette, each $6. Open Monday through Friday, for lunch, from 11:30 a.m. to 2:30 p.m., and for dinner from 5 to 10 p.m.; and Saturday for dinner only from 5:30 to 10:30 p.m. CC's accepted: AE, MC, and V.

About four miles east of Dover past several cornfields is the town of Little Creek, on the Mahon and Little Rivers off Delaware Bay, and the home of the **Village Inn**, Route 9, Little Creek (tel. 734-3245). Founded 20 years ago and still run by a local family named Roe, this restaurant has built its reputation on an ever-fresh seafood menu. The interior is a cheery blend of nautical and floral décor, with local handcrafts and grapevine wreaths. Lunch, priced from $3.75 to $6.95, consists mainly of sandwiches (try the oyster club or soft-shell crab on a toasted bun), salads, and seafood platters. House specialty on the dinner menu is fresh flounder, served stuffed with crab, breaded, poached, or whatever way you wish. Other seafood entrees range from oyster pot pie, lobster Thermidor, crab cakes, and stuffed butterflied gulf shrimp to a steamed seafood pot (king crab legs, clams, scallops, and shrimp). Steaks, chicken, and prime ribs are also featured. All entrees, which include salad, two vegetables, and fresh-baked breads, run from $9.95 to $18.95, with most under the $14 mark. Open Tuesday through Friday for lunch from 11 a.m. to 2 p.m., and for dinner from 4:30 to 10 p.m.; Saturday from 11 a.m. to 10 p.m.; and Sunday from noon to 9 p.m. Reservations are a must. CC's accepted: MC and V.

Moderately Priced Dining

One of Dover's newest restaurants, **W. T. Smithers,** 140 S. State St. (tel. 674-8875), has been named in honor of a colorful citizen who was, at various times, an ace baseball player, a lawyer, a member of the Constitutional Convention of Delaware of 1897, and one of Teddy Roosevelt's Rough Riders. To add to the historical aura, the building that houses the restaurant is actually the last home of this local hero. Handsomely redecorated and renovated to convey a Victorian ambience, the restaurant offers a choice of eight different appropriately furnished dining rooms including a library, a parlor, a tavern, a trophy room, a balcony loft, and an "anniversary room," ideal for special dinners for two to four persons. The menu at lunch features double-decker sandwiches, burgers, pasta, and vegetarian platters, priced from $2.75 to $4.95. Dinner entrees, which run from $7.95 to $14.95, include steaks, chicken Cordon Bleu, capon-and-scampi skewer, and a creatively presented seafood mosaic (lobster, shrimp, crab, and scallops). Accompaniments are a house salad, two vegetables, and potato or rice. Open daily from 11 a.m. to 2 p.m. for lunch, and from 5 to 9 p.m. for dinner, with raw bar and light dishes available all day until 1 a.m. CC's accepted: AE, D, MC, and V.

For more than 30 years, Doverites have enjoyed **The Hub** at Route 13 and Loockermann Street (tel. 734-7571). Located next to the Comfort Inn, this is basically a steak and lobster house with a relaxing décor of subdued lighting and dark wood. Lunch features salads, sandwiches, and hot entrees, priced from $2.95 to $13.95; a hot and cold buffet including dessert is also usually available for $4.95. Dinner entrees, which range from $8.95 to $19.95, with most choices under $14, include whole lobster, seafood combination platters, teriyaki shrimp and steak, prime ribs, and chicken Cordon Bleu. Homemade breads, open salad bar, and potato or vegetable come with the main course. On Fridays, there is a bountiful seafood buffet for $14.95. The Hub is also known for its disco, which operates at the rear of the restaurant, and for specialty drinks, priced from $2 to $3, such as cold buttered rum (butter pecan ice cream and rum); toasted almond (Amaretto, Kahlúa, and ice cream with crushed almonds); and frosted banana (bananas, ice cream, Amaretto, and crushed almonds). Open Monday to Saturday from 11:30 a.m. to 2 p.m. for lunch, and from 5 to 10 p.m. for dinner. CC's accepted: AE, MC, and V.

Budget Meals

A favorite stop at any time of day for travelers along the Delaware coast is **Captain John's,** 518 Bay Rd. at Route 113 (tel. 678-8166). Breakfast, served at all hours, includes an omelet bar, country platters, pancakes, and "the best waffles in Delaware," priced from $2.50 to $4.95. Lunch items, such as sandwiches and burgers, fall into the same price range. Dinner entrees, which include a 60-item salad bar, are priced from $6.95 to $11.95, for such dishes as fried chicken, seafood platter (shrimp, scallops, and flounder), crab imperial, steaks, and prime ribs. Captain John's is also famous for its all-you-can-eat buffets, such as Friday and Saturday surf-and-turf nights ($9.95). Open 24 hours a day on Friday and Saturday, and from 6 a.m. to midnight Sunday through Thursday. CC's accepted: MC and V.

Mort's Country Store and Eating House, 25 Loockerman St. (tel. 734-

9701), has been a Dover fixture for over 25 years, mainly because of Mort, a friendly and obliging chef/host. The menu, described as a blend of Israeli and Italian dishes, includes cheese steaks, salads, hot and cold sandwiches, subs, and "Mort's Special," corned beef with cole slaw and Russian dressing, all priced from $2 to $5. Breakfast items are also available until 11 a.m. each day (try the eggs and salami for a fast start). Open Monday to Friday from 6 a.m. to 5 p.m., and Saturday from 6 a.m. to 4 p.m. No CC's are accepted.

THE TOP ATTRACTIONS: Dover is centered around a park-like square, simply called "The Green," laid out in 1722 in accordance with William Penn's order of 1683. From the beginning, it was the site of public meetings, farmers' markets, and fairs. Today it is also the focus of activity for both the county seat and state capital. Most of Dover's landmark buildings surround the Green and the Visitor's Center is just a few steps away.

Chief among these historic sites is the **Delaware State House,** South State Street (tel. 736-4266), located on the east side of The Green. Built in 1792, the second-oldest state house in continuous use in America, this building was restored in 1976 as part of Delaware's Bicentennial celebration. It contains a courtroom, a ceremonial governor's office, legislative chambers, and county offices. Although the Delaware General Assembly moved to nearby Legislative Hall in 1934, the State House still remains Delaware's symbolic capitol. Open to the public, free of charge, Tuesday through Saturday from 10 a.m. to 4:30 p.m., and Sunday from 1:30 to 4:30 p.m.

The nearby **State Museum Complex,** 316 S. Governors Ave. (tel. 674-8818), contains three important buildings, the Meetinghouse Gallery, formerly a Presbyterian church, built in 1790, now the home of rotating exhibits highlighting life in Delaware; the 1880 Gallery, a showcase for turn-of-the-century crafts; and the Johnson Memorial Building, a tribute to Dover-born Eldridge Reeves Johnson, inventor and founder of the Victor Talking Machine Company, known today as RCA. The third museum, actually located one block west of the other two buildings at Bank Lane and New Street, is designed as a 1920s Victrola dealer's store, with an extensive collection of talking machines; early recordings; and an oil painting of "Nipper," the dog that made the RCA trademark, "His Master's Voice," household words in the early 20th century. All three museums are open, free of charge, Tuesday to Saturday from 10 a.m. to 4:30 p.m., and Sunday from 1:30 to 4:30 p.m.

Heading over to Route 13, you'll find the **Delaware Agricultural Museum,** 866 N. du Pont Highway (tel. 734-1618). Opened in 1980, this museum preserves and interprets 200 years of Delaware's agricultural heritage. All tours of the museum start in a replica of a large barn that houses a collection of antique farm machinery and tools; a short audio-visual presentation about 19th- and 20th-century farming activities is also shown here. Outdoor exhibits include an 1850 one-room schoolhouse, an 1893 farmhouse, a gristmill, a sawmill, a blacksmith and wheelwright shop, a granary, a wagon shed, and a meathouse. Special events are held throughout the year on the museum grounds, and basket-makers, quilters, and other craftsmen often demonstrate their skills; fiddle and string bands also play old tunes for dancing. Open from April through December, Tuesday through Saturday, from 10 a.m. to 4 p.m.; with additional Sunday hours from 1 to 4 p.m. in July, August, and September. Admission charges are $3 for adults, $2 for children aged 10 to 16, and free for children under 10.

Five miles south of Dover is **Dover Air Force Base,** Route 113 (tel. 678-6881), home of the giant C-5 Galaxy airplanes, the world's largest aircraft and the equivalent of an eight-lane bowling alley. This base is Dover's second largest industry and the biggest aerial port facility on the East Coast, with a 6,000-plus work force. The base is not normally open to the public, but if you plan a visit for the "open-house days" on the third Saturday in June, July, or August, you can get a look at the C-5's, with crew members on board to answer questions. On these days you can enter the base at the North Gate on U.S. 113 from 10 a.m. to 2 p.m. There is also an Airbase Museum displaying flight jackets, World War II memorabilia, and other flight materials.

If you continue southward on Route 113 and turn onto Route 68, you'll come to the **John Dickinson Plantation,** Kitts-Hummock Road (tel. 736-4266), the onetime home of Delaware's foremost statesman of the Revolutionary and Federal periods, John Dickinson. This fine example of Delaware plantation architecture was built around 1740. Open to the public, free of charge, Tuesday through Saturday from 10 a.m. to 4:30 p.m., and Sunday from 1:30 to 4:30 p.m.

SHOPPING: Since the state of Delaware charges no sales tax, many people find shopping here a wise expenditure. This area is best known for the Dover Mall, a sprawling complex on Route 13. This giant shopping plaza has four major department stores and more than 100 smaller boutiques and shops, selling everything from clothes and carpets to appliances and art works.

For something a little different, you should also plan a visit to **Spence's Bazaar,** Queen Street and New Burton Road (tel. 734-3441), a Dover institution for over 50 years. This big red building, formerly a tomato cannery, is a combination farm stand, flea market, and auction house. Local craftsmen and entrepreneurs gather here to sell, as do the Amish who bring homemade breads, pies, cheeses, and sausage. Open every Tuesday and Friday, from 8 a.m. to 9 p.m.

Dover's Amish community, located west of the city, also operates an excellent craft shop in the heart of farming countryside. Drive west on Loockerman Street and follow Route 8W to Route 198, also known as Rose Valley Road; one mile to the left is the **Rose Valley Quilt Shop.** You'll find an assortment of colorful items, from quilts and pillows to potholders and baby booties, all handcrafted in neighboring homes by Amish and Mennonite women. If you don't see what you want, special orders are gladly taken. Open daily (except Thursday and Sunday) from 9 a.m. to 6 p.m.

SPORTS AND ACTIVITIES: Dover's beautiful Silver Lake is the core of a parkside recreation area in the heart of the city. Walking, biking, jogging, boating, swimming, waterskiing, and picnicking are among the facilities available. Open each day from 8 a.m. until one hour before sundown, with entrances on State Street, Washington Street, and Kings Highway. Complete information can be obtained from the **Kent County Parks and Recreation Department,** 414 Federal St., Dover, DE 19901 (tel. 736-2090).

Car racing fans flock to the **Dover Downs International Speedway,** Route 13, P.O. Box 843, Dover, DE 19903 (tel. 302/674-4600 or 302/734-RACE), described as the world's most challenging high-banked superspeedway and the home of the "Delaware 500" auto races. Traditionally held during the third weekend in May and September, the "500" draws 40 of the top stock-car drivers of the world. Ticket prices for adults range from $18 for general admission on Saturday to reserved seat tickets of $22 to $80 on Sunday. Mail orders are filled and MC and V credit cards are accepted. In addition, from December through the first week of April, this track is open for a full program of harness racing. Post time is 8 p.m. Tuesday through Saturday and at 1 p.m. on Sunday.

EVENTS: Old Dover Days, the city's premier celebration, is held each year on the first weekend in May. On these two days, Dover's leading Colonial, Federal, and Victorian homes, mostly private residences, are all opened to the public. This "open-door" celebration has been held for over 50 years, making it the longest-running house-and-garden tour in the state. These 18th- and 19th-century homes, many clustered around The Green, include the Ridgely House, the Hughes-Jackson House, and the Carey House, as well as the governor's house. Hostesses in period costumes greet visitors and answer questions. The buildings are open from 10 a.m. to 4:30 p.m., and there are parades, music, maypole dancing, refreshments, and traditional crafts on sale on The Green. For advance information, contact the **Visitor Center** or **Friends of Old Dover,** P.O. Box 44, Dover, DE 19901 (tel. 734-2655).

A VISIT TO NEARBY MILFORD: Eighteen miles south of Dover, at the gateway to the Delaware beaches and the junction of Routes 113 and 1, is the town of Milford on the banks of the Mispillion River. Dating back to the mid-1700s, Milford was originally known for its gristmill and later for shipbuilding. But today Milford is more readily recognized as the home of World Championship Weakfish Tournament, a competition that offers $100,000 in prizes. Held in late May or early June each year, this event draws thousands of fishermen from more than a dozen states. Complete information about the tournament is available from **The Milford Chamber of Commerce,** 204 N.E. Front St., P.O. Box K, Milford, DE 19963 (tel. 302/422-3300 or toll-free 800/345-4444).

Not surprisingly, Milford also enjoys a reputation as a place to eat fresh seafood and at least three restaurants are worth a quick trip from Dover for a memorable meal.

A restaurant that combines an historic setting with fine food is the **Banking House Inn,** 112 Northwest Front St., Milford (tel. 422-5708). Dating back to 1787, the east wing of this building was constructed by one of the founders of Milford, Joseph Oliver, and later served as a stagecoach inn, while the west wing, erected in 1811, started as a bank. The two structures were joined in 1879 and restored in a Victorian style that is preserved today in the format of a restaurant and country inn. Stroll around the house, as Colonial music plays in the background, and enjoy the open fireplaces, mounted wildlife, century-old lodge chairs, hurricane lamps, crystal chandeliers, chiming grandfather clocks, antique sideboards, and heirloom silver. An inlaid parquet floor, said to be a duplicate of one in the White House, is a special feature of the dining room, which has a floral-motif setting of salmon pink, peach, and mint tones. Lunch fare ranges from homemade seafood chowders and casserole dishes to croissant and club sandwiches, salads, quiches, and omelets, priced from $3.75 to $6.95. Dinner entrees, which run from $9.95 to $16.95, include a host of fresh fish dishes as well as chicken boxwood (sautéed in herbs with creamy sherry sauce), duck Amaretto, and veal and beef dishes. Lunch is served daily from 11 a.m. to 2:30 p.m., and dinner from 5 to 9 p.m., and until 10 p.m. in the summer months. Innkeepers Charles Kable and Hubbard Macklin also have five refurbished and air-conditioned bedrooms available on a B&B basis, starting at $60 for a double (two with private bath and three with shared baths). CC's accepted: MC and V.

Since 1964, **Geyer's,** 556 S. du Pont Blvd., Milford (tel. 422-5327) has been synonymous with good eating in this area. Located at the junction of Routes 36 and 113, this is an ideal stop for traffic heading to or from Delaware's beaches. The restaurant started as a one-room operation but has since grown to three distinct dining areas, using contemporary, Colonial, and art-deco themes.

Lunch features a variety of hot and cold sandwiches, customized burgers, hot entrees, and bountiful salads, priced from $2.95 to $6.95. Steaks and seafood dominate the evening menu with such dishes as crab au gratin, lobster tails, seafood Norfolk (sautéed shrimp, crab, and scallops), prime ribs, and house steak (tenderloin filets topped with melted provolone cheese and sautéed mushrooms). Entrees, priced from $8.95 to $16.95, with most around the $12 mark, come with cheese and crackers, freshly baked bread, and two vegetables. Open Monday through Thursday from 11:30 a.m. to 8:30 p.m., and Friday and Saturday from 11:30 a.m. to 9 p.m. CC's accepted: MC and V.

A waterfront location overlooking the Mispillion marina is a prime attraction of **Oliver's Meeting House,** Routes 1 and 36, Milford (tel. 422-8877). Using an Americana theme for both its cuisine and décor, this restaurant is a showcase for old quilt hangings, farm implements, and Colonial-style curtains and furniture. The lunch menu features hot and cold sandwiches, salads, and hot seafood platters, priced from $1.95 to $5.95. More than a dozen seafood entrees are available for dinner including a "sea harvest" combination (petit lobster tail, jumbo shrimp, flounder filet, and crab imperial), as well as beef, veal, and chicken dishes. A "shore dinner" of chicken, country ham, and crab cake is also featured. The prices range from $8.95 to $20.95, with most dishes in the under-$14 bracket; included with the entrees are potato, salad, vegetable, and homemade muffins. Open Tuesday through Thursday from 11 a.m. to 9 p.m., on Friday from 11 a.m. to 10 p.m., and on Saturday from 5 to 10 p.m. CC's accepted: MC and V.

2. The Delaware Beaches

Often called the "Delmarvelous Beaches," Delaware's Atlantic coastal region stretches for more than 20 miles, a third of the entire state shoreline. Because Delaware's ocean beaches share the same peninsula with Ocean City, Maryland, and Virginia's Eastern Shore, the whole tri-state area is usually referred to as "Del-Mar-Va" or simply "Delmarva."

The most popular beaches in Delaware's stretch of the Delmarva peninsula begin at Lewes and continue along the ocean to Fenwick Island, the southern edge of the state.

LEWES: Situated at the tip of Cape Henlopen, between the Atlantic Ocean, Delaware Bay, and the Lewes-Rehoboth Canal, Lewes (pronounced "Lewis") is often described as the first town of the first state. This claim is supported by Henry Hudson's discovery of Delaware Bay in 1609 and a subsequent settlement in 1631 by the Dutch who sought to establish a whaling center here called "Zwaanendael" (meaning "Valley of the Swans"). Ever since then the Lewes area has been generally recognized as Delaware's first European colony.

In later years, Lewes was known by various names (from Whorekill to Port Lewes), and ruled alternately by the Dutch and the English, until it finally rested under William Penn's control in 1682, and evolved into a prosperous maritime town and seaport, occasional county seat, and leading fish-processing center.

Today's Lewes (pop.: 2,600) is still involved with the sea, as a beach resort, a boating marina, and as a port for dozens of amateur fishing tournaments. Also located here is the College of Marine Studies of the University of Delaware with its own shoreline park, harbor, and two research vessels.

The town's other claims to fame include being the home of the Barcroft plant, which manufactures and bottles Maalox, and the southern terminus of the Cape May–Lewes Ferry system. On an adventurous note, the waters off Lewes were also the site of the 1984 discovery of the fabled HMS *deBraak,* a reputedly treasure-laden British brig that was sunk off the coast of Cape Henlopen in 1798.

The Ferry

Many visitors come to Lewes via the Cape May–Lewes Ferry, a convenient 70-minute Delaware Bay mini-cruise that connects southern New Jersey to mid-Delaware and saves considerable driving mileage for north- or south-bound passengers along the Atlantic coast.

In operation since 1964, this ferry service maintains a fleet of five vessels, each holding up to 800 passengers and 100 cars. Departures are operated daily year round, from early morning till evening, with almost hourly service in the summer months from 7 a.m. until midnight.

Passenger rates begin at $4 per trip; vehicle fares, calculated by car length, range from $17 to $50, with reduced prices for motorcycle and bicycle passengers. A drive-on, drive-off service is operated, so reservations are not necessary. The Lewes Terminal is next to the Cape Henlopen Park entrance, about a mile from the center of town. Further information can be obtained by calling 609/886-2718 (in Cape May) or 302/645-6313 (in Lewes).

Visitor Information

For travel brochures about this area, contact the **Lewes Chamber of Commerce,** P.O. Box 1, Lewes, DE 19958 (tel. 302/645-8073). The chamber's offices are housed in the Fisher-Martin House, a charming gambrel-roofed structure at Kings Highway, next to the Zwaanendael Museum. Moved from its original location at Coolspring, this structure was once owned by Joshua Fisher who is credited with charting Delaware Bay and River. This is one of almost 50 houses in Lewes, many transported from surrounding areas, that are now fully restored and in present-day use in the town. Summer hours are from 10 a.m. to 3 p.m. on Monday through Saturday, and from noon to 3 p.m. on Sunday, with a reduced schedule during the rest of the year.

Getting Around Lewes

The best way to see Lewes is to bring your car. If you do take the ferry on foot from Cape May on a day trip, however, you can avail of local taxi and sightseeing services operated by **Kane Transport,** 217 Monroe Ave. (tel. 645-8100).

In addition, cars can be rented from **Diver Auto Rental,** Route 1 (tel. 645-6221).

Where to Stay

Lewes' choice of accommodations is limited primarily to modern motels, all within the moderate price range in high season and some in the budget range at other times of the year. It is best to check what rate is in effect at the time you plan to visit and if two- or three-day minimum stays are required; reservations are certainly necessary in the summer months and recommended at other times since the total room capacity barely exceeds 100. All of the motels described here are clustered at the entrance to the town near the canal and wharf areas, but not directly on the beach.

One of the oldest lodging establishments in the area, the **Angler's Motel,** Angler Road and Market Street, P.O. Box 511, Lewes, DE 19958 (tel. 302/645-2831), is very well kept and a favorite with fishing guests. Most of the 25 rooms enjoy views of the wharf and marina and there is a very pleasant open sundeck for the use of guests. All units have one or two double beds, color cable television, and air conditioning. Doubles range from $50 to $60 between mid-May and mid-September, with a three-day minimum stay on weekends. Reduced rates apply at other times of the year. CC's accepted: AE, MC, V.

Note: This is one of several properties in town using the name Angler. There is also a restaurant, not associated with the motel, using the name, as well as a marina and a road. For a community so involved with fishing, the frequent use of the word Angler is understandable, although it can be a bit confusing for visitors.

The **Cape Henlopen Motel,** Savannah and Angler Roads, Lewes, DE 19958 (tel. 302/645-2828), is a modern two-story L-shaped structure with 28 units. Each room is fully carpeted, with air conditioning, telephone, and color TV; upstairs rooms also have balconies. The rate for a double runs from $40 to $75 on Friday and Saturday, and from $35 to $70 from Sunday through Thursday, with a two-night minimum on weekends and a three-night minimum during holiday weekends. Open all year. CC's accepted: AE, MC, and V.

At the edge of the canal is the **Vesuvio Motel,** 105 Savannah Rd., Lewes, DE 19958 (tel. 302/645-2224), a modern two-story structure with a red brick façade. The 16 rooms enjoy views of the bay and canal and all have air conditioning, color TV, and phone. The price for a room with one double bed ranges from $25 to $60; a room with two double beds runs $30 to $65 per night. Open all year. CC's accepted: AE, MC, and V.

A Bed-and-Breakfast Alternative: The ambience of a bygone era is what Dick and Susan Stafursky offer to guests who come to stay at the **Savannah Inn,** 330 Savannah Rd. (Route 9), Lewes, DE 19958 (tel. 302/645-5592). A gracious old brick semi-Victorian house with wrap-around enclosed porch, this bed-and-breakfast facility is conveniently situated in the heart of midtown Lewes. There are seven bedrooms of varying size and décor, all with shared baths. Prices range from $40 to $55 per night for one or two persons, and some rooms can accommodate three or four persons, at a rate of $47 to $60. Open from late May until early September, this inn accepts reservations only for a two-night minimum on weekends and a three-night minimum on holidays. The rates include breakfasts of local fruits, juices, homemade breads and muffins, jams, granola, and a choice of hot beverages. No CC's are accepted.

Where to Dine

Like the lodging choices, the restaurants of Lewes nearly all fall into the moderate category, with a few variations. Because Lewes is a seaport, most of the restaurants offer water's edge locations, whether by the beach, the canal, or the marina. Seafood, understandably, is also the star of most menus.

Starting right at the beachfront, a top choice is **Kupchick's,** 3 East Bay Ave. (tel. 645-0420). This restaurant, opened in 1985, carries on a tradition of fine food started in 1913 when the present owners' grandparents, immigrants from Romania, began the first "Kupchick's" in Toronto and later added a second restaurant of the same name in Montreal. There are two dining rooms on the ground floor, each with a European ambience and décor, and a more casual upper-level open deck for sea-view meals on warm summer days. Lunch choices range from chili, salads, seafood platters, sandwiches, and burgers to omelets, priced from $3.75 to $7.95, with most dishes under $5. Dinner prices are mostly moderate, with entrees averaging between $12 and $16, for crab imperial, flounder breaded with almonds, shrimp scampi, or chicken Samuel (whole breast stuffed with bay scallops and shrimp). Many gourmet selections, however, like rack of lamb, stuffed quail, lobster, fresh swordfish, Chateaubriand and certified Angus steaks, run from $18 to $22 a person. All entrees include a relish tray, salad, homemade breads, potato or pasta, and vegetable. Kupchick's is also known for its "delmarvelous" chowder ($2.75 a bowl) and desserts such as key lime cheesecake, chocolate walnut pie, and raspberry soufflé, priced at $2.75 to $3.75 a serving. Light jazz is featured on weekends. Open year round, Kupchick's serves lunch from 11 a.m. to 4 p.m. Monday through Sunday; and dinner from 5 to 10 p.m. from Sunday through Thursday, and until 11 p.m. on Friday and Saturday, with slightly shorter hours in the winter. All major CC's are accepted.

Next door to Kupchick's is **The DeBraak Inn,** 2 Bay Ave. (tel. 645-2271), also situated right across from the beach, but with relatively few windows and little emphasis on panoramic views. Although it bears the name of the famous sunken ship, this restaurant has no direct seafaring connections other than a nautical décor and a collection of memorabilia relating to the treasure hunting in nearby waters. The emphasis here is quite simply on good food, with all dishes prepared to order. Lunch features seafood and a large selection of sandwiches, salads, and burgers, as well as waist-trimmer choices; the price range is from $3.25 to $6.50. The menu at dinner offers prime rib, veal or chicken Cordon Bleu, and a wide range of crab, flounder, shrimp, and lobster dishes. The DeBraak also claims to be "the home of veal Oscar" (made with veal cutlet, sautéed crab imperial, fresh asparagus, and hollandaise sauce). Entrees range from $7.95 to $17.95, with most dishes averaging about $12, including house salad, and potato or vegetable. An added feature on Wednesday through Sunday is live entertainment, described as "good for dancing but not too loud for talk"; no cover charge. During the summer months, "early-bird" dinners, offered from 4 to 6 p.m., also include a free twilight cruise aboard the charter boat *Angler.* Open all year, Monday through Friday from 11 a.m. to 1 a.m., and on Saturday and Sunday from 9 a.m. to 1 a.m. CC's accepted: MC and V.

One of the most unique dining spots in Lewes is **Desmond's,** 134 Market St., Canal Square (tel. 645-9339). The creation of owner John Desmond, this restaurant consists of a refurbished diving boat anchored on the marina, attached to a renovated chicken coop on the dock. Although it sounds outlandish, the result is a charming harborfront structure with a trendy open deck bar and several small dining rooms furnished with ladderback chairs, antique tables, and collectibles. An outdoor garden area, complete with roses and caged birds, offers extra seating in the summertime. Lunch choices, priced from $4.75 to $6.95, include crabmeat Benedict, homemade quiche, croissant sandwiches, and summer salads. The dinner menu, although limited to four or five blackboard selections, is a tribute to the small kitchen—from a most memorable spicy crab soup ($2.50) to succulent charbroiled soft-shell crabs, tender tuna and swordfish steaks, as well as prime beef. Entree prices, which include salad and vegetable, range from $9.95 to $14.95. Desmond's is also known for its unusual "Canal Bar" drinks ($3.50 to $4) such as frozen Irish coffee, and "Daphne Divine's Deluxe Dixie Daiquiri," a frozen blend of strawberries, Southern Comfort, and Amaretto. Open daily year round (except January), serving lunch from noon to 3 p.m., dinner from 6 to 10 p.m. CC's accepted: MC and V.

Some of the best wide-windowed harborside views can be enjoyed at the oldest eatery in town, the **Angler's Restaurant,** Angler Road (tel. 645-9931). Originally built as a local fishermen's clubhouse in 1937, it was converted into a restaurant on the marina in 1946. The décor is still decidedly nautical with mounted fish, ropes, and nets hanging on the walls. A favorite with fishing folk, Angler's is known for the casual atmosphere that pervades both the inner dining room and the enclosed outside porch. Lunches, which range from burgers and sandwiches to seafood salads, average between $2.95 and $6.95. Dinner entrees, priced from $8.95 to $16.95, include salad or cole slaw and a choice of vegetable. House specials are frogs' legs, imperial crab, and an assorted seafood platter (white fish, scallops, oysters, shrimp, and soft-shell crab). Open from May to mid-October, daily from 11 a.m. to 10 p.m. From July through Labor Day Weekend, an "early-bird" dinner special is in effect, offering customers a free cruise on the *Angler* boat after dinners served between 3 and 6 p.m. CC's accepted: MC and V.

Just down the road is **Fisherman's Wharf Lighthouse Restaurant,** by the Drawbridge (tel. 645-6271), also big on nautical décor and views of the marina. An all-day menu features soups, salads, sandwiches, and platters, priced from $2.50 to $10.95; especially worth trying are the seaside salads (greens topped with sautéed shrimp, scallops, and crab) at $4.95. The dinner menu also emphasizes a selection of fish dishes, such as seafood gumbo, crab cakes, combination platters, and lobster. Entrees, which include potato and vegetable, range from $9.95 to $19.95, with most choices around $13.95. Open from 11:30 a.m. to 5 p.m. for lunch, and from 5 to 9:30 p.m. for dinner weekdays, and until 10 p.m. on Friday, Saturday, and Sunday. CC's accepted: MC and V.

For a change of pace and scene, try the downtown setting of the **Rose and Crown Restaurant and Pub,** 108 Second St., in the historic 1930s Walsh Building. There is a choice of three separate eating areas—a bright and plant-filled front room with large windows overlooking busy Second Street; a clubby bar area with brass fixtures, seafaring scenes, skylit ceiling, and wall hangings from England and Ireland; and a cozy back room with dark wood trim, exposed brick walls, and a tin ceiling. Lunch fare includes pub salads, homemade soups, sandwiches, quiches, shepherd's pie, Welsh rabbit, and fish and chips. Most selections average under $6. Dinner entrees, priced from $8.95 to $10.95, include local seafood, London broil, mixed grill, Sussex Hot Pot (a delicately seasoned stew of lamb, potatoes, and garden vegetables), or "Toad in the Hole" (English sausages baked in a delicate Yorkshire pudding batter). All entrees come with a pub salad and choice of two side dishes. If all this hearty food gives you a thirst, remember that this pub is also known for its large selection of imported ale, beer, and stout from England, Ireland, and continental Europe, averaging $2.50 a bottle or mug. Open daily, serving lunch from 11:30 a.m. to 4 p.m., and dinner from 5 to 10 p.m. CC's accepted: AE, MC, and V.

A Budget Choice: The **Salad Shed,** 124 Second St. (tel. 645-7325), is a bright and cheery eatery in the heart of town, serving breakfast and lunch. The ever-changing blackboard menu consists of salads, homemade soups, "super" sandwiches, and a 14-foot 40-item salad bar, with eat-in and take-out services. Most sandwiches are in the $3 range and the salads are sold by the pound ($2.25 to $3.75). Open Monday through Saturday from 7 a.m. to 3 p.m. No CC's are accepted.

A Word About Breakfast: Since Lewes is a motel port, unless you carry a portable coffeemaker, you'll have to venture out for breakfast. Not all restaurants are open for breakfast, so here are the ones to remember:

Fisherman's Wharf Lighthouse Restaurant serves breakfast daily from "opening" (before the fishing boats go out at 7 a.m.) to 11:30 a.m. on weekdays, and until 1 p.m. on Saturdays and Sundays. Pancakes with fruit, three-egg omelets, and breakfast sandwiches are popular here, with prices ranging from $1.95 to $4.95.

Angler's Restaurant also offers a choice of egg dishes, hot cakes, omelets, or egg sandwiches, priced from $2 to $4.50, with an "all you can eat" buffet on Saturday and Sunday ($5.95 for adults; $3.95 for children). It's also open from early morning (before 7 a.m.) to 11 a.m.

The Salad Shed has a variety of breakfast items from egg dishes to sticky buns and fresh fruits, available each morning from 7 a.m. to 10 a.m., Monday through Saturday.

On Saturday and Sunday only, you can also try **DeBraak's,** popular for its creative country breakfasts including French toast, eggs Benedict, gourmet omelets, steak and eggs, and creamed chipped beef. Prices range from $2.50 to $6.50. Breakfast is served from 9 a.m. to noon.

The Top Attractions

Most visitors are drawn to Lewes by the beaches and marina, but you will find that many other intriguing attractions are well worth a visit once you come to this friendly and historic town.

Throughout the streets of Lewes, you'll see beautifully restored 17th-, 18th-, and 19th-century structures functioning as private homes, shops, churches, and public buildings, such as the visitor information center at the Fisher-Martin House (circa 1730). To guide you around, the Lewes Chamber of Commerce has designed a free pocket-sized brochure detailing a self-guided "Walking Tour" of the town. Some of the highlights include:

Zwaanendael Museum, Kings Highway and Savannah Road (tel. 645-9418). Designed in memory of Lewes' first Dutch settlers, this museum was built in 1931 to duplicate the architectural style of the town hall of Hoorn, Holland. The exhibits inside the Zwaanendael explore the rich and varied history of the area from the original colony to the present. Open Tuesday through Saturday from 10 a.m. to 4:30 p.m., and on Sunday from 1:30 p.m. to 4:30 p.m. Free admission.

Shipcarpenter Square is a complex of historic buildings, administered by the Lewes Historical Society, Third and Shipcarpenter Streets (tel. 645-6708). The buildings include an early plank house, a country store, and the Burton-Ingram House (circa 1789). This home, known for its fine collection of early-American furniture, is constructed of hand-hewn timbers and cypress shingles and also has cellar walls made of stones and bricks once used as a ship's ballast. The entire complex is open on weekends from 1 to 3 p.m. in April, May, and June, and from Tuesday through Saturday from 10 a.m. to 3 p.m.; admission is $2.50 for the whole project or $1 for individual buildings. In addition, guided tours, priced at $3.50 per person, are conducted on Thursday, Friday, and Saturday at 10:30 a.m., during July, August, and September.

A recent focus of visitor attention has been the *deBraak*—the treasure-laden, 18th-century British ship that was discovered off the coast of Lewes in 1984. A Nevada-based company called "Sub-Sal" used side-scan sonar to track the craft under the seas and raised it in August of 1986. If you are interested in having a look at some of the well-preserved artifacts and solid gold coins, inquire at the Lewes Chamber of Commerce to arrange an appointment.

Sports and Activities: With easy access to both Delaware Bay and the Atlantic, Lewes offers a wide variety of sportfishing opportunities. The fishing season starts when the ocean fills with huge schools of mackerel in late March through April; large sea trout (weakfish) invade the waters in early May and June; and flounder arrive in May and remain throughout the summer, as do bluefish and shark. As the ocean warms up in June, it is also time for off-shore species such as tuna, marlin, and dolphin. Bottom fishing in the bay for trout, flounder, sea bass, and blues continues all summer, with late August through September often providing the largest catches. October and November also bring porgies, shad, and blackfish.

From April through November, head boats leave every morning at 7 a.m. from the docks at Lewes harbor. A full day's fishing (eight hours) costs $23 per person. In addition, from May 30 to October 1st, additional boats go out for half-day trips, either from 8 a.m. to 1 p.m. or 1:30 to 6 p.m. ($14 per person), and, from July to Labor Day, there is a six-hour trip (priced at $18 each), leaving at 9 a.m. and returning at 3 p.m. From May through Labor Day, night trips also operate from Wednesday through Sunday, leaving at 7 p.m. and returning at 3 a.m. ($30). Half-price rates apply in most cases for children under 12. No license is required for most deep-sea fishing; rod rental is $4 to $5, depending on length of trip, and free bait is supplied. Arrangements can be made through **Fisherman's Wharf,** at the **Drawbridge,** (tel. 645-8862 or 645-8541), or the **Angler's Fishing Center** at the end of Angler Road (tel. 645-8212, 645-5775 or 645-6080).

Boat cruises—A good way to see the Delaware Bay and the Lewes Canal harbor is to take a boat cruise. Two-hour narrated sightseeing excursions are operated by the **Angler's Fishing Center** at the end of Angler Road (tel. 645-5775) on weekdays at 3, 5, and 7 p.m.; weekends at 7 p.m. In addition, another 7 p.m. cruise leaves from Fisherman's Wharf at the Drawbridge (tel. 645-8862) each evening. Prices are $5 for adults and $3 for children under 12, from June 30 to Labor Day.

Sailing—Fisherman's Wharf is also the base for a 50-foot ketch called *Iridescence.* Half-day sails cost $40 per person and can be arranged by calling Capt. John Nelson (tel. 645-5872), or by stopping by the boat when it is at the dock.

A selection of 15-foot fiberglass boats with a small outboard are available from **U-Drive-Em Boat Rentals, Rod & Reel Boat Rentals,** Fisherman's Wharf (tel. 645-8862). Rates, which range from $25 for a two-hour rental to $55 for an eight-hour day, include oars, one tank of gas and oil, life jackets and/or safety flotation cushions, and a map of the bay.

Windsurfing—Equipment can be rented at **Salty Dog Windsurf,** 26 Henlopen Dr. (tel. 645-5300 or 645-8384).

Bicycling—Lewes' historic streets and shoreline paths are also ideal for cycling. If you haven't brought your own, hire a bike from **New Happy Holiday Boatel,** 209 Savannah Rd. (tel. 645-8904). Although it deals primarily in boating supplies, this shop also rents bicycles from 9 a.m. to 5 p.m. seven days a week, June through Labor Day, and on weekends during the rest of the year. Charges average $7 for a weekend or $20 a week.

Other Sports—**Cape Henlopen State Park,** one mile east of Lewes, is a 2,500-acre outdoor playground for local residents and visitors alike. Bordered on one side by the Atlantic and on another by Delaware Bay, this is just the spot to enjoy beach swimming, tennis, picnicking, nature trails, bayshore crabbing, and pier fishing. This is also the home of the famous "walking dunes," and the 80-foot Great Dune, the highest sand dune between Cape Hatteras and Cape Cod. For those who enjoy a good climb, a refurbished World War II observation tower (115 steps) offers some of the best coastal views for miles. In addition, there are also 155 campsites, available from April 1 through October 31, on a first-come, first-served basis. Admission charges to the park are $2 for Delaware cars, and $4 for all out-of-state cars, plus 50¢ for each person in addition to a car's driver. For further information on the park's attractions, contact the **Cape Henlopen State Park,** 42 Cape Henlopen Drive, Lewes, DE 19958 (tel. 302/645-8983).

Events: Throughout the summer, Lewes is the setting for a number of **fishing tournaments** including competitions for trout (late May); shark (late June); tuna (mid-July); marlin (early August), and blackfish (during entire month of October). Whether you want to cast a line or just watch the action, complete details can be obtained in advance from the **Lewes Chamber of Commerce,** P.O. Box 1, Lewes, DE 19958 (tel. 302/645-8073). When you are in town, you can always get an update on the tournaments by calling the **Lewes Harbor Marina** (tel. 645-6227).

REHOBOTH BEACH AND DEWEY BEACH: Rehoboth Beach is a small year-round coastal community (pop.: 4,000) less than ten miles south of Lewes. Selected over 120 years ago as the site for Methodist camp meetings, Rehoboth was founded on strong religious traditions. Even the name, "Rehoboth," is biblical in origin (meaning "room enough").

Today, although the camp meetings have long since disappeared, there is still "room enough" for lots of visitors; more than 100,000 flock to this family-oriented resort in an average summer. Because Rehoboth has long been favored as a vacation retreat by leading politicians and lawmakers from the Washington, D.C., area, it is often referred to as "the nation's summer capital."

Rehoboth's popularity owes much to its idyllic location: a pleasant tree-shaded strip of land, bordered on the east by the Atlantic, on the west by the Rehoboth-Lewes Canal, and on the south by a natural waterfowl refuge called Silver Lake.

Neighboring Dewey Beach is also known for its magical setting. Nestled just south of Rehoboth on the lower shore of Silver Lake, Dewey is a unique stretch of real estate, only two blocks wide and divided by Route 1. No matter where you are in Dewey, just turn your head in one direction to see the Atlantic or the other way to enjoy Rehoboth Bay. In contrast to Rehoboth, Dewey is the state's youngest town and a lively nighttime spot, making it a great favorite with the young, single, and professional crowd.

Visitor Information

General sightseeing brochures, maps, descriptions of accommodations, and restaurant listings are available from the **Rehoboth Beach–Dewey Beach Chamber of Commerce,** Municipal Building, 73 Rehoboth Ave., P.O. Box 216, Rehoboth Beach, DE 19971 (tel. 302/227-2233 or toll-free 800/441-1329). The office is open year round Monday through Friday, from 9 a.m. to 4:30 p.m.; in addition, from Memorial Day through Labor Day there are Saturday hours from 9 a.m. to noon.

Getting Around

There is more to Rehoboth than its beach and boardwalk, and the best way to see the town's highlights is to take a ride on the **Jolly Trolly,** a 10-mile narrated sightseeing tour. Operating on weekends in May and September, and daily from June through August, the trolly departs regularly, from 9:30 a.m. through 8:30 p.m., from the Boardwalk at Rehoboth Avenue. The fare is $2; free for children under 5. The trolly is a subsidiary of **Kane Transport,** 217 Monroe Ave., Lewes (tel. 645-8100), a company that also provides local taxi service.

For people interested in visiting the Rusty Rudder Restaurant and its affiliated attractions at Dewey Beach, **Ruddertowne Transit Trolly Service** (tel. 227-3888) operates a continuous and complimentary daily shuttle from the Boardwalk at Rehoboth Avenue to Dewey and back, from noon to 1 a.m., Memorial Day to Labor Day, and on weekends in May and September.

Parking: Parking in Rehoboth Beach can be difficult. Metered parking is in effect (30 minutes, hourly, and up to 12 hours, with the majority of machines programmed for the first two time limits). This system operates from 10 a.m. to 10 p.m., seven days a week, May 1 to one week after Labor Day; head-in or parallel parking only is permitted. The number of spaces can rarely accommodate the demand, and consequently, you can waste a lot of time looking for a parking spot when you could be basking on the beach or relaxing at a restaurant. To ease the situation, most lodging places offer free parking to their guests and many people choose to park their car and leave it at the hotel or motel until departure for home. Rehoboth is small enough that walking usually proves to be the best way to get around.

Where to Stay

Most of the accommodations in Rehoboth and Dewey fall into the moderate motel bracket, although in July and August it is hard to find any room (single or double occupancy) near the beach for under $90 a night. If you must be beside the water, be ready to pay top dollar, or better yet, try traveling here in May, June, September, or October. And if you must come in the summer, be prepared to accept lodgings on side streets without views of the water and with compulsory minimum stays. In any case, reservations are always necessary in the summer and strongly recommended at other times.

Rehoboth Beach—Luxury Lodgings: First choice on the beach is the **Henlopen Hotel,** Lake Avenue and the Boardwalk, P.O. Box 16, Rehoboth Beach, DE 19971 (tel. 302/227-2551 and toll-free 800/441-8450). At the north end of the boardwalk, this gracious eight-story tower has a tradition that dates back to 1879 when the first Henlopen Hotel was built on this site. The present modern structure has 92 rooms (12 ocean front, 80 with ocean views), each with its own railed balcony, two double beds, air conditioning, and color TV. Rates for a double range from $55 to $85 in the spring and fall to $98 to $140 in the summer months, and include underground car parking. Two-night minimums apply for all weekend bookings and three-night minimums are required for holiday weekend reservations; the hotel is open from the end of March through September. Whether you are staying at the Henlopen or not, be sure to visit the hotel's rooftop restaurant and lounge, The Horizon Room (direct line: tel. 227-3373). It's got the best view in town (on a clear day you can see New Jersey) with floor-to-ceiling windows on three sides of the dining room and a menu that includes a variety of seafood and steak items as well as pasta and chicken dishes, priced from $9.95 to $18.95. Entrees are accompanied by soup or salad and choice of vegetable or potato. In the evenings, there is music at the piano bar, with dancing on Saturdays. Dinner is served Tuesday through Saturday from 5 to 10 p.m., and Sunday brunch from 10 a.m. to 1 p.m. All major CC's are accepted at the hotel and restaurant.

A few doors away is Rehoboth's largest lodging facility, the **Atlantic Sands Motel,** Boardwalk at Baltimore Avenue, Rehoboth Beach, DE 19971 (tel. 302/227-2511 or toll-free, 800/422-0600). This recently expanded five-story inn has 114 rooms, including four new efficiency suites, and is the only oceanfront property in Rehoboth with an outdoor pool. Each modern guest room has air conditioning, color TV, and a direct-dial phone. Open all year, doubles range from $50 to $130, depending on the time of year and if a room is "ocean front" or "ocean view." At certain periods, a four-night minimum applies. Facilities include a café, an elevator, and parking. All major CC's are accepted.

Rehoboth's Moderate Choices: Newly opened in 1986, the **Sandcastle Motel,** 61 Rehoboth Ave., Rehoboth Beach, DE 19971 (tel. 302/227-0400 or toll-free 800/372-2112), is a handsome five-story building right off the main thoroughfare, two blocks from the beach. Each of the 60 fully-carpeted and designer-furnished rooms has air conditioning, a private balcony, color cable TV, a direct-dial phone, and a wet bar with refrigerator. Facilities include an elevator, enclosed parking garage (free for guests), an elevated sundeck, and an indoor/

outdoor swimming pool with lifeguard. The Sandcastle is open all year, with doubles ranging from $40 to $95, depending on season. CC's accepted: AE, MC, and V.

The **Oceanus Motel,** 6 Second St., P.O. Box 324, Rehoboth Beach, DE 19971 (tel. 302/227-9436), is located two blocks from the beach, just off Rehoboth Avenue in a quiet neighborhood. It is an L-shaped, three-story building with 38 rooms, some with balconies. Each unit is outfitted with rattan furniture, air conditioning, a telephone, and color cable TV. Guest facilities include an outdoor swimming pool and free morning coffee. Open from the end of March to mid-October, rates for a double range from $30 to $80; at certain periods, weekend supplements of $10 to $20 a night prevail. CC's accepted: AE, MC, and V.

The **Admiral Motel,** 2 Baltimore Ave., Rehoboth Beach, DE 19971, (tel. 302/227-2103 or toll-free 800/428-2424), is admirably situated just off the boardwalk and one block from Rehoboth Avenue in the heart of the beach district. Open year round, this modern 66-unit motel has its own outdoor swimming pool, an elevator, and free parking for guests. Rates for a double range from $35 to $95, with a three-night minimum in the summer and supplementary charges for some peak or holiday weekends. All rooms have double or king beds, partial ocean views, direct-dial phones, color cable TV, air conditioning, and in-room coffee equipment; most rooms have a private balcony. CC's accepted: AE, Ch, MC, and V.

A Little Easier on the Budget: Atlantic Budget, Route 1, P.O. Box 630, Rehoboth Beach, DE 19971 (tel. 302/227-0401 or toll-free 800/245-2112), is located about 1½ miles from the beach on the main highway that connects Delaware's beach resorts. This modern two-story contemporary structure offers eight motel rooms and 56 efficiency suites, each with color TV, air conditioning, a direct-dial phone, and many with individual balconies. Guests amenities include an outdoor pool, free parking, and a shuttle service to the beach. Open from early April until September, double occupancy rates for the motel rooms go from $32 to $65, and from $40 to $85 for the efficiency suites. A three-night minimum applies for weekends in season. Major CC's are accepted.

Adjacent to the Atlantic Budget, you'll find the newly constructed **Econo Lodge Resort,** 4361 Route 1, Rehoboth Beach, DE 19971 (tel. 302/227-0500 or toll-free 800/446-6900). It has 77 units, each with color TV, a direct-dial phone, and air conditioning. Most rooms have a balcony, and some rooms are adjoining, ideal for families. Facilities including an outdoor pool, shuttle service to beach, and a guest launderette. In addition, free coffee and ice cream are available throughout the day. Doubles range from $33.95 to $65.95, with slightly higher prices on weekends. CC's accepted: AE, Ch, MC, and V.

Dewey Beach Moderate Choices: The ideal place to watch the sun go down on Rehoboth Bay is **The Bay Resort,** Bellevue Street, P.O. Box 461, Dewey Beach, DE 19971 (tel. 302/227-6400 or toll-free 800/922-9240). As its name implies, this relatively new (1983) motel and efficiency complex is right on the water at Rehoboth Bay and just two blocks from the ocean on the other side of the land strip. Facilities include an outdoor pool, a private beach, a 250-foot pier on the bay, and free parking. Each of the 68 units has designer-decorated furnishings, a balcony, a direct-dial phone, color cable TV, and extra-length double or king-size beds. All guest rooms face either the pool or the bay, with slightly higher charges for the latter and for efficiency units with kitchenettes. Doubles range from $34 to $80; depending on the time of year, there can also be a weekend surcharge of $15 to $25 per night and a three-night minimum on holidays. CC's accepted: AE, MC, and V.

The main north-south beach highway is the setting for two motels that enjoy equal views and distance from the bay or the ocean (both about one block away). The **Atlantic Oceanside,** 1700 Route 1 at McKinley St., Dewey Beach, DE 19971 (tel. 302/227-8811 or toll-free 800/245-2112), is a modern three-story structure with 60 rooms, all with color TV, air conditioning, direct-dial phones, and in-room coffee equipment. Open from April to October, doubles range from $35 to $85, with weekend surcharges in effect at certain periods and a three-night minimum required for summer weekends. All major CC's are accepted.

Just a block north of the Atlantic Oceanside is one of Dewey Beach's newest (opened in 1986) motels, the **Sand Palace,** Route 1 at Dagsworthy St., Dewey Beach, DE 19971 (tel. 302/227-4000). Each of the 47 rooms has a king-size or two double beds, a refrigerator, color TV, air conditioning, and a direct-dial phone. Guest amenities include a pool, free parking, and courtesy coffee service. Doubles range from $35 to $85, with a three-night minimum in the summer. CC's accepted: AE, Ch, MC, and V.

If you prefer to be right on the beach, then try the **Adams Ocean Front Motel,** 4 Read Ave., Dewey Beach, DE 19971 (tel. 302/227-3030). This modern 23-room property provides free morning coffee and donuts to guests in addition to all ocean front rooms, air conditioning, color TV, and free parking. Open from mid-March through October, the rates for a double range from $30 to $85, with a three-night minimum on summer weekends. CC's accepted: AE, MC, and V.

Where to Dine in Rehoboth

The Top Choices: Although this area is full of good restaurants, the closest you'll come to French country inn décor, cuisine, and service is **Chez La Mer,** at the corner of Second and Wilmington Avenues (tel. 227-6494). Specialties of the house include veal sweetbreads (Monday and Tuesday), soft-shell crabs (Wednesday and Thursday), and a spicy bouillabaisse (available every night for a minimum of two persons). Entrees range from $12 to $20, with most dishes around the $15 level; and are served with fresh vegetables and bread. All dishes are cooked to order, and special diets, such as low sodium, can be catered for. Open from mid-May to mid-October for dinner only, Chez La Mer is very popular and its three intimate little dining rooms fill up quickly, so don't dream of going without a reservation; proper attire is also a must. Open from 5:30 to 10 p.m. on weekdays, and until 10:30 on Friday and Saturday. All major CC's are accepted.

Away from the beach, and along the main north-south road, is the **Garden Gourmet,** 421 Route 1 (tel. 227-4747), a converted 100-year-old farmhouse surrounded by gardens on its own grounds (with parking lot). Furnished with antiques, crystal lamps, and chandeliers, the décor of this restaurant blends a touch of Williamsburg with Victorian style, plus lots of contemporary leafy plants and flowers. The imaginative dinner-only menu includes mako steakfish piccata, flounder à l'orange, veal à la creme, duckling with green peppercorns, and crab bake (twin crab cakes). Most entrees are priced from $13.50 to $17.50, and a 20% discount is given on all meals ordered by 6 p.m. Hours are 5 to 9 p.m. daily, year-round. CC's accepted: Ch, MC, and V.

For straightforward quality food and hefty portions, it's hard to beat the **Sea Horse,** Rehoboth Avenue and State Road (tel. 227-7451). This is a plush and welcoming dining room with sturdy captain's chairs, copper lanterns, a huge stone fireplace, and historical prints, with modern accents of burgundy wall coverings and panels of mirrors. Lunch ranges from burgers to crab imperial ($3.95 to $7.95). Dinner offers a wide selection of beef (from baked tenderloin of beef to Chateaubriand), and seafood (monkfish, salmon, flounder, Cajun blackened fish, lump crab, and rock lobster tails), with prices from $9.95 to $18.95. All entrees include salad, vegetable, and potato. Open year round, from 11:30 a.m. to 10 p.m. on weekdays, and until 11 p.m. on Friday and Saturday; there is also a huge guest parking lot. CC's accepted: MC, V.

A classy café ambience prevails at **Club Potpourri,** 110 Rehoboth Ave. (tel. 227-4227), an oasis for fans of live jazz as well as good food. The décor blends brass, globe lanterns, skylights, mirrored walls, and lots of garden plants. The dinner menu ranges from scampi Créole, coquilles St-Jacques, and crab-stuffed lobster to veal saltimbocca, Oriental chicken, or beef Wellington. All entrees are priced from $12 to $22, with most around the $16 mark; the accompaniments include home-baked breads, salad, and vegetables. Open year round for dinner, from 5 to 11 p.m., and until midnight on Friday and Saturday. CC's accepted: MC and V.

Moderately Priced Dining: It's hard to top the value at the **Dinner Dell Inn,** 2 Christian St. (tel. 227-2561), an area landmark that also happens to be celebrating its 50th anniversary in 1988. Surrounded by flowering gardens, the restaurant is furnished in a patio-style theme, with white lattice work, wrought iron, rattan, floral wallpaper, exposed beams painted green and white, tropical fans, and Polynesian-style chairs. Lunch, which focuses on light fare as well as burgers and sandwiches, runs from $2.95 to $7.95, but the star value here is dinner. Each evening brings a wide choice of meat dishes including Delaware panned chicken, Virginia baked ham, and prime rib cut to order, as well as a dozen fresh seafood selections from scallops to swordfish. For those who like to sample a few dishes, you can't beat the Captain's Plate (shrimp and crab au gratin, crab imperial, and seafood Newburg), or the Neptune Platter (broiled fish, lobster tail, clams, steamed shrimp, and king-crab legs). Entrees run from $7.95 to $18.95, with the majority under $15—and that includes two vegetables, salad, and hot rolls from the on-premises bakery. In addition, daily dinner "specials" average $12.95 for a complete dinner including soup, dessert, and coffee. Open from April through September, for lunch from noon to 2 p.m.; and for dinner weekdays from 5:30 to 9:30 p.m., and from 5 to 10 p.m. on Friday and Saturday. CC's accepted: AE, MC, and V.

The casual ambience of Key West dominates the scene at the **Back Porch Café,** 21 Rehoboth Avenue (tel. 227-3674). The décor is a mix of indoor alcoves with three outdoor decks, all furnished with an eclectic collection of plants, stained-glass, recycled theater seats, and sewing machine tabletops. Lunch items, priced from $3.50 to $7.50, include crab and spinach omelet, basil ratatouille, and salad sampler (choice of three different garden-fresh varieties). Dinner entrees, priced from $14 to $18, range from shrimp curry stir-fry, medallions of lamb loin, and blackened Cajun-spiced pork to marinated duck breast. Lunch is served from 11 a.m. to 3 p.m., and dinner from 6 to 11 p.m. CC's accepted: MC and V.

For more than 20 years, visitors have enjoyed a blend of nautical and garden ambience at the cottage-style restaurant known as **Café on the Green,** 93 Rehoboth Ave. (tel. 227-0789). Lunch fare ranges from seafood platters to croissant sandwiches, quiche, burgers, and salads, priced from $2.95 to $6.95. Seafood predominates in the evening with such dishes as flounder florentine, homemade crab cakes, golden fried oysters, and seafood au gratin, priced from $9.95 to $13.95. The menu also features surf-and-turf to fit various budgets (filet mignon and lobster for $17.95, or chopped sirloin and shrimp for $11.95). All entrees include salad and two accompaniments. Open May through October for lunch and dinner, from noon to 1 a.m. CC's accepted: AE, MC, and V.

Three miles north of town is **The Lamp Post,** Routes 1 and 24 (tel. 645-9132), a convenient restaurant if you are in transit along the beach coast or staying in one of the motels on the highway. Founded in 1953 by award-winning restaurateur Ruth Steele, this friendly spot has been enhanced and expanded by three generations of the Steele family. Tables are hand-crafted from authentic hatch-cover tops from the Liberty ships of World War II. Many entrees are priced under $10, for such dishes as broiled flounder, mussels marinara, grilled beef liver, steak en sauce, or "Delmarvelous" fried chicken. Other choices, in the $11.95 to $18.95 range, include prime rib, surf-and-turf, veal and crab, or scallops au gratin. All entrees come with soup, salad bar, and potato or vegetable. Open daily year round for lunch and dinner, from noon to 9 p.m. on Sunday through Thursday, and until 10 p.m. on Friday and Saturday; there is also live entertainment on weekends. CC's accepted: MC, V.

Budget Meals: Obie's By the Sea, on the Boardwalk at Olive Avenue (tel. 227-6261), is the closest you'll get to oceanside dining. A casual and beachy atmosphere prevails here, day and night, with an all-day menu of sandwiches, burgers, ribs, salads, and clam bakes (steamed clams, spiced shrimp, barbecued chicken, corn on the cob, and muffins). Prices range from $2.95 to $12.95, with most items under $10. Open daily May through September, from 11:30 a.m. to 1 a.m., with DJ music and dancing on weekends. Major CC's are accepted.

For light fare and refreshing snacks, try the **Royal Treat,** 4 Wilmington Ave. (tel. 227-6277), a restored Rehoboth landmark next to the Boardwalk with an ice-cream-parlor ambience. Most items on the menu average $2 to $4. Open from 8 a.m. to 11:30 a.m., and from 1 to 11:30 p.m. No CC's are accepted.

Dining in Dewey

The center of activity for the young (and young at heart) at Dewey Beach is the **Rusty Rudder,** at Route 1 and Dickinson St., (tel. 227-3888), a restaurant and entertainment spot right on the bay. Opened in 1979, the Rusty Rudder is a modern California-style eatery of indoor and outdoor dining rooms, open decks, and terraces. Success has also brought the recent development of the adjacent "Ruddertowne," a beachside complex of galleries, shops, seafood carry-outs, snackeries and bars. Rusty Rudder lunches, priced from $3.95 to $5.95, range from salads and sandwiches to Cajun catfish and other fish specials. Dinner entrees, which include unlimited trips to the bountiful salad bar, are mostly priced in the $9.95 to $15.95 range. Some favorites include chicken teriyaki, pan-fried backfin crab cakes, flounder amandine, and prime ribs. There is nightly entertainment with frequent big-name concerts on weekends. Open year round for lunch from 11:30 a.m. to 5 p.m., and for dinner from 4 to 11 p.m., with "early-bird dinners" served between 4 and 5 p.m. CC's accepted: AE, MC, and V.

A Word About Breakfast: Since many motels do not have restaurants, here are some of the leading venues for a morning meal: **Dinner Bell Inn** (8 a.m. to 11 a.m.); **Royal Treat** (8 a.m. to 11:30 a.m.); **Café on the Green** (8 a.m. to 2 p.m.); the **Lamp Post** (8 a.m. to 11 a.m.); and the **Horizon Room** at the Henlopen Hotel (8 a.m. to 11 a.m.).

The Top Attractions

Most of Rehoboth's activity centers around the mile-long boardwalk and

Rehoboth Avenue, the main street that runs perpendicular to the boardwalk at its center point. The **Boardwalk** itself is just right for strolling and to sample the variety of amusements, games, fast-food concessions, and shops. When the mood strikes, don't miss two unique Rehoboth experiences: **Dolle's Taffy** (established 1927) and **Grotto's Pizza** (since 1960). On weekend evenings in summer, concerts and other musical events are held (usually at 8 p.m.) at the **Bandstand** on Rehoboth Avenue, adjacent to the Boardwalk. Check with the Chamber of Commerce for an up-to-date schedule for the time of your visit.

A good place to gain a perspective on Rehoboth and its early days is the **Anna Hazzard Museum** at Martin's Lawn (tel. 422-8161). A "Camp Meeting Era" building, named for a former owner and civic leader, this house now serves as a museum for the area. It's open to the public free of charge on weekend afternoons, Memorial Day through Labor Day, from 1 to 4 p.m.

Sports and Activities

Swimming and sunning on Rehoboth's wide sandy beaches are the top activities. All the beaches have public access and offer a wide range of daily rental services: umbrellas, $5; chairs, $2.50; and rafts, $5.

Bay Sports, 11 Dickinson St., Dewey Beach (tel. 227-7590) rents pedal boats, windsurfers, sunfish, and jet skis by the half hour, hourly, or by the day. Rates for pedal boats start at $6 for a half hour; hourly charges for a windsurfer or sunfish are $12; and jet skis are $10. Sailing and windsurfing lessons are also arranged.

For a selection of water sports, plan to visit the **Delaware Seashore State Park,** Route 1 (tel. 227-2800), located two miles south of Rehoboth Beach. This beachland paradise offers both the crashing surf of the Atlantic and the gentle waters of Rehoboth Bay. Facilities include lifeguard-supervised swimming, surfing, and fishing. In addition, there is a full-service boating marina and a bayshore campground with 295 sites for tents and trailers. Admission to the park is $2 for Delaware cars and $4 for out-of-state vehicles.

Bicycling: The flat Rehoboth terrain and cool sea breezes also make bicycling popular here. Bikes are allowed on the boardwalk during the hours of 5 a.m. to 10 a.m. from May 15 to September 15. You can rent all types of equipment from **Boardwalk Bikes,** on the Boardwalk at 1 Virginia Ave., Rehoboth Beach, open daily from 7 a.m. to 5 p.m.; rates range from $2 to $4 an hour and $5 to $10 a day. Also try **Bob's Rentals,** N. First St., at Maryland Avenue, Rehoboth Beach, for two- and three-wheelers by the hour, day, or week.

Events: Highlight of the summer calendar is the **Annual Rehoboth Beach Sandcastle Contest,** usually the first Saturday of August. Held at Fishermen's Beach, just north of the Henlopen Hotel, this competition is open to all, free of charge; divisions include sand castle, whale sculpture, and free form, all in children's and adult categories. If outdoor fairs and antique shows interest you, plan a visit to Rehoboth in the spring or fall. **Sidewalk sales,** held along Rehoboth Avenue during the second weekend of May and the third weekend of September draw enthusiastic followers. The Chamber of Commerce is the best source for information on all of these gatherings.

Children's Corner: A **Summer Children's Theatre** is operated at the All Saints Parish Hall, Olive Avenue (tel. 227-6766). Curtain is at 7:30 p.m., and prices for all seats are $2.50. The repertoire includes *Snow White, The Magic Flute,* and *Peter Pan.*

Rehoboth Beach has two summertime Boardwalk family amusement areas, **Funland,** situated off Delaware Avenue, with rides and games (opens at 1 p.m. daily); and **Playland,** off Wilmington Avenue, which features video games for all ages (open from 10 a.m. to midnight). About 1½ miles north of town there is also **Sports Complex,** Route 1 and Country Club Road. This is a family fun park with go-kart tracks, miniature golf, a waterslide, bumper boats, kiddie canoes, and other outdoor rides.

Just in case it rains, you can take the children to **Bad Beach Day Matinees** at the Midway Palace Multi-Theatre, Midway Shopping Centre, Route 1 (tel. 645-0200). On wet days, this complex offers family-oriented movies at 1 p.m.

BETHANY BEACH AND FENWICK ISLAND: Bethany Beach and Fenwick Island comprise a thin and mostly finger-like stretch of land between the Delaware Seashore State Park and the Maryland border. This southernmost tip of Delaware is fittingly and accurately referred to as the land of "The Quiet Resorts."

With the Atlantic Ocean on its eastern shore and various stretches of inland waters (from the Indian River Bay to the Little Assawoman Bay) to the west, these "quiet resorts" are relatively undeveloped, compared to the side-by-side condos, towering hotels, and nightlife meccas of nearby Ocean City, Maryland. The contrast when you cross the border is astonishing, like another world. Certainly, you'll find the best of both worlds all within a short drive.

Like Rehoboth, Bethany was named after a biblical place (Bethany was the home of Lazarus). Also like Rehoboth, Bethany Beach got its start when it was chosen as a site for 19th-century gatherings of a religious group (the Christian Church Conference).

Of more recent origin, Fenwick, one mile north of the Maryland/Delaware border, is actually divided into two distinct areas. The southern section is unincorporated and county-zoned (multi-family dwellings, such as motels, are allowed) and the northern section is an incorporated town with building codes that call primarily for single-family residences.

Both Bethany and Fenwick pride themselves on being "quiet" family-style resorts. These communities are still very much residential, with strict control on the height and size of any new buildings. You won't find any large resort hotels, major lodging chains, sophisticated tourist attractions, or entertainment complexes here. With almost everything geared to a tranquil atmosphere and a low-key pace, Bethany and Fenwick are unique finds, almost undiscovered by the average East Coast beach traveler. And the people who live here intend to keep the "quiet resorts" just the way they are.

Visitor Information

The **Bethany-Fenwick Area Chamber of Commerce,** P.O. Box 502, Bethany Beach, DE 19930 (tel. 302/539-2100), is situated on Route 1, otherwise known as Ocean Highway, adjacent to the Fenwick Island State Park at the Fenwick Line. In keeping with the shoreline ambience of the area, the office is designed like a beach house with wide windows overlooking the ocean and snow-white sands. The Chamber publishes a very helpful booklet called *The Quiet Resorts,* and also stocks brochures from leading motels, restaurants, and other visitor services. Hours are from 10 a.m. to 5 p.m. Monday through Friday, and from 10 a.m. to 2 p.m. on Saturday, Sunday, and holidays; in winter, from 10 a.m. to 4 p.m. Monday through Friday.

Getting Around

Since Bethany Beach and Fenwick Island are within five miles of each other, the predominant mode of transport is car. Most visitors bring their own vehicles or hire cars from nearby rental stations in Ocean City, Maryland; or the upstate cities of Dover and Wilmington. Like Rehoboth, many Bethany and Fenwick streets are subject to meter or permit parking and the rules are strictly enforced. Fortunately, all the motels provide free parking for guests and most of the restaurants also have access to plentiful parking for customers.

Where to Stay

Like the other Delaware coastal resorts, Bethany Beach and Fenwick Island depend on the summer season when the beaches are at their best. Rooms are not only booked out months in advance for July and August, but they are also at the highest rate levels, often with weekend surcharges and two- or three-night minimums. Motels that would otherwise be considered in a moderate or budget category at other times of the year will run between $70 and $100 for a double. If you'd like to keep the costs reasonable, try to come during midweek or consider a visit in May, June, September, or October when the weather can be almost as warm and the sea breezes just as balmy as the high season.

Motels in the Bethany Area: Bethany Arms Motel and Apts., Atlantic Avenue and Hollywood Street, P.O. Box 29, Bethany Beach, DE 19930 (tel. 302/539-9603). This modern five-building complex offers a choice of basic motel units with two double beds and a refrigerator, or several types of efficiencies with fully equipped kitchens, double or queen-sized beds, and many with ocean-front views. All units have air conditioning, color cable TV, and parking privileges. Two buildings are right on the boardwalk and the other three are situated just behind the first two, between the boardwalk and Atlantic Avenue; all are two- or three-stories high. Open from early March to mid-December, rates for a double range from $45 to $80 in the motel rooms, and from $60 to $120 for the apartments, depending on the season and the type of unit chosen. A two-night minimum is in effect on summer weekends; holiday periods (such as Memorial and Labor Day weekends) often have three-night minimums and some surcharges. CC's accepted: MC and V.

Nearby is **Sea Crest Motel,** 99 Garfield Parkway, Bethany Beach, DE 19930 (tel. 302/539-7621), situated next to the Boardwalk and the Holiday House Restaurant. A Bethany favorite for more than 40 years, this small Colonial-style motel has 14 spacious rooms, all air-conditioned, fully-carpeted, with color cable TV, and free continental breakfast. The lobby level also houses a unique boutique selling one-of-a-kind jewelry, watercolors, and unusual seacraft gifts. Open all year, rates for a double range from $50 to $70 in the high season, with lower rates at other times. CC's accepted: Ch, Disc, MC, and V.

The **Harbor View Motel,** Route 1, R.D. 1, P.O. Box 102, Bethany Beach, DE 19930 (tel. 302/539-0500), is located two miles north of Bethany Beach, on the bay side, but with views of both bay and ocean. This modern two-story building offers 60 motel rooms, priced from $40 to $75, and eight efficiencies, from $50 to $80, with some weekend surcharges and three-day minimums in season. All units have color TV, air conditioning, telephone, and some have individual Jacuzzis. Guest facilities include complimentary continental breakfast, an outdoor swimming pool, a sundeck on the bay, and a launderette. Open from March to December; CC's accepted: AE, Ch, MC, and V.

Condo Rentals by the Week or Weekend: Sea Colony, Middlesex, Drawer L, Bethany Beach, DE 19930 (tel. 302/539-6961 or toll-free 800/732-2656), is a condominium resort comprised of 10 different buildings, many as high as 14 stories. It is the only high-rise residential property in the area, built before current restrictions were put into effect. Although most of the units are for sale, a limited number are available for short-term rentals. Accommodations (with a choice of one to four bedrooms) range from oceanfront apartments to secluded townhouse villas in garden, seaside, or tennis community settings. Rental rates per unit range from $125 to $400 for a weekend and $250 to $1200 for a week, depending on size and season. Guest amenities include a half mile of beachfront, 37 acres of gardens and greenery, seven swimming pools, a sauna and health club, 21 tennis courts, and a full program of social activities. No CC's are accepted.

Fenwick Island Motels: The only accommodations right on the beach in Fenwick are at **The Sea Charm,** Oceanfront and Bunting Avenue, Fenwick Island, DE 19944 (tel. 302/539-9613), a vintage three-story house with wraparound porches on two levels. Fully renovated and converted into 15 individual air-conditioned units, this family-run inn offers a choice of motel rooms from $40 to $70; oceanfront efficiencies from $50 to $80; and one-bedroom oceanview apartments from $50 to $85. There is also one three-bedroom apartment, which rents for $60 to $100 a day. Open from mid-May to October, a three-night minimum reservation is required throughout the season and some surcharges apply on weekends. Facilities for guests include color cable TV in all units, balconies with some rooms, and the use of a ground-level patio/deck with picnic furniture and outdoor grills. CC's accepted: MC and V.

Sands Motel, Route 1 (Ocean Highway) at James Street, Fenwick Island, DE 19944 (tel. 302/539-7745 or 302/539-8200 and from December to March 301/289-2152), is situated on the oceanside of the highway, but not directly on the oceanfront. It is a modern building offering a choice of 18 doubles, priced from $30 to $65; eight efficiencies, from $40 to $80; or 10 apartments, from $45 to $90. Each unit has air conditioning, color cable TV, and an AM/FM radio; rooms on the second floor also have balconies and views of the bay or ocean. Facilities include a large kidney-shaped pool and easy access to the beach. Open from March through November, rates are subject to a three-day minimum stay in season, holidays, and weekends; surcharges also apply for certain weekend bookings. All major CC's are accepted.

Opened in 1985, the **Fenwick Islander,** Route 1 and South Carolina Avenue, Fenwick Island, DE 19944 (tel. 302/539-2333), is a bright and modern three-story efficiency motel on the bay side of the highway. There are 63 units, each pleasantly furnished in pastels and fully carpeted, with a direct-dial phone, color cable TV, a refrigerator, and kitchenette facilities; second- and third-floor rooms also have balconies. Guest amenities include a guarded outdoor swimming pool and a launderette. Open from April through October, doubles range from $40 to $90 per night; weekend and holiday rates are subject to surcharges. CC's accepted: AE, Ch, MC, and V.

Where to Dine

The restaurants of the Bethany Beach and Fenwick Island area provide a pleasant blend of waterside and inland dining, and all at fairly moderate prices. Because these two resorts are very popular with families, there are also some fine examples of lower-priced restaurants that offer a high level of quality, ambience, and creative cooking. Most restaurants serve liquor, unless otherwise noted; also note that in Bethany, alcoholic beverages are only available in restaurants—there are no bars.

Moderately Priced Bethany Area Dining: For oceanfront dining, don't miss **Holiday House Seafood Restaurant,** Garfield Parkway and the Boardwalk, Bethany Beach (tel. 539-7298). Light fare, sandwiches, and salads are available for lunch, mostly under the $5 mark. The menu at dinner, priced from $8.95 to $21.95, includes prime rib, Delaware fried chicken, and veal and pork dishes. But the emphasis is on seafood—from sautéed shrimp scampi and broiled scallops to local soft-shell crabs and broiled crab-stuffed flounder. If you'd like to try a little of everything, this is the ideal place; a nightly "all you can eat" seafood smorgasbord, priced at $16.95, is also available. Help yourself to a dozen varieties of seafood, from whole steamed crabs to crab legs and claws, oysters, shrimp, clams, and an array of locally caught fish, along with roast beef, fried chicken, and the "largest salad bar on the shore." Open for lunch from 11:30 a.m. to 2 p.m., and for dinner from 5 to 9 p.m. CC's accepted: AE, MC, and V.

South of Bethany, just opposite the Sea Colony, is the small cottage-style **Peppermill Restaurant,** Route 1, Bethany Beach (tel. 539-4722). The cheery décor includes a welcoming fireplace, hanging plants, colored glass, lantern lights, etched-glass globes, framed prints, and a giant working peppermill in the center of the room. Lunch, which primarily focuses on salads, sandwiches, omelets, and pastas, is priced from $2.95 to $6.95. Dinner entrees, which range from $10.95 to $19.95, are a gourmet's delight: from beef Wellington and French pepper steak to sautéed veal and crab; stuffed breast of capon; duckling in raspberry sauce; scallops in champagne; flounder en croûte; lobster medallions in triple mustard sauce; and "seafood peppermill" (scallops, shrimp, crab, and flounder, sautéed in a light garlic and lemon sauce). All dishes are served with salad, vegetable, potato, and freshly baked onion bread. Finish off a meal with one of the three dozen different Peppermill specialty coffee drinks such as "girl scout cookie" (white crème de menthe, dark crème de cacao, and cream), "nutty Irishman" (Bailey's Irish Cream, Frangelico, and cream), or "Tennessee mud" (Jack Daniels, Amaretto, and cream). Open daily year round, for lunch from 11 a.m. to 3 p.m. Monday to Saturday; dinner from 5 to 10 p.m. Monday to Thursday, and until 11 p.m. on Friday and Saturday. CC's accepted: AE, Ch, MC, and V.

About two miles northwest of Bethany Beach on Indian River Bay is **Topside,** White Creek County Route 360, Ocean View (tel. 539-7983), a waterfront restaurant with a deck overlooking the marina and an ideal spot to see some of Delaware's dramatic sunsets. Lunch, from $3.95 to $5.95, features light fare such as sandwiches, omelets, and salads. Dinner entrees, which come with a bountiful salad bar and potato, are priced from $9.95 to $19.95, with most about $13.95. Choices include surf-and-turf, London broil, prime ribs, seafood platters, and fresh daily fish specials. Open daily, serving lunch from 11:30 a.m. to 3 p.m., and dinner from 4:30 to 10 p.m. CC's accepted: MC and V.

The ambience of the Carolinas is the main feature of **Magnolia's Restaurant,** Cedar Neck Road, Ocean View (tel. 539-5671). There are no great sea views or wide windows here, but an elegant décor of lace curtains and tablecloths, light woods, ceiling fans, colored glass, and lots of leafy plants and flowers. The dinner menu, with entrees priced from $8.95 to $15.95, is a medley of dishes influenced by the old South—from baked Dixie chicken, lobster Savannah, or a broiled seafood "plantation platter," to Cajun-style shrimp New Orleans, flounder veranda (with crab and artichoke hearts in a mornay sauce), and veal magnolia (topped by buttered crab sauce and shrimp). Open daily from 5 to 11 p.m. for dinner; a light menu of "fun foods" is also available from 11 a.m. to midnight for lunch or snacks in an adjacent pub room, priced from $2.75 to $5.95. CC's accepted: AE, MC, and V.

North of central Bethany and adjacent to the Harbor View Motel is the **Harbor Lights Restaurant,** Route 1, Bethany Beach (tel. 539-3061), in an ideal location with views of the bay, the ocean, and adjacent sand dunes. There is a lively lounge on the lower level with entertainment most evenings from 10 p.m.

to 1 a.m., and an upstairs restaurant with a contemporary and open décor featuring ceiling hangings of colorful kites and windsocks. Lunch, mainly salads, sandwiches, and burgers, ranges from $2.95 to $5.95. At dinner there is a wide choice of bay and ocean seafood entrees including soft-shell crabs, swordfish, flounder florentine, shrimp and scallop scampi, and a house special of seafood crêpes. Meat dishes range from veal Oscar to steaks. Prices run from $9.95 to $17.95, with most entrees under $14. Accompaniments include a complimentary cheese tray or vegetable crûdités, salad, potato or vegetable, and a basket of freshly baked breads. Open daily, April to October, for lunch and dinner from 11 a.m. to 9 p.m. on weekdays, and until 10 p.m. on weekends. CC's accepted: MC and V.

For light meals and snacks with an international flair, try the **Dream Café,** Pennsylvania Avenue and Campbell Place, Bethany Beach, (tel. 539-1588). This small restaurant is a combination sidewalk café and gourmet delicatessen, featuring a variety of foods made fresh daily on the premises—from salads (try the tuna curry with grapes), to croissant sandwiches, pastas, and cheeses from around the world. Sweet treats include berry pies and homemade ice cream (chocolate hazelnut, zabaglione, and black currant sorbetto are favorites). Prices of most items range from $2.95 to $5.95. Open daily from 8 a.m. to 10 p.m., with eat-in or carry-out services. CC's accepted: MC and V.

Moderately Priced Fenwick Dining: Dining in Delaware with views of Maryland is all part of the experience at **Harpoon Hanna's,** Route 54 and the Bay, Fenwick Island (tel. 539-3095), located on Assawoman Bay near the state border. This is a large and lively nautical-style restaurant, with a half-dozen dining rooms of various sizes, lots of window tables with views of the water, plenty of outdoor deck seating, boat docking facilities, and live music, with dancing nightly. Lunch, priced from $3.95 to $7.95, ranges from sandwiches and salads to omelets (try the Harpoon Seafood Omelet, overflowing with shrimp, crab, mild Cheddar, tomatoes, and sautéed mushrooms). In the evening fresh fish leads the menu—from swordfish and sea trout to tuna and tile, as well as a wide selection of shrimp, crab, and lobster dishes. Entrees, accompanied by freshly baked bread and muffins, salad, and vegetable, range from $7.95 to $17.95, with most around the $13 or $14 level. No reservations are accepted, so get there early. Open daily year round, from 11 a.m. to 4 p.m. for lunch, and from 4 to 11 p.m. for dinner. CC's accepted: AE, Ch, MC, and V.

Mussels are the specialty at **The Feed Bag,** Route 1, Fenwick Island (tel. 539-3526). This rustic and casual restaurant is part of the Village of Fenwick, a complex of shops and boutiques near the historic lighthouse and overlooking the waters of the Lighthouse Cove canal. There is a choice of indoor and outdoor deck seating, with an all-day menu that ranges from sandwiches and salads, priced from $3 to $5.95, to more substantial evening fare. Dinner entrees, many with an Italian slant, are priced from $8.95 to $16, and include assorted breads and spaghetti or fries. A variety of mussel dishes is available, as well as a half-dozen pastas, veal parmigiana, seafoods, ribs, and charbroiled steaks. Open daily, May through September, from 11:30 a.m. to 1 a.m. The busy bar specializes in frozen drinks such as "summer smoothie" (strawberries, Amaretto, and cream) and frozen Irish coffee. CC's accepted: AE, Ch, MC, and V.

Budget Meals at Fenwick: A favorite for all ages is **Libby's,** Route 1, Fenwick Island (tel. 539-7379), known far and wide for its polka-dot façade and huge breakfasts, served from 7 a.m. until 3:30 p.m. Choices include "pancakes with personality" such as royal cherry, Georgia pecan, chocolate chip, and old-fashioned buckwheat cakes, priced from $2.65 to $3.95, as well as omelets, waffles, French toast, and lo-cal breakfasts (all priced under $5). Lunch, which features a wide variety of overstuffed sandwiches, burgers, and salads, costs from $1.95 to $4.95. Dinner entrees, which come with salad bar, are priced mostly under $10, and range from soft-shell crabs and steaks, to shrimp or chicken "in the basket." Open from Easter to the end of October, lunch is available from 11:30 a.m. to 3:30 p.m., and dinner from 3:30 to 10 p.m. Cocktails are served with meals and also in the upper deck lounge. CC's accepted: MC and V. Since 1985, Libbys also operates a branch in the heart of Bethany Beach at 116 Garfield Parkway (tel. 539-4500).

For more than 20 years, wholesome cooking at reasonable prices has also been the trademark of **Warren Station,** Coastal Highway (Route 1), Fenwick Island (tel. 539-7156), a homey and casual restaurant. Recently renovated to duplicate the look of the old Indian River Coast Guard Station, the décor features light woods, lots of windows, and bright blue canvas dividers. Sandwiches, burgers, soups, and salads are available for lunch, priced from $1.50 to $3.95. At dinner, turkey is the specialty of the house, roasted fresh daily and hand-carved to order, priced from $7.50 for a complete dinner. Other entrees include "Delmarvelous fried chicken," sugar-cured ham with raisin sauce, charbroiled T-bone steaks, crab cutlets, and flounder stuffed with crab imperial. Complete dinners, with appetizer or soup, salad, two vegetables, and beverage, range from $7 to $13 with most choices $10 and under. Open daily, from early May to late September, serving lunch from 11 a.m. to 4 p.m.; dinner from 4 to 9 p.m. on Sunday to Thursday, and until 10 p.m. on Friday and Saturday. No reservations are taken and no alcohol is served. CC's accepted: MC and V.

A Word About Breakfast: Since most motels in Bethany and Fenwick, like the other shore resorts, do not serve breakfast, here is a short list of places open for morning meals. The top spot, as indicated above, is **Libbys,** which claims to offer "the largest selection of breakfast items on the shore" from 7 a.m. to 3:30 p.m. Other choices are **Warren Station,** which serves breakfast from 8 to 11 a.m.; and **Holiday House,** which has a "breakfast bar" from 8 to 11:30 a.m. from Monday through Saturday, and a Sunday buffet brunch from 9 a.m. to 1 p.m. Sunday brunches are also served at **Harpoon Hanna's** from 10 a.m. to 3 p.m. and at the **Peppermill** from 10 a.m. to 2 p.m.

The Top Attractions

The mile-long **Bethany Beach Boardwalk,** relatively free of commercial enterprises, is an attraction in itself for those who enjoy a quiet beachside walk and unobstructed views of the wide-open strand. The locals also claim that this is the only boardwalk where you can actually sit safely beneath it. The boardwalk is the focal point of the town and most of the shops and fast-food eateries are located on Garfield Parkway, the street that runs perpendicular to the center of the boardwalk.

Fenwick, while lacking a boardwalk, has a wide-open beach with gentle dunes. There are no concessions or fast-food outlets along the shoreline, only private homes and rental properties. Most of the shops and business enterprises are concentrated one block inland along Route 1, also known as the Coastal Highway.

Chief among the sights here is the **Fenwick Island Lighthouse** on the Mason Dixon Line, Route 54, approximately one-quarter mile west of Route 1. Built in 1859, this is one of the Delaware shore's oldest landmarks still in operation today, with beams that can be seen for 15 miles.

On the south side of the lighthouse, you'll see the **Mason Dixon Monument,** between Routes 1 and 54, literally on the Delaware and Maryland border. This is the first marker that was laid as a result of the historic survey conducted in 1751. Delaware's southern and western borders are formed by the Mason and Dixon line, making it the only state to lie both north and east of the line.

Sports and Activities: Ideal for swimming and sunning, **Bethany Beach** is a free public facility for all to enjoy. **Steen's Beach Service** (tel. 539-9160) operates a rental concession on the beach offering 8-foot umbrellas, surf mats, and boogie boards, for $1.50 an hour or $5 a day; highback or lounge chairs, $1 an hour or $2 a day.

In addition, **Resort Rentals,** York Beach Mall, Bethany Beach (tel. 539-6679), one mile south of Sea Colony, specializes in combination rentals (such as a large umbrella and two sand chairs for $20 a week).

Harry's Bait and Tackle Shop, 201 Central Blvd. and Pennsylvania Avenue, Bethany Beach (tel. 539-6244), also has a full line of beach accessories, as well as fishing and crabbing supplies, plus a fleet of bicycles, from $2 an hour or $6 per day. (This shop is also the Carolina Trailways Bus Depot for the area).

A paradise for water-sports enthusiasts is **Fenwick Island State Park,** Route 1 (tel. 539-9060), just south of Bethany Beach. With the Atlantic on one side and Little Assawoman Bay on the other, this park is comprised of three miles of seacoast beaches and dunes as well as 344 acres of parkland and open bayfront, ideal for fishing, crabbing, and boating. The facilities include a boardwalk with picnic tables, gift shop, and refreshments; shower and changing rooms; a first-aid room, and lifeguards. Surfing is permitted here and access is allowed for fishermen's four-wheel-drive vehicles. In addition, bird watchers will find rare seabirds, such as tern, piping plover, and black skimmer, nesting in protected areas. Admission is $4 for out-of-state cars and $2 for Delaware cars.

Adjacent to the park on the bayside is **Sailing Inc.,** Route 1, Fenwick Island (tel. 539-7999), a source for rentals of sailboards and paddleboats, from $15 an hour; and catamarans in three sizes, from $25 to $35 an hour. Sailing lessons are also available from $50 for two hours.

Events: For the past ten years, the Bethany area's major happening has been the **Boardwalk Arts Festival.** Held on the third Saturday in August, this show attracts craftsmen, artisans, and spectators from near and far, taking up the entire length of the boardwalk. This is a juried show of original creations in woodcarving, photography, handmade jewelry, batik, metal sculpture, calligraphy, oil and watercolor painting, toys, dolls, and painted porcelain. Hours are 10 a.m. to 5 p.m.; a full program is available in advance from the Bethany Beach Chamber of Commerce.

Children's Corner: The **Fenwick Island Boardwalk,** Routes 1 and 54, Fenwick Island (tel. 539-8129), is an inland amusement park across the street from the Fenwick Island Lighthouse. This summertime attraction features a water slide, miniature golf, and go-cart rides.

INTRODUCTION TO MARYLAND

1. Welcome to the Old Line State
2. Getting to Maryland
3. Getting Around Maryland
4. Useful Facts

AMERICA IN MINIATURE is the way Maryland is often described. From its snow-capped Allegheny mountains and the sandy Ocean City beaches to the booming metropolis of Baltimore and the fertile horse farms of Frederick, Maryland is a state of many sights and experiences.

"Truly a delightsome land" are the words Captain John Smith used to describe this area as he sailed up the Chesapeake Bay into the Potomac in June of 1608. Twentieth-century visitors would be hard-pressed to say it any better.

1. Welcome to the Old Line State

Maryland had its beginnings in 1634 as an English province when Lord Baltimore's brother, Leonard Calvert, christened the land at the mouth of the Potomac in honor of the second name of Henrietta Maria, wife of King Charles I. The first settlement on the new land was also appropriately called "St. Marie's Citty" (or St. Mary's City).

From its earliest days, Maryland was at the forefront of the original 13 colonies and led the way in many Revolutionary War encounters. It was the courageous action of Marylanders in the battles of Chesapeake, Brandywine, and Long Island that led to the state's nickname. When the valor of the "regular troops of the line" from Maryland was commended, the phrase "old line state" was coined.

Maryland's place in American history continued throughout the War of 1812 (when the "Star Spangled Banner" was composed at Baltimore) and during the Civil War (when the bloodiest battle was fought at Antietam).

It's no wonder that Maryland today is a fascinating state to visit, with more than 150 historical sites. Maryland was also the birthplace of American railroading and the pathway for much of this country's first national pike.

Best of all, Maryland preserves its past and melds it into 20th-century diversity. From Annapolis to Princess Anne, Cambridge to Cumberland, and Salisbury to Sharpsburg, you'll find gracious southern mansions and restored

Federal town houses doing double duty as restaurants, bed-and-breakfast inns, and sightseeing attractions for today's travelers.

A state bordered by Virginia and West Virginia to the south and west, and by Pennsylvania and Delaware to the north and east, Maryland enjoys characteristics common to both sides of the Mason-Dixon line. You'll find hi-tech industry and manufacturing plants side-by-side with sprawling tobacco farms, meandering apple orchards, and mammoth poultry farms. The terrain ranges from sandy seashore beaches to mountain ski slopes.

With a total area of about 10,000 square miles and a population of over four million friendly folk, Maryland is big enough (over 200 miles at its widest) to offer a great variety of attractions, and small enough (two miles at its narrowest point) to get to know easily.

2. Getting to Maryland

Situated in the middle of the eastern seaboard, Maryland extends from the Atlantic Ocean and the Chesapeake Bay on the east to the Allegheny Mountains on the west, offering easy access from many eastern seaboard cities. Maryland is within a 300-mile radius of New York City, Buffalo, Philadelphia, Pittsburgh, Norfolk, and Richmond; and Cleveland, Toronto, and Charleston are less than 400 miles away.

BY PLANE: The gateway to Maryland is the **Baltimore-Washington International Airport,** situated ten miles south of Baltimore and 20 miles north of the state capital at Annapolis. Hundreds of domestic and international flights land and depart from this gateway every day. In addition, commuter flights also operate into **Salisbury Airport** and **Ocean City Airport** on Maryland's eastern shore, and into the regional airports in the western part of the state, such as Cumberland and Hagerstown.

BY TRAIN: **Amtrak** offers convenient daily Metroliner service into Baltimore from New York and Washington, with onward passenger links from Boston, Florida, and points west. The beautifully restored beaux arts–style station in downtown Baltimore is conveniently located close to major hotels and other visitor facilities.

BY BUS: Both **Greyhound** and **Trailways** serve major points in Maryland such as Baltimore, Ocean City, Salisbury, Easton, Cambridge, Hagerstown, and Cumberland.

BY CAR: Interstate-95, the eastern seaboard's major north-south link from Maine to Florida, passes through the state via Baltimore and central Maryland before continuing on to Wilmington and Philadelphia to the north, or to Washington, D.C., Virginia, and points southward. Other interstate highways that traverse Maryland are I-83 from Pennsylvania, I-81 between West Virginia and Pennsylvania, and I-70 in an east-west direction. Route 40, part of the original National Pike, also runs from Baltimore westward via Frederick, Hagerstown, and Cumberland. U.S. Routes 50 and 301 connect Maryland's eastern and western shores via the William Preston Lane Memorial Bridge over the Chesapeake Bay. The Eastern Shore is also served by U.S. Route 13 between Delaware and Virginia.

Major car rental firms are well represented throughout Maryland in such cities as Baltimore, Salisbury, Ocean City, Cambridge, Easton, and Hagerstown.

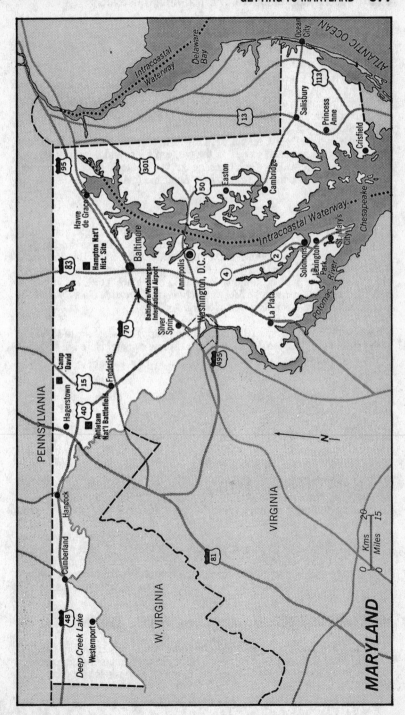

3. Getting Around Maryland

BY PLANE: Commuter flights within the state are operated from Baltimore International Airport to several smaller airports, such as Salisbury, Ocean City, Hagerstown, and Cumberland.

BY CAR: In addition to the major interstate highways and routes, Maryland is well served with local roads, such as Routes 2, 4, and 5, which lead southward toward St. Mary's City; Route 413, which will take you to Crisfield; and Route 219, which leads to Deep Creek Lake. Driving in Maryland is a pleasant experience with fertile farmland scenes on the western shore and dozens of seaport towns on the eastern side of the Chesapeake. As Route 40 leads west beyond Hagerstown, it is also the gateway to panoramic mountain vistas.

4. Useful Facts

VISITOR INFORMATION: For comprehensive brochures, maps, and lists of events for the whole state, contact the **Maryland Office of Tourism Development,** 45 Calvert St., Annapolis, MD 21401 (tel. 301/269-3517). This office publishes a very useful *Maryland Travel Guide,* a magazine-style brochure chock full of sightseeing and accommodations facts. If you are interested in sports, parks, or camping, request the *Maryland Outdoor Recreation Guide.* All of this excellent literature is supplied free of charge.

CLIMATE: With an elevation that ranges from 0 along the seashore to 3,360 feet in the mountains, Maryland has an equally diverse climate. Here is a sampling of what you can expect:

Climate

	Av. Summer Temp.	Av. Winter Temp.	Rainfall	Snow	Frost-Free Days
Baltimore Area	77°F	37°F	41 in.	23 in.	232 days
Central MD	72–74	32–36	40–46	22–36	194
Western MD	65–72	28–32	36–47	35–82	122–168
Southeast Shore	75	38	46	14.7	201

MARYLAND OUTDOORS: With 4,000 man-made lakes, 3,190 miles of tidal shoreline, and a coast that touches the Atlantic, Chesapeake, and Potomac, Maryland is a paradise for water sports from fishing and crabbing to boating and swimming. To add to the natural riches, Maryland is also the home of over 50 state parks and forests and is a prime area on the Atlantic Flyway for wintering waterfowl. The Maryland office of tourism development publishes a number of booklets that give specific names and addresses for sporting arrangements—from where to get licenses to how to rent equipment. Start by requesting a copy of the *Maryland Outdoor Guide*—it's free and can be obtained from any visitor information office throughout the state.

MARYLAND SEAFOOD: If you like seafood, you'll find ambrosia in the state of Maryland.

The Chesapeake waters surrounding Maryland's eastern shore yield no less than 29 million pounds of hard-shell crabs per year, not to mention another two million pounds of soft-shell crabs, two million bushels of oysters, and 500,000 bushels of clams.

Everywhere you go in this state, you'll find fresh seafood on the menu. The king of Maryland cuisine, however, is crab (in season from April through December). Crab is to Maryland what the peanut is to Georgia, the grapefruit to Florida, or the pineapple to Hawaii. To get the most out of crab cuisine, here are a few tasty tips.

First of all, crab is at its best served "au natural," that is, fresh from the bay, steamed, and lightly spiced in the shell. Many restaurants feature crab this way, but be prepared to work for your dinner—cracking and breaking open the shells (mallets and other helpful utensils, and paper towels, are always supplied!) So, dress casually, and settle down to an evening of serious crab-cracking.

Soft-shell crabs are also plentiful and served in many ways, from a simple sauté to amandine, or stuffed with succulent lump crabmeat. In Maryland, soft-shell crabs are simply known as "soft" crabs.

For those who don't want to crack shells and work for their dinner, the dish to choose is crab imperial. This is usually in casserole form with lots of lump or backfin crabmeat topped with a creamy white sauce, either mornay or béchamel, and often with a touch of sherry or other "secret recipe" ingredients.

Last but not least, there are crab cakes. Although they vary from restaurant to restaurant, a classic crab cake is basically a scoop of crab (either lump or backfin) formed into the size of a hamburger. The crab is usually mixed with breadcrumbs, a bit of ham, green and red pepper, or other compatible ingredients, and then deep-fried or broiled. The secret of a good crab cake is lots of crab and very little other fillers. Some of the best crab cakes are dished up at Crisfield on Maryland's eastern shore, otherwise known as the "Seafood Capital of the World."

AREA CODE: The entire state is part of the 301 telephone area code.

SALES TAX: All hotel room charges, meals, and purchases within the state of Maryland are subject to a 5% sales tax; some other local or county taxes often also apply. It is best to check in the course of your travels to see what tax will be added to your bill.

Chapter XXII

BALTIMORE

1. Getting to Baltimore
2. Overview of Downtown
3. Getting Around Baltimore
4. Where to Stay
5. Where to Dine
6. The Top Attractions
7. Nightlife
8. Sports and Activities
9. Events

MIDWAY BETWEEN NORTH AND SOUTH, Baltimore is a city proud of its heritage and even more enthusiastic about its present. Founded in 1729, incorporated in 1797, and named after Lord Baltimore of England, this key port in the Mid-Atlantic has many claims to fame.

Birthplace of the "Star Spangled Banner" and the famous Baltimore clipper ships, this city was briefly the nation's capital; it was also the starting point for the first railroad in the U.S. and the site of the first railroad passenger and freight station. The first telegraph communication ("What hath God wrought") was beamed to Baltimore in 1844 and the nation's oldest cathedral is also here. Over the years, Baltimore has been home to a parade of leading personalities from Edgar Allan Poe and H.L. Mencken to Babe Ruth, Eubie Blake, Wallis Warfield Simpson (Duchess of Windsor), and Saint Elizabeth Ann Seton.

Situated on the Patapsco River off Chesapeake Bay, Baltimore today is a world-class seaport with 45 miles of waterfront, the third largest in the U.S., ideally located 33 miles north of Washington and 95 miles south of Philadelphia. With a 79-mile square area, it is also Maryland's major city (pop.: 786,000), and a prime economic and manufacturing center.

As a travel destination, Baltimore has been called "The Cinderella City" because of its "rags-to-riches" renewal. In the last 20 years, this city has been artfully transformed from a scruffy megalopolis into a spiffy urban blend of futuristic skyscrapers, overhead walkways, cascading fountains, open-air plazas, and a bustling harborside recreational area. Best of all, this renaissance has paid proper homage to the gracious Federal homes and rowhouses, amiably blending the city's old-world charm with the new cosmopolitan ambience. So successful has Baltimore been in rejuvenating itself that tourism is now the city's number-three industry, attracting more than 20 million visitors a year.

VISITOR INFORMATION: For maps, brochures, and useful pamphlets to help

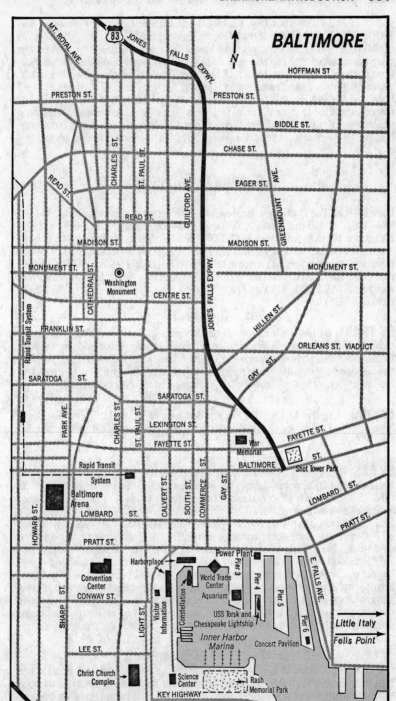

you plan and enjoy your trip, contact the **Baltimore Office of Promotion and Tourism,** 34 Market Place, Suite 310, Baltimore, MD 21202 (tel. 301/837-4636 or 301/837-INFO). Once you are in town, there are several visitor centers in busy travel areas that are manned daily for on-the-spot inquiries. These locations include a booth next to the Light Street Pavilion, Harborplace; a kiosk in the main lobby of the Pennsylvania Railroad Station, 1525 N. Charles St.; and booths at the Baltimore-Washington International Airport at Pier C (main entrance) and Pier D (international terminal). In addition to general sightseeing brochures, all offices distribute copies of the *Baltimore Good Times,* a comprehensive 16-page newspaper-style guide to what's happening in and around the city.

1. Getting to Baltimore

BY PLANE: The **Baltimore-Washington International Airport,** Route 46 (tel. 859-7100), is 10 miles south of downtown Baltimore, off I-695 and the Baltimore-Washington Parkway (I-295). Each day hundreds of flights from both domestic and international points land at this airport. Some useful local airline telephone numbers are: **American** (tel. 850-5800); **Delta** (tel. 768-9000); **Eastern** (tel. 768-3100); **Northwest Orient** (tel. 837-6663); **Pan Am** (tel. 685-2115); **Piedmont** (tel. 761-5402); **TWA** (tel. 338-1156); **United** (tel. 850-4557); and **USAir** (tel. 727-0825).

BY TRAIN: Baltimore is a stop on the main East Coast corridor of Amtrak, between Wilmington and Washington, D. C. All trains arrive and depart from Baltimore's **Pennsylvania Station,** 1525 N. Charles St. (tel. 539-2112), on the north side of the city. Recently restored to the tune of $3.5 million, this building is a beaux-arts gem and the sixth-busiest station in the Amtrak system.

BY BUS: Regular bus service is provided to and from Baltimore via **Greyhound,** 601 N. Howard St. (tel. 744-9311), and **Trailways,** 201 W. Fayette St. (tel. 752-2115).

BY CAR: From the northeast and south, I-95 has access to downtown areas via I-695 and the Baltimore-Washington Parkway (I-295). From the north, exit 23 off I-95 South will lead straight into the center of town. Traffic from the west approaches downtown from I-70, I-695, and Route 40. Southbound access is via I-83. The newly completed Fort McHenry Tunnel (I-895) is the final connection of I-95 through Baltimore, running under the Patapsco River and providing easy access from the north to downtown Baltimore. Opened in November of 1985, this eight-lane structure is the widest tunnel in the world and one of the largest public works developments in history; the toll per car is $1. Once you arrive, you'll find that many hotels provide indoor parking; otherwise, public metered lots and street parking are available throughout the city. Rates at the numerous commercial lots and garages average about $2 an hour. Most maps produced by the tourism office clearly indicate public parking places.

2. Overview of Downtown

You'll hardly be in Baltimore an hour before you will be drawn to see the Inner Harbor at the city's southern edge. With its dazzling pavilions of boutiques, markets, and restaurants, and its modern museums, open-air concert decks, state-of-the-art convention center, and boats of all sizes, the Inner Harbor is a showplace of Baltimore at its best. Once a row of abandoned warehouses and factories, this vibrant waterfront is the epitome of successful urban restoration.

Although much emphasis is justifiably put on the Inner Harbor, there is a lot more to the city beyond this recreational development. The main downtown area radiates around the Charles Center, a 33-acre complex incorporating apartments, office buildings, hotels, shops, landscaped plazas, and a theater, all connected by an overhead walkway. Begun in 1956, this center is the cornerstone of Baltimore's downtown renaissance, and a model for urban-renewal projects. It is bounded by Liberty, Saratoga, Lombard, and Charles Streets, the latter of which divides Baltimore from east to west.

Also within this perimeter is Baltimore Street, which divides the city from north to south. Almost all downtown streets run only one way, although the important exceptions are Howard and Eutaw Streets. All of Baltimore's numbered streets run east and west.

Toward the northern end of Charles Street is an area known as Mount Vernon, dominated by a 178-foot monument dedicated to George Washington. Laid out in 1827, Mount Vernon was once the city's most fashionable residential district, and it is still a delight, with its elegant town houses and four park-like squares. This is also the location of many of the city's oldest churches and cultural institutions including the Peabody Conservatory of Music, one of the leading music schools in the world, and the Walters Art Gallery.

To the east of the Inner Harbor is Little Italy, one of Baltimore's most colorful and self-contained ethnic neighborhoods and the location of about two dozen fine Italian restaurants. Here you will also see some fine examples of neighborhood rowhouses, with their gleaming white marble front stoops which the residents still scrub daily. In this section, as in many of the Baltimore ethnic neighborhoods, the practice of window-screen painting is still carried on by craftsmen. Passersby can't see in, but window sitters can see out.

Moving still more to the east is the Fells Point section, the old seaport where Baltimore originally started. Fells Point today is an old-world area with brick-lined streets and more than 350 original residential structures reflecting the architecture of the American Federal period.

3. Getting Around Baltimore

PUBLIC TRANSPORT: Baltimore's **Mass Transit Administration (MTA)** operates a network of buses that connect all sections of the city. The base fare is 90¢ and exact change is necessary. For information and schedules call 539-5000. Although Baltimore does have a subway system, The Metro, at the moment it serves primarily as a link from downtown to the northwestern suburbs such as Owens Mills. The minimum fare is also 90¢; for more information call 333-2700. All taxis in the city are metered; the three largest fleets are **Yellow Cab** (tel. 685-1212); **Sun Cab** (tel. 235-0300); and **Diamond Cab** (tel. 947-3333). For airport trips, call **BWI Airport Cab** (tel. 859-7545).

THE TROLLEY: The mode of transport most frequently used by visitors to Baltimore is the trolley. The current fleet is composed of new motorized trolley buses, replicas of Baltimore's original cabled vehicles. These colorful trolleys operate continuously along Charles Street in the heart of the city and throughout the Inner Harbor. The Charles Street route runs Monday through Saturday from 11 a.m. to 7 p.m., from Conway Street along Charles Street to Lafayette Avenue and back via Maryland Avenue. The Inner harbor circuit operates Sunday through Thursday from 11 a.m. to 10 p.m., and Friday and Saturday from 11 a.m. to 11 p.m., leaving Little Italy, west on Pratt Street, and around the harbor and back. The trolleys run at seven- to ten-minute intervals and stop every two blocks. The fare is 25¢ and exact change is required. For further information, call Baltimore Trolley Works (tel. 396-4259).

CAR RENTAL: There are many car rental firms with offices in downtown Baltimore and at Baltimore-Washington International Airport, including: **American International,** 819 E. Fayette St. (tel. 752-0303); **Avis,** 4 E. Lombard St. (tel. 685-6000) and at the airport (tel. 859-1680); **Budget,** 200 S. Paca St. (tel. 837-6955) and at the airport (tel. 859-0850); **Dollar,** 100 Hopkins Place (tel. 539-4224) and at the airport (tel. 859-8950); **Hertz,** 501 W. Lombard St. (tel. 322-0015) and at the airport (tel. 850-7400); and **National,** 300 W. Lombard St. (tel. 752-1127) and at the airport (tel. 859-8860).

ESCORTED TOURS: Good Time Tours, Light Street and Key Highway (tel. 539-3330), operates regularly scheduled bus tours of Baltimore of two- and three-hour durations. A basic two-hour orientation tour, which departs at 10 a.m. and 1 p.m. on Saturday, Sunday, and Monday, covers the city highlights from Fort McHenry and the Star Spangled Banner House to the Carroll Mansion; the cost is $6.50. Two different three-hour tours operate on Thursday and Friday, either at 9 a.m. or 1 p.m., and are priced from $11.75 to $13.50, depending on itinerary. Tour tickets are available at most hotels, the Good Time Tours Office, or the Baltimore Box Office, Pier 4, 601 E. Pratt St.

    Baltimore-Rent-A-Tour, 3414 Philips Dr. (tel. 653-2998), designs tours to suit any request, from walking rambles to insomniac late-evening jaunts about town. Prices vary according to itinerary; reservations are necessary.

WALKING TOURS: Two self-guided downtown walking tours with maps are outlined in the *Baltimore Good Times* newspaper, published by the Baltimore Office of Promotion and Tourism. Copies are available, free of charge, at all visitor outlets, public transport depots, and hotels.

AUTO TOURS: For sightseeing by automobile, Tour Tapes of Baltimore offers three self-guided cassette tapes, designed to be used in your own car at your own pace; driving directions and maps are included in the package. The itineraries break the city down into three areas (east; west; and north and county). The tapes are available from various sources throughout the city including the **Baltimore Office of Promotion and Tourism,** 34 Market Place, Suite 310 (tel. 837-4636); each casette is $9.95; a complete set of three costs $25.

HARBOR CRUISES: See Baltimore from its harbor on board a variety of nautical craft. The twin-deck *Patriot* offers 1½-hour narrated cruises from Constellation Dock, Pratt and Light Streets (tel. 685-4288). The schedule is April 15 through April 30, at 11 a.m., 1, and 3 p.m.; May through September, hourly departures from 11 a.m. through 4 p.m.; and in October at 11 a.m., 1, and 3 p.m. Additional evening cruises are also scheduled on some summer weekends. The cost is $4.40 for adults and $2.20 for children aged 2 to 11.

    In addition, another company, **Harbor Cruises,** 301 Light St. (tel. 727-3113) operates more extensive excursions on board two 450-passenger cruise ships. The first, *Port Welcome,* departs Harborplace for scenic all-day trips as follows: to Annapolis, every Wednesday through Saturday, from June 25 to August 30, priced at $13.90 for adults and $7.60 for children; to St. Michaels, once or twice monthly at 9:30 a.m., at $16.95 for adults and $8.95 for children; and to the Chesapeake and Delaware Canal for fall foliage viewing, at 9:30 a.m. on selected weekends in October, at $14.75 for adults and $7.85 for children. The *Port Welcome* also schedules additional trips to Annapolis in May and September and occasional evening music-theme cruises. The second ship, *The Lady Baltimore*, offers a "showboat" experience with dining and entertainment (lunch or dinner with a full musical revue) in a cruise-ship setting. Lunch cruises, which operate Tuesday through Sunday, from noon to 2 p.m., are priced at $14.20 per person (half-price for children on weekends). Dinner cruises leave from 7 to 10 p.m., on Tuesday through Thursday at $19.70 per person, and on Friday through Sunday at $21.90 per person. In addition, "moonlight cruises" are available from 11 p.m. to 1:30 a.m. on Friday and Saturday, at $9.80 per person. Most major CC's are accepted.

SAILING CRUISES: The *Clipper City*, a 158-foot replica of an 1854 topsail schooner and the largest tall ship licensed to carry passengers in the U.S., offers three-hour sea excursions from the Inner Harbor in the summer months, at 11 a.m. daily (except Monday), with a sailing at 7 p.m. on Friday and Sunday evenings. Cost is $15 per person for adults and $7.50 for children. To reserve a place, contact **Clipper City Inc.,** 720 Light Street (tel. 539-6277).

WATER SHUTTLES: **Maryland Tours Inc.** (tel. 752-1515) operates water-shuttle services between the Inner Harbor's Finger Pier and Fort McHenry or Fells Point via two 85-passenger vessels, *The Baltimore Defender* and *The Guardian.* After each ride, passengers disembark, tour these historic areas, and return to the Inner Harbor via a later boat. This shuttle service, in operation from Memorial Day through Labor Day, leaves the Inner Harbor every half hour from 11 a.m. to 5:30 p.m.; returning from Fort McHenry or Fells Point every half hour from 11:30 a.m. to 6 p.m. Ticket prices are $3.30 round-trip ($2.20 one-way) for adults and $2.20 round-trip ($1.65 one-way) for children under 12. Three-stop tickets, allowing travel from the Inner Harbor to both Fort McHenry and Fells Point, are available for $4.40 for adults and $3.30 for children under 12.

WATER TAXIS: Small water-taxi boats operate in the Baltimore Inner Harbor every 15 minutes from mid-April through mid-October. This service provides a water link between Harborplace and such attractions as the Maryland Science Center, Pier 6, and Little Italy. The fare is $1.25 and the schedule runs from 11 a.m. to 11 p.m., Sunday through Thursday; and from 11 a.m. to midnight on Friday and Saturday. For more information, call 547-0090.

SKYWALK: Although Baltimore is an easy city to walk, the trek from downtown Charles Center to the Inner Harbor is made even easier by a new elevated pedestrian walkway called Skywalk. Following an indoor-outdoor path, the well-signposted route begins at Charles and Saratoga Streets and ends at Harborplace, connecting commercial buildings, shops, theaters, pedestrian plazas, the Baltimore Convention Center, restaurants, and hotels (Omni, Lord Baltimore, Sheraton, and Hyatt) along its safe and traffic-free route.

4. Where to Stay

Ten years ago, Baltimore was known as a destination of low-to medium-grade hotels with no more than 1,500 rooms available. Thanks to the city's overall urban renewal, the current hotel picture has changed dramatically. Modern new hotels have sprung up, especially around the Inner Harbor, and the grand older properties have been restored, renovated, and refurbished. There are now more than 5,000 hotel rooms in this city and the majority fall into the first-class and deluxe caliber. This means that it can be hard to find a double for under $100 during the week; happily, most hotels offer special weekend rates that represent savings of 35% to 50% off normal Sunday through Thursday tariffs. So, don't be scared off by your first look at the room prices; try to time your visit for a weekend and remember to ask if a reduced rate applies. In the coming year, more hotels will continue to spring up; look for the new 620-room Stouffer property scheduled to open soon next to Harborplace.

Unless we indicate otherwise, the Baltimore hotels that follow have restaurants that serve meals throughout the day, from 7 a.m. through 2 or 3 p.m. for breakfast and lunch, and from 5 or 6 until 10 or 11 p.m. for dinner; we'll make note when a hotel dining room is a standout. Another point to remember about most hotels in this city is that they subscribe rather strictly to a policy of no check-ins before 3 p.m.

THE NEW AND MODERN HOTELS: Influenced by the remarkably successful Harborplace and the Charles Center, most of the city's new hotels are located close to the Inner Harbor.

The best location so far belongs to the **Hyatt Regency Baltimore,** 300 Light St., Baltimore, MD 21202 (tel. 301/528-1234 or toll-free 800/228-9000), right on the Inner Harbor and adjacent to the convention center. This ultra-modern 490-room hotel has an exterior of mirrored glass that reflects both the passing boats and the myriad activities of Harborplace. The bedrooms are contemporary in style, equipped with every modern convenience from color cable TV to air conditioning, but with emphasis on wide windows and dramatic views of the water or the city (even the elevators that connect the floors provide spectacular views). Doubles range from $124 to $165, with a flat weekend rate of $85. Guest amenities include an outdoor pool, tennis courts, a jogging track, and direct access to the Skywalk. Even if you don't stay here, visit the rooftop restaurant/nightspot called Berry and Elliot's, which really comes alive when the city lights shine. The Hyatt also boasts a gourmet eatery called The Trellis Garden which is romantically designed with its own indoor lake, trees, and foliage. The dinner entrees, priced from $13.95 to $17.95, include Black Angus beef, rack of lamb, veal and crab, quail champignon, shrimp, and pasta. All major CC's are accepted.

Next door is the **Sheraton,** 30 S. Charles St., Baltimore, MD 21201 (tel. 301/962-8300 or toll-free 800/325-3535), close to Harborplace, the Convention Center, and on the Skywalk route. Although the harbor views are also an attraction here, art from across America, with emphasis on Maryland artists, is the main focus of this hotel's décor. The 334 modern rooms offer a choice of styles, with the usual color TV, air conditioning, and direct-dial phones. Doubles range from $114 to $150. Guest facilities include an indoor pool, a health club, a sauna, the option of non-smoking rooms, a lobby-level piano bar, a high-energy multi-level video disco called Impulse, and a top-notch restaurant called McHenry's. Known for its Cajun dishes and Maryland seafood specialties, this dining spot offers entrees ranging from crabmeat cannelloni and lobster in pastry to beef jambalaya, priced in the $13.95 to $21.95 bracket. All major CC's are accepted.

Previously known as the Hilton, the **Omni International,** 101 West Fayette St., Baltimore, MD 21201 (tel. 301/752-1100 or toll-free 800/THE-OMNI), has just undergone a $13 million renovation. With 714 rooms, this is the largest hotel in Maryland, consisting of two beige towers, 27 and 23 floors in height, and situated opposite the Charles Center and the Baltimore Arena. Most bedrooms are L-shaped with mirrored closets, double or queen beds, air conditioning, cable TV, and two phones. Doubles range from $99 to $120, although a 50% weekend discount is usually in effect. Other facilities include an outdoor swimming pool, a fitness center, and a bistro-style restaurant called Jacqueline. This trendy eatery features the cuisines of different European countries, with dinner entrees in the $9.95 to $18.95 category. Major CC's are accepted.

Equally convenient to the Charles Center and the Convention Center is the **Baltimore Marriott Inner Harbor,** Pratt and Eutaw Streets, Baltimore, MD 21201 (tel. 301/962-0202). New in 1985, this 10-story crescent-shaped tower started as the Baltimore Plaza, a deluxe Howard Johnson, but was taken over by Marriott in 1986. The lobby area is very appealing, with a cascading waterfall and a serene décor of soft-salmon pink and beige tones. The 356 bedrooms are also designed in restful shades, with customary air conditioning, color cable TV with radio, and direct-dial phones. Doubles range from $100 to $115. Other services include a restaurant and cocktail lounge, an indoor swimming pool, a game room, and a fitness center with saunas and whirlpool. This hotel also overlooks the city's historic Bromer Seltzer Clock. All major CC's are accepted.

THE GRAND OLD-WORLD HOTELS: A distinguished clientele ranging from Clark Gable and Henry Fonda to the Duke of Windsor and Archbishop Desmond Tutu have all known the delights of **The Belvedere,** 1 East Chase St., Baltimore, MD 21202 (tel. 301/332-1000 and toll-free 800/692-2700). Located in the northern part of the city's historic Mount Vernon district, at the corner of Charles and Chase Streets, this "grande dame" of Baltimore hotels first opened its doors with a flourish in 1903. The grounds were originally part of an estate once owned by American Revolutionary War hero John Edgar Howard. Recently refurbished, this 12-story landmark has 180 rooms, decorated in an old-world style but with every modern convenience including air conditioning, color cable TV, and direct-dial phones. Doubles range from $80 to $120. Guest amenities include an enclosed pool, a health center, and racquetball courts. Public rooms include the medieval-style Owl Bar for light fare; the John Edger Howard Room, a full-service restaurant with an impressive décor of hand-painted wall murals, antique chandeliers, and a baby grand piano; a rooftop entertainment lounge; and a lobby-level Japanese restaurant. Major CC's are accepted.

Also in the heart of the Mount Vernon district is the **Peabody Court,** 612 Cathedral St., Baltimore, MD 21201 (tel. 301/727-7101 or toll-free 800/732-5301). First opened as a hotel in 1930, later converted into an apartment building, and now back as a hotel since 1985, this building has undergone a total renovation and rejuvenation, earning it a place on the roster of Leading Hotels of the World. As you step inside the lobby, dominated by a six-foot 500-pound Baccarat crystal chandelier, a sense of grandeur greets you. The décor in the public rooms features period furniture, hand-loomed carpeting, and original art. Each of the 105 guest rooms has a marble bathroom, color cable TV, a direct-dial phone, and air conditioning. Rates range from $135 to $175 for a double, with considerable reductions on weekend nights. There are two restaurants, the second-floor Brasserie for moderate meals, including fixed-price theater-suppers, and the glass-enclosed rooftop Conservatory, for gourmet French cuisine. All major CC's are accepted.

Located near the Charles Center, the **Lord Baltimore Quality Royale,** 20-30 W. Baltimore St., Baltimore, MD 21202 (tel. 301/539-8400 or toll-free 800/228-5152), is another vintage hotel, recently renovated (1986) and restored to its 1920s elegance. The entrance is particularly impressive with rich tones of green, brown, and gold; marble columns; hand-carved artwork; brass fixtures; and a massive central chandelier. The 440 bedrooms, many of which are non-smoking, offer a choice of double, queen, or king size beds. While decorated in an old-world theme, each room is also outfitted with all the modern amenities ranging from color cable TV to air conditioning and a direct-dial phone. Doubles range from $90 to $145. Facilities include a health club with sauna and exercise room, and Maestro's Restaurant for fine dining. All major CC's are accepted.

BED-AND-BREAKFAST INNS: For a homey atmosphere, try the 15-room **Society Hill,** 58 W. Biddle St., Baltimore, MD 21201 (tel. 301/837-3630), a bed-and-breakfast inn located in the fashionable Mount Vernon district. Opened in 1984, this gracious town house is within walking distance of leading cultural attractions. The bedrooms, each individually furnished, feature king, queen, or double beds, many with canopies or brass headboards, as well as antique furnishings, books, and plants; all have private bath, air conditioning, color cable TV, and phone. The rates for a double range from $80 to $95 and include a continental breakfast delivered to each room; reduced rates often apply in the summer months. There is also a two-room restaurant on the lower level, with a concert-hall theme enforced by a décor of musical instruments mounted on the walls; and a greenhouse solarium area with lots of plants. The innovative kitchen prepares dinner entrees in the mostly moderate bracket ($9.95 to $15.95), with dishes such as shrimp stir-fry; veal with escargot; and canard avante-garde (duck with choice of raspberry champagne or orange Cointréau sauces). Society Hill has recently opened two other Baltimore B&B locations (at 1125 N. Calvert St. 21202, tel. 301/752-7722, and at 3404 St. Paul St., Baltimore, MD 21218, tel. 301/235-8600). CC's accepted: AE, D, MC, and V.

In the Fells Point section of the city is the **Admiral Fell Inn,** 888 S. Broadway, Baltimore, MD 21231 (tel. 301/522-7377 or toll-free 800/BXB-INNS). This inn is composed of three buildings, dating from 1850–1910, a blend of Victorian and Georgian architectures. Originally a boardinghouse for sailors, later a YMCA, and then a vinegar bottling plant, this delightful facility was completely renovated and refurbished in 1985. The public areas include a homey antique-filled lobby, an atrium, a library, and a courtyard. The 37 guest rooms are individually decorated, many with four-poster beds, and named after a particular historical character (such as the Carroll Room or the Calvert Room); all rooms have private bath and modern amenities such as air conditioning, color TV, and direct-dial phone. The inn also offers little extras such as a free shoeshine service, complimentary transport to the downtown area, and daily newspapers. Rates range from $90 for a double to $140 for suites with Jacuzzis. CC's accepted: AE, MC, and V.

EASY ON THE BUDGET: One of the best bargains you'll find downtown is the new **Days Inn,** 100 Hopkins Place, Baltimore, MD 21202 (tel. 301/576-1000 or toll-free 800/325-2525), conveniently situated between the Arena and Convention Center. This nine-story hotel is built with a brick façade that conveys an old-world Baltimore charm, while offering every modern amenity from air conditioning and direct-dial phones to color cable TVs in the 251 bedrooms. Doubles range from $69 to $80. Amenities include an outdoor heated pool, a patio courtyard, and a full-service restaurant. All major CC's are accepted.

Between Charles Center and Mount Vernon Place is **The Comfort Inn,** 24 W. Franklin St., Baltimore, MD 21201 (tel. 301/576-8400 or toll-free 800/228-

5150), at the corner of Cathedral and Franklin Streets. This is a former YMCA, an historic landmark dating back to 1907 (with a picture in the lobby to prove it). Now totally renovated, it has 200 modern rooms, furnished in a contemporary style, with a choice of double, queen, king, or extra-long beds. Each room has color TV, AM/FM radio, free in-room movies, a direct-dial telephone, and air conditioning. Some non-smoking rooms are available, as are bi-level suites with Jacuzzis. Doubles range from $55 to $75. Other on-premises facilities include a guest launderette and Michael's Pub for light fare. All major CC's are accepted.

5. Where to Dine

Often referred to as "Crabtown," Baltimore is well known for its excellent seafood restaurants. The recent development of the Inner Harbor has provided both an impetus and an ideal setting for more eateries emphasizing the sea's bounty.

As Maryland's major metropolis, Baltimore is also home to a wide diversity of restaurants featuring regional and ethnic cuisines, and traditional steakhouses. In addition to the waterfront, you'll find clusters of restaurants downtown along Charles Street (known locally as "restaurant row") and in the older neighborhood sections of the city such as Little Italy and Fells Point.

INNER HARBOR AREA: Here is a sampling of our favorites in the newly developed Inner Harbor Area.

The Top Choices

Of the 14 restaurants and sidewalk cafés located in the festive Harborplace development, a special choice is **Gianni's**, Pratt Street Pavilion, Upper Level, Harborplace (tel. 837-1130). With emphasis on Northern Italian cuisine, this is a combination of a formal inside dining room with art-deco tones and an open-air veranda overlooking the waterfront and very much with the feel of Venice. As befits such a prime setting, the prices are not cheap, but the food, service, and atmosphere are well worth the tab. Lunch selections, priced from $5.95 to $12.95, include salads, burgers, sandwiches, homemade pasta, and light dishes such as lasagne with seafood and ricotta. Dinner entrees range from seafood cioppino with lobster over linguine to crabmeat cannelloni and scaloppine of veal with black mushrooms. The prices fall into the $9.95 to $19.95 category, with most entrees over $15; salads, appetizers, and pasta are all extra. Nightly specials tend to be more in the moderate bracket. A wise choice is the weekend champagne brunch at $13.95, which includes antipasto, a main course, pasta, dessert, and coffee. Open daily, for lunch from 11:30 a.m. to 3 p.m., and for dinner from 6 to 11:30 p.m.; Saturday and Sunday brunch from noon to 4 p.m. CC's accepted: AE, MC, and V.

Moderately Priced Dining

Just east of Harborplace is the **Chart House**, 601 E. Pratt St. Pier 4 (tel. 539-6616), right on the water's edge. Originally a warehouse for the nearby power plant, this building has been tastefully converted into a bi-level restaurant with an outside deck. The décor is appropriately nautical, with ship replicas and carvings, and photos of the sea and of the old Baltimore waterfront. Lunch, priced from $2.95 to $6.95, features super-deli sandwiches (from crab salad to smoked turkey) and raw-bar selections, such as cream of crab soup, oysters, shrimp, clams, and other shellfish treats. Entrees at dinner, in the $10.95 to $21.95 range, include baked stuffed flounder, lobster tails, chicken teriyaki, and steaks. All main courses are served with homemade breads and a "portable" salad bar that moves from table to table. Open for lunch Monday through Saturday from 11:30 a.m. to 2:30 p.m.; dinner Monday through Thursday from 5 to 10:30 p.m.; Friday and Saturday from 5 p.m. until midnight, and Sunday from 3 to 10 p.m. CC's accepted: AE, MC, and V.

One of the busiest restaurants on the waterfront is **Phillips Harborplace,** Lower Level, Light Street Pavilion, Harborplace (tel. 685-6600), a branch of the very successful establishment of the same name that has been an Ocean City, Maryland, landmark since 1956. Lunches here, priced from $3.95, focus mainly on creative sandwiches, burgers, and light dishes, but dinner is a feast of fresh seafood. Entrees are priced from $8.95 to $19.95, and feature crab in many forms including soft-shell crabs that are stuffed with a tasty mixture of lump crab and ham; and a "clam bake for two" (lobster, crab clusters, clams, shrimp, mussels, and corn on the cob). This is a fun restaurant with a lively sing-along piano bar and entertainment at night. Open daily from 11 a.m. to 11 p.m. CC's accepted: AE, Ch, MC, and V.

Nearby, a French-bistro atmosphere prevails at **Jean Claude's Café,** lower level, Light Street Pavilion, Harborplace (tel. 332-0950), also facing the water. Lunch, priced from $3.95 to $8.95, concentrates on light dishes such as quiches, salads, and seafood. Dinner entrees, in the $9.95 to $15.95 bracket, include crêpes Bretonne (shrimp and scallops in white wine and cream sauce); soft-shell crab amandine; noisette of beef tenderloin with wild mushrooms and Madeira sauce; and chicken dijonnaise. Open for lunch Monday through Sunday from 11:30 a.m. to 2:30 p.m.; and for dinner Monday through Thursday from 5:30 to 10:30 p.m., Friday and Saturday until 11 p.m., and on Sunday until 9 p.m. CC's accepted: AE, D, MC, and V.

Across the street from Harborplace and the Convention Center is **Cinnabar,** 100 S. Charles St. (tel. 727-3377), a convenient stop on the overhead skyway. Although the menu concentrates on Szechuan and Hunan cuisines, the atmosphere is contemporary Baltimore. A bright and plant-filled conservatory is the setting for two levels of plush blue-and-beige banquette seating. Business people and tourists alike flock here at lunchtime to enjoy a sumptuous "all-you-can-eat" buffet of Chinese specialties for $6.95. Individual dishes are also available from $4.95 to $9.95 (including Hunan duck, lemon chicken, and shrimp with lobster sauce). Dinner entrees, priced from $7.95 to $20.95, with most under $10, range from Mongolian lamb and Peking duck to orange-flavored beef, chicken with pine nuts, or sweet-and-sour pork. Open Monday through Thursday from 11 a.m. to 11:30 p.m., Friday and Saturday until midnight, and Sunday until 10 p.m. CC's accepted: AE, MC, and V.

Just a block north of Pratt Street and Harborplace is the **Water Street Exchange,** 110 Water St. (tel. 332-4060), an authentic Victorian setting on a brick-lined courtyard. Once a parking garage, this old building has been beautifully restored into a multi-level restaurant with original brick walls, tile floors, tin ceiling, etched glass, brass fixtures, and a huge mahogany bar. American cuisine is the focus at lunch with items ranging from salads and crêpes to croissantwiches and omelets, priced from $4.95 to $8.95. Dinner entrees, in the $12.50 to $20.95 price bracket, with most under $15, have a more international flair, with such dishes as veal saltimbocca, coq au vin, veal Cordon Bleu, shrimp curry, mixed grill, and steak au poivre. Tableside service is also a feature, with Caesar salad ($4.35) and flaming desserts such as cherries jubilee and baked Alaska ($3.50 to $5). Open Monday through Saturday from 11:30 a.m. to 11 p.m. CC: AE, MC, Ch, and V.

Budget Meals

For more than 50 years, **Burke's Restaurant,** 36 Light St. at Lombard Street (tel. 752-4189), has been a downtown fixture. Located opposite Harborplace, this tavern eatery is known for its pub atmosphere and exotic cocktails (there is a separate drink menu with over 80 listings from melon-ball sours to Kahlua coladas, mostly priced from $2 to $3). A long bar dominates the décor, which also features lots of dark wood, ceiling fans, old barrels, pewter tankards, and booth and stool seating. The food is particularly good here; the menu is not extensive, but you can't go wrong with the crab cakes at any time of day. Lunch choices also include sandwiches, burgers, and crab melts, priced from $2.25 to $5.95. Dinner entrees, in the $5.75 to $13.95 range, with most under $10, include steaks, crab cakes, spare ribs, barbecued chicken, and a delicious soft-crab imperial (sautéed soft-shell crabs covered in lump crab meat and topped with mornay sauce). All main courses are accompanied by salad and potatoes. Open daily from 11:30 a.m. to 3 p.m. for lunch, and from 5:30 to 11 p.m. for dinner. CC's accepted: MC and V.

CHARLES STREET AND DOWNTOWN: Try any of these when you're in the Charles Street/downtown area.

The Top Choices

Ever since 1961, **Danny's,** 1201 N. Charles St. (tel. 539-1393) has been known for serving "cuisine for the gourmet." This is a family-run restaurant, the pride and joy of Danny and Beatrice Dickman, located in the fashionable Mount Vernon section of the city, between Biddle and Preston Streets. There are four dining rooms, with seating ranging from 15 to 100, and a plush contemporary décor with lots of mirrors, leather seating, and wood paneling. Lunch, priced from $5.95 to $12.95, includes petit steaks, seafood, crêpes, salads, and sandwiches. The main focus, however, is on dinner when you can get just about anything your heart desires. You can start with an appetizer of fresh steamed mussels ($7) or you can blow the budget and opt for the Beluga caviar ($50). Entrees, priced from $17 to $28, range from lobster and Dover sole to Chateaubriand, steak Diane flambé, beef Wellington, and prime ribs (all prime Black Angus beef). Everything is à la carte, so figure another $10 for salad and vegetables. Top it all off with a bottle of wine from the 8,000-bottle cellar. Open Monday through Friday for lunch and dinner from 11:30 a.m. to 11 p.m., and on Saturday from 5 p.m. to midnight. All major CC's are accepted.

Just two blocks away is another great place for beef, the **Prime Rib,** 1101 N. Calvert St. (tel. 539-1804), between Biddle and Chase Streets. This restaurant, a fixture since 1965, is open only for dinner. In addition to aged midwestern beef, fresh Chesapeake Bay seafood is a specialty of the chef who has won accolades from the prestigious Chaine des Rotisseurs. Most people start a meal here with the house trademark, Greenberg potato skins ($3.95), named after a regular customer. Entrees, priced from $13.95 to $23.95, include a panorama of prime ribs, steaks, rack of lamb, veal chops, and such seafood dishes as blackened swordfish, crab cakes, and lobster tails. All main courses are accompanied by potatoes. Open daily from 5 p.m. to 2 a.m. All major CC's are accepted.

Moderately Priced Dining

The Mount Vernon area is also home to the **Brass Elephant,** 924 N. Charles St. (tel. 547-8480), a restaurant in a restored 1861 town house, originally the home of Baltimore businessman Charles Stuart. The décor carries on the 19th-century tradition with high ceilings, open fireplace, gold-leaf trim, chandeliers, and, as its name implies, lots of brass fixtures. Gentle shades of blue and classical background music add to the serene atmosphere. The cuisine is a blend of American and Northern Italian. Lunch, priced from $4.95 to $6.95, ranges from open-faced sandwiches and omelets to pastas and entrees such as veal francese, osso buco, or rainbow trout. Dinner pastas are priced from $9.75 to $10.95, and main courses from $12.95 to $18.95. Choices include seafood cioppino, veal saltimbocca, and sirloin pizzaiola. In addition, early-bird diners can avail of a fixed-price theater-supper that offers a complete dinner including appetizer for $14.95. Open for lunch Monday through Friday from 11:30 a.m. to 2 p.m.; and for dinner Monday through Thursday from 5:30 to 9:30 p.m., Friday and Saturday from 5:30 to 10:30 p.m., and Sunday from 5 to 9 p.m. Major CC's are accepted.

California cuisine is the keynote of **Pacifica,** 326 N. Charles St. (tel. 727-8264), in the heart of the Charles Street "restaurant row." Baltimore's original mesquite-wood fire-grill restaurant, this spot is also known for its homemade pastas and for its innovative use of fresh regional produce. Gourmet pizzas are the feature at lunch, as well as smoked seafood, burgers, and other light dishes, all in the $4.95 to $7.95 price bracket. Dinner choices, priced from $7.95 to $15.95, include mesquite-grilled steaks, salmon, swordfish, brochette of seafood, baby quail, and sweetbreads. Open for lunch Monday through Friday from 11:30 a.m. to 2:30 p.m., and for dinner Monday through Saturday from 5:30 to 11 p.m. CC's accepted: AE, D, MC, and V.

Budget Meals

As its name implies, **Louie's Bookstore Café,** 518 N. Charles St. (tel. 962-1222) is a blend of bookstore and bistro, also on "restaurant row." Staffed by local artists and musicians, this unusual eatery is decorated with paintings by local talent and an eclectic blend of furniture, with chamber music emanating from the background. Lunch choices, priced from $3.95 to $6.95, feature creative salads (such as artichoke and feta with spinach), as well as filet of fish, steak sandwiches, and charbroiled chicken marinated in a curry. Dinner entrees, in the $6.95 to $9.95 bracket, include steaks, vegetable stir-fry, crab, shrimp casserole, and chicken stuffed with oysters and ham. Open for lunch and dinner Tuesday through Saturday from 11:30 a.m. to 2 a.m., Sunday from 10:30 a.m. to midnight, and Monday from 11:30 a.m. to midnight. CC's accepted: MC and V.

THE NEIGHBORHOODS: Baltimore's ethnic neighborhoods are wonderful to explore at mealtime. Choose from German, northern and southern Italian, and historic waterfront cuisine.

A Bit of Bavaria in Baltimore

In the German section of east Baltimore known as Highland Town, you'll find **Haussner's,** 3244 Eastern Ave. (tel. 327-8365), started in this city in 1926 by Bavarian-born William Henry Haussner. Moved to its present location in 1936, this restaurant is still carried on by the founder's widow Frances and family. A Baltimore institution that you have to see to believe, this is not only a great place to go for good value and good food (the main dining room seats 500), but it is also an art and antique gallery, with wall-to-wall and floor-to-ceiling paintings, porcelains, sculptures, clocks, figurines, and old plates. Everywhere you look there is art, collected over the years by the Haussners; even the menu features sample paintings. You're apt to forget that you came to eat, until you look at the menu. Lunch choices, priced from $2.95 to $13.50, include sandwiches, seafood salads, omelets, and hot dishes, but dinner is the pièce de résistance with over 70 entrees, all fresh and delicious daily. The price range is $6.95 to $17.95, with most entrees priced at $12 and under, and usually including a choice of two vegetables. The selection embraces all kinds of meats and seafoods as well as unique choices such as frogs' legs, finnan haddie, bouillabaisse, sweetbreads, wiener schnitzel, baked rabbit, pigs' knuckles, and ox tongue. With its own bakery on the premises, Haussner's is also known for its desserts (over 30 varieties, ranging from strawberry pie and apple strudel to honey almond cake, $1.75 to $2.95). Only lunch reservations are accepted, so get there early for dinner. Open for lunch from 11 a.m. to 4 p.m. Tuesday through Friday, and from 11 a.m. to 2 p.m. on Saturday; for dinner from 4 to 11 p.m. Tuesday through Saturday. CC's accepted: AE, MC, and V.

Mostly Moderate Dining in Little Italy

Just east of the Inner Harbor area is **Little Italy,** with at least 15 good restaurants including a long-time (since 1916) favorite, **Chiapparelli's,** 237 S. High St. (tel. 837-0309). Southern Italian dishes are the trademark here with special plaudits for Mom Chiapparelli's raviolis (stuffed with spinach and ricotta). Lunch, priced at $5 and up, also includes sandwiches, antipasto platters, omelets, and salads. Dinner is the main event, with entrees priced from $9.95 to $24, with most choices under $15. Veal, cooked at least a dozen different ways, is the star of the menu, along with tasty chicken dishes and such classics as lobster fra diavolo and steak Italiana. All main courses are served with salad. Open Sunday through Thursday from 11 a.m. to 11 p.m., on Friday until 1 a.m., and on Saturday until 2 a.m. Major CC's are accepted.

Both northern and southern Italian cuisine are featured at **Sabatino's Restaurant,** 901 Fawn St. (tel. 727-9414), with a façade distinguished by its colorful painted window scenes. This is a particularly good late dining spot since it is open every day from noon to 3 a.m. Dinner entrees, priced from $9.95 to $24.95, include veal francese, shrimp scampi, calamari marinara, beef pizzaiola, and two dozen pastas such as spaghetti with broccoli and anchovy sauce. CC's accepted: Ch, MC, and V.

If you like music with your meal, head to **Da Mimmo,** 217 S. High St. (tel. 727-6876), a small candlelit restaurant with nightly piano entertainment. Lunch is also available here, from $4 to $8, for sandwiches, pastas, and seafood dishes. Dinner pastas are priced from $6 to $9, and entrees from $11 to $24. The varied menu features everything from chicken cacciatore, lobster pizzaiola, and filet mignon to the "Mimmo seafood special" for two (shrimp, clams, calamari, and mussels in marinara sauce on a bed of linguine). Da Mimmo's is also very obliging for special orders, and encourages patrons to call ahead and advise preferences. Open Monday through Thursday from 11:30 a.m. to 11:30 p.m., on Friday until 1 a.m., on Saturday from 5 p.m. to 1 a.m., and on Sunday from 2 p.m. to 1 a.m. All major CC's are accepted.

Fell's Point

Still farther east of Little Italy is **Fells Point,** the waterfront neighborhood where Baltimore began. One restaurant you should not miss in this area is **Bertha's,** 734 S. Broadway (327-5795), a fun place known for its mussels and music. The décor is a blend of yesteryear, with original brick walls, antique prints, old wine bottles, and nautical bric-a-brac. You'll also see musical instruments fashioned into chandeliers and wall hangings, a reminder that traditional and folk music is on tap here most weekend nights. Lunch, priced from $1.95 to $10.95, includes shepherd's pie, seafood, salads, omelets, burgers, and fish cakes. Mussels are featured at dinner (fixed at least a dozen different ways); other entrees range from paella or curried seafood to a vegetable platter with brown rice or chicken staccato (boneless breast with kumquats and peanuts). All main courses are priced from $5.95 to $16.95. This restaurant, which also serves a very respectable afternoon tea in the best British tradition, has a tempting array of desserts in the $2.50 bracket, from pecan butter tart to Scottish trifle. Reservations are only accepted for parties of six or more and for afternoon tea (from 3 to 5 p.m. each day). Open Sunday through Thursday from 11:30 a.m. to 11 p.m.; Friday and Saturday until midnight. CC's accepted: Ch, MC, and V.

Just two blocks away is the **The Admiral's Cup,** 1645–47 Thames St. (tel. 675-6988), a tradition along this historic waterfront since 1916. This restaurant is actually composed of two adjoining houses, restored and furnished in a cozy 18th-century style. Salads, sandwiches, and seafood are featured at lunch, priced from $4.95 to $8.95. Dinner entrees, priced from $9.95 to $17.95, with most under $15, include soft-shell crabs, shad roe, lobster, and steaks. All main courses come with house salad and vegetables. Open for lunch Tuesday through Saturday from 11:30 a.m. to 2:30 p.m.; dinner Tuesday through Sunday from 5 to 11 p.m. CC's accepted: AE, Ch, MC, and V.

6. The Top Attractions

Harborplace is located in the heart of the Inner Harbor, adjacent to the city's dazzling Convention Center. As its name so aptly indicates, Harborplace is positioned right on the edge of the waterfront. It occupies two full blocks along Light and Pratt Streets, and is the keystone to the revitalization of Baltimore as a tourist mecca.

Built in 1981, Harborplace is to Baltimore what Station Square is to Pittsburgh, Faneuil Hall to Boston, and Ghirardelli Square to San Francisco—it is a bright and airy complex of restaurants, food markets, curiosity shops, and trendy boutiques, side-by-side in a milieu of music, camaraderie, and good times.

Designed to duplicate the look of an early steamship pier headquarters, Harborplace is made up of two pavilions, each named after the streets they occupy. The **Light Street Pavilion,** the more informal of the two, is composed of 45 specialty vendors (from bonbons and books to spices and silks), arranged along colonnades on two split levels. The upper level houses a food hall of ethnic eateries plus the **Sam Smith Market,** a street-fair arrangement featuring the works of local artists and craftsmen, from scrimshaw and silver to pottery and puppets.

The **Pratt Street Pavilion** is a bi-level emporium of designer shops (from Laura Ashley and Crabtree and Evelyn to Pappagallo) as well as collectibles (music boxes, ornaments, rare prints, brass, crystal, and imported clothing). The two pavilions also provide a setting for more than a dozen top-class restaurants and over 50 fast-food vendors (from crabs to croissants). Open Monday through Thursday from 10 a.m. to 9:30 p.m.; Friday and Saturday from 10 a.m. to 10 p.m.; and Sunday from noon to 8 p.m.; with dining most nights until 2 a.m.

Note: When you first walk into Harborplace, it can be a little overpowering. To help you adjust and get your bearings, there is a handy pocket-size guide available free of charge. You can pick up a copy from the tourist office or from the various vendors at Harborplace. This booklet not only gives a description of all the restaurants and shops but also pinpoints their locations with mini-maps and floor plans.

If you are new to Baltimore and want to get a sweeping overview of the whole harbor and city, head for the **Top of the World,** 401 E. Pratt St. (tel. 659-4545). This is Baltimore's sky-high observatory, located on the 27th floor of the pentagonal World Trade Center, just opposite Harborplace. In addition to a look at the cityscapes below, you can acquire a bit of background about Baltimore from the sky-high exhibits, hands-on displays, and multi-media presentations at this facility. Admission is $1.50 for adults and $1.25 for children aged 5 to 15. Hours are 10 a.m. to 5 p.m. daily, except Saturday when it is open from 10 a.m. to 10 p.m.

One of the Inner Harbor's biggest draws is the U. S. Frigate *Constellation,*

Constellation Dock, Pier One, Pratt Street (tel. 539-1797). Launched from Baltimore in 1797, this was the first ship that the U. S. Navy put to sea and the first to defeat an enemy man-of-war; it has been continuously afloat longer than any other ship in the world. With a long history of travels to the Barbary Coast, England, France, and many other ports throughout the world, the *Constellation* is now permanently at home in Baltimore and welcomes 20th-century mates on board to inspect her decks. Open daily June 15 through Labor Day from 10 a.m. to 8 p.m.; the day after Labor Day until October 14, from 10 a.m. to 6 p.m.; October 15 to May 14 from 10 a.m. to 4 p.m.; and May 15 to June 14 from 10 a.m. to 6 p.m. Admission is $1.75 for adults and 75¢ for children aged 6 to 15.

A spectacular seven-level glass and steel structure, the **National Aquarium,** Pier 3, 501 E. Pratt St. (tel. 576-3810) contains over a million gallons of water and more than 5,000 specimens of mammals, fish, rare birds, reptiles, and amphibians. All the creatures are on view in settings that re-create their natural habitats, including a South American rain forest, an Atlantic coral reef, and an open-ocean tank. Moving belts and ramped bridges carry visitors from one exhibit level to the next. Open from mid-May to mid-September, Monday through Thursday from 9 a.m. to 5 p.m., Friday through Sunday until 8 p.m.; and the rest of the year, daily from 10 a.m. to 5 p.m., except until 8 p.m. on Friday. Admission charge is $6.75 for adults, $5 for students over 12, and $3.75 for children aged 3 to 12.

Nearby is the **Baltimore Maritime Museum,** Pier 4, foot of Pratt Street, (tel. 396-3854). This outdoor complex is the home of the submarine U.S.S. *Torsk,* which sank the last warship in World War II, and the lightship *Chesapeake,* a floating lighthouse built in 1930. Both vessels are moored at the dock and are open to visitors. Hours are from 10 a.m. to 5 p.m. Thursday through Monday, during November through April; and daily from 10 a.m. to 8 p.m., from May through October. Admission is $2.50 for adults and $1 for children 12 and under.

Another popular attraction of the Inner Harbor area is the **Maryland Science Center and Davis Planetarium,** 601 Light St. (tel. 685-2370). The geological aspects of the Chesapeake Bay and Baltimore City are illustrated in contemporary hands-on displays, science arcades, computer games, and movies, geared to visitors of all ages. In addition, journeys through time and space and star shows are featured in the adjacent Davis Planetarium. Open June through September, from 10 a.m. to 8 p.m. on Monday through Saturday, and from noon to 6 p.m. on Sunday; and the rest of the year from 10 a.m. to 5 p.m. on Monday through Thursday, from 10 a.m. to 10 p.m. on Friday and Saturday, and from noon to 6 p.m. on Sunday. Admission is $3.50 for adults and $3 for students (children under 5 not permitted). Admission to the planetarium is an additional $1 per person.

One of Baltimore's great historic houses is the **Carroll Mansion,** 800 E. Lombard St. (tel. 396-3523), an early 19th-century merchant's house built in 1812. This house is also associated with Charles Carroll of Carrollton, the Maryland patriot who signed the Declaration of Independence. Carroll wintered here during the last 12 years of his life (1820–1832), when he was the focus of much attention because he was the last surviving signer of the Declaration. Today the building is filled with early-American furniture, decorative arts, and paintings from the late 18th century through the 1840s. Open, free of charge, Tuesday through Sunday from 10 a.m. to 4 p.m.

A trailblazer in American railroading, this city is also the setting of the **Baltimore and Ohio (B & O) Railroad Museum,** 901 W. Pratt St. (tel. 237-2387). Often called a railroad university, this museum has hundreds of exhibits ranging from double-decker stagecoaches on iron wheels and early diesels to steam locomotives and the 1830 Mount Clare Station, the nation's first passenger and freight station, as well as the 1844 round house with the original B & O tracks and turntable. Peter Cooper built and tested his famous Tom Thumb on this site and Samuel Morse strung his first telegraph wires through this depot. A visit here will chug you along on a 300-year round-trip through the annals of American train travel. Hours are from 10 a.m. to 4 p.m. Wednesday through Sunday (except major holidays). Admission charge is $2.50 for adults and $1.50 for children under 12.

The tiny house where **Edgar Allan Poe** began his writing career is located in the heart of Baltimore at 203 N. Amity St. (tel. 396-7932). Poe lived here for three years (1832–1835) while courting his cousin, whom he later married. The building contains Poe memorabilia plus period furniture, ever-changing exhibits, and a video presentation of leading Poe works. Open Wednesday through Saturday, April through July, and October to mid-December, from noon to 4 p.m.; on Saturday only in August and September, from noon to 4 p.m. Closed from mid-December through March. Admission is $1 for adults and 50¢ for children under 12.

One of the most-visited landmarks in the city is the **Fort McHenry National Monument and Historic Shrine,** E. Fort Avenue (tel. 539-FORT), birthplace of our national anthem. It was the sight of our flag flying over this star-shaped fort during the 1814 Battle of Baltimore that inspired Francis Scott Key to write the words of the "Star Spangled Banner." Not only was the song written, but the American forces were successful against the British and the fort never again came under attack. It remained an active military base for many years, however, until 1925, when it became a national park. To assist visitors in touring the fort, there are historical and military exhibits; a 15-minute film, shown every half hour; explanatory maps; and, during the summer months, guided walks are regularly scheduled. The park is open daily from 9 a.m. to 5 p.m., and from 9 a.m. until 8 p.m. from Memorial Day through Labor Day (except Christmas and New Year's Day). Admission is $1 per person.

After seeing Ft. McHenry, the obvious place to go is to the **Flag House and 1812 Museum,** 844 E. Pratt St. (tel. 837-1793). This is the home of Mary Pickersgill, the seamstress who made the 30×42-foot red, white, and blue Ft. McHenry flag, the symbol that motivated Francis Scott Key to write the "Star Spangled Banner." This Federal-style (1793) house is full of period furnishings and a collection of early-American art. Outside the building is an unusual garden featuring a map of the continental United States made of stones native to each state. Open Monday to Saturday from 10 a.m. to 4 p.m., and Sunday from 1 to 4 p.m.; closed Sundays in December, January and February. Admission $1.50 for adults, $1 for students aged 13 to 18, and 50¢ for children aged 6 to 12.

Baseball fans of all ages enjoy a visit to the **Babe Ruth Birthplace and Museum/Maryland Baseball Hall of Fame,** 216 Emory St. (tel. 727-1539), where the great player was born on February 6, 1895. This restored house and adjoining museum contain personal mementos of George Herman "Babe" Ruth, otherwise known as "the sultan of swat." The exhibits, which focus on the Baltimore Orioles and Maryland baseball as well as the great Babe, include "touchable" items such as hats, bats, and gloves; there is also an audio-visual presentation on baseball, world series film highlights, and a wall mural of famous baseball personalities. Open daily April through October from 10 a.m. to 5 p.m.; and November 1 through March 31 from 10 a.m. to 4 p.m. daily (except Easter, Thanksgiving, and Christmas Eve and Day). Admission charge is $2.50 for adults and $1.25 for children aged 12 and under.

Baltimore is home to seven different **city markets,** all more than 100 years in operation. The oldest (1782) and largest, the Lexington Market, at Lexington, Paca and Eutaw Streets (tel. 685-6169), is perhaps the most colorful, with over 160 stalls featuring seafood, poultry, ethnic foods, raw bars, produce, meats, and specialty items. All of the markets, each with its own neighborhood flavor, are open Monday through Saturday from 8 a.m. to 6 p.m. A complete lists of markets and addresses is included in the *Baltimore Good Times* newspaper. No admission charges.

7. Nightlife

BALTIMORE BOX OFFICE: Tickets to just about all events, from concerts and theatrical productions to sports, can all be purchased from one handy source in the midst of the Inner Harbor, **The Baltimore Box Office,** 601 E. Pratt St., Pier 4 (tel. 576-9333). This is the city's one-stop ticket shop, open Monday through Saturday from 10 a.m. to 6 p.m. Tickets to many events can also be purchased at the **Baltimore Arena,** 201 W. Baltimore St. (tel. 347-2010). If you prefer to order your tickets by phone, the local "TeleCharge" number is 625-1400.

THEATERS: Broadway's home in Baltimore is how critics describe the **Morris Mechanic Theater,** 25 Hopkins Plaza (tel. 625-1400), an ultra-modern showplace in the heart of midtown's Charles Center. This theater stages contemporary plays with original casts en route to or from the Great White Way; recent productions have included *Cats, The Tap Dance Kid,* and *Singin' in the Rain.* The curtain is at 8 p.m. Monday through Saturday, with matinees at 2 p.m. on Wednesday and Saturday. The box office is open from 10 a.m. to 8:30 p.m. Ticket prices average $15 to $25 for most shows. CC's accepted: AE, Ch, MC, and V.

Award-winning musicals from *Annie* and *Show Boat* to *Can-Can* are the focus at the **Fells Point Theater,** 511 S. Broadway (tel. 522-4126). The program includes a show performed by resident professionals and a gourmet dinner, with choices ranging from filet mignon and bouillabaisse to chicken with shrimp. Open all year, Wednesday through Sunday, with dinner from 6 to 7:30 p.m. and showtime at 8 p.m.; on Sundays, there is a matinee with meal at noon and show at 2:30 p.m. Prices range from $22 to $26 per person and the box office is open from 10 a.m. to 10 p.m. CC's accepted: AE, Ch, MC, and V.

MUSIC AND DANCING: Housed in the building that once served as the source of electricity for Baltimore's streetcars in the early 1900s, the **P.T. Flagg's Musical Time Machine,** 601 E. Pratt St., Pier 4 (tel. 347-7521) is the latest addition to Baltimore's nighttime scene. By day, this building, known simply as "The Power Plant," is a multi-faceted amusement center for children, but, once 6 o'clock comes, it is the setting for a dazzling live musical revue from ragtime to rock and roll. The evening also includes Baltimore's only laser show, musical entertainment on 17 video screens, and dancing. Open Tuesday through Sunday from 6 p.m. to 2 a.m. Drinks and light food available. Cover charge is $3.95 per person.

Jazz singer Ethel Ennis is the tour de force behind **Ethel's Place,** 1225 Cathedral St. (tel. 727-7077), a modern multi-level nightclub. In addition to Ms. Ennis' frequent spots, other leading artists appear regularly, in an ever-changing program of jazz, bluegrass, folk, classical, and mellow rock. Open Tuesday through Saturday, show times are at 8 and 10 p.m., often with an extra midnight show on weekends. The cover charge varies from $5 to $20, depending on the star. Drinks, bar snacks, and wine are available at additional cost and there is also a full-service restaurant on the premises. CC's accepted: AE, MC, and V.

The showplace of the Inner Harbor is the **Pier Six Concert Pavilion,** Pier 6 and Pratt Street (tel. 727-5580). This is a 3,000-seat outdoor facility perched at the end of one of Baltimore's old-fashioned harbor piers. Pier Six is the setting for frequent open-air concerts throughout the summertime, such as the annual two-month Harbor Lights Festival (see "Events"). The Baltimore *Good Times* newspaper is the best source of up-to-date program information.

8. Sports and Activities

WATER SPORTS: Several concessions along the Harborplace dock rent small craft for individual use (two people per vessel). Electric boats can be hired for $9 per one-half hour; and paddleboats are available at $4.25 for a half hour, and $7.50 for a full hour's splash. Cruise vessels, sailboats, and water taxis also operate throughout the summer season (see "Getting Around").

HORSE RACING: Maryland's oldest thoroughbred track and the site of the annual Preakness Stakes is **Pimlico Race Course,** Park Heights and Belvedere Avenues (tel. 542-9400), about five miles from the Inner Harbor on the city's northwest side. The full racing season extends from mid-March to the end of May, mid-July to mid-August, and from early September to early October. Post time is 1 p.m., and admission charges are $3 for the grandstand and $5 for the clubhouse, plus $1 per car for parking. Pimlico is also the home of the **National Jockey's Hall of Fame,** open from 9 to 11 a.m. during the racing season, free of charge.

BASEBALL: The Baltimore Orioles play their April–October season at **Memorial Stadium,** 33rd Street and Ellerslie Avenue (tel. 338-1300). Ticket prices range from $4.75 for adult general admission ($2.50 for children under 12) to $9.50 for a field box seat. In addition to the stadium, tickets are on sale at the **Baltimore Box Office,** 601 E. Pratt St., Pier 4; the **Baltimore Civic Center,** 201 W. Baltimore St.; the **Orioles Fanfare Store,** Light Street Pavilion, Harborplace; and at the **Hecht Department Store,** Howard and Lexington Streets.

9. Events

HARBOR LIGHTS FESTIVAL: The highlight of the summer calendar in Baltimore is the **Harbor Lights Music Festival,** Pier Six Concert Pavilion, Pier 6 and Pratt Street, Baltimore Inner Harbor (tel. 727-5580). Running from late June through August, this is a series of evening open-air concerts featuring big names in popular, folk, symphony, jazz, and bluegrass music. In recent years, the program has included Harry Belafonte, Tony Bennett, Ella Fitzgerald, Crystal Gayle, Peter, Paul and Mary, Pia Zadora, Ferrante and Teicher, and Rosemary Clooney. The final event of the schedule is always a jazz festival dedicated to Baltimore-born Eubie Blake. Reserved seats are priced from $10 to $18 and lawn tickets go for $6 to $9. Tickets can be purchased at the Pier 6 Box Office and the Pier 4 Box Office, and at other outlets throughout the city. Most major CC's accepted.

PREAKNESS FESTIVAL: Probably the most well-known of Baltimore's annual celebrations is the **Preakness Festival Week,** held in mid-May. This city-wide event pays tribute to the race called the "Preakness Stakes" at the Pimlico Race Course (1988 will be the 113th running). The middle jewel in horse racing's Triple Crown, the Preakness is regarded as one of the prime sporting events in the world and annually adds more than $18 million to the local economy. The week-long hoopla surrounding the race begins on the previous weekend and includes hot-air-balloon races, crab derbies, boating races, food-eating contests, and other waterside activities, based mostly in the Inner Harbor area. On the eve of the race, there is also a Preakness Festival Parade of Lights, with lighted floats, giant helium balloon characters, and marching bands. More than 80,000 people usually attend the race itself; post time is approximately 5:30 p.m. All seats are reserved at the Pimlico Race Course on Preakness Day (phone 301/542-9400 or toll-free 800/638-3811 for further information).

Chapter XXIII

WESTERN MARYLAND

1. **Frederick**
2. **Hagerstown**
3. **Cumberland**
4. **Deep Creek Lake**

FROM THE SHORES OF THE POTOMAC to the Allegheny mountain tops, western Maryland is a panorama of fertile farmlands and historic hillsides. Jutting out like a panhandle beyond Baltimore and wedged in between Pennsylvania and West Virginia, this land was the westward gateway of our forefathers as they headed their covered wagons for Ohio and beyond.

Route 40, this country's first National Pike, still meanders over the entire length of this countryside, connecting Frederick to Hagerstown, Cumberland, and other points east and west. This area was also the path for the great feat of mid-19th-century ingenuity, the 184½-mile-long Chesapeake and Ohio Canal (the C&O) linking Georgetown to Cumberland.

Western Maryland is the home of Francis Scott Key and Barbara Fritchie; and the site of Antietam National Battlefield, Fort Cumberland, and Fort Frederick. It is also the setting for Lilypons Water Gardens; the "Antiques Capital of Maryland" at historic New Market; and "Camp David," the retreat of U.S. presidents since Franklin Roosevelt.

With an elevation ranging from 490 feet to 3,650 feet, this 225-mile stretch of land extends from the rolling hills of Frederick's horse country to the dramatic ski slopes of Wisp Mountain in Garrett County.

In addition to the trusty pavements of old Route 40, a network of modern interstate highways will bring you to this relatively undiscovered corner of the Old Line State. Interstate-70 runs from Baltimore to Frederick and Hagerstown before it crosses up into the Pennsylvania border toward Breezewood. Interstate-270 connects Washington, D.C., to Frederick, and Interstate-81 skirts Hagerstown as it runs in a north-south direction between Pennsylvania and West Virginia.

1. Frederick

The gateway to western Maryland, Frederick is just an hour's drive from Baltimore or Washington, D.C. It is situated in the heart of Maryland's prime horse country, the seat of one of America's richest agricultural counties.

Frederick is also a city of beautifully preserved 18th- and 19th-century town houses, landmark church spires, and gracious Victorian gardens. Perhaps Frederick is best known, however, as the birthplace of Francis Scott Key, the author of our national anthem, and Barbara Fritchie, legendary heroine of the Civil War. It also lies in the shadow of the Catoctin Mountains, the home of the presidential retreat "Camp David."

Named for Frederick Calvert, sixth Lord of Baltimore, this proud city was founded in 1745 by English and German settlers. Initially a frontier settlement en route to the West, then a Colonial crossroads on the National Pike, and later during the Revolutionary and Civil Wars, Frederick always played a pivotal role in our nation's progress.

Today, with a population 35,000, Frederick is a shining example of a prosperous 20th-century city that melds its history into everyday life. Horse-drawn carts still pass by Frederick's squares and courtyards; rows of craft shops and antique galleries line the streets. Old brick homes are enjoying a second life as trendy restaurants, and abandoned factories are being recycled into chic shopping boutiques.

VISITOR INFORMATION: The **Tourism Council of Frederick County** operates a very efficient and helpful visitor center at 19 E. Church St., Frederick, MD 21701 (tel. 301/663-8703). This office not only supplies maps, brochures, and listings of accommodations and restaurants, but it will also arrange walking tours of the historic district. The very helpful staff espouse the motto "We're glad you're here!" and they really mean it. In addition to this full-service office, tourist information booths are also located in the rest areas of the Frederick exits of I-70 East and U.S. 15 South. All of these facilities are open seven days a week from 9 a.m. to 5 p.m.

GETTING TO AND AROUND FREDERICK: Greyhound operates regular services to Frederick into its depot on East All Saints Street (tel. 663-3311), between South Market and Carroll Streets.

Locally, the **Frederick City Bus Transit Service** connects major downtown points to the various shopping malls for a flat fare of 60¢. **Taxis** do not cruise the city, but are available by phone; two reliable firms are **Citycab** (tel. 662-2250) and **AB's Taxi** (tel. 663-8200).

For **self-drive cars, Budget Rent-a-Car** maintains an office at 6001 Urbana Pike (tel. 663-8255).

Bicycle rentals are available from **The Wheel Base,** 229 N. Market, St. (tel. 663-9288).

Horse and Carriage Tours: The best way to savor the sights and the ambience of historic Frederick is to take a horse-drawn carriage ride. Tours with commentary are operated daily from Old City Hall by **Frederick Carriage and Livery,** 112 Monroe Ave. (tel. 301/695-7433). Complete information, schedules, and reservations are also available at the Visitor Center at 19 E. Church St. The cost for a 30-minute tour is $3 for adults and $2 for children.

Walking Tours: If you prefer to see the sights on foot, walking tours of the Frederick Historic District are conducted by certified guides, May through October, at 11 a.m. and 1 p.m. on Saturdays and holidays and at 1:30 p.m. on Sundays. All tours, which last for 1½ hours, depart from the Frederick Visitor Center at 19 E. Church St. and reservations and tickets may also be obtained there; the charge is $2 for adults and free for children under 12 with an adult. Tours at other times and days can also be arranged, with advance notice. In addition, the Visitor Center provides a free folder that maps out a self-guided walk around the city.

WHERE TO STAY: The hotels and motels of Frederick are primarily located on major roads (Routes 40, 15, and 85) leading into the city, although there are plans in the next few years to restore old buildings in the downtown area for use as up-to-date hotels. For the moment, however, here are some of the best places to stay close to the city or within a short drive.

Mostly Moderate Choices

Just one-half mile west of the city center is the **Holiday Inn,** 999 W. Patrick St. (Route 40), Frederick, MD 21701 (tel. 301/662-5141 or toll-free 800/ HOLIDAY). This modern three-story hotel has 159 recently refurbished rooms, each with double or king-size beds, air conditioning, a direct-dial phone, and color cable TV. Rates for a double range from $55 to $75; over-sized king leisure rooms with executive work areas go for $75 to $85. Other amenities include a full-service restaurant called Foxberry's, valet service, an outdoor swimming pool, a patio, and an adjacent complex of movie theaters. Lunch, priced from $3.95 to $6.95, focuses on burgers, deli-style sandwiches, pasta, salad bar, and omelets. Dinner entrees, which range from $8.95 to $16.95, include flounder amandine, veal parmigiana, Maryland fried chicken, steaks, crab cakes, and a tasty seafood Marechiaro (shrimp, clams, mussels, and scallops in a light marinara sauce with pasta). Open from 11:30 a.m. to 2 p.m. for lunch, and from 5 to 10 p.m. for dinner (9 p.m. on Sunday); breakfast is available from 6:30 a.m. on weekdays and from 7 a.m. on weekends. All major CC's are accepted.

Route 85, the home of the Francis Scott Key Shopping Mall, is the newest "hotel row" in the area and the setting for the **Quality Inn,** 7400 Quality Court, Frederick, MD 21701 (tel. 301/694-7704 or toll-free 800/228-5151). Opened in 1986, this modern six-story hotel is nestled beside a man-made lake and Hooper's Island Lighthouse, a unique 80-seat gazebo lounge connected by footbridge to the hotel. There are 170 rooms, with a choice of double, queen, or king-size beds, and many with views of the lake. Each room has air conditioning, a direct-dial phone, and 50-channel cable TV; 32 rooms are also equipped for computer work and there is a complete non-smoking floor. Doubles range from $55 to $80. Guest amenities include valet service, an outdoor pool, a spa, a sauna, and an exercise room. The nautical-style restaurant, The Chesapeake Room, overlooks the water and lighthouse and offers a delectable raw bar throughout the day. Lunch, priced from $4.95 to $6.95, also features hot and cold sandwiches, eggs Benedict, omelets, burgers, and a wide range of salads (try the tuna trimmer, the cashew chicken, or the marinated mushroom for a light meal). Dinner choices range from regional cooking to international dishes, such as Maryland country ham or fried chicken, roast pork tenderloin, prime ribs, and filet of sole, as well as chicken chasseur, salmon with dill sauce, veal Oscar, chicken Kiev, and marinated beef and vegetable brochettes. The prices, from $8.95 to $21.95, include a salad and vegetable selection. Lunch is served from 11:30 a.m. to 2:30 p.m., and dinner from 5 to 10 p.m. Major CC's are accepted.

Also near the Francis Scott Key Mall and south of Frederick off Route 85 is the **Sheraton,** 5400 Sheraton Dr., Frederick, MD 21701 (tel. 301/694-7500 or toll-free 800/325-3535). Situated in a well-landscaped garden setting, this modern two-story brick structure has 155 rooms, each with a double or king bed, air conditioning, a direct-dial phone, and color cable TV. Doubles range from $66 to $84 per night. Other facilities include an enclosed indoor pool, a whirlpool, and a sauna, as well as a game room, miniature golf, and evening entertainment with dancing. There are two restaurants, the Village Green, set in a tropical courtyard overlooking the pool for light snacks, and Harrigan's, a smartly decorated multi-level dining room with rich burgundy tones. Sandwiches, salads, and burgers are available at lunchtime, priced from $3.95 to $5.95. Dinner entrees, which run from $8.95 to $16.95, include crab imperial, shrimp stir-fry, sautéed scallops, chicken au whisky, veal piccata, and tournedos Marseille (a luscious combination of filet mignon with crab, asparagus, and hollandaise). Lunch is served from 11:30 a.m. to 2:30 p.m., and dinner from 5 to 10 p.m. (until 11 p.m. on Friday and Saturday). All major CC's are accepted.

Budget Range

Two miles north of Frederick is **Beckley's Motel,** Route 15 and Willow Road, Frederick, MD 21701 (tel. 301/662-2126), a favorite lodging place with families. This Colonial-style inn has 25 modern units, each with color TV, air conditioning, and a telephone; all rooms are on the ground level and some also have kitchenettes. Doubles range from $30 to $40. Guest facilities include an outdoor swimming pool, a snack bar, and a family restaurant that is open seven days a week from 8 a.m. to 10 p.m. Specialties on the menu range from pan-fried chicken to pot pies, with prices under the $10 level for a complete meal. This motel is also known for its old-fashioned country store, selling items from all 50 states, including matchbox toys, bells, cut glass, cast-iron skillets, stone crocks, sugar-cured country ham, homemade honey, apple butter, and jelly and stick candy. CC's accepted: MC and V.

Another popular place with families is the **Cozy Motel and Restaurant,** 103 Frederick Rd., Thurmont, MD 21788 (tel. 301/217-4301), located about 15 miles north of Frederick at the base of the Catoctin Mountains. Founded in 1929, this is a bustling complex of motel and cottage units, a restaurant with a choice of nine dining rooms, a pub, a bakery, and a village of shops. The basic motel rooms, furnished with one or two double beds, wall-to-wall carpeting, color TV, and air conditioning, are priced from $28 to $35. Deluxe cottages, each with two queen-size beds, a fireplace, and a small refrigerator, average $60 a night for up to 4 people. Weekend rates are slightly higher in all cases. The Cozy restaurant (direct line: 271-7373) is known for its lunchtime smorgasbord-style "souper salad bar" which includes soups, salads, sandwich fixings, and dessert ($4.75 per person) or salad bar only ($3.50). Regular sandwiches are also available. Dinner entrees, priced from $5.95 to $9.95, include country-fried chicken, baked ham, roast turkey, crab cakes, and steaks. Evening buffets are also available, with different nightly specials (all buffets include a giant groaning board), priced from $7.95 to $10.95, depending on selection. Lunch is served between 11:15 a.m. and 4 p.m. Monday through Saturday; dinners from 4 p.m. to closing Monday through Saturday, and from noon to 8 p.m. on Sunday. CC's accepted: MC and V.

WHERE TO DINE: Downtown Frederick is a mecca for fine food; the area around Market and Patrick Streets alone boasts more than 20 good restaurants. Here are some of the best:

The Top Choice

One of Frederick's newest restaurants is **The Bull on Market,** 611 N. Market St., (tel. 695-8183), a bright and modern dining room that carries out a stock-market theme in its décor and menu. Lunch, priced from $3.95 to $6.95, features sandwiches with stock-market names like "the merger" (smoked Virginia ham and Maryland lump crabmeat) or the "prime rate" (prime rib on sourdough roll with mushrooms), as well as salads, raw-bar choices, and daily specials. Dinner, with a similarly clever menu, offers a variety of gourmet dishes from veal Oscar, breast of chicken Rollantine (stuffed with ham, Swiss cheese, and aspargus, all flamed in cognac), and lob-ka-bob (chunks of lobster and beef tenderloin) to Virginia ham, lump crab sauté, and scallops alla marsala, as well as prime rib cut to order. Entrees, priced from $11.95 to $16.95, are served with appropriate fresh vegetables. This restaurant also has its own pastry chef and maintains a distinguished wine list, with labels from leading Maryland vineyards, as well as from California and France, at $12 to $80 a bottle. The service is extremely attentive and enthusiastic. Open daily for lunch from 11 a.m. to 4 p.m.; and for dinner from 4 to 10 p.m. on Sunday through Thursday, and from 4 to 11 p.m. on Friday and Saturday. CC's accepted: AE, MC, and V.

Other Moderately Priced Places

A nautical theme prevails at the **Brown Pelican,** 5 E. Church St., (tel. 695-5833). Housed in the basement of an old brick building, this restaurant is decorated with vibrant sea tones, driftwood, and yachting collectibles. Lunch features sandwiches, burgers, salads, pasta, and hot entrees, costing from $3.95 to $9.95. Dinner, priced in the $9.95 to $16.95 range, includes a variety of interesting dishes from walnut bourbon chicken, coq au vin, flounder à l orange, shrimp and lobster alla marsala, scallops au gratin, and roast duckling to ever-popular steaks. All entrees are served with appropriate vegetables and house salad. Open for lunch Monday through Saturday from 11:30 a.m. to 3 p.m.; and for dinner Monday through Thursday from 5:30 to 9:30 p.m., Friday and Saturday from 5:30 to 10 p.m., and on Sunday from 5 to 9:30 p.m. CC's accepted: AE, MC, and V.

As its name implies, the **Louisiana Purchase,** 101 N. Market St. (tel. 663-1266), brings the atmosphere of New Orleans to the heart of Frederick. Open seven nights a week for dinner only, this restaurant is an oasis of Cajun cuisine, with such dishes as blackened redfish, seafood gumbo, chicken and crab jambalaya, shrimp étouffée, and Cajun-spiced prime rib. Traditional choices, from steaks and lobster tails to shrimp Diane and stuffed chicken, are also available. The prices run from $12.95 to $21.95, with most under $15. All entrees are served with a hearty house salad topped with crabmeat, vegetables, and a choice of potato, red beans, or rice. Open nightly from 6 p.m. to midnight, with a piano bar on weekends. Major CC's are accepted.

Bushwallers Seafood Saloon, 209 N. Market St. (tel. 694-5697), is housed in an 1840s building that was used variously as a private home, a drugstore, and a dry-goods shop before becoming a restaurant. Retaining its 19th-century atmosphere, the décor incorporates many Frederick family mementoes as well as old pictures, newspaper front pages, and turn-of-the-century political cartoons. Lunch items, which run $3.95 to $6.95, include salads, pasta, chili, sandwiches, burgers, and raw-bar items. Dinner entrees, priced from $7.95 to $14.95, focus on such seafood dishes as yellowtail flounder filets stuffed with lump crab, calamari sauté, flounder francese, and baby Coho salmon with Dijon and honey sauce, as well as meat choices ranging from veal scaloppine topped with imported brie, or steak Diane to Italian sausage with linguine. Lunch is served from 11:30 a.m. to 3 p.m., and dinner from 5 to 10 p.m. Sunday dinner is available from 3 to 10 p.m. CC's accepted: MC and V.

Another old Frederick house, circa 1767, is the setting of **The Province,** 129 N. Market St. (tel. 663-1441). This restaurant consists of a small bistro-style front room and a bright brick-walled room in the rear. The latter overlooks the herb garden, which produces ingredients for the kitchen. The furnishings range from snowshoe chairs to handmade quilt hangings and paintings by local artists. Lunchtime selections, which run from $1.95 to $3.95, focus on salads, quiches, omelets, crab cakes, and "creative American" sandwiches (such as fried oyster and bacon, or country sausage and Cheddar). Dinner entrees, from $5.95 to $10.95, change daily but two favorite dishes are scallops with Irish Mist and chicken breast with artichokes and mushrooms. Open for lunch Tuesday through Saturday from 11:30 a.m. to 3 p.m.; for dinner Tuesday through Thursday from 5:30 to 9:30 p.m., Friday and Saturday from 5:30 to 10 p.m., and on Sunday from 4 to 8 p.m. Brunch is also served on Saturday and Sunday from 11:30 a.m. to 2:30 p.m. Major CC's are accepted.

The cuisine of Italy thrives in Frederick at **di Francesco's,** 26 N. Market St. (tel. 695-5499), a restaurant decorated like a country villa with whitewashed walls and lots of leafy plants. Lunch features salads, sandwiches, omelets, pizzas, and pastas ($2.95 to $4.95). Dinner is more elaborate with over a dozen pastas ($5.95 to $8.95), available in full or half orders, such as fettuccine with smoked salmon, spaghetti with anchovies and garlic, cannelloni, and lasagne. Entrees, priced from $8.95 to $13.95, include chicken saltimbocca, shrimp marinara, clams with linguine, veal Florence (with prosciutto, asparagus, and crab), and filet mignon Christina (with basil, pine nuts, and garlic). Lunch is served from 11:30 a.m. to 3 p.m., and dinner from 5:30 to 10 p.m. Monday through Friday; dinner only is available on Saturday and Sunday from 3 to 10 p.m.; and brunch on Sunday from 11:30 a.m. to 3 p.m. CC's accepted: AE, MC, and V.

THE TOP ATTRACTIONS: The focus of Frederick is its 33-block **Historic District.** Not only have many of the buildings been carefully restored, but the streetscape today is much as it was in the early days. With Court House Square and Old Frederick City Hall at its heart, this city is a showcase of stately mansions and elegant brick town houses. The vista also includes a panorama of 18th- and 19th-century church spires, graceful Victorian parks and gardens, and the oldest and largest ginkgo tree in the U.S. The Frederick Visitor Center distributes a map of the district and also coordinates a full program of walking and horse-drawn carriage tours.

One of the highlights of the district is the **Barbara Fritchie House and Museum,** 154 W. Patrick St. (tel. 663-3833), a replica of the original home of the woman who was the heroine of Frederick during the Civil War. After bravely waving the Stars and Stripes in the path of Confederate soldiers, 95-year-old Barbara was immortalized in a poem by John Greenleaf Whittier as the "bravest of all in Frederick-town." A visit to the house includes a slide and tape presentation; a first-hand look at a collection of mementos including quilts and linens made by Barbara; her caps, shawls, and dresses; and her desk, tables, chairs, and china. Open from 1 to 4 p.m. on Sunday and from 10 a.m. to 4 p.m. during the rest of the week (except Tuesday); admission is $1.25 for adults and $1 for children aged 5 to 12.

Another house, built in 1799, linked to famous Frederick citizens is the **Roger Brooke Taney Home and Francis Scott Key Museum,** 123 S. Bentz St. Roger Brooke Taney (prounced Taw-nee) was chief justice of the U.S. Supreme Court and swore in seven presidents, including Lincoln. He is also remembered for writing the Dred Scott Decision, an opinion that led to Civil War by ruling that slavery was justifiable and legal under the Constitution. Taney was a brother-in-law of Francis Scott Key, the Frederick lawyer who has gone down in history for writing the poem that became our national anthem, "The Star Spangled Banner." The museum in this house is dedicated to Key and includes many items associated with his life. Admission must be arranged by appointment through the **Tourism Council of Frederick County** (tel. 663-8703). The **Francis Scott Key grave and monument** is located in nearby Mt. Olivet cemetery, South Market Street, near I-70.

On the western edge of town is **Schifferstadt,** 1110 Rosemont Avenue (tel. 663-6225), the oldest house in Frederick and one of America's finest examples of German Colonial architecture. Built in 1756 by the Brunner family who named it for their homeland in Germany, this house is made of sandstone walls 2½ feet thick, and hand-hewn beams of native oak pinned together with wooden pegs. Unusual original features include an enclosed staircase, a vaulted cellar and chimney, a unique five-plate cast-iron stove, and a squirrel-tail bake oven. A tour of the house includes a slide show and a self-guided tour leaflet. Donation is $1 for adults and 50¢ for children; open from 10 a.m. to 4 p.m. daily from April through mid-December (except Easter and Thanksgiving). The adjacent gallery is an artisan's co-operative, selling crafts fashioned from clay, wood, fibers, metal, and glass.

Eight miles south of Frederick is **Lily Pons Water Gardens,** 6800 Lilypons Rd., Lilypons (tel. 874-5133). The opera singer Lily Pons lent her name to these beautiful gardens when she visited here in 1935. One of the largest suppliers of ornamental fish and aquatic plants in the world, this site has acres of water lilies and goldfish ponds. The lilies are at their blooming peak in May. Open daily March 15 through September (except Easter) from 9 a.m. to 4 p.m., and weekdays only October through May from 10 a.m. to 3 p.m. No admission charge.

Less than a half-hour drive north of Frederick is the **National Shrine of St. Elizabeth Ann Seton,** 333 S. Seton Ave., Emmitsburg (tel. 447-6606). The home of the U.S.'s first canonized saint, this complex includes the Stone House, where Mother Seton established her religious community in 1809, and the White House, where she began the first parochial school in America. A visit here includes a six-minute slide show of historical background and an opportunity to take a self-guided tour of the grounds. Open daily from 10 a.m. to 5 p.m. (except the last two weeks of January; Mondays from November through April; and Christmas). No admission charge.

NIGHTLIFE: In the months of June, July, and August there are free open-air concerts at the **Baker Park Bandshell,** Second and Bentz Streets. (tel. 662-5161, ext. 247). Concerts are scheduled for 7:30 p.m. on Sunday evenings and feature a variety of local and military bands.

Throughout the year, the **Weinberg Center for the Arts,** 20 W. Patrick St. (tel. 694-8585), presents an ever-changing program of drama, dancing, and concerts. This old world theater is the home of the Fredericktowne Players and also welcomes visiting troupes. Tickets are priced from $7 and can be obtained at the box office Tuesday through Friday from 10 a.m. to 5 p.m., Saturday from 10 a.m. to 2 p.m., and one hour before all shows. CC's accepted: MC and V.

SHOPPING: For many years, **West Patrick Street** (Route 40) has been known as the "Golden Mile" because of its many shopping and commercial opportunities. The continuing restoration of downtown, however, has also led to a renewed shopping interest in city center streets.

Today Frederick is home to more than 30 antique shops, located mainly in the midcity historic district, and known collectively as the "Guild of Antique Shops of Frederick." Merchandise on sale ranges from furniture, diamonds, coins, baseball cards, vintage clothing, books, postcards, porcelains, glass, clocks, and dollhouse miniatures to lamps and linens. A complete list of shops, with a map, addresses, and hours of business, is available from the Frederick Visitor Center.

Another pocket of good shopping is historic **Shab Row,** East Street (between 2nd and Church Streets). This section is made up of 200-year-old buildings that were once the homes of local tradesman and artisans. In the early 20th century, these small dwellings fell into disrepair and were abandoned, until their recent restoration into specialty shops and craft centers.

The most exciting shopping development of all is **Everedy Square,** a 2½-acre nine-building complex between East Street and Patrick Street, originally the site of the Everedy Bottle Capping Company, founded in 1920 and one of the largest businesses in Frederick. More than $2 million has been spent to transform these old industrial buildings into a cluster of courtyards, craft shops, boutiques, restaurants, and galleries, all scheduled to be in full swing by 1988.

SPORTS AND ACTIVITIES: Of the many parks in the Frederick area, the **Catoctin Mountain Park** (on Routes 77 and 15) is the most famous because it is home to Camp David. Located 3 miles west of Thurmont and about 15 miles north of downtown Frederick, this is a 5,769-acre park, administered by the National Park Service. Highlights include a 42-acre lake for swimming, waterfalls, hiking trails, fishing, boating, riding, mountain climbing, camping, and picnic facilities. A Visitors Information Center is operated daily, from 8 a.m. to 5 p.m. A unique attraction on the grounds is the **Blue Blazes Still,** a genuine still relocated after Prohibition Days and operated as an interpretive program (open for tours only on Saturday and Sunday from 11 a.m. to 5 p.m., from Memorial Day to October). For complete information call 663-9330.

CHILDREN'S CORNER: A "touch and see" theme prevails at the **Rose Hill Manor Children's Museum,** 1611 N. Market St. (tel. 694-1646). Built in the 1790s, this Georgian mansion was the home of Maryland's first governor, Thomas Johnson. Now a museum of state and national heritage, it is designed so that children can experience many of the facets of early-American life such as combing unspun wool, throwing a shuttle on the loom, and adding a few stitches to a quilt. Other activities include soap-making, candle-dipping, quilting bees, barn raisings, and apple-butter boiling. More than 300 items are on display over 43 acres in the authentic settings of a manor house, a carriage museum, a blacksmith shop, a log cabin, herb and flower gardens, and a farm museum. Walk-in tours are conducted by costumed guides April through October from 10 a.m. to 4 p.m., Monday through Saturday; and from 1 to 4 p.m. on Sundays. During March, November, and December, the museum is open only on weekends and it is closed during January and February. Admission is $1 for those over 18; children are free.

Animal lovers of all ages enjoy the **Catoctin Zoo Park,** 13019 Catoctin Furnace Rd., Thurmont (tel. 271-7488). This is a wildlife, breeding, and petting zoo in a 30-acre woodland setting, home to more than 500 animals, of 120 varieties. Open daily from 9 a.m. to 6 p.m. throughout the summer months, and from 9 a.m. to 5 p.m. after September. Admission is $4.50 for adults and $2.95 for children aged 2 to 12; children under 2 are admitted free. CC's accepted: MC and V.

AN EXCURSION TO NEW MARKET: Six miles east of Frederick is historic **New Market,** founded in 1793 as a stop for travelers on the National Pike. Today this beautifully preserved Federal-style town (pop.: 300) is listed on the National Register of Historic Places and is also known as "The Antiques Capital of Maryland." More than 40 different antique shops line both sides of the half-mile-long main street. To guide visitors, the New Market Antique Dealers Association publishes a handy guide/map of the town which is available free of charge throughout the town.

A sampling of shops and their wares includes:

Maria's Chalet Antiques, 2 E. Main St. (tel. 865-5225), for German steins, teddy bears, old rugs, and clocks. Accepts: MC and V.

Thomas' Antiques, 60 W. Main St. (tel. 831-6622), for oak furniture, brass and copper items, and weather-vanes. Accepts: MC and V.

Fromer's Antiques, 52 W. Main St. (tel. 831-6712), for antique and woodworking tools, Victorian furniture, prints, china, and glass. Accepts: MC and V.

Shaw's of New Market, 22 W. Main St. (tel. 831-6010), for vases, chandeliers, grandfather clocks, china dolls, and brass lamps. Accepts: MC and V.

Victorian Manor, 33 W. Main St. (tel. 865-3083), for jewelry and silver, and oak furniture. Accepts: MC and V.

Stone House Gallery, 25 W. Main St. (tel. 865-3451), for antique toys and primitive paintings. No CC's accepted.

Parkside Antiques, 21 W. Main St. (tel. 831-6111), for antique kitchen lamps and utensils. No CC's accepted.

MacNair's Corner Shop, 1 W. Main St. (tel. 831-6882), for country antiques, fine soaps and candles, and old chests. CC's accepted: MC and V.

Shop hours are usually Saturdays and Sundays from 1 to 5 p.m., and at other times by appointment. In addition to the antique shops, New Market is also home to a top-class Scottish clothing import store, **The House of Kindness Thistle Stop,** 5 W. Main St. (tel. 865-3140). Housed in an 1840s building that was once a hotel, a stage office, a tavern, a post office, a library, and a general store, this shop stocks a wide range of Scottish kilts, skirts, sweaters, handknits, jewelry, and Prince Charles-type jackets. No CC's accepted.

STAYING OVER IN NEW MARKET: This antique collectors' town is home to two excellent bed-and-breakfast houses. The oldest (opened in 1973) is the **Strawberry Inn,** 17 Main St., P.O. Box 237, New Market, MD 21774 (tel. 301/865-3318), a lovingly restored 120-year-old home. Innkeepers Jane and Ed Rossig offer five antique-furnished rooms, all with private bath and air conditioning. Each room is individually decorated according to a special theme, such as the Strawberry or Blueberry Room, or the 1776 Room. There are no TVs and credit cards are not accepted. Ground floor rooms are available. Rates for a double range from $55 to $65, including a continental breakfast delivered to each room on a butler's tray.

The **National Pike Inn,** 9–11 Main St., P.O. Box 299, New Market, MD 21774 (tel. 301/865-5055), is named after the road that passes through the town. Opened as a B&B in 1986, this sturdy Federal house was built in the early 1800s; a unique widow's watch was added in 1900. Recently restored by owners Tom and Terry Rimel, this cozy house has four charmingly decorated guest rooms, all air-conditioned (two with private bath and two that share a bath). Doubles range from $60 to $65 and include a hearty continental breakfast served to the room or in the dining room. No television and no credit cards accepted.

DINING IN NEW MARKET: Even if you can't stay in New Market, it's worth a trip just to dine at **Mealey's,** 8 W. Main St. (tel. 865-5488), a handsome two-story brick building dating back to 1793. Like a Colonial house, this restaurant offers several small parlor-size rooms as well as the Pump Room, a large main dining room built around a wooden water pump that dates back to 1800. The overall décor includes exposed brick walls, stone fireplaces, ladderback chairs, brass fixtures, lanterns, and candlelight. The current owners, the Jefferies family, have built a reputation for fine food as well as Colonial ambience. Lunch, priced from $2.95 to $8.95, ranges from sandwiches and hot platters to steaks. Dinner entrees, which cost from $7.95 to $16.95, feature a blend of Colonial and contemporary cuisine: chicken livers supreme (cooked in an old iron skillet), a half spring chicken country-style, crab imperial, jumbo fantail shrimp, crab cakes, prime ribs, and reef-and-beef (N.Y. strip steak and a selection of seafood items). All main courses are served with a relish tray, salad, potato, vegetable, hot bread, and fritters. Lunch is available Friday and Saturday from 11:30 a.m. to 3 p.m.; dinner on Tuesday through Saturday from 5 to 9 p.m., and Sunday dinner from 11:30 a.m. to 8 p.m. CC's accepted: AE, MC, and V.

2. Hagerstown

Known as the "hub" city of the Cumberland Valley, Hagerstown is at the crossroads between two major interstate highways (81 and 70) and a half dozen other state and local roads. It is not only at the center of Maryland but it is also sandwiched in between Pennsylvania, Virginia, and West Virginia.

Hagerstown is consequently an ideal base—within an hour's drive of Gettysburg, Harper's Ferry, Antietam, Frederick, and other historic destinations, not to mention its own landmark attractions.

Hagerstown's annals go back to 1762 when it was founded by a German immigrant, Jonathan Hager, who courageously settled the area on his own in the 1730s. Hager also served in the Revolutionary War under General Braddock and was later elected to the General Assembly in Annapolis of 1773. His house still stands and is one of the town's many buildings of significant heritage.

A city of 35,000 people, Hagerstown today is also a busy hub of agricultural and industrial activities.

VISITOR INFORMATION: Brochures and maps detailing Hagerstown's attractions are available from the **Washington County Tourism Office,** Court House Annex, Hagerstown, MD 21740 (tel. 301/791-3130). This office also operates a 24-hour tourism information hotline (tel. 301/797-8800). Be sure to ask for a copy of the *Walking Tour of Downtown Hagerstown,* a handy leaflet that describes the most significant public buildings, churches, and sights in the historic district.

GETTING TO AND AROUND HAGERSTOWN: Greyhound Bus, 31 E. Antietam Rd. (tel. 739-7420) links Hagerstown to other cities and towns within Maryland and beyond.

In addition, the city is served by **Washington County Regional Airport,** Route 11 (tel. 733-5200), five miles north of downtown. Scheduled flights are operated by **Allegheny Commuter** (tel. toll-free 800/428-4253) and **Piedmont** (tel. 733-5380).

A local bus service, the **County Commuter,** connects Hagerstown to neighboring communities within the perimeters of Washington County such as Boonsboro and Sharpsburg. For information, call 791-3047.

Rent-a-car offices are operated in the Hagerstown area by **Avis,** 735 Potomac Ave. (tel. 733-1277); **Hertz,** Washington County Airport (tel. 739-6117); and **National,** Maugans Avenue at I-81 (tel. 797-7119). A reliable local taxi service is **Turner's Taxi** (tel. 733-7788).

WHERE TO STAY: Most of Hagerstown's hotels and motels are on Route 40, also known locally as the "Dual Highway." Located between the southern edge of downtown and the entrance to Route 70, this wide strip is also home to many of the area's restaurants, fast-food chains, and commercial enterprises.

One of the closest hotels to the center of town is the **Best Western Venice**

Inn, 431 Dual Highway, Hagerstown, MD 21740 (tel. 301/733-0830 or toll-free 800/528-1234). This modern and recently expanded hotel offers 240 rooms, some in a high-rise tower and others laid out in a motel format. Each room is decorated in a contemporary style, with one or two double beds, air conditioning, a direct-dial phone, and cable color TV. King suites with whirlpools and rooms with kitchenettes are also available. Guest facilities include valet service, an outdoor Olympic swimming pool, and entertainment with dancing from Monday through Saturday nights. Doubles range from $42 to $58; king suites from $75 to $100; and kitchenettes from $50 to $75. The on-premises restaurant, Avellino's (direct line: tel. 739-5700), is known for its lunchtime antipasto bar of Italian savories (select as many choices as you wish for one price, $4.35). Other lunch items, priced from $2.95 to $6.95, include sandwiches and salads, as well as a variety of hot light fare (such as turkey chow mein, seafood omelet, or shrimp Créole). Dinner entrees, which cost from $5.95 to $14.95, with most under $10, range from pastas and veal parmigiana to filet mignon with mushrooms, broasted chicken (quick fried under pressure), and Maryland local crab and seafood. All main courses come with choice of salad or vegetable and potato. Lunch is served from 11 a.m. to 2 p.m. and dinner from 5 to 10:30 p.m. The restaurant also offers a sumptuous Sunday brunch from 11 a.m. to 3 p.m., priced at $6.95 adults and $4.95 for children. Regular breakfast is also served from 6:30 to 11 a.m. Monday through Saturday, and from 7 to 11 a.m. on Sunday. All major CC's are accepted.

In a shady garden setting is the **Holiday Inn,** 900 Dual Highway, Hagerstown, MD 21740 (tel. 301/739-9050 or toll free 800/HOLIDAY). This modern motel-style facility has 140 rooms (some are non-smoking), each with two double beds or a king-size bed, air conditioning, color TV, and a direct-dial phone. Doubles range from $41 to $67. Other amenities include a swimming pool, an exercise room, a guest laundry, and a lively lounge with music called Plums Food and Drink Emporium, offering snacks, salads, and light fare throughout the day, priced from $2.95 to $7.95. There is also a full-service restaurant, The Landing, which features salads, burgers, sandwiches, pastas, and light seafood for lunch (priced from $3.95 to $5.95). Dinner entrees focus on such dishes as southern fried chicken, steaks, pasta and meatballs, crab cakes, pasta primavera and shrimp, and pot roast, a house specialty. Each main course, priced from $7.95 to $12.95, includes unlimited salad bar. All major CC's are accepted.

The closest hotel to I-70 is the **Sheraton Inn,** 1910 Dual Highway, Hagerstown, MD 21740 (tel. 301/790-3010 or toll-free 800/325-3535). This is also a modern motel-style property in a leafy garden setting. The 140 rooms are equipped with a choice of double, queen or king-size beds, color cable TV, air conditioning, and a direct-dial phone. Doubles range from $50 to $56. Guest facilities include a swimming pool, a health spa, a game room, and a lounge with evening entertainment. This inn is also the home of Nick's Other Place, a top-class restaurant associated with the original Nick's at the airport. Overlooking the tropical setting of the hotel pool, this dining room is decorated in a Colonial blue-and-white motif. Featured dishes at dinner include charbroiled steaks, prime ribs, chicken in pastry, and seafood symphony (king-crab legs, scallops, crab imperial, and stuffed flounder). The main courses, accompanied by salad, vegetable, and potato, are priced from $8.95 to $16.95. Open from 5 to 10 p.m. for dinner, as well as 11:30 a.m. to 2:30 p.m. for lunch, and 7 to 10 a.m. for breakfast. All major CC's are accepted.

The newest full-service hotel in the area (opened 1985) is a six-story **Howard Johnson,** 107 Underpass Way, Halfway Boulevard Exit of I-81, Hagerstown, MD 21740 (tel. 301/797-2500 or toll-free 800/654-2000). Situated about a mile southwest of the downtown area, in a quiet grassy setting opposite the Valley Mall, this sleek modern hotel has 170 rooms, each with contemporary furnishings, air conditioning, an in-room refrigerator and coffee maker, color cable TV, and a direct-dial phone; non-smoking rooms are also available. Doubles range from $48 to $60. Other guest amenities include a heated indoor pool with spa and sauna, a fitness room, and the trendy Sir Walter Raleigh Restaurant. Mostly light fare and sandwiches are served at lunchtime, in a $4.95 to $5.95 price range. Dinner choices, which cost from $8.95 to $19.95, include prime ribs, scallops en casserole, king-crab legs, barbecue ribs, and chicken. Meal times are lunch from 11:30 a.m. to 2 p.m. Monday through Saturday; and dinner Monday through Thursday from 5 to 9:30 p.m., Friday and Saturday from 5 to 10 p.m., and Sunday from noon to 9 p.m. Breakfast is also available from 6:30 to 9:30 a.m. Monday through Saturday, and from 7:30 to 10:30 a.m. Sunday. All major CC's are accepted.

WHERE TO DINE: The busy Dual Highway, which is the location for most of Hagerstown's hotels, is also home to many fast-food establishments. We have therefore chosen a few restaurants that are a little off the beaten track but well worth the extra effort. All of these listed generally fall into the moderate category.

The reputation for the best food in the area belongs to **Nick's Airport Inn,** Middleburg Pike (Route 11) (tel. 733-8560). Located five miles north of downtown, at the entrance to Hagerstown's small airport, this dining room proves that airport restaurants can be outstanding in their own right. Recently renovated in a bright conservatory style, Nick's is such an institution in the Hagerstown area that it has produced a clone (in the Sheraton Inn). The lunch menu features hearty sandwiches and salads as well as hot dishes like crab imperial, fried shrimp, or prime ribs of beef, in the $2.95 to $10.95 price range. The extensive dinner menu, priced from $10.95 to $21.95 (most choices under $15), focuses on seafood choices such as crab au gratin, stuffed flounder, lobster tails, bay or sea scallops, a variety of steak cuts, rack of lamb, and veal and chicken dishes with an Italian or French finesse. All entrees are accompanied by salad, potato or vegetable, and rolls, and there is a very extensive wine list. Lunch is served from 11 a.m. to 2:30 p.m. Monday through Saturday; dinner from 5 to 10 p.m. Monday through Friday, and from 4:30 to 10:30 p.m. on Saturday. CC's accepted: AE, MC, and V.

South of Nick's and slightly closer to downtown along Route 11 is the **Pleasant View Inn,** 2373 Pennsylvania Ave., (tel. 733-2414), a Hagerstown tradition since 1930. Designed on two levels, with a décor of brick walls, open beams, pitched ceilings, a big stone fireplace, antique furnishings, and windows that frame distant mountain views, this restaurant has a limited but reliable menu. Lunch, priced from $1.95 to $4.95, features salads, sandwiches, and soups. Dinner entrees, priced from $9.95 to $14.95, focus on steaks and prime ribs as well as seafood selections, such as shrimp-and-scallop kebab, crab cakes, seafood au gratin, or crab imperial. All main courses come with potatoes or rice and a medley of vegetables. Open Monday through Saturday for lunch from 11:30 a.m. to 2:30 p.m., and dinner from 5 to 10 p.m., with dinner music from 6 to 10:30 p.m. on Friday and Saturday nights. CC's accepted: AE, MC, and V.

About a 20-minute drive southeast of Hagerstown is the **Old South Mountain Inn,** Route 40 Alt., Boonsboro (tel. 371-5400 and 432-6155), perched atop Turner's Gap along the Appalachian Trail. Erected in 1732, this landmark building served variously over the years as a wagon stand, a stagecoach stop, a wayside inn, a tavern, and a private residence; it was visited by several presidents and was a favorite stop of Henry Clay and Daniel Webster. Since 1981, it is a Colonial-style restaurant with modern American cuisine, in the hands of Russell and Judy Schwartz. The beautifully preserved stone building is augmented by an outdoor terrace, ancient trees, gardens, a wishing well, and panoramic mountain views. Now serving dinner every day but Monday, the restaurant offers such entrees as steak au poivre vert, chicken Cordon Bleu, cured country ham, fettuccine primavera, center-cut pork, and local seafood, priced from $9.95 to $19.95. There is also an extensive wine list, priced from $10 a bottle, including a few fine Maryland wines. Dinner hours are from 5 to 9 p.m. Tuesday through Friday, from noon to 10 p.m. on Saturday, and from noon to 8 p.m. on Sunday; a hearty country brunch, priced at $7.95, is also served on Sunday from 10:30 a.m. to 2 p.m. All major CC's are accepted.

THE TOP ATTRACTIONS: To get your bearings in Hagerstown, take a walk around the **Historic District,** a four-block square area of 18th- and 19th-century buildings, centered around Potomac Street. This downtown cluster, made up primarily of structures listed on the National Register of Historic Places, includes City Hall, the Washington County Court House, Federal-style homes, museums, churches, and the Maryland Theatre, a rococo landmark built in 1915. A descriptive walking tour leaflet with map is available free of charge from the tourist office.

The next place to see is the **Hager House,** 19 Key St. (tel. 739-8393), the home of Jonathan Hager, founder of Hagerstown. Situated on the northern edge of Hagerstown's City Park, this 3½-story structure was built in 1740 by Hager himself, using uncut fieldstones on a site over a cool-water spring. It is styled in the German tradition, with a large chimney at its center and 22-inch-thick walls. Now completely restored and outfitted with authentic furnishings of the period, this house is open to the public. Next door is the **Hager Museum,** a collection of hundreds of farm implements, coins, household items, clothing, and other artifacts from the Hagerstown area. Admission to both the house and museum is $1 for adults and 50¢ for children under 12. Open April through December from 10 a.m. to 4 p.m. on Tuesday through Saturday, and from 2 to 5 p.m. on Sunday.

One of the state's oldest markets also operates regularly in Hagerstown and is worth a look if you happen to be in town on a Wednesday or Saturday. More than 50 farmers, craftsmen, and exhibitors sell all kinds of local vegetables, fruits, meats, country crafts, and home-baked goods at this gathering, which has been a tradition since 1875, first at City Hall and in its present location since 1928. Look for the Old Farmers' Markets, 11 W. Church St. (tel. 733-6486 Monday through Friday and 739-9772 on Saturday mornings), June through December, on Wednesday from 11 a.m. to 4 p.m., and year round on Saturday from 6 to 11 a.m.

Ten miles southwest of Hagerstown along a winding country farm road is **Fort Frederick,** Routes 56 and 65, Big Pool (tel. 842-2155), the cornerstone of Maryland's frontier defense during the French and Indian War. This strong stone fortress, which was also used in the Revolutionary War and the Civil War, is a showcase of 18th-century military life. Some of the most interesting displays include the fort's massive stone wall, a garrison garden, cannons, barracks, bastions, and a wooden catwalk that originally spanned the entire inner perimeter of the fort wall. The fort and its surrounding parklands are open to the public year round, free of charge, from 8 a.m. to dusk; and the barracks and visitor center are open May 1 to October 1 from 8:30 a.m. to 5 p.m. In addition, from 9 a.m. to 5 p.m., Memorial Day through Labor Day, costumed guides are on duty to answer questions and explain the fort's layout. A free walking-tour brochure is also available.

The **Antietam Battlefield,** the scene of the bloodiest battle of the Civil War, is 12 miles south of Hagerstown near Sharpsburg along Routes 34 and 65 (tel. 432-5124). More than 23,000 men were killed or wounded on this site which commemorates where the Union forces met and stopped the first Southern invasion of the North on September 17, 1862. Clara Barton, who was to found the Red Cross 19 years later, attended to the wounded at a field hospital on the battlefield. Start your visit at the visitor center, located north of Sharpsburg on Route 65. Administered by the National Park Service and open daily except for major holidays, this office provides free information, literature, and suggested tours of the battlefield and cemetery. There are also helpful historical exhibits and an 18-minute audio-visual (shown every half hour). During May and September musket and cannon demonstrations and historical talks are scheduled. Admission charge is $1 per person.

NIGHTLIFE: No visit to Hagerstown is complete without a night at the magnificent **Maryland Theatre,** 21 S. Potomac St. (tel. 790-2000). Originally built in 1915 and rebuilt after a 1974 fire, this revered landmark has provided a stage for all types of entertainment from acrobats to opera, choirs to country western concerts, and personalities ranging from Will Rogers and John Philip Sousa to Lowell Thomas and Anna Pavlova. Recent productions have included *Up With People, Evita, Chorus Line,* and the Miss Maryland Pageant. The Maryland Symphony Orchestra, under the direction of French master hornist Barry Tuckwell, is also headquarted here. The curtain is usually at 8 p.m., but exact schedules and prices vary with each production. Check at the box office, which is open Monday through Friday from 10 a.m. to 5 p.m. CC's accepted: MC and V.

For dinner-theater, you need only cross the street to the **Washington County Playhouse,** 44 N. Potamac St. (tel. 739-SHOW). With a repertoire that includes such productions as *Caberet, I Do, I Do, The Fantasticks,* and *My Fair Lady,* this theater presents a buffet on stage before each show. Performances are Thursday, Friday, and Saturday evenings ($19.95), and Sunday matinees ($16.95). CC's accepted: MC and V.

SPORTS AND ACTIVITIES: Hagerstown's outdoor life is centered in and around **City Park,** Virginia Avenue (tel. 739-4673), rated among the nation's most beautiful natural city parks. This idyllic 50-acre setting includes a man-made lake that is home to hundreds of ducks, swans, and geese; flower gardens; wooded picnic areas; softball fields; tennis courts; and an open-air bandshell, site of frequent summer concerts. For the last ten years, a two-day arts, crafts, and entertainment festival has also been staged here on the last weekend in June. Admission is free.

EVENTS: A major highlight of the calendar each year is the **Great Hagerstown Fair,** held in early September, at the Hagerstown Fairgrounds, between Routes 11 and 70. This is a six-day country fair and agricultural show with big-name entertainment nightly. Attractions include displays of antique steam tractors and farmers' engines, parades, arts, and crafts. Admission is $2 per person and parking is $1, with supplementary charges of $5 to $10 for evening shows. Further information can be obtained from the Hagerstown Fairgrounds, Mulberry Street, Hagerstown, MD 21740 (tel. 301/739-5550). CC's accepted for evening concerts: Ch, MC, and V.

CHILDREN'S CORNER: Corridors of limestone with jeweled stalactites and stalagmites are the unique underground attractions at the **Crystal Grottoes Caverns,** Route 34, Boonsboro, (tel. 432-6336). Maryland's only commercial underground caverns, these formations were created by millions of years of chemical and mineral action beneath the earth's surface. Open daily, March through November, from 9 a.m. to 6 p.m.; and on weekends in December, January and February from 11 a.m. to 5 p.m. Admission, which includes the services of a well-informed guide, is $5 for adults, $3 for children aged 5 to 11, and free for those 4 and under.

3. Cumberland

The most westerly of Maryland's cities, Cumberland lies between West Virginia and Pennsylvania along the shores of the Potomac and in the heart of the Allegheny Mountains. First known as Ft. Cumberland (called after the English duke of the same name), this part of the state served as a western outpost in Colonial times for generals like George Washington and Edward Braddock.

In the 1800s Cumberland's importance grew as it became a gateway to the American West. It was not only chosen as a terminus for the first National Pike (also known as the Cumberland Road and now Route 40), but it also became a focal point for both the Western Maryland Railroad and the Chesapeake & Ohio Canal.

Today the railroad and the canal have ceased to function and Route 40 has been overshadowed by wider highways, but Cumberland still draws visitors, particularly those with an interest in history and Victorian architecture.

A city of 26,000 people, Cumberland is centered around a pedestrian downtown mall, lined with shops and commercial outlets, in a park-like setting of shade trees, flowers, benches, brick walks, and fountains.

VISITOR INFORMATION: Walking-tour folders, maps, and brochures of Cumberland are available from the **Allegany County Tourism and Public Relations Office,** Western Maryland Station Center, Canal Street, Cumberland, MD 21502 (tel. 301/777-5905).

GETTING TO CUMBERLAND: Cumberland is served by the **Cumberland Municipal Airport,** Route 28, Virginia Avenue, which is actually just over the border in West Virginia. Flights are operated by **Cumberland Airlines,** connecting this western part of the state to Baltimore and Ocean City. The telephone number for both the airport and the airline is 304/738-8640.

In addition, **Greyhound** operates regular bus service into Cumberland, stopping at 201 Glenn St. (tel. 722-6226).

WHERE TO STAY: With only one hotel in the center of town and a few motels on the outskirts, Cumberland is obviously not a city of great lodging choices. The two best bets can both be classified in the moderate category.

The city's only full-scale hotel is the **Holiday Inn,** 111 S. George St., Cumberland, MD 21502 (tel. 301/724-8800 or toll-free 800/238-5400). Located in the heart of town, this modern, six-story structure has 131 rooms, each decorated in a contemporary style with a double or king bed, air conditioning, a direct-dial phone, and color cable TV. Doubles range from $57 to $70. Guest facilities include an outdoor swimming pool, private parking, a lounge with entertainment every night except Sunday, and a lively restaurant called Harrigan's. Lunch items, priced from $3.95 to $8.95, include a dozen different salads, overstuffed sandwiches, burgers, and pastas. Dinner entrees, from $9.95 to $15.95, range from chicken Dijon and veal Oscar, shrimp piccata, and Norwegian salmon fillet to Cajun-style dishes. Lunch is served from 11 a.m. to 2 p.m., and dinner from 5:30 to 10 p.m. Breakfast is also available from 7 a.m. each day. In the summer months, the Holiday Inn is also the venue for occasional locally produced dinner-theater productions, usually priced in the $12 to $15 range, including show and buffet. All major CC's are accepted.

A tree-shaded country setting adds to the rural atmosphere at the **Best Western Braddock Motor Inn,** 1268 National Highway, Route 40A, LaVale, MD 21502 (tel. 301/729-3300 or toll-free 800/528-1234). Located about five miles west of downtown Cumberland, this motel is near the historic LaVale Toll Gate. The 110 modern units are tastefully furnished with double, queen, or king size beds, color cable TVs, air conditioning, and phones. Guest facilities include an indoor swimming pool with a Jacuzzi and exercise room. Doubles range from $55 to $60. All major CC's are accepted.

WHERE TO DINE IN CUMBERLAND: The following are our restaurant selections for the Cumberland area. Let us know if you find others.

Moderately Priced Dining

The aura of Cumberland's early days prevails at **Ed Mason's 1890 Restaurants,** Routes 40 and 48, (tel. 722-6155). Located one mile east of downtown, this restaurant complex was established in 1954 as a roadside diner and has been growing ever since. Today Ed Mason offers his customers a choice of two dining settings—a casual saloon-style room downstairs and an authentic old-world barn décor upstairs. The saloon, known as J.B.'s, offers an all-day sandwich and snack menu, with most items priced under $5. The Barn, a full-service restaurant, also features sandwiches, pizzas, salads, and light fare, from 11 a.m. to 5 p.m. each day, in the $1.95 to $6.95 range. From 5 to 11 p.m., the Barn's dinner menu features a medley of fine steak and seafood dishes including oyster imperial, lobster tails, flounder, shrimp, perch, and a half dozen varieties of local Maryland crab dishes. Entrees, priced from $5.95 to $22.95, fall mostly in the $12-and-under category; salad bar, vegetable, and hot rolls accompany each main course. Besides the dependably good food, part of the attraction of this restaurant is in browsing at the eclectic collection of antiques and memorabilia from the area, and also in meeting Ed, who is always in attendance. CC's accepted: AE, MC, and V.

A French provincial ambience is the keynote of **The Bistro,** Downtown Cumberland Mall, 37 N. Centre St. (tel. 777-8462). With a décor of brick walls, stained glass, and leafy plants, this restaurant offers four dining rooms, ranging from a Victorian parlor to a garden setting. Lunch, priced from $2.95 to $4.95, focuses on simple fare such as sandwiches, burgers, and casseroles (such as beef and mushroom béarnaise). Dinner, usually in the $8.95 to $14.95 range, includes such entrees as frogs' legs, chicken breast with sherry, filet mignon, or lobster. Lunch is served Monday through Thursday from 11:30 a.m. to 2:30 p.m., and Friday and Saturday from 11:30 a.m. to 3 p.m.; and dinner Monday through Saturday from 6 to 10:30 p.m. Sunday brunch is also available from 11 a.m. to 3 p.m. If you prefer a picnic, the same management also operates an in-house gourmet shop, Monday through Saturday from 10 a.m. to 6 p.m. Major CC's are accepted.

Budget Meals

Shoppers or strollers find a delightful respite and repast at **The Green House,** Lazarus Department Store, Downtown Cumberland Mall (tel. 724-6500). Located on the third floor of a fashionable ladies clothing store, this restaurant is the perfect venue to enjoy a light lunch in a garden setting of flowers, birds, Tiffany lamps, and trellises. Choices, which range from seafood crêpes, quiches (crab or jalapeno), and burgers to salads, are mostly priced under $5. Serving lunch only, Monday through Saturday from 11 a.m. to 2:30 p.m. CC's accepted: AE, MC, and V.

THE TOP ATTRACTIONS: The highlight of a visit to Cumberland is a stroll through the **Victorian Historic District,** primarily along Washington Street on the western side of town. This area includes the site of the original Fort Cumberland (now the Emmanuel Episcopal Church) and more than 50 residential and public buildings, built primarily in the 1800s when Cumberland was at its economic peak. Placed on the National Register of Historic Places in 1973, this street is a showcase of homes with elaborate stained-glass windows, graceful cupolas, and sloping mansard roofs. You'll see architectural styles ranging from Federal, Romanesque, Queen Anne, Empire, Colonial Revival, Italianate, and English Country Gothic to Georgian Revival, Gothic Revival, and Greek Revival. Most of the houses are not open to the public, but a self-guided walking tour of the neighborhood has been plotted out and is described in a booklet available free from the tourist information office.

One building that is open to the public in this district is the appropriately named **History House,** 218 Washington St. (tel. 777-8678), originally built as a private residence in 1867 for the president of the C & O Canal. Now in the hands of the Allegany County Historical Society, this restored 18-room dwelling contains a variety of antique furnishings such as a Victorian courting couch and an 1840 square grand piano. Other features include a genealogical research room, an early 19th-century brick-walled garden, and a basement kitchen with authentic cooking utensils, fireplace, coal stove, dishes, pottery, and crocks. Open May through October, on Tuesday through Saturday from 11 a.m. to 4 p.m., and on Sunday from 1:30 to 4 p.m. Admission is $1 for adults and 25¢ for children over 12.

The recently restored **Western Maryland Station Center,** Canal Street (tel. 777-9137), is a focal point in Cumberland history. Built in 1913, when American railroad power was at its peak, this imposing building was an important stop on the state's rail system for both passenger and freight traffic. It now houses a railroad museum, an arts gallery, a visitor center, and the local tourist office. Railroad buffs will particularly enjoy the exhibits of early train memorabilia including lanterns, photographs, tools, ties, and timetables. Administered by the Allegany County Arts Council, this former train station is also now the venue for an on-going program of events and entertainment. Open to the public, free of charge, Monday and Tuesday from 9 a.m. to 3 p.m., Wednesday through Saturday from 9 a.m. to 5 p.m., and Sunday from 1 to 4 p.m.

A log cabin associated with the first president of the U.S. is designated as **George Washington's Headquarters,** in Riverside Park, Greene Street, at the junction of Wills Creek and Potomac River. This simple structure, believed to be the only remaining section of the original Fort Cumberland, was used by Washington as his official quarters during the French and Indian War. The cabin is not open to the public, but does have a viewing window and a tape-recorded description that plays when activated by a push-button.

A full-scale replica of a **19th-century canal boat** that traversed the 184-mile route between Georgetown and Cumberland is on view at the C & O National Historical Park, North Branch, off Route 51. Located five miles south of Cumberland at the C & O Canal Lock No. 75, this site is administered by National Park Service Rangers who conduct guided tours of the area on afternoons from June through August. Inside the boat, you can see a captain's cabin furnished in the 1828–1924 period, a hay house, and an on-board mule stable. A restored log-cabin lock house is located nearby. No admission charge.

When this country's first national road was built, it was also the first to be constructed with federal funds. Ownership was then turned over to the states and tolls had to be collected. In Maryland, the **first toll gate** was built near Cumberland in 1836; this same building is now the last to remain in the state. Located four miles west of Cumberland on Route 40A (the old National Road), at LaVale, this original Toll Gate House is open (now free of charge) May through August from 1 to 4 p.m. on Sunday, Wednesday, and Friday. For further information call 726-8538 or 729-1210.

SPORTS AND ACTIVITIES: One of Cumberland's leading outdoor attractions is **Rocky Gap State Park,** Route 1, Box 90, Flintstone, MD 21530 (tel. 301/777-2138). Located six miles east of the city off US 40, this facility is a paradise for fishing, hiking, biking, and walking. There is also a 243-acre lake with two beaches for swimming and a 278-unit campsite. Open May through October from 6 a.m. to 9:30 p.m., and mid-October through April from 9 a.m. to 6 p.m. The entrance charge is $3 per car and 50¢ for walk-ins. Camping fees are $10 a night for regular sites, $15 for waterfront sites, and $1 additional a night for out-of-state cars. Reservations are accepted.

EVENTS: Continuous country music and old-time cooking are the main features of the **C & O Canal Boat Festival** scheduled on the next-to-last weekend of August each year. Held at the North Branch of the C & O Canal Park, 5 miles south of Cumberland on Route 51, this gathering also focuses on arts and crafts of American frontier life, such as embroidery, quilting, chair-caning, leather-crafting, and antique carpentry. Other activities include walking tours of the canal, guided tours of the canal boat, and horse and buggy rides. Contact the tourist office for complete details and a program.

4. Deep Creek Lake

Maryland's largest freshwater lake is Deep Creek, nearly 12 miles in length with a shoreline of 65 miles and covering nearly 3,900 acres. Located in the heart of Garrett County, on the state's western border, Deep Creek is completely man-made, a 1925 work project of the Youghiogheny Electric Company, which sold it to the Pennsylvania Electric Company in 1942. It is now leased to the Maryland Inland Fish and Game Commission for the nominal fee of $1 a year, and is managed by the Maryland Department of Natural Resources.

Nestled in the heart of the Allegheny Mountains, and with an elevation of 2,462 feet, Deep Creek Lake has long been a popular year-round recreational area. Summer temperatures average 65.9°F, ideal for boating and water sports. In the winter months, however, Deep Creek Lake really comes into its own, as Maryland's premier ski resort (with an average temperature of 28°F and a yearly snowfall of over 80 inches).

You can reach Deep Creek Lake by heading westward along Route 48 to Keyser's Ridge and then following Route 219 south. It's about an hour's drive from Cumberland. The two principal towns in the area are Oakland, the county seat of Garrett County, and McHenry, named for Col. James McHenry of Baltimore who was an aide to General Washington during the Revolutionary War and a signer of the Constitution.

VISITOR INFORMATION: The **Deep Creek Lake-Garrett County Promotion Council** is located at the Garrett County Court House, Oakland, MD 21550 (tel. 301/334-1948). From Memorial Day through Labor Day, an Information

Booth is located on Route 219, at Deep Creek Lake, south of Deep Creek Lake Bridge, (tel. 301/334-1948). In the winter, a telephone snow report service is operated (tel. 301/387-4000).

WHERE TO STAY AND DINE: The center of activity on Deep Creek Lake is the **Wisp Resort,** Marsh Hill Road, McHenry, MD 21541 (tel. 301/387-5581). This modern condo-hotel property currently has 70 units, with plans for an additional 470. All regular bedrooms have a queen-size bed, queen-size sofa bed, and a small refrigerator, plus the usual heat/air conditioning facilities, a direct-dial phone, and color cable TV. Some rooms also have small kitchenettes or fireplaces. Rates for a double range from $60 to $75. Other amenities include an indoor swimming pool and a whirlpool, handball and racquetball courts, and an 18-hole championship golf course. The Wisp is also Maryland's largest ski area with major ski runs, lifts, and snow-making operations in the winter months. Throughout the year there is a lively cocktail lounge with entertainment and a restaurant called The Gathering. Open for lunch from 11:30 a.m. to 2 p.m. each day, the menu ranges from sandwiches and salads to hot platters, priced from $1.95 to $3.95. Dinner, which is served from 5:30 to 10 p.m. each evening, ranges in price from $7.95 to $14.95. Entrees include chicken breast à l'orange, crab imperial, baby back ribs, duck pasta in brown sauce, veal with lemon, and prime ribs. All choices are accompanied by a salad and vegetables. Breakfast is also served each morning from 7 to 11 a.m. Future developments at the Wisp also include tennis courts, a heated outdoor pool, and an indoor ice-skating rink. Golf and ski packages are also available at reduced rates. CC's accepted: MC and V.

The **Point View Inn,** Route 219, P.O. Box 100, McHenry, MD 21541 (tel. 301/387-5555), is situated on the shores of Deep Creek Lake. The 20 motel-style bedrooms each have two double beds or a king-size bed, and many have porches or private terraces overlooking the lake. Rates for a double range from $35 to $50; efficiency units are available from $60 to $75. Facilities for guests include a boat dock and a private beach. There is also a lounge called The Keg Room, and a full-service lakeside restaurant, The Trellis Room, open to the public from 7 a.m. to 10 p.m. Dinner specialties include Garrett County roasted turkey, fresh rainbow trout, Maryland crab cakes, steaks, and a variety of German dishes such as wiener schnitzel, sauerbraten, bratwurst, or knockwurst. Entrees, priced from $7.50 to $15.95, are accompanied by salad and potatoes or vegetables. CC's accepted: AE, MC, and V.

Views of the lake and mountains are part of the charm at the **Alpine Village Inn,** Glendale Bridge Road, Star Route 1, P. O. Box 114, Oakland, MD 21550 (tel. 301/387-5534). Located just off Route 219 south of McHenry, this facility has 29 lodge-style rooms and 14 chalets in a secluded wooded setting. Doubles, which range from $30 to $60 a day, have queen-size beds, color TV, heat/air conditioning, and sun decks. Many rooms have cathedral ceilings, fireplaces, and kitchenettes. The chalets, which have living rooms, patios, and complete kitchens, in addition to at least two bedrooms, can accommodate up to six persons and range from $80 to $100 daily, with weekly rates available. Guests also enjoy docking facilities, beach swimming, and a heated outdoor pool (in the summer). Major CC's are accepted.

Adjacent to the Alpine Village is the **Silver Tree,** Glendale Bridge Road, Oakland (tel. 387-4040), a lakefront restaurant and cocktail lounge with an 1890s décor of knotty-pine walls, beamed-ceilings, colored-glass lamps, and open fireplaces. Wide picture windows add a contemporary touch, framing views of the lake and surrounding woodlands. Open for dinner seven days a week, the specialty here is Italian food with such dishes as veal parmigiana, chicken à la formaggio, lasagne, and manicotti. In addition, there is a wide range of seafood entrees, ranging from crab imperial and crab soufflé to seafood Newburg and fish combination platters; prime ribs and char-broiled steaks are also on the menu. Entrees, priced from $6.95 to $16.95, come with salad and two vegetables or a side dish of spaghetti. A special after-dinner feature of this restaurant is its selection of old-fashioned ice-cream-parlor desserts, at turn-of-the-century prices of 5¢ or 10¢ each. Hours are from 5 to 10 p.m., Monday through Thursday, from 5 to 11 p.m. on Friday and Saturday, and from 4 to 10 p.m. on Sunday. No reservations are taken. CC's accepted: AE, MC, and V.

Note on Sunday dining: Garrett County liquor regulations prohibit restaurants from selling or serving any alcoholic beverages, including wine, on Sundays.

SPORTS AND ACTIVITIES: A complete year-round resort, Deep Creek Lake is equally at its best in summer or winter.

Boating: Summer activities focus on water sports with every type of boat from sailboat to speedster on the lake. Nearly all marinas around the lake have craft for rent, seven days a week. Pedal boats or canoes average $5 an hour; fishing boats, $8 an hour; pontoon boats, from $15 to $25 an hour; sailboats, $9 an hour; skiboats and runabouts, from $12 to $25 an hour, depending on horsepower. Some of the leading firms are **Echo Marina,** White Oak Drive, Swanton (tel. 387-5910); **Bill's Marine Service,** Glendale Road, Oakland (tel. 387-5536); and **Crystal Waters,** Route 219, Oakland (tel. 387-5515). Echo and Bill's accept MC and V, but Crystal Waters does not accept credit cards.

Golf: The **Wisp Resort Golf Course,** Marsh Hill Road, McHenry (tel. 387-5581) is an 18-hole championship facility nestled between the Allegheny Mountains and Deep Creek Lake. Open from April through mid-October, the course welcomes guests seven days a week. Greens fees are $9 for nine holes throughout the week; $12 for 18 holes on weekdays, and $15 for 18 holes on weekends. Golf carts can be rented for $9 for nine holes or $16 for 18 holes and there is a fully stocked pro shop on the grounds. In addition, the **Oakland Country Club,** Sang Run Road, Oakland (tel. 334-3883), invites visitors to play on its 18-hole championship course on weekdays. Greens fees are $10 to $12 for 18 holes; after 4 p.m., the rate is $9. Golf carts are available for $8 for nine holes and $12 for 18 holes.

Horseback Riding: Seeing the mountain and lakeside sights from a saddle is a popular activity in the Deep Creek area. For nearly 30 years, the **Double GG Ranch** has operated a year-round equestrian center on Route 219 in McHenry (tel. 387-5481). Horses are available for rental by the hour ($8) or half hour ($5). Trail rides and hay rides are arranged in the summer season and horse-drawn sled rides in the winter. In addition, the Double GG offers more than 100 campsites in a working-ranch atmosphere. Rates start at $10 a night including electricity, water, sewer, and air conditioning or heat. CC's accepted: MC and V.

Swimming: Deep Creek Lake State Park, south of McHenry on State Park Road, features an 800-foot sandy beach with lifeguards on duty.

Skiing: Deep Creek Lake is the home of Maryland's largest ski area. With an elevation of 3,080 feet and a vertical rise of 610 feet, the **Wisp Resort** offers 16 major ski runs and challenging trails on 220 acres of mountainside. The longest single run is two miles. Facilities include double-chair lifts, rope-tow, and poma lifts; snow-making; and night skiing. Slope fees range from $19 on weekdays to $25 on weekends, with reduced rates for night skiing, two-day tickets, and for children. The ski season opens at the end of November and closes in mid-March. The Wisp also operates an on-premises ski school, rental service, and ski shop. For full information, contact the Wisp Resort, Marsh Hill Road, Deep Creek Lake, MD 21541 (tel. 301/387-5581). CC's accepted: MC and V.

ANNAPOLIS

A GEM OF COLONIAL ARCHITECTURE, Annapolis is home to an historic district of more than 1,500 buildings. Situated at the confluence of the Chesapeake Bay and the Severn River, this picturesque port is also the capital of Maryland.

First settled in the mid-1600s, Annapolis was initially known as Providence, and later called Anne Arundel Town, after the wife of Cecilius Calvert, the second Lord Baltimore who sponsored the area's first English settlers. It was an Englishman, Francis Nicholson, who laid out the city's streets in 1695 according to a pattern of radiating throughfares. In 1694 the name of Annapolis was chosen, in honor of Princess Anne, who later became the Queen of England.

With all of its lofty connections, it is no wonder that Annapolis has led a charmed existence. A prosperous seaport due to the tobacco trade, Annapolis had its golden years from 1750 to 1790, as the commercial, political, and social center of Maryland. The first library in the colonies as well as the first theater are believed to have been founded in Annapolis during those years, as was St. John's College, one of the first public schools in America.

Between November 1783 and August 1784, Annapolis was also the first peacetime capital of the U.S. It was during that period that the city served as the site for the ratification of the Treaty of Paris, the document in which Great Britain formally recognized the independence of the United States, ending the Revolutionary War.

As you stroll down the streets of Annapolis today, you can't help but think that not much has changed here since those glorious days. Except for the cars, it is almost as if time has stood still. The city is a vista of 18th-century mansions, churches, and public buildings. The original layout is still in place—narrow brick streets fanning out from two round throughfares, State Circle and Church

Circle. Colonial names are everywhere: King George Street, Duke of Gloucester Street, Compromise Street, and Shipwright Street, to name a few.

This charming seaport city (pop.: 30,000) does have newer claims to fame, of course. It is the home of the U.S. Naval Academy and the government of the state of Maryland. With 16 miles of waterfront, tiny Annapolis is also the pleasure-boating capital of the eastern U.S. and a tourism destination renowned for its landmark sights, historic inns and restaurants, convivial taverns, trendy shops, and relaxed atmosphere.

VISITOR INFORMATION: There are two main sources for tourist brochures and maps of Annapolis: the **Visitors Center,** Maryland State House, State Circle, Annapolis, MD 21401 (tel. 301/269-3400); and the **Tourism Council of Annapolis and Anne Arundel County,** 152 Main St., Annapolis, MD 21401, (tel. 301/268-8687). Once you are in town, you can also stop by an information booth at the foot of the City Dock for on-the-spot directions and assistance.

1. Getting To Annapolis

BY CAR: Located in the center of Maryland's Chesapeake Bay coast, Annapolis is about 30 miles south of Baltimore (via Route 2), and 40 miles east of Washington, D.C. (via Routes 50/301). Annapolis is also accessible from the east via the William Preston Lane Memorial Bridge, locally known as "the Bay Bridge."

BY PLANE: Annapolis is served by **Baltimore-Washington International Airport.** More than 300 flights a day land at this northern Maryland gateway, located 20 miles northwest of Annapolis. Minibus transfer services between the airport and the major hotels of Annapolis are operated by **BWI Airport Limo,** a division of Holliday Taxi-Limo Inc., 111 Dominoe Rd. (tel. 266-8494). The fare is $12 one-way and $22 round-trip. Transfer by taxi is approximately $22 one-way.

2. Getting Around Annapolis

PUBLIC TRANSPORT AND PARKING: True to its 18th-century style, midtown Annapolis is very compact, with lots of narrow streets; consequently, parking in the historic district is limited. Visitors are encouraged to leave their cars in a park-n-ride lot, located on the edge of town, off Rowe Boulevard, on the west side of the Navy-Marine Corps Stadium. Trolley-style shuttle buses depart from this field every 15 minutes for the short ride into the historic district. This limited form of public transport is operated every day except Sundays; the one-way fare is 60¢. For up-to-date information on this shuttle service, call 263-7964.

TAXIS: Once you are in town, if you need transport, call **Annapolis Taxi** (tel. 266-8494); **Blue Cab** (tel. 268-1323); or **Yellow Cab** (tel. 266-8835 and 268-3737).

WALKING TOURS: Although you can easily walk around Annapolis, you'll enjoy twice the fun (and twice the history) if you put yourself in the hands of a qualified guide. One of the leading guide services is operated by **Historic Annapolis Tours,** Old Treasury Building, State Circle (tel. 267-8149), the organization that has been very influential in saving and preserving many of the city's landmark buildings. Using a "museum without walls" theme, this company conducts 90-minute walks around the historic district and the U.S. Naval Academy. Tours depart from the Historic Annapolis office, weekdays at 10 a.m. and 1:30 p.m., with daily departures and an additional tour at 3 p.m. in the summer months. The fee is $4.50 for adults and $2.50 for children aged 6 to 18. Historic Annapolis also has several excursions designed specifically for adults, such as a 90-minute "waterfront and tavern" tour ($4.50); and a three-hour exploration of the interiors of the city's great mansions ($10.50). Tailor-made tours focusing on preservation and the decorative arts can also be arranged. The regularly scheduled tours are operated on a "walk-in" basis, but reservations are required for the specialized tours.

Another firm, **Three Centuries Tours of Annapolis,** 48 Maryland Ave. (tel. 263-5401), is known for its well-versed guides in Colonial costume. These tours, which cover the highlights of the historic district and the Naval Academy, are two hours in length and are operated on a "turn-up-and-go" basis, with no reservations needed. From April through October, there is a daily "early-bird" departure at 9:30 a.m. from Hilton Inn lobby. During the May through September period, there is an additional tour, a "summer stroll," departing daily at 1:30 p.m. from the Harbormaster Building at City Dock. The price for either tour is $4 for adults and $2 for students. Three Centuries Tours also offers pre-planned and tailor-made tours by reservation, focusing on such topics as Colonial life (for young visitors), historic mansions, and bay cruises.

The **U.S. Naval Academy Guide Service,** Ricketts Hall (tel. 267-3363), provides guided walking tours of the academy, March 1 through May 31, daily from 10 a.m. to 2 p.m., on the hour; from June through Labor Day Weekend, from 9:30 a.m. to 4 p.m., every half hour; and after Labor Day, on weekends only through Thanksgiving weekend, from 10 a.m. to 3 p.m., on the hour. The charge is $2 for adults and $1 for children under 12.

BOATING TOURS: Chesapeake Marine Tours, Slip 20, City Dock (tel. 268-7600), operates various sightseeing cruises of Annapolis Harbor. Unless indicated otherwise, these trips are available daily from Memorial Day through Labor Day; on weekends from mid-April to Memorial Day and after Labor Day to mid-October. Children's rates apply for youngsters aged 2 to 12.

The Harbor Queen—a 40-minute narrated cruise that covers the highlights of Annapolis Harbor, the U.S. Naval Academy, and the Severn River. Operates hourly from 11 a.m. to 5 p.m.; the charge is $3.50 for adults and $1.75 for children.

Little Miss Anne—this is a 40-minute tour focusing on the historic Annapolis harbor and residential waterfront along Spa Creek. Trips depart at quarter past the hour starting at 12:15 p.m. until 9:15 p.m.; the charge is $3.50 for adults and $1.75 for children.

Lady Sarah—a 90-minute outing leaving Annapolis Harbor, past the U.S. Naval Academy and up the Severn River, considered one of the most scenic bodies of water of the Chesapeake Bay. Operates Wednesday through Sunday only during the summer season, and on weekends only from mid-May to Memorial Day and after Labor Day to early October. Departures are at 1:30 and 3:30 p.m.; the charge is $7 for adults and $4 for children.

Annapolitan II—On Wednesday through Sunday, this boat offers a full-day on the bay (7½ hours), departing from Annapolis and cruising to St. Michaels, an historic fishing port on the Eastern Shore. On Tuesday, June through August, this vessel heads in the opposite direction upstream to Baltimore's Inner Harbor. (The St. Michaels' excursion also operates on weekends only from mid-May to Memorial Day and after Labor Day until early October). Both trips include three hours of on-shore sightseeing time before the return trip to Annapolis. In all cases, boarding is at 9:30 a.m., returning to the city dock at approximately 5:30 p.m.; the price is $25 for adults and $15 for children.

3. Where to Stay

The main accommodations choices in Annapolis are concentrated in or near the downtown area. Consequently, most hotels and inns are within walking distance of the major attractions, shopping and restaurants. Convenience is costly, however, and, except for a few motels on the outskirts of town, it is hard to find a double-occupancy room in Annapolis under $75, and even more of a coup to find one under $50. To lessen the dent to your wallet, many properties offer packages at specially reduced rates; be sure to inquire if a package rate applies at the time you intend to visit.

HISTORIC INNS: Thanks to the efforts of a local preservationist and developer, Paul Pearson, five of Annapolis' most historic buildings were purchased and saved from destruction over 20 years ago. With the guidance and encouragement of the non-profit local group Historic Annapolis Inc., Pearson has since turned the properties into five elegant inns with a total of 138 guest rooms. Clustered around Annapolis' two key city circles, these landmark buildings are now collectively known as the Historic Inns of Annapolis. Double-occupancy rates at these beautifully restored and antique-furnished inns range from $85 to $125; suites from $110 to $200. To reserve a room or a meal at any one of the locations, contact the central office of **Historic Inns of Annapolis,** 16 Church Circle, Annapolis, MD 21401 (tel. 301/263-2641 or toll-free 800/847-8882). All major CC's are accepted, and parking facilities are available. Here is a thumbnail sketch of each of these distinctive inns:

The first to be restored, and the veritable "flagship" of the group is **The Maryland Inn,** 16 Church Circle. Wedged into a busy triangular intersection, this four-story flatiron-shaped structure has been operating as an inn ever since it was built in the 1770s. It has been carefully restored and is now decorated in period furnishings ranging from antique fireplaces, rush-seated chairs, electrified lantern fixtures, brass candlesticks, and country hunt prints to Queen Anne and Louis XIV pieces. Each of the 44 bedrooms has a private bath, air conditioning, color cable TV, and a direct-dial phone. This is also the home of the Treaty of Paris restaurant, a 70-seat Colonial style dining room with the ambience of a country inn and a menu that emphasizes nouvelle and regional cuisines. Lunch, priced from $4.95 to $7.95, ranges from sandwiches, steaks, and salads, to seafood omelets, fruit plates, and crêpes. Candlelight dinners feature a variety of entrees, priced from $12.95 to $17.95. House specialties include lamb chops with wild elderberries and green peppercorns; redfish garnished with roasted pecans in Cajun butter sauce; duck with cranberry and apple-honey glaze; baked oysters with crabmeat; seafood sausage (a chilled blend of lobster, scallops, crab, and shrimp in tomato-basil cream); veal chop stuffed with oyster, spinach and Smithfield ham in a red wine and sage sauce; chicken colonial (simmered in ginger snap gravy); and an artful beef Wellington. All main courses are served with a choice of spinach or tossed green salad, and vegetables of the day. Lunch is served from 11:30 a.m. to 3 p.m., and dinner from 6 to 9:30 p.m.

The nearby **Governor Calvert House,** 58 State Circle, is both a conference center and a hotel, composed of several restored and integrated Colonial and Victorian residences. Dating back to 1727, one of the public rooms, partially built on the site of the old Calvert family greenhouse, contains an original hypocaust (a warm-air heating system), now covered with a huge sheet of tempered glass and used as a museum display area. Also furnished with antiques, the 51 bedrooms of this inn each have a private bath, air conditioning, color cable TV, and a direct-dial phone. Other facilities include underground parking and a sunny ground-floor atrium.

The **Robert Johnson House,** 23 State Circle (1765), consists of three adjoining Georgian homes, dating back to 1773, overlooking the Governor's mansion and the Maryland State House. The 30 guest rooms, artfully restored and furnished, are individually decorated with four-poster beds and antiques; each unit also has a private bath, air conditioning, color cable TV, and a direct-dial phone. A hearty continental breakfast is delivered to guest rooms each morning, in true bed-and-breakfast style.

The **State House Inn,** 201 Main St., off State Circle, also operates as a bed-and-breakfast inn. Each bedroom key also unlocks the main door of this (1820) four-story mansard-roof building. Like the other properties, the nine rooms here are all furnished with antiques and yet equipped with every modern convenience. The Hampton House restaurant occupies the main floor, although it is operated by a separate management.

The newest addition (opened in 1986) to the Historic Inns family is the **Reynolds Tavern,** 7 Church Circle (tel. 263-6599). Built by William Reynolds in 1737, it was first a location of a hat business and in 1747 it was used as an ordinary inn called the "The Beaver and Lac'd Hat." After a meticulous seven-year restoration, the fully air-conditioned Reynolds Tavern now offers four deluxe suite-style rooms upstairs with heirloom furniture, quilted decorations, and stenciled walls. On the ground floor is a 70-seat restaurant, with four Colonial-style dining rooms, plus a garden terrace that is sheltered by the boughs of 100-year-old magnolias and great Persian walnut trees. The lunch menu, priced from $3.50 to $7.95, offers salads and unusual sandwiches (such as beef and brie or smoked turkey and Stilton), as well as light seafood entrees (a bowl of shrimp and crab chowder or crab cakes). Dinner entrees, which run from $8.95 to $13.95, range from fresh filet of catfish and "seafood pye" (scallops and shrimp with sherry and cream, baked in puff pastry) to slow-roasted boneless breast of duck and steaks. All main courses are served with breads and biscuits baked on the premises, salad, and vegetable. Lunch hours are from 11:30 a.m. to 2 p.m.; and dinner from 5 to 10 p.m. on weekdays, on Friday and Saturday until 11 p.m., and Sunday from 11:30 a.m. to 8 p.m.

LUXURY LODGINGS: Of all the full-service hotels in town, the best location belongs to the **The Annapolis Hilton Inn,** Compromise and St. Mary's Streets, Annapolis, MD 21401 (tel. 301/268-7555), right on the harbor beside the city dock. This modern six-story hotel, built of brick with a Colonial motif, has 135 rooms, many with balconies, overlooking either the harbor or the town. Each room has two double beds, a desk, lounge chairs, color TV, a direct-dial phone, and air conditioning. Doubles range from $90 to $191; and deluxe suites go for $325 to $445 a day. Guest amenities include reduced-rate parking ($2 a day), a harborside open-deck bar, an outdoor swimming pool, a sundeck, a 200-foot boardwalk, boat-docking facilities, and a penthouse restaurant, The Ward Room. With windows on three sides, the restaurant is the ideal spot to enjoy fine food with sweeping views of Annapolis. Lunch selections, priced from $4.95 to $7.95, include pastas, salads, sandwiches, burgers, omelets, quiches, and light seafood dishes. The dinner menu focuses on tableside service (with such dishes as Caesar salad and steak Diane), and abundant seafood selections such as shrimp fra diavolo, filet of sole casino, trout meunière, and delicacies of the Chesapeake (shrimp, scallops, crab, and clams, in wine and herbs). Entrees, which average $10.95 to $15.95, are served on an à la carte basis, so allow at least another $5 for salad and vegetable. Lunch is served from 11:30 a.m. to 2:30 p.m., and dinner from 6:30 to 10:30 p.m. All major CC's are accepted.

The newest and largest (215-room) property in town is the **Annapolis Hotel,** 126 West St., Annapolis, MD 21401 (tel. 301/263-7777 or toll-free 800/351-5656). Situated several blocks west of State Circle, this modern six-story hotel is within walking distance of all the major historic sites and the city dock. A $12 million development, it is richly appointed with a spacious courtyard entrance, a four-story atrium lobby, teak floors, and plush carpeting of teal and other nautical blues. Model sailing vessels on display in the public rooms convey a yacht-club ambience. The bedrooms have an equally rich décor, with double or king beds, air conditioning, color cable TV, direct-dial phones, and separate dressing and sitting areas. Doubles start at $105; suites from $175. The nautical-style West Street Café Coffee Shop serves breakfast and light meals throughout the day. The main restaurant, Basil's, is furnished in a panorama of green, white, and gold tones. The gourmet menu includes entrees of grilled red snapper, roast breast of duckling, sliced loin of veal, baby halibut, and seared salmon, all in the $18 to $24 price bracket. Dinner is served from 6 to 10 p.m. Valet parking is available for guests, and all major CC's are accepted.

Outside of the downtown area, the top choice is the **Ramada Inn,** 173 Jennifer Rd., Annapolis, MD 21401 (tel. 266-3131 or toll-free 800/351-9209), about three miles from midcity at the intersection of Routes 50 and 301. Opened in 1985, this modern 197-room hotel features a contemporary décor. Each bedroom has a queen, a king, or two double beds, air conditioning, color cable TV, and a direct-dial phone. Doubles range from $79 to $99. Other guest facilities include an indoor/outdoor swimming pool, a sauna, a Jacuzzi, free parking, evening entertainment/music in Secrets lounge, and a trendy skylit restaurant, Lester's. Selections at lunch, priced from $4.95 to $8.95, range from hot and cold sandwiches, mesquite burgers, quiches, crêpes, omelets, and seafood to pasta dishes. The dinner menu features such entrees as prime rib cut to order; sirloin and shrimp; breast of duck in sweet currant sauce; charbroiled pork chops with teriyaki and honey sauce; veal Dijon; Chesapeake chicken (with lump crab and hollandaise); rainbow trout with toasted pecans; and blackened red snapper. All main courses, priced from $9.95 to $17.95, are accompanied by fresh breads and vegetables. Lunch is served Monday through Saturday from 11 a.m. to 2 p.m.; dinner Monday through Friday from 5 to 10 p.m., Friday and Saturday until 11 p.m., and Sunday until 9 p.m. A buffet breakfast is also available Monday through Saturday, and brunch on Sunday. All major CC's are accepted.

MODERATE CHOICES: A reasonably priced bed-and-breakfast choice is the **Prince George Inn,** 232 Prince George St., Annapolis, MD 21401 (tel. 301/263-6418), a 100-year-old Victorian town house in the heart of the city, just a block from State Circle. Converted into a guest home in the early 1980s by Bill and Norma Grovermann, this three-story brick building offers a cozy parlor with a fireplace and a pleasant screened-in side porch that serves as a breakfast room. Four guest rooms are available, all with shared bath; some rooms have air conditioning. Doubles start at $53 and include a buffet breakfast of fresh fruit, juices, coffee, tea, and freshly baked breads and muffins. No on-site parking facilities are available, and no CC's are accepted.

About three miles from the historic district is the **Thr-rift Inn,** 2542 Riva

Rd., Annapolis, MD 21401 (tel. 301/224-2800 or toll-free 800/638-5179). Located just off Routes 50 and 301, this two-story motel has 149 rooms, each featuring either a king-size bed, or one and two double beds, wall-to-wall carpeting, a vanity area, color TV, a direct-dial phone, and air conditioning. Some non-smoking rooms are available, and nine units have kitchenettes. Doubles range from $50 for a double to $56 for a king-size leisure room; or $62 for an efficiency unit. Free parking is provided, and major CC's are accepted.

About eight miles from downtown, and just west of the Bay Bridge that leads to the Eastern Shore, is the **Econo Lodge,** 591 Revell Hwy. (Routes 50 and 301), Annapolis, MD 21401 (tel. 301/974-4440 or toll-free 800/446-6900). This modern motel has 74 rooms, each with one or two double beds, air conditioning, color cable TV, and a direct-dial phone. Guest amenities include some non-smoking rooms, free parking, a launderette, and a "small pets allowed" policy. Doubles range from $43.95 to $48.95. CC's accepted: AE, MC, and V.

4. Where to Dine

Annapolis is well known for its excellent restaurants—from Colonial dining rooms and taverns to romantic bistros and waterside seafood houses. As outlined above, many choice dining spots are also located in the city's hotels and restored inns. In addition, for families and travelers on-the-go, Annapolis is home to a **Restaurant Park,** a fast-food and family-style complex of eateries located on Routes 50 and 301, about three miles from downtown and opposite the Annapolis Shopping Plaza.

THE TOP CHOICES: A touch of old Europe is thriving in Annapolis at the **Hampton House,** 201 Main St. (tel. 268-7898), a small dining room in a restored 1820 town house right in the heart of midtown. Combining a selection of light French and Hungarian dishes, this elegant restaurant is one of *the* places to dine for a truly memorable meal. The dinner menu features such entrees as Hungarian Platter (medallions of pork and chicken in paprika) and Wiener Schnitzel Modena (veal, cured ham, and cheese in pimento sauce), as well as veal Oscar; chicken Cordon Bleu; sole en papillote; lobster and shrimp Newburg en croûte; and steak au poivre. The price range for all main courses is from $14.95 to $19.95. Starters average between $3.95 and $4.95 for such authentic treats as Hungarian gulyas soup or stuffed cabbage. Simpler fare, priced from $4.95 to $6.95, is presented at lunch with choices ranging from assorted sandwiches and burgers to hot dishes (such as Budapest burger or pork paprika). Lunch is served Tuesday through Saturday from 11:30 a.m. to 2:30 p.m.; dinner Monday through Thursday from 6 to 9:30 p.m., and until 10 p.m. on Friday and Saturday. Reservations are essential. CC's accepted: AE, Ch, MC, and V.

Creative American cuisine is the trademark of **Capers,** 210 Revell Hwy. (tel. 757-0200), a spacious bilevel restaurant in a wooded setting on Route 50, about three miles from town. The modern décor includes varying tones of gray and blue furnishings, a large open fireplace, knotty wood walls, and lots of leafy plants. Lunch focuses on salads, pastas, sandwiches, and light entrees like seafood strudel, apple and Cheddar crêpes, or Oriental beef sauté, in the $5.95 to $8.95 bracket. Dinner entrees, priced from $13.95 to $19.95, include shrimp au poivre vert; pasta cioppino (with mussels, scallops, shrimp, and sole); chargrilled filet mignon with Shiitake mushroom sauce; roast loin of lamb; duck with strawberry sauce; and chicken chasseur (sautéed with parmesan cheese and topped with a shallot, tomato, and mushroom sauce). All main courses are accompanied by breads and pumpkin muffins baked on the premises. An award-winning wine list also offers more than two dozen vintage wines by the glass and bottle. Lunch is served from 11:30 a.m. to 2:30 p.m. Monday through Saturday, and dinner from 5:30 to 9:30 p.m. Monday through Saturday. A sumptuous Sunday brunch (priced at $12.95) is also available from 10:30 a.m. to 2:30 p.m. CC's accepted: AE, MC, and V.

The place to go for maritime views while you dine is **The Harbour House,** 87 Prince George St., (tel. 268-0771), overlooking the city dock. Opened in 1960 and expanded over the years to a 350-seat capacity, this nautical-style restaurant is manned by two generations of the Phillips family. Seafood selections dominate the lunch menu with such dishes as crab quiche, salmon strudel, and seafood pie, as well as sandwiches and burgers, all priced from $4.95 to $6.95. Soups, such as cream of crab with sherry or crab vegetable, are also very popular at any time of day ($2.50 to $3.50 a bowl). Dinner entrees, priced between $11.95 to $18.95, include a host of crab creations as well as bouillabaisse seafood stew; blackened or regular prime rib; butterfly shrimp; lobster Thermidor; and steaks. All main courses come with potato or rice, and salad or vegetable. In the summer months, meals are also served on an outside terrace. An extensive wine list is offered (from $9 to $30 a bottle) which features labels from Maryland, California, and Europe, as well as "house wines" produced at the restaurant's own winery in Hammonton, N.J. Open daily all year for lunch from 11:30 a.m. to 3 p.m., and for dinner from 3 to 10 p.m. No reservations are taken; CC's accepted: AE, MC, and V.

MODERATELY PRICED DINING: A favorite haunt of legislators is **Harry Browne's,** 66 State Circle (tel. 263-4332), a midtown eatery with a genuine tin ceiling, nautical chandeliers, globe lights, large framed mirrors, and an "old Maryland" ambience. For a change of pace, there is also an art-deco cocktail lounge upstairs and an outdoor brick-floored courtyard café. Lunch, priced from $3.95 to $5.95, includes an interesting array of salads, quiches, crossantwiches, burgers, chili, Welsh rarebit, and pâté and cheese platters. Entrees at dinner, priced from $12.95 to $17.95, range from blackened swordfish, shrimp scampi, and seafood pasta to "veal birds" (cutlets rolled with oysters and sage stuffing in white wine sauce), and chicken breast with asparagus mousse. Top off your meal with a flambé dessert (such as bananas Foster and cherries jubilee, from $7.50 to $9 for two). Lunch is served from 11:30 a.m. to 3 p.m.; dinner from 5:30 to 11 p.m. on Sunday through Thursday, and until midnight on Friday and Saturday. Sunday brunch is available from 10:30 a.m. to 3 p.m. All major CC's are accepted.

Established by Horatio Middleton as "an inn for seafaring men" in 1750, the **Middleton Tavern,** 2 Market Space and Randall St. (tel. 263-3323), has had many prominent patrons including George Washington, Thomas Jefferson, and Benjamin Franklin. Today this city dock landmark is enjoyed equally by men and women and has been restored and expanded over the years. The lunch menu, priced from $3.95 to $9.95, focuses on sandwiches, salads, and hot specialties such as chili, fish and chips, and barbecued seafood kebabs. Dinner entrees, priced from $9.95 to $23.95, with most under $15, include crêpes Middleton (shrimp, scallops, and crab in a light Newburg sauce); lobster Luicci (lightly breaded lobster tails broiled in herbs and butter); filet of sole stuffed with crab, spinach, and mushrooms; duck à l'orange flamed at tableside; steak tartare; and Chateaubriand for two. All main courses are served with salad, potato, and vegetable. Lunch is served daily from 11 a.m. to 4 p.m.; dinner Sunday through Thursday from 5 to 10 p.m., and Friday and Saturday until 11 p.m. CC's accepted: MC and V.

Riordan's, 26 Market Space (tel. 263-5449) is an early-American tavern with an Irish ambience, as evidenced by an illuminated shamrock at its entrance and the Irish flag on its ceiling. The eclectic décor also includes a tin ceiling, tile floors, Tiffany lamps, ceiling fans, vintage pictures and posters, and colorful stained-glass. Light choices (overstuffed sandwiches, burgers, pastas, and salads) are available at lunch, priced in the $3.95 to $7.95 bracket. The regular dinner menu, priced at $7.95 to $13.95, includes crab-stuffed flounder, prime ribs, pork ribs, steamed shrimp, broiled swordfish, and steaks. All entrees come with a garden salad and potato. In addition, on Friday and Saturday nights, an upstairs dining room, overlooking the Annapolis city dock, also offers candlelight dining and gourmet fare at slightly higher prices ($12.95 to $15.95). Choices upstairs include prime rib and crab; veal Christopher (with avocado, dill sauce, and shrimp); stuffed soft-shell crabs; lamb with zinfandel sauce; and grouper with raspberry butter sauce. Each entree is accompanied by creamy potatoes in a crock, salad, and fresh vegetable. Lunch is served from 11 a.m. to 2 p.m. and dinner from 6 to 11 p.m. (until midnight on Friday and Saturday). CC's accepted: AE, Ch, MC, and V.

Just west of downtown is **The Rustic Inn,** 2029 West St. (tel. 263-2626), a little hideaway with a décor that befits its name. Established in 1982, this restaurant is known for its fresh seafood, Iowa choice beef, and Provimi milk-fed veal. In addition, all dressings, sauces, and accompaniments are made on the premises. Lunch, priced from $4.95 to $7.95, consists of hearty sandwiches (served on thin-sliced beer bread), salads, pastas, and hot dishes. A good way to start dinner is with a unique "raw bar sampler" (an array of oysters, shrimp, clams, and scallops for $5.95). Entrees, which run from $10.95 to $17.95, include scallops champignon (baked in Marsala wine with fresh mushrooms, and grated Cheddar); oyster imperial and crab imperial; veal (marsala, piccata, or francese); chicken Divan; steak béarnaise; and "salty strip" (strip steak covered with freshly shucked sautéed oysters and mushrooms). All dishes include salad, breads, and potato. Lunch is served Tuesday through Saturday from 11:30 a.m. to 1:30 p.m.; dinner Tuesday through Thursday and on Sunday from 5 to 10 p.m., and Friday and Saturday from 5 to 11 p.m. CC's accepted: AE, MC, and V.

BUDGET MEALS: Conveniently situated between State Circle and Prince George Street, the **Little Campus Inn,** 61–63 Maryland Ave. (tel. 263-9250), has been a favorite midtown restaurant since 1924. The second generation of the Nichols family now runs this homey restaurant, known for its hearty home-style food and a décor of original brick, dark woods, and murals of early Annapolis. Lunch, priced from $2.95 to $5.95, includes sandwiches, burgers, and hot dishes, such as fried chicken, omelets, and breaded veal steak. Dinner selections range from beef or lamb shish kebab, corned beef and cabbage, and spaghetti with meatballs to soft-shell crabs, chicken Kiev, and seafood samplers (crab, lobster, scallops, shrimp, crab claw, fish filet, and clams casino). All entrees, priced from $6.95 to $13.95, with most under $10, are served with vegetables, potato, and salad. Most major CC's are accepted.

For a look at an Annapolis tradition, stop into **Chick and Ruth's Delly,** 165 Main St. (tel. 269-6737), a "ma and pa" establishment run by two generations of the Levitt family for more than 20 years. This small storefront deli-restaurant is famous for sandwiches named after local politicians and attractions of the area, such as the "Main Street" (corned beef and cole slaw), the "President Reagan" (6-ounce steak, cheese, and onions), and the "Golda Meir" (lox, cream cheese, onion, and tomato, on a bagel); platters and salads are also available. Breakfast and lunch are served all day; prices range from $1.50 to $3.95. No CC's accepted.

5. The Top Attractions

The entire midcity area of Annapolis is a National Historic District with more than 1,500 restored and preserved buildings. Since the streets are narrow, the ideal way to see the sights is on foot. Several guided walking tours are available (see "Getting Around"); self-guided walking-tour maps are also available free of charge from the various tourist offices.

Plan to spend some time in the area around the City Dock along the Annapolis waterfront. This is a yachting hub, with hundreds of craft of all sizes in port. Various sightseeing cruises of the harbor are available (see "Getting Around") in the spring, summer, and fall months. The City Dock is also home to a parade of fine seafood restaurants, lively bars, specialty shops, galleries, and a summer theater. Other highlights of this area include **Market House,** a central farmers' produce station built in 1784 and again in 1858. Today it still retains much of the flavor of the open stalls with a variety of foods, although the wares now fall mostly into the fast-food category (open Monday through Thursday from 9 a.m. to 6 p.m., Friday and Saturday from 9 a.m. to 7:30 p.m., and Sunday from 10 a.m. to 6 p.m.). Also located here is **Maritime Annapolis,** an historical triorama housed in the Victualling Warehouse, 77 Main St. (tel. 268-5576). This exhibit will give you an idea of what the waterfront looked like in 1751–1791 when the port of Annapolis was in its heyday. Hours are 11 a.m. to 4:30 p.m. daily (except Thanksgiving and Christmas); admission charge is 50¢ for adults and 25¢ for children aged 6 to 18.

In the center of Annapolis, you'll find the **Maryland State House,** on State Circle (tel. 269-3400), the oldest U.S. state capitol in continuous legislative use (built 1772–1779). This building also served as the capitol of our country from November 26, 1783 to August 13, 1784. As you step inside the Old Senate Chamber, you'll be in the historic spot where George Washington resigned his commission as Commander-in-Chief of the Continental armies. This was also the setting for the ratification of the Treaty of Paris which ended the Revolutionary War. The dome of this building, the largest of its kind constructed entirely of wood, is made of cypress beams and held together by wooden pegs. You can stroll throughout the State House on your own, examining the various exhibits that depict life in Annapolis in Colonial times, or you can avail of guided tours that depart on the hour, 10 a.m. to 4 p.m. (except 1 p.m.), from the Visitors Center on the first floor. Open daily (except Thanksgiving, Christmas, and New Year's Day) from 9 a.m. to 5 p.m.; admission and tours are free.

Annapolis is also synonymous with the **U.S. Naval Academy,** King George and Randall Streets (tel. 263-6933). Founded in 1845, this is the Navy's undergraduate professional college and a national historic site spread over 300 acres along the Severn River on the eastern edge of town. Visitors are welcome to stroll the grounds at leisure and to see such sights as the chapel and crypt of John Paul Jones, and the Preble Hall Museum containing fascinating collections of nautical relics, paintings, ship models, and other historic items relating to the Navy's role in wars, global exploration, and space. **Commissioning Week,** usually the third week in May, is a colorful time of full-dress parades; it is also a busy period for Annapolis hotels as relatives and friends of the cadets pour into the city. The grounds are open Monday through Saturday from 9:30 a.m. to 5 p.m., and on Sunday from noon to 5 p.m., except January 1 and December 25; no admission charge. Guided tours are also available, departing daily from Ricketts Hall at Gate 1, March 1 through May 31, from 10 a.m. to 2 p.m. on the hour; June 1 through Labor Day Weekend, from 9:30 a.m. to 4 p.m., every half hour; after Labor Day through Thanksgiving weekend, from 10 a.m. to 3 p.m., on the hour. The charge for tours is $2 for adults and $1 for children under 12.

Among the great historic residences to see in Annapolis is the **William Paca House and Garden,** 186 Prince George St., at Martin Street (tel. 263-5533). Built between 1763 and 1765, this was the home of William Paca, a signer of the Declaration of Independence and a governor of Maryland during the Revolutionary period. Restored by Historic Annapolis Inc. from 1965 to 1976, it is a five-part structure, with a stalwart central block, hyphens and wings, and a total of 37 rooms. Guided tours of the house are available, Tuesday through Saturday from 10 a.m. to 4 p.m., and Sundays and holidays from noon to 4 p.m.; the charge is $3.00 for adults and $2 for children aged 6 to 18. Another attraction of the Paca estate is the adjacent two-acre pleasure garden with blooms for all seasons. The layout includes five elegant terraces, a fish-shaped pond, a Chinese Chippendale bridge, a domed pavilion, and a wilderness garden. If you are not touring the house first, you can enter the garden directly through a **Visitor Center** at 1 Martin St. (tel. 269-0601). Garden tours are conducted Monday through Saturday from 10 a.m. to 4 p.m.; Sundays, from noon to 5 p.m., May through October; and from noon to 4 p.m. during the rest of the year. A tour of the gardens only is $1.50 for adults and $1 for children. Combination packages, covering both the house and the garden, are $4 for adults and $2.50 for children.

Hammond-Harwood House, 19 Maryland Ave., at King George Street (tel. 269-1714), is considered to be one of the finest examples of Georgian architecture in the U.S. Built in 1774, this house is also an outstanding example of the Maryland five-part plan that connects the central section by hyphens to semioctagonal wings. Famous for its center doorway of tall Ionic columns, this house is also a showcase of interior decorative ornamentation and woodcarvings. It is named for its first and last owners: Matthias Hammond, a Maryland member of the Provincial Assembly, and the Harwood family who owned the house in recent years before it became a museum. Open April through October, Tuesday through Saturday from 10 a.m. to 5 p.m., and on Sunday from 2 to 5 p.m.; November through March, Tuesday through Saturday from 10 a.m. to 4 p.m., and on Sunday from 1 to 4 p.m. Closed on January 1, Thanksgiving, Christmas. Admission charge is $2.50 for adults and $1.50 for children aged 6 to 18.

6. Nightlife

As the state capital, a college town, and a yachting center, Annapolis is a lively place at night. One of the top spots for music is the **King of France Tavern** in the Maryland Inn, 16 Church Circle, (tel. 263-2641 or toll-free 800/847-8882). The former Colonial kitchens of this landmark inn have been transformed into a jazz club, the home base of guitarist Charlie Byrd. In addition to jazz, the nightly program also offers occasional classical and chamber music, and dinner/cabaret shows featuring songs of the '30s and '40s.

For Broadway musicals, the place to go is the **Annapolis Summer Garden Theater,** at the corner of Main and Compromise Streets (tel. 268-0809), near the City Dock. Once a blacksmith shop, this theater was established in 1966, with productions ranging from *Pippin* to *The Sound of Music.* Curtain is at 8:45 p.m., Thursday through Sunday, Memorial Day through Labor Day. Tickets are priced from $6 and $8; no CC's accepted.

Be prepared for an authentic "disappearing act" at the **Annapolis Theatre of Magic,** 46 State Circle, Annapolis, MD 21401 (tel. 301/263-7469). Located in the beautifully restored former Circle Theatre (1920), right opposite the State House, this production features award-winning illusionists Wayne and Sandy

Allen. It's a show of magic, music, and dance from the roaring '20s to the dazzling '80s. Staged on Friday and Saturday evenings at 8 p.m., and on Sunday at 2 p.m.; tickets range from $8 to $12. Major CC's accepted.

Annapolis is also a town of trendy pubs, often featuring live music, entertainment, or dancing. Most of the "in" spots are clustered around the waterfront area, such as **McGarvey's Saloon,** on the City Dock (tel. 263-5700), **Riordan's Saloon,** City Dock (tel. 263-5449), **Armadillo's,** City Dock (tel. 268-6680), **Fran O'Brien's,** 113 Main St. (268-6288), and **Mum's,** 136 Dock St. (tel. 263-3353).

7. Shopping

Annapolis is a good shopping and browsing town. Although boutiques and shops line all of the main streets, Maryland Avenue is fast developing a reputation as the most unique "shopping row." Here is a sampling of the wares you'll find on this one street:

The **Charing Cross Book Shop,** 88 Maryland Ave. (tel. 268-1440), a wide selection of volumes on Maryland and Annapolis history, maps, and seafood cookbooks; and new and used books. Open Monday through Saturday from 10:30 a.m. to 5:30 p.m. and on Sunday from 9 a.m. to 4 p.m. CC's accepted: AE, MC, and V.

The **Gift Horse,** 77 Maryland Ave. (tel. 263-3737), is an emporium of unusual crystal, glass, brass, pewter, armetale, oil lamps, figurines, prisms, mobiles, and paper weights. Open Monday to Saturday from 10 a.m. to 5:30 p.m.; and during spring, summer and fall months, on Sunday from noon to 5 p.m. All major CC's accepted.

The **Ship Shop,** 75 Maryland Ave. (tel. 268-1141), sells metal models and miniatures of the army, navy, and marines; and Canadian mounted police; as well as toy soldiers; and models of cars, ships, trains, and planes. Open Monday to Saturday from 10:30 a.m. to 5:30 p.m. and on Sunday from noon to 5:30 p.m. CC's accepted: AE, MC, and V.

Annapolis Country Store, 53 Maryland Ave. (tel. 269-6773) is the oldest and largest wicker shop in Maryland; also stocks pottery, mugs, jams, baskets, and kitchen accessories. Open Monday to Saturday from 10 a.m. to 6 p.m. and on Sunday from noon to 5 p.m. CC's Accepted: AE, Ch, MC, and V.

Walnut Leaf Antiques, 50 Maryland Ave. (tel. 263-4885), specializes in period and oak furniture, European and Oriental porcelain, cut glass, linens, and vintage costume jewelry. Open seven days a week from noon to 5 p.m. CC's accepted: AE, MC, and V.

8. Events

Various events might attract you to Annapolis at certain times of the year. Conversely, if you have no interest in a particular happening, you might want to avoid visiting during peak periods when hotel rooms will be hard to find and often subject to a surcharge. For example, October is a time of year when the boating world converges on this city for the U.S. Sailboat Show, the world's largest in-the-water boat show, and the U.S. Power Boat Show, the largest show of its kind with more than 300 boats on display in and out of the water. For information on either of these events, contact the **Greater Annapolis Chamber of Commerce,** 152 Main St., Annapolis, MD 21401 (tel. 301/268-7676).

This city is also busy in mid-June when the Annapolis Arts Festival takes place along the City Dock. A fixture for more than 25 years, this event includes open-air concerts and arts and craft exhibits. For a program, contact the **Annap-**

olis **Fine Arts Foundation,** P.O. Box 228, Annapolis, MD 21404 (tel. 301/267-7922).

If you love seafood, plan ahead to come to Annapolis in early September for the **Maryland Seafood Festival.** Started in 1966, this event is held at Sandy Point State Park, about eight miles from downtown. The program includes three days of continuous live entertainment and lots of good eating (steamed crabs, oysters, crab cakes, steamed shrimp, fried fish, and clam chowder). Complete information is available from the Greater Annapolis Chamber of Commerce (see above).

9. Excursion to St. Mary's City and Solomon's Island

ST. MARY'S CITY: After you have seen the current capital of Maryland, you really should have a look at the state's first capital, St. Mary's City (known initially as "St. Marie's Citty"). Leaving Annapolis, head southward on Route 2. This road wends its way through Anne Arundel County and Calvert County until it becomes Routes 2 and 4. You'll pass through flat farmland, the heart of Maryland's tobacco country.

After crossing over the Patuxent River, change to Route 235 and follow the road south until you see signs for St. Mary's City. It sounds complicated, but it really is an easy two-hour drive, continually heading south. When you arrive in St. Mary's City, don't expect a panorama of Colonial buildings like Annapolis. Don't even expect to find a city in the same format as we know it.

Nestled between the Potomac and the Chesapeake, this secluded corner of Maryland is almost as it was in 1634. That was the year *The Ark* and *The Dove* arrived from England with the first 140 colonists under a royal charter from Lord Baltimore. These stalwart settlers set up a community that served as the beginning of Maryland and the state's first capital until 1694. Among the many achievements of this early city was the enactment of the first laws recognizing religious tolerance.

Today's St. Mary's City is a "living history" outdoor museum spread out over 850 acres of Tidewater landscape. Thanks to years of archeological excavations, St. Mary's City has been authentically re-assembled to show a typical tobacco farm plantation, a waterfront preserve, and woodland nature trails. The first State House has also been reconstructed as has the "Farthing's Ordinary," a primitive tavern that today serves light lunches of yeast-bread sandwiches, garden salads, hearty soups, and seafood stews (at 20th-century prices of $3 to $6; and accepts MC and V credit cards).

Any tour of St. Mary's City starts at the **Visitor Center.** Here you will pay the general admission charge ($3 for adults and $1.50 for children) and see a five-minute introductory audio-visual. This building also houses a number of exhibits that provide useful background on what life was like in these parts 350 years ago.

Plan to spend at least two hours outside to explore the various buildings and the grounds and to see the *Maryland Dove,* a replica of Lord Baltimore's square-rigged ship.

The **St. Mary's City Visitor Center** (tel. 862-1634) is open daily year round, from 10 a.m. to 5 p.m. (except Thanksgiving, Christmas, and New Year's Day). The outdoor attractions are open daily Memorial Day through Labor Day from 10 a.m. to 5 p.m.; and on weekends from 10 a.m. to 5 p.m., from late March through May and again from early September through November.

In addition, during summer evenings (mid-June through mid-August), St.

Mary's City provides an outdoor stage for weekend **Shakespeare productions.** Curtain is at 8 p.m. and tickets are priced from $6 to $9 (Ch, MC, and V are accepted).

SOLOMON'S ISLAND: While you are in the neighborhood or as you travel back to Annapolis, plan to stop at **Solomon's Island,** a busy yacht- and boat-building center and the home of the **Calvert Marine Museum,** Route 4 (tel. 326-2042).

Established in 1970, the museum is housed in a former schoolhouse, on a seven-acre site in the heart of town on the Patuxent River. The chief indoor exhibits include a maritime history room with models of boats such as bugeyes, schooners, and skipjacks; a watermen's room illustrating the various techniques of harvesting fish, oysters, and crabs; a fossil room with specimens dating back millions of years; and an estuarine gallery with mounted fish and waterfowl.

Among the outdoor exhibits in this complex is the **Drum Point Lighthouse,** built in 1883 and moved to this site in 1975; a boat basin and salt marsh walk; and a boat-building skills preservation center. In addition, one-hour cruises around Solomon's Inner Harbor are available on the *William B. Tennison,* the oldest certified passenger-carrying vessel on the Chesapeake Bay. Cruises leave the museum dock at 2 p.m., Wednesday through Sunday, Memorial Weekend through October.

The **Calvert Marine Museum** is open daily (except Thanksgiving, Christmas, and New Year's Day). Summer hours are in effect from May through September, Monday through Saturday from 10 a.m. to 5 p.m., and Sunday from noon to 5 p.m. Winter hours are in effect from October through April, Monday through Friday from 10 a.m. to 4:30 p.m., and Saturday and Sunday from noon to 4:30 p.m. The cruises on the *William B. Tennison* cost an additional $3.50 for adults and $2.50 for children aged 5 to 12 years, with a $12 maximum charge per family.

STAYING OVER: The best place to stay in this part of southern Maryland is the **Patuxent Inn,** P.O. Box 778, Highway 235, Lexington Park, MD 20653 (tel. 301/862-4100), a modern three-story hotel with a country-inn ambience. The 120 spacious rooms are tastefully furnished in a contemporary-Colonial style with two double or king-size beds. Each room has wall-to-wall carpeting, air conditioning, a direct-dial phone, and color cable TV with free HBO. Other amenities include a swimming pool, lighted tennis courts, a jogging/fitness trail, free parking, and a guest launderette, plus a very obliging and efficient staff. Doubles start at $60. All major CC's are accepted.

WHERE TO EAT: With its great marine traditions, Solomon's Island is a natural setting for good seafood restaurants. One of the best is the **Lighthouse Inn,** Route 4 (tel. 326-2444), right on the harbor, with floor-to-ceiling views of the water. The nautical décor includes a bar that is fashioned out of a sailboat, paintings of classic sailboats, captain's chairs, ships' lanterns, and driftwood trim. Lunch choices, priced from $2.95 to $7.95, focus on seafood sandwiches, salads, and burgers. The extensive dinner menu features such seafood delights as lobster tails; scallops champignon; oysters topped with crab imperial; flounder stuffed with crab imperial; and a bountiful mariner's platter that offers a little of everything (fantailed shrimp, soft-shell crab, crab cake, filet of fish, and scallops lightly breaded and fried or broiled). Beef and chicken dishes are also available, as is surf-and-turf and "seafood strip" (steak topped with sautéed seafood). Main courses, which are priced from $7.95 to $19.95, with most under $15, are accompanied by freshly baked bread, potato, and salad. Open daily for lunch from 11 a.m. to 4 p.m., and for dinner from 4 to 10 p.m. (slightly later on Friday and Saturday nights). CC's accepted: MC and V.

Chapter XXV

MARYLAND'S EASTERN SHORE

1. Easton
2. Cambridge
3. Crisfield
4. Salisbury
5. Ocean City

A PENINSULA bordered on one side by the Atlantic and on the other by Chesapeake Bay, Maryland's Eastern Shore is almost an island. For centuries, this eastern portion of the state was linked to the rest of Maryland's mainland only by a northeasterly spit of land closer to Wilmington than to Baltimore.

It wasn't until 1952, when the William Preston Lane Bridge was built from Annapolis over the Chesapeake Bay, that the Eastern Shore really became easily accessible to the rest of the state.

Back-to-back with Delaware and nudging Virginia's coastal strip, these eastern Maryland counties have developed a personality of their own, as part of the Delmarva peninsula. Much of James Michener's novel *Chesapeake* was inspired by the everyday lifestyle of these rural coastal communities.

Two of Maryland's most active ports, Cambridge and Salisbury, are located on the Eastern Shore and some of the state's oldest towns and early shipbuilding centers are also here.

Most of all, this part of the world is known for its good eating. A haven for crabs, oysters, and other seafood, Crisfield is modestly called "The Seafood Capital of the World," and the Salisbury area, home of Perdue farms, is readily recognized as one of the nation's leading poultry producers. Top-class restaurants line the shore, in settings ranging from picturesque Victorian buildings and converted crab shacks to wide-windowed marina decks.

Added to all of this is Ocean City, the Eastern's Shore premier beach resort, with ten miles of sandy beach, a three-mile boardwalk, and hundreds of hotels, restaurants, and amusements. In contrast, this part of Maryland is also the home of the Blackwater National Wildlife Refuge, one of the chief resting areas for migrating wildfowl along the Atlantic Flyway.

The best way to reach the Eastern Shore from the west is via Route 50 and the bridge over the bay. Once you arrive, Route 50 will take you to Easton, Cambridge, Salisbury, and all the way over to Ocean City. If you are approaching from Delaware on the north or from the south via Virginia's coast, then

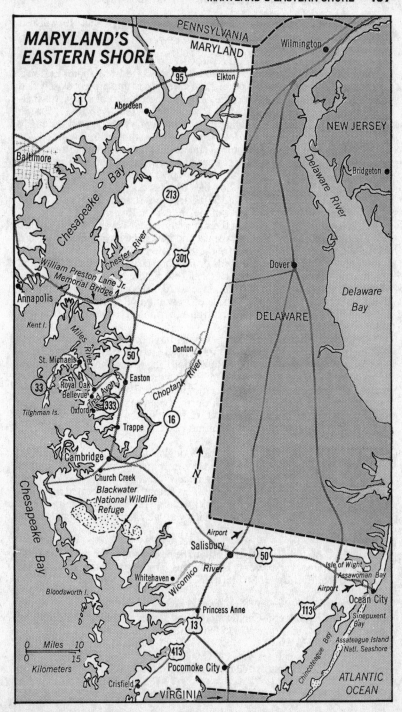

MARYLAND'S
EASTERN SHORE

PENNSYLVANIA
MARYLAND

95   Elkton

1

Aberdeen

Wilmington

NEW JERSEY

Baltimore

Chesapeake Bay

213

Chester River

Bridgeton

Delaware River

301

William Preston Lane Jr.
Memorial Bridge

Dover

Delaware Bay

Annapolis

Kent I.

DELAWARE

Miles River

St. Michaels

Denton

50

33

Royal Oak

Easton

Choptank River

Bellevue

Tred Avon R.

Oxford   333

16

Tilghman Is.

Trappe

Cambridge

Church Creek

Blackwater
National Wildlife
Refuge

N

Chesapeake Bay

Airport

Salisbury

50

Isle of Wight

Whitehaven

Wicomico River

Assawoman Bay

Bloodsworth I.

Airport

Ocean City

Princess Anne

113

Sinepuxent
Bay

13

Assateague Island
Natl. Seashore

0   Miles   10

413

Chincoteague Bay

0   15
Kilometers

Pocomoke City

Crisfield

VIRGINIA

ATLANTIC
OCEAN

Route 13 is the most direct road. Route 13 and its off-shoot, Route 413, will also bring you to Crisfield.

1. Easton

Once known as the Colonial Capital of Maryland's eastern shore, Easton is today a quiet little community (pop.: 7,500), with a past and present closely tied to nearby waters. Directly facing the center of the Chesapeake Bay, yet sheltered by the many coves of the Miles River and the Tred Avon River, Easton was an ideal locale for shipbuilding in the 18th century and now it is equally perfect as a haven for those who love to savor the sea or to sample seafood.

Easton is also the gateway to several neighboring maritime retreats. We like to picture Easton as the inner core or heart of the area, with two arms stretching out toward the Chesapeake. The upper (and longest) arm takes you to the village of St. Michaels on the Miles River and to Tilghman Island, dangling right on the Chesapeake. The lower arm goes straight to Oxford, a sheltered town nestled along the shores of the Tred Avon River.

Called after the archangel of the same name, St. Michaels was one of the oldest settlements along the Chesapeake and flourished in Colonial times as a shipbuilding center (the birthplace of the illustrious Baltimore clipper). Today it is an aesthetic delight—no billboards or fast-food chains; just quiet tree-lined streets, rows of boutiques housed in graceful old restored buildings, and a marina so clean that it seems to sparkle. At least 20,000 boats a year pull into this idyllic harbor just seven miles outside of Easton (via Route 33). Another 15 miles will bring you to Tilghman Island, an important base for fishermen of oysters, crabs, clams, and fin fish.

Oxford, also one of the oldest towns in Maryland, was the Colonial home of Robert Morris Jr., the man who befriended George Washington and then used his own savings to finance the Revolution. The Morris family home is now a first-rate inn and restaurant which in itself is worth the ten miles from Easton to Oxford (via Route 333). The most enjoyable way to reach Oxford, however, is to take the Tred Avon ferry across from the Bellevue section of St. Michaels. No matter how you come, don't miss Oxford—it's a town that time has hardly touched, with a pervasive quiet charm and views of the water at every turn.

VISITOR INFORMATION: For complete lodging and restaurant information, maps and brochures about Easton and the surrounding communities, contact the **Talbot County Chamber of Commerce,** 7 Federal St., P.O. Box 1366, Easton, MD 21601. (tel. 301/822-4606). This helpful office is located in a landmark building once known as the "Brick Hotel," the leading hostelry on the Eastern Shore in the 19th century, which was later to become a bank and a meeting hall before its present usage.

GETTING TO AND AROUND EASTON: The best way to get to the Easton area is by car. For those who prefer to take the bus, **Trailways** offers regular service into its depot at East Dover Street (tel. 822-0280).

　　Car Rental: If you haven't brought your own car to the Easton area, you can rent one from **Avis Rent-a-Car,** Route 50 and Dover Street (tel. 822-5040), or **Discount Rent-a-Car,** Route 50 and Dover Street (tel. 822-8446).

　　Taxis: For local cab service, try **Cecil's Taxi** (tel. 822-8533), **Rasin's Taxi** (tel. 822-1048), or **Thomas's Yellow Top Cabs** (tel. 822-1121).

　　Walking Tours: With a couple of day's notice, you can arrange a guided walking tour of Easton's historic district. Make a reservation by contacting the **Historical Society of Talbot County**, 25 S. Washington St., P.O. Box 964, Easton, MD 21601 (tel. 301/833-0773). The prices are $2 for adults and 50¢ for students.

Ferry Service: For the trip between St. Michaels and Oxford or just for a scenic and satisfying experience, don't miss a ride on the **Oxford Bellevue Ferry** (tel. 226-5408 or 745-9023). Established in 1683, this is America's oldest privately operated ferry. Crossing the Tred Avon River, the distance is just a mile wide and seven minutes in duration. You can catch the ferry either from Bellevue, off Routes 33 and 329, near St. Michaels, or at Oxford (off Route 333). Operating year round, with continuous service every 20 minutes, the ferry schedule is May 1 to Labor Day, on Monday through Friday from 7 a.m. to 9 p.m., and on weekends from 9 a.m. to 9 p.m.; Labor Day to May 1, on Monday through Friday from 7 a.m. to sunset, and weekends from 9 a.m. to sunset (closed Christmas Day). Rates for a car and two persons are $3.50 one way and $5.50 round-trip; extra car passenger, 25¢; walk-on passengers, 50¢.

Harbor Cruises: See the highlights of the Easton area from the water on board *The Patriot*, a 65-foot sightseeing vessel operated by **Patriot Cruises Inc.**, P.O. Box 1206, St. Michaels, (tel. 745-3100). These 90-minute narrated cruises ply the waters of the Miles River and the shoreline off St. Michaels. The boats, which have snack and bar services, depart daily from the dock at the Chesapeake Bay Maritime Museum, St. Michaels. The schedule is May through September, at 11 a.m., 1, and 3 p.m.; the cost is $5 for adults and $2.50 for children under 12.

WHERE TO STAY: The Easton–St. Michaels–Oxford area offers a range of modern and old-world accommodations. Most of these fall into the moderate category, although suites and luxury rooms can certainly be classified in the expensive range. Rates on weekends are often subject to surcharges; and summer prices are usually the highest. One exception to this is the waterfowl hunting season (October through January) when top rates can also apply at many places. It is always best to check in advance with the lodging of your choice to see what rate will be in effect during the time of your visit.

If you want to stay right in the heart of Easton, then the ideal place is the **Tidewater Inn**, Dover and Harrison Streets, P.O. Box 359, Easton, MD 21601 (tel. 301/822-1300). Built in 1949 in the tradition of old public houses of Colonial days, this four-story hotel exudes an old-world feeling, thanks to its décor of dark woods, arched doorways, hurricane lamps, electric candles, flagstone floors, open fireplaces, and paintings of 18th-century Easton. The 120 bedrooms blend early-American-theme furnishings with modern comforts like computer-card room keys, direct-dial phones, private baths, and color TVs, as well as a choice of twin, double, queen, or king beds. Doubles range from $56 to $75 and suites from $140 to $210. Other amenities include a swimming pool, valet service, entertainment on Saturday evenings, and a full-service restaurant. Lunch, which ranges from crêpes and crab cakes to burgers, hot platters, and salads, is priced from $5.95 to $10.95. Dinner entrees, from $12.95 to $23, include Maryland turkey, sugar-cured ham in champagne sauce, breast of capon, crab imperial, prime ribs, and surf-and-turf. Lunch is served daily from 11:30 a.m. to 2:30 p.m., and dinner from 5 to 10 p.m.; breakfast is also available from 7 a.m. each day. CC's accepted: AE, D, MC, and V.

If you enjoy views of the water and boats, then it's hard to beat **St. Michaels Harbor Inn,** 101 N. Harbor Rd., St. Michaels, MD 21663 (tel. 301/745-9001). Opened in 1986, this is not only the newest lodging development in this area, but it is also one of the best. Situated right along the marina, this modern hotel offers 46 rooms and suites, all with sweeping wide-windowed views of the water and most with private balconies or terraces. Each room has one or two queen beds, a direct-dial phone, remote control cable TV, a digital clock radio, plush wall-to-wall carpeting, and contemporary furnishings in soft pastel sea tones. The suites also have kitchenettes, wet bars, and sitting rooms. Other amenities include short-term berthing for guest boats on a 60-slip marina, an outdoor swimming pool, an exercise room, guest laundry, and an Old English–style restaurant overlooking the harbor. Rates for a double range from $40 to $88; and suites (which sleep four) run from $58 to $135. The restaurant is particularly romantic at dinner as the sun sets over the marina. Entrees, which cost from $8.95 to $16.95, range from crab cakes and scampi Chesapeake to chicken Oscar, medallions of veal, and filet of beef. CC's accepted: Ch, MC, and V.

Another star in this region is the **Robert Morris Inn,** N. Morris Street and The Strand, P.O. Box 70, Oxford, MD 21654 (tel. 301/226-5111), once the home of the man who financed the Continental Army during Revolutionary times, and now the focal point of one of Maryland's loveliest towns. Situated on the banks of the Tred Avon River, this historic (1710) building was constructed by ships' carpenters with wooden-pegged paneling, ships' nails, and hand-hewn beams, all of which remain today. The house still has much of its original flooring, fireplaces, and murals. Offering a choice of twin, double, or king-size beds, the guest rooms of this renovated facility are spread out among the original house and nearby cottages and lodges, making a total of 31 units, 25 with private bath. Many of the rooms have river views, private porches, and sitting rooms; and some non-smoking units are available. Rates for two people run from $40 to $60 with shared bath; and from $70 to $120 for rooms with private bath. The dining room, which is open to the public, serves lunch daily, with prices from $3.95 to $15.95. Choices include sandwiches, omelets, burgers, and hot entrees ranging from prime rib and steaks to elaborate seafood platters and salads. Dinner entrees are priced from $8.95 to $22.95, with most dishes under $15. The house specialties include baked seafood au gratin cakes; baked stuffed shrimp; prime rib supreme (topped and broiled with crabmeat); chicken breast stuffed with assorted seafoods; and a hefty seafood platter (with nine different crab, shrimp, scallop, and fish selections). All main courses come with assorted relishes, muffins, and a choice of vegetables. Lunch is served from noon to 3 p.m., and dinner from 6 to 9 p.m. (except Sunday when the kitchen is open all day from noon to 8 p.m.). *Note:* the inn is closed Christmas and from mid-January to mid-March. CC's accepted: AE, MC, and V.

Among the many motels in the region, a good choice is the **St. Michaels Motor Inn,** Route 33 and Peaneck Road, P.O. Box 437, St. Michaels, MD 21663 (tel. 301/745-3333). Situated on the road between Easton and St. Michaels (not directly on the water), this facility has 93 units, each with two double beds or a queen bed, color TV, and a direct-dial phone. The rooms are decorated in contemporary style with a hunting and wildfowl theme. Guest amenities include an outdoor swimming pool and free pick-up for boaters who overnight at the motel. Rates for a double range from $57 to $66. CC's accepted: AE, MC, and V.

A Bed-and-Breakfast Choice

A turn-of-the-century atmosphere prevails at **Hambleton on-the-Harbour,** 202 Cherry St., St. Michaels, MD 21663 (tel. 301/745-3350), a lovely bed-and-breakfast inn facing the harbor. Innkeepers Aileen and Harry Arader have completely renovated this historic antique-filled retreat and furnished each of the five guest rooms with an individual style and décor. All rooms have a view of the waterfront, private bath facilities, air conditioning, and wall-to-wall carpeting; some rooms also have fireplaces and two are on the ground-floor level. A lovely enclosed porch is also available for guests as a relaxing lookout to watch the boats go by. Doubles range from $70 to $90 per night, including a substantial continental breakfast. Open all year. CC's accepted: MC and V.

In the Budget Range

The **Easton Manor Inn,** Route 50, Easton, MD 21601, (tel. 301/822-2200), is situated right on the main north-south road between Easton and points south. This modern two-story facility, with an outdoor swimming pool, has 102 rooms, decorated in a contemporary style, each with one or two double beds, color TV, and a phone. Rates for two people start at $38 on weekdays and $43 on weekends. Because it is so centrally located, this motel is usually booked out way in advance during waterfowl season. All major CC's are accepted.

WHERE TO DINE: Seafood lovers, this is the place! The Easton area is the heart of Maryland's crab, oyster, and fish country. Crab is the prime attraction, whether it is served as "crab imperial" in a rich creamy sauce, rolled up in plump crab cakes, floating in crab chowder, as crab claws, soft-shell crabs, or the just plain hard-shell variety, this is the place to eat crab. So, come and have your fill; the crab is plentiful and the price is right. Almost all restaurants here fall into the mostly moderate category.

Top Spots for Crabs

The **Salty Oyster,** Route 33 and Peaneck Road, St. Michaels (tel. 745-5151), is crab heaven. Although not perched right on the water, this restaurant is thoroughly nautical with a décor of ship ropes, lanterns, model boats, divers' helmuts, and fishing nets. There is seating both indoors and out, depending on the weather. Lunch choices, priced from $3.95 to $4.95, feature sandwiches and crabwiches, burgers, seafood salads, and soups (crab vegetable and cream of crab are divine). Crab is also the main focus at dinner, with entrees priced from $9.95 to $15.95. Selections include an "all-you-can-eat crab feast," hard crab of all sizes, soft-shell crabs, king-crab legs, crab imperial, Chesapeake surf-and-turf (two crab cakes and two pieces of fresh fried chicken), and oysters Chesapeake (stuffed with crab imperial). Different varieties of shrimp, scallop, and steak dishes are always also on the menu. All main courses are served with salad and vegetables. Open every day from 11:30 a.m. to 9:30 p.m. (10 p.m. on weekends). CC's accepted: Ch, MC, and V.

If you'd like a view of the harbor when you feast on seafood, a good choice is **Longfellows,** Mulberry Street, St. Michaels (tel. 745-2624). Located in a gracious old home, this restaurant features dining on two levels indoors; meals are also served on a sheltered outdoor patio and on an adjacent deck; there is also a piano bar for dancing on Saturday and Sunday. Salads, burgers, omelets, and pita sandwiches are featured at lunchtime, all in the $3.95 to $7.95 price range. Dinner entrees, which cost from $8.95 to $15.95, focus on an ever-changing selection of crab dishes and seafood platters, as well as steaks, roast lamb, pasta, chicken, and pork choices. Open daily year round, with lunch from 11 a.m. to 4 p.m., and dinner from 4 to 10 p.m. CC's accepted: MC and V.

Right next door is the **Town Dock Restaurant,** 305 Mulberry St., St. Michaels (tel. 745-5577), directly on the marina. The emphasis here is on casual open-air dining, with a small (air-conditioned) nautical interior, and a large outdoor area lined with picnic tables and umbrellas. The building itself dates back to the 1830s, when it was an oyster-shucking shed, and the patio bricks outside were kilned in St. Michaels during the late 1800s. Lunch choices, priced from $3 to $7, include oyster stew, shrimp and crab salads, crab and meat sandwiches, quiches, and seafood platters. An international flavor dominates the dinner menu, with such dishes as swordfish au gratin, cold-water lobster tails, parma (shrimp, scallops, and lobster in sherry cream sauce over fettuccine), cioppino (shrimp, clams, flounder, lobster, and scallops), rack of lamb, veal alla marsala, wiener schnitzel, oyster-stuffed chicken breast, and veal Simone (with cream sauce and shrimp). Priced $8.95 to $16.95 with most entrees under $10, all choices are served with two vegetables. Open daily year round (except for January and February), lunch is served from 11:30 a.m. to 4 p.m., and dinner from 4 to 10 p.m. CC's accepted: MC and V.

Downtown Easton should also not be overlooked for fine-dining choices. The first to catch your eye will probably be **Chambers Restaurant,** 22 W. Dover St., Easton (tel. 822-5522), located across the street from the landmark Talbot County Courthouse. The restaurant building itself has a storied past—constructed in 1892, it was previously a harness shop, a dry goods store, and a grocery store, and it retains much of its original walls. A favorite of visiting celebrities such as author James Michener and TV commentator Walter Cronkite, this restaurant offers a choice of four dining rooms, each with a décor reflecting its name, from the oak-paneled Tavern Room and Gas Light Bar to the book-filled Library and Gallery with original paintings. Lunch, priced from $3.95 to $5.95, consists mainly of burgers, sandwiches, and specialty dishes (like ham and asparagus rarebit or beer-batter fish). Charbroiled steaks are featured at dinnertime, as well as such varied dishes as grilled lemon chicken breast, prime ribs, Créole-style chicken and shrimp pasta, crab cakes, coquilles St-Jacques, veal Lamanna (sautéed in white wine and garnished with lump crab), or beef and shrimp stir-fry. Prices run from $8.95 to $19.95 and include vegetables. Lunch is available Monday through Saturday from 11 a.m. to 4 p.m.; dinner Monday through Thursday from 5:30 to 9:30 p.m., Friday and Saturday from 5:30 to 10:30 p.m., and Sunday from 4 to 9 p.m. CC's accepted: Ch, MC, and V.

Also near the Courthouse is newcomer **Peach Blossoms,** 6 Washington St., Easton (tel. 822-5220), a bright café-style restaurant and wine bar, with a décor of leafy plants and light caned furniture. Everything is made on the premises, from tangy salad dressings to breads, pastries, and desserts. Lunch features salads, sandwiches, omelets, and pastas, in the $3.95 to $4.95 bracket. Dinner choices, priced from $9.95 to $15.95, include grilled duck breast with apple-raspberry chutney, seafood cannelloni, shrimp and scallops sauté, boneless beef fore-rib, veal Provençal, and grilled swordfish. Open Wednesday through Saturday from 9 to 11 a.m. for coffee; from 11:30 a.m. to 2:30 p.m. for lunch; and from 5:30 to 9:30 p.m. for dinner; plus Sunday brunch from 10:30 a.m. to 2:30 p.m. CC's accepted: AE, MC, and V.

The **Rustic Inn,** Talbottown Shopping Center, Easton (tel. 820-8212) is an affiliate of the restaurant of the same name in Annapolis. Situated in the midst of a string of shops, this restaurant can easily be overlooked, but is well worth finding, especially for families. The décor befits its name with a fascinating display of early farm implements, tobacco-growing tools, and old newspapers. Lunch, priced from $4.95 to $7.95, consists of hearty sandwiches (served on thin-sliced beer bread), salads, pastas, and hot dishes. A good way to start dinner is with a unique "raw bar sampler" (an array of oysters, shrimp, clams, and scallops for $5.95). Entrees, which run from $10.95 to $17.95, include scallops champignon (baked in marsala wine, with fresh mushrooms and grated Cheddar); oyster imperial and crab imperial; veal (marsala, piccata, or francese); chicken Divan; steak béarnaise; and "salty strip" (strip steak covered with freshly shucked sautéed oysters and mushrooms). All dishes include salad, breads, and potato. Lunch is served Tuesday through Saturday from 11:30 a.m. to 1:30 p.m.; dinner Tuesday through Thursday and on Sunday from 5 to 10 p.m., and on Friday and Saturday from 5 to 11 p.m. CC's accepted: AE, MC, and V.

Budget Meals

Seafood in the rough is the specialty of the **Crab Claw,** Navy Point by Maritime Museum, St. Michaels (tel. 745-2900), a favorite restaurant here for almost 25 years. There is no air conditioning, just ceiling fans and lots of bay breezes in this casual indoor and outdoor eatery on the lower end of the waterfront. The all-day menu ranges from $4.95 to $14.95, with most dishes under $10. The emphasis is on crabs, served all ways, from hot, steamed, and seasoned to fried hard crab, backfin crab cake, crab chowder, soft crab, "crab dogs" (on a roll), and crab imperial; other seafoods and fried chicken are also available. Open mid-March to mid-November, Tuesday through Saturday from 11 a.m. to 10 p.m.; lunch only on Mondays from April through Labor Day. No CC's accepted.

THE TOP ATTRACTIONS: Start with a stroll around Easton's **Historic District,** centered around Washington Street. Here you will find more than 40 beautifully restored and preserved public buildings, churches and private homes, all dating back to the 18th and 19th centuries. Centerpiece of the district is the **Talbot County Courthouse,** on Washington between Dover and Federal Streets. First built from 1710 to 1712, and then again in 1791, and remodeled in 1958, this impressive structure is the symbol of Easton. Among its claims to fame is the fact that its main portion was used as a sub-capital of Maryland for the Eastern Shore. In addition, a document called the "Talbot Reserves," adopted on the Courthouse grounds in May of 1774, was the first public airing of the sentiments that were later embodied in the Declaration of Independence.

Another highlight of the historic district is the **Talbot County Museum,** 25 S. Washington St. (tel. 822-0773), housed in a renovated 19th century building, under the auspices of the Historical Society of Talbot County. This is a three-gallery museum of permanent and changing exhibits depicting the rich heritage of the area. The museum also embraces a 1795 Quaker cabinetmaker's house and an 1810 brick Federal town house, both restored and situated around a Federal-style garden. In addition, a newly restored 1795 building serves as a museum shop with displays of handcraft work and unusual gifts. Open Tuesday through Saturday from 10 a.m. to 4 p.m.; and Sundays from 1 to 4 p.m. (except January and February). Admission charge is $2 per adult, and 50¢ for children.

Chesapeake Bay Maritime Museum, Mill Street, Navy Point (tel. 745-2916). Dedicated to the preservation of maritime history, this waterside museum consists of 18 buildings on six acres of land. Some of the highlights are an authentic 110-year-old Chesapeake Bay lighthouse, a comprehensive bay-craft collection, a boat restoration shop, an extensive waterfowl decoy collection, and an aquarium featuring life from local waters. There are also floating exhibits, including a skipjack and a restored log-bottom bugeye. Open daily from 10 a.m. to 5 p.m. (until 7 p.m. on Saturdays) in the summer months; and daily from 10 a.m. to 4 p.m. in other months (and weekends only January to mid-March). Admission charge is $4 for adults, $3 for college students, and $1 for children aged 6 to 16. Guided tours of the museum are conducted at 11 a.m. and 2 p.m. at no extra charge.

SHOPPING: The newest shopping development in Easton is **Talbottown,** a Colonial-style complex of shops, restaurants, and boutiques, adjacent to historic Pitt's Bridge, off N. Washington Street.

Antique shops are also plentiful in this region; one particularly worth noting is **Dover Antiques,** 7 E. Dover St., Easton (tel. 822-9190). It's a fascinating emporium of period and country furnishings, fine art, pottery, and brass, as well as duck decoys and guns. Open from 9:30 a.m. to 4 p.m. every day except Wednesday; CC's accepted: MC and V.

Seafaring clothes and collectibles are the specialty of the **Ship's Store,** 202 Bank St., Oxford (tel. 226-5113). One of the most well-stocked chandleries on the Eastern shore, this shop's wares range from nautical necessities and yachting apparel to gifts and games. Open all year, daily from 8 a.m. to 6 p.m. (closed Sundays in the winter). CC's accepted: MC and V.

Creative cooks flock to the **The Tender Herb,** 100 W. Division St., Oxford (tel. 226-5503) for all kinds of home-grown herbs and spices. This shop also stocks herb gifts, art, prints by regional artists, and carved duck decoys. Open daily from 10 a.m. to 5 p.m. (except Wednesdays and the months of January through mid-March). CC's accepted: MC and V.

SPORTS AND ACTIVITIES: Much of the focus of outdoor life in the Easton–St. Michaels–Oxford area is in and around the water. Whether you have your own boat or not, you'll always find lots of activity at **St. Michaels Town Dock Marina,** 305 Mulberry St., St. Michaels, (tel. 745-2400). You can rent sailboats from $18 for two hours; pedal boats for $5 a half hour, or $8 an hour; and runabouts with outboard engines for $55 for the first two hours and $15 for each hour thereafter. If you have your own craft, you can also dock it here. Overnight dockage charges are 80¢ per foot (with a $28 minimum) on weekdays and $1 per foot (with a $35 minimum) on weekends. Some smaller slips are also available and there is hourly dockage, with a $3 minimum. If you prefer terra firma, you can also rent bikes here at $3 a hour, $5 for two hours, or $16 for a full day. CC's accepted: AE, Ch, MC, and V.

At Oxford you can also rent Boston Whaler 15-foot power boats and other types of craft from **Crockett Brothers Boatyard,** Bank Street (tel. 226-5113). Rates start at $75 for a half day or $100 for a full day (MC and V accepted). In addition, the **Eastern Shore Yacht Charters,** Tilghman Street, Oxford (tel. 226-5000)rents sailboats from April to mid-November (No CC's accepted).

Hunting: Maryland's Eastern Shore is considered by many to be the finest duck- and goose-hunting region on the Atlantic Flyway. Every year, over 500,000 migratory game birds winter on the fields, marshes, rivers, tidal flats, and waters of Maryland. More than 20 local organizations conduct regular guided waterfowl hunts for Canada geese (late November through late January), ducks (late November through mid-January), and sea ducks (early October through mid-January). Some quail and pheasant hunting is also available. Goose hunting for two people ranges from about $240 to $260 a day plus licenses; and quail and pheasant rates are based on the number of birds caught. Two reliable sources of more information are **Richard D. Higgins,** Box 365, Neavitt, MD 21652 (tel. 301/745-2433) and **Tom Knox** at Grey Sky

Hunting Service, Route 1, Box 232A, Centreville, MD 21617 (tel. 301/758-2016).

Bicycle Rentals: In addition to bike rentals at St. Michaels Town Dock Marina, you can also get two-wheelers of all sorts (from 3-speeds to tandems) at **Oxford Mews,** 105 Morris St., Oxford (tel. 820-8222) daily except Wednesday, from $1.75 an hour with a $3.50 minimum; $7 a day; or $35 a week. No CC's accepted.

EVENTS: One of Easton's most noteworthy gatherings is the annual **Waterfowl Festival,** held each mid-November since 1971. This three-day event is attended by waterfowl artists, carvers, sculptors, photographers, collectors, and anyone with an interest in waterfowl. Activities include duck- and goose-calling contests, workshops, auctions of antique decoys, dog trials, and exhibits of waterfowl paintings, artifacts, books, carvings, duck stamps, and memorabilia. Admission charges are $5 for one day and $10 for 3 days; children under 10 with an adult are admitted free. There are small additional charges for auctions and calling contests; all proceeds go to waterfowl conservation causes. For complete information, contact the Waterfowl Festival, P.O. Box 929, Easton, MD 21601 (tel. 301/822-4567).

2. Cambridge

Founded in 1684, Cambridge is situated on the Choptank River, just off Chesapeake Bay. As Maryland's second-largest deep water port (after Baltimore), Cambridge today (pop.: 11,700) has an active harbor, supplying ocean-going vessels and coastal freighters with grain and seafood cargo.

For visitors, the Cambridge marina provides opportunities to stroll in grassy bayfront public parks. The town is also known for its restored Victorian buildings downtown and its scenic drives along the river. Gracious old homes line the shoreline, including a house originally built for Annie Oakley.

Twelve miles southeast of Cambridge is the Blackwater National Wildfowl Refuge, one of the chief wintering areas for Canada geese and ducks along the Atlantic Flyway.

VISITOR INFORMATION: Maps, walking-tour folders, and brochures on Cambridge are available from the **Dorchester County Tourism Office,** Dorchester Office Building, Room 107, Court Lane, P.O. Box 307, Cambridge, MD 21613 (tel. 301/228-3234) or from the **Chamber of Commerce Office,** 203 Sunburst Hwy. (Route 50), P.O. Box 205, Cambridge, MD 21613 (tel. 301/228-3575).

GETTING TO AND AROUND CAMBRIDGE: The best way to get around Cambridge is to bring your own car and then to walk the streets and the riverfront at your leisure. Walking-tour folders and driving routes are available from the tourist office and chamber of commerce.

Bus service: For those who prefer not to drive, regular bus service is operated to Cambridge by **Trailways** into its depot at 216 Dorchester Ave. (tel. 228-4626).

Car rentals: Two major firms are represented in Cambridge, **Avis,** 324 Sunburst Hwy. (tel. 228-4088) and **Hertz,** 206 Cedar St. (tel. 228-1688).

Taxis: Reliable services are operated by **Bay Country Cab** (tel. 228-7177), **Blue's Cab** (tel. 228-1449), **City Taxi** (tel. 228-6354), and **Mills Taxi** (tel. 228-0985).

WHERE TO STAY: Most of Cambridge's lodging facilities lie on the outskirts of the city, either along Sunburst Highway (Route 50) or eastward along the Choptank River. All choices fall into the moderate category.

Just eight blocks from downtown is the **Quality Inn,** Route 50 (Sunburst Highway), P.O. Box 311, Cambridge, MD 21613 (tel. 301/228-6900), near two major shopping areas, the Shoals Creek Mall and Cambridge Plaza. This modern two-story motel is decorated in a Colonial motif; each of the 60 rooms has one or two double beds, air conditioning, color TV, a direct-dial phone, and wall-to-wall carpeting. Doubles range from $40 to $45. Guest amenities include an outdoor pool, a coffeeshop (open from 7 a.m.), and The Shoals Restaurant (direct line: 228-7599), which serves dinner nightly. With a rustic country atmosphere, the restaurant features such varied dishes as flounder stuffed with cheese, crab cakes, lobster tails, seafood mixed platters, prime rib, steaks, and baked Virginia ham. The main courses are priced from $6.95 to $14.95 and include salad, vegetable, and rolls. Open Monday through Thursday from 5 to 9 p.m., Friday and Saturday from 5 to 10 p.m., and Sunday from 3 to 9 p.m. Major CC's are accepted.

A little farther south is the **Econo Lodge,** Route 50 and Oak Hill Rd., P.O. Box 1107, Cambridge, MD 21613 (tel. 301/221-0800 or toll-free 800/446-6900), near the road leading to the Blackwater National Wildlife Refuge. This modern two-story motel has 101 rooms, each with double or queen-size beds, wide picture windows, air conditioning, and color TV; some rooms also have individual Jacuzzis. Doubles range from $40.95 to $48.95. Facilities include an indoor swimming pool, an exercise room, and a sauna. CC's accepted: AE, MC, and V.

If you prefer a bed-and-breakfast home, then **Lodgecliffe,** 103 Choptank Terrace, Cambridge, MD 21613 (tel. 301/228-1760), is an ideal choice. Mrs. F. W. Richardson welcomes guests to her gracious old Victorian-style home on the Choptank River. Two rooms are available, with either twin or double beds, shared or private bath. Situated in a quiet residential section of Cambridge, this house also boasts a comfortable screened-in porch, the perfect spot to watch the sailboats breeze by. Doubles start at $50 and include a continental breakfast. Open all year; no CC's are accepted.

WHERE TO DINE: Both choices here fall into the moderate category.

After operating for more than 100 years as Clayton's Seafoods, it was a natural (and most welcome) progression when the same family opened a seafood restaurant in 1985. Located on the water, **Clayton's on the Creek,** 108 Commerce St. (tel. 228-7200), is a bright and modern restaurant, with indoor and outdoor deck seating. The same menu is in effect all day, for lunch and dinner. Light-meal choices range from seafood sandwiches (such as oyster poorboy, crab, or fish filet), crab burgers and beef burgers to seafood salads (priced from $3.95 to $5.95). Main course entrees (which range from $8.95 to $13.95) feature crabs (imperial, cakes, soft, hard, and lump meat), shrimp, oysters, clams, scallops, and seafood kebabs. Non-seafood dishes include ribs, steaks, and Eastern shore fried chicken. Clayton's is open daily year round, from 11:30 a.m. to 9 p.m. If you'd like to order some crabs-to-go from the adjacent seafood shop, you can get a dozen steamed crabs from $9 a dozen. CC's accepted: AE, MC, and V.

A Victorian theme prevails at the **Cator House,** 411 Muse St. (tel. 221-0300), a lovely old three-story home in the heart of downtown Cambridge. Fresh flowers, candlelight, and semi-classical music add to the gentle ambience of this country house restaurant. Lunch, priced from $3.95 to $7.95, features quiches, sandwiches, salads, and light entrees (like seafood casserole or chicken Dijon). The menu at dinner changes often but among the house favorites are lemon chicken, crab imperial, veal alla marsala, prime steaks, baked stuffed oysters, shellfish combinations, and calves' liver. All main courses are priced from $9.95 to $14.95, and are accompanied by freshly baked breads and muffins, apple butter and other relishes, and two vegetables. For early birds, a "twilight dinner" menu is also offered (from 5 to 6:30 p.m.) with a price range of $7.95 to $9.95 for such entrees as petite sirloin, crab cake, fried shrimp, and seafood au gratin. Lunch is served from 11:30 a.m. to 2:30 p.m., and dinner from 4:30 to 9 p.m., daily except Tuesday. CC's accepted: MC and V.

THE TOP ATTRACTIONS: Historic **High Street** is the focal point of Cambridge. This two-block area is lined with dozens of houses from the 18th and 19th centuries. Most were built as private homes, but some were inns, cottages, rectories, or meeting places. A free walking-tour brochure describing the history and architecture of these homes is available from the tourist office and the Chamber of Commerce.

Local county history is the focus of the **Dorchester Heritage Museum,** Horn Point Road, off Route 343, Cambridge (tel. 228-5530). This working museum contains maritime, farming, natural resource, and Indian exhibits, all reflecting the development of the area. Open from April 15th to October 30th, on Saturday and Sunday from 1 to 4:30 p.m., and by appointment. Free admission.

The **Meredith House,** 902 Greenway Drive at Maryland Avenue, Cambridge (tel. 228-7953), is a restored Georgian-style residence (1760) under the auspices of the Dorchester County Historical Society. The exhibits include a Governor's Room honoring six men from the county who became governors of Maryland. There is also an antique doll collection. The adjacent Neild building contains exhibits on local maritime and industrial development, and farm life including an original McCormick reaper (circa 1834). Other attractions on the property are formal gardens, an herb garden, a smokehouse filled with culinary wares, and a combination wheelwright/blacksmith shop. Open Friday from 9 a.m. to 3 p.m., and by appointment; admission charge is $2 per person.

Eight miles southwest of Cambridge is the **Old Trinity Church,** Route 16, Church Creek (tel. 228-2940 or 228-3161). Built circa 1675 and meticulously restored to its original condition, this is said to be the oldest Episcopal church in active use in the U.S. Open from March through December, on Wednesday through Saturday from 9 a.m. to 5 p.m. and on Sunday from noon to 5 p.m.; also in January and February on Sunday only from 11 a.m. to 4 p.m. No admission charge.

More than 300,000 visitors a year come to this area to see the **Blackwater National Wildlife Refuge,** Key Wallace Street, off Route 335, Church Creek (tel. 228-2677), about 12 miles southeast of Cambridge. Established in 1932, this is a 14,000-acre site of rich tidal marsh, freshwater ponds, and woodlands. It serves as a resting and feeding area for migrant and wintering wildfowl including huge flocks of Canada geese (numbering approximately 60,000) and ducks (exceeding 35,000) at the peak of fall migration, usually in November. The grounds are also the home of some endangered species such as the bald eagle, Delmarva fox squirrel, migrant peregrine falcon, and red-cockaded woodpecker. Facilities for visitors include an observation tower, a five-mile wildlife drive, and walking and biking trails. Self-guided walking- and driving-tour leaflets are also provided free of charge. A **Visitors Center** is open Monday through Friday from 7:30 a.m. to 4 p.m., and from 9 a.m. to 5 p.m. on Saturday and Sunday (except for weekends during June, July, and August; Labor Day Weekend; and Christmas). The wildlife trail and other outdoor facilities are open daily, all year, dawn to dusk. Admission is free.

3. Crisfield

Legend has it that Crisfield is built almost entirely on oyster shells. It's a likely story, considering that this tiny town (pop.: 2,900) has long laid claim to the title of "Seafood Capital of the World."

Tucked into the most southerly corner of Maryland's Eastern Shore along the Chesapeake, Crisfield has relied on the sea for its livelihood for over 100 years.

Stroll the city dock or marina—you'll see everything from the fish-laden head boats to the crab-picking, oyster-shucking, and seafood-packing plants. Better still, breathe in the salty air and amble into one of the town's restaurants to taste the maritime bounty.

Although many types of seafood are caught in the waters off Crisfield, crab is unquestionably king in this port—there is even a crab derby festival staged here at the end of each summer.

VISITOR INFORMATION: For brochures, maps, and all sorts of helpful information about Crisfield and the surrounding countryside, contact the **Somerset County Tourism Office,** Route 13, Princess Anne, MD 21853 (tel. 301/651-2968); or the **Crisfield Chamber of Commerce,** J. Millard Tawes Museum, Somers Cove Marina, Crisfield, MD 21817. (tel. 301/968-2500).

WHERE TO STAY: Choosing where to stay is easy in Crisfield. There are only two motels in town, both in the moderate category.

For almost 30 years, the **Pines Motel,** N. Somerset Avenue, P.O. Box 106, Crisfield, MD 21817 (tel. 301/968-0900), has offered fine lodging in a quiet residential setting of tall pine trees. The 28 modern ground-level units each have contemporary furnishings, two double beds, color TV, air conditioning, wall-to-wall carpeting, and views of the adjacent outdoor swimming pool and picnic area. Doubles range from $34 to $65; two efficiencies are available at $7 extra per room. Open all year; no CC's accepted.

Views of the water are part of the setting at the **Somers Cove Motel, Inc.,** R.R. Norris Drive, P.O. Box 387, Crisfield, MD 21817 (tel. 301/968-1900). Opened in 1979, this modern facility has 40 rooms, each with one or two double beds, color cable TV, a telephone, and air conditioning; some units also have balconies. Guest amenities include an outdoor heated swimming pool, patios, picnic tables, barbecue grills, boat-docking facilities, and ramps. Open all year, doubles range from $26 to $56; seven efficiencies are available for $7 extra per room. CC's accepted: MC and V.

WHERE TO DINE: The focus of attention here is simply seafood—and plenty of it. From crab omelets for breakfast and crab soup and crabwiches for lunch to crab cooked in a dozen different ways for dinner, this is the place to have your fill of this tasty and succulent crustacean. Most all restaurants in town serve breakfast, with choices usually priced from $1 to $5, starting at 5:30 to 6 a.m. to cater to the resident and visiting fishermen. Beer, wine, and cocktails are available at most restaurants, unless noted otherwise. Reservations are particularly necessary on weekends.

Moderately Priced Dining

The ideal place to watch the boats moving in or out of the harbor is the **Captain's Galley,** West Main Street at the City Dock (tel. 968-1636), a bright and contemporary-style restaurant with wide windows overlooking the water. The sweeping view is only the beginning; this is also the home of "the world's best crab cake." After tasting them (solid and succulent sweet crabmeat), we think you'll agree. This critically acclaimed dish is available at lunch or dinner, along with a host of other items from the sea's bounty. At lunch, the choice, priced from $1.95 to $4.95, includes sandwiches (such as the illustrious crab cake, or oyster fritter, crab imperial, soft crab, fish square, shrimp or tuna salad, as well as meats). The dinner entrees range from a gargantuan "Eastern Shore Dinner" (soft crab, crab cake, fish filet, scallops, shrimp, and oysters) to the famous crab cakes, crab imperial, crab au gratin, plus steaks and fried chicken. All entrees, which run from $4.95 to $14.95, include salad bar and vegetable. Open for lunch from 11:30 a.m. to 2:30 p.m., and for dinner from 5 to 10 p.m. CC's accepted: MC and V.

On the other side of the waterfront, you'll find **The Harbor View,** 8th Street and Broadway (tel. 968-3367), overlooking Somers Cove Marina. The décor here is also nautical with a wide-windowed emphasis on the vistas outside. Lunch, which concentrates on sandwiches, burgers, and salads, is priced from $1.95 to $4.95. Dinner entrees feature such seafood delights as whole stuffed flounder, clam strips, crab and shrimp bake, and seafood platter (shrimp, scallops, flounder, and crab cake), plus steaks, fried chicken, and smoked ham. The main courses, which run from $5.95 to $14.95, are all served with salad bar and vegetables. Lunch is served from 11 a.m. to 2 p.m., and dinner from 5 to 10 p.m. daily. CC's accepted: MC and V.

Although the **Watermen's Inn,** 9th and Main Streets (tel. 968-2119), does not boast such great water views, the food is equally good as The Harbor View's. Lunchtime fare, priced from $1.95 to $5.95, includes overstuffed sandwiches, burgers, and salads. Dinnertime choices focus on such specialties as baked stuffed jumbo soft crabs, crab cake fluff, regular crab cakes, baked stuffed flounder, jumbo fantail shrimp, crab Crisfield (scallops in butter topped with crab imperial), crab au gratin, fried chicken, imported baby back ribs, charbroiled steaks, and the "bull and the bay" (Delmonico steak and jumbo crab cake). Priced from $5.95 to $15.95, all dinners include salad and vegetable. Open daily for lunch from 11:30 a.m. to 2:30 p.m., for dinner Monday through Saturday from 5 to 10 p.m., and Sunday from 5 until 9 p.m. CC's accepted: Ch, MC, and V.

Budget Meals

Aunt Em's, Richardson Avenue at Route 413 (tel. 968-0353), is a favorite with families and with fishermen who come for an early breakfast and also to order a home-style and hefty boxed lunch ($5.95). Regular lunchtime selections, priced from $2 to $4, include pizzas, burgers, subs, salads, and sandwiches (ranging from oyster and crabwiches to cheese steaks). Featured dishes at dinnertime include crab and oyster dishes, plus stuffed flounder, prime ribs, fried chicken, steaks, and veal cutlet. The entrees run from $5.95 to $10.95, with most under $9. Open daily for lunch from 11:30 a.m. to 2:30 p.m.; and for dinner from 5 to 10 p.m. on weekdays, and from 5 to 11 p.m. on weekends. No CC's are accepted.

The **Barrel Wharf,** 1008 W. Main St. (tel. 968-2693), is located near the town dock but not on the water. Like most of the restaurants in town, lunches are priced under $5 and feature sandwiches and light fare. Dinner entrees, priced from $4.95 to $8.95, include crab and seafood dishes plus steaks, prime ribs, fried chicken, chicken imperial, pork chops, and ham steaks. The lunch counter is open Monday through Saturday from 11 a.m. to 2:30 p.m., the dining room is open Friday and Saturday evenings from 5 to 9 p.m., and Sunday from noon to 7 p.m. CC's accepted: MC and V.

THE TOP ATTRACTIONS: The **J. Millard Tawes Museum,** on the Somers Point Marina (tel. 968-2500), was founded in 1982 to honor a Crisfield-born former governor of Maryland. The headquarters of the Chamber of Commerce offices, this museum is a good place to start a walk around the town. The exhibits will give you useful background about the history of Crisfield and the development of the city's seafood industry; there is also a fascinating wildfowl woodcarving workshop on the premises. Open daily from 10 a.m. to 6 p.m. Admission charge is $1.

About 15 miles north of Crisfield on Route 13 is **Princess Anne,** a well-preserved Colonial town created in 1733. The highlight is the **Teackle Mansion,** built in 1801–1803 and patterned after a Scottish manor house. This was the residence of Littleton Dennis Teackle, an associate of Thomas Jefferson and one of the principal transoceanic shipping magnates of the 18th century. He also is credited with establishing Maryland's first public school system and the first public commercial bank on the American continent. With two entrances, one fronting the Manokin River and one facing the town, this grand house measures nearly 200 feet in length and is symmetrically balanced throughout. The house is open for guided tours every Sunday from 2 to 4 p.m. Some of the things you will see include elaborate plaster ceilings, mirrored windows, a seven-foot fireplace and beehive oven, American Chippendale furniture, Della Robia (fruit-designed) ceilings, a Tudor-Gothic pipe organ, an 1806 silk world map, and a 1712 family bible. The admission and tour charge is $2 per person.

In addition, about 20 other houses in this charming town open their doors one weekend a year (in mid-October), as part of the **Olde Princess Anne Days' celebration.** The structures, which are both private and public buildings, range from Federal, Victorian, Italianate, and Georgian mansions to cottages and the town's oldest inhabited dwelling (1705). Self-guided tour folders are provided to all visitors; fee for the day-long open-house event is $7 per person.

SHOPPING: Besides its copious crab, this area's other claim to fame is being the home of the **Carvel Hall Factory Outlet,** Route 413, Crisfield (tel. 968-0500), a division of Towle Manufacturing Company. Carvel Hall was started in 1895 when a young blacksmith hammered out his first seafood harvesting tools on a borrowed anvil. Today discounts of up to 50% are given on brand-name cutlery, made entirely in this Crisfield plant, plus hundreds of other nationally known gift items such as glassware, pewter, sterling silver, plated hollowware, brass, woodenware, and crystal. Open Monday through Saturday from 9 a.m. to 5 p.m. (closed Sundays and major holidays). CC's accepted: Ch, MC, and V.

SPORTS AND ACTIVITIES: The **Somers Cove Marina** (tel. 968-0925), a $30 million development built on the site of a farm started in 1663 by Benjamin Somers, is one of the largest facilities of its kind in Maryland. The marina is ultra-modern, able to accommodate all types of vessels from 10 feet to 150 feet. There are 272 boat slips, boat ramps, deluxe tiled showers, a laundry room, a swimming pool, boat storage, electricity and water, and a fuel dock.

Head boats leave from the marina and from the nearby town dock each day on **fishing trips** in pursuit of flounder, trout, spot, drum, and blues. For further information, walk along the waterfront and talk with the various boatmen on duty or call any of the following: **Capt. Curtis Johns** (tel. 623-2035); **Capt. James Landon** (tel. 968-0177); **Capt. Joe Asanovich** (tel. 957-2562); **Capt. Lionel Daugherty** (tel. 968-0947); or **Capt. John E. Sterling** (tel. 968-0975).

Most visitors to Crisfield also take cruises to the nearby off-shore islands of Smith and Tangier, featured in the 1986 National Geographic TV film, *Chesapeake Borne*. Both are approximately one hour away by boat and all vessels usually depart Crisfield's marina or town dock at 12:30 p.m., returning between 5 and 5:30 p.m. Reservations are not required, but are recommended in the busy summer months. Rates range between $9 and $14 for a round-trip boat ride, to $22 to $25 for a trip that includes sightseeing on the islands and a bountiful lunch.

For a trip to Smith Island, contact **Capt. Tyler** at Somers Cove Marina (tel. 425-2771); **Capt. Gordon Evans** at the Somers Cove Marina (tel. 425-5571), or **Capt. Jason** at the City Dock (tel. 425-5421 and 425-2351). Tangier Island Cruises can be arranged through **Capt. Rudy Thomas** at the City Dock (tel. 968-2338).

EVENTS: Ever since 1947, the **Annual Hard Crab Derby and Fair** has been a major fixture on the Crisfield calendar (each Labor Day weekend). Highlight of this three-day event is a crab race that has crustaceans from other states (as far as Hawaii) try to match the speed of the Eastern Shore crabs. Other activities include crab-cooking and crab-picking competitions, boat-docking contests, a tennis tournament, a dock party, a fishing tournament, a 10k marathon, a beauty contest, fireworks, a parade, and lots of crab eating. Daily admission charges are $3 for adults and $1 for children. For a full program and information, contact the **Crisfield Chamber of Commerce**, P.O. Box 215, Crisfield, MD 21817 (tel. 301/968-2500 or 968-2682).

4. Salisbury

Originally a settlement at the intersection of Indian trails, Salisbury has long been considered the crossroads of Chesapeake Country. Nestled on the banks of the Wicomico River, this "hub city" of today lies at the junction of Routes 13 and 50, equidistant between Cambridge and Ocean City.

In addition, Salisbury (pronounced: Salls-berry) is the largest city (pop.: 17,000) and second-largest port on Maryland's Eastern Shore, and it is also widely recognized as a major trade and transport center for the entire Delmarva Peninsula. An abundance of seafood and fresh produce of all kinds is part of everyday living in Salisbury.

As the business headquarters and home of Frank Perdue, Salisbury is also known as the "poultry capital of the world." No visit to this area is complete without a "down home"–style dinner of fried chicken, fresh crab, oyster fritters, hush puppies, and sweet-potato pie.

Equally positioned in the heart of wildfowl country, this bustling city is also home to the world's largest collection of contemporary and classic wildfowl art, the North American Wildfowl Carving and Art Museum.

VISITOR INFORMATION: Lodging and restaurant directories, brochures and walking-tour maps are available from the **Wicomico County Convention and Visitors Bureau,** Civic Center, Glen Avenue, Salisbury, MD 21801 (tel. 301/548-4914). This office also operates a tourism information hotline during non-business hours: 301/749-TOUR.

GETTING TO AND AROUND SALISBURY: Salisbury/Wicomico County Airport, Airport Road (tel. 548-5827), is the second-largest airport in Maryland. It is a gateway for scheduled passenger flights operated by **Henson (Piedmont Regional) Airlines** (tel. 749-0633), and **Allegheny Commuter** (tel. 749-7105).

Bus service: For those who prefer to travel by bus, **Greyhound** operates regular service into its Salisbury depot at Snow Hill Road and Lincoln Avenue (tel. 749-5502); and **Trailways** also serves Salisbury, with its terminal at 431 E. Main St. (tel. 749-4121).

Car rental: Four major car-rental firms are represented in the Salisbury area, all with desks at the Salisbury-Wicomico Airport: **Avis** (tel. 742-8566), **Dollar** (tel. 742-9448), **Hertz** (tel. 749-2235), and **National** (tel. 749-2450).

Taxis: Reliable taxi services are operated by the following companies: **Allied Taxi** (tel. 749-4500), **Gene's Taxi** (tel. 742-4444), **Ideal Taxi** (tel. 742-3200), and **Salisbury Taxi** (tel. 742-6666).

WHERE TO STAY: Most all of Salisbury's hotels are located along Route 13 (known locally as Business Route 13 or Salisbury Boulevard), a commercial strip that runs north-south along the eastern edge of downtown.

Mostly Moderate Choices

The closest hotel to the Historic District and the midtown Plaza area is the **Sheraton Salisbury Inn,** 300 S. Salisbury Blvd. (Route 13), Salisbury, MD 21801 (tel. 301/546-4400 or toll-free 800/325-3535). Delightfully located along the edge of Salisbury's Riverwalk Park, this recently renovated (1987) five-story property has 160 rooms (20 are non-smoking). Each room is furnished in contemporary style, with two double beds or a king bed, color cable TV, air conditioning, and a direct-dial phone. Doubles range from $72 to $90. Guest amenities include an indoor swimming pool, an exercise room and aerobic classes, a jogging trail, valet service, an entertainment lounge, and a multi-tiered restaurant with a view of the water. Lunch, priced from $4.95 to $8.95, focuses on quiches, salads, pita sandwiches, burgers, hot dishes, and vegetarian platters. Dinner entrees, which include such dishes as lobster Thermidor, almond chicken, red snapper Créole, steaks, prime ribs, and surf-and-turf, are priced from $8.95 to $15.95. Lunch is served from 11:30 a.m. to 2 p.m., and dinner from 5 to 10 p.m.; breakfast is also available from 6:30 to 11:30 a.m. Monday through Friday, and from 7 a.m. on weekends. All major CC's are accepted.

Six blocks north of downtown is the **Best Western Statesman,** 712 N. Salisbury Blvd., Salisbury, MD 21801 (tel. 301/749-7155 or toll-free 800/528-1234). This modern two-story motel has 94 units, each with double or king beds, color cable TV, air conditioning, and a direct-dial phone. Guest amenities include free morning coffee in the lobby, valet service, and a large outdoor swimming pool. Doubles range from $38 to $54. All major CC's are accepted.

Three miles north of the city is the **Holiday Inn,** Route 13 at Route 6, Box 415, Salisbury, MD 21801 (tel. 301/742-7194 or toll-free 800/HOLIDAY). This modern two-story hotel has 123 rooms, each with a double or king bed, color cable TV, air conditioning, and a direct-dial phone; many rooms also feature in-room steambaths. Rates for two people run from $52 to $78. Other facilities include an outdoor swimming pool and a restaurant, the Greenhouse Café, with a tropical garden atmosphere. Sandwiches, croissantwiches, omelets, salads, and burgers are featured at lunch, priced from $2.95 to $6.95. Dinner entrees, which run from $6.95 to $15.95, include steak imperial (filet mignon with crab imperial), crab cakes, seafood combination (crab cake, shrimp, oysters, scallops, and flounder), and shore-style fried chicken. All main courses are accompanied by a salad, potato, or vegetable. Lunch is served from 11:30 a.m. to 2:30 p.m., and dinner from 5 to 10 p.m.; breakfast is available from 7 a.m. daily. All major CC's are accepted.

Nearby is the **Lord Salisbury Motel,** Routes 13 and 6, Box 415AA, Salisbury, MD 21801 (tel. 301/742-3251 or toll-free 800/238-2564). This modern two-story motel, decorated with a Colonial motif, has 50 rooms, all situated back from the main highway in a sheltered setting with an outdoor swimming pool. Each unit has one or two double beds, color cable TV, an AM/FM radio, and air conditioning; some rooms have queen or king beds. The price for two people ranges from $39.95 to $45. Family rooms with kitchenettes are also available from $55. All major CC's are accepted.

Budget Range

A hunting-lodge atmosphere prevails in the lobby of the **Temple Hill Motel,** S. Salisbury Boulevard, Salisbury, MD 21801 (tel. 301/742-3284 or toll-free 800/ 835-7427, ext. 680), located two miles south of downtown, and within walking distance of the wildfowl museum. The décor is rich in knotty pine, with a selection of old Salisbury collectibles ranging from deer heads, ships' models, and oak chests to an antique cash register (1888). The 62 bedrooms, much more modern in style, each have one or two double beds, color TV, in-room coffee facilities, a direct-dial phone, and air conditioning. The property also includes an outdoor swimming pool, a barbecue patio, a playground, and a guest launderette; small pets are welcome. Doubles range from $30 to $52. Major CC's are accepted.

WHERE TO DINE: In the heart of seafood, chicken, and farm country, Salisbury has many fine restaurants at all price levels. Route 13 is the location of most of the fast-food eating spots, while the more distinctive restaurants are spread out from the heart of downtown well into the suburbs. The restaurants described here fall into the mostly moderate category.

Creative décor and cuisine are the keynotes at **Christophers,** 213-219 W. Main St. (tel. 546-3104), a new restaurant in the center of the historic downtown Plaza. An artist's pallette of colors sweeps over the furnishings and walls of this trendy plant-filled dining room. In addition to lunch and dinner, food is available throughout the day from breakfast to an all-day lounge menu of light items, priced from $2.95 to $6.95 (served until midnight). Lunch, priced from $4.95 to $7.95, focuses on salads, open sandwiches, burgers, quiches, omelets, crab balls, pastas, and vegetarian platters. The choices at dinner range from beef Wellington, steak Diane, and rack of lamb to seafood Newburg en croûte, tarragon-poached chicken, veal Oscar, and "seafood Margarette" (scallops and shrimp glazed with hollandaise). The entrees, which are accompanied by a salad and an array of seasonal vegetables, are priced from $11.95 to $18.95, with most under the $15 mark. Lunch is served from 11:30 a.m. to 2:30 p.m., and dinner from 5 to 10 p.m., Monday through Saturday. A breakfast buffet is available from 7 to 10 a.m., Monday through Friday. CC's accepted: AE, Ch, MC, and V.

Johnny and Sammy's, 670 S. Salisbury Blvd. (tel. 742-1116), can best be described as a Salisbury tradition. In business since 1946, this restaurant is actually two eateries in one, a diner-style coffeeshop and a gourmet restaurant with a Bavarian theme. The coffeeshop features sandwiches, burgers, and salads at lunchtime, in the $1.95 to $6.95 price range, and wholesome dinner entrees (beef, pork, veal, ham, and seafood dishes) for $6.95 to $12.95. The adjacent Alpine Room, decorated like a European chalet, offers a serene candlelight atmosphere with live music on Tuesday through Saturday evenings. Dinner selections, priced from $6.95 to $18.95, include roast Maryland turkey, fried chicken, crab au gratin, surf-and-turf, Eastern Shore combination (turkey, glazed ham, and crab cake), roast duckling, broiled seafood trio (filet of flounder, lobster tail, and stuffed shrimp), prime ribs, steaks, and skewered filet mignon flambé. All main courses come with soup or salad, potato, and a choice of vegetables. Light lunches (such as burgers, crab cakes, and salads), are also available in the Alpine Room from noon to 4 p.m. Dinner is served from 5 to 10 p.m., Monday through Thursday, and until 11 p.m. on Friday and Saturday. CC's accepted: AE, MC, and V.

A rustic atmosphere prevails at **The Shanty,** 835 E. Main St., (tel. 742-9901), located on Route 50 one-half mile east of downtown. Open for dinner only, this restaurant is known for its beef selections; all entrees are cooked and seasoned to order. In addition to aged prime rib and various cuts of steak, the menu features chicken Oscar, crab-stuffed flounder, shrimp scampi, surf-and-turf, and seafood Norfolk (lobster, shrimp, king-crab legs, scallops, and backfin of crab, sautéed in butter and topped with mushrooms). Prices range from $9.95 to $19.95, with most dishes under $15. All entrees come with salad, vegetable, and fresh-baked breads. Open from 4 to 10 p.m. on Sunday through Thursday, and until 11 p.m. on Friday and Saturday. CC's accepted: AE, Ch, MC, and V.

Budget

The ideal spot to try country-style fried chicken, hush puppies and sweet-potato biscuits with apple butter is **English's Family Restaurant,** 735 S. Salisbury Blvd. (tel. 742-8182). Founded in Salisbury in 1933, this is actually one of a chain of 16 restaurants of the same name along the Eastern Shore throughout Maryland and Delaware. Lunch choices, priced from $1.95 to $4.95, include chicken filet sandwiches, salads, burgers, omelets, and an assortment of seafood and meat sandwiches. Dinner offers a half dozen varieties of chicken, plus seafood, steaks, honey-glazed ham, and Maryland turkey. Entree prices, which range from $5.95 to $8.95, include vegetables, hush puppies, and sweet potato biscuits. Sweet-potato pie is also on the menu ($1.50 a slice). Open all day for lunch and dinner until 10 p.m. Sunday through Thursday, and until midnight on Friday and Saturday. CC's accepted: MC and V.

A Special Choice Outside of Town

One of the most delicious (and most fun) dining experiences in all of Maryland is **The Red Roost,** Clara Road, Whitehaven (tel. 546-5443). Located about a half hour's drive from Salisbury, you can reach this unusual restaurant by taking Route 50 west and then going south on Route 349 to Route 352 which leads to the Red Roost. It's well signposted, and so popular with the locals that you can usually just follow the patterns of traffic on this scenic country road, past the corn and soybean fields. Located in a refurbished (and now air-conditioned) Perdue chicken house, this restaurant was founded over a dozen years ago by the Palmer family who are still enthusiastically in charge. A relaxed casual atmosphere prevails and the only dress code is "comfortable." The menu includes whole steamed fish, steamed shrimp, fried chicken, porterhouse steak, and baby back ribs, but the overwhelming dinner choice is crab, crab, crab. Steamed in huge vats and dipped in a spicy blend of seasonings, crabs here are served as an all-you-can-eat experience, with mallets and picks provided to crack and extract the succulent crab from its shell. Piles of crabs are placed on the table (on the disposable brown paper tablecloth) and ample supplies of paper towels are supplied. The Palmers stroll around the restaurant and are eager to offer crab-cracking advice as are most of the other more-experienced patrons. If you don't mind working for your dinner, the Red Roost is a thoroughly delightful and delicious dining experience. Most meals come with hush puppies, shrimp or clam crisps, corn on the cob, and salad. Beer and wine and wine-based cocktails are also available. Open for dinner only, daily from mid-May to Labor Day; and Thursday through Sunday from April to mid-May and again from September through mid-November. Hours vary slightly in the different seasons, but are usually from 6 to 10 p.m. on week nights, from 4 or 5 to 10 p.m. on Saturdays, and from 4 to 8 or 9 p.m. on Sundays. Entree prices range from $5.95 to $10.95. No reservations are accepted, so get there early. CC's accepted: Ch, MC, and V.

THE TOP ATTRACTIONS: As a city chartered in 1732, Salisbury boasts two significant historic areas. The first is its two-block Downtown Plaza, located on Main Street in the heart of the city's business district. It is a picturesque open-air pedestrian walkway, lined with trees, fountains, and shops housed in Victorian buildings dating back to the 1880s.

Nearby is the six-block **Newtown Historic District,** Elizabeth Street and Poplar Hill Avenue, north of Salisbury Parkway (Route 50). The homes on these streets reflect architecture that spans two centuries, from Victorian and Queen Anne to Greek Revival, Colonial Revival, and Second Empire. Twenty-seven of these buildings are described in a self-guided walking-tour leaflet, available free of charge from the tourist office.

One of the few buildings in the Newtown district that is opened to the public is the **Poplar Hill Mansion,** 117 Elizabeth St. (tel. 749-1776). This is said to be the oldest property in the city, circa 1805, and is built of Georgian and Federal-style architecture. The prime features to see are a second-story Palladian window, several bull's-eye windows, dentil molding, and a fan-shaped window over the front doorway, as well as a fine collection of period furniture, original fireplaces and mantels, and large brass locks on the doors. Open free of charge on Sunday from 1 to 4 p.m., and by appointment.

Two miles south of the city on the campus of the Salisbury State College is the **North American Wildfowl Art Museum,** Holloway Hall, 655 S. Salisbury Blvd. (tel. 742-4988). This is a prime showcase for displays of decoys of ducks and geese and carvings of songbirds. The exhibits include an evolutionary history of decoy-making, antique hunting decoys, modern carved decoratives, paintings, and sculpture of wildfowl art, as well as prints of wild birds. The museum also sponsors an annual (October) workshop for woodcarvers; and an on-premises shop also sells unique wildfowl-related gifts. Open Tuesday through

Saturday from 10 a.m. to 5 p.m., and Sunday from 1 to 5 p.m. Admission charge is $1 for adults and free for children under 12 years of age. The shop accepts MC and V.

NIGHTLIFE: A year-long performing-arts program of drama, chamber music, symphony concerts, ballet, jazz, and top-name entertainment is coordinated by the Salisbury Wicomico Arts Council, based at the new **Wicomico Youth and Civic Center,** Glen Avenue, P.O. Box 884, Salisbury, MD 21801 (tel. 301/543-ARTS). Tickets range from $3 to $20, depending on the event and the venue (which can range from hotels and high schools to the main hall of the 6,000-seat Civic Center itself). The **Civic Center box office** (direct line: 301/742-3201) is open from 9 a.m. to 5 p.m., and on weekends when there is an event scheduled. CC's accepted: MC and V.

SHOPPING: Since wildlife art is a trademark of this part of Maryland, the Salisbury area is home to many artists specializing in local bird and water scenes, including award-winning F. Wayne Taylor. Wayne's studio is located next to the Red Roost Restaurant, Clara Road, Whitehaven (direct line: 873-2658), about a half hour from Salisbury. If you are dining at the Red Roost (and everyone should), then don't miss visiting Wayne's studio before or after dinner. You'll find him hard at work, Friday and Saturday from 5 to 10 p.m., and on Sunday from 5 to 9:30 p.m. CC's accepted: Ch, MC, and V.

With its proud Victorian heritage, Salisbury is also alive with good antique shops. One of the most interesting is **The Windfall,** on the Downtown Plaza (tel. 742-6681), a haven for antique silver, brass, china, crystal, furniture, prints, and paintings. Open Monday through Saturday from 10 a.m. to 5 p.m. CC's accepted: Ch, MC, and V.

SPORTS AND ACTIVITIES: Outdoor activity in Salisbury is centered in **City Park** (tel. 548-3188), a delightful sylvan setting in the southwest corner of town near the Civic Center. Surrounded by shady ancient pines, the park winds around Beaver Creek Dam, part of the south prong of the Wicomico River. Facilities include an outdoor zoo, footbridges, a picnic island with gazebo, jogging and walking trails, duck ponds, and a horseshoe pavilion. There are four tennis courts on the grounds, for use free of charge. Paddleboats are also available on the waterways ($3 for a half hour and $5 for an hour), daily from June through Labor Day, and on weekends from Easter until cold weather. In the evenings, music concerts are held every Sunday at 7 p.m.

Walkers and joggers also enjoy Riverfront Walk, the path that meanders along Salisbury's downtown district.

CHILDREN'S CORNER: The **Salisbury Zoological Park,** 750 S. Park Dr. (tel. 742-2123) is a 12-acre open-air zoo in the heart of City Park. Appealing to all ages, this zoo houses more than 200 mammals, birds, and reptiles in naturalistic habitats among shade trees and exotic plantings. Major exhibits include spectacled bears, monkeys, jaguars, bison, bald eagles, and waterfowl, all native to North, South, and Central America. There is no admission charge to the zoo, which is open from 8:30 a.m. to 7:30 p.m. daily, Memorial Day to Labor Day; and from 8:30 a.m. to 4:30 p.m. during the rest of the year.

5. Ocean City

The narrow peninsula known as Ocean City is Maryland's star attraction along the Atlantic. A ten-mile strip of white sandy beach, Ocean City is a lively and well-developed vacationland, sandwiched in between the "quiet" Delaware resorts of Fenwick Island and Bethany Beach to the north and the equally tranquil Assateague Island and the Virginia border to the south.

In addition to its seafront side to the east, Ocean City is also rimmed on its west by a series of picturesque bays with memorable names like Assawoman, Montego, Isle of Wight, and Sinepuxent. To add to its glories as a summer mecca, Ocean City's wide expanse of free beach is complimented by a three-mile-long boardwalk, lined with hotels, restaurants, shops, and amusements. It's no wonder that the city's small resident population of 7,000 easily swells to over 200,000 on July and August weekends.

Like other destinations in Maryland, Ocean City also has a proud history. Officially opened as a beach resort on July 4, 1875, Ocean City was first reached by stagecoach from Salisbury, Philadelphia, and Baltimore. Turn-of-the-century sun-seekers thought nothing of long train journeys from as far away as Wilmington to reach Ocean City's shores. In 1910, when the first permanent boardwalk was laid, its length was just five blocks; today it spans 27 blocks.

The beach itself has been developed to a 145-block length. The lower section, which was the original Ocean City, is home to the boardwalk, the amusement parks, and most of the older hotels. The upper section, from about 40th Street to 145th Street, is rich in modern motels and rows of towering condominiums.

One road, Route 1 (otherwise known as Coastal Highway) spans the entire length of the beach from north to south. This road divides Ocean City into two halves, the ocean front and the bay side. The city is connected to the Maryland mainland by two bridges, the Route 50 bridge (which crosses over into First Street at the southern tip of Ocean City) and the Route 90 bridge (which brings you midway into the city at 62nd Street).

VISITOR INFORMATION: Ocean City has a very active and enthusiastic tourist office that stocks all kinds of helpful information, maps, and brochures. It is located right in the heart of town and is open daily all year, with extended evening hours on summer weekends. Be sure to head for the **Ocean City Visitors and Convention Bureau,** 4001 Coastal Highway, Ocean City, MD 21842 (tel. 301/289-8181). The bureau also publishes a *Daily Info* sheet, a "what's on" listing of events and sports schedules; this handy one-page bulletin is distributed free at hotels, restaurants, and other public places.

GETTING TO OCEAN CITY: By Plane: The **Ocean City Municipal Airport,** Stephen Decatur Memorial Road, off Route 611 (tel. 289-0927), is located three miles west of town. This facility handles regularly scheduled commuter flights to and from Baltimore and Cumberland via **Cumberland Airlines** (tel. 304/738-8640 or toll-free 800/624-0070).

By Bus: Trailways has daily services into Ocean City from points north and south, stopping at 2nd and Philadelphia Streets (tel. 289-9307).

GETTING AROUND OCEAN CITY: Public Transport: Regular daily bus services are operated up and down Coastal Highway (Route 1) by **The Ocean City Municipal Bus Service,** 65th Street and the Bay (tel. 723-1606/7). In the summer months, the schedule is every ten minutes, 24 hours a day. From October 1st until Memorial Day, buses run every half hour. The fare is 75¢, one way, and exact change is required.

Boardwalk Train: Starting at South First Street, a tram-type train runs along the boardwalk every 20 minutes up to 27th Street. The trip lasts about a half hour and is an ideal way to get an orientation on the hotels, restaurants, and shops along the boardwalk. You can also signal the conductor by raising your hand and disembark at any point you wish before the end of the line. The fare is 75¢ and you pay as you board after the train arrives at the starting point. If there is room, the tram will also pick up new passengers along the route, but the fare remains the same. The train runs from Memorial Day through Labor Day.

Car Rental: The car-rental firms represented in this area include **Avis,** 60th Street and Coastal Highway (tel. 524-2824), **Dollar,** Ocean City Airport (tel. 289-2421), and **Hertz,** Ocean City Airport (tel. 289-8355).

Taxis: If you need a ride, call **O.C. Cab Co.** (tel. 289-8164) or **Resort Taxi** (tel. 524-9339).

Parking: Parking is difficult, particularly at the height of the season. Many public facilities, such as shopping centers and restaurants, usually offer ample free parking to patrons. There are also public parking lots in certain areas near the beach such as the Inlet on South First Street. Otherwise, parking is by meter on the streets. Most hotels and motels have their own parking lots or garages and supply their guests with parking permits that usually allow one free parking space per room.

Bay Cruises: Since Ocean City is surrounded by the waters of the ocean and bay, sightseeing by boat is especially popular. Most vessels operate from Memorial Day weekend to September. Daytime excursions usually last between 1½ to two hours. Some of the services available are the *Bay Queen,* Talbot Street Pier, Talbot Street and the Bay (tel. 289-9125), which cruises the Sinepuxtent, Assawoman, and Isle of Wight Bays, departing at 10:30 a.m., 12:15 p.m., and 2 p.m.; the fare is $5 for adults and $3 for children. Cruises to Assateague Island are operated on board *The Misty,* by Bahia Marina, 21st Street and the Bay (tel. 289-7438), departing at 2 and 4 p.m., at $6 for adults and $4 for children.

In addition, the *Ocean City Belle,* an authentic paddlewheeler, is the vehicle for 1½-hour bay sightseeing cruises, at 1:30, 4, and 7 p.m.; the cost is $7 for adults and $3.50 for children. On Wednesday and Saturday evenings, 2½-hour dinner-dance cruises are also offered at $27.50 per person (reservations necessary). Contact the *Belle* at Shanty Town Village, on the west side of Route 50 Bridge (tel. 289-5400).

Other evening and sunset cruises of the bay and ocean coast, usually priced at $4 for adults and $2 for children, are operated on *The Angler,* docked at Talbot Street on the Bay (tel. 289-7424), at 7 and 9 p.m.; on *The Captain Bunting,* 307 Dorchester St. and the Bay (tel. 289-6720), at 7:30 p.m.; on *The Mariner,* at Talbot Street Pier, Talbot Street and the Bay (tel. 289-9125), at 7:30 p.m.; on *Miss Ocean City,* leaving from 308 First St. and the Bay (tel. 289-8234), at 7:10 and 8:55 p.m.; on *The Taurus* at South Harbour Road, Route 1, West Ocean City (tel. 289-2525), at 8 p.m.; and on board *The Misty* and *Taylor Maid,* out of Bahia Marina, 21st Street on the Bay (tel. 289-7438), at 7 p.m. Most of these firms accept MC and V.

WHERE TO STAY: With more than 8,500 hotel rooms (and 6,000 condo units), a description of Ocean City's lodgings could easily fill a fat guidebook on its own. It is impossible to do justice to all of the hotels and motels in this short section, but we'll give you some of the highlights. We'll tell you about some of the large and the small, the old and the new, and a few on the ocean and a few on the bay, to help you get your bearings. If you have never been here before, you might find it best to pick a place to stay by relying on your favorite hotel chain (Best Western, Econo Lodge, Holiday Inn, Quality Inn, and Sheraton are all well represented here).

First, here are some helpful ground rules for Ocean City accommodations: Most properties depend on a five-month season, and the summer months (especially July and August) command the highest rates, often with supplements on weekend nights as well. In many cases, minimum stays of two or three nights may apply, so it is always best to check the rates in advance. Reservations are certainly a must in the summer and a wise idea at other times.

In almost all cases, the larger hotels offer money-saving package plans, particularly in the late-spring or early-autumn seasons, when Ocean City can be equally as lovely as the peak of summer (and a lot less crowded). Although it is a great treat to overlook the ocean, rooms with partial or no views of the water often cost considerably less than those with "oceanfront" prices.

Luxury Lodgings

Of all the hotel chains in this beachfront community, we'll mention only one because it is in a class by itself—the **Sheraton Fontainebleau Inn and Spa,** 10100 Ocean Highway, Ocean City, MD 21842 (tel. 301/524-3535 or toll-free 800/325-3535). It is located right on the ocean at 101st Street, far from the boardwalk and in the midst of the residential high-rise condo section of Ocean City. Recently (1986) renovated to the tune of $5 million, this 16-story tower has 250 oversized rooms and suites, all with views of the ocean and bay. Each room has also its own private balcony, brand new contemporary furnishings, plush wall-to-wall carpeting, color TV, a direct-dial phone, a refrigerator, and air conditioning. Guest amenities include restaurants and lounges overlooking the ocean, evening entertainment, a beach-side terrace, valet services, an arcade of shops, a convention center, a video game room, an indoor heated pool, and a complete spa with Jacuzzi, workout room, steam room, sauna, whirlpool, and sun rooms. In many ways, this hotel is a complete resort in itself. Rates for rooms with two double beds range from $50 to $175; studios with king beds and sleep sofas from $90 to $160; and bilevel suites with kitchenettes from $120 to $455 a day. All major CC's are accepted.

Moderate Choices

One of the newest (1987) hotels on the ocean is the **Dunes Manor,** 28th Street and the Ocean, Ocean City, MD 21842 (tel. 301/289-1100). Situated on its own stretch of beach just north of the boardwalk, this hotel is designed with a Victorian façade including a grand open porch with rockers and a private mini-boardwalk facing the ocean. Each of the 171 modern rooms has "ocean-front" views with a balcony, two double beds, a refrigerator, cable color TV, and a direct-dial telephone. The guest amenities include an indoor/outdoor pool, a Jacuzzi, an exercise room, and a sundeck. Doubles range from $55 to $75; and kitchenette suites run from $100 to $135. Open year round; all major CC's are accepted.

Another modern property on the beach north of the boardwalk with a striking exterior is **Castle in the Sand,** Ocean Front at 37th Street, Ocean City, MD 21842 (tel. 301/289-6846). As its name implies, this hotel has a mock-castle look, complete with turrets. Open from April through October, there are 36 regular rooms and 137 efficiency units; a standard hotel room with two double beds is priced from $40 to $90, and oceanfront efficiencies with balconies are priced from $60 to $125 a day. All units have direct-dial phones, color cable TV, air conditioning, and modern furnishings. Outdoor amenities include an Olympic-size swimming pool, a private beach, and an oceanfront patio. CC's accepted: AE, Ch, MC, and V.

Moving down the beach to the lower end of the boardwalk, you'll find a lovely Victorian hotel that epitomizes the charm of Ocean City of earlier days, the **Majestic,** on the Ocean at 7th Street, Ocean City, MD 21842 (tel. 301/289-6262). Open only from mid-May through mid-September, this well-kept four-story hotel has a picture-window lobby that looks out over the ocean. Its adjacent outside porch hugs the boardwalk as guests relax in vintage rocking chairs to enjoy the sea breezes. Each of the 57 up-to-date bedrooms has wall-to-wall carpeting, ceramic tile baths, color cable TV, and a direct-dial telephone. Other guest facilities include a heated pool, a sun terrace, and an elevator. Doubles with oceanfront views are priced from $44 to $75; and rooms not directly on the sea cost from $40 to $70. CC's accepted: Ch, MC, and V.

This mid-boardwalk point is also home to several other old-world-style properties, such as the **Phillips Beach Plaza Hotel,** 13th Street and Boardwalk, P.O. Box K, Ocean City, MD 21842 (tel. 301/289-9121 or toll-free 800/638-5920). Open year round, this hotel boasts an elegant Victorian lobby with crystal chandeliers, wrought-iron fixtures, and graceful statuary, plus a long open porch overlooking the ocean, and a top-notch on-premises seafood restaurant, Phillips By the Sea (see "Where to Dine" below). For guest comfort, the sleeping accommodations are housed in an attached modern five-story bedroom block with 60 rooms and 26 apartments (with an elevator). Each room has air conditioning, color TV, an AM/FM radio, and a direct-dial phone. Doubles with oceanfront views are priced from $36 to $88; rooms facing in other directions go from $33 to $80; and efficiency apartments average $80 to $110 a day in the high season or $45 to $60 in the off-season. Major CC's are accepted.

One of the city's landmarks, dating from 1930, is the **Commander Hotel,** on the Ocean at 14th Street, Ocean City, MD 21842 (tel. 301/289-6166). This gracious old Victorian treasure has been renovated and kept up-to-date over the years. Each of its 93 guest bedrooms has twin, double, or king beds, color TV, air conditioning, and a telephone. Doubles range from $60 to $90 a day, depending if the view is full oceanfront, partial, or northern exposure. Other guest amenities include an elevator, a heated swimming pool, a sun terrace, a shuffleboard court, and an on-premises dinner theater in the summer evenings (see "Nightlife" below). Open April to October; CC's accepted: MC and V.

A colonial décor and atmosphere prevails at **Harrison Hall,** Boardwalk and 15th Street, P.O. Box 160, Ocean City, MD 21842, (tel. 301/289-6222 or toll-free 800/638-2106). Open from April through October, this 97-room hotel has a long front porch with rocking chairs, directly on the boardwalk. Each modernized guest room has Posturepedic bedding, color TV, an AM/FM radio, air conditioning, and wall-to-wall carpeting. Other amenities include an Olympic-size swimming pool, an elevator, and complimentary coffee, fresh fruit, and newspapers each morning in the lobby. Rates range from $35 to $65 for side rooms with one double bed; from $45 to $85 for a room with two double beds; and from $45 to $90 for an oceanfront room with a queen-size bed. All major CC's are accepted.

If you prefer a motel, then a good choice is the **Sandyhill,** 18th Street at Boardwalk, P.O. 427, Ocean City, MD 21842 (tel. 301/289-6151). This modern two-story facility faces the beach and has units with direct ocean views and some at side angles. Open from March to October, there are 28 motel bedrooms and 30 efficiencies. Rates range from $34 to $80 for an oceanfront double with a kitchenette, and $25 to $65 for standard rooms not facing the ocean. All units have two double beds, air conditioning, color TV, wall-to-wall carpeting, and a direct-dial phone; some rooms also have a balcony. Outdoor facilities include a swimming pool and a tropical patio with a gazebo. CC's accepted: Ch, MC, and V.

A motel not directly on the beach but a block away is **The Tides,** 7100 Coastal Highway, P.O. Box 540, Ocean City, MD 21842 (tel. 301/524-7100 or toll-free 800/638-1600). One of the newest motels along the strip (opened in 1986), this three-story property is on 71st Street along the upper end of the main north-south artery. Just as it is one block from the ocean, if you cross the Coastal Highway, it is also one block from the bay. Each of the 54 units is a fully equipped efficiency with a kitchenette, air conditioning, carpeting, color cable TV, and a telephone. An outdoor pool is also part of the amenities. Doubles range from $38 to $70. Open from May to mid-September; CC's accepted: Ch, MC, and V.

Budget Range

A small motel on the bayside of the highway is **Taka-A-Mitsia,** 401 11th Street, Ocean City, MD 21842 (tel. 301/289-3200). Furnished with an Oriental décor, each of the nine rooms enjoys open views of the bay and a private terrace, as well as full kitchen facilities, two double beds, wall-to-wall carpeting, color cable TV, and air conditioning. Small pets are welcome, which is unusual in most lodgings in this area, and boat slips are available for motel guests who arrive by water ($10 a day). Rates range from $25 to $45. Open all year; no pool, no in-room phones, and no CC's are accepted.

Just a block from the ocean at 12th Street is the **King Charles Hotel,** 1209 Baltimore Avenue, Ocean City, MD 21842 (tel. 301/289-6141). This small (21 rooms) and friendly facility offers air-conditioned rooms, each with ceramic tiled bath and shower, but no in-room phones or televisions. Open April to November, doubles go from $35 to $48. CC's accepted: MC and V.

WHERE TO DINE: At last count, there were well over 100 restaurants in Ocean City, plus at least 60 fast-food establishments. Understandably, seafood is a favorite here and, for the most part, a casual atmosphere prevails, although it is always wise to make a reservation in the better restaurants and to check on the dress code. During the summer months, restaurants are rarely closed. Some start as early as 5 a.m., dishing up hearty breakfasts for fishermen, and continue serving meals right through until 10 or 11 p.m. Unless we give specific hours, you can be fairly certain that lunch will start at 11 a.m. or 11:30 a.m. and continue throughout most of the afternoon and then a dinner menu will be in effect from 5 p.m. until closing. Most all restaurants have full-bar facilities. Just to be safe, you should obtain a copy of the Ocean City Visitor Bureau's guide to restaurants; it gives descriptions, hours of opening, and price guidelines for at least 50 of the best eateries.

Top Choices

The Phillips seafood restaurants that are so famous in Baltimore, Norfolk, and Washington, D.C., all owe their origin to a small crab carry-out that was started here by Shirley and Brice Phillips in 1956. That family enterprise is today known as **Phillips Crab House,** 21st Street and Philadelphia Avenue (tel. 289-

6821), an Ocean City tradition and the town's largest restaurant, seating 1,300 people in 11 different dining rooms. Like the menu of 30 years ago, seafood is the focus and crab is still king. Lunchtime choices, which are priced from $4.95 to $7.95, include crab sandwiches and salads. Dinner entrees offer an extensive crab repertoire including crab au gratin and imperial; crab cakes; soft-shell crabs; crab with Smithfield ham; and special "Phillips crab bounty" (crab vegetable soup, crab cake, soft-shell crab, petite crab imperial, and souvenir crab mallet). Lovers of salmon, shrimp, flounder, scallops, oysters, and lobster will also find their favorites here, prepared in a variety of ways, as well as steaks, filet mignon, and fried chicken. Prices range from $8.95 to $23.95, with the majority under $15; and all main courses are served with a choice of two vegetables or a salad. Open April through October; reservations are not taken, so get there early. CC's accepted: AE, Ch, MC, and V.

In recent years, Ocean City visitors have enjoyed the Phillips seafood cuisine so much that two additional restaurant locations were opened to serve the demand. In 1973 business began at **Phillips by the Sea,** in the Phillips Beach Plaza Hotel, Oceanfront at 13th Street and the Boardwalk (tel. 289-9121); and in 1977 came the addition of **Phillips Seafood House,** 141st St. and Coastal Highway (tel. 250-1200). Both of these restaurants are open year round and maintain similar menus (and prices) as the 21st Street landmark.

One of the loveliest places to dine while watching the sun set is **The Hobbit,** 81st Street and the Bay (tel. 524-8100). Open all year, this restaurant is right on the bay, and not too big (seating for about 160 plus outside decks). The emphasis is on continental cuisine, and lacy tablecloths dominate the décor. Lunch, priced from $4.95 to $6.95, features such choices as seafood pasta, burgers, quiches, salads, stews, and crab-stuffed artichoke hearts. Dinner entrees, priced from $12.95 to $18.95, include flounder stuffed with lobster; rainbow trout stuffed with shrimp and crab; steak Diane; duck à l'orange; and shrimp or scallops francese. Open every day year round. CC's accepted: Ch, MC, and V.

Moderately Priced Dining

Ever since 1938, **Capt. Bill Bunting's Angler,** Talbot Street and the Bay (tel. 289-7424 and 289-6980), has been a favorite restaurant on the marina of Ocean City. With a rustic and nautical décor, this spacious restaurant features an air-conditioned main dining room plus an outdoor patio deck overlooking the bay. It's an ideal spot to see the boats sailing by or to watch the fishermen bring back their bounty. Lunch, priced from $3.95 to $7.95, focuses on tempting raw bar selections, fishwiches, salads, and burgers. The extensive dinner menu includes coquilles St-Jacques, shrimp scampi, flounder francese, surf-and-turf, roast turkey, fried chicken, and a popular "admiral's feast" that features a little of everything (flounder, scallops, shrimp, crab cakes, oysters, and lobster). All dishes, priced from $9.95 to $22.95, come with soup, salad bar, and vegetable. In addition, Capt. Bill provides a free evening cruise of the bay at 7 or 9 p.m. as part of the dinner price. For early risers, this is one of the restaurants that opens its doors at 5 a.m. for breakfast and continues serving meals throughout the day and night. CC's accepted: Ch, MC, and V.

Fager's Island, 60th Street In the Bay, (tel. 524-5500), is not actually in the water, as its address implies, but it is perched on the edge of the bay and surrounded by three outside decks, a pier, and a gazebo. With wide wrap-around windows, this establishment was made for watching sunsets and is very popular at cocktail hour, although food is served all day. Overstuffed sandwiches and heaping salads are available from 11 a.m. until 10 p.m. Serious dining is on tap from 5:30 p.m. with a menu that has a Cajun slant: blackened redfish and blackened prime rib, as well as char-grilled scallops with tarragon sauce, and a shrimp and ribs combination. Priced from $11.95 to $23.95, all main courses include salad and vegetable; an award-winning wine cellar also offers more than 400 labels. Most major CC's are accepted.

Moving away from the bay, you'll get a spectacular open view of the ocean and nearby Assateague Island at **Harrison's Harbor Watch,** Boardwalk South overlooking Inlet (tel. 289-5121). As its address states, this new (1986) restaurant is situated at the boardwalk's southernmost point before crossing the inlet. It's a large complex (seating 400), with various levels of seating, tile floors, lots of leafy plants, and a Colonial-nautical décor. Lunch, from $2.95 to $7.95, emphasizes light fare (sandwiches and salads). A bountiful raw bar is the focus of attention at dinner, and a popular appetizer choice is a "sampler platter" ($20.95 for two) with such delights as steamed spiced shrimp, oysters baked in champagne, crab claws, and clams casino. Dinner entrees, priced from $7.95 to $17.95, include hickory-barbecued shrimp, whole local lobster, lobster linguine, crab legs, swordfish with crab imperial, steaks, and fried chicken. All main courses come with salad and vegetables. Open all year. CC's accepted: MC and V.

A lovingly restored 100-year-old Victorian building known locally as "Mount Vernon" is the home of **Kate Bunting's Seafood House,** 10 Talbot St. (tel. 289-1441). This restaurant is located on a quiet side street, just off the boardwalk. There are no water views but a gentle old-world ambience prevails both in the upstairs dining room and on the front porch open-air deck. The menu is rather simple, just crabs, scallops, shrimp, clams, oysters, and lobster tails, all prepared to suit your desires, whether it be au gratin, barbecued, with imperial sauce, or au natural. Chicken and steaks are also available for non-fish eaters. The price range is $6.95 to $19.95, with most choices under $15, and that includes two vegetables. Open year round. Major CC's are accepted.

Although it is on the bay side of the road, views are not the attraction at the **BonFire,** 71st Street and Coastal Highway (tel. 524-7171). This is a large (seats 475), elaborately decorated restaurant with a choice of four different rooms and two totally different menus. With a huge oval bar in the center of the complex, the eclectic furnishings include captain's chairs, plush leatherette banquettes, leaded- and etched-glass windows, gas lanterns, original oil paintings, and tree-size plants. Open only for dinner, the BonFire has been known for over 15 years for its charcoal-broiled steaks, aged prime ribs, and beef Wellington, as well as its baby back ribs, crab-stuffed chicken, duckling à l'orange, and veal dishes. A recent innovation is its additional menu of 25 Chinese dishes ranging from Szechuan shrimp and pepper steak to roast pork with snow peas and lobster Cantonese. Both menus fall into the $10.95 to $23.95 range, and both come with appropriate accompaniments. The music of a live band is also featured seven nights a week. Open year round; all major CC's are accepted.

One of the most creative kitchens in Ocean City belongs to **The Bayside Skillet,** 77th Street and Coastal Highway (tel. 524-7950), a place you would probably pass by unless you were in the mood for a crêpe or omelet. While it's true that crêpes, omelets, and light dishes are served throughout the day ($2.95 to $8.95), this modern restaurant also offers a wide range of other dinner entrees, such as baked shrimp and ratatouille provençal; seafood mornay (flounder, scallops, shrimp, and crab); filet of flounder stuffed with crabmeat and avocado; and shrimp scampi. The crêpes are also worth a try at any hour: with fillings such as coquilles St-Jacques; chicken with mushrooms in Madeira sauce; or bacon, spinach, and hollandaise. Priced from $6.95 to $14.95, all entrees are served with fresh vegetables and salad. This wide-windowed eatery also features tall beamed ceilings, knotty-pine walls, pink linens, hanging plants, and some of the best sunset views along the bay. Open year round, 24 hours a day; BYOB. CC's accepted: MC and V.

Budget Meals

All-you-can-eat meals are featured at the **Mug and Mallet,** Second and Boardwalk (tel. 289-5995). Complete crab dinners average $9.95 and pancake breakfasts cost $3.95. Seating is indoors and outside, in a casual atmosphere; beer and wine are available. There are two other locations: at 15th Street and Boardwalk (tel. 289-5901) and at 94th Street Plaza (tel. 524-5959). All major CC's are accepted.

Nearby is **The Paul Revere Smorgasbord,** Second Street and the Boardwalk (tel. 524-1776). With eight Colonial-style dining rooms, this huge restaurant can accommodate up to 700 diners. One price ($6.99) also prevails here; with a buffet array of more than 100 items ranging from soups, salads, roast beef, turkey, fried chicken, ribs, seafood, and pasta to a tempting dessert bar. Open from 4 to 10 p.m., April through October. Beer and wine served. CC's accepted: MC and V.

If you yearn for something different (like a pineapple pizza), try **Granny's,** 1609 Philadelphia Ave. (tel. 289-4084). The all-day menu consists mainly of sandwiches, burgers, salads, and creative pizzas. The price range is $1.95 to $10. Granny's also has a branch at 125th Street and Coastal Highway (tel. 723-2433). Open all year; CC's accepted: MC and V.

THE TOP ATTRACTIONS: To give yourself a proper feel for Ocean City, a stroll along the **boardwalk** is a must. You'll see lots of amusements and shops and some food concessions that have become traditions, like Dumser's Dairyland (since 1939); the Alaska Stands (since 1933); and Thrasher's French Fries (since 1929). Your eyes will also be drawn to the unique **Ocean Gallery World,** at Second Street and Boardwalk. Famous for its fine art at close-out prices, this colorful emporium is chock full of art posters and original oil paintings.

At the southern tip of the boardwalk is the **Ocean City Life-Saving Station Museum** (tel. 289-4991), founded in 1878. In addition to exhibits on the U.S. life-saving service from 1875–1914, this museum offers a fascinating display of dollhouse models depicting Ocean City in its early days, and a pictorial history of the fishing industry in Ocean City. There are also two 300-gallon saltwater aquariums that contain marine life indigenous to this area and a unique collection of fossils and beachcomber finds. Hours of operation are June through September, daily from 11 a.m. to 10 p.m.; May and October, daily from 11 a.m. to 4 p.m.; and weekends only during the rest of year, from noon to 4 p.m. Admission charge is $1 for adults and 50¢ for children under 12.

Just south of Ocean City is **Assateague Island National Seashore and State Park,** a 32-mile-long island, belonging jointly to Maryland and Virginia. The state of Maryland owns 680 acres containing two miles of ocean frontage, divided into two equal sections, with a beautiful white sandy beach and dunes (ranging from 14 to 22 feet) on one side, and salt marsh on the other. There is a visitor center, a boardwalk, a bath house with changing rooms and lockers, a tackle shop, charcoal grills and tables, a picnic area, some primitive campsites, nature walks, and lots of room for swimming, surfing, and fishing. Assateague's greatest claim to fame, however, is its resident wild ponies that roam the island. Descended from domesticated stock that grazed here as early as the 17th century, these shaggy and sturdy ponies are smaller than horses, and well adapted to their harsh seashore environment with marsh and dune grasses supplying the bulk of their food. They are a thrill to see, but visitors are warned to keep a safe distance. For further information, contact the Park Superintendent, Assateague State Park, Route 2, P.O. Box 293, Berlin, MD 21811 (tel. 301/641-2120).

NIGHTLIFE: Many restaurants and dining spots feature live entertainment and dancing in the evenings; among the most popular are **Capt. Bill Bunting's Angler Restaurant,** Talbot Street and the Bay (tel. 289-7424); **The BonFire,** 71st Street and Coastal Highway (tel. 524-7171); and **Fager's Island,** 60th Street in the Bay (tel. 524-5500).

The **Ocean City Convention Hall,** 40th Street and Coastal Highway (tel. 289-8311), also presents a year-long program of top entertainers (from Bob Hope to Jermaine Jackson), big-name dance bands, and other live shows. Tickets usually range from $11 to $15. Check with the visitors bureau for the latest schedule.

Broadway musicals such as *Annie, Camelot, The Sound of Music,* or *Hello, Dolly* are presented in a dinner-theater format at the **Commander Boardwalk Cabaret,** 14th Street on the Boardwalk (tel. 289-6166). Staffed by young professionals who not only sing and dance but also serve the meal, this show is available during the ten weeks of summer, Tuesday through Saturday, with dinner seating at 7:30 p.m. Total cost for the dinner and show is based on the price of dinner (entrees range from lobster, crab and shrimp Newburg, prime ribs, and crab cakes to ham steak), with a $19 minimum. Depending on space, seating is sometimes available at 9 p.m. for cocktails/show only, with a $10 minimum. Reservations are a must. CC's accepted: MC and V.

SPORTS AND ACTIVITIES: The variety of activities available include fishing, sailing, swimming, bicycling, and tennis.

Fishing: The waters surrounding Ocean City are ideal for deep-sea fishing (for mackerel, sea bass, sea trout, and blues). One of the leading sources for fishing equipment is **Bahia Marina,** on the Bay between 21st and 22nd Streets (tel. 289-7438). Open April through October, 24 hours a day in season, Bahia rents everything from rods (from $4) to boats (from $28 an hour) for fishing. This company also operates deep-sea fishing trips on 78-passenger head boats from April through September, departing at 8 a.m. and returning at 2 or 3 p.m.; priced from $15 for adults and $7 for children. Morning or afternoon bay-fishing trips are also organized; from $15 for adults and $8 for children. CC's accepted: MC and V.

Several other companies also send out their head boats for seven-hour (7 a.m. to 2 p.m.) fishing excursions each morning from the piers along the bay. The price on board these trips generally runs from $22 for adults and $11 for children, with rod rental at $4 and bait furnished free. Some of the names to contact are Capt. Bill Bunting, *The Angler,* Talbot Street and the Bay (tel. 289-7424); Capt. Orlando Bunting, *The Captain Bunting,* 307 Dorchester St. and the Bay (tel. 289-6720); the Talbot Street Pier, *The Mariner,* Talbot Street and the Bay (tel. 289-9125); and Capt. Jack Bunting, *Miss Ocean City,* 308 First St. and the Bay (tel. 289-8234). Another operator, across the bay west of the Route 1 bridge, offers four-hour morning or afternoon trips priced at $14 for adults and $7 for children; contact Capt. Howard Cleaver on *The Taurus,* South Harbour Road, West Ocean City (tel. 289-2525).

Sailing: The 30-foot cutter *Therapy* offers half-day or evening cruises of the Ocean City waters, from $25 per person (maximum 6 passengers). Half-day cruises depart at 9 a.m. and 1 p.m., and evening sails go out at 5:30 p.m., returning after sunset. The operator is **Hook, Line and Sinker,** Shanty Town Marina, off Route 50 Bridge, West Ocean City (tel. 289-8818).

Swimming: The entire ten-mile stretch of Ocean City beach is open to the public, free of charge. Numerous beachfront concessions rent various equipment such as chairs ($2.50 a day) and umbrellas ($5 a day).

Bicycling: Ocean City is ideal for bicycling, particularly early in the morning before heavy traffic hours. Boardwalk biking is also allowed between 6 and 10 a.m. Rates vary according to the type of bike, but you can expect to pay between $2 and $4 an hour for a two-wheeler, $5.50 an hour for a tandem, and $6.50 an hour for a tri-tandem. Some of the best sources are **Sunburst Bike Rental** at 16th Street and Coastal Highway; **Pedal Pusher,** 609 N. Boardwalk (tel. 289-6865); and **Trimpers Cycle Center,** 603-A, S. Baltimore Ave. (tel. 289-5442).

Tennis: Local public courts, offering free tennis on a first-come basis, are located at 14th, 94th, and 136th Streets. Two other public courts, at 41st and 61st Streets, are operated on a reservation basis, at $4 per hour (tel. 524-8337).

EVENTS: Among its many claims to fame, Ocean City is known as the "White Marlin Capital of the World." Two summertime competitions draw white-marlin enthusiasts from far and wide: the annual **White Marlin Tournament** (started in 1958), on the last weekend of August, sponsored by the Ocean City Marlin Club, 201 S. St. Louis Ave. (tel. 289-6363); and the **White Marlin Open,** held in mid-August, offering $40,000 in prizes, and organized by Harbour Island Marina, 14th and the Bay (tel. 289-7991).

Other highlights of the Ocean City calendar include **The Great Board Walk,** a five-mile walk along the boardwalk from the inlet to 27th Street and back again, held in late May; and **PolkaMotion on the Ocean,** a mid-September festival of continuous polka music, polka dance groups, free dance lessons, and merriment. Contact the visitor's bureau for complete details on all of these Ocean City events.

CHILDREN'S CORNER: Ocean City is home to several amusement parks and child-oriented activities. Some of the leading spots include:

Trimper's Park, on the Boardwalk near the Inlet, between South Division and South First Streets (tel. 289-8617). Established in 1887, this is the granddaddy of Ocean City's amusement areas, with over 100 rides and attractions for the whole family, including a 1902 merry-go-round with all hand-carved animals. Most rides are 30¢; open daily, May through September, from 11 a.m. to midnight.

Jolly Roger, 30th Street and Coastal Highway (tel. 289-3477) is home to Ocean City's largest roller coaster, mini-golf courses, a petting zoo, water slides, and a children's theater called the Parker Playhouse. Admission is $3.50 for golf and 30¢ for rides; the water park is extra at $5 per hour or $10 a day. The theater presents such shows as *Jack and the Beanstalk* and *Little Red Riding Hood,* at 7 p.m. each evening, Monday through Friday, and matinees on Wednesday at 1 p.m. The general admission charge is $2.75. The entire park is open daily from noon to midnight, May through September.

Frontier Town and Rodeo, Route 1, West Ocean City (tel. 289-7877), is a western theme park. Set on 38 acres of woodland, this park includes a replica of a western town of the 1860s, genuine rodeos, cowboy- and dance-hall shows, stagecoach rides, riverboats, a steam train, and a giant waterslide. Children can also go trail riding, panning for gold, and visit a petting zoo. Open every day from 10 a.m. to 6 p.m., mid-June through Labor Day, the admission charge is $7 for adults and $6 for children aged 13 and under. To facilitate customers, a free van service is operated each morning and afternoon between the park and downtown Ocean City.

WASHINGTON, DISTRICT OF COLUMBIA

ETCHED FROM A CORNER OF MARYLAND overlooking the Potomac River, the site for our nation's "federal city" was chosen in 1790 by the man for whom it was named, George Washington.

Identified as Washington, District of Columbia, this national capital city was originally a ten-mile square that crossed the Potomac into Virginia, but the Virginia part was turned back to that state in 1846. The city was designed by Major Pierre Charles L'Enfant, who planned it, with great foresight, to have the wide tree-lined streets, squares, circles, and quadrants that we still enjoy today.

1. The Nation's Capital

Washington, D.C., became our country's official capital in 1800 when the members of Congress moved from Philadelphia. The White House was also readied in that same year, and John Adams moved in as its first presidential occupant. The rest indeed is history.

At the start, Washington had 130 federal employees; today there are over 300,000. With the economy of the area so solidly based on the workings of the U.S. government, it is not startling to note that federal employment accounts for 21% of greater Washington's work force.

What may be surprising, however, is that tourism ranks as the second-largest industry in the city, producing more than $1 billion and nearly 20 million visitors annually. Although Washington is readily identified with the government, our nation's seat of power, it is also a very appealing city, and ideal for

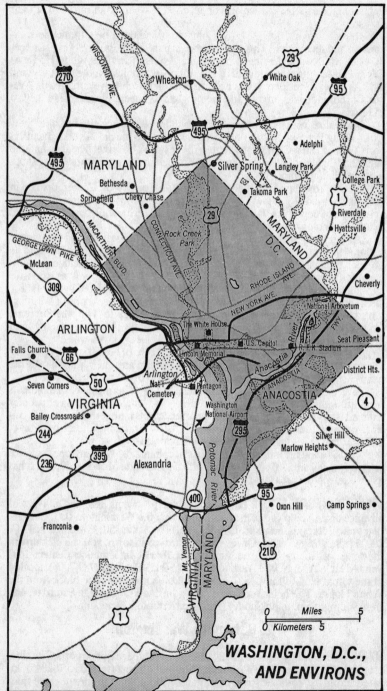

WASHINGTON, D.C., AND ENVIRONS

sightseeing vacations, particularly on weekends, when hotel rates are at their lowest.

In recent years, downtown Washington has undergone a tremendous expansion and renovation. This was spurred, in part, by President John F. Kennedy who, as he walked along Pennsylvania Avenue from the White House to Capitol Hill on the morning of his inauguration, was quick to note that the grand old "Avenue of Presidents" was badly in need of a facelift. A Pennsylvania Avenue Corporation was formed and the progress has been remarkable in the last 25 years.

Now alive with new plazas, office buildings, and restaurants, the "new look" along Pennsylvania Avenue also includes the much ballyhooed and reborn Willard Inter-Continental Hotel, the restored National Theatre, and the landmark Old Post Office Building, transformed into a trendy three-story shopping and dining complex.

Nearby, the new $100 million Washington Convention Center, opened in 1982, has served as a catalyst for much of the downtown area's growth, including dozens of new and refurbished hotels, and a "Techworld" complex devoted to high technology and world trade.

As we go to press, historic Union Station itself is gearing up to become a major attraction. Extensive restoration work has returned this landmark to its original grandeur, and some new attractions are being added, including a complex of 100 fashionable shops, restaurants, and cinemas, as well as extensive parking facilities. The entire project is expected to be completed by late 1988.

These new developments only serve to enhance the backbone of Washington's basic appeal—the aura of the White House, Capitol Hill, the Supreme Court, the Mall, the museums, and the monuments. There are literally hundreds of attractions, most of them free, available seven days a week.

Although Washington is the governmental core of our 50 states, reflecting all aspects of our country, it is totally different from any one state. This district has a cosmopolitan personality of its own, a blend of the nation as a whole.

Washington is also a truly international city, a gathering place of diplomats from around the world. You'll hear a myriad of languages and meet peoples from all lands. Even the city's restaurants reflect this multi-ethnic mix, with cuisines ranging from African to Austrian, British to Brazilian, Cuban to Chinese, and Mexican to Middle Eastern, just to mention a few.

Considering the influence and impact it commands, Washington, D.C., is a relatively small area, 63 square miles, with a population of about 650,000. It has its own telephone area code (202).

VISITOR INFORMATION: For brochures, maps, events lists, and all types of advance data to help you plan your trip, contact the **Washington, D.C. Convention and Visitors Association,** 1575 Eye St. NW, Suite 250, Washington, D.C. 20005 (tel. 202/789-7000). Once you have arrived in town, you can pick up on-the-spot particulars from the **Washington Tourist Information Center,** 1400 Pennsylvania Ave. N.W., Washington, D.C. 20230 (tel. 202/789-7000), located in the Great Hall of the U.S. Department of Commerce, one block from the White House. The hours are 9 a.m. to 5 p.m. Monday through Saturday, and from 9 a.m. to 5 p.m. on Sunday (from April through October).

2. Getting to Washington

BY PLANE: The city is served by 24 carriers and three major airports. The closest airport to downtown is **Washington National Airport** (tel. 703/557-2045), located across the Potomac River in Virginia, a 3½-mile or 15-minute drive from downtown Washington. This is a strictly domestic airport, used by more than 20 carriers including the shuttle flights from New York and Boston. Fares to downtown are approximately $7 by taxi, $5 by multipassenger limousine vans, or 80¢ via Metrorail.

Dulles International Airport (tel. 703/471-7838), is located 25 miles west of downtown near Herndon, Virginia, about a 45-minute drive from downtown. Twenty-four transcontinental and international carriers use this facility. The taxi fare to downtown Washington is approximately $30 to $35; limousine van service is $10.

Baltimore-Washington International Airport (tel. 301/859-7100), is approximately 34 miles northeast, off the Baltimore-Washington Parkway, and about 45 minutes from downtown. Serving both the capital and Baltimore, this airport is a gateway for 19 carriers. The taxi fare to Washington is approximately $35 to $40 and it is suggested that you agree on the price with the taxi driver before you leave the airport. Limousine van service operates every 45 minutes and is $10 one way or $18 round-trip.

For information on airport limousine service to and from and among the three airports, call **The Washington Flyer** (tel. 202/683-1400).

Some of the local numbers for the leading carriers include **American** (tel. 393-2345); **Continental** (tel. 628-6666); **Delta** (tel. 920-5500); **Eastern** (tel. 393-4000); **Northwest** (tel. 737-7333); **Pan Am** (tel. 845-8000); **TWA** (tel. 737-7400); **United** (tel. 893-3400); and **USAir** (tel. 783-4500).

BY TRAIN: Amtrak, the national railway passenger system, links major metropolitan areas throughout the country to **Washington's Union Station,** 50 Massachusetts Avenue NE (tel. 484-7540 or toll-free 800/872-7245), conveniently located near the U.S. Capitol and adjacent to the Metro. Hundreds of trains a day arrive here from other eastern corridor cities between Boston and Florida, and from all points westward.

To assist capital-city visitors, **Amtrak** operates a three-day vacation package. Priced from $114 per person when purchased in conjunction with an Amtrak rail fare to Washington, this money-saving plan includes two nights' hotel accommodations, based on double occupancy, choice of sightseeing excursions, and a special information packet.

BY BUS: Bus transportation into Washington is provided by **Trailways** 1005 1st St. NE (tel. 737-5800) and **Greyhound,** 1110 New York Ave. NW (tel. 565-2662).

BY CAR: The "Capital Beltway" is an expressway that encircles the city and interchanges with all major approach routes. The eastern portion of the beltway is part of I-95, the major artery that links Baltimore to the north and Richmond to the south. The remainder of the beltway is numbered I-495. Route 1 and the Baltimore-Washington Parkway (I-295) approach the city from the north; Routes 50, 4, and 5 come from western and southern Maryland. Leading into the city from the south, via Alexandria and Arlington, Virginia, are Route 1 and I-395. From the north, I-270 links the metropolitan area with I-70 at Frederick. From the south, I-66 and Route 50 connect with the Virginia part of I-495 on its approach to Washington.

3. Overview of the City

The U.S. Capitol is the geographic center of Washington, and all major streets are identified in relation to that point. With the Capitol as the core, the city is therefore divided into four sections—Northwest, Northeast, Southwest, and Southeast, and the dividing lines are North Capitol Street, South Capitol Street, East Capitol Street, and the Mall, radiating like spokes of a wheel from the Capitol itself.

North-south streets are numbers. East-west streets are letters in alphabetical order (but there are no J, X, Y, or Z streets). With the exception of I ("Eye") Street, all others are indicated simply by the alphabetical letter itself. For the most part, avenues all have state names, such as Rhode Island or Pennsylvania, and all of these avenues are diagonals. Circles and squares occur at the intersections of diagonal avenues and numbered and lettered streets.

When looking for an address, always check the quadrant indicator (for example, NW, NE, SW, or SE) before setting out to find it. Remember that an address such as 500 C Street, for example, can be found in four different locations, in the NW, NE, SW, and SE quadrants of the nation's capital.

Fortunately, the majority of sights of interest to visitors fall into the NW quadrant, including most museums, the downtown area, the White House, Dupont Circle, Embassy Row, and Georgetown. Many of the museums and buildings around the Mall fall into the SW quadrant, but the attractions in the immediate vicinity of the Capitol are likely to fall into any of the four quadrants. The Capitol is probably the most tricky area to negotiate, so be sure to check which quadrant you are looking for, and then double-check with a map, to help you get your bearings.

Once you have mastered this pattern, you'll find it quite simple to get around Washington, either on foot or via the easy-to-follow Metro system.

The main areas that you'll most likely want to see first are as follows:

The Capitol—Probably the best place to start a tour, since walking around here will help you to get your bearings. It is also within the reach of four different Metro stops, so you'll have no trouble moving on. The Capitol Hill area is not only home to the U.S. Senate and House of Representatives, but the Library of Congress and the Botanic Gardens are also located here, as well as Union Station.

The Mall—Moving directly west of Capitol Hill, you'll come to The Mall, the grassy 14-block-long strip that lies between the Capitol and the Washington Monument. The Mall is one of the oldest federal parks, but is best known for the Smithsonian Museums that line each side of its wide corridor. We'll cover these fully in the "Top Attractions" section. Before you leave the Mall area, you may wish to explore the adjacent Tidal Basin which not only holds the Jefferson Memorial but is also home to hundreds of Yoshino and Akebono cherry trees, gifts from Japan in 1912. These trees usually come into full bloom in early April and the famous **Cherry Blossom Festival** is held to mark the occasion.

The White House Area—If you proceed from the Washington Monument directly northward, you eventually come to the White House. After visiting the presidential mansion, you then have many options. Going east, you can stop at the Tourist Information Center (if you have not already been there), and then explore Pennsylvania Avenue. Here you'll also find the Federal Triangle, home of such institutions as the Internal Revenue Service and the F.B.I.

Four blocks northeast of the White House is the new **Washington Convention Center,** a $100 million facility, opened in 1982, which is revitalizing the area that surrounds it. Adjacent to it is the city's two-block **Chinatown** (between Sixth and Eighth, around G and H Streets).

Alternatively, you can go directly northward from the White House and come to Connecticut Avenue, lined with fashionable hotels, restaurants, and shops. The route westward along Pennsylvania Avenue also leads to many fine restaurants, hotels, George Washington University, and then to the West End and Georgetown.

Dupont Circle—This is the point where Connecticut Avenue intersects Massachusetts Avenue. A major Metro stop, it is the gateway to "embassy row" which basically runs along Massachusetts Avenue NW, west of Dupont. More than 150 embassies and chanceries are located in this region. In this vicinity, you'll find elegant Victorian row houses mixed in with hotels, restaurants, and cafés of all nations, boutiques, bookshops, art galleries, and a generally cosmopolitan aura. North of Dupont, between 18th Street and Kalorama Park NW, along Columbia Road, is the area designated as "Adams-Morgan." This is the "united nations" of Washington, a multi-cultural neighborhood with specialty shops, galleries, ethnic grocery stores, and street vendors.

The West End—This is the neighborhood surrounding the intersection of Virginia and New Hampshire Avenues. Once a marshy lowland docking region for trader clipper ships, this area was christened "Foggy Bottom" because it was the lowest part of town (generally below sea level) and usually foggy. Now it is looked on more as the emerging "West End" of town, between the White House area and Georgetown. Among the highlights here are the John F. Kennedy Center for the Performing Arts and the Watergate complex, as well as Federal row houses dating back to the 1800s. The State Department, George Washington University, and the Pan American Union are also located here.

Georgetown—Along the banks of the Potomac River, this is the city's oldest and most famous neighborhood. The starting point for the C & O Canal and a vibrant commercial port in Colonial days, Georgetown today is a magnet for visitors, with its panorama of nightclubs, restaurants, specialty boutiques, and beautifully restored Federal-period homes. It also offers all the bohemian qualities of a college town, with Georgetown University tucked in its northwest corner. This popular section of the city is located west of downtown and on the other side of Rock Creek.

4. Getting Around Washington

PUBLIC TRANSPORT: The **Washington Metropolitan Transit Authority,** or **Metro,** operates the bus and subway systems within the District. The Metro subway, which began in 1976, operates underground within the city and above ground in the suburbs of Maryland and Virginia. The entire system will be fully operational in early 1990, with a total of 101 miles of track and 86 stations throughout the Greater Washington area.

Visitors find the **Metro subway** of particular benefit in seeing the city's sights. It is a safe, spotless, and speedy rapid transit system. The four lines of the subway are color-coded and follow a transport pattern that is easy to master, even if it is your first day in Washington.

The fare system is computerized and farecards are purchased from vending machines at each station (the machines make change up to $5). You simply check what the fare will be to your destination and buy a ticket for that amount. Fares are based on distance traveled and time of day, ranging from 80¢ to $2.75. Most trips within the downtown area fall into the 80¢ level. You simply put your farecard through the turnstiles on entering and leaving the subway.

Metro trains run every 10 minutes, from 6 a.m. to midnight, Monday through Friday; from 8 a.m. to midnight on Saturday; and from 10 a.m. to midnight on Sunday. Metro station entrances are marked by an "M" located atop a tall brown pillar.

Metrobus picks up where the Metrorail ends. The city operates a fleet of 1,825 modern buses that travel throughout Greater Washington. During peak

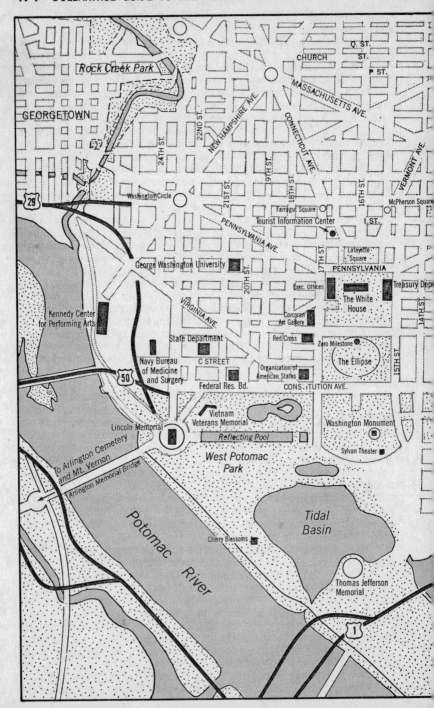

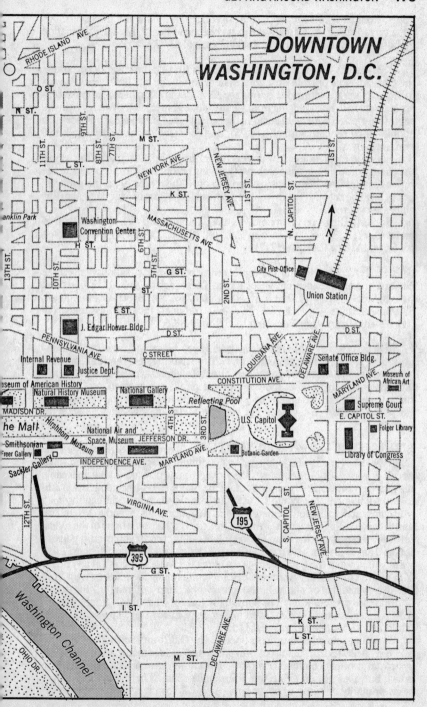

DOWNTOWN WASHINGTON, D.C.

hours, from 6 to 9:30 a.m. and from 3 to 6:30 p.m., minimum fare is 80¢; off-peak fares are 75¢. You must have exact change to board. For full information on both subway and bus schedules and fares, call 637-7000.

TAXIS: The city has more than 9,000 taxicabs that can be hailed anywhere in the city. All taxis operate on a zone system within the city limits; most downtown locations are within one or two zones. Zones are numbered from the center outward with rates ranging from $2.10 for one zone or $3 for two zones in the central city to $8.05 for eight zones in the outer limits. Surcharges apply for each additional passenger (normally $1.25), and for travel between 4:30 and 6:30 p.m. (usually 65¢).

City taxi regulations allow drivers to pick up additional fares on the way to the client's destination, with each party paying his or her share according to the zones they traverse. For trips beyond the downtown area or to the suburbs, prices must be set with the driver before boarding. Taxis in Maryland and Virginia are metered.

Some leading taxi companies include: **Capitol Cab** (tel. 546-2400); **Diamond Cab** (tel. 387-6200); **Eastern Cab** (tel. 829-4222); **Liberty Cab** (tel. 544-6666); and **Yellow Cab** (544-1212).

CAR RENTAL: Most leading car-rental firms operate rental stations at the three airports and at other downtown locations. These include **Avis,** 1722 K St. NW (tel. 467-6588); **Budget,** 1200 K St. NW (tel. 628-2750); **Hertz,** Union Station, 50 Massachusetts Ave. NE (tel. 789-0460); **National,** 12th and K Streets NW (tel. 824-1000); and **Ugly Duckling,** 1400 Rhode Island Ave. NE (tel. 529-7900).

PARKING: When in Washington, the best way to get around is via public transportation. If you must drive in the city, read the parking signs carefully, because all parking regulations are strictly enforced. In general, parking is extremely limited on city streets, but there are ample public garages and lots. Charges range from $5 to $10 a day. If your hotel provides parking, it is best to leave your car parked while you sightsee, and take the Metro or sightseeing vehicles for touring.

SIGHTSEEING TRAMS AND TROLLEYS: **Tourmobile Sightseeing,** 1000 Ohio Dr. SW (tel. 554-5100) operates a continuous two-car tram service on a circuit covering 18 historic sites. The driver-guides provide a knowledgeable narration en route. The tram stops at all the major sights (including the Washington Monument, the White House, the Lincoln Memorial, the Smithsonian Museums, and Arlington Cemetery), and passengers are invited to disembark and tour individual attractions. You are free to get off at some or all of the sights, or you can remain on the tram for the full two-hour trip. If you get off, you can reboard any tram whenever you wish at the designated Tourmobile signs. Likewise, you can join the tram at any point along the route and finish at any point. You buy the ticket from Tourmobile ticket booths along the route or right from the driver and he or she will also give you a map outlining all the stops. Tourmobiles operate every half hour, daily (except Christmas), from 9 a.m. to 4:30 p.m. and until 6:30 p.m. from mid-June to Labor Day. The cost is $7 for adults and $3.50 for children aged 3 to 11.

Another convenient service is operated by **Old Town Trolley Tours,** 3150 V St. NE (tel. 269-3020). Using colorful green-and-orange motorized trolleys, this system also offers continuous transit connections between major sightseeing areas, but does not duplicate the Tourmobile route. The trolleys make their stops primarily at hotels or at shopping areas, following a route that runs be-

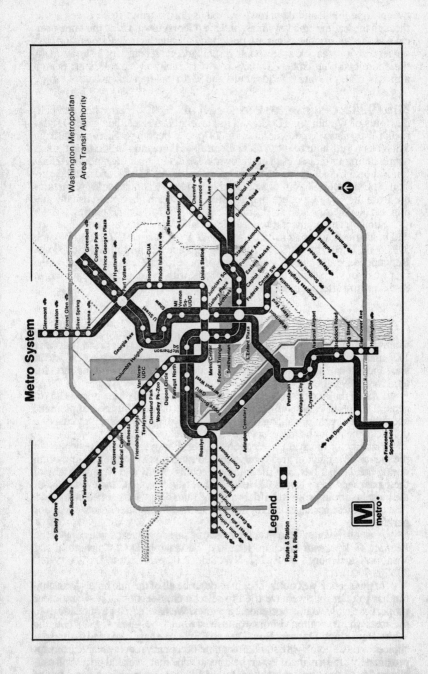

tween Capitol Hill and downtown as well as northward to Rock Creek Park, through the leading embassy areas, and into Georgetown. Using the same principle as the Tourmobile, signs are posted to indicate the trolley stops, and passengers can join the ride at any point, disembark and reboard, or just stay on for the entire two-hour circuit. Trolleys run year round, every half hour, from 9 a.m. to 4 p.m. The fare is $8 for adults and $3 for children under 12.

BUS TOURS: Gray Line, 333 E St. SW (tel. 479-5900), operates full- and half-day tours of Washington, D.C., and its surroundings, including general sightseeing trips and visits to the interiors of public buildings. Fares range from $13.80 for a four-hour tour to $22.95 for an all-day program. In addition, there is a nine-hour tour that takes in downtown Washington, plus Alexandria, Arlington National Cemetery, and Mt. Vernon, priced from $31.95, and other excursions to Colonial Williamsburg and the Shenandoah National Park. Departures are from the Gray Line terminal and from selected major hotels, usually at 9 a.m. for all-day trips, and at 9 a.m. or 2:30 p.m. for half-day itineraries.

Similar general-interest tours and special-interest itineraries (such as arts and industries), are conducted by **All About Town Tours,** 519 6th St. NW (tel. 393-3696). Prices start at $12 for half-day trips and $22 for full-day excursions. Reductions are also given if you take two or more tours. Departures begin at the tour office or via pickups from leading hotels, with morning tours beginning at 8:45 a.m. and afternoon sections at 1:30 p.m.

5. Where to Stay

The greater Washington area has the fourth-largest concentration of hotel rooms (over 43,000) available in a major city anywhere in the world. Between 1976 and 1986, the metropolitan area acquired more than 44 new hotels, and at least another half dozen are under construction, with planned opening dates for the 1988–1989 period.

Like all major cities, hotel rates fall into the high end of the price scale. In general, hotels in Washington cater to a large international business, diplomatic and lobbyist clientele, making midweek rates particularly steep. The cost of a double at the major luxury properties is rarely below $150 to $200 a night.

Happily for the average vacation traveler, however, nearly every hotel in the greater Washington area offers reduced rates on the weekends, and often during holiday periods, and the summer months of July and August. Many of these packages are as low as $20 to $30 per person per night, and even some of the most luxurious properties offer weekend rates below $50 per person a night. Best of all, these packages usually include "extras" like theater tickets, meals, or parking.

As soon as you start to plan your visit, be sure to request a free copy of the *Washington Weekends* brochure from the Washington, D.C. Convention and Visitors Association, 1575 Eye St. NW, Suite 250, Washington, DC 20005 (tel. 202/789-7000).

In this section we couldn't begin to describe all of the fine hotels Washington has to offer, but we have tried to select a cross-section of new and older properties that have the most moderate rates. We have confined our choices to the areas where vacation visitors would most want to be—near Capitol Hill, the White House, and Embassy Row/Dupont Circle. We have also tried to limit the choices to those hotels with standard double-occupancy rates available from approximately $150 a night or lower, bearing in mind that weekend prices will usually be $40 per person per night or less. In addition, we have included a few of the top-price luxury hotels, such as the new Willard and the grande dame Ritz

Carlton, because it would be hard to write a chapter on the capital without mentioning them.

In all cases, an extra 10% District of Columbia sales tax and $1 per room occupancy tax will be added to your bill.

To avoid too much repetition, we have primarily chosen lodging properties that have full-service restaurants offering three meals daily. Unless otherwise indicated, you can assume that breakfast would be available from 6:30 or 7 a.m. to 10 or 11 a.m.; lunch from 11:30 a.m. or noon to 2:30 or 3 p.m.; and dinner from 5:30 or 6 to 10 or 11 p.m. You can also assume that all of the hotels below offer accommodations that include air conditioning, color cable TV, and direct-dial phones. We'll try to specify only those features that are unique or different.

CAPITOL HILL AREA: If you are looking for a genteel oasis that is convenient to all parts of the city, the best choice is the **Phoenix Park,** 520 N. Capitol St. NW, Washington, DC 20001 (tel. 202/638-6900 or toll-free 800/824-5419), three blocks from Capitol Hill. Best of all, it's one block from Union Station, putting Metro or Amtrak traveling practically at the front door. Recently restored and totally refurbished, this 87-room gem is named after Dublin's main parkland and brings a touch of the Emerald Isle's friendliness and charm to downtown Washington. The décor reflects an 18th-century Irish country inn, with fittings of mahogany and marble, leaded glass and crystal, and country flowers at every turn. The guest rooms are decorated in subtle jade or rose tones, with reproduction furniture. Doubles start at $157. Facilities include complimentary morning newspapers, valet parking, and the Powerscourt, a restaurant that features specialties with Irish recipes or ingredients. Dinner entrees, priced from $16.95 to $21.95, include such dishes as oak-smoked salmon, steak flamed with Jamison whiskey, and Dublin mixed grill. Lunch items run from $6.95 to $15. All major CC's are accepted.

The **Loews L'Enfant Plaza Hotel,** 480 L'Enfant Plaza SW, Washington, DC 20024 (tel. 202/484-1000 or toll-free 800/223-0888), is ideally situated within six blocks of the Capitol and two blocks from the heart of the Mall's museum row. Built in 1968 and named for Washington's architect, this modern 12-story tower is part of a shopping and office complex of the same name which also has its own Metro station. The modern 372 guest rooms offer sweeping views of the Washington skyline or the Potomac waterfront; all units have fully stocked bars and refrigerators. Doubles start at $135. Guest facilities include a rooftop swimming pool and atrium, a greenhouse-style café, and a lounge with nightly music. There is also a gourmet restaurant, The Apple of Eve, known for its blend of continental dishes and mesquite-style cookery. Lunch entrees are priced from $6 to $17, and dinner from $15 to $23. All major CC's are accepted.

Two blocks north of the U.S. Capitol building is the **Quality Inn Capitol Hill Hotel,** 415 New Jersey Ave. NW, Washington, DC 20001 (tel. 202/638-1616 or toll-free 800/228-5151), a modern ten-story property with 340 rooms. Most guest rooms have separate vanity areas and feature reproduction-style furniture, with floral prints and decorative headboards. Doubles run from $95 to $120. Amenities include free enclosed parking, a rooftop pool and sundeck, and a complimentary walking-tour map. There is also a full-service restaurant, the Coach and Parlor, which conveys a turn-of-the-century railroad ambience. The menu features American regional seafoods and meats, and a variety of pastas, with prices in the $4.95 to $8.95 range for lunch and from $7.95 to $16.95 for dinner entrees. All major CC's are accepted.

The **Capitol Hill Hotel,** 200 C St. SE, Washington, DC 20003 (tel. 202/543-6000 or toll-free 800/424-9165), is located in a quiet residential neighborhood, two blocks east of the Capitol building and one block from a Metro station. A former apartment building converted into a hotel, this property is ideal for extended stays. Most of the 153 units are small suites and outfitted with Queen Anne–style furnishings. Double-occupancy rates for guest rooms are priced from $95 and suites with kitchenetes from $105. All major CC's are accepted.

Five blocks south of the Capitol is the **Best Western Skyline Inn,** 10 Eye St. at South Capitol Street SW, Washington, D.C. 20024 (tel. 202/488-7500 or toll-free 800/528-1234), conveniently situated just off the intersection of I-295 and I-395. This seven-story motor inn has 203 recently refurbished rooms, decorated in a modern motif of gold and beige autumn tones; some rooms offer views of the Capitol and others overlook the pool. Doubles range from $72 to $95. Guest amenities include free indoor and outdoor parking, a swimming pool, and a lounge with nightly entertainment and dancing. In addition, the Board 'n' Bottle dining room offers French-American cuisine, with entrees priced from $4 to $12 at lunch and from $6 to $18 at dinner. All major CC's are accepted.

WHITE HOUSE AREA: Just two blocks from the White House, the hotel now known as the **Willard Inter-Continental,** 1401 Pennsylvania Ave. NW, Washington, DC 20004 (tel. 202/628-9100 or toll-free 800/327-0200), has a proud history dating back to 1850. Originally a 100-room hotel built by Henry Willard, it was transformed into a grand beaux-arts property in the early 1900s. Over the years, the Willard thrived as the meeting place of the mighty, and the home of presidents (chief executives from Lincoln to Eisenhower slept here). Time took its toll, however, and the hotel fell into disrepair and closed its doors in 1968. Preservation-minded citizens came to the fore, however, and the Willard was not only saved from the wrecking ball, but was enhanced with a $73 million restoration, reopening its doors with much fanfare in 1986. Now on the National Register of Historic Places, the Willard today has 394 deluxe rooms, designed in more than 100 different configurations and each individually decorated in elegant turn-of-the-century fashion. Doubles range from $180 to $255. The public rooms have also been returned to their former splendor, including the marble-floored Peacock Alley Promenade that runs through the length of the hotel. With the official seals of all 50 states hanging from its ceiling, the lobby is a showcase of plush red-and-gold tones, marble granite columns, crystal chandeliers, mosaic tiles, and solid brass fixtures. It was here that the term "lobbyist" is said to have been coined, as 19th-century gentlemen who represented special interests congregated in the lobby to corner politicians who were staying at the hotel. Modern-day visitors and locals also gather in the chic Round Robin Bar, under the sketches of former patrons like Howard Taft, Woodrow Wilson, and Nathaniel Hawthorne. The main dining room is a masterful restoration of oak beams, paneled walls, etched-glass dividers, and brass lamps. The upscale menu features American cuisine, with dinner entrees mostly in the $15 to $25 bracket, and wines from the 39 wine-producing states of the union. For lighter and more moderate fare, there is also an all-day café called The Expresso. All major CC's are accepted.

The closest you can be to the White House without a key to the front door is **The Hay-Adams,** One Lafayette Square, Washington, DC 20006 (tel. 202/638-6600 or toll-free 800/424-5054). Situated at 16th and H Streets NW, on a parklet directly opposite the executive mansion, this recently restored gem is named for John Hay and Henry Adams, two prominent 19th-century Washingtonians whose homes originally occupied this site. Designed in Italian Renaissance style, the hotel was built in 1927, and over the years has been a favorite with visiting statesmen and celebrities. Thanks to the attentive and eager tuxedo-clad staff, every guest is made to feel like a star. This is a place where you can relax and sip afternoon tea in a grand setting of oak- and walnut-paneled walls, gilt moldings, hand-woven tapestries, and fine English antiques. The 155 guest rooms are individually furnished with antique reproductions, plush floral fabrics, and marble baths; some units have balconies or fireplaces, and many have views of Lafayette Square, the White House, and the Washington Monument. Doubles range from $140 to $275. Dining facilities include a grill room, the sunlit Adams Room for light meals, and the gourmet enclave called the John Hay Room for dinner, where entrees at lunch range from $15 to $30 and from $20 to $50 at dinner. All major CC's are accepted.

Another grande dame in this lofty neighborhood is the **Mayflower,** 1127 Connecticut Ave. NW, Washington, DC 20036 (tel. 202/347-3000 or toll-free 800/468-3571), situated in the heart of town amid a row of chic shops and restaurants. Just four blocks from the White House, between L and M Streets, it is also next to a Metro stop. Now a Stouffer hotel, this 1925 landmark was recently restored and updated to the tune of $65 million. The spacious lobby is a study in light marble tones, polished brass fixtures, and gilt-edge trim. The 724 guest rooms are furnished in rich mahogany and oak reproductions, and plush pastel fabrics. Doubles range from $95 to $205. Guest facilities comprise an arcade of shops including a barber, a lounge with nightly music, and the Promenade Café, serving moderately priced meals all day. In addition, in the evening, there is Restaurant Nicholas, noted for blending the flavors of Europe with Asia and America. The dinner entrees, priced from $17.50 to $25.50, include filet of salmon with Enoki mushrooms; fricassee of Maine lobster; breast of Wisconsin duck with cabernet sauce; and western beef with sweet onion and stone-ground mustard. All major CC's are accepted.

A former apartment building is the setting for the **Hotel Lombardy,** 2019 Eye St. NW, Washington, DC 20006 (tel. 202/828-2600 or toll-free 800/424-5486), at the corner of Pennsylvania Avenue and 21st Street. This gracious and homey property is four blocks from the White House, two blocks from the Metro, and directly across from George Washington University. There are 125 units, many equipped with small kitchens. Doubles range from $85 to $130; and small suites with kitchens go from $90 to $130. Facilities include a small all-day café offering moderately priced meals. All major CC's are accepted.

One of the best values in the midtown area is the **Days Inn,** 12th and K Streets NW, Washington, DC 20005 (tel. 202/842-1020 or toll-free 800/325-2525), six blocks from the White House, and two blocks from the Convention Center. Formerly a Travel Lodge property, this modern hotel has 218 rooms, many with views of the Capitol or the Washington Monument. Doubles range from $64 to $75. Guest facilities include free parking, a rooftop pool, and a lounge with live music. The on-premises restaurant, Buckleys, specializes in mesquite-grilled meats and fish, at moderate prices; lunch items range from $2.95 to $8.95, and dinner entrees from $8.95 to $15.95. All major CC's are accepted.

DUPONT CIRCLE AND EMBASSY ROW AREA: In the heart of the tree-lined embassy district is the **Ritz Carlton,** 2100 Massachusetts Ave. NW, Washington, DC 20008 (tel. 202/293-2100 or toll-free 800/424-8008), a lovely eight-story Georgian brick building with a pervasive old-world charm. Originally known as the Fairfax, it came into its present ownership in 1982 and has recently undergone a thorough renovation. The 240 extra-large guest rooms are outfitted with 18th-century-style American and English furniture, crafted curtains of imported chintz, and printed linens. Doubles range from $175 to $240. Facilities include a lounge bar and an afternoon tea service, but the Ritz-Carlton is probably best known for its classic American restaurant, the Jockey Club. Staffed by a core of experienced and enthusiastic wait-persons, this is a clubby setting of half-timbered walls, red-leather banquettes, horsey and sporting pictures, and red-checker tablecloths. Prices at lunch range from $10.75 to $20, and from $18 to $27 at dinner; specialties include crab cakes, Chateaubriand, and rack of lamb. All major CC's are accepted.

No hotel summary would be complete without mentioning the city's largest property, the 1,505-room **Sheraton Washington,** 2660 Woodley Rd. at Connecticut Avenue NW, Washington, DC 20008 (tel. 202/328-2000 or toll-free 800/325-3535). Situated on a 12-acre, tree-shaded hilltop in a resort-like setting, this modern 11-story property is slightly off the beaten track, about a mile north of Dupont Circle, but has its own Metro stop. This is basically a residential neighborhood near leading embassies, adjacent to Rock Creek Park, and four blocks from the National Zoo. Although the hotel officially dates back only to 1980, it has an historical side as well, since it incorporates a wing of the landmark Wardman Park Hotel, built in 1918, and part of the 1950s Sheraton Park hotel. The majority of guest rooms are wide-windowed and decorated with modern art, beige- and gold-toned furnishings, and individual vanity/desk wall units. Doubles range from $135 to $165. Guest facilities include two heated outdoor pools and a sundeck, a fitness room, beauty and barber shops, a gift shop, a game room, and valet or self-parking garages ($7 a day for registered guests). There are also three lounges, offering live-band entertainment and dancing, three café and snack shops, and a formal dining room, Americus. This art deco–inspired restaurant is known for its seafood, steaks, and American regional cuisine, with dinner entrees in the $11.95 to $23 range. All major CC's are accepted.

The **Dupont Plaza Hotel,** 1500 New Hampshire Ave. NW, Washington, DC 20036 (tel. 202/483-6000 or toll-free 800/421-6662), is located on Dupont Circle, a major Metro station. This is where Massachusetts and Connecticut Avenues meet, in a neighborhood of three-story Victorian row houses, foreign embassies, bookstores, boutiques, and outdoor cafés. A modern eight-story property, the Dupont has 308 wide-windowed rooms, each outfitted with wet bar, refrigerator, and an extra phone in the bathroom. Doubles run from $125 to $170. Amenities include a valet parking garage, a lounge, and Stephanie's Restaurant. This old-world dining room specializes in continental and Viennese-style cuisines, served to the tunes of strolling violinists and a resident pianist. Lunch items cost from $4.95 to $8.95, and dinner entrees run from $9.95 to $18.95. All major CC's are accepted.

Three blocks from Dupont Circle is the **Hotel Anthony,** 1823 L St. NW, Washington, D.C. 20036 (tel. 202/223-4320 or toll-free 800/424-2970), a small 99-unit hotel with a fashionable art deco lobby. The guest rooms are actually small suites, with reproduction furnishings, a living area, a dressing room, and either a wet bar or a small kitchen. Doubles range from $98 to $108 and that includes continental breakfast and a morning newspaper. There is also a small restaurant offering lunch and dinner in the moderate price range. All major CC's are accepted.

Last, but certainly not least, is one of our favorite hotels in the whole city, the **Normandy Inn,** 2118 Wyoming Ave. NW, Washington, DC 20008 (tel. 202/483-1350 or toll-free 800/424-3729), situated in a residential area seven blocks north of Dupont Circle. This small five-story property offers top-class comforts at affordable prices. The 77 guest rooms are tastefully decorated in beige and peach tones, with reproduction furnishings. Doubles are priced at $83. There is no restaurant, but continental breakfast is available each morning. Other facilities include underground parking ($4 a night), and the services of a very friendly and obliging staff. CC's accepted: AE, MC, and V.

6. Where to Dine

As the capital of our country and an international meeting place of the world, Washington boasts a wide variety of American regional and ethnic eating places. Many D.C. restaurants are top award winners and culinary classics in their own right, certainly fit for presidents, prime ministers, potentates, and the powerful of all levels.

Consequently, downtown Washington restaurants are largely geared to expense-account business and diplomatic dining. With few exceptions, visitors seeking budget-priced meals are best advised to stick to the museum cafeterias and fast-food courts.

The restaurants listed below have been selected to represent a cross-section of moderate to expensive dining, in the main parts of the city where visitors tend to go—Capitol Hill, the White House area, and Dupont Circle/ Embassy Row. In addition, we have included a few restaurants in the trendy region that Washingtonians also favor in the evening—Georgetown and the emerging West End. We have tried to compile a sampling of different types of cuisines, and a blend of old traditional spots as well as innovative newcomers.

A note about parking: Many midtown restaurants offer free or reduced-rate parking in the evening for dinner patrons. Be sure to check when you make your reservation, as you could save at least $5 to $8 in the process.

CAPITOL HILL AREA: A favorite of U.S. congresspeople is **La Colline,** 400 N. Capitol St. NW (tel. 737-0400), a restaurant named for its Capitol Hill clientele ("la colline" means "hill" in French). Located just a block from the legislative power center, this bright and modern dining room is decorated with walls of paintings (for sale) by local artists, while the entrance area is lined with a collage of pictures of governmental celebrities who dine there. The French cuisine menus are quite similar for lunch and dinner, and prices do not vary greatly, although the selections do change each day. This is not a place to come for lunch if you want a quick sandwich, but if you'd like bouillabaisse, frogs' legs, tripe, or a rib-eye steak, you'll be well satisfied. Lunch usually costs $7.95 to $13.95. In the evening, choices range from $13.25 to $17.95, and often include such dishes as Dover sole meunière; half pheasant with sherry port and cognac cream sauce; filet mignon béarnaise; noisettes of venison; gratin of lump crab Thermidor; or shrimp Toulouse-Lautrec (with lobster sauce and Pernod). If you don't mind a more limited choice, this restaurant also offers great value in nightly fixed-price dinners, priced from $14.50, for a complete meal of appetizer, entree, salad, and dessert cart (don't miss the house special of strawberry and chocolate mousse cake with raspberry sauce). Lunch is served Monday through Friday from 11:30 a.m. to 3 p.m.; dinner Monday through Saturday from 6 to 10 p.m.; and Sunday from 5 to 9 p.m. All major CC's are accepted.

Also a block from the Capitol in an eastward direction is **The Monocle,** 107 D St. NE (tel. 546-4488), a congressional favorite since 1960. Housed in a 100-year-old building, this restaurant has an eclectic décor including classic sketches of monocle-wearing characters, flashy glass-and-mirror trim, and a sturdy old fireplace. The straightforward menu concentrates on aged American beef and regional seafood. Lunch, priced from $4.95 to $10.95, includes sandwiches, salads, omelets, and light entrees such as London broil, Maryland crab cakes, or veal scaloppine. Entrees at dinner are priced in the $12.50 to $17.95 range, for such choices as prime ribs, steaks, calves' liver, salmon, swordfish, and shellfish. Open Monday through Friday from 11:30 a.m. to midnight, and Saturday from 5 p.m. to midnight. All major CC's are accepted.

Southwest of Capitol Hill is the Washington channel waterfront area where you'll find a number of dockside restaurants, primarily known for great views and seafood menus. The best way to get here is by taxi or take the Metro to L'Enfant Plaza and walk three blocks. A dining tradition in this area is **Hogates,** 9th Street and Maine Avenue SW (tel. 484-6300), established in the neighborhood in 1938 and in this location since 1972. From the moment you put your hands on the lobster-shaped door handles and step inside past the huge shellfish tanks and the on-premises fish store, you know you're in the right spot for the freshest of seafood. You'll also enjoy some panoramic harbor views, with most tables facing wide curved windows, amid a décor of authentic brass portholes, fishing nets, ships' bells and wheels, harpoons, oars, and diving helmets. There is indoor seating for 600 and an outside terrace that holds 300 in the summer. Lunch, priced from $4.95 to $9.95, offers salads, sandwiches, burgers, and daily fish specials such as lemon sole, Cape bluefish, yellowfin tuna, or king salmon. Dinner entrees, priced from $8.95 to $23.95, with most choices under $15, feature whatever is freshest, from Florida mahi mahi, red snapper, or sea trout to lobster. Many people opt for the bountiful "Hogate's Original 1938 Mariner Platter," available for lunch or dinner at $15.95 (flounder, oysters, scallops, clams, shrimp, crab cake, shrimp salad, cole slaw, and potatoes). All other items are accompanied by the restaurant's famous rum buns and potato or rice. Open from 11 a.m. to 11 p.m. Monday through Thursday; from 11 a.m. to midnight on Friday; from noon to midnight on Saturday; and on Sunday from 10:30 a.m. to 2:30 p.m. for brunch and from noon to 10 p.m. for dinner. All major CC's are accepted.

A block away is **Phillips Flagship,** 900 Water St. SW (tel. 488-8515), an affiliate of the original Ocean City, Maryland, restaurant founded in 1956, and the Baltimore Inner Harbor branch. This particular location opened in 1985 and offers similar menus and a décor reflective of a southern mansion. In the summer the huge glass windows that face the water are simply rolled up and the whole restaurant becomes an open-air dining room. At lunchtime you can order light items like sandwiches and salads, priced from $4.95 to $7.95, or any selection from the full-dinner menu. The dinner entrees are in the $7.95 to $23.95 price bracket, and include lobsters, crab dishes, shrimp, flounder florentine, Coho salmon, sea scallops, and fried oysters, as well as steak, ham, and veal. All main courses come with vegetable or salad, and potato. Open daily from 11 a.m. to 11 p.m. All major CC's are accepted.

In the budget bracket, you'll enjoy the **American Café,** 227 Massachusetts Ave. NE (tel. 547-8500), three blocks from the Capitol and two blocks from Union Station. A modern eatery with emphasis on fresh ingredients, the kitchen also bakes all its own breads (from croissants to sourdough, whole wheat, and pumpernickel). Lunch items, such as sandwiches, salads, and chili, are in the $3.95 to $9.95 bracket. Dinner entrees feature seafood and beef grilled over mesquite, as well as chicken tarragon, Portland tuna, and applewood-smoked turkey. Prices fall into the $5.95 to $14.95 range. Open Sunday from 10:30 a.m. to 1 a.m.; Monday through Thursday from 11 a.m. to 1 a.m.; Friday and Saturday from 11 a.m. to 3 a.m. Also located downtown at 1300 F St. NW (tel. 626-0770) and in Georgetown, 1211 Wisconsin Ave. NW (tel. 944-9470). All major CC's are accepted.

WHITE HOUSE AREA: Just a block west of the White House is **Maison Blanche,** 1725 F St. NW (tel. 842-0070), located in Liberty Plaza, a brick courtyard with its own pond, directly opposite the Old Executive Office Building. From its name (the French equivalent of "white house"), to its grand style and very continental menu, this restaurant is assuredly French, but you can have a menu printed in English if you wish. Said to be a favorite with those who frequent the presidential residence, this place has an equally impressive décor of crystal chandeliers, plush leather seating, walnut paneling, etched glass, and textured wallpaper of golden tones. The menu is similar for lunch and dinner, with slightly larger portions and higher prices in the evening (midday entrees range from $9 to $14, while main courses at night go for $17.50 to $25.95). The selections include breast of duckling on an Arctic berry sauce with fresh ginger root; beef tenderloin sautéed with cognac and truffles; roast fresh squab with sauce of foie gras; loin of young rabbit with cèpes; braid of Dover sole and salmon; and lobster flan with jumbo lump crabmeat. Lunch is served from noon to 2:30 p.m., Monday through Friday; and dinner from 6 to 11 p.m., Monday through Saturday. All major CC's are accepted.

There's never a dull moment at **Dominique's,** 1900 Pennsylvania Ave. NW, (tel. 452-1126), at 20th Street, in the ground level of the Thomas Edison Building. With an eclectic décor of French paintings, leafy plants, exposed brick walls, etched-glass, and cozy alcoves, this restaurant is a favorite of government and show-business celebrities, as you'll see by the many signed photographs that also line the walls. The pièce de résistance is the illustrated 21-page menu, guaranteed not to be boring, with such choices as Florida alligator, quail pâté, smoked buffalo, venison sausages, rattlesnake salad, and U. S. Senate bean soup, which is so popular it is sold in cans-to-go. The best seller, however, is usually rack of lamb for two, but rainbow trout, duck, and lobster tails are also popular choices. Entree prices at lunch average $8.95 to $14.95, with dinner portions between $12.95 and $21.95. Appetizers run from $2.95 to $13.95, and there is also a fixed-price dinner of $12.95 for pre- and post-theatergoers. Open for lunch Monday through Friday from 11:30 a.m. to 2:30 p.m.; and for dinner Monday through Thursday from 5:30 p.m. to midnight, and until 1 a.m. on Friday and Saturday. All major CC's are accepted.

One of Washington's oldest restaurants is **Harvey's,** 1101 18th St. NW (tel. 833-1858), at the corner of K Street. Originally started in a converted blacksmith shop by Thomas Harvey in 1858, this popular seafood house has continued to operate ever since, with a few changes of location, moving to its present address in 1970. The décor reflects its earlier days, from beamed ceilings and carved woods to wrought-iron candlelight lanterns. The lunch items, priced from $7.95 to $13.95, include seafood soups and sandwiches, burgers, salads, crab or lobster omelets, and daily fish catches. The extensive menu at dinner is priced from $14.95 to $27.95, with most dishes between $15 and $20. Featured entrees are crab imperial, fish stew, red snapper, Coho salmon, king crab, shrimp Norfolk, broiled whole flounder, grilled tuna, and a half dozen lobster choices. Open Monday through Friday, for lunch and dinner, from 11:30 a.m. to 10:30 p.m.; Saturday and Sunday, dinner only, from 5 to 10:30 p.m. (closed Sundays in the summer). All major CC's are accepted.

Sports pictures and trophies dominate the décor at **Duke Zeibert's,** 1050 Connecticut Ave. NW (tel. 466-3730), on the mezzanine level of the Washington Square Building, opposite the Mayflower Hotel. Although it is housed in modern new quarters with outdoor courtyard seating in the summer, the "Duke's" has been a Washington institution for over 35 years, having moved to its present location recently to make way for the Metro. Lunch, priced from $8.95 to $12.95, offers hefty helpings of steaks, omelets, roast-beef hash, corned beef and cabbage, short ribs of beef, curry of chicken, and seafood casseroles. Similar fare is on tap at dinner plus seafood platters, beef Stroganoff, goulash, or stew. The dinner entrees are priced from $13.95 to $20.95 with most under $17, and include vegetable and potato. Open Monday through Saturday from 11:30 a.m. to 11:30 p.m., and Sunday from 5 to 10 p.m. (closed Sundays in July and August). All major CC's are accepted.

An old brick town house is the setting for **Le Gaulois,** 2133 Pennsylvania Ave. NW (tel. 466-3232), five blocks west of the White House and close to the city's West End. Both décor and menu convey a Parisian ambience with a small bistro-style interior and sidewalk-café seating outdoors. A similar menu is offered for lunch and dinner, with most entrees in the $8.75 to $14.95 range. The choices, which change daily, often include coquilles St-Jacques; squid casserole; pepper steak; rabbit casserole; duck and lamb casserole with pork sausage and beans; or veal sweetbreads with imported mushrooms. The desserts are also very tempting, including a luscious black-currant and passion-fruit mousse cake ($2.75). Open for lunch from 11:30 a.m. to 2:30 p.m., Monday through Friday; and for dinner from 5:30 to 11 p.m., Monday through Thursday, and until midnight on Friday and Saturday. CC's accepted: AE, Ch, MC, and V.

A Washington landmark, the **Old Ebbitt Grill,** 675 15th St. NW, (tel. 347-4801), has been frequented by past presidents and politicos. Housed in a restored vaudeville theater opposite the Treasury Building and a block from the White House, this popular eatery is decorated with D.C. memorabilia, ranging from lace curtains and muraled ceilings to leather and velvet booths with etched-glass dividers; stuffed animal heads; and marble, gilt, and brass trim. Lunch items are priced from $5 to $10, and dinner entrees go for $9.95 to $15.95. Featured dishes include beef stew, trout parmesan, leg of lamb, chicken paillard, steaks, and pastas. Open for lunch from noon to 3 p.m., Monday through Friday; and for dinner from 4 p.m. to 2 a.m., Sunday through Thursday, and from 4 p.m. to 3 a.m., Friday and Saturday. All major CC's are accepted.

The menu of new American cuisine changes twice a day at **Prime Plus,** 727 15th St. NW, (tel. 783-0166), a basement-level eatery between New York Avenue and H Street, three blocks from the White House. The décor is a blend of raspberry, pink, and lavendar tones, with glass dividers and modern light woods. Prices at lunch usually fall into the $6.50 to $11.50 range with dinner entrees in the $8.50 to $17.50 bracket. Specialties include seafood waffles; veal scallops with chanterelles, bacon, and port; grilled pheasant stuffed with mushrooms; sautéed Norwegian salmon; grilled black bass with sage; sautéed halibut with cockles and cucumbers; and sautéed quail with pecan bourbon sauce. Lunch is served Monday through Friday from 11:30 a.m. to 2:30 p.m.; dinner Monday through Thursday from 5 to 10 p.m., and Friday and Saturday until 11:30 p.m. CC's accepted: AE, Ch, MC, and V.

One of the top dining spots in the Old Post Office Pavilion is **Fitch, Fox, and Brown,** 1100 Pennsylvania Ave NW (tel. 289-1100), a pubby bilevel eatery. Named after three college athlete friends who traveled the world, the menu reflects some of their itineraries, with Indian, Greek, Italian, and Chinese dishes. Lunch is priced from $4.95 to $9.95, mostly for sea or meat salads, sandwiches, and burgers. Dinner entrees, which fall into the $8.95 to $16.95 category, feature stir-fry dishes, pastas, curries, southeast seafoods, steaks, and spareribs with mustard-honey glaze. Open from 11:30 a.m. until 10 p.m. on Sunday and Monday, and until 11 p.m. Tuesday through Saturday. All major CC's are accepted.

DUPONT CIRCLE AND EMBASSY ROW: Since 1949, **Gusti's,** 19th and M Streets NW (tel. 331-9444), has been a favorite in this neighborhood two blocks south of Dupont Circle. Famous for its Italian cuisine and its treasure-trove of things Italian, this large white building resulted from the joining of four private houses, dating back to the 1800s. It now offers a choice of ten dining rooms and alcoves on three floors, in a setting of giant paintings of Rome and Venice, antique tapestries, old bottles, statuary, and artifacts, including a Venetian ice-cream cart (circa 1916), and vintage cappuccino machines. In the summertime, seating expands to an outdoor garden café. A similar menu prevails throughout the day, with lunch items priced in the $2.95 to $6.95 bracket and dinner entrees priced from $5.95 to $14.95. The selections include scampi, calamari, pastas, saltimbocca, veal cacciatore, chicken parmigiana, and filet mignon en brochette. All main courses come with spaghetti and vegetable. Open daily from 11 a.m. to midnight. All major CC's are accepted.

Around the corner, the emphasis is on classic American cuisine at **Gary's,** 1800 M St. NW (tel. 463-6470), a midtown restaurant situated off a brick courtyard near 18th Street. With a Steinway piano and its entrance and walls lined with cartoons and fun pictures, Gary's is a relaxed contemporary setting for uncomplicated food. Lunch, priced from $6.50 to $11.50, offers prime-rib sandwiches, chopped steak, executive salads, and seafoods. Dinner entrees, priced from $13 to $21, include aged prime steaks, prime ribs, rack of lamb or rack of pork, veal chops, and swordfish or scallops. Open Monday through Friday from 11:30 a.m. to 11 p.m. and Saturday from 6:30 to 11 p.m. All major CC's are accepted.

An off-street pathway leads to the **Iron Gate Inn,** 1734 N St. NW (tel. 737-1370), a converted 18th-century stable that has been a Middle Eastern restaurant since 1957. Besides the cozy mews-like interior, on warm days you can dine in the romantic sheltered courtyard, amid flowering magnolias and a grape arbor. Throughout the day the menu presents such dishes as rock Cornish hen kebab; lamb, shrimp, or vegetarian curries; and grape leaves stuffed with ground lamb and rice. The most popular choice is an Arabian Knights Platter that offers a little of everything including couscous, lamb meatballs, and stuffed squash and eggplant. The entree prices range from $7.95 to $12.95 for lunch or dinner. Open from 11:30 a.m. to 10:30 p.m. daily. All major CC's accepted.

Across the street is the **Tabard Inn,** 1739 N St. NW (tel. 785-1277), with a slightly overgrown outside garden, but a manicured old-world interior including a handsome skylit dining room. Lunch, priced from $5.95 to $9.95, focuses on such items as turkey pot pie, herb lamb loaf, grilled rockfish, and salads. Dinner entrees, in the $10.95 to $13.95 bracket, usually include such innovative dishes as grilled duck breast with chutney; oven-braised salmon with horseradish mustard cream sauce; and breast of chicken with apples, Jarlsburg cheese, and cider sauce. Lunch is served from 11:30 a.m. to 2:45 p.m., Monday through Friday; dinner from 6 to 10:30 p.m. Monday through Wednesday, until 11 p.m. Thursday through Saturday, and until 10 p.m. on Sunday. CC's accepted: MC and V.

A pub atmosphere prevails at the **Brickskeller,** 1523 22nd St. NW (tel. 293-1885), housed in a sturdy building (circa 1888), between P and Q Streets, two blocks west of Dupont Circle. Called "Brick's" by the locals, this restaurant's main claim to fame is that it features more than 500 American and imported beers, and has many antique beer cans displayed along the original unfired brick walls. Lunch items, priced from $3.50 to $4.95, are mainly burgers, sandwiches, and cheeseboard selections. Dinnertime entrees, in the $5.95 to $13.95 bracket, are more extensive, with such dishes as rainbow trout, South Dakota buffalo steaks and stews, baby back ribs, and vegetable tempura. This is also a fun place to come for a game of darts or backgammon. Open Monday through Friday from 11:30 a.m. to 2 a.m.; Saturday from 6 p.m. to 3 a.m.; and Sunday from 6 p.m. to 2 a.m. All major CC's are accepted.

A block from Dupont Circle, you'll find **Afterwords Café,** 1517 Connecticut Ave. NW (tel. 387-1462), tucked in the back of the Kramerbooks Store. This is a café-cum-bookstore, which also offers full bar service. You can browse among the best sellers or pick through the paperbacks to work up an appetite. Open throughout the day, lunch items include salads, sandwiches, and nacho platters ($4.75 to $7.75). Dinner entrees, averaging $8.75 to $10.75, feature Cajun shrimp; pork or chicken stir-fry; pastas; and hearty dinner salads. Open daily for lunch and dinner, from noon to midnight. CC's accepted: AE, MC, and V.

THE WEST END—FROM FOGGY BOTTOM TO GEORGETOWN: It's hard to imagine, but the classy 1,200-seat restaurant with a New Orleans motif known as **Blackie's House of Beef,** 1217 22nd St. and M Street NW (tel. 333-1100), was started in 1946 as a small quick-service grill by "Blackie" Auger and his family. After a few changes in location and much expansion, the Augers are still in charge and they have lined the walls with pictures of the famous guests they have welcomed. The eclectic décor also features mementos collected over the years, from a hand-carved organ and a cash register with saw-tooth oak, to a glass-enclosed case of world currency, and a live UPI newswire that constantly prints out the latest headlines and stock reports. The selection at lunch features sandwiches, cold plates, salads, steaks, burgers, and ribs, in the $3.95 to $9.95 price bracket. Colorado steaks, prime beef, and seafood are the main attractions on the dinner menu, priced from $9.95 to $19.95. After a hearty meal, you can also dance the night away in the adjacent Deja Vu lounge, a showcase of music from the 1950s and 1960s. Open Monday through Saturday from 11 a.m. to 10:30 p.m. and Saturday from 4 to 10:30 p.m. All major CC's are accepted.

One of Washington's newest eateries is the **City Café,** 2213 M St. NW (tel. 797-4860), an art-deco modern restaurant in the heart of the Foggy Bottom section. With a bilevel layout, the geometric décor is a blend of blacks and whites, pinks and grays, lots of mirrors, triangular tables for two, and square tables for larger parties. The cuisine features biodynamic food, with emphasis on freshness and no chemical additives; all ingredients come from nearby farms. Lunch items, priced from $4.50 to $8.50, include salads, pastas, and light entrees, like roasted peppers and goat cheese, or smoked peppered bluefish. The dinner entrees, priced from $6.50 to $11.50, offer stir-fry dishes, gourmet pizzas, pastas, free-range chicken, West Virginia rainbow trout, bunless burgers, and marinated pork. Open for lunch Monday through Friday from 11:30 to 2:30 p.m.; for dinner, Monday through Thursday from 5:30 p.m. to midnight, on Friday and Saturday until 1 a.m., and on Sunday from 5:30 to 11 p.m. No CC's are accepted.

If you would like to dine in elegance in Georgetown, there's no better place than **1789,** 1226 36th St. NW (tel. 965-1789), a beautifully restored 18th-century house, located in a hilly residential section next to Georgetown University. With three cozy dining rooms, the décor offers a touch of the Colonial, with open fireplaces, gas lamps, candlelight, oil paintings of hunt scenes, and framed etchings depicting scenes of early Washington. Open primarily for dinner, the menu ranges from Shenandoah Valley trout, char-grilled Alaskan salmon, veal sweetbreads, and Maryland pheasant to aged Black Angus strip steak. Entrees are priced from $17 to $25. Open for dinner, from 6 to 11 p.m. Monday through Thursday, and until midnight on Friday and Saturday. Brunch is also available on Sunday from 11 a.m. to 3 p.m., in the $8 to $13 price bracket. All major CC's are accepted.

A favorite spot with well-known Washingtonians is **Glorious Café,** 3251 Prospect St. NW (tel. 333-0200), located in Georgetown Court, one block from Wisconsin and M Streets, the heart of the shopping district. Nestled in a brick courtyard, this is a very pleasant setting of floor-to-ceiling windows, tree-size plants, marble tables, and rattan chairs, with classical music in the background. New American cuisine is featured on the menu, and the extensive wine list changes every four months. Lunch or brunch, priced from $6.50 to $14, includes such dishes as seafood crêpes, pasta primavera, creamed chicken on toast, and steak and eggs. Evening entrees, priced from $9 to $16, range from rack of veal or seafood casserolettes to striped bass, café burgers, or cold herbed loin of lamb with wild rice salad and ratatouille. Open Monday through Saturday from noon to midnight; and Sunday from 11 a.m. to 3 p.m. for brunch, and from 6 to 10 p.m. for dinner. CC's accepted: AE, MC, and V.

The newest dining spot in Georgetown is **Potomac on the River,** K and Thomas Jefferson Streets NW (tel. 944-4200), a glitzy creation of New York restaurateur Warner LeRoy (of Maxwell Plum's fame). Situated right on the river in the new Washington Harbour condominium project, this 1,000-seat bilevel restaurant is a splashy showcase of 20-foot circular windows, a jeweled ceiling, mirrors, flowers, and oversized crystal chandeliers. If the other sights aren't enough to hold your attention, an all-brass miniature electric train set encircles the balcony of the main dining room. The lunch menu, priced from $5.95 to $21, offers pastas, omelets, and salads. Entrees at dinner, averaging $9.50 to $22, include pizzas made from a wood-burning stove, roasted free-range chicken, Cajun shrimp, prime ribs, and lobster. Open for lunch, Monday through Friday from 11:30 a.m. to 4 p.m.; for dinner, Sunday through Thursday from 5 p.m. to midnight, and Friday and Saturday from 6 p.m. to 1 a.m. Brunch is also available on Saturday and Sunday from 10 a.m. to 4 p.m. All major CC's are accepted.

A Georgetown favorite with Washingtonians and visitors alike, **Clyde's,** 3236 M St. NW (tel. 333-9180), is basically a pub that serves good food. At lunch and brunch, Clyde's is famous for its omelets, with fillings that range from chili to bacon and spinach. The quiches and pastas are also popular at midday, when the price range is $5.75 to $6.75. Dinner entrees cost between $8.95 and $14.95, and include steak tartare (except Sunday), London broil, beer-batter shrimp, bay scallops, and rock shrimp. Open all day from 7:30 a.m. to 2 a.m., Monday through Thursday; from 7:30 a.m. to 3 a.m. on Friday; from 9 a.m. to 3 a.m. on Saturday; and from 9 a.m. to 2 a.m. on Sunday. All major CC's are accepted.

As its name implies, **The Foundry,** 1050 30th St. NW (tel. 337-1500), is a restaurant housed in an old (1856) foundry building. Situated in a delightful part of Georgetown just south of M Street and overlooking the towpath of the C&O Canal, this historic landmark also served as a veterinary house for the mules working on that famous waterway in the 1870s. Today its exposed brick walls have been enhanced by blond woods, hanging plants, and a skylit ceiling. In the summer months, there is also seating on an outdoor patio overlooking the canal. Sandwiches, salads, and pastas are the focus at lunchtime, in the $4.95 to $7.95 price bracket. The dinner menu, priced from $11.95 to $21.95 with most items under $15, includes mesquite-grilled swordfish, blackened redfish, lobster tails, rock Cornish hen, and Idaho brook trout. Open Monday through Saturday, for lunch from 11:30 a.m. to 5 p.m.; and for dinner from 5:30 to 11 p.m. All major CC's are accepted.

Waiters who move from table to table on roller skates are the main attraction at **La Niçoise,** 1721 Wisconsin Ave NW, (tel. 965-9300), a unique north Georgetown restaurant. The colorful murals on the wall depict scenes from Nice and the Cote d'Azur and set the tone for the mostly French menu at this novel dinner-only eatery. Specialties include veal niçoise; stuffed baked mussels; bouillabaisse, and poulet tarragon, as well as rabbit in mustard sauce, and Virginia trout sautéed with mussels and baby shrimp. Most entrees are priced between $13.75 to $19.95. After dinner, the entire restaurant staff usually performs a spontaneous adult cabaret show for guests. Open daily from 5:30 to 11 p.m. All major CC's are accepted.

The many cuisines of Asia are the keynote at **Germaine's,** 2400 Wisconsin

Ave. NW (tel. 965-1185), a modern second-floor restaurant in north George-town. Simply described as pan-Asian, the menu blends dishes from Vietnam, China, Thailand, Japan, Korea, and Indonesia in a bright and airy setting of beige woods, cane furniture, textured walls, leafy plants, and Oriental screens. Featured dishes are similar throughout the day, with lunch prices in the $7.95 to $12.95 bracket and dinner entrees costing $11.95 to $19.95. The tasty ensemble includes teriyaki chicken, basil beef, Peking pork, curry lamb, Szechuan lob-ster, three-colored shrimp, pinecone fish, and scallops with seaweed. Lunch is served, Monday through Friday from noon to 2:30 p.m.; and dinner, Sunday through Friday from 6 to 10 p.m., and Saturday from 6 to 11 p.m. Major CC's are accepted.

7. The Top Attractions

Washington is a sightseer's dream, with dozens of museums and galleries, famous houses and government buildings, historic churches and shrines, parks, and gardens open to the public. Best of all, most of these places are open seven days a week, year round, and with no admission fees. The Washington Convention and Visitors Bureau publishes a handy pocket-size *Attractions* brochure, free of charge, which describes about 100 of the leading sights, along with hours of admission and special features. In the meantime, we'll describe a small sampling, our own personal favorites, to get you started.

Anxious to see the magnificent furnishings and paintings or perhaps to catch a glimpse of the president, more than one million people a year line up to see **The White House,** 1600 Pennsylvania Ave. NW (tel. 456-2200). Home to every U.S. President since John Adams in 1800, this 132-room mansion was designed by Irishman James Hoban and is fashioned after Leinster House in Dublin. Five rooms are open to the public, including the State Dining Room, and can be toured Tuesday through Saturday from 10 a.m. to noon. All tours begin at the East Gate on East Executive Avenue. Tickets for specific times are required for tours from Memorial Day through Labor Day, and can be obtained, free of charge, at the Ellipse booth at Constitution Avenue, from 8 a.m. until noon. Closed Christmas, New Year's Day, and for Presidential functions. No admission charge.

Perched on top of Capitol Hill in a beautiful 200-acre park is **The United States Capitol,** National Mall (tel. 225-6827), an imposing 540-room structure where all of our elected senators and representatives meet to shape U.S. legislative policy. The Capitol is literally the center of the city, the point from which all streets are numbered. The symbol of our government, this building is easily recognized by its 180-foot white dome, which can be seen from all parts of Washington. The highlights include the Rotunda, which is lined with pictures and murals of America's great statesmen; Statuary Hall, which has two statues from each state; the House of Representatives, the largest legislative chamber in the world; the Senate, with its famous reception room; and the Crypt, the original Supreme Court chamber. The building is open daily (except Thanksgiving, Christmas, and New Year's Day) from 9 a.m. to 4:30 p.m., and until 10 p.m. during Easter to Labor Day; free half-hour tours are conducted from 9 a.m. to 3:45 p.m. All tours begin at the Rotunda and depart every 20 minutes. No admission charge.

The **Smithsonian Institution** is the world's largest museum complex, with 13 distinct buildings or units, 11 of which are located on or near the National Mall (between the Capitol Building and the Washington Monument), and two others, including the National Zoo, located in other parts of Washington. All museums are open daily, except Christmas Day, with slightly varying hours, but usually at least from 10 a.m. to 5:30 p.m., and with extended spring/summer hours. Admission to all Smithsonian Museums is free, and free walk-in "highlights" tours are usually available to the public in most museums. For visitor information, call 357-2700 daily, 9 a.m. to 5 p.m.; or for 24-hour recorded information, dial 357-2020.

The best place to start a tour of this mammoth complex is at the **Smithsonian Institution Building,** 1000 Jefferson Dr. SW (tel. 357-2700), popularly known as the "Castle," the oldest member of the group, built in 1855. This reddish-colored building houses the Smithsonian Information Center and the crypt of James Smithson, founder of the Smithsonian Institution.

Adjacent to the "Castle" in the Quadrangle area of the Smithsonian is the **National Museum of African Art,** 950 Independence Ave. SW (tel. 357-4600), the only museum in the U.S. devoted to the art and culture of Africa. To the immediate west is the **Freer Gallery of Art,** Jefferson Drive at 12th Street SW (tel. 357-2104), one of the world's finest collections of Oriental art, with works from the Near and Far East. In addition, this collection focuses on paintings by late-19th- and early-20th-century artists, including James McNeill Whistler, Winslow Homer, and others. This is where you'll find Whistler's famous Peacock Room.

In the other direction, to the east of the Smithsonian Castle, are the **Arts and Industries Building,** 900 Jefferson Dr. SW (tel. 357-1481), which includes working steam engines and other machines of the Victorian era; and the **Hirshhorn Museum and Sculpture Garden,** Independence Avenue at 7th Street SW (tel. 357-3235), a striking cylindrical structure that houses changing exhibits of contemporary and modern art.

Continuing east toward the Capitol, the next building is the **National Air and Space Museum,** 6th Street and Independence Avenue SW (tel. 357-1400), the most visited museum in the world. It contains 23 galleries showcasing the evolution of aviation and space technology, including the original 1903 *Wright Flyer;* Lindbergh's *Spirit of St. Louis;* John Glenn's *Friendship 7* space capsule; the Apollo II command module; a space station, and touchable moon rocks. Visitors can also enjoy exhilarating films in the **Langley Theatre** on a special screen which is 50-feet high and 70-feet wide. Admission to the museum is free, but there is a $1.50 charge for the theater.

Directly across the Mall are the East and West buildings of the **National Gallery of Art,** 4th Street between the Mall and Constitution Avenue NW (tel. 737-4215), a showcase for European and American paintings, sculpture, and graphic arts, from the 13th century to the present. Although the National Gallery was created as a bureau of the Smithsonian, it is governed by a separate board of trustees, and has slightly different hours on Sunday (noon to 9 p.m.).

Continuing westward on the north side of the Mall, you'll come to the **National Museum of Natural History,** 10th Street and Constitution Avenue NW (tel. 357-2747), a collection of more than 81 million items documenting man and his natural environment, from dinosaur displays to the 45½-carat Hope Diamond; and the **National Museum of American History,** 14th Street and Constitution Avenue NW (tel. 357-1481), an all-American display of memorabilia including the original Star-Spangled Banner, gowns of the First Ladies, and Henry Ford's first Model-T.

Two components of the Smithsonian are located outside the Mall but close by: the **National Portrait Gallery,** 8th and F Streets NW (tel. 357-2920), which contains portraits of famous Americans from Pocahontas to President Jimmy Carter; and the **Renwick Gallery,** Pennsylvania Avenue at 17th Street NW (tel. 357-3111), featuring American crafts, design, and decorative arts.

In addition, in southeast Washington, you'll find the **Anacostia Neighborhood Museum,** 2405 Martin Luther King Jr. Ave. SE (tel. 287-3369), which presents changing exhibits on the history and art of Afro-Americans. It is open weekdays from 10 a.m. to 6 p.m., and on weekends from 1 to 6 p.m.

The final gem of the Smithsonian group is the **National Zoological Park,** 3000 block of Connecticut Avenue NW (tel. 673-4717), located in the city's upper northwest, about a half-hour subway ride or drive from the National Mall. More than 3,000 animals representing 400 species live here, including the giant pandas, Ling-Ling and Hsing-Hsing (gifts from China), as well as American bison, and exotic reptiles and birds. Hours are from 8 a.m. to 6 p.m. for the grounds, and from 9 a.m. to 4:30 p.m. for the buildings, during mid-Septemer to the end of April. In the summer months (May to mid-September) the grounds stay open until 8 p.m. and the buildings until 6 p.m.

Note: Excellent cafeterias are located in the National Gallery of Art, National Air and Space Museum, National Museum of American History, and the National Museum of Natural History.

When you are in the area of the National Mall, you should also take time to visit the **Washington Monument,** at 15th Street NW (tel. 426-6841), the tallest masonry structure in the world (555 feet). Opened in 1888 and dedicated to the memory of the first U.S. President in 1885, this majestic 90,000-pound stone obelisk is more than just a landmark. Its 897 steps and 50 landings lead to an observation deck where you can enjoy a panoramic view of the city and the Potomac River. If you are hale and hearty, you can climb to the top, but most folks prefer the speed of the elevator (70 seconds to ascend, and 60 seconds to come down). Open daily from 9 a.m. to 5 p.m. year round (except Christmas), with extended hours until midnight from April through Labor Day. A visit here has been free for the past 100 years, although there is a possibility that a $2 charge might be levied, starting in 1988. Check in advance.

Other monuments that should not be missed include:

● **The Lincoln Memorial,** West Potomac Park at 23rd Street NW (tel. 426-6841), overlooking the Reflecting Pool on the National Mall. This grand tribute to Abraham Lincoln is shaped like a Grecian Temple and features a 19-foot statue of the sixteenth President plus words from his most famous speeches. Open daily except Christmas, 24 hours a day. Free admission and free tours available on request.

● **The Jefferson Memorial,** Tidal Basin (South Bank), West Potomac Park, contains a classical dome and colonnade, dedicated to Thomas Jefferson, third President of the U.S. The site includes a 19-foot bronze statue of Jefferson plus quotes from the Declaration of Independence and other of his writings. Open daily, except Christmas, 24 hours a day, with tours from 8 a.m. to midnight. Free admission.

● **The Vietnam Veterans Memorial,** Constitution Avenue between Henry Bacon Drive and 21st Street NW (tel. 426-6841), is a modern V-shaped tribute listing the names of the 58,022 people who died or remain missing in the Vietnam War. Built with the private contributions of American citizens, this memorial is open daily, 24 hours, free of charge.

Among the favorite indoor attractions is the **The National Archives,** 8th Street and Constitution Avenue NW (tel. 523-3183), a building housing many of America's original documents, including the Declaration of Independence, the Constitution, and the Bill of Rights. You can also trace your own family roots in the Research Room. Open daily (except Christmas) from 10 a.m. to 5:30 p.m., with extended hours until 9 p.m. from April 1 to Labor Day.

Near the Capitol building is **The Supreme Court,** 1st Street and Maryland Avenue NE (tel. 479-3000), the highest court in the land. Housed in a classical white-marble building dating back to 1935, the court is in session two weeks of every month (October to June). The building is open year round (except national holidays) Monday through Friday from 9 a.m. to 4:30 p.m., with tours conducted from 9 a.m. through 3:30 p.m. No admission charge.

The **National Geographic Society,** Explorer's Hall, 17th and M Streets NW (tel. 857-7588), contains exhibits of famous scientific expeditions in anthropology and oceanography, as well as explorations of outer space. The main permanent exhibit is the world's largest free-standing globe, 11 feet in diameter. Open Monday through Saturday from 9 a.m. to 5 p.m.; and on Sunday from 10 a.m. to 5 p.m. (closed Christmas). No admission charge.

Billions of U.S. dollars and stamps are churned out each year at the **Bureau of Engraving and Printing,** 14th and C Streets SW (tel. 447-9709). Visitors can take a self-guided tour and watch high-speed presses print more than 7,000 sheets of paper currency an hour. Naturally, there is strict security and photography is not allowed. Open Monday through Friday from 9 a.m. to 2 p.m.; admission is by ticket, distributed free at the entrance, on a first-come basis. Closed on national holidays and the week between Christmas and New Year's.

The **Federal Bureau of Investigation (FBI) Headquarters,** 9th and Pennsylvania Avenues NW (tel. 324-3447), provides visitors with an insight into modern crime-fighting techniques. You can take a free one-hour tour that includes a look at the "ten most wanted" posters, entrance into a crime laboratory, and a live firearms demonstration, viewed from behind bulletproof glass. Open Monday through Friday from 8:45 a.m. to 4:15 p.m.; closed all federal holidays. No admission charge.

One of Washington's newest additions is the **National Museum of Women in the Arts,** 13th Street and New York Avenue NW (tel. 337-2615), two blocks from the White House. Opened in the spring of 1987, this is the first museum in the world devoted exclusively to the creations of women artists. The works of 200 women from 20 countries, dating from the Renaissance to the present, are represented in paintings, sculpture, prints, drawings, photographs, books, and pottery. Open from 10 a.m. to 5 p.m., Tuesday through Saturday, and from noon to 5 p.m. on Sunday. No admission charge.

8. Nightlife

PERFORMING ARTS: The premier showplace in Washington is the **John F. Kennedy Center for the Performing Arts,** New Hampshire Avenue at Rock Creek Parkway, Washington, D.C. 20566 (tel. 202/254-3600), opened in 1971. Located in Washington's West End section, next to the Watergate complex and overlooking the Potomac, the Kennedy Center is worth a visit, even if you don't have time for a show (free tours are conducted daily from 10 a.m. to 1 p.m.). A complex the size of four football fields, it contains works of art that were gifts from heads of state from around the world. Presenting a varied program of nightly drama, dance, music, and film, the center has five performing venues, including an opera house, a concert hall, and legitimate theater stages, plus four restaurants of varying price ranges. This is the home of the National Symphony, the American National Theatre, the Washington Opera, and the American Film Institute; many Broadway musicals play here prior to or after New York. Ticket prices depend on seat location and the nature of the event, but average between $10 and $35. An advance ticket bulletin, *Two On the Aisle,* is published bimonthly and is available free. You can purchase tickets at the box office (open Monday through Saturday from 10 a.m. to 9 p.m., and Sunday from noon to 9 p.m.), by mail, or by phoning Instant-Charge (tel. 202/857-0900). All major CC's are accepted.

Ford's Theatre, 511 10th St. NW, Washington, D.C. 20004 (tel. 202/426-6924), is best known as the scene of Abraham Lincoln's assassination, but today it is also the stage for modern touring shows. Performances are usually on Tuesday through Sunday at 7:30 p.m., with matinees on Sunday at 3 p.m.; seat prices average $18 to $22. Tickets can be obtained at the box office or by calling Chargit (tel. 202/385-0044). All major CC's are accepted. (*Note:* Guided tours of the theater itself are available daily from 9 a.m. to 5 p.m., on the half-hour, except 12:30 p.m. The fee is $1 per person).

The **National Theatre,** 1321 Pennsylvania Ave. NW, Washington, D.C. 20004 (tel. 202/783-3370), is one of this country's oldest continually operating theaters, opened in 1835. Located two blocks from the White House, it is known as the Theatre of Presidents, because every president since 1850 has attended a performance here. The National is a venue for Broadway-bound shows, scheduled Tuesday through Sunday at 8 p.m., with matinees at 2 p.m. on Saturday, and at 3 p.m. on Sunday. Tickets range from $18 to $35 and all major CC's are accepted. A special feature of this facility is that it offers performances of music, comedy, and dance, for free admission on Monday nights. All shows are at 7 p.m. and 8:30 p.m. but reservations must be made by calling 202/783-3372, one week in advance. A similar arrangement works for performances on Saturday mornings at 9:30 and 11 a.m., also free with a one-week advance reservation. Contact the theater or check with the Washington Convention and Visitors Association for the upcoming schedules of free events.

Note: For shows at the above theaters and many others in the Washington area, you can obtain half-price tickets on the day of a performance at **Ticketplace,** F Street Plaza, 12th and 13th Streets NW (tel. 842-5387). This facility is open on Monday from noon to 2 p.m., and Tuesday through Saturday from 11 a.m. to 6 p.m. (tickets for Sunday can be purchased on Saturday). No CC's are accepted. You can also buy tickets for future dates here, but each ticket will be full price and subject to $1 surcharge. CC's are accepted for advance sales only: AE, MC, and V.

An entertainment highlight outside the city is the **Wolf Trap Foundation for the Performing Arts,** 1624 Trap Rd., Vienna, Virginia 22180 (tel. 703/255-1900). This is the nation's only farm park devoted to the performing arts, featuring jazz, dance, musicals, theater, opera, and other performances in an outdoor setting during the summer months, daily from 7 a.m. to dusk. Admission to the park is free, but shows range from $5 to $25; and all major CC's are accepted. From October through mid-May, performances are held indoors at **The Wolf Trap Barns,** two authentic 18th-century farm buildings converted into a 350-seat performance hall, with daytime weekend shows for children (at 11 a.m. and 1 p.m.) and evening concerts for adults. The Barns operate a separate box office on their premises at 1325 Trap Rd., Vienna, Virginia 22180 (tel. 703/938-2404). Tickets range in price from $4 for children and $10 to $12 for adults. CC's accepted: MC and V.

CLUBS AND CABARETS: Washington has a number of music clubs and cabarets, open most nights from Monday through Saturday. For humorous revues, political satire, and other live entertainment, try **Chez Artiste,** 1201 Pennsylvania Ave. NW (tel. 737-7772). There is no cover charge, and light meals are served from 5:30 p.m. to midnight. All major CC's are accepted. Another cabaret club is **D.C. Space,** 433 7th St. NW (tel. 347-1445), which features everything from poetry readings to jazz, reggae, rock, new wave, and classical performers. Cover charge is $7.50, with a $5 minimum; open until 1:30 a.m. on weekdays and 3 a.m. on weekends. CC's accepted: AE, MC, and V.

The décor and mood change seasonally at **Mirage,** 1330 19th St. NW (tel. 463-8888), a New York–style dance club, where a D.J. plays the top-40 disco tunes. Open Wednesday and Thursday from 9 p.m. to 2 a.m., with a $4 cover charge; Friday and Saturday from 9 p.m. to 4 a.m., with a $4 cover charge until 10 p.m., and then $8. All major CC's are accepted.

For a laugh or two, try the **Comedy Café,** 1520 K St. NW (tel. 638-JOKE), which features top national and local comedy acts. Showtimes are Friday at 8:30 and 10:30 p.m.; Saturday at 7:30, 9:30, and 11:30 p.m., with an open mike every Thursday at 8:30 p.m. Cover charge is $6 on weekends; $2.49 special on Thursday. Major CC's accepted.

Among the many clubs in the Georgetown area is **Blues Alley,** 1073 Wisconsin Avenue at M Street NW (tel. 337-4141), which attracts major jazz artists. This club operates on a dinner-show basis, with two shows (at 8 and 10 p.m.) Sunday through Thursday, and three shows (8 p.m., 10 p.m., and midnight) on Friday and Saturday. Cover charge ranges from $8 to $25. All major CC's are accepted.

9. Shopping

Washington prides itself on being one of the top fashion capitals of the world, with a generous selection of sleek new shopping complexes, as well as specialty boutiques. Many of these exclusive and unique shops line Connecticut Avenue or are housed in converted landmarks such as the **Old Post Office Pavilion,** 1100 Pennsylvania Ave. and 12th Street NW (tel. 289-4224). The former city post office, this spendid Romanesque building (1899) was restored and opened in 1983 as the home of more than 50 trendy shops, selling everything from crystal to chocolates, watches to women's wear, and souvenirs to stationery, and, quite appropriately, stamps for the collector. This midcity emporium also contains a medley of restaurants and a fast-food court. Open Monday through Saturday from 10 a.m. to 9:30 p.m., and Sunday from noon to 8 p.m., with later hours for restaurants. All major CC's are accepted in most shops and restaurants.

One of the city's busiest shopping clusters is **Georgetown Park,** 3222 M St. NW (tel. 342-8190), a former warehouse turned into a very classy trilevel skylit mall in the heart of Georgetown. There are 75 restaurants and shops including the fashionable and the famous, such as Abercrombie and Fitch, Ann Taylor, Crabtree and Evelyn, F.A.O. Schwartz, Garfinkels, and Godiva, to name a few. Open Monday through Saturday from 10 a.m. to 9 p.m.; and on Sunday from noon to 6 p.m. All major CC's are accepted. While you are in the neighborhood, stop into the new **Georgetown Court,** 3251 Prospect Ave. NW, (tel. 298-6323), a smaller but equally chic complex featuring such names as Carroll Reed and Jaeger. This complex is just a block away, follows the same hours, and also accepts major CC's.

The museum shops of the Smithsonian are also a "must" in Washington. Largely reflecting the contents of the various museums in which they are housed, these shops follow the normal opening hours, usually from 10 a.m. to 5 p.m. daily. CC's accepted: AE, MC, and V. Start your shopping spree with these: **National Portrait Gallery,** 8th and F Streets NW (tel. 357-1447); **National Museum of American Art,** 8th and G Streets NW (tel. 357-1545); **National Museum of Natural History,** 10th Street and Constitution Avenue NW (tel. 357-1536); **National Museum of American History,** 14th Street and Constitution Avenue NW (tel. 357-1528); the **National Air and Space Museum,** 6th Street and Independence Avenue SW (tel. 357-1387); and the **Hirshhorn Museum and Sculpture Garden,** 7th Street and Independence Avenue SW (tel. 357-1429).

KEY BRIDGE

George Washington University

Watergate Complex

NEW HAMPSHIRE AVE
VIRGINIA AVE
H ST.
G ST.
23RD. ST.

LEE HIGHWAY
29
U.S. NAVY
66
LEE HIGHWAY

KEY BLVD.
19TH ST.
MOORE ST.
FT. MYER DR.
18TH ST.
WILSON DR.
17TH ST.

Theodore Roosevelt Memorial

Theodore Roosevelt Island

Little River

WASHINGTON MEMORIAL PARKWAY

J. F. Kennedy Center

T. ROOSEVELT BRIDGE

50

50
ARLINGTON BLVD.
MEADE ST.
14TH
FT. MYER DR.
12TH ST.

Marine Corps War Memorial

Potomac River

Vietnam Veterans Memorial

Lincoln Memorial

ARLINGTON MEMORIAL BRIDGE

Lady Bird Johnson Park

N

WASHINGTON MEMORIAL PARKWAY

ORD & WEITZEL DR.

SHERMAN DR.

MEMORIAL DR.

JEFFERSON DAVIS HIGHWAY

Kennedy Graves

Robert E. Lee Memorial

Arlington House

MCCLELLAN DR.

ROOSEVELT DR.

GRANT DR.

EISENHOWER DR.

MEMORIAL DR.

ARLINGTON
NATIONAL
CEMETERY

YORK DR.

BRADLEY DR.

Boundary Channel

WASHINGTON BLVD.

110

Maine Memorial

Tomb of the Unknown Soldier

GRANT DR.

MACARTHUR CIRCLE

WEST END AND ARLINGTON

Pentagon

10. Attractions Near Washington

The attractions that surround Washington are almost as abundant as those within the city itself. After spending at least three or four days seeing the sights downtown, you could easily spend another day or more on the outskirts. Here are the two favorites which should not be missed:

Just south of Washington on the other side of the Potomac is **Arlington National Cemetery,** Arlington, Virginia (tel. 703/692-0931). This is the final resting place of 175,000 American soldiers who fought from the Revolutionary War to the present. It can be reached via the Metro and is usually on the itineraries of most tours of Washington. Perhaps the most well-known sight here is the flickering eternal flame over the **grave of President John F. Kennedy.** Others buried here include Washington's architect, Pierre Charles L'Enfant, Robert F. Kennedy, William Howard Taft, Oliver Wendell Holmes, boxer Joe Louis, and astronaut Virgil Grissom. On a hillside, you can also see **Arlington House, a** memorial to Robert E. Lee. In addition, try to take in the hourly changing of the guard at the **Tomb of the Unknown Soldier.** Open daily from 8 a.m. to 5 p.m., with extended hours to 7 p.m. during the April to September period. No charges.

Mount Vernon, Mount Vernon, Virginia (tel. 703/780-2000), the home of George Washington, is located 16 miles south of Washington, on the other side of the river, off Mount Vernon Memorial Highway (Route 235). Surrounded by 30 acres of pastoral fields, manicured lawns and shrubs, and flowering gardens, this gracious mid-Georgian-style mansion was designed and enlarged by Washington from the 1½-story farmhouse of his youth. Visitors can tour 14 rooms of the house, plus the gardens and surrounding cottages and workshops; the tomb of George and Martha Washington is also located here. Open daily from 9 a.m. to 5 p.m., March through October, and from 9 a.m. to 4 p.m. during the rest of the year. Admission charge is $4 for adults and $2 for children aged 6 to 11.

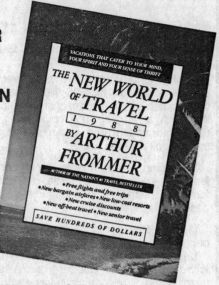

Date_____

FROMMER BOOKS
PRENTICE HALL PRESS
ONE GULF + WESTERN PLAZA
NEW YORK, NY 10023

Friends:

Please send me the books checked below:

FROMMER'S $-A-DAY GUIDES™

(In-depth guides to sightseeing and low-cost tourist accommodations and facilities.)

☐ Europe on $30 a Day $13.95	☐ New Zealand on $40 a Day $10.95
☐ Australia on $25 a Day $10.95	☐ New York on $50 a Day............. $10.95
☐ Eastern Europe on $25 a Day $10.95	☐ Scandinavia on $50 a Day........... $10.95
☐ England on $40 a Day.............. $11.95	☐ Scotland and Wales on $40 a Day..... $11.95
☐ Greece on $30 a Day................ $11.95	☐ South America on $30 a Day $10.95
☐ Hawaii on $50 a Day $11.95	☐ Spain and Morocco (plus the Canary
☐ India on $25 a Day $10.95	Is.) on $40 a Day $10.95
☐ Ireland on $30 a Day................ $10.95	☐ Turkey on $25 a Day............... $10.95
☐ Israel on $30 & $35 a Day $11.95	☐ Washington, D.C., & Historic Va. on
☐ Mexico on $20 a Day $10.95	$40 a Day $11.95

FROMMER'S DOLLARWISE GUIDES™

(Guides to sightseeing and tourist accommodations and facilities from budget to deluxe, with emphasis on the medium-priced.)

☐ Alaska $12.95	☐ Cruises (incl. Alaska, Carib, Mex,
☐ Austria & Hungary $11.95	Hawaii, Panama, Canada, & US) $12.95
☐ Belgium, Holland, Luxembourg $11.95	☐ California & Las Vegas $11.95
☐ Egypt............................ $11.95	☐ Florida............................ $11.95
☐ England & Scotland $11.95	☐ Mid-Atlantic States $12.95
☐ France $11.95	☐ New England $12.95
☐ Germany $12.95	☐ New York State $12.95
☐ Italy.............................. $11.95	☐ Northwest $11.95
☐ Japan & Hong Kong $12.95	☐ Skiing in Europe $12.95
☐ Portugal (incl. Madeira & the Azores) . $12.95	☐ Skiing USA—East $11.95
☐ South Pacific...................... $12.95	☐ Skiing USA—West $11.95
☐ Switzerland & Liechtenstein $12.95	☐ Southeast & New Orleans............ $11.95
☐ Bermuda & The Bahamas............ $11.95	☐ Southwest........................ $11.95
☐ Canada $12.95	☐ Texas............................ $11.95
☐ Caribbean $13.95	

TURN PAGE FOR ADDITIONAL BOOKS AND ORDER FORM.

THE ARTHUR FROMMER GUIDES™

(Pocket-size guides to sightseeing and tourist accommodations and facilities in all price ranges.)

☐ Amsterdam/Holland	$5.95	☐ Mexico City/Acapulco	$5.95
☐ Athens...........................	$5.95	☐ Minneapolis/St. Paul................	$5.95
☐ Atlantic City/Cape May	$5.95	☐ Montreal/Quebec City	$5.95
☐ Boston...........................	$5.95	☐ New Orleans	$5.95
☐ Cancún/Cozumel/Yucatán	$5.95	☐ New York.........................	$5.95
☐ Dublin/Ireland	$5.95	☐ Orlando/Disney World/EPCOT........	$5.95
☐ Hawaii...........................	$5.95	☐ Paris	$5.95
☐ Las Vegas	$5.95	☐ Philadelphia.......................	$5.95
☐ Lisbon/Madrid/Costa del Sol........	$5.95	☐ Rome	$5.95
☐ London	$5.95	☐ San Francisco	$5.95
☐ Los Angeles	$5.95	☐ Washington, D.C...................	$5.95

FROMMER'S TOURING GUIDES™

(Color illustrated guides that include walking tours, cultural & historic sites, and other vital travel information.)

☐ Egypt............................	$8.95	☐ Paris	$8.95
☐ Florence	$8.95	☐ Venice	$8.95
☐ London	$8.95		

SPECIAL EDITIONS

☐ A Shopper's Guide to the Caribbean...	$12.95	☐ Motorist's Phrase Book (Fr/Ger/Sp) ...	$4.95
☐ Bed & Breakfast—N. America	$8.95	☐ Swap and Go (Home Exchanging)	$10.95
☐ Guide to Honeymoons (US, Canada, Mexico, & Carib)..................	$12.95	☐ The Candy Apple (NY for Kids).......	$11.95
		☐ Travel Diary and Record Book........	$5.95
☐ How to Beat the High Cost of Travel ...	$4.95	☐ Where to Stay USA (Lodging from $3 to $30 a night)	$9.95
☐ Marilyn Wood's Wonderful Weekends (NY, Conn, Mass, RI, Vt, NH, NJ, Del, Pa)	$11.95		

☐ Arthur Frommer's New World of Travel (Annual sourcebook previewing: new travel trends, new modes of travel, and the latest cost-cutting strategies for savvy travelers) $12.95

ORDER NOW!

In U.S. include $1.50 shipping UPS for 1st book; 50¢ ea. add'l book. Outside U.S. $2 and 50¢, respectively.

Enclosed is my check or money order for $_____

NAME _____

ADDRESS _____

CITY _____ STATE _____ ZIP _____

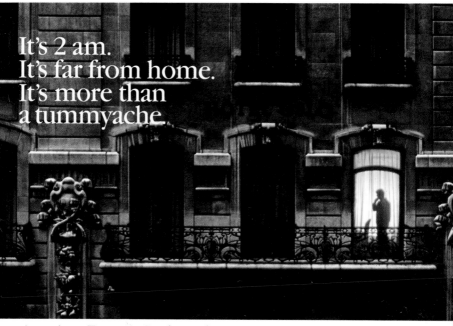

It's 2 am.
It's far from home.
It's more than
a tummyache.

American Express Cardmembers can get emergency medical and legal referrals, worldwide. Simply by calling Global Assist.℠

What if it really is more than a tummyache? What if your back goes out? What if you get into a legal fix?

Call Global Assist – a new emergency referral service for the exclusive use of American Express Cardmembers. Just call. Toll-free. 24 hours a day. Every day. Virtually anywhere in the world.

Your call helps find a doctor, lawyer, dentist, optician, chiropractor, nurse, pharmacist, or an interpreter.

All this costs nothing, except for the medical and legal bills you would normally expect to pay.

Global Assist. One more reason to have the American Express® Card. Or, to get one.

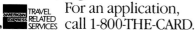 For an application, call 1-800-THE-CARD.

Don't leave home without it.®

If you lose cash on vacation, don't count on a Boy Scout finding it.

Honestly.

How many people can you trust to give back hundreds of dollars in cash? Not too many.

That's why it's so important to help protect your vacation with American Express® Travelers Cheques.

If they're lost, you can get them back from over 100,000 refund locations throu out the world. Or you can hope a Boy Sc finds it.

Protect your vacation.

AMERICAN EXPRESS **Travelers Cheques**